SQL Queries 2012 Joes 2 Pros® Volume 4

Query Programming Objects for SQL Server 2012

(SQL Exam Prep Series 70-461 Volume 4 of 5)

By

Rick A. Morelan
MCDBA, MCTS, MCITP, MCAD, MOE, MCSE, MCSE+I

Pinal Dave
Founder of SQLAuthority.com

© Pinal Dave/Rick A. Morelan
All Rights Reserved 2011

ISBN: 1481118765
EAN: 978-1481118767

Rick A Morelan
Info@Joes2Pros.com

Table of Contents

About the Authors 11
   Rick A Morelan 11
   Pinal Dave 11
Acknowledgements 12
Preface 13
Introduction 13
Skills Needed for this Book 14
About this Book 14
How to Use and Download Companion Files 15
DVD or Videos as a Companion 16
What this Book is Not 17

Chapter 1. Constraints 18
Data Types 18
Primary Keys 19
   Duplicate ID values 19
   Creating Primary Keys on Existing Tables 21
CHECK constraints 23
   Creating CHECK constraints 24
   Changing Existing CHECK constraints 26
Lab 1.1: Introduction to Constraints 28
Points to Ponder - Introduction to Constraints 31
Unique Constraints 32
   Creating Unique Constraints 33
   Unique Constraint Considerations 34
Lab 1.2: Unique Constraints 36
Points to Ponder - Unique Constraints 38
Default Constraints 39
Creating and Using Default Constraints 39
   Dynamic Defaults 43
   Overriding Default Constraints 44
   Removing Default Constraints 45
Lab 1.3: Default Constraints 46
Points to Ponder - Default Constraints 48
Data Integrity 49
   Domain Integrity 50
   Entity Integrity 52

Referential Integrity 55
Foreign Key Constraints 56
    Using the WITH NOCHECK Option 61
Lab 1.4: Foreign Key Constraints 65
Points to Ponder - Foreign Key Constraints 67
Creating Tables with Constraints 68
Lab 1.5: Creating Table Constraints 71
Points to Ponder - Creating Table Constraints 72
Chapter Glossary 73
Review Quiz - Chapter One 74
    Answer Key 77
Bug Catcher Game 78

Chapter 2. After Triggers 79
Insert Triggers 79
    Coding the After Insert Trigger 83
    Enabling and Disabling Triggers 86
Lab 2.1: Insert Triggers 89
Points to Ponder - Insert Triggers 90
Delete Triggers 91
    Creating Delete Triggers 91
    Running Delete Triggers 92
    Using Triggers for Data Integrity 93
Lab 2.2: Delete Triggers 97
Points to Ponder - Delete Triggers 99
Update Triggers 99
    Creating Update Triggers 99
    Running Update Triggers 101
    Update Triggers and Data Integrity 102
Lab 2.3: Update Triggers 106
Points to Ponder - Update Triggers 109
Chapter Glossary 110
Review Quiz - Chapter Two 111
    Answer Key 113
Bug Catcher Game 113

Chapter 3. Other Triggers 115
The "Instead Of" Trigger 115
    Creating "Instead Of" Triggers 116
    Running "Instead Of" Triggers 117
    After Trigger Abstraction Layer 118
    Putting Multiple Events on One Trigger 120
Lab 3.1: "Instead Of" Triggers 122

- Points to Ponder - "Instead Of" Triggers 124
- Nesting Triggers 125
  - Using @@NESTLEVEL 127
- Lab 3.2: Nested Triggers 130
- Points to Ponder - Nested Triggers 131
- DDL Triggers 133
  - Creating DDL Triggers 134
  - Trigger Event Details 136
  - Using Rollback 138
- Lab 3.3: DDL Triggers 141
- Points to Ponder - DDL Triggers 142
- Chapter Glossary 143
- Review Quiz - Chapter Three 144
  - Answer Key 152
- Bug Catcher Game 153

Chapter 4. Views 154
- Using Views 154
  - Creating Views with Management Studio 155
  - Creating Views Using T-SQL Code 158
- Analyzing Existing Views 160
- Lab 4.1: Creating Views 163
- Points to Ponder - Creating Views 165
- Altering Views 166
- Nesting Views 167
- Lab 4.2: Altering Views 171
- Points to Ponder - Altering Views 173
- View Options 174
  - View Rules 174
  - Encrypting Views 176
  - Schemabinding Views 179
- Lab 4.3: View Options 185
- Points to Ponder - Altering Views 187
- Chapter Glossary 188
- Review Quiz - Chapter Four 189
  - Answer Key 190
- Bug Catcher Game 191

Chapter 5. Updating and Maintaining Views 193
- Manipulating Data through Views 194
  - Selecting Data through Views 194
  - Updating Records through Views 195
  - Inserting Records through Views 196

Lab 5.1: Manipulating Data through Views 201
Points to Ponder - Manipulating Data through Views 203
View Modification Restrictions 204
    Inserting Data through Views 204
    Deleting Data through Views 205
    Updating Data through Views 206
    Using Check Option 211
Lab 5.2: View Modification Restrictions 218
Points to Ponder - View Modifications 220
Indexed Views Overview 221
    Creating an Index on a View 221
    Materialized Views 226
    Indexed View Requirements 229
    Space Used by Indexed Views 237
Lab 5.3: Indexed Views 239
Points to Ponder - Indexed Views 240
Chapter Glossary 241
Review Quiz - Chapter Five 242
    Answer Key 245
Bug Catcher Game 246

Chapter 6. Stored Procedures 248
Stored Procedures Recap 248
    Basic Stored Procedures 249
    Stored Procedure Parameters 250
    Scalar Result Sets 254
Lab 6.1: Stored Procedures Recap 256
Points to Ponder - Stored Procedure Recap 257
Stored Procedure Return Values 257
    Creating Return Values 258
    Using Return Values 261
    Using Default Values 264
Lab 6.2: Return Values 267
Points to Ponder - Return Values 268
Output Parameters 269
    Creating Output Parameters 271
Using Output Parameters 273
Lab 6.3: Output Parameters 275
Points to Ponder - Output Parameters 276
Chapter Glossary 277
Review Quiz - Chapter Six 278
    Answer Key 279

Bug Catcher Game 279
Chapter 7. Stored Procedure Techniques 281
Stored Procedure Execution Options 281
   Inserting Data with Stored Procedures 281
   Capturing Stored Procedure Return Data 283
   SCOPE_IDENTITY() 285
   @@IDENTITY 287
   IDENT_CURRENT() 289
   @@ROWCOUNT 289
   Lab 7.1: Stored Procedure Options 291
Points to Ponder - Stored Procedure Options 292
Table-Valued Stored procedure Parameters 293
   Declaring Table Types as Variables 293
   Table Types 296
   Using Table Types as Variables 296
   Table-Valued Parameters 300
Lab 7.2: Table-Valued Stored Procedure Parameters 303
Points to Ponder - Table-Valued Stored Procedures 304
Chapter Glossary 305
Review Quiz – Chapter Seven 306
   Answer Key 307
Bug Catcher Game 308

Chapter 8. String Functions 310
Basic String Functions 310
   Using LEN() 311
   Returning Parts of Strings 312
   Changing Strings 314
   Casting to Strings 316
Lab 8.1: Basic String Functions 320
Points to Ponder – Basic String Functions 322
New 2012 String Functions 323
   CONCAT 323
   FORMAT with Dates 324
   FORMAT with Months 328
   FORMAT with Money 330
Lab 8.2: New 2012 String Functions 331
Points to Ponder - New 2012 String Functions 333
Viewing Table and Field Metadata 334
Lab 8.3: Viewing Table and Field Metadata 341
Points to Ponder - Table and Field Metadata 342
Chapter Glossary 343

Review Quiz - Chapter Eight 344
    Answer Key 346
Bug Catcher Game 347

Chapter 9. Time Functions 349
System Time Functions 350
    Returning DateTime from Time Functions 350
Lab 9.1: System Time Functions 353
Points to Ponder – System Time Functions 354
Time Calculation Functions 355
    Using DatePart 355
    Using DateAdd 359
Lab 9.2: Time Calculation Functions 363
Points to Ponder - Time Calculation Functions 364
New SQL 2012 Time Functions 365
    DATEFROMPARTS 365
    TIMEFROMPARTS 367
    DATETIMEFROMPARTS 370
    EOMONTH 371
Lab 9.3: New SQL 2012 Time Functions 374
Points to Ponder - New SQL 2012 Time Functions 376
Chapter Glossary 377
Review Quiz - Chapter Nine 378
    Answer Key 380
Bug Catcher Game 382

Chapter 10. Logical and Analytical Functions 384
Logical Functions 385
    Using ISNULL 385
    Using CASE 389
    COALESCE 391
    Using IIF 394
Lab 10.1: Logical Functions 397
Points to Ponder - Logical Functions 400
New SQL 2012 Analytical Functions 401
    Using CUME_DIST and PERCENT_RANK 401
    Using FIRST_VALUE and LAST_VALUE 403
    Using LEAD 405
    Using LAG 407
Using PERCENTILE_CONT 409
    Using PERCENTILE_CONT with PARTITION 411
Lab 10.2: New SQL 2012 Analytical Functions 413
Points to Ponder - New SQL 2012 Analytical Functions 416

Chapter Glossary 417
Review Quiz - Chapter Ten 418
   Answer Key 419
Bug Catcher Game 420

Chapter 11. User-Defined Functions 421

Functions versus Stored Procedures 421
Scalar Functions 422
   Creating and Implementing Scalar Functions 422
   Using Functions with Queries 424
   Functions with Multiple Parameters 425
   Aggregate Functions Recap 426
Lab 11.1: Scalar Functions 432
Points to Ponder - Scalar Functions 433
Table-Valued Functions 435
   Creating and Implementing Table-Valued Functions 435
   Views versus Parameterized Table-Valued Functions 437
Lab 11.2: Table-Valued Functions 440
Points to Ponder - Table-Valued Functions 442
Function Determinability 443
   Using Deterministic Functions 443
   Deterministic Functions in Views 444
   Non-Deterministic Functions in Views 445
   User-Defined Function Determinability 447
Lab 11.3: Function Determinability 450
Points to Ponder - Function Determinability 452
Chapter Glossary 452
Review Quiz - Chapter Eleven 453
   Answer Key 454
Bug Catcher Game 455

Chapter 12. SQL Error Messages 456

SQL Server Error Messages 456
   Errors in SQL Statements 456
   Custom Error Messages 460
   Error Severity 463
   Using Error Message Variables 465
Lab 12.1: SQL Server Error Messages 470
Points to Ponder - SQL Server Error Messages 472
SQL Error Actions 473
   Statement Termination 473
   Scope Abortion 474
   Batch Abortion 474

- Connection Termination 475
  - Testing Error Actions 475
  - XACT_ABORT 483
- Lab 12.2: SQL Error Actions 485
- Points to Ponder - SQL Error Actions 487
- Chapter Glossary 487
- Review Quiz - Chapter Twelve 489
  - Answer Key 490
- Bug Catcher Game 491

Chapter 13. Error Handling 493

- Structured Error Handling 493
  - Anticipating Potential Errors 494
  - The TRY Block 495
  - The CATCH Block 496
  - Structured Error Handling Summary 500
  - Transactions in Structured Error Handling 500
- Lab 13.1: Structured Error Handling 508
- Points to Ponder - Structured Error Handling 509
- THROW 510
  - Introduction to THROW 510
  - Using THROW with TRY/CATCH 511
- TRY/CATCH in Stored Procedures 513
- Nesting Structured Error Handling 515
- THROW the Calling Code 518
- Lab 13.2: THROW 520
- Points to Ponder - THROW 522
- Chapter Glossary 523
- Review Quiz - Chapter Thirteen 524
  - Answer Key 527
- Bug Catcher Game 528

Chapter 14. Dynamic SQL 529

- Exec Dynamic SQL 530
  - Dynamic DML statements 530
  - Dynamic DDL statements 532
- Lab 14.1: Exec Dynamic SQL 536
- Points to Ponder - Exec Dynamic SQL 538
- sp_executesql 539
  - Using sp_executesql 539
  - sp_executesql Parameters 540
  - sp_executesql Performance 541
- Lab 14.2: sp_executesql 543

- Points to Ponder - sp_executesql 545
- Dynamic Admin Tasks 546
  - Database Backup Statement 548
  - Dynamic Date Stamps 554
- Exec Dynamic SQL Drawbacks 555
- SQL Injection 555
- Dynamic SQL Performance 558
- Dynamic SQL with Stored Procedures 558
- Lab 14.3: Dynamic Admin Tasks 562
- Points to Ponder - Dynamic Admin Tasks 562
- Chapter Glossary 563
- Review Quiz - Chapter Fourteen 564
  - Answer Key 567
- Bug Catcher Game 567

Chapter 15. Cursors 569
- Using Cursors 570
  - Automation Challenges 571
  - Automating Tasks from a Table 572
- Using Cursors 573
  - @@FETCH_STATUS 575
  - Capturing a Variable from a Cursor 577
  - Automating Tasks with a Cursor 577
  - Looping with @@FETCH_STATUS 579
- Lab 15.1: Using Cursors 584
- Points to Ponder - Using Cursors 586
- Cursor Types 587
  - FORWARD_ONLY and SCROLL Cursors 587
  - Dynamic Cursors 589
  - Static Cursor 591
  - Cursor Variables 593
- Lab 15.2: Cursor Types 594
- Points to Ponder - Cursor Types 595
- Chapter Glossary 595
- Review Quiz - Chapter Fifteen 597
  - Answer Key 598
- Bug Catcher Game 599

Chapter 16. Summary of Volume 4 600
- What's next 601
- Index 603

About the Authors

We write each book in this series to help anyone seeking knowledge about SQL Server – whether an intermediate looking to fill gaps in their knowledge, an expert looking for new features in the 2012 version of SQL Server, or even a developer picking up SQL Server as their second or third programming language. At the heart of the mission as an educator remains the dedication to helping people with the power of SQL Server. The goal of education is action.

Rick A Morelan

In 1994, you could find Rick Morelan braving the frigid waters of the Bering Sea as an Alaskan commercial fisherman. His computer skills were non-existent at the time, so you might figure such beginnings seemed unlikely to lead him down the path to SQL Server expertise at Microsoft. However, every computer expert in the world today woke up at some point in their life knowing nothing about computers.

Making the change from fisherman seemed scary and took daily schooling at Catapult Software Training Institute. Rick got his lucky break in August of 1995, working his first database job at Microsoft. Since that time, Rick has worked more than 10 years at Microsoft and has attained over 30 Microsoft technical certifications in applications, networking, databases and .NET development.

His books are used the world over by individuals and educators to help people with little experience learn these technical topics and gain the ability to earn a Microsoft certification or have the confidence to do well in a job interview with their new found knowledge.

Rick's speaking engagements have included SQL Saturdays and SQL Server Intelligence Conferences. In addition to these speaking engagements Rick gives back to the community by personally teaching students at both Bellevue College and MoreTechnology in Redmond, WA.

Pinal Dave

Pinal Dave is a technology enthusiast and avid blogger. Prior to joining Microsoft, his outstanding community service helped to earn several awards, including the Microsoft Most Valuable Professional in SQL Server Technology (3 continuous years) and the Community Impact Award as an Individual Contributor for 2010.

Playing an active role in the IT industry for over eight years, his career has taken him across the world working in both India and the US, primarily with SQL Server Technology, from version 6.5 to its latest form. His early work experience includes being a Technology Evangelist with Microsoft and a Sr. Consultant with SolidQ, and he continues to work on performance tuning and optimization projects for high transactional systems.

Pinal's higher education degrees include a Master of Science from the University of Southern California, and a Bachelor of Engineering from Gujarat University. In addition to his degrees, Pinal holds multiple Microsoft certificates and helps to spread his knowledge as a regular speaker for many international events like TechEd, SQL PASS, MSDN, TechNet and countless user groups.
At the time of this writing, Pinal has co-authored three SQL Server books:

- o SQL Server Programming
- o SQL Wait Stats
- o SQL Server Interview Questions and Answers

Pinal's passion for the community drives him to share his training and knowledge and frequently writes on his blog http://blog.SQLAuthority.com covering various subjects related to SQL Server technology and Business Intelligence. As a very active member of the social media community it is easy to connect with him using one of these services:

- o Twitter: http://twitter.com/pinaldave
- o Facebook: http://facebook.com/SQLAuth

When he is not in front of a computer, he is usually travelling to explore hidden treasures in nature with his lovely daughter, Shaivi, and very supportive wife, Nupur.

Acknowledgements

As a book with a supporting web site, illustrations, media content and software scripts, it takes more than the usual author, illustrator and editor to put everything together into a great learning experience. Since my publisher has the more traditional contributor list available, I'd like to recognize the core team members:

Editor: Lori Stow
Technical Review: Tony Smithlin
User Acceptance Testing: Sandra Howard
Index: Tony Smithlin

Thank you to all the teachers at Catapult Software Training Institute in the mid-1990s. What a great start to open my eyes. It landed me my first job at Microsoft by August of that year. A giant second wind came from Koenig-Solutions, which gives twice the training and attention for half the price of most other schools. Mr. Rohit Aggarwal is the visionary founder of this company based in New Delhi, India. Rohit's business model sits students down one-on-one with experts. Each expert dedicates weeks to help each new IT student succeed. The numerous twelve-hour flights I took to India to attend those classes were pivotal to my success. Whenever a new generation of software was released, I got years ahead of the learning curve by spending one or two months at Koenig.

Dr. James D. McCaffrey at Volt Technical Resources in Bellevue, Wash., taught me how to improve my own learning by teaching others. You'll frequently see me in his classroom because he makes learning fun. McCaffrey's unique style boosts the self-confidence of his students, and his tutelage has been essential to my own professional development. His philosophy inspires the *Joes 2 Pros* curriculum.

Preface

We write each book in this series to help anyone seeking knowledge about SQL Server – whether an intermediate looking to fill gaps in their knowledge, an expert looking for new features in the 2012 version of SQL Server, or even a developer picking up SQL Server as their second or third programming language.

Introduction

Many SQL Server developer job openings refer to skills with larger databases or complex databases. A database can be complex without being very large, and *vice versa*. If you have ever seen a database that has no user input and does not allow any updates (just inserts from feeds), then you know sometimes a giant database is little more than a big relational storage area. Many companies need to track updates, approvals, time changes, historical changes, and currency conversions based on real time market rates. In short, every database is a combination of data and actions and tells a story about the business or organization it represents.

Most actions within a database take place many times to satisfy many customers or partners. The SQL developer needs to be able to create processes for the working database by using one of many programming objects (like functions, stored procedures, constraints, or triggers). By creating objects that talk with SQL Server, you control the way other programs (like applications or web pages) can interconnect. These external programs only need to call on the names of your programming objects by name rather than needing to submit large pieces of advanced code. This limited number of handshakes to SQL often represents a safe and pre-set way into SQL and keeps data better protected.

Programming objects are the building blocks for software and business intelligence applications. Throughout your SQL development career, most of the code you write will be contained in these objects.

Once you learn how programming objects work in SQL Server, you are in control of how things run on your system. These objects become tools you wield in order to enforce business rules within your database. Sometimes a valid SQL statement might be one you never want to run. Some tables may have data that is not allowed to be changed or duplicated. With objects like constraints and triggers, you can make your own rules about which actions are allowed – and which are forbidden – within your database.

Skills Needed for this Book

If you have no SQL coding knowledge, then I recommend you first get into the groove of the first three volumes of *SQL Queries 2012 Joes 2 Pros* book series. I have carefully sequenced the chapters and topics to build upon each other. However, intermediates and developers with a good handle on T-SQL and SQL query writing should be able to approach the programming topics without much difficulty.

About this Book

My understanding of the engine in my car is very limited, yet I benefit every day from its underlying complexity because I know how to operate the pedals, steering wheel, and other devices of the car. I don't need to be an expert at a car's construction to use it effectively. Very few people in the company will actually want or need direct access to SQL Server. Rather, their goal will be to have your work benefit them, their people, and their business but without needing to understand the complexity of SQL Server or T-SQL. By developing programming objects that their applications get to use, very advanced perspectives of the data will be used by many people within your company.

Data needs to be useful to a business. In the *SQL Queries 2012 Joes 2 Pros Volume 1* book the very first chapter talked about turning data into information. For the most part we saw how to do that in the *SQL Queries 2012 Joes 2 Pros*

Volume 2 book. Data has been around for thousands of years but quick business information (reports) from that data has only become instantaneous in the last few decades. Having access to the right information is complex but crucial to business. SQL Programming is your chance to bridge this critical gap of information to the right people.

Most of the exercises in this book are designed around proper database practices in the workplace. The workplace also offers common challenges and process changes over time. For example, it is good practice to use numeric data for IDs. If you have ever seen a Canadian postal code (zip code), you can understand the need for character data in relational information. You will occasionally see an off-the-beaten-path strategy demonstrated, so you know how to approach a topic in a job interview or workplace assignment.

Note: For purposes of keeping code examples as short and readable as possible for students, in many cases throughout the series I use simple naming when calling database objects, including referenced objects. However, the recommended best practice is to use two-part naming (particularly when calling stored procedures and referenced tables) because it consumes fewer SQL Server system resources.

I'm often asked about the Points to Ponder feature, which is popular with both beginners and experienced developers. Some have asked why I don't simply call it a "Summary Page". While it's true that the Points to Ponder page generally captures key points from each section, I frequently include options or technical insights not contained in the chapter. Often these are points which I or my students have found helpful and which I believe will enhance your understanding of SQL Server.

The *Joes 2 Pros* series began in the summer of 2006. The project started as a few easy-to-view labs to transform the old, dry text reading into easier and fun lessons for the classroom. The labs grew into stories. The stories grew into chapters. In 2008, many people whose lives and careers had been improved through my classes convinced me to write a book to reach out to more people. In 2009 the first book began in full gear until its completion (*Beginning SQL Joes 2 Pros*, ISBN 1-4392-5317-5) and the adventure continues.

How to Use and Download Companion Files

To help get you started, the first three chapters are in video format for free downloading. Videos show labs, demonstrate concepts, and review Points to Ponder along with tips from the appendix. Ranging from 3-15 minutes in length, they use special effects to highlight key points. You can go at your own pace and pause or replay within these lessons as needed. To make knowing where to start even easier, the videos are numbered. You don't even need to refer to the book to know what order they should be viewed in. There is even a "Setup" video that shows you how to download and use all other files.

Clear content and high-resolution multimedia videos coupled with code samples will take you on this journey. To give you all this and save printing costs, all supporting files are available with a free download from www.Joes2Pros.com. The breakdown of the offerings from these supporting files is listed below:

Training videos: To get you started, the first three chapters are in video format for free downloading. Videos show labs and demonstrate concepts. Ranging from 3-15 minutes in length, they use special effects to highlight key points. There is even a "Setup" video that shows you how to download and use all other files. You can go at your own pace and pause or replay within lessons as needed.

Answer Keys: The downloadable files also include an answer key. You can verify your completed work against these keys. Another helpful use is these coding answers are available for peeking if you get really stuck.

Resource files: If you are asked to import a file into SQL Server, you will need that resource file. Located in the resources sub-folder from the download site are your practice lab resource files. These files hold the few non-SQL script files needed for some labs. Please note that no resource files are needed this book.

Lab setup files: SQL Server is a database engine and we need to practice on a database. The Joes 2 Pros Practice Company database is a fictitious travel booking company whose name is shortened to the database name of JProCo. The scripts to set up the JProCo database can be found here.

Chapter Review Files: Ready to take your new skills out for a test drive? We have the ever popular Bug Catcher game located here.

DVD or Videos as a Companion

Training videos: These books are also available for sale as video books. In these videos I guide you through the lessons of each section of the book. Every lab of every chapter of this book series has multimedia steps recorded into videos. The content of the five book series fits into 10 DVDs. When comparing prices, you will find the costs are much less than the existing ad-hoc options on the market today.

If you have done some shopping around you will have noticed there are video training sets that cost over $300. You might also have seen single certification books for $60 each. Do the math and you see one book from other leading publishers will set you back nearly $400.

What this Book is Not

This is not a memorization book. Rather, this is a skills book to make preparing for the certification test a familiarization process. This book prepares you to apply what you've learned to answer SQL questions in the job setting. The highest hopes are that your progress and level of SQL knowledge will soon have business managers seeking your expertise to provide the reporting and information vital to their decision making. It's a good feeling to achieve and to help at the same time. Many students commented that the training method used in *Joes 2 Pros* was what finally helped them achieve their goal of certification.

When you go through the *Joes 2 Pros* series and really know this material, you deserve a fair shot at SQL certification. Use only authentic testing engines to measure your skill. Show you know it for real. At the time of this writing, MeasureUp® at http://www.measureup.com provides a good test preparation simulator. The company's test pass guarantee makes it a very appealing option.

Chapter 1.   Constraints

When I was a little kid, the watchwords "buckle up" could always be heard whenever we got into the family car. Public service ad campaigns were popular at that time, and I recall commercials and billboards with slogans like "always wear safety belts" or "use your safety constraints".

Nowadays, it's a well-known fact that safety constraints (like seat belts) in automobiles or airplanes save lives. Emergency response teams and healthcare professionals save the lives of individuals rescued from accidents, even if people did not use their safety constraints. However, the best practice is to buckle up and try to prevent calamities from occurring in the first place.

The same is true with databases. Utilizing database constraints can help you avoid "accidents" which can harm your data. Constraints can save you time, because you won't need to spend time removing bad data from your system. Like vehicle safety constraints, they are designed to prevent bad things from happening.

This chapter will explore the types of constraints that help keep your database safe and also help maintain data integrity. Since the syntax for adding most of these constraints at the time of table creation is fairly straightforward (e.g., we've already added primary keys to most of the tables we created in Volumes 2 and 3 of the *Joes 2 Pros SQL Series*), we will examine each constraint in the more advanced context of modifying existing tables and constraints. The final section of the chapter will demonstrate the syntax and tips for creating each of the constraints on brand new tables.

READER NOTE: *Please run the script SQLQueries2012Vol4Chapter1.0Setup.sql in order to follow along with the examples in the first section of Chapter 1. All scripts mentioned in this chapter may be found at* **www.Joes2Pros.com**.

Data Types

Suppose we use the SMALLMONEY data type for a field called HourlyRate. Just to test this, try entering the word 'Peanuts' into the PayRate.HourlyRate field (Figure 1.1). *SQL Server rejects this entry because the SMALLMONEY data type will only allow numeric values into this field.*

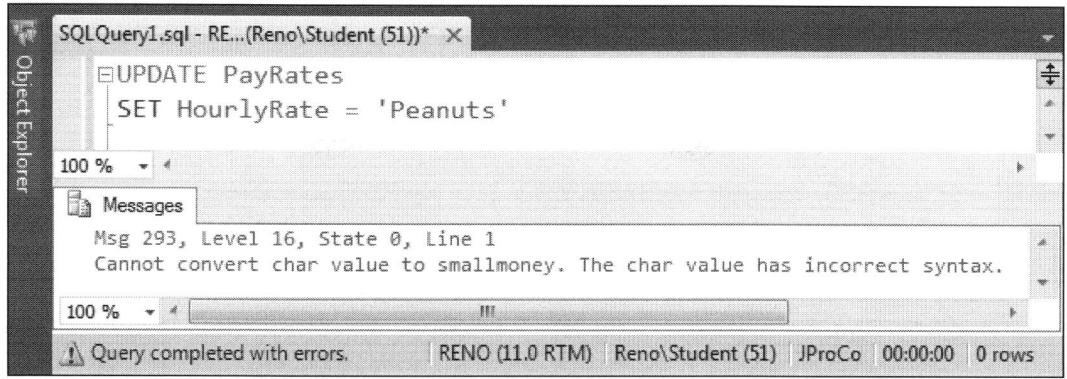

```
SQLQuery1.sql - RE...(Reno\Student (51))*  ×
UPDATE PayRates
SET HourlyRate = 'Peanuts'

Messages
Msg 293, Level 16, State 0, Line 1
Cannot convert char value to smallmoney. The char value has incorrect syntax.
```

Figure 1.1 The SMALLMONEY data type constrains the values that can be entered into the field.

Notice that entering the letter P in Peanuts (and all the other letters) will be rejected by the HourlyRate field. In this situation, data types are the first line of defense in constraining bad data and ensuring field inputs are valid.

Data types are the simplest and most frequently used **constraints**. They are the only constraint which can blanket every field in every table of your database.

Primary Keys

Perhaps the most commonly used and talked about constraint is the primary key. A primary key prevents duplicates and ensures that all records have their own distinct values. Primary keys don't allow NULLs, so you are guaranteed that each record has its own unique populated value.

Duplicate ID values

A glance at the dbo.StateList table of the JProCo database shows us we have 63 records. All states and territories listed in this table have values for the StateID field, the StateName field, the RegionName field, and the LandMass field.

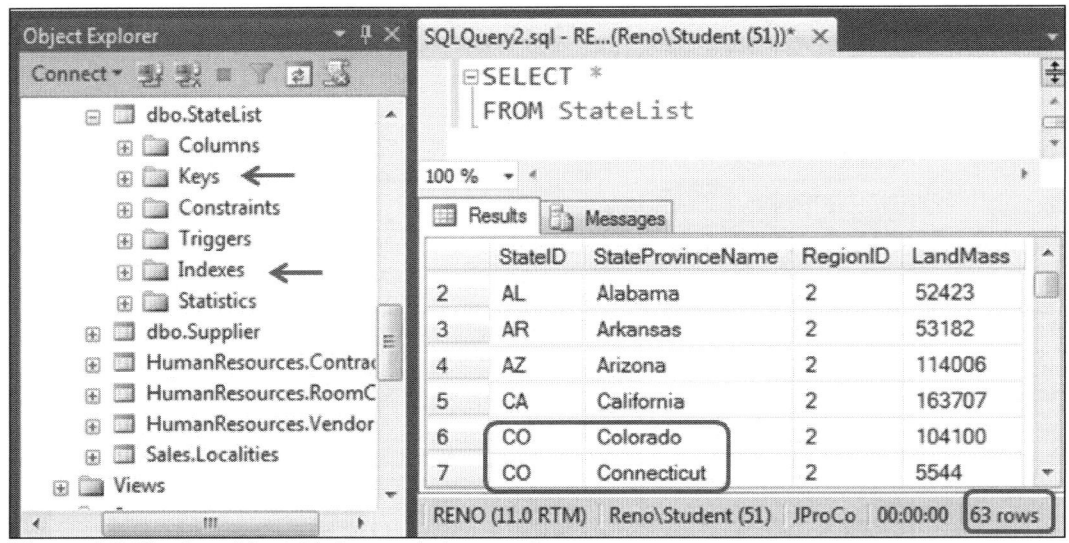

Figure 1.2 The StateList table has no indexes or keys.

If we looked at the metadata for this table, we would see it has no keys and no indexes. That can be risky, as evidenced by the mistakes shown in Rows 6 and 7. In Figure 1.2 you can see both Colorado and Connecticut are abbreviated as "CO". There are no constraints preventing duplicate StateID records from being entered into this table.

The NH-New Hampshire record is also listed twice (Figure 1.3). It's clearly time to scrub this data and remove duplicates from the StateList table.

```
SELECT *
FROM StateList
```

StateID	StateName	RegionName	LandMass
30 NE	Nebraska	USA-Continental	77358
31 NH	New Hampshire	USA-Continental	9351
32 NJ	New Jersey	USA-Continental	8722
33 NH	New Hampshire	USA-Continental	9351
34 NM	New Mexico	USA-Continental	121593
35 NV	Nevada	USA-Continental	110567

63 rows

Figure 1.3 The NH–New Hampshire record is duplicated in the StateList table.

Creating Primary Keys on Existing Tables

Let's fix the CO Colorado/Connecticut problem and the New Hampshire duplicate with two different statements. The following UPDATE statement corrects the StateID of Connecticut to be abbreviated as CT:

```
UPDATE StateList SET StateID = 'CT'
WHERE StateProvinceName = 'Connecticut'
```

To ensure we get rid of just one of the two New Hampshire records, we will combine a DELETE statement with the TOP keyword (Figure 1.4).

```
DELETE TOP (1)
FROM StateList
WHERE StateID = 'NH'
```

Messages
(1 row(s) affected)

0 rows

Figure 1.4 Use TOP (1) with DELETE to eliminate one of the two NH–New Hampshire records.

Our StateList data is now scrubbed but we need to prevent bad records (e.g., duplicate StateID records) from entering the table in the future. A primary key on the StateID field of the StateList table would have prevented the duplicate values issue. With this primary key added, SQL Server will not allow any accidental or intentional duplication of values in the StateID field.

Since this table is used constantly, we'd prefer to add the constraint to the existing table in production (versus dropping and re-building the table). We will alter the table and add a primary key constraint on the StateID field. A good naming convention is to use PK for "primary key" plus the table name and the field name. In this case, we will name the primary key **PK_StateList_StateID**. You can also specify whether this primary key will create a clustered or non-clustered index, as well as whether to sort StateID values in ascending or descending order. We will add this primary key as a clustered index in ascending order.

(*Note:* If no clustered index already exists on the table, then adding a primary key constraint will generate a clustered index by default. However, you may choose to specify a non-clustered index for the primary key.) The following code puts the PK_StateList_StateID primary key on the StateID field of the StateList table:

```
ALTER TABLE StateList
ADD CONSTRAINT PK_StateList_StateID
PRIMARY KEY CLUSTERED(StateID ASC)
```

After running the code, open Object Explorer to find the primary key we just created. Beneath the JProCo database, expand the Tables folder and navigate to the dbo.StateList table. Expand the Keys or Indexes folder and note that the primary key PK_StateList_StateID is present (Figure 1.5). Right-click dbo.StateList to refresh its folders, as needed. As well, observe that the Indexes folder has a new clustered index named for the primary key.

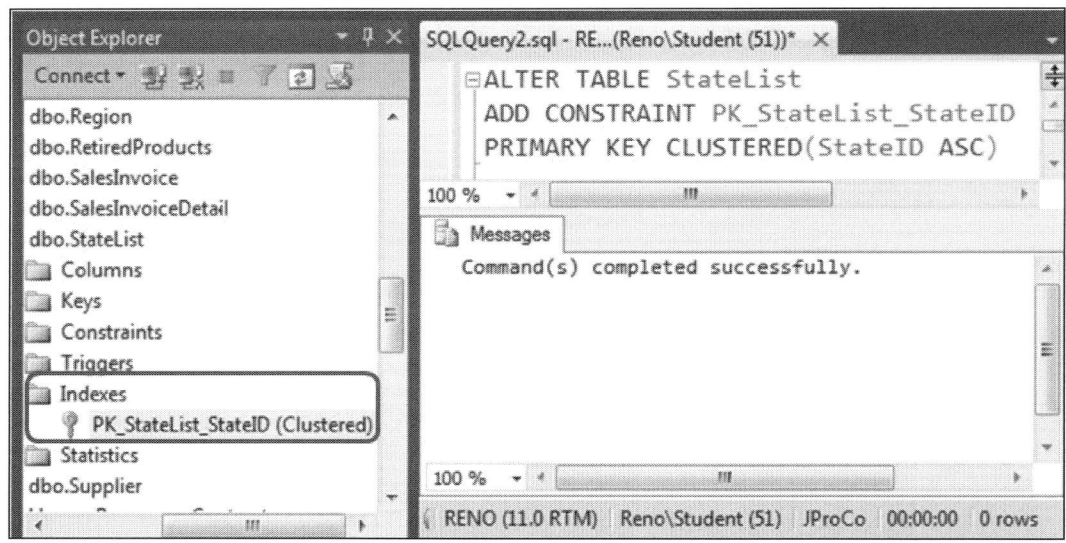

Figure 1.5 The Object Explorer shows us the creation of the primary key and a clustered index.

The purpose of PK_StateList_StateID is to prevent duplicate StateID values from entering our table. To confirm whether this really protects the StateList table, Figure 1.6 attempts to change the StateList.StateID field of the Connecticut record back to CO with the following code:

```
UPDATE StateList
SET StateID = 'CO'
WHERE StateProvinceName = 'Connecticut'
```

```
Messages
Msg 2627, Level 14, State 1, Line 1
Violation of PRIMARY KEY constraint 'PK_StateList_StateID'. Cannot insert
duplicate key in object 'dbo.StateList'. The duplicate key value is (CO).
The statement has been terminated.
                                                                    0 rows
```

Figure 1.6 PK_StateList_StateID prevents duplicate StateID values in the StateList table.

The error message demonstrates that PK_StateList_StateID has detected a violation and will prevent the update from running (Figure 1.6).

CHECK constraints

My old track coach would tell us to give 110% effort. However, had my math teacher heard this, he would have explained that a percentage value exceeding 100% in this context is actually a hyperbolic, exaggerated figure. It implies that you will give all you have, but then somehow you will give 10% more than "all". Does that mean 110% is always an incorrect value? No, it depends on the situation. For example, this year's sales could be 110% of last year's sales. The range of acceptable values defined for a field depends upon the context.

Let's consider negative numbers for a moment. If a form asked for my height in inches, and I wrote -67.5, you would think this was either a typo or a joke. That figure would be easily accepted by a decimal or float data type, but in the context of height, a negative number simply isn't acceptable. A person's height will always be a positive number, never a negative number. For that reason, a "Height" field in a database should be restricted to only positive values. If you want to add your own logic on top of a data type, you can use what is known as a **check constraint**.

Returning to the StateList table, all is well with respect to protection from the risk of duplicate StateID values. But there are other possible erroneous updates or inserts we haven't yet prevented. For example, the "District of Columbia" consists of 68 square miles of land. However, we see a negative LandMass value for a few records, including the District of Columbia, in the StateList field (Figure 1.7).

```
SELECT *
FROM StateList
WHERE LandMass < 0
```

	StateID	StateName	RegionName	LandMass
1	DC	District of Columbia	USA-Continental	-68
2	DE	Delaware	USA-Continental	-2489
3	RI	Rhode Island	USA-Continental	-1545

3 rows

Figure 1.7 Some records (e.g., District of Columbia) show a negative LandMass number.

Similar to the concept of height, there really is no such thing as a negative land mass (coastal erosion anomalies aside) We know that the absolute value for each LandMass number in our table is correct, so we essentially just need to change any negative figures to positive numbers (e.g., -68 should be 68). The following UPDATE statement (Figure 1.8) multiplies the LandMass value by -1 where the existing LandMass value is < 0 (less than zero). The SELECT query in Figure 1.8 shows that no negative LandMass values remain following the update.

```
UPDATE StateList SET LandMass = LandMass * -1
WHERE LandMass < 0

SELECT *
FROM StateList
WHERE LandMass < 0
```

StateID	StateName	Region	LandMass

0 rows

Figure 1.8 There are no negative LandMass values remaining in the StateList table.

Creating CHECK constraints

Our LandMass data has been scrubbed and now we want to create the check constraint to maintain this field's data integrity during future inserts or updates. Last time, we used a primary key to prevent bad entries in StateID, but that won't solve the LandMass problem. A primary key wouldn't prevent negative values. As well, a primary key would enforce uniqueness of each LandMass value. This would be incorrect business logic because it is perfectly acceptable for two states to have the same LandMass.

We want SQL Server to say "Yes" to duplicate LandMass values but "No" to any update or INSERT Statement resulting in a negative LandMass value. The check constraint in Figure 1.9 will check to see if the value is positive before accepting the transaction. The preferred naming convention for the check constraint is similar to the primary key convention. CK for check (constraint) plus the table name and the fieldname, with each part separated by an underscore: CK_StateList_LandMass.

```
ALTER TABLE StateList
ADD Constraint CK_StateList_LandMass
CHECK(LandMass >=0)
```

Messages
Command(s) completed successfully.

0 rows

Figure 1.9 Use an ALTER TABLE statement to add a new constraint to an existing table.

To prove that our check constraint will prevent DML statements which try to introduce negative LandMass numbers, we will run a quick test. Below, you see an UPDATE statement which attempts to change some of the LandMass values into negative numbers. The CK_StateList_LandMass check constraint guards against updates which would result in invalid LandMass values (Figure 1.10).

```
UPDATE StateList SET LandMass = -1
WHERE LandMass BETWEEN 68 AND 5000
```

```
Messages
Msg 547, Level 16, State 0, Line 1
The UPDATE statement conflicted with the CHECK constraint
"CK_StateList_LandMass". The conflict occurred in database "JProCo", table
"dbo.StateList", column 'LandMass'.
The statement has been terminated.
0 rows
```

Figure 1.10 Trying to update the LandMass field to a negative number no longer works.

Figure 1.11 shows the CK_StateList_LandMass check constraint that we just added. In Object Explorer, expand the "Tables" folder of the JProCo database and expand Constraints. *Note:* You may need to right-click to refresh the Constraints folder and see newly created items.

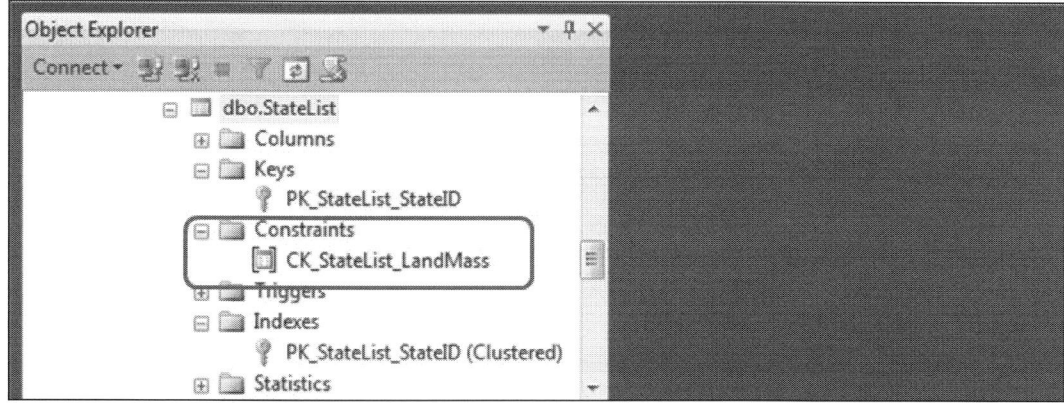

Figure 1.11 The CK_StateList_LandMass check constraint is inside the Constraints folder (a.k.a., the Constraints node) of the StateList table.

Let's consider other errors which could occur in our LandMass data. Our largest current LandMass is Alaska at just over 650,000 square miles. A typo adding one or two extra zeros would really be a problem (i.e., distorting Alaska's LandMass to either 6 million or 65 million miles). Let's attempt a bad UPDATE to help us recognize that our check constraint isn't currently protecting our table from these kinds of mistakes:

```
UPDATE StateList
SET LandMass = 65642500
WHERE StateID = 'AK'
```

Since the UPDATE succeeded, our StateList table now incorrectly indicates that Alaska's LandMass exceeds 65 million square miles. While constraints can't guard against all potential data integrity problems, we should constrain the upper limit of the LandMass field to disallow such glaringly large, erroneous values.

Before proceeding, let's reset Alaska's LandMass back to its proper value:

```
UPDATE StateList
SET LandMass = 656425
WHERE StateID = 'AK'
```

Changing Existing CHECK constraints

We want to add another condition to CK_StateList_LandMass, our existing check constraint for the LandMass field. Note: While SQL Server Management Studio (SSMS) offers some options for adding, modifying, and deleting check constraints by clicking through the Object Explorer interface, all of our solutions will be based in T-SQL code.

There isn't a T-SQL statement which allows us to directly modify our existing check constraint. But we can easily accomplish our purpose by dropping the current constraint object and then rebuilding it with both conditions (values for LandMass must be non-negative and less than 2 million square miles).

Run the DROP CONSTRAINT statement:

```
ALTER TABLE StateList
DROP CONSTRAINT CK_StateList_LandMass
GO
```

Re-create CK_StateList_LandMass with expressions covering both of the conditions which we want the constraint to prevent (LandMass >= 0 and LandMass < 2000000) use the following code:

```
ALTER TABLE StateList
ADD CONSTRAINT CK_StateList_LandMass
CHECK(LandMass >=0 AND LandMass < 2000000)
```

To test whether our revised constraint works, let's reattempt our earlier UPDATE statements seen in the following code:

```
UPDATE StateList
SET LandMass = 65642500
WHERE StateID = 'AK'

UPDATE StateList
SET LandMass = 656425
WHERE StateID = 'AK'
```

Our first condition (LandMass >= 0) is enforced by the revised check constraint. Non-negative values are disallowed for the LandMass field (Figure 1.12).

```
UPDATE StateList SET LandMass = LandMass * -1
WHERE LandMass BETWEEN 68 AND 5000
```

```
Messages
Msg 547, Level 16, State 0, Line 1
The UPDATE statement conflicted with the CHECK constraint
"CK_StateList_LandMass". The conflict occurred in database "JProCo", table
"dbo.StateList", column 'LandMass'.
The statement has been terminated.
                                                                    0 rows
```

Figure 1.12 The check constraint blocks any DML statement which would place negative values in the LandMass field.

Our second requirement (LandMass < 2000000) is similarly enforced by the revised check constraint. Values in excess of 2 million (square miles) are disallowed for the LandMass field (Figure 1.13).

```
UPDATE StateList
SET LandMass = 65642500
WHERE StateID = 'AK'
```

```
Messages
Msg 547, Level 16, State 0, Line 1
The UPDATE statement conflicted with the CHECK constraint
"CK_StateList_LandMass". The conflict occurred in database "JProCo", table
"dbo.StateList", column 'LandMass'.
The statement has been terminated.
                                                                    0 rows
```

Figure 1.13 The check constraint blocks any DML statement which would place values greater than 2 million in the LandMass field.

You may also wish to perform additional testing to observe the check constraint allows valid transactions into the StateList table. Afterward, remember to rerun the setup script SQLProgrammingChapter1.0Setup.sql (i.e., to reset your StateList table) before performing any examples involving the StateList table.

Lab 1.1: Introduction to Constraints

Lab Prep: Each lab has one or more Skill Checks. Start with Skill Check 1 and proceed until reaching the Points to Ponder section.

Before beginning this lab, verify that SQL Server 2012 is properly installed and operating. Before running the lab setup script for resetting the database (SQLQueries2012Vol4Chapter1.1Setup.sql), please make sure to close all query windows within SSMS. An open query window pointing to a database context can lock that database preventing it from updating when the script is executing. A simple way to assure all query windows are closed, is to exit out of SSMS, then open a new instance of SSMS, and lastly run the setup script.

Skill Check 1: Create a primary key constraint called PK_RetiredProducts_ProductID on the RetiredProducts table, that duplicates are prevented from occurring in the ProductID field. Make sure the primary key also creates a clustered index. As shown in Figure 1.14.

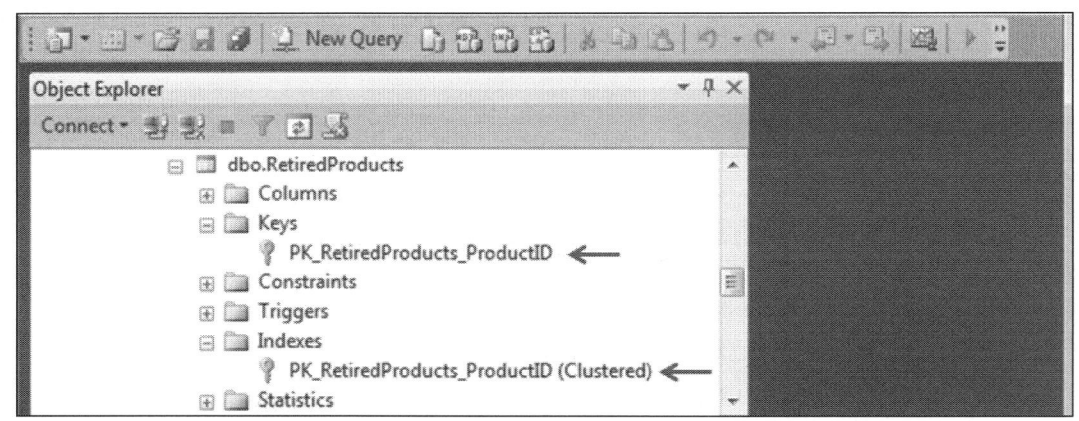

Figure 1.14 Skill Check 1 Object Explorer.

Skill Check 2: Create a primary key constraint on the R_ID field of the HumanResources.RoomChart table. Make sure the primary key also creates a clustered index.

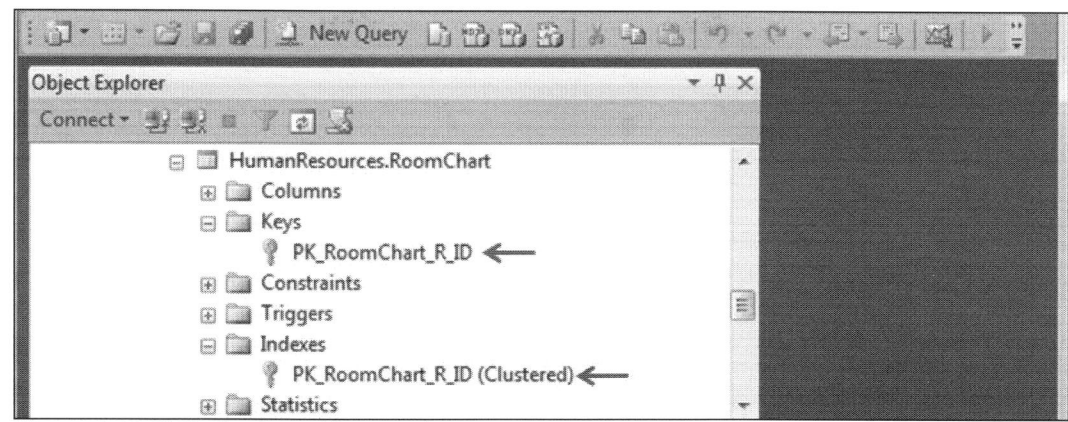

Figure 1.15 Skill Check 2 Object Explorer.

Skill Check 3: Create a CHECK constraint to make sure that the UnitDiscount field of the SalesInvoiceDetail table does not allow negative values. Test your constraint by trying to update the UnitDiscount field with a negative value as seen in Figure 1.16.

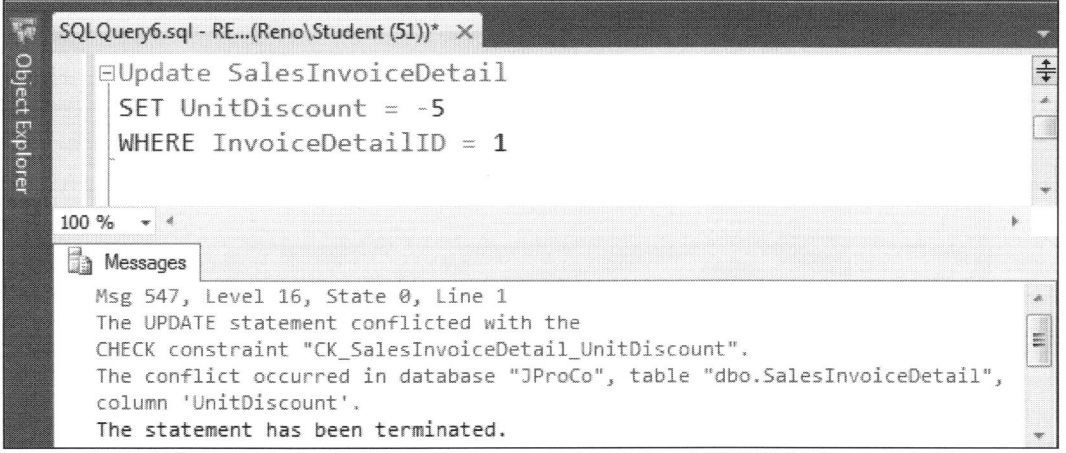

Figure 1.16 Skill Check 3 result does not allow negative values in the UnitDiscount field.

Skill Check 4: Create a constraint called CK_SalesInvoice_PaidDate, for the SalesInvoice table, which checks to see that the PaidDate is never earlier than the OrderDate. The PaidDate can be the same as the OrderDate or it can be any date subsequent to the OrderDate. Test your code by trying to update a PaidDate value to occur before the OrderDate for InvoiceID 1.

Skill Check 5: On the MgmtTraining table, create a check constraint called CK_MgmtTraining_ApprovedDate that only allows ApprovedDate values of '1/1/2006' or newer.

Answer Code: The T-SQL code to this lab can be found in the downloadable files in a file named Lab1.1_IntroductionToConstraints.sql.

Points to Ponder - Introduction to Constraints

1. Data integrity is the consistency and accuracy of the data which is stored in a database.
2. Good data integrity produces high quality, reliable data.
3. A constraint is a table column property which performs data validation. Using constraints, you can maintain database integrity by preventing invalid data from being entered.
4. Constraints can be added to, or dropped from, tables using the ALTER TABLE statement.
5. You can add constraints to a table that already has data.
6. A table can only have one primary key.
7. Primary keys cannot accept NULL values, but unique indexes can.
8. A check constraint restricts the values that users can enter into a particular column during INSERT and UPDATE statements.
9. Column level check constraints restrict the values that can be stored in a column.
10. Table level check constraints reference multiple columns in the same table to allow for cross-referencing and comparison of values.
11. A check constraint can be any logical expression that returns true or false.
12. Tip: If necessary, you can temporarily disable a CHECK constraint. However, data integrity will not be enforced while the constraint is disabled. Disabling and enabling constraints is outside of the scope of this book.

Unique Constraints

Since we created a primary key on the StateID field, no StateID value can be repeated. Thus, we have ensured each StateID value will be unique. In other words, two states will never have the same StateID (Figure 1.17).

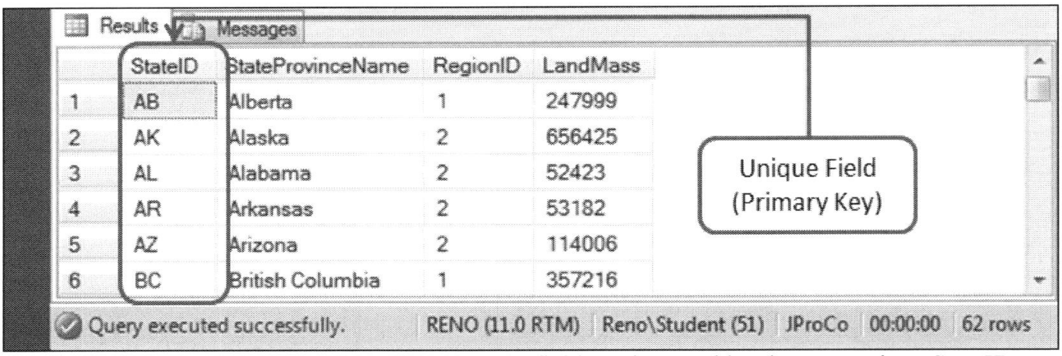

	StateID	StateProvinceName	RegionID	LandMass
1	AB	Alberta	1	247999
2	AK	Alaska	2	656425
3	AL	Alabama	2	52423
4	AR	Arkansas	2	53182
5	AZ	Arizona	2	114006
6	BC	British Columbia	1	357216

Figure 1.17 With the primary key on the StateID field, each record has its own unique StateID.

However, there is no constraint on the StateProvinceName field. Currently the only requirement for a StateProvinceName value is that it be compatible with a VARCHAR(50) data type or that it be NULL. We would like to ensure uniqueness for each StateProvinceName value. Since a table may only have one primary key, and StateList already has a primary key (StateID), we'll need another way to ensure uniqueness of this field.

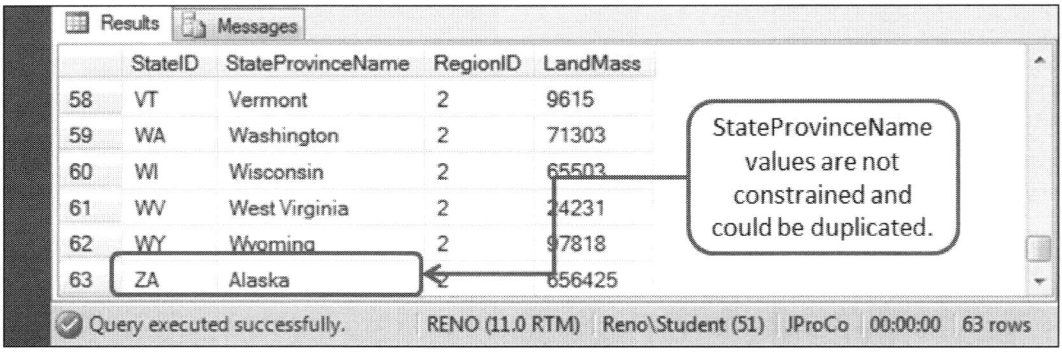

	StateID	StateProvinceName	RegionID	LandMass
58	VT	Vermont	2	9615
59	WA	Washington	2	71303
60	WI	Wisconsin	2	65503
61	WV	West Virginia	2	24231
62	WY	Wyoming	2	97818
63	ZA	Alaska	2	656425

Figure 1.18 We want to ensure uniqueness of the StateProvinceName field.

While tables are limited to a single primary key field, SQL Server allows multiple *unique constraints* to be added to a table.

Comparing Unique Constraints to Primary Keys

Unique constraints have two main differences versus primary keys:
- o Unique constraints will allow a NULL value. If a field is nullable then a unique constraint will allow at most one NULL value (i.e., since all values must be unique).
- o SQL Server allows many unique constraints per table where it allows just one primary key per table.

Creating Unique Constraints

Now let's write the statement which will add a unique constraint to the StateProvinceName field. Our object name will begin with UQ (for **unique constraint**) but otherwise will follow the naming convention for the other constraints which we've built in this chapter: The code to create the UQ_TableName_FieldName constraint is seen in the following code:

```
ALTER TABLE StateList
ADD CONSTRAINT UQ_StateList_StateProvinceName
UNIQUE(StateProvinceName)
GO
```

Let's test our new constraint by attempting to insert a record which would duplicate the StateProvinceName Alaska. Success! The constraint disallows the insert.

```
INSERT INTO StateList VALUES('ZA', 'Alaska', 2, 656425)
```

```
Messages
Msg 2627, Level 14, State 1, Line 1
Violation of UNIQUE KEY constraint 'UQ_StateList_StateProvinceName'. Cannot
insert duplicate key in object 'dbo.StateList'. The duplicate key value is
(Alaska).
The statement has been terminated.

                                                                      0 rows
```

Figure 1.19 The unique constraint does not allow you to insert 'Alaska' twice.

Let's turn to the RoomChart table for our next example. An earlier Skill Check exercise added a primary key constraint to the R_ID field. Suppose we are given a new requirement that no two RoomDescription values should be duplicated in the RoomChart table (Figure 1.20).

```
SELECT *
FROM HumanResources.RoomChart
```

R_ID	R_Code	RoomName	RoomDescription	RoomNotes	RoomLocation
1	1	RLT	Renault-Langsford...	This room is designed for Customer Previews	NULL	NULL
2	2	QTX	Quinault-Experience	Parties and Moral events get top priority	NULL	NULL
3	3	TQW	TranquilWest	Misc	NULL	NULL
4	4	XW	XavierWest	NULL	NULL	NULL
5	5	YRD	Yard	Industrial Yard Space	Outdoor	0x0000000...
6	6	WRS	Warehouse	Company Main Warehouse	Indoor	0x0000000...

Figure 1.20 No two RoomDescription fields can be the same in the RoomChart table.

We need to add a unique constraint to the RoomDescription field. Our new unique constraint, UQ_RoomChart_RoomDescription, will prevent duplicate descriptions from appearing in this field:

```
ALTER TABLE StateList
ADD CONSTRAINT UQ_RoomChart_RoomDescription
UNIQUE(RoomDescription)
GO
```

Unique Constraint Considerations

Open Object Explorer and look at the details for the HumanResources.RoomChart table. The Columns folder contains the specifics for each field in the RoomChart table (field name, data type, and nullability)

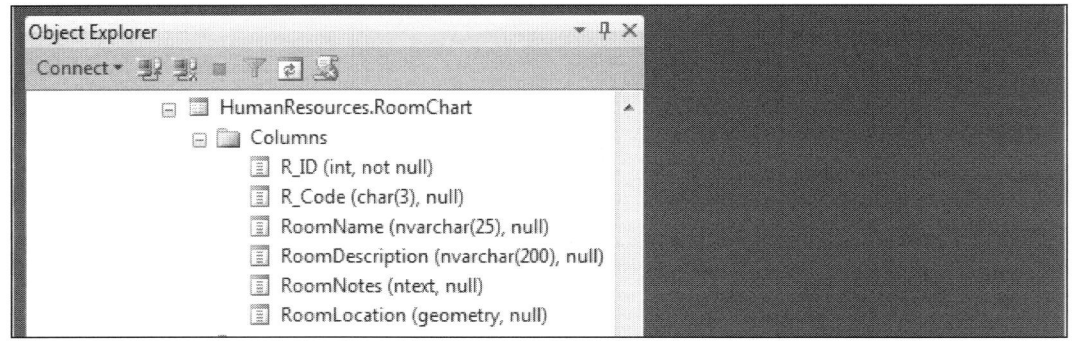

- HumanResources.RoomChart
  - Columns
    - R_ID (int, not null)
    - R_Code (char(3), null)
    - RoomName (nvarchar(25), null)
    - RoomDescription (nvarchar(200), null)
    - RoomNotes (ntext, null)
    - RoomLocation (geometry, null)

Figure 1.21 RoomDescription is an NVARCHAR(200) field that can take up to 400 bytes in your memory page.

We just added a unique constraint to the RoomDescription field, which is an NVARCHAR(200). Thus far, that's the biggest field to which we've added a unique constraint. Each value in this field could take up to 400 bytes.

Suppose we receive an additional requirement saying that no two RoomNotes values may be duplicated. The RoomNotes field is an NTEXT data type. When you try to run the ALTER TABLE statement adding the unique constraint, you get an error message which references a problem with the data type. You cannot put a unique constraint on a field having a data type over 900 bytes.

```
ALTER TABLE HumanResources.RoomChart
ADD CONSTRAINT UQ_RoomChart_RoomNotes
UNIQUE(RoomNotes)
GO
```

```
Messages
Msg 1919, Level 16, State 1, Line 1
Column 'RoomNotes' in table 'RoomChart' is of a type that is invalid for use
as a key column in an index.
Msg 1750, Level 16, State 0, Line 1
Could not create constraint. See previous errors.
                                                                    0 rows
```

Figure 1.22 A unique constraint can't be added to a field with a data type over 900 bytes.

Unique constraints are limited to data types that are 900 bytes, or less. Examples of data types that cannot be made into a unique constraint are: TEXT, NTEXT, IMAGE, GEOGRAPHY, NVARCHAR(MAX) and VARCHAR(MAX), VARCHAR (901) and higher, and NVARCHAR(451) and higher.

Lab 1.2: Unique Constraints

Lab Prep: Each lab has one or more Skill Checks. Start with Skill Check 1 and proceed until reaching the Points to Ponder section.

Before beginning this lab, verify that SQL Server 2012 is properly installed and operating. Before running the lab setup script for resetting the database (SQLQueries2012Vol4Chapter1.2Setup.sql), please make sure to close all query windows within SSMS. An open query window pointing to a database context can lock that database preventing it from updating when the script is executing. A simple way to assure all query windows are closed, is to exit out of SSMS, then open a new instance of SSMS, and lastly run the setup script.

Skill Check 1: Create a unique constraint called UQ_RoomChart_RoomName on the RoomName field of the RoomChart table. Verify the new constraint in the Keys folder Object Explorer.

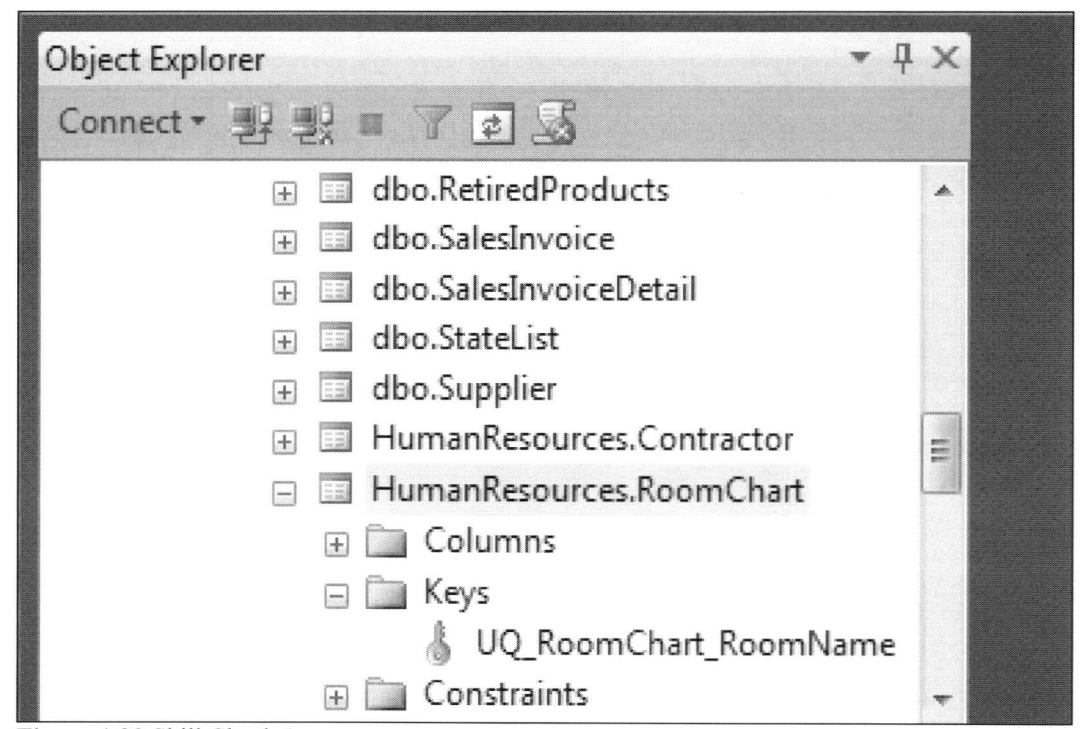

Figure 1.23 Skill Check 1.

Chapter 1. Constraints

Skill Check 2: Create a unique constraint called UQ_MgmtTraining_ClassName on the ClassName field of the MgmtTraining table. Verify the new constraint in the Keys folder Object Explorer.

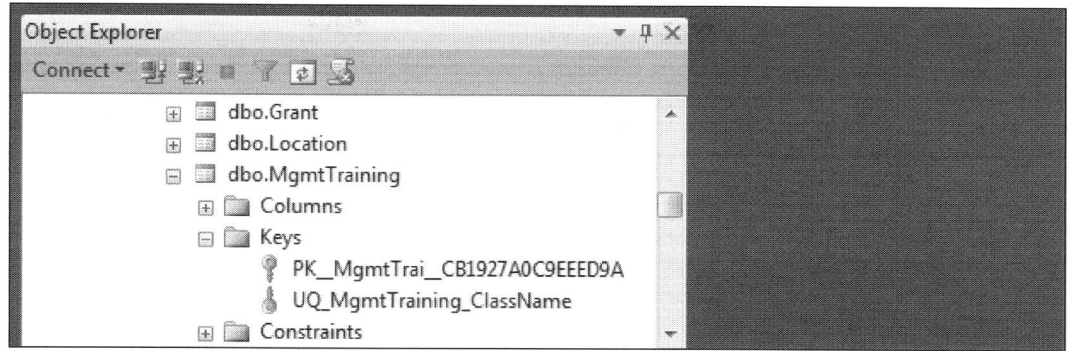

Figure 1.24 Skill Check 2

Skill Check 3: Management wants unique constraints on the HumanResources.Vendor table. They say the Email will never be duplicated and neither will Description. Write the code to create one of these constraints and a comment on why the other is not possible *(READERNOTE: There is no result figure for Skill Check 3, since it would give away the answer).*

Answer Code: The T-SQL code to this lab can be found in the downloadable files in a file named Lab1.2_UniqueConstraints.sql.

Points to Ponder - Unique Constraints

1. Unique constraints ensure a column will never contain duplicate values.
2. Unique constraints will allow up to one NULL value.
3. If your data type does not allow NULLs and you put a unique constraint on it, then your field will have no NULL values.
4. A table can have only one primary key but it may have many unique constraints.
5. Unique constraints on fields cannot include LOB types like TEXT, VARCHAR(max), IMAGE, and XML.
6. Unique constraints cannot be placed on fields using the sparse data type feature (The sparse data option is covered in *SQL Queries 2012 Joes 2 Pros Volume 3*, Chapter 4.).
7. Unique constraints can be applied on a composite of multiple fields to ensure uniqueness of records.
   Example: City + State in the StateList table.

Default Constraints

Another useful tool for protecting table data is the establishment of **default values** wherever possible.

Until this point in the *Joes 2 Pros* series, most of the values we've entered into empty fields have been our own user-supplied values or a function (e.g., CURRENT_TIMESTAMP). The only alternative we've seen is the possible use of a NULL value (i.e., assuming the field is nullable). Non-nullable fields are helpful for steering your users into providing data, rather than leaving null values. A field having some data is usually preferable to no data, but you have no guarantee the data will be clean (i.e., free of typos or errors) or even meaningful.

Even if the default value is a temporary placeholder (as we will see in our first example), supplying a default value reduces the likelihood of NULL values in your data because you've offered users a reasonable value for those fields.

Defaults are the only type of constraints which don't actually restrict data entry. Unless the default value is the only possible value for a field, users are able to enter their own value.

Creating and Using Default Constraints

A default constraint may be added to a field in an existing table (using ALTER TABLE), or it may be added to a field at the time you create a table (using CREATE TABLE – this will be shown in the final section of this chapter).

Our first example will add a default constraint to the Status field of the Employee table. As we can see from the current dataset, the status for most of our employees is "Active" (Figure 1.25). Recall that the newest hires (i.e., Janis Smith and Phil Wilconkinski) arrived two years ago. Both employees were hired in 2009 andJProCo is currently experiencing an upswing in activity and needs to hire a number of additional people. They have developed a thorough orientation and onboarding process to ramp up new hires on the company's businesses and processes, as well as role-specific training.

The new Status category "Orientation" has been added to the business requirements for the Employee table. All new hire records will receive the "Orientation" Status by default. After each employee completes the extensive onboarding process, the Status will be upgraded to "Active".

```sql
SELECT *
FROM Employee
```

Figure 1.25 The Status field of the Employee table is upgraded to 'Active' after Orientation.

First we will alter the Employee table to add this default constraint on the Status field. Then we will add several of JProCo's new hires to the Employee table.

The syntax to add the *default constraint* is similar to the other constraints we create in this chapter. We begin with an ALTER TABLE statement, an ADD CONSTRAINT clause which names the constraint (DF_TableName_FieldName), and finally a clause which defines the specific behavior of the constraint. In this case, the specific behavior is that "Orientation" will be the default value for the Status field. See the following code:

```sql
ALTER TABLE dbo.Employee
ADD CONSTRAINT DF_Employee_Status
DEFAULT 'Orientation' FOR [Status]
GO
```

When you type this code into your query window, try removing the delimiting brackets around the keyword Status and notice that it turns blue. This is because Status is a reserved keyword. In this instance, SQL Server will allow the statement to complete even without the brackets. But because this isn't always the case, the best practice recommendation is to bracket reserved words when you use them as names of database objects (e.g., the State field, the Grant table, and the Status field). This also helps keep the color scheme of your coding consistent (e.g., keywords appear in one color, database objects appear in another color, and so forth).

Before we see DF_Employee_Status in action, let's briefly look at the changes visible in SSMS following the creation of this new default constraint (Figure 1.26). The only change to the Object Explorer tree appears to be the addition of

DF_Employee_Status in the Constraints folder of the Employee table. The design view of the Employee table hasn't changed (Figure 1.26). However, the Column Properties tab now shows the Default Value or Binding ("Orientation").

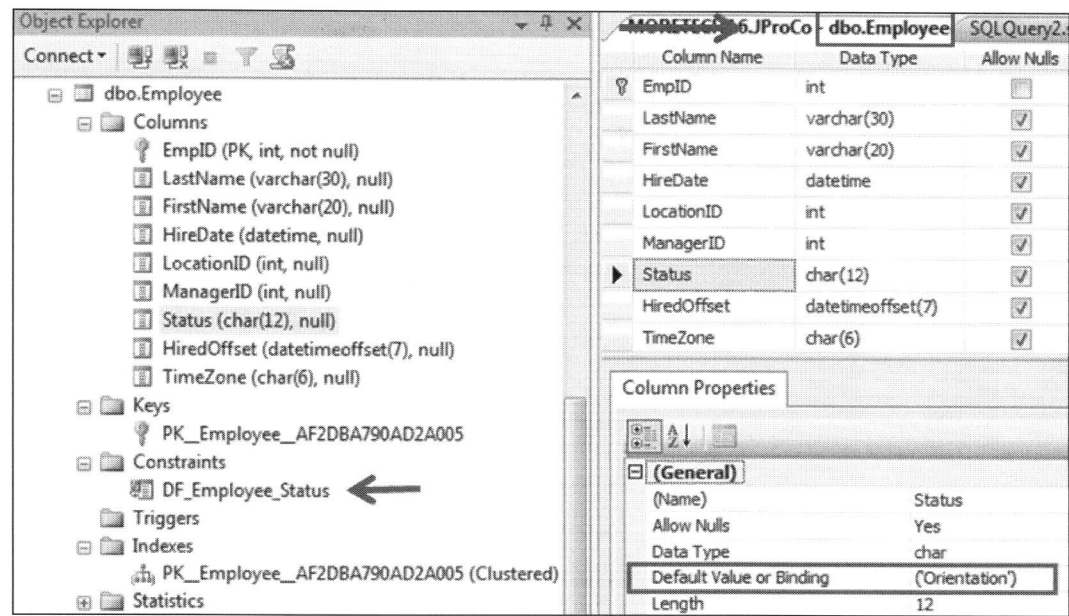

Figure 1.26 The Object Explorer tree and the design view of dbo.Employee following creation of the default constraint DF_Employee_Status.

Let's begin by adding the newest JProCo hire and see the effect of our new default constraint (Figure 1.27). Tess Jones is the employee and she will work in the Seattle office (Location 1) for Manager 11. Since Tess hasn't yet completed the orientation process, her Status must be the default value ("Orientation").

In order to better visualize each field and value, we've copied the Column names from the Object Explorer (click and drag the Columns folder icon into the query window) and are inserting the values by name, instead of position (Figure 1.27). *READERNOTE:* Inserting values by name and by position is covered in *SQL Queries 2012 Joes 2 Pros Volume 2*, Chap 3, p. 116.

After running the INSERT INTO statement, we run the SELECT query (shown in the lower query window) to see all 15 Employee records, including Tess Jones and her Status value of "Orientation" (Figure 1.27).

```
INSERT INTO Employee
(EmpID, LastName, FirstName, HireDate, LocationID,
ManagerID, [Status], HiredOffset, TimeZone)
VALUES
(15, 'Jones', 'Tess', CURRENT_TIMESTAMP, 1, 11,
DEFAULT, NULL, '-08:00')
SELECT * FROM Employee
```

	EmpID	LastName	FirstName	HireDate	LocationID	ManagerID	Status	HiredO
10	10	O'Haire	Terry	2004-10-04…	2	3	Active	2004-
11	11	Smith	Sally	1989-04-01…	1	NULL	Active	1989-0
12	12	O'Neil	Barbara	1995-05-26…	4	4	Has Tenure	1995-0
13	13	Wilconki…	Phil	2009-06-11…	1	4	Active	2009-0
14	14	Smith	Janis	2009-10-18…	1	4	Active	2009-
15	15	Jones	Tess	2012-10-04…	1	11	Orientation	NULL

Figure 1.27 Using the Default keyword in this INSERT Statement has the same effect as explicitly inserting the value "Orientation" into the Status field.

Notice that the TimeZone field indicates that nearly all of JProCo's employees work in the same TimeZone (-08:00, signifying GMT minus 8 hours, which corresponds to Pacific Time and includes the west coasts of the U.S. and Canada).

Before we add our next new hire record, we will add the default value of -08:00 to the TimeZone field. The ALTER TABLE statement to accomplish this is similar to the statement we ran to create the default constraint on the Status field. Run the code you see here to create DF_Employee_TimeZone:

```
ALTER TABLE dbo.Employee
ADD CONSTRAINT DF_Employee_TimeZone
DEFAULT '-08:00'
FOR TimeZone
GO
```

When we add our next new hire record (for Nancy Biggs), we're able use both of our defaults. Nancy's initial status is Orientation, and she will work in the Seattle Headquarters, which is in the -8:00 time zone. The second default keyword will use the value from the DF_Employee_TimeZone default constraint (Figure 1.28).

```
INSERT INTO Employee
(EmpID, LastName, FirstName, HireDate, LocationID,
ManagerID, [Status], HiredOffset, TimeZone)
VALUES
(16, 'Biggs', 'Nancy', CURRENT_TIMESTAMP, 1, 11, DEFAULT,
NULL, DEFAULT)
```

```
Messages
(1 row(s) affected)
```
                                                                                            0 rows

Figure 1.28 We want -08:00 to be the default value for the last field of the Employee table.

Let's run a SELECT statement to see all 16 records in the Employee table, including the new record for Nancy Biggs. Notice that Nancy's TimeZone value is -08:00, as we expected (Figure 1.29).

```
SELECT * FROM Employee
```

	EmpID	LastName	FirstName	HireDate	LocationID	ManagerID	Status	HiredOffset	TimeZone
11	11	Smith	Sally	1989-04-01...	1	NULL	Active	1989-04-01...	-08:00
12	12	O'Neil	Barbara	1995-05-26...	4	4	Has Tenure	1995-05-26...	-08:00
13	13	Wilconkinski	Phil	2009-06-11...	1	4	Active	2009-06-11...	-08:00
14	14	Smith	Janis	2009-10-18...	1	4	Active	2009-10-18...	-08:00
15	15	Jones	Tess	2012-10-04...	1	11	Orientation	NULL	-08:00
16	16	Biggs	Nancy	2012-10-04...	1	11	Orientation	NULL	-08:00

Query executed successfully.   RENO (11.0 RTM)   Reno\Student (51)   JProCo   00:00:00   16 rows

Figure 1.29 Nancy Biggs' record shows both default values, Orientation and -08:00.

Dynamic Defaults

You may notice that each employee record includes their HireDate as well as a HiredOffset value, which is a combination of HireDate + TimeZone.

A default constraint can make coding of dynamic values much easier for reuse. Our next step will be to add a default constraint to the HiredOffset field. Being able to type "Default" in an INSERT statement rather than a lengthy expression saves us a significant number of keystrokes and is a great use of the default constraint.

Alter the Employee table to add a constraint named **DF_Employee_HiredOffset** where the value will be an expression using the ToDateTimeOffset function with the CURRENT_TIMESTAMP property:

```
ALTER TABLE dbo.Employee
ADD CONSTRAINT DF_Employee_HiredOffset
DEFAULT TODATETIMEOFFSET(CURRENT_TIMESTAMP,'-08:00')
FOR HiredOffset
GO
```

We will now add the next new JProCo employee, Wendy Downs. Since Wendy will also work in the Seattle Headquarters office, we can use all three default values in her INSERT INTO statement:

```
INSERT INTO Employee
VALUES (17, 'Downs', 'Wendy', CURRENT_TIMESTAMP, 1, 11,
DEFAULT, DEFAULT, DEFAULT)
```

Let's rerun a SELECT statement to see all 17 records in the Employee table (Figure 1.30). We see all of Wendy's values appearing, as expected.

```
SELECT * FROM Employee
```

	EmpID	LastName	FirstName	HireDate	LocationID	ManagerID	Status	HiredOffset	TimeZone
12	12	O'Neil	Barbara	1995-05-26...	4	4	Has Tenure	1995-05-26...	-08:00
13	13	Wilconki...	Phil	2009-06-11...	1	4	Active	2009-06-11...	-08:00
14	14	Smith	Janis	2009-10-18...	1	4	Active	2009-10-18...	-08:00
15	15	Jones	Tess	2012-10-04...	1	11	Orientation	NULL	-08:00
16	16	Biggs	Nancy	2012-10-04...	1	11	Orientation	NULL	-08:00
17	17	Downs	Wendy	2012-10-04...	1	11	Orientation	2012-10-04...	-08:00

Figure 1.30 Wendy's record appears as we expected. The default value was inserted for 3 fields.

Overriding Default Constraints

To insert a record with a value other than the default, simply include the explicit value in the INSERT statement.

We will test this by attempting to insert a test record with "HIRE DELAYED" as the value for the Status field:

```
INSERT INTO Employee
VALUES (98, 'Test98', 'InsertRecord98', CURRENT_TIMESTAMP,
1, 11, 'HIRE DELAYED', DEFAULT, DEFAULT)
```

Our test inserted the value, as we expected. The Status value of our test record is "HIRE DELAYED" (Figure 1.31).

```
SELECT * FROM Employee
WHERE EmpID = 98
```

EmpID	LastName	FirstName	HireDate	LocationID	ManagerID	Status	HiredOffset
98	Test98	InsertRecord98	2012-10-04...	1	11	HIRE DELAYED	2012-10-04 13:32:30

Figure 1.31 Our explicit value HIRE DELAYED overrode the default.

Removing Default Constraints

The code syntax shown here will remove a default constraint, in case you no longer wish to have the default enabled on your field:

```
ALTER TABLE dbo.Employee
DROP DF_Employee_Status
GO

ALTER TABLE dbo.Employee
DROP DF_Employee_HiredOffset
GO
```

This inserted test record includes the default keyword for the two fields (Status and HiredOffset) which no longer have default constraints using the following code:

```
INSERT INTO Employee
VALUES (99, 'Test99', 'InsertRecord99', CURRENT_TIMESTAMP,
1, 11, DEFAULT, DEFAULT, DEFAULT)
```

The keyword "Default" in the INSERT Statement results in a NULL value for both fields (Figure 1.32).

```
SELECT * FROM Employee
WHERE EmpID = 99
```

EmpID	LastName	FirstName	HireDate	LocationID	ManagerID	Status	HiredOffset	TimeZone
99	Test99	InsertRecord99	2012-10-04...	1	11	NULL	NULL	-08:00

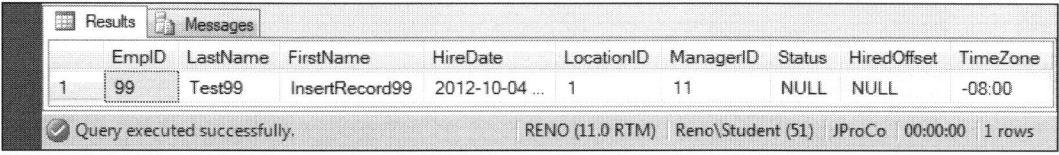

Figure 1.32 The default keyword added NULLs to the fields after 2 default constraints were removed.

Chapter 1. Constraints

Lab 1.3: Default Constraints

Lab Prep: Lab Prep: Each lab has one or more Skill Checks. Start with Skill Check 1 and proceed until reaching the Points to Ponder section.

Before beginning this lab, verify that SQL Server 2012 is properly installed and operating. Before running the lab setup script for resetting the database (SQLQueries2012Vol4Chapter1.3Setup.sql), please make sure to close all query windows within SSMS. An open query window pointing to a database context can lock that database preventing it from updating when the script is executing. A simple way to assure all query windows are closed, is to exit out of SSMS, then open a new instance of SSMS, and lastly run the setup script.

Skill Check 1: Create a default constraint named DF_Employee_LocationID that sets the default for the LocationID field of the Employee table to 1.

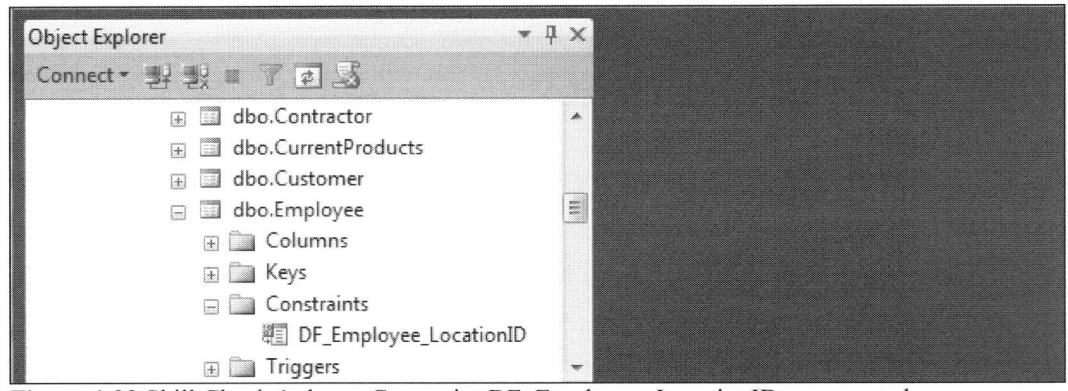

Figure 1.33 Skill Check 1 shows Constraint DF_Employee_LocationID was created.

Skill Check 2: Create a default constraint that sets the UnitDiscount field of the SalesInvoiceDetail table to 0 (zero). Use proper naming conventions for your constraint.

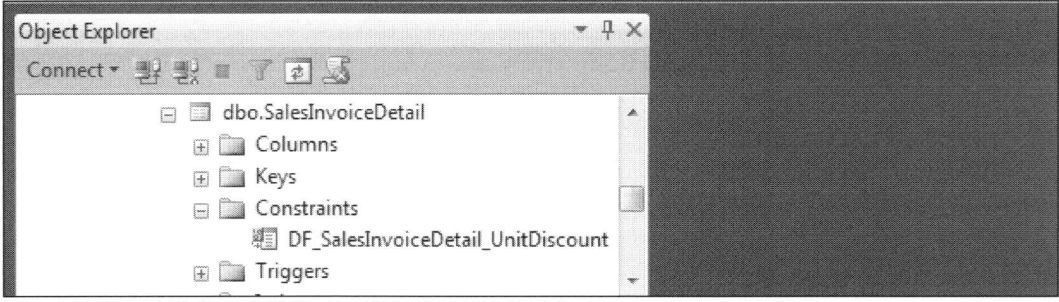

Figure 1.34 Skill Check 2 Shows Constraint DF_SalesInvoiceDetail_UnitDiscount was created.

Skill Check 3: Create a default constraint that sets the OrderDate field of the SalesInvoice table to the current date and time using the CURRENT_TIMESTAMP property.

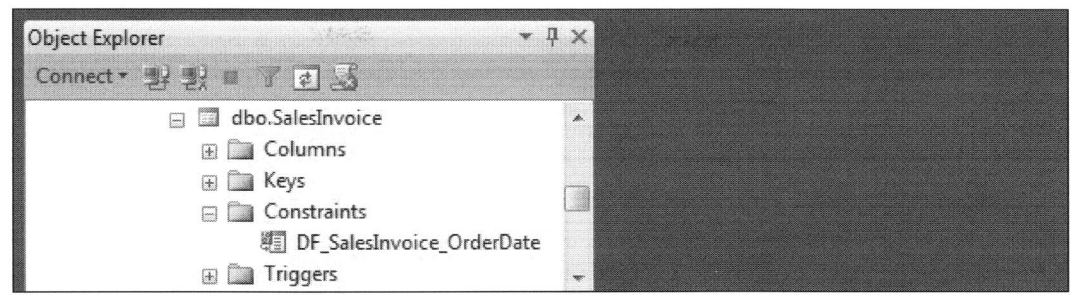

Figure 1.35 Skill Check 3 Shows Constraint DF_SalesInvoice_OrderDate was created.

Answer Code: The T-SQL code to this lab can be found in the downloadable files in a file named Lab1.3_DefaultConstraints.sql.

Points to Ponder - Default Constraints

1. A default constraint enters a value in a column when one is not specified in an INSERT or UPDATE statement.
2. The ALTER TABLE statement modifies a table definition by altering, adding, or dropping columns and constraints, reassigning partitions, or disabling or enabling constraints and triggers.
3. Default constraints can be created on fields in your table.
4. The DEFAULT keyword defines a value that is used if the user doesn't specify a value for the column.
5. Defaults may not be added to timestamp data types or to identity fields.
6. Defaults are the only type of constraints which don't actually restrict data entry.

Chapter 1. Constraints

Data Integrity

Dictionary definitions of the term "integrity" include helpful terms like incorruptibility, soundness, and wholeness. In the world of relational databases, the term "data integrity" denotes a system of processes and constraints established to ensure that data remains intact, adheres to business rules, and is not adversely impacted (i.e., corrupted) by user input or by database operations. The specific requirements to uphold data integrity will vary from database to database according to the purpose of the database and its attendant level of complexity and criticality.

Constraints are objects which support and enforce data integrity. Each of the constraints we've explored in this chapter plays a role in your data integrity strategy, which should be executed on three levels: *domain integrity*, *entity integrity*, and *referential integrity*.

- o **Domain integrity.** Only values which meet the criteria of the column should be allowed into the table. In other words, *domain integrity* is achieved when constraints ensure that each value allowed to be inserted into a column falls within the *domain* of acceptable values for the column. CHECK constraints help enforce domain integrity by rejecting any DML statement which would introduce unacceptable values.
- o **Entity integrity.** This principle defines each row as a unique entity in a table. Primary keys and unique constraints enforce *entity integrity*. They evaluate each proposed value, compare it to the set of existing values, and disallow any statement which would introduce an unacceptable value (i.e., NULL or non-unique).
- o **Referential integrity.** This principle involves fields which are present across your database tables. The foreign key constraint enforces the rule that columnar values referenced by another column (often within another table) must be in sync with the chief instance of the field. This is frequently accomplished with the help of lookup or mapping tables. *Example:* Each record in the Employee table includes the LocationID for the site where the employee works. LocationID is a primary key in the Location table. The Location table is the source of the master Location data – any column which references location data must look to the Location table in order to ensure that it contains accurate location data. The LocationID field in the Employee table is a foreign key. This foreign key ensures that only values from Location.LocationID will be allowed into the Employee.LocationID field. The foreign key constraint will reject

any DML statement which introduces a LocationID not found in Location.LocationID.

Since we've become well-versed in the various types of data constraints (data types, primary keys, check constraints, unique constraints, and default constraints). This will speed our comprehension of implementing data integrity methodology in our data model and database design. This section will also demonstrate the mechanics of foreign key constraints.

Domain Integrity

Recall the check constraint we enabled earlier on the StateList table, CK_StateList_LandMass. It allows only non-negative (>=0) values and those which are less than 2 million (square miles).

These constraints enforce our rules for valid data which should be allowed into the StateList table – good data is allowed in and bad data is kept out. This constraint preserves domain integrity in the StateList table (Figure 1.36).

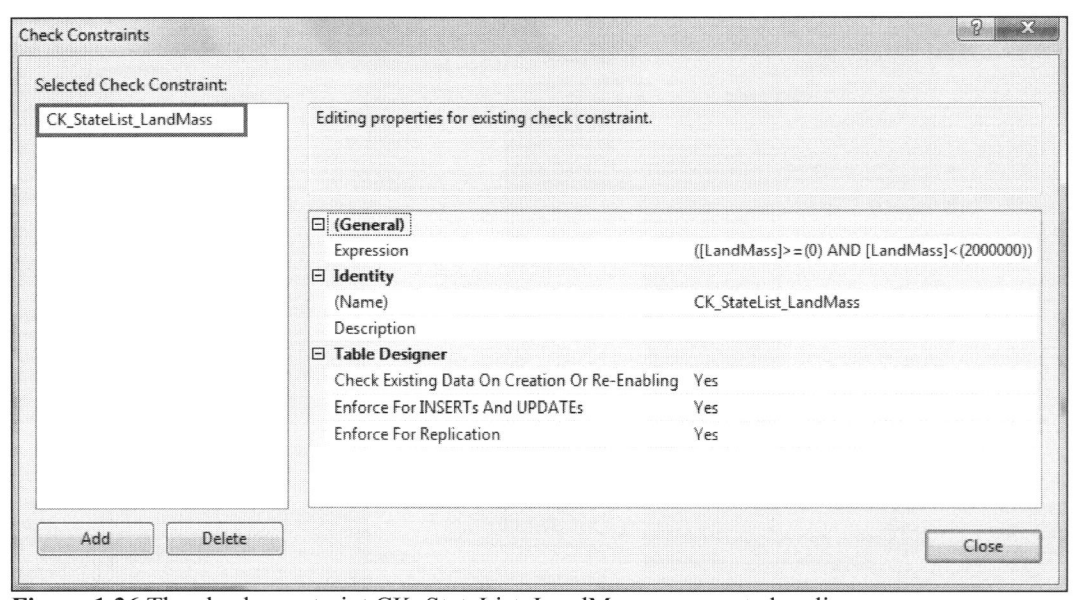

Figure 1.36 The check constraint CK_StateList_LandMass was created earlier.

(*Note:* The CHECK constraints dialog showing the properties may be seen by right-clicking the constraint in Object Explorer > Modify.)

The check constraint CK_StateList_LandMass blocks any DML statement which would place values greater than 2 million in the LandMass field.

```
UPDATE StateList
SET LandMass = 65642500
WHERE StateID = 'AK'
```

```
Messages
Msg 547, Level 16, State 0, Line 1
The UPDATE statement conflicted with the CHECK constraint
"CK_StateList_LandMass". The conflict occurred in database "JProCo", table
"dbo.StateList", column 'LandMass'
The statement has been terminated.

                                                                    0 rows
```

Figure 1.37 The check constraint enforces domain integrity.

Before the CK_StateList_LandMass check constraint allows a value into the LandMass field, it confirms whether the proposed value meets the criteria.

	StateID	StateProvinceName	RegionID	LandMass
8	CO	Colorado	2	104100
9	CT	Connecticut	2	5544
10	DC	District of Columbia	2	68
11	DE	Delaware	2	2489
12	FL	Florida	2	65758
13	GA	Georgia	2	59441

Is -68 valid? (NO)
Is 68 valid? (yes)

Query executed successfully. RENO (11.0 RTM) Reno\Student (51) JProCo 00:00:00 62 rows

Figure 1.38 Negative numbers are not valid values for the LandMass field.

Negative values and values >2 million are not allowed. This check constraint enforces *domain integrity*.

```
SELECT * FROM StateList
```

	StateID	StateProvinceName	RegionID	LandMass
1	AB	Alberta	1	247999
2	AK	Alaska	2	656425
3	AL	Alabama	2	52423
4	AR	Arkansas	2	53182
5	AZ	Arizona	2	114006
6	BC	British Columbia	1	357216

62 rows

Figure 1.39 A partial view of the dataset contained in the StateList table, which is protected by a check constraint. It is also protected by a primary key and unique constraint, which enforce *entity integrity*.

Entity Integrity

Because we've been focused on domain integrity, thus far we have ignored the primary key constraint which is also protecting the StateList table (Figure 1.37). Primary keys and unique constraints enforce *entity integrity*. Whereas *domain integrity* is concerned with protecting single values in a column, entity integrity is about protecting a table by ensuring the uniqueness of each record.

PK_StateList_StateID is responsible for ensuring that each StateID value is unique and non-null. With each value you attempt to add to the StateID field, the primary key checks all the existing values to confirm that the proposed value isn't already present in the field.

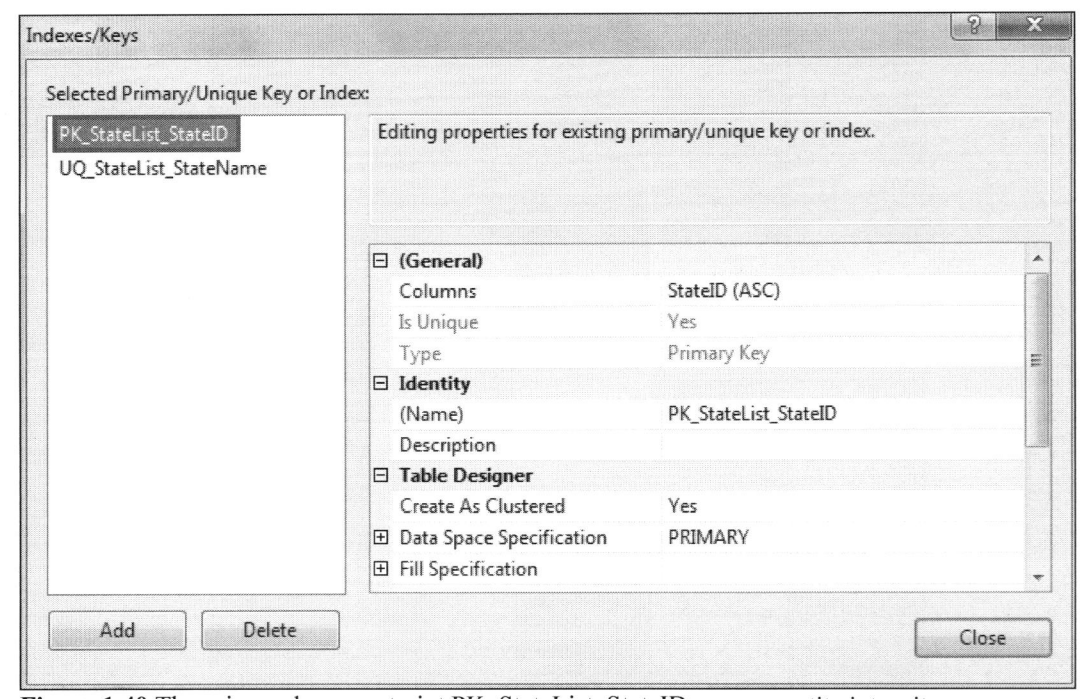

Figure 1.40 The primary key constraint PK_StateList_StateID ensures *entity integrity*.

The Indexes/Keys dialog (Figure 1.40 and Figure 1.41) may be seen by Opening **Databases** > **JProCo** > **dbo.StateList** > right-click and **Design** > then right-click in the design table UI > choose **Indexes/Keys**.

Chapter 1. Constraints

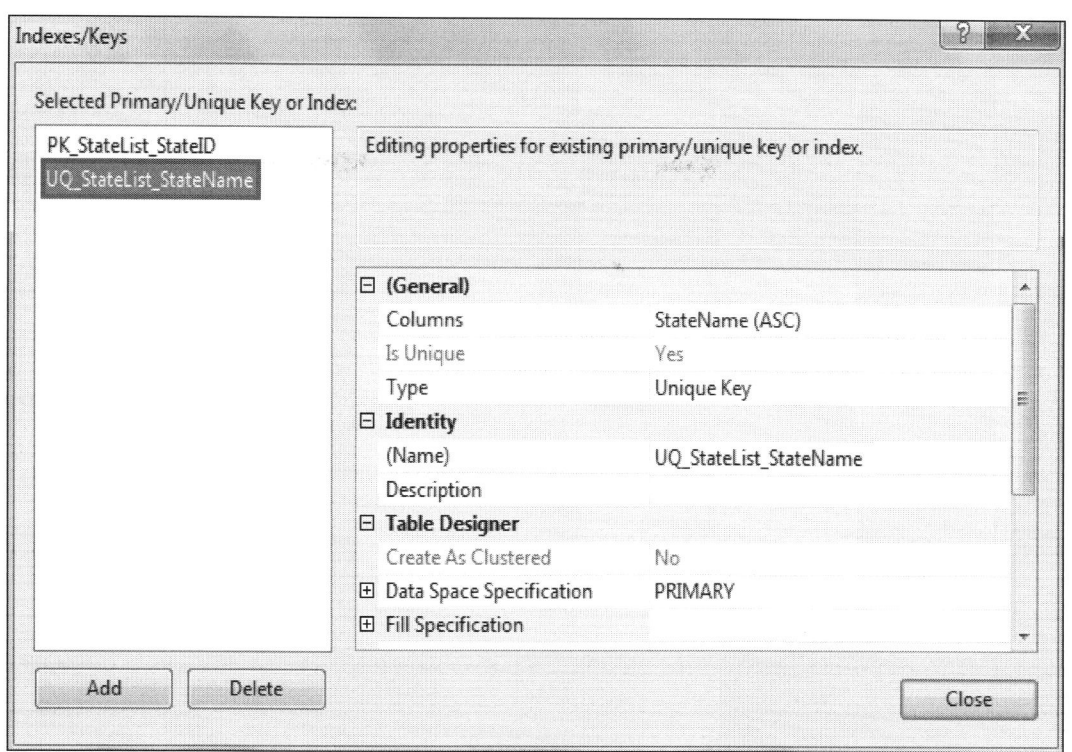

Figure 1.41 The unique constraint UQ_StateList_StateName was originally created earlier.

Readers who have previously worked hands-on with relational databases will already be aware of the heavy emphasis placed on having a primary key for every table in your database. By ensuring uniqueness and non-nullability for each value of the StateID field, we eliminate the possibility of duplicate records in the StateList table. This ensures the integrity of the StateList entity. Later in the discussion of referential integrity, we will also see that assuring integrity of the StateList entity at the field and table levels also helps ensure integrity of StateList in relation to other entities in the database.

As we saw earlier, this primary key constraint (PK_StateList_StateID) violation prevented the duplicate StateID value "CO" from entering the StateList table. The primary key rejects the value and effectively disallows the update (Figure 1.42).

```
UPDATE StateList SET StateID = 'CO'
WHERE StateProvinceName = 'Connecticut'
```

```
Message
Msg 2627, Level 14, State 1, Line 1
Violation of PRIMARY KEY constraint 'PK_StateList_StateID'. Cannot insert
duplicate key in object 'dbo.StateList'. The duplicate key value is (CO).
The statement has been terminated.

                                                                    0 rows
```

Figure 1.42 PK_StateList_StateID rejects this duplicate StateID value.

Notice the possible insert shown here (Figure 1.43) and consider whether this insert would be allowed. Currently there is no "TU" value existing in the StateID field; neither is there a "Tuskani" value in the StateName field. The value of 84,956 (square miles) fulfills the criteria for the LandMass field.

Yes, this insert would be allowed. Despite the fact that three of four fields each have constraints, an incorrect record could still slip into our table. Yikes!

StateID	StateProvinceName	RegionID	LandMass
TU	Tuskani	3	84956
1 AB	Alberta	1	247999
2 AK	Alaska	2	656425
3 AL	Alabama	2	52423
4 AR	Arkansas	2	53182
5 AZ	Arizona	2	114006
6 BC	British Columbia	1	357216

Figure 1.43 The primary key will check for an existing value 'TU' in the StateID field to enforce entity integrity.

This example illustrates that even a well-devised plan for data integrity can't prevent all unforeseen data. This brings us back to our seatbelt analogy. Implementing constraints as part of a comprehensive data integrity strategy is necessary – just as wearing seatbelts is legally required. If you reside someplace where this isn't a legal requirement, you should be smart and wear them anyway! But protecting your data also requires human intelligence and review – in the workplace, these are known as "sanity checks" of your data.

A helpful way of thinking about *entity integrity* is that "entities" are the main players in your business and thus are represented by the major tables in your database. For example, the entities in JProCo are Employee, Location, Customer, CurrentProducts, Grant, and Supplier. Fields are attributes of the entities (e.g., the attributes of each employee record are Name, ManagerID, HireDate, etc.). The

Employee table is the definitive source of information for our employees, so it's important that there be no duplicate records and that the data remain clean. The same is true for Location, Customer, and so forth.

The same is just as true for our StateList table, even though it is essentially a resource table. Other tables or objects relying on the StateList table depend upon the StateList data to be accurate. Adhering to the guideline that each table in your database should have a primary key is a smart way to keep your data safe and ensure uniqueness of each record in every table.

Referential Integrity

The concept of *referential integrity* is tied closely to our next topic, *foreign keys*. Whereas *domain integrity* is concerned with protecting the values in a column, and *entity integrity* requires that each record in a table be unique, *referential integrity* is about ensuring that your clean entity data (i.e., table data) remains just as squeaky clean and intact when it appears in other tables – in other words, when it is *referenced* by columns which most often are in other tables. Later you will see that foreign keys work hand-in-glove with primary keys in their enforcement of referential integrity.

Let's look at two related tables, Employee and Location shown respectively in the upper and lower portions of Figure 1.44.

```
SELECT * FROM Employee
SELECT * FROM Location
```

Figure 1.44 Employee records may only use LocationID values which exist in the Location table.

The Location table is the definitive source for location information in the JProCo database. Any location data which is referenced by other tables must originate in the Location table. JProCo currently has six office locations. If the address or other vital information for a location changes (e.g., a new office is added, an office is closed). The data must first be updated in the Location table before it can cascade out to the other tables.

As illustrated in Figure 1.44, any value added to Employee.LocationID must be contained in the Location.LocationID field. In other words, the only legitimate values for LocationID are 1 through 6. Thus, if we enter a new employee record with a LocationID of 9, that data would be incorrect.

Similarly, the only legitimate values for the Employee.ManagerID field are those contained in the Employee.EmpID field. If an insert to the Employee table were to accept a non-existent ManagerID (e.g., 111), then the Employee table data would become incorrect (i.e., unusable due to invalid data) and referential integrity would be violated.

For a database to have sound data integrity, the principles of domain integrity, entity integrity, and referential integrity must be upheld. Since SQL Server is an RDMS (relational database management system), it offers many tools and prompts for enforcing data integrity in as systematic a way as possible.

Foreign Key Constraints

Foreign key constraints enforce *referential integrity*. The referential integrity topic mentioned that foreign keys and primary keys work hand-in-glove. The foreign key builds upon the primary key and *entity integrity* you have established in each of your database tables.

A simple way to think of a foreign key is that, essentially, it is another field which has a corresponding primary key field. Every foreign key field refers to another column which is a primary key field, most often in another table. The Employee.LocationID field references the Location.LocationID field (the Employee table is the *referencing table* and Location is the *referenced table* – the one which contains the definitive instance of the Location data).

Compare the two instances of the LocationID field in Figure 1.45 (Location.LocationID and Employee.LocationID). One noticeable difference between the primary key (Location.LocationID) versus the foreign key (Employee.LocationID) is that the values are non-unique in the foreign key. The master version of the location data in the Location table (i.e., the *referenced table*) contains one unique record for each JProCo office. However, the Employee table (i.e., the *referencing table*) naturally reflects many employees working at each location. In other words, the Location and Employee entities have a 1:Many relationship ("one-to-many relationship"). Notice that the same is true for Employee and Grant – one employee may have many grants (Figure 1.45).

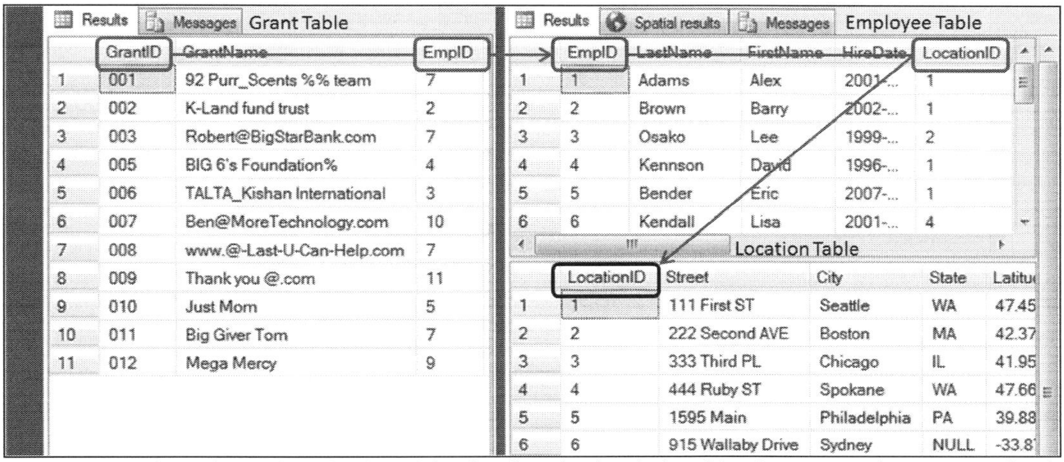

Grant Table

	GrantID	GrantName	EmpID
1	001	92 Purr_Scents %% team	7
2	002	K-Land fund trust	2
3	003	Robert@BigStarBank.com	7
4	005	BIG 6's Foundation%	4
5	006	TALTA_Kishan International	3
6	007	Ben@MoreTechnology.com	10
7	008	www.@-Last-U-Can-Help.com	7
8	009	Thank you @.com	11
9	010	Just Mom	5
10	011	Big Giver Tom	7
11	012	Mega Mercy	9

Employee Table

	EmpID	LastName	FirstName	HireDate	LocationID
1	1	Adams	Alex	2001-...	1
2	2	Brown	Barry	2002-...	1
3	3	Osako	Lee	1999-...	2
4	4	Kennson	David	1996-...	1
5	5	Bender	Eric	2007-...	1
6	6	Kendall	Lisa	2001-...	4

Location Table

	LocationID	Street	City	State	Latitu
1	1	111 First ST	Seattle	WA	47.45
2	2	222 Second AVE	Boston	MA	42.37
3	3	333 Third PL	Chicago	IL	41.95
4	4	444 Ruby ST	Spokane	WA	47.66
5	5	1595 Main	Philadelphia	PA	39.88
6	6	915 Wallaby Drive	Sydney	NULL	-33.8

Figure 1.45 The primary key (PK) and foreign key (FK) relationships between columns contained in the Grant, Employee, and Location tables.

Currently we don't actually have a foreign key constraint added to the Employee.LocationID field. But irrespective of whether this field does or doesn't contain the foreign key constraint object, the rules of a relational database require that the field must logically behave in the same fashion. In other words, the Employee.LocationID field may contain only those values found in the Location.LocationID field. If a location is removed from the Location table (e.g., if JProCo closed its Boston office), then no employee records in the Employee table could legitimately have Boston (LocationID 2) as their location. If a new JProCo location is added, then that value becomes available for use by the Employee table.

Before we look at the mechanics of adding the foreign key to the Employee table, let's attempt to add some incorrect data, so that we can get a better sense of how foreign keys can protect our data. We will attempt to add an employee record having a LocationID value of 11, which we know doesn't exist (Figure 1.46). Since JProCo doesn't yet have a Location 11, this record should be disallowed.

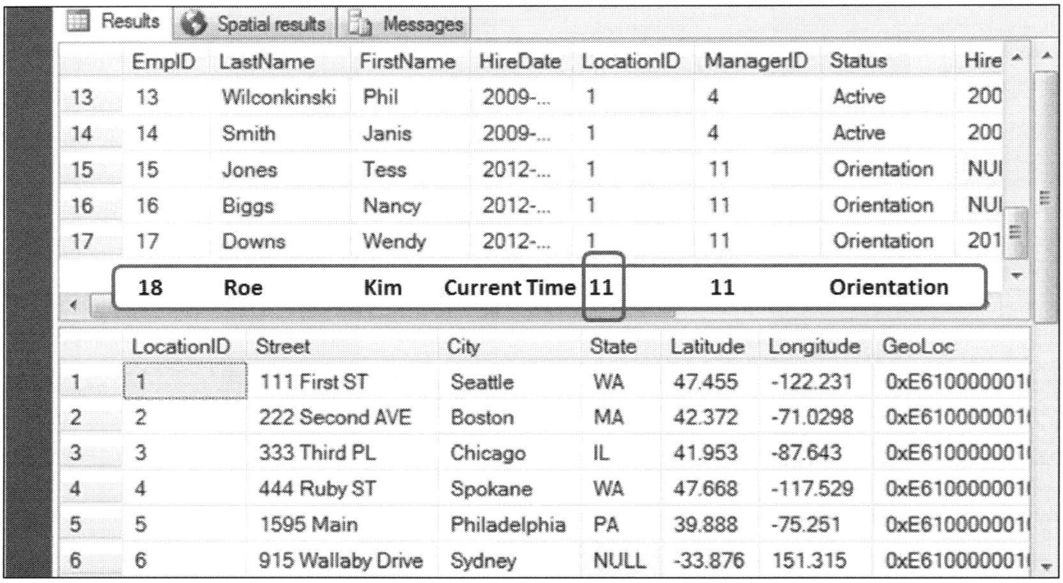

	EmpID	LastName	FirstName	HireDate	LocationID	ManagerID	Status	Hire
13	13	Wilconkinski	Phil	2009-...	1	4	Active	200
14	14	Smith	Janis	2009-...	1	4	Active	200
15	15	Jones	Tess	2012-...	1	11	Orientation	NUI
16	16	Biggs	Nancy	2012-...	1	11	Orientation	NUI
17	17	Downs	Wendy	2012-...	1	11	Orientation	201
	18	**Roe**	**Kim**	**Current Time**	**11**	**11**	**Orientation**	

	LocationID	Street	City	State	Latitude	Longitude	GeoLoc
1	1	111 First ST	Seattle	WA	47.455	-122.231	0xE610000001
2	2	222 Second AVE	Boston	MA	42.372	-71.0298	0xE610000001
3	3	333 Third PL	Chicago	IL	41.953	-87.643	0xE610000001
4	4	444 Ruby ST	Spokane	WA	47.668	-117.529	0xE610000001
5	5	1595 Main	Philadelphia	PA	39.888	-75.251	0xE610000001
6	6	915 Wallaby Drive	Sydney	NULL	-33.876	151.315	0xE610000001

Figure 1.46 We are going to attempt to insert LocationID 11 for a new employee, knowing there is no LocationID 11 existing in the Location table.

However, the Employee table allows the bad data to be inserted into the LocationID field. Because the LocationID field of the *referencing table* contains a value not found in the LocationID field of the *referenced table*, referential integrity has been violated.

```
INSERT INTO Employee
VALUES (18,'Roe','Kim', CURRENT_TIMESTAMP, 11, 11,
DEFAULT, DEFAULT, DEFAULT)

SELECT * FROM Employee
```

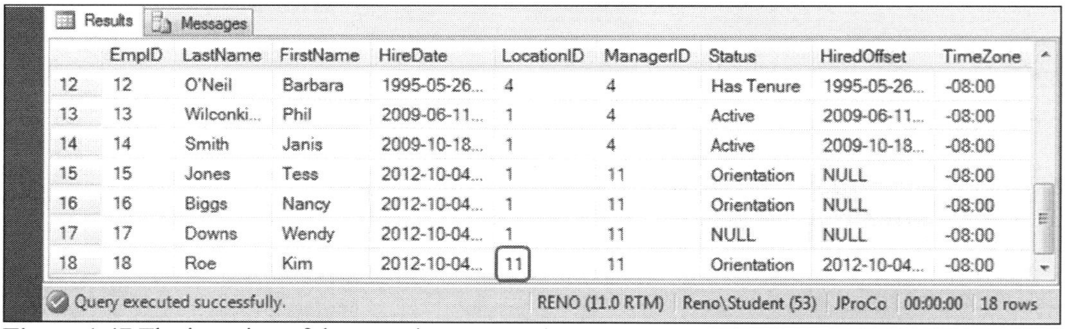

	EmpID	LastName	FirstName	HireDate	LocationID	ManagerID	Status	HiredOffset	TimeZone
12	12	O'Neil	Barbara	1995-05-26...	4	4	Has Tenure	1995-05-26...	-08:00
13	13	Wilconki...	Phil	2009-06-11...	1	4	Active	2009-06-11...	-08:00
14	14	Smith	Janis	2009-10-18...	1	4	Active	2009-10-18...	-08:00
15	15	Jones	Tess	2012-10-04...	1	11	Orientation	NULL	-08:00
16	16	Biggs	Nancy	2012-10-04...	1	11	Orientation	NULL	-08:00
17	17	Downs	Wendy	2012-10-04...	1	11	NULL	NULL	-08:00
18	18	Roe	Kim	2012-10-04...	11	11	Orientation	2012-10-04...	-08:00

Figure 1.47 The insertion of the LocationID 11 value was allowed since there is no foreign key to enforce referential integrity.

Delete the Employee 18 record, so that we can create the foreign key by using the following code:

```
DELETE FROM Employee
WHERE EmpID = 18
```

Run this code to add the FK_Employee_Location_LocationID constraint to the Employee table and disallow invalid inserts:

```
ALTER TABLE Employee
ADD CONSTRAINT FK_Employee_Location_LocationID
FOREIGN KEY (LocationID)
REFERENCES Location(LocationID)
GO
```

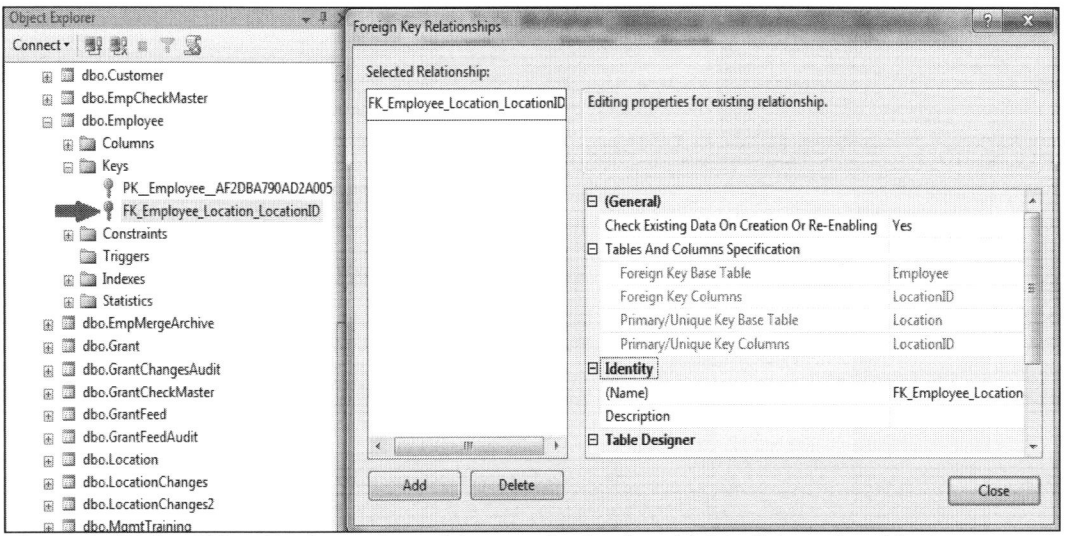

Figure 1.48 The Object Explorer view of the new foreign key (right-click on the object > Modify).

After you create the foreign key constraint, it's worth taking a moment to view it in Object Explorer. The foreign key has a grey key icon and has been created in the Keys folder of the Employee table. The **Foreign Key Relationships** dialog displays metadata about the constraint and its options.

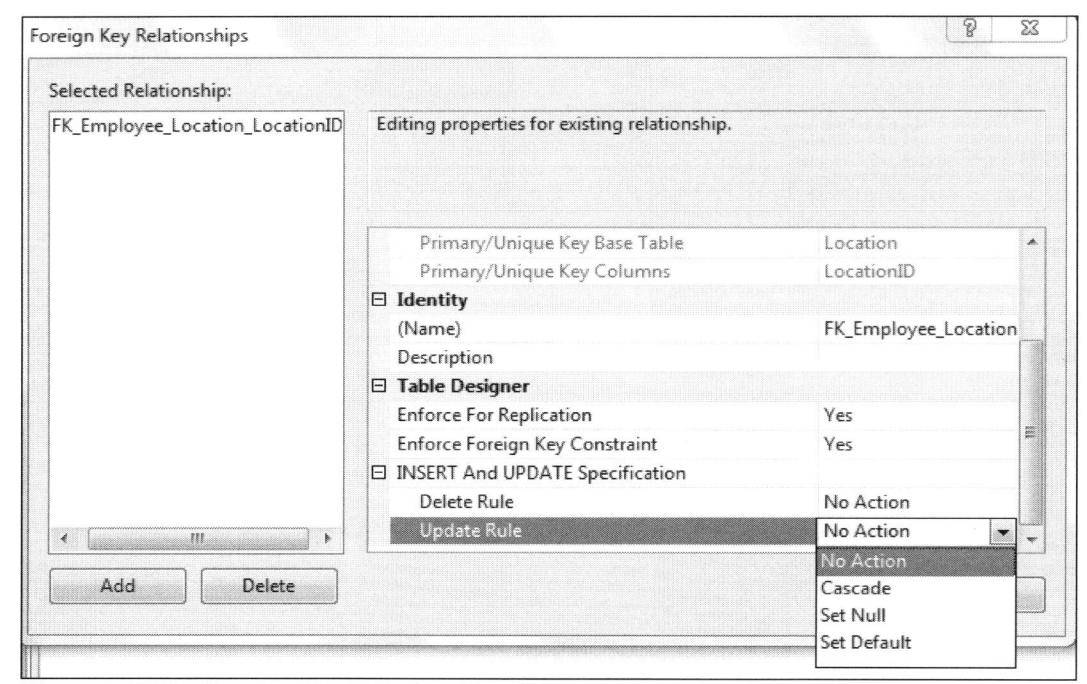

Figure 1.49 The **Foreign Key Relationships** dialog.

(*Note:* Because the footprint of the **Foreign Key Relationships** dialog doesn't fully expand, it's difficult to adequately display these options in a figure.)

Following the creation of FK_Employee_Location_LocationID, each update to a LocationID value in the Employee table will only be allowed by this foreign key constraint if it is in agreement with the Location.LocationID field.

With our new foreign key in place and establishing referential integrity on the Employee.LocationID field, the Employee table is protected against false LocationID data. Observe that when you reattempt to insert the bad LocationID into the Employee table, it disallows the insert (Figure 1.50).

```
INSERT INTO Employee
VALUES (18,'Roe','Kim', CURRENT_TIMESTAMP, 11, 11,
DEFAULT, DEFAULT, DEFAULT)
```

```
Message
Msg 2627, Level 16, State 0, Line 1
The INSERT statement conflicted with the FOREIGN KEY constraint "
FK_Employee_Location_LocationID" The conflict occurred in database "JProCo:",
table "dbo.Location", column 'LocationID'
The statement has been terminated.

                                                                    0 rows
```

Figure 1.50 The FK_Employee_Location_LocationID constraint will not insert LocationID 11.

Using the WITH NOCHECK Option

Recall that earlier in Figure 1.48 and Figure 1.49 we looked at the Foreign Key Relationships dialog in SSMS (SQL Server Management Studio) and we reviewed the metadata for FK_Employee_Location_LocationID.

You may have noticed the Yes/No option that determines whether or not to "Check Existing Data On Creation Or Re-Enabling" (Figure 1.51). This option defaults to "Yes" – at the time you create the constraint, it first checks the existing data to confirm that all values in the field are legitimate.

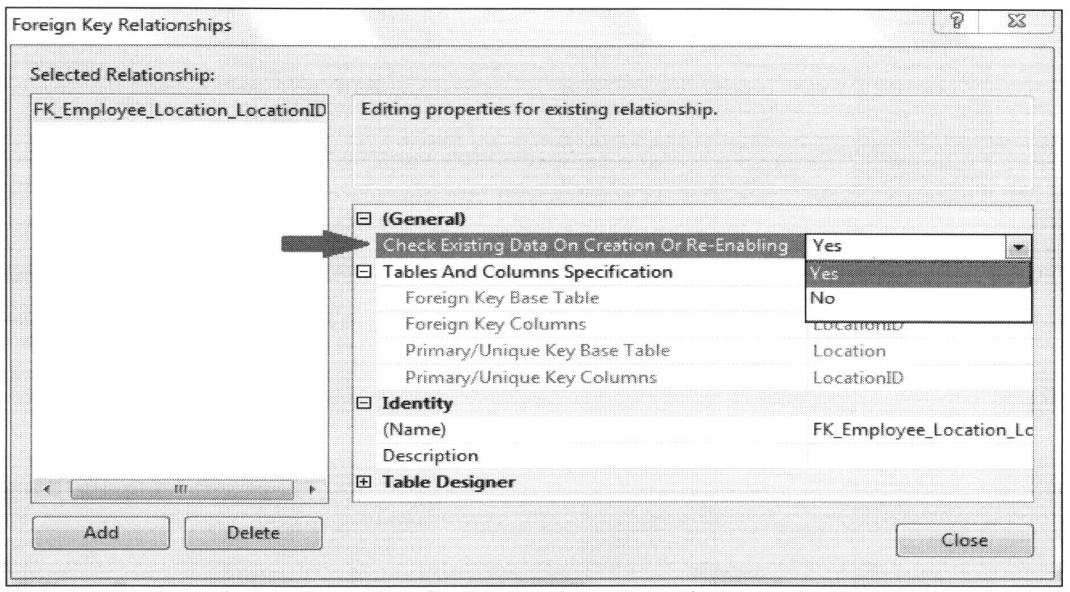

Figure 1.51 The options and metadata for FK_Employee_Location_LocationID.

Prior to creating the foreign key constraint, we removed the record containing false data (i.e., LocationID 11).

Our next example will take us back to the point prior to the creation of the constraint. We want to create the constraint again, but this time we will have it skip the step of validating the existing data before creating the foreign key. Run the following code to remove the foreign key constraint:

```
ALTER TABLE Employee DROP CONSTRAINT
FK_Employee_Location_LocationID
GO
```

Run this code which inserts some bad data into the Employee table. As we know, the value of 13 is not an actual LocationID, but we are intentionally inserting it in order to demonstrate the WITH NOCHECK option (Figure 1.52).

```
INSERT INTO Employee
VALUES (19, 'Testing', 'Data', CURRENT_TIMESTAMP, 13, 11,
DEFAULT,DEFAULT,DEFAULT)
```

	EmpID	LastName	FirstName	HireDate	LocationID	ManagerID	Status	HiredOffset	TimeZone
13	13	Wilconkinski	Phil	2009-06-11 0...	1	4	Active	2009-06-11 00:00...	-08:00
14	14	Smith	Janis	2009-10-18 0...	1	4	Active	2009-10-18 00:00...	-08:00
15	15	Jones	Tess	2012-11-16 1...	1	11	Orientation	NULL	-08:00
16	16	Biggs	Nancy	2012-11-16 1...	1	11	Orientation	NULL	-08:00
17	17	Downs	Wendy	2012-11-16 1...	1	11	Orientation	2012-11-16 11:38...	-08:00
18	18	Roe	Kim	2012-11-16 1...	11	11	NULL	NULL	-08:00
19	19	Testing	Data	2012-11-16 1...	13	11	NULL	NULL	-08:00

Figure 1.52 Because we've temporarily removed the protection of the foreign key, the Employee table allowed the insertion of our bad data (i.e., LocationID 13).

Create the foreign key constraint using WITH NOCHECK:

```
ALTER TABLE Employee
WITH NOCHECK
ADD CONSTRAINT FK_Employee_Employee_ManagerID
FOREIGN KEY (ManagerID)
REFERENCES Employee(EmpID)
GO
```

When we check the Object Explorer, we see the newly created constraint. The WITH NOCHECK option allowed FK_Employee_Location_LocationID to be created, despite the invalid value (13) present in the Employee.LocationID field. The Foreign Key Relationships dialog now shows a "No" for the Check Existing Data option.

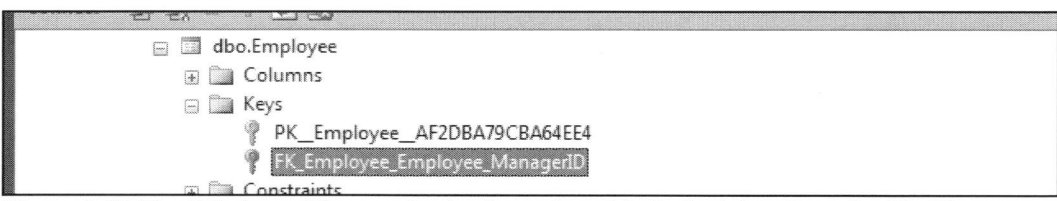

- dbo.Employee
  - Columns
  - Keys
    - PK_Employee__AF2DBA79CBA64EE4
    - FK_Employee_Employee_ManagerID
  - Constraints

Figure 1.53 The OE view of the new foreign key, alongside the bad data (LocationID 13).

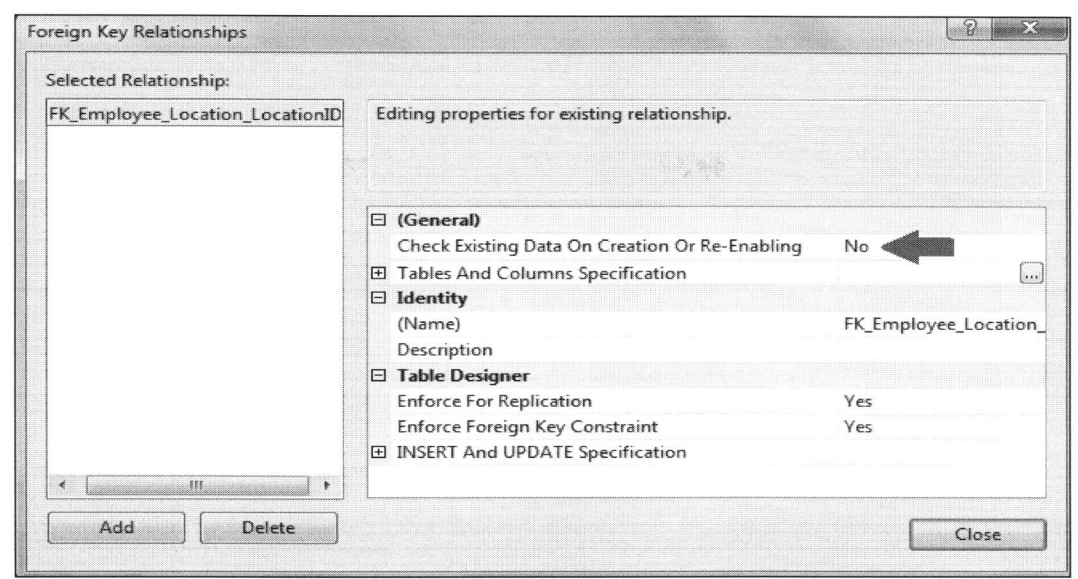

Figure 1.54 The FK Relationships dialog showing "Check Existing Data" option is "No".

Our demonstration is complete – we now have the foreign key constraint enabled on the Employee.LocationID field, and we have one bad record in our Employee table. Let's consider how this unusual situation may occur in our database within a production environment – in other words, how the WITH NOCHECK may come in handy in the workplace setting.

We know the best practice is to establish data constraints as early as possible in the life cycle of our tables. However, we don't always encounter "best case" scenarios with our data or databases. For example, if your database is dependent upon data coming from other systems, new schema or data changes may be requested which require new tables or modification of your existing data constraints. Our demonstration simulates a situation where you discover bad data coming into a field. You need to add a constraint to the field, but if you stop and attempt to scrub out the bad data prior to adding the constraint, even more bad data could enter your table while you take the time needed to investigate and scrub the data.

The flexibility of the WITH NOCHECK option allows you to add the constraint immediately without having to first correct all of your data. This immediately halts the flow of bad data into the field. Obviously you should also correct the existing data as quickly as possible, but the more pressing urgency is to stop more bad data from entering your table.

This is not unlike the classic leaky rowboat analogy. When triaging a complex data issue, often you need multiple steps in order to fully handle the problem.

Think of the option of enabling a data constraint WITH NOCHECK as a way to plug the leak, so that water stops coming into the boat. Once that perilous situation is stopped, then you can bail the water out of the boat. In the case of your database, that's when you can take the time you need for analysis and remediation or removal of the bad data from your table.

Finally, we will remove the bad record (LocationID 13) from the Employee table using the following code:

```
DELETE FROM Employee
WHERE EmpID = 19
```

Lab 1.4: Foreign Key Constraints

Lab Prep: Lab Prep: Each lab has one or more Skill Checks. Start with Skill Check 1 and proceed until reaching the Points to Ponder section.

Before beginning this lab, verify that SQL Server 2012 is properly installed and operating. Before running the lab setup script for resetting the database (SQLQueries2012Vol4Chapter1.4Setup.sql), please make sure to close all query windows within SSMS. An open query window pointing to a database context can lock that database preventing it from updating when the script is executing. A simple way to assure all query windows are closed, is to exit out of SSMS, then open a new instance of SSMS, and lastly run the setup script.

Skill Check 1: Create a foreign key relationship called FK_Grant_Employee_EmpID that ensures all EmpID values entered into the Grant table are from valid values listed in the Employee table.

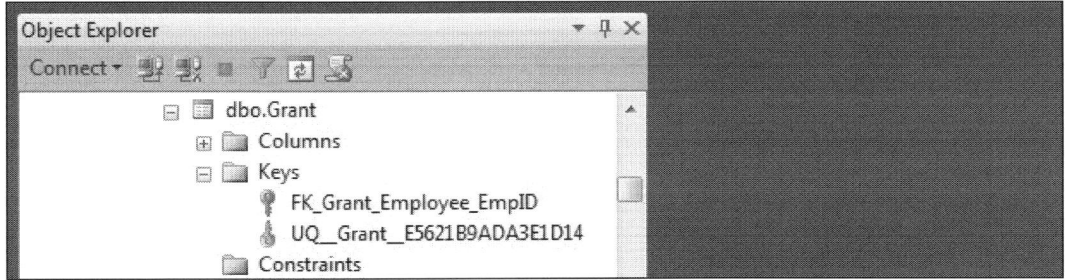

Figure 1.55 Skill Check 1 shows FK_Grant_Employee_EmpID was created.

Skill Check 2: You notice that your invoice numbers range from 1 to 1885. Someone entered a record into the SalesInvoiceDetail table referring to Invoice 2000. Tomorrow you will investigate what to do with that record. In the meanwhile, establish referential integrity between SalesInvoice and SalesInvoiceDetail, so that only InvoiceID values listed in SalesInvoice will be allowed into the SalesInvoiceDetail table. Name the constraint FK_SalesInvoiceDetail_SalesInvoice_InvoiceID.

Chapter 1. Constraints

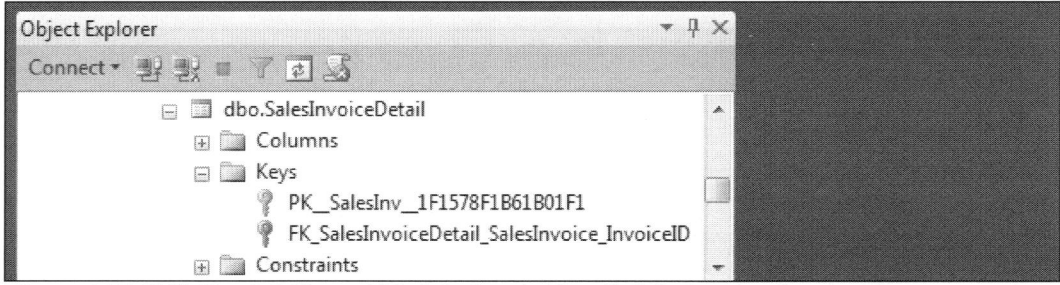

Figure 1.56 Skill Check 2 Shows FK_SalesInvoiceDetail_SalesInvoice_InvoiceID was created.

Skill Check 3: Add a foreign key called FK_SalesInvoiceDetail_CurrentProducts_ProductID, so the ProductID field of the SalesInvoiceDetail table references the ProductID of the CurrentProducts table.

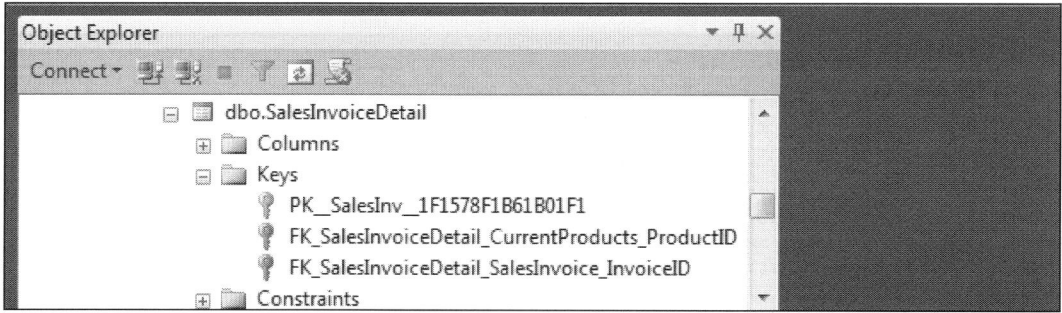

Figure 1.57 Skill Check 3 shows foreign key FK_SalesInvoiceDetail_CurrentProducts_ProductID was created.

Answer Code: The T-SQL code to this lab can be found in the downloadable files in a file named Lab1.4_ForeignKeyConstraints.sql.

Points to Ponder - Foreign Key Constraints

1. Foreign keys are constraints that compare values between one column and another.
2. Setting up a foreign key relationship enforces what is known as referential integrity.
3. The foreign key field of a table must be the same data type when referencing the primary key table. For example, the LocationID field of the Employee table is a CHAR(3), if the LocationID of the Location table was an INT then you could not create this reference.
4. You can use a FOREIGN KEY to specify that a column allows only those values contained in the referenced table (a.k.a., the base table).
5. Data integrity is the consistency and accuracy of the data which is stored in a database. In relational databases, the three types of data integrity are:
    - Domain Integrity (data type, check constraint)
    - Entity Integrity (primary key, unique constraint)
    - Referential Integrity (handled by foreign key constraint)
6. If you don't want to check the existing data at the time you create the foreign key, then specify WITH NOCHECK.

Creating Tables with Constraints

Our earlier examples created or modified constraints on existing tables. This section will demonstrate the code syntax for creating these constraints at the time you create your tables.

PK_TravelTrip_TripID is a primary key constraint on the TripID field. We know the CLUSTERED keyword specifies that the records of the table will be physically ordered by TripID. Substitute the NONCLUSTERED keyword, if you do not wish the records to be physically ordered by TripID:

```
CREATE TABLE Sales.TravelTrip
(TripID INT NOT NULL, TripName VARCHAR(100), EmpID INT NULL,
CONSTRAINT PK_TravelTrip_TripID PRIMARY KEY CLUSTERED
(TripID ASC))
GO
```

An alternate syntax for adding a primary key in your CREATE TABLE statement is shown in the following example. This syntax also specifies a unique constraint (UQ_TravelTrip_TripName), so that the values of the TripName field will be unique:

```
CREATE TABLE Sales.TravelTrip
(TripID INT NOT NULL, TripName VARCHAR(100) CONSTRAINT
UQ_TravelTrip_TripName UNIQUE, EmpID INT NULL, CONSTRAINT
PK_TravelTrip_TripID PRIMARY KEY CLUSTERED (TripID ASC))
GO
```

Note: If you want to run this code make sure you first drop the Sales.TravelTrip table [DROP TABLE Sales.TravelTrip]. Observe that we chose not to customize the name for our primary key on the TripID field. Instead we allowed SQL Server to create the key using its own convention (PK_*First8CharOfTableName_AlphanumericID*). If you later wish to customize the appearance of your key (i.e., to include the FieldName), right-click on the key in Object Explorer and choose the Rename option. As you change the name of the key (or constraint), SQL Server will follow suit and automatically rename the index to match your custom name (Figure 1.58).

Chapter 1. Constraints

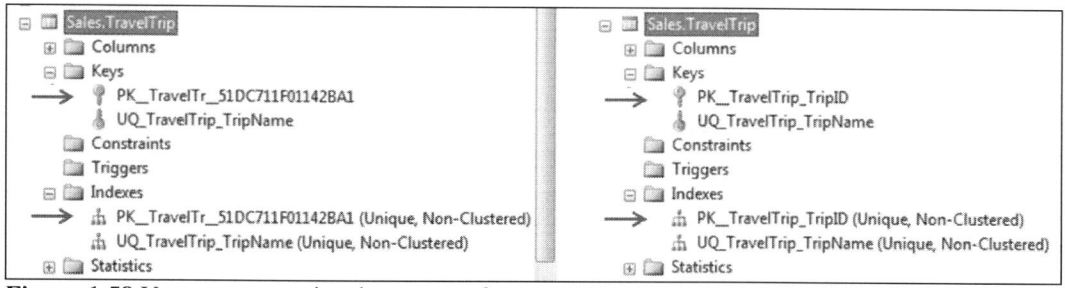

Figure 1.58 You can customize the names of your Keys and Constraints in Object Explorer.

Default constraint values may be defined at the time of table creation as seen in the following code:

```
CREATE TABLE Sales.TravelerProfile
(First_Name CHAR(30), Last_Name CHAR(60), Mailing_Address
CHAR(50) DEFAULT 'Unknown', City CHAR(50) DEFAULT 'Seattle',
Country CHAR(30), Birth_Date DATE)
GO
```

After creating the Sales.TravelerProfile table, the values for the default constraints (Mailing_Address 'Unknown', City 'Seattle') may be seen by opening **Object Explorer** > **Databases** > **Tables** > right-click **Sales.TravelerProfile** > **Design**. Click the City field in the design interface in order to display the Column Properties tab for the City field (Figure 1.59).

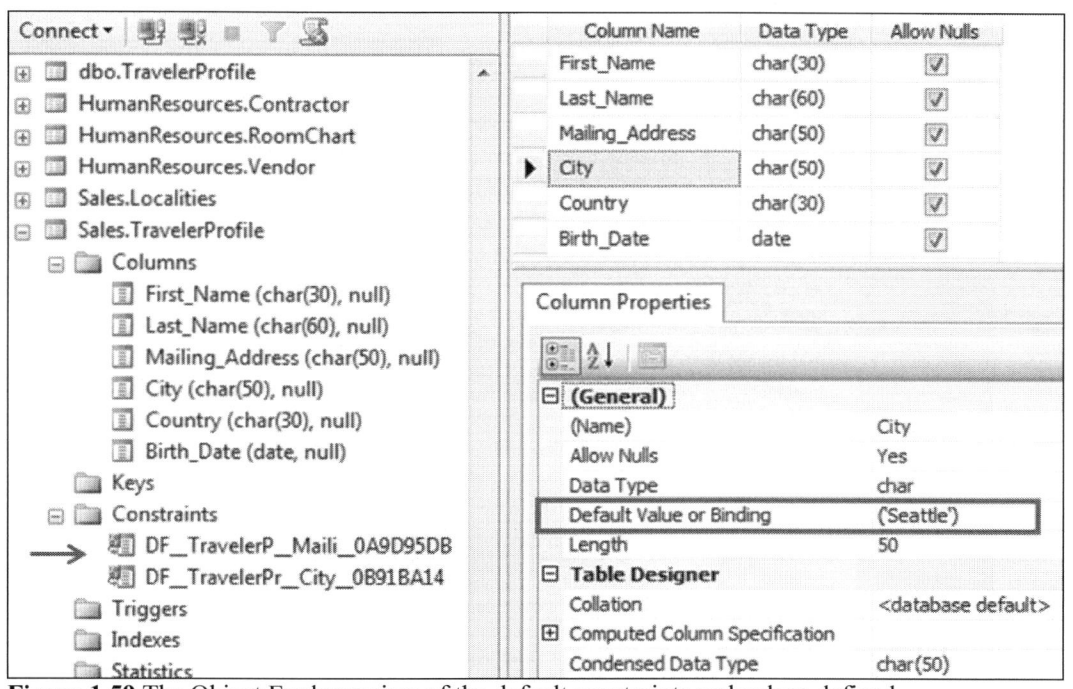

Figure 1.59 The Object Explorer view of the default constraints and values defined.

CHECK constraints may also be added to a table at the time of its creation. Below we add the CK_TravelTrip_EndDate check constraint, which ensures that the EndDate for a trip can't occur earlier than the StartDate:

```sql
DROP TABLE Sales.TravelTrip
GO

CREATE TABLE Sales.TravelTrip
(TripID INT NOT NULL, TripName VARCHAR(100)
CONSTRAINT UQ_TravelTrip_TripName UNIQUE, StartDate DATETIME
NOT NULL, EndDate DATETIME NOT NULL, Complaint BIT NOT NULL,
EmpID INT NULL,
CONSTRAINT PK_TravelTrip_TripID PRIMARY KEY CLUSTERED
(TripID ASC),
CONSTRAINT CK_TravelTrip_EndDate CHECK (EndDate>=StartDate))
GO
```

Foreign key constraints may also be added at the time of table creation. Here we see FK_TravelTrip_Employee_EmpID added as a foreign key referencing the EmpID field of the Employee table. For this to run, the Employee table must already have been created:

```sql
DROP TABLE Sales.TravelTrip
GO

CREATE TABLE Sales.TravelTrip
(TripID INT NOT NULL, TripName VARCHAR(100)
CONSTRAINT UQ_TravelTrip_TripName UNIQUE, StartDate DATETIME
NOT NULL, EndDate DATETIME NOT NULL, Complaint BIT NOT NULL,
EmpID INT NULL,
CONSTRAINT PK_TravelTrip_TripID PRIMARY KEY CLUSTERED
(TripID ASC),
CONSTRAINT CK_TravelTrip_EndDate CHECK (EndDate>=StartDate),
CONSTRAINT FK_TravelTrip_Employee_EmpID FOREIGN KEY (EmpID)
REFERENCES Employee(EmpID))
GO
```

If the Employee table does not exist, then you would get an error.

Lab 1.5: Creating Table Constraints

Lab Prep: Lab Prep: Each lab has one or more Skill Checks. Start with Skill Check 1 and proceed until reaching the Points to Ponder section.

Before beginning this lab, verify that SQL Server 2012 is properly installed and operating. Before running the lab setup script for resetting the database (SQLQueries2012Vol4Chapter1.5Setup.sql), please make sure to close all query windows within SSMS. An open query window pointing to a database context can lock that database preventing it from updating when the script is executing. A simple way to assure all query windows are closed, is to exit out of SSMS, then open a new instance of SSMS, and lastly run the setup script.

Skill Check 1: Create the dbo.Contestant table and insert the three records seen in the Figure 1.60.

Your checklist to complete this code should include the following:

- All fields should not allow nulls.
- The ContestantID should be the primary key using the naming convention of PK_*Tablename_Fieldname*.
- A check constraint on the Gender field should only allow an F or an M.
- Test your check constraint by attempting to insert Sam Haas with a gender value of 'O' and verify that it fails.

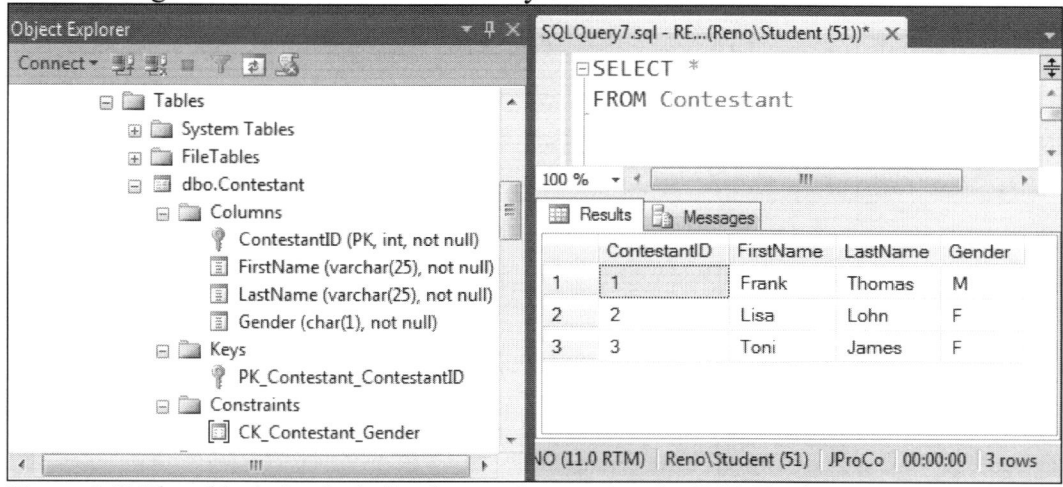

Figure 1.60 The table design including keys and constraints for Skill Check 1.

Test the check constraint to prevents the gender value of 'O' from being entered using the following INSERT statement (Figure 1.61).

```
INSERT INTO Contestant VALUES ('Sam', 'Haas', 'O')
```

```
Messages
Msg 547, Level 16, State 0, Line 1
The INSERT statement conflicted with the CHECK constraint
"CK_Contestant_Gender". The conflict occurred in database "JProCo", table
"dbo.Contestant", column 'Gender'.
The statement has been terminated.
                                                                    0 rows
```

Figure 1.61 Test the check constraint which prevents the gender value of 'O' from being entered.

Answer Code: The T-SQL code to this lab can be found in the downloadable files in a file named Lab1.5_CreatingTablesWithConstraints.sql.

Points to Ponder - Creating Table Constraints

1. You can create constraints while creating a new table using the CREATE TABLE statement.

2. When an INSERT, UPDATE, or DELETE statement violates a constraint, then the statement is terminated with an error.

3. Creating a unique constraint creates an index. By default this index will be non-clustered.

4. Creating a primary key constraint creates an index. By default this index will be clustered.

5. Foreign keys are constraints that compare values between columns (usually, but not always, of different tables).

7. You can create constraints using:
    - The CONSTRAINT keyword in the CREATE TABLE statement at the time you create the table.
    - The CONSTRAINT keyword in the ALTER TABLE statement after you have created the table.

Chapter Glossary

CHECK constraint: An object on a SQL Server table that places a condition to verify valid data during inserts or updates.

Composite key (also known as *compound key*): Two or more fields that when combined uniquely identify a row.

Condition: A rule which you want a constraint to enforce. E*xamples:* all height values must be positive; LandMass values must be non-negative and < 2 million; a numeric data type can ensure that no character data is entered into a number field.

Data integrity: The consistency and accuracy of the data which is stored in a database.

Default constraint: Inserts a specific value into a field when the input is left blank for the field.

Domain integrity: Every accepted value is verified by the rules set forth on the field.

Foreign key: Constraints that compare values between other fields.

Primary key: An object on a SQL Server table that specifies which fields must have unique, non-NULL values for each record.

Referenced table: Also known as *base table*. This specifies an enumerated set of acceptable values that can be used.

Referencing table: A table that is being used by another object in SQL Server.

Referential integrity: A guideline that says valid values are only values from a referenced table.

Table constraint: Object on a table that disallows unacceptable data from entering the table.

Unique constraint: SQL Object that ensures that no duplicate values are entered in specific columns.

WITH NOCHECK: An option available when creating a constraint that allows existing data to be out of compliance with the constraint. All new data coming in will be in compliance with the constraint.

Review Quiz - Chapter One

1.) Data types help to enforce what type of data integrity?

   O a. Entity Integrity
   O b. Domain Integrity
   O c. Referential Integrity

2.) How many primary keys can a table have?

   O a. Depends on your ANSI NULL settings
   O b. Up to 1
   O c. Up to as many fields as you have
   O d. No limit

3.) A check constraint

   O a. must be present on every table in your database.
   O b. can be a logical expression.
   O c. must be purchased from Microsoft as a middleware component from a third party before you can use it.

4.) Foreign keys are used to enforce referential integrity. What does referential integrity do?

   O a. Assigns values between tables to save the user time.
   O b. Compares values to different fields to run complex calculations in place of methods.
   O c. Compares values between the fields of two tables to limit the acceptable values which may be used.

5.) Which column cannot have a unique constraint?

   O a. ISBN **INT** NULL
   O b. ISBN **NCHAR(100)** NULL
   O c. ISBN **NVARCHAR(100)** NULL
   O d. ISBN **NVARCHAR(max)** NULL

Chapter 1. Constraints

6.) You tried to set up a foreign key constraint to limit LocationID values of your Employee table to valid values listed in the Location.LocationID field. Where do you place the foreign key?

   O a. On the Employee.LocationID field.

   O b. On the Location.LocationID field.

7.) You have a database with two tables named Employee and Location. Both tables have a field called LocationID. You need to ensure that all Locations listed in the Employee table have a corresponding LocationID in the Location table? How do you enforce this type of integrity?

   O a. JOIN

   O b. DDL Trigger

   O c. Foreign key constraint

   O d. Primary key constraint

8.) You have a table named Feedback that contains every record of how a customer felt about their purchase. One field is called Complaint, where 0 is no complaint and 1 is a complaint. You also have a field called Rating that ranges from 0 to 100. If a customer complains they should not be giving a perfect rating of 100. If they complain then they can enter a score between 0 and 90. If they don't then it can be between 1 and 100. Which check constraint would you use?

   O a. `CHECK (Rating BETWEEN 1 and 100)`

   O b. `CHECK (Rating <=90 AND Complaint = 1)`

   O c. `CHECK ( (Rating BETWEEN 1 and 90 AND Complaint = 1) )`
      `OR ( Rating BETWEEN 1 and 100 AND Complaint = 0) )`

   O d. `CHECK ( (Rating BETWEEN 1 and 90 AND Complaint = 1)`
      `AND ( Rating BETWEEN 1 and 100 AND Complaint = 0) )`

Chapter 1. Constraints

9.) You have a table named Customer. You need to ensure that customer data in the table meets the following requirements:

- Credit limit must be zero unless customer identification has been verified.
- Credit limit must be less than 25,000.

Which check constraint should you use?

- a. **CHECK (CreditLimit BETWEEN 1 AND 25000 AND 0)**
- b. **CHECK (PreApproved = 1 AND CreditLimit BETWEEN 1 AND 25000)**
- c. **CHECK ((CreditLimit = 0 AND PreApproved = 0) OR (CreditLimit BETWEEN 1 AND 25000 AND PreApproved = 1))**
- d. **CHECK ((CreditLimit = 0 AND PreApproved = 0) AND (CreditLimit BETWEEN 1 AND 25000 AND PreApproved = 1))**

10.) Which two column definitions could have a unique constraint?

- a. **NVARCHAR(100) NULL**
- b. **NVARCHAR(max) NOT NULL**
- c. **NVARCHAR(100) NOT NULL**
- d. **NVARCHAR(100) SPARSE NOT NULL**

11.) You have a table named Customer. The Customer table has a field called [CreditLimit]. You need to ensure that the credit limit be zero if the customer identification has not yet been verified. The field that stores the values for verified customers is called [PreApproved] and is set to 1 if yes and 0 if no. All verified customer must have a credit limit of 5,000 or less. All approved customers will have a value of at least 100. Which check constraint will do this?

- a. **CHECK (CreditLimit BETWEEN 100 AND 5000)**
- b. **CHECK (PreApproved = 1 AND CreditLimit BETWEEN 100 AND 5000)**
- c. **CHECK ((CreditLimit = 0 AND PreApproved = 0) AND (CreditLimit BETWEEN 100 AND 5000 AND PreApproved = 1))**
- d. **CHECK ((CreditLimit = 0 AND PreApproved = 0) OR (CreditLimit BETWEEN 100 AND 5000 AND PreApproved = 1))**

12.) You are developing a new database with two tables named SalesInvoiceDetail and CurrentProducts. You need to ensure that all ProductID's referenced in the SalesInvoiceDetail table have a corresponding record in the ProductID field of the CurrentProducts table. Which method should you use?

O a. JOIN

O b. DDL Trigger

O c. CHECK constraint

O d. Foreign key constraint

O e. Primary key constraint

Answer Key

1.) Data types prevent improper values from being entered into a field based solely on its value. They do not look at the values of other rows (entities), so (a) is incorrect. They also do not look at other fields like Referential Integrity, so (c) is also wrong. Domain Integrity only looks at the value itself, therefore (b) is correct.

2.) There is only 1 primary key allowed per table, so (a), (c), and (d) are all incorrect. Therefore (b) is the correct answer.

3.) CHECK constraints are optional, so (a) is incorrect. They come free with SQL Server, so (c) is wrong. They are based on a logical expression, making (b) the correct answer.

4.) Foreign keys do not assign values but they do check the validity of values being entered, so (a) is incorrect. Foreign keys check values in other fields for a match and don't run any calculations, so (b) is wrong, making (c) the correct answer.

5.) Unique constraints can only be on smaller data types, so (a) is wrong. You can't put a unique constraint on a max data type field, making (d) the correct answer.

6.) You place the foreign key on the table that you want to restrict the value. We are trying to control the values entered into the Employee table, making (a) the correct answer.

7.) Since we want to compare two different fields and primary keys and DDL triggers can't do that (b) and (d) are both wrong. A join can compare values and, so can a foreign key but a join does not limit values (it only shows matching values) therefore (a) is incorrect, making (c) is correct.

8.) We want to allow any rating from 1 to 100 and limit the values of complaint to 1 or 2 based on the rating. Answer (a) is incorrect since it does not limit the complaint values. Answer (b) is wrong since it never allows us to rate over 90 and we need to go up to 100. Answer (d) is wrong because it's impossible to have a 0 and a 1 value at the same time on the same record. The correct answer is (c) because it allows either a 1 to 90 complaint or a 1 to 100 non-complaint.

9.) Answer (a) is wrong because you can't have the AND keyword twice with just one BETWEEN keyword. We must allow credit limits from zero to 25,000 and (b) is wrong since it does not allow zero. To allow for no credit or high approved credit the only correct answer is (c).

10.) You can't put unique constraints on sparse or max columns, so (b) and (d) are incorrect. Nullability does not matter, so both (a) and (c) are the correct answers.

11.) Answer (a) and (b) are wrong since they must allow credit limits from zero to 5,000 and they don't go below 100. To allow for no credit or high approved credit the only correct answer is (d).

12.) We want referential integrity between the SalesInvoiceDetail and CurrentProducts table. Primary keys, Joins and DDL triggers can't do referential integrity, making (a), (b), and (e) incorrect. CHECK constraints can do referential integrity, but not very well, and this question said should, so (c) is incorrect. Foreign keys are the master of referential integrity, making (d) the correct answer.

Bug Catcher Game

To play the Bug Catcher game, run the file SQLQueries2012Vol4BugCatcher1.pps from the BugCatcher folder of the companion files found at www.Joes2Pros.com.

Chapter 2.   After Triggers

Back in high school during Track & Field competition, I knew to listen for a starting siren or whistle to cue me that it was time to take off running. Of all the noises coming from the outdoors, the stadium, the team, or the crowd, I was focused and listening intently for that one sound. You could say there was a **trigger** in my head waiting for that event.

In this analogy, the starting sound was the *event* and in my mind was a *trigger* that fired off a command telling my legs to take me as fast as possible down and around the track. I never ran before that starting sound event for fear of disqualification.

Based on events which take place in your database, you can have SQL Server "listen" for just the ones that should signal when it's time for actions to run automatically. **AFTER triggers** are essentially stored procedures that run after an event occurs.

There are three types of AFTER triggers: after insert triggers, after delete triggers, and after update triggers. For short, these are referred to as insert triggers, update triggers, and delete triggers. In this chapter we will examine all three types of AFTER triggers.

READER NOTE: *Please run the script SQLQueries2012Vol4Chapter2.0Setup.sql in order to follow along with the examples in the first section of Chapter 2. All scripts mentioned in this chapter may be found at* ***www.Joes2Pros.com***.

Insert Triggers

The first type of trigger we will examine is the **insert trigger**. Since our first examples will be based on the Employee table data, query your Employee table and confirm you have the same 17 employee records (Figure 2.1). If not, please run the setup script SQLProgrammingChapter2.0Setup.sql. Our most recent hire is Employee 17 (Wendy Downs), who is still in orientation.

```
SELECT * FROM Employee
```

	EmpID	LastName	FirstName	HireDate	LocationID	ManagerID	Status	HiredOffset	TimeZone
1	1	Adams	Alex	2001-01-01...	1	11	Active	2001-01-01...	-08:00
2	2	Brown	Barry	2002-08-12...	1	11	Active	2002-08-12...	-08:00
3	3	Osako	Lee	1999-09-01...	2	11	Active	1999-09-01...	-05:00
4	4	Kennson	David	1996-03-16...	1	11	Has Tenure	1996-03-16...	-08:00
5	5	Bender	Eric	2007-05-17...	1	11	Active	2007-05-17...	-08:00
6	6	Kendall	Lisa	2001-11-15...	4	4	Active	2001-11-15...	-08:00

Query executed successfully. RENO (11.0 RTM) Reno\Student (51) JProCo 00:00:00 17 rows

Figure 2.1 Our most recent employee is EmpID 17, Wendy Downs.

We want to have two identical tables called Employee and EmployeeHistory. Attempting to query the EmployeeHistory table (which does not yet exist) gets an error message (Figure 2.2). We can confirm in the Object Explorer that we see an Employee table but no EmployeeHistory table.

```
SELECT * FROM EmployeeHistory
```
```
Messages
Msg 208, Level 16, State 1, Line 1
Invalid object name 'EmployeeHistory'.
                                                                    0 rows
```

Figure 2.2 There is no table called EmployeeHistory in the JProCo database.

One way to create the Employee table would be to run a CREATE TABLE statement and then insert the records. An easy way to obtain the code for an existing table is to right click it in Object Explorer > Script Table as > CREATE To > New Query Editor Window. This gives you the table's structure, and then you need to insert the values. However, a SELECT INTO statement is a quicker process and is a commonly used technique for quickly copying a table (including all its data). Be aware that the SELECT INTO statement doesn't support the creation of clustered indexes. Our trigger example in this section would work fine without a clustered index, but we will briefly digress to show you this useful technique.

Recall that the Employee table has a primary key on the EmpID field. In Object Explorer, expand the dbo.Employee object and notice the primary key (Figure 2.3). Alternatively, you can right click dbo.Employee to see the design of the Employee table where the key symbol denotes the primary key on the EmpID field.

Chapter 2. After Triggers

Figure 2.3 There is a primary key constraint on the EmpID field of the Employee table.

Run the SELECT INTO statement you see in Figure 2.4. The ORDER BY clause isn't essential. However, it will make our creation of the clustered index on the EmployeeHistory table run more quickly. This is because inserting tables in order on a clustered index doesn't cause page splits.

```
SELECT * INTO EmployeeHistory
FROM Employee ORDER BY EmpID
```

```
Messages
(17 row(s) affected)

                                                                    0 rows
```

Figure 2.4 The EmployeeHistory table is a copy of the Employee table and all its records.

We have successfully created the EmployeeHistory table, which is a copy of the Employee table and all of its records. At this point, we could move ahead with our main example, which is to create a trigger (In many cases in the job setting, once you've completed the SELECT INTO statement, you can roll forward). However, since the EmployeeHistory table doesn't contain a clustered index, any new records added will not necessarily be ordered by EmpID.

If we check Object Explorer, we will see the EmployeeHistory table shows no primary key and no clustered index (Figure 2.5).

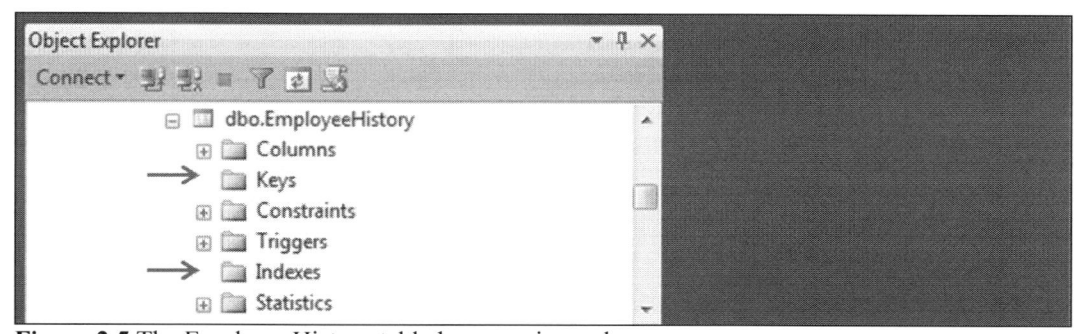

Figure 2.5 The EmployeeHistory table has no primary key.

Our next step will be to add a primary key on EmpID. Adding this clustered index will ensure records in the EmployeeHistory table will always appear in order according to EmpID:

```
ALTER TABLE EmployeeHistory
ADD PRIMARY KEY (EmpID)
GO
```

(*Note:* If for some reason we didn't want EmpID to be a primary key, we could accomplish our goal by creating a unique clustered index on EmpID.)

The two tables are currently in sync and each contains precisely the same 17 records. If we inserted an 18th record into the Employee table but did not take the time to write the same insert for the EmployeeHistory table, they would no longer be in sync.

To demonstrate how these two tables can get out of sync with an INSERT statement, let's add a new record to the Employee table. A new employee named Rainy Walker (EmpID 18) was hired on January 1, 2010. Rainy will work for Manager 11 in Location 1. To keep things simple, we will use the default values for the last three fields of this record:

```
INSERT INTO Employee VALUES
(18,'Walker','Rainy', '1-1-2010', 1, 11, DEFAULT,
DEFAULT, DEFAULT)
```

After you get the "1 row(s) affected" message, you should see 18 records in the Employee table. A SELECT query confirms it has 18 records, and the EmployeeHistory table still has 17 records (Figure 2.6). The EmployeeHistory should have the same number of records as the Employee table, so we need to identify and deal with the missing record.

```
SELECT * FROM Employee
SELECT * FROM EmployeeHistory
```

Figure 2.6 EmpID 18 is in the Employee table but not the EmployeeHistory table.

We know exactly which record is missing, since we caused the mismatch. But in the real world you won't always be so lucky. If you inherited this asynchronous data problem and needed to find out which record was missing, it would take some investigation. You can always run an unmatched query. A left outer join of the Employee table to the EmployeeHistory table on the EmpID field will get all matching and non-matching records. To look for every record where the Employee table does not have a matching record in the EmployeeHistory table, we look for a NULL in the EmployeeHistory table. The result of the unmatched query shows that the one missing record is EmpID 18 (Figure 2.7).

```
SELECT em.*
FROM Employee AS em
LEFT OUTER JOIN [EmployeeHistory] AS eh
ON em.EmpID = eh.EmpID
WHERE eh.EmpID IS NULL
```

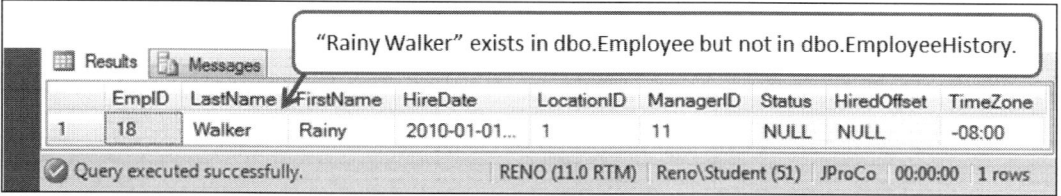

Figure 2.7 The unmatched query shows the record missing from the Employee table.

Employee 18's record needs to be inserted into the EmployeeHistory table. A quick way to accomplish this is to simply add an INSERT statement to our existing query:

```
INSERT INTO [EmployeeHistory]
SELECT em.*
FROM Employee AS em LEFT OUTER JOIN [EmployeeHistory] AS eh
ON em.EmpID = eh.EmpID
WHERE eh.EmpID IS NULL
```

To confirm your tables are back in sync, you can repeat the mismatch query (Figure 2.7). You can also repeat the SELECT queries (Figure 2.6).

Coding the After Insert Trigger

The Employee and EmployeeHistory tables were out of sync for a short period of time. Two INSERT statements were needed because we have two tables that need the same records. The first INSERT statement put the record in the Employee table; the second INSERT statement put the same record into the EmployeeHistory table. To ensure that the data for these two tables remains synchronized, we would need the two INSERT statements to run at the same time. *Therefore, our goal is to have all inserts from the Employee table also affect the EmployeeHistory table.*

We can tell the Employee table, that as soon as it encounters an insert, it should immediately invoke another INSERT statement to the EmployeeHistory table. An object that runs an action after an event (e.g., after an insert to the Employee table) is known as an **AFTER trigger**. An **AFTER trigger** is actually a stored procedure which runs after a specified event occurs. In this example, the specified event will be an insert into the Employee table.

We're going to create a trigger called trg_InsertEmployee which awaits an insert to the Employee table. This trigger will run after the insert happens. The following code outlines what we will need for this trigger:

```sql
CREATE TRIGGER trg_InsertEmployee
ON dbo.Employee
AFTER INSERT AS

BEGIN

--Insert Code to run here

END
GO
```

Between the BEGIN and END keywords, we're going to write code to INSERT INTO dbo.EmployeeHistory the same records which are inserted into the Employee table. Behind the scenes, all rows affected by the insert to dbo.Employee will go into the "Inserted" table. Thus, we can pull those same rows from the Inserted table in order to populate the EmployeeHistory table:

```sql
CREATE TRIGGER trg_InsertEmployee
ON dbo.Employee
AFTER INSERT AS

BEGIN
INSERT INTO dbo.EmployeeHistory
SELECT * FROM Inserted
END
GO
```

The inserted table is a memory resident table created during an event. This is covered with more detail in Volume 2. Once you see the "Command(s) completed successfully" confirmation, the trigger will be visible in Object Explorer.

Chapter 2. After Triggers

This trigger should run the moment after we insert any records into the Employee table. It's always a good idea to test your code, which we will do by inserting a new record.

Figure 2.8 Our new trigger shows in Object Explorer.

Figure 2.9 shows an insert for a new record, Employee #19. Notice we see two "1 row(s) affected" confirmation messages. The first reflects our insert into the Employee table. The second message is confirmation that the record was inserted into the EmployeeHistory table as a result of the trigger.

```
INSERT INTO dbo.[Employee]VALUES
(19, 'Beckman', 'Sandy', '1-15-2010', 1, 11,
DEFAULT, DEFAULT, DEFAULT)
```

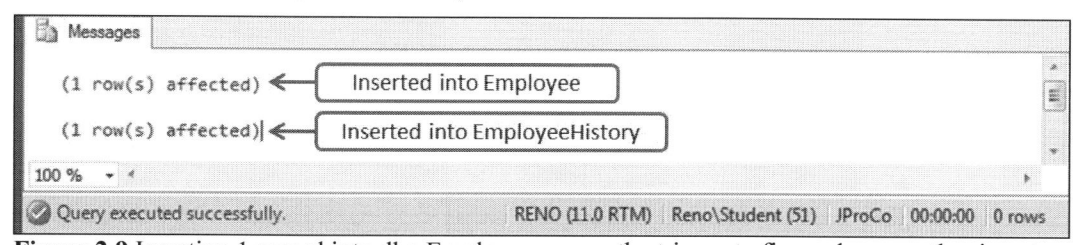

Figure 2.9 Inserting 1 record into dbo.Employee causes the trigger to fire and run another insert.

When we re-query both tables, we see that our trigger worked perfectly. When we inserted Sandy Beckman's record into the Employee table, the trigger immediately inserted a copy of her record into the EmployeeHistory table (Figure 2.10).

```
SELECT * FROM Employee
SELECT * FROM EmployeeHistory
```

Figure 2.10 Our trigger worked perfectly – EmpID 19 now appears in both tables.

Enabling and Disabling Triggers

To prevent a trigger from running, you can either get rid of the trigger or you can temporarily disable the trigger. If you test fictitious data which you will later delete, you must delete it from two tables (i.e., because you created an insert trigger). For example, testing an insert from a new process creates an employee called "Dummy One" with EmpID 999. This is acceptable data for our test team, but it's not data we plan to keep or use in production. In fact, once this dummy record gets into the Employee table, our test is done and we will delete the record. Unfortunately, we risk leaving this legacy data behind in dbo.EmployeeHistory because trg_InsertEmployee is constantly monitoring the Employee table and will fire each time an INSERT statement is run against this table. We have the option of disabling the trigger. We won't need to delete test data from our history table, because the trigger simply won't fire:

```
ALTER TABLE dbo.Employee
DISABLE TRIGGER trg_InsertEmployee
GO
```

Now that trg_InsertEmployee is disabled, we will run a test by attempting to add some dummy data into the Employee table. If we successfully disabled the trigger, then we will expect to see just one transaction ("1 row(s) affected"), which will add one record to the Employee table and zero records to EmployeeHistory.

```
INSERT INTO Employee VALUES
(999, 'Dummy', 'One', '2-2-2222', 1, 11,
DEFAULT, DEFAULT, DEFAULT)
```

```
Messages
(1 row(s) affected)
                                                                  0 rows
```

Figure 2.11 We are inserting this dummy data into dbo.Employee to confirm the trigger is disabled.

The confirmation of a single transaction (i.e., "1 row affected" shown in Figure 2.11) meets our expectations. Our insert of the dummy data affected only the Employee table. A SELECT COUNT query also confirms that the Employee table has increased to 20 records, but the EmployeeHistory table still contains just 19 records (Figure 2.12).

```
SELECT COUNT(*) FROM Employee
SELECT COUNT(*) FROM EmployeeHistory
```

(No column name)
20

(No column name)
19

1 rows

Figure 2.12 Due to the disabled insert trigger, dbo.EmployeeHistory still contains just 19 records.

It's now time to delete that one fictitious record from the Employee table. Run this DELETE statement to remove the dummy test record from your Employee table:

```
DELETE FROM Employee WHERE EmpID = 999
```

Now let's re-enable the trigger so that any data coming into dbo.Employee will be copied into dbo.EmployeeHistory:

```
ALTER TABLE dbo.Employee
ENABLE TRIGGER trg_InsertEmployee
GO
```

You can also disable the trigger directly. The following code shows the alternate syntax, which will disable trg_InsertEmployee.

```
DISABLE TRIGGER trg_InsertEmployee ON Employee
GO
```

With the trigger disabled, it won't function. Re-check the trigger in Object Explorer and notice that the trigger's icon now includes a small downward arrow, which indicates that the trigger has been disabled (Figure 2.13).

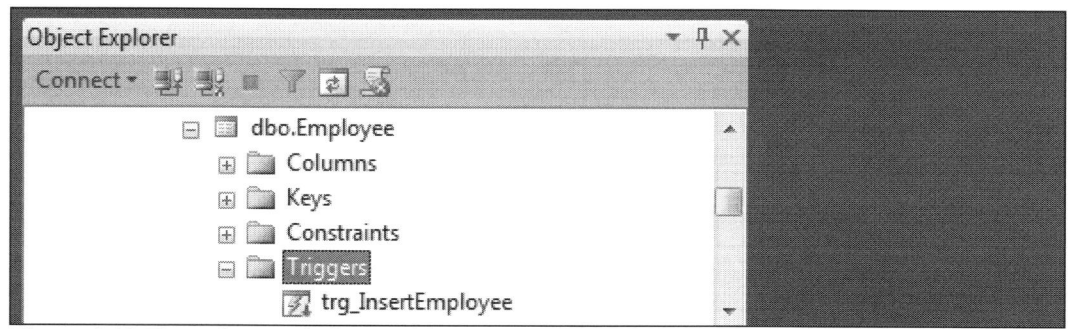

Figure 2.13 The red arrow indicates this trigger is disabled.

Now let's re-enable the trigger using the alternate code syntax:

```
ENABLE TRIGGER trg_InsertEmployee ON Employee
```

In your Object Explorer notice in Figure 2.14 that after you refresh, the red disable arrow disappears.

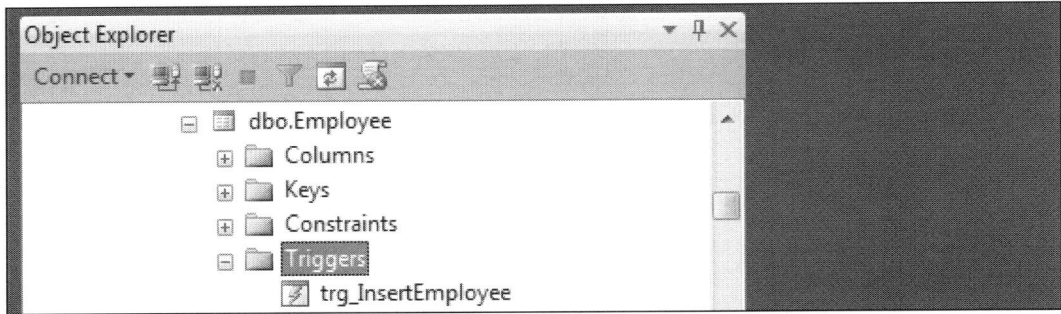

Figure 2.14 Refresh your trigger in Object Explorer to see its latest status.

Lab 2.1: Insert Triggers

Lab Prep: Lab Prep: Each lab has one or more Skill Checks. Start with Skill Check 1 and proceed until reaching the Points to Ponder section.

Before beginning this lab, verify that SQL Server 2012 is properly installed and operating. Before running the lab setup script for resetting the database (SQLQueries2012Vol4Chapter2.1Setup.sql), please make sure to close all query windows within SSMS. An open query window pointing to a database context can lock that database preventing it from updating when the script is executing. A simple way to assure all query windows are closed, is to exit out of SSMS, then open a new instance of SSMS, and lastly run the setup script.

Skill Check 1: Currently there is a PayRates table that has no records. Create a trigger called trg_InsertPayRates that takes inserted records into the PayRates table and copies them into the PayRatesHistory table (Figure 2.15). Test your trigger by inserting a pay of $45,000 per year for Employee 1 (Figure 2.16).

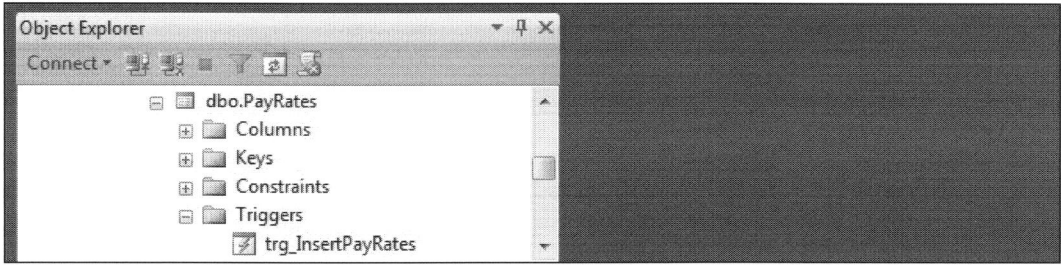

Figure 2.15 Object Explorer shows Trigger trg_InsertPayRates was created.

```
INSERT INTO dbo.PayRates VALUES
(15,45000,null,null)
```

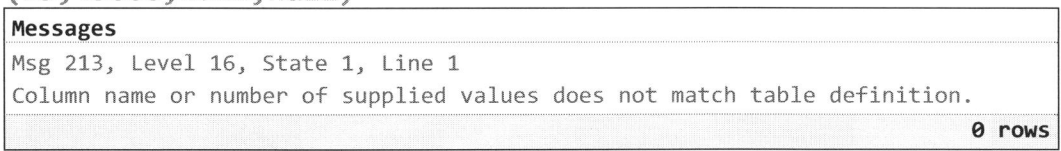

```
Messages
Msg 213, Level 16, State 1, Line 1
Column name or number of supplied values does not match table definition.
                                                                    0 rows
```

Figure 2.16 Skill Check 1.

Answer Code: The T-SQL code to this practice lab can be found in the downloadable files in a file named Lab2.1_InsertTriggers.sql.

Points to Ponder - Insert Triggers

1. A trigger is a special type of stored procedure that is not called directly by a user.
2. A trigger is like a stored procedure that executes when an INSERT, UPDATE, or DELETE event modifies data in a table.
3. When an insert trigger fires, it guarantees two things have occurred:
    a. You have at least one record in the Inserted table.
    b. You have at least one new record in the table that the insert trigger is on.
4. The Inserted table is a memory resident table (sometimes referred to as a "magic table" or a "special table") that holds a copy of the rows which have been inserted.
5. The trigger can examine the Inserted table to determine whether the trigger action(s) should be executed.
6. You can reference data from the Inserted table without having to store the data in @variables.
7. Triggers have access to the features of T-SQL and can therefore enforce complex business logic beyond constraints or rules.
8. Constraints can use system messages only for reporting errors. With triggers, you can customize error messages and mechanisms (More information on constraints may be found in Chapter 1).

Delete Triggers

We've learned that insert triggers run their code after an insert is made to a table. Similarly, an **(after) delete trigger** runs its code after a delete event occurs on a table. You will more commonly hear an after delete trigger simply referred to as a **delete trigger**.

Creating Delete Triggers

JProCo is a young company and thus far hasn't had anyone leave the company. We still have our original 19 employees. Since we someday may need to permanently delete a record from our Employee table, we need a history table to hold the records of employees who have left the company. In the JProCo database we have such a table, which is called dbo.FormerEmployee. Currently there are no records in the dbo.FormerEmployee table, because no one has been deleted (Figure 2.17).

```
SELECT * FROM dbo.Employee
SELECT * FROM dbo.FormerEmployee
```

EmpID	LastName	FirstName	HireDate	LocationID	ManagerID	Status	HiredOffs
1	Adams	Alex	2001-01-01...	1	11	Active	2001-01
2	Brown	Barry	2002-08-12...	1	11	Active	2002-08
3	Osako	Lee	1999-09-01...	2	11	Active	1999-09
4	Kennson	David	1996-03-16...	1	11	Has Tenure	1996-03
5	Bender	Eric	2007-05-17...	1	11	Active	2007-05
6	Kendall	Lisa	2001-11-15...	4	4	Active	2001-11

EmpID	LastName	FirstName	HireDate	LocationID	ManagerID	Status	HiredOffset	TimeZone

Figure 2.17 The Employee table and the FormerEmployee table have the same fields, but the FormerEmployee table is unpopulated since no one has left the company.

A delete trigger creates the Deleted table.

READER NOTE: The memory resident Inserted and Deleted tables were covered in SQL Queries 2012 Volume 2 along with the OUTPUT clause.

The moment a delete is made from the Employee table, we want the deleted record logged automatically into the dbo.FormerEmployee table. This shows the trg_DelEmployee trigger on the Employee table which will run following a DELETE statement. This trigger will take the records from the Deleted table (which is based on what was deleted from the Employee table) and insert those records into the FormerEmployee table.

```
CREATE TRIGGER trg_DelEmployee ON dbo.Employee
AFTER DELETE AS
BEGIN
INSERT INTO [FormerEmployee]
SELECT * FROM Deleted
END
GO
```

After you see the "Command(s) completed successfully" confirmation, check the Object Explorer and notice that this new trigger is visible in the Triggers folder of the Employee table (Figure 2.18). This is our second trigger on the Employee table. This first one was the trg_InsertEmployee trigger we created in the last section. Even though you can have many triggers on one table, you can only have one of each event type. The three possible event types are: insert, update, and delete. For example, we can't have two delete triggers on the Employee table.

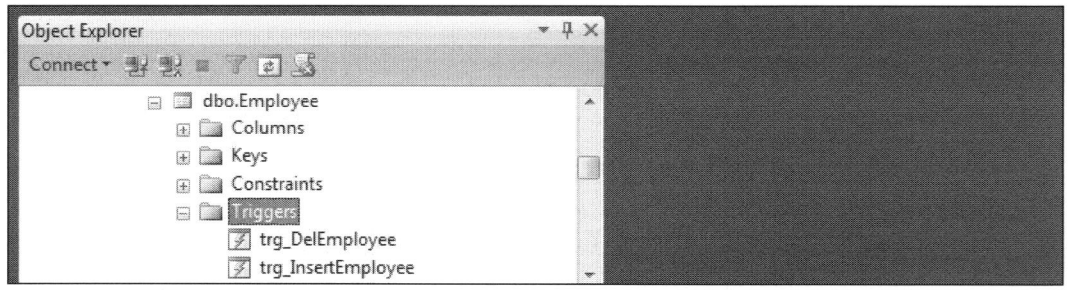

Figure 2.18 The insert and delete triggers can be seen in the Object Explorer.

Running Delete Triggers

To truly test this trigger, we should delete a record from the Employee table. Suppose that EmpID 19 (Sandy Beckman) is leaving. Running a DELETE statement should display "1 row(s) affected" twice in your messages tab.

```
DELETE FROM dbo.Employee WHERE EmpID = 19
```

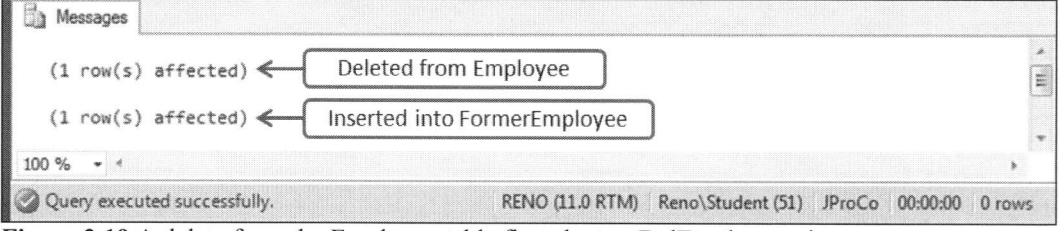

Figure 2.19 A delete from the Employee table fires the trg_DelEmployee trigger.

When you query each of the tables, you will notice that there are only 18 records in the Employee table instead of 19. The EmpID 19 row has been removed from the Employee table and now appears in the FormerEmployee table (Figure 2.20).

```
SELECT * FROM dbo.Employee
SELECT * FROM dbo.FormerEmployee
```

	EmpID	LastName	FirstName	HireDate	LocationID	ManagerID	Status	HiredOffset
17	17	Downs	Wendy	2012-10-04...	1	11	Orie...	2012-10-04 20:3!
18	18	Walker	Rainy	2010-01-01...	1	11	NULL	NULL

	EmpID	LastName	FirstName	HireDate	LocationID	ManagerID	Status	HiredOffset	TimeZ
1	19	Beckman	Sandy	2010-01-15...	1	11	NULL	NULL	-08:00

Figure 2.20 Sandy Beckman's record was deleted and now appears in the FormerEmployee table.

Note: In order to keep the focus on triggers, we used an extremely simplified version of a "history table" here. A historical record would also track additional data points, such as the employee's departure date.

Using Triggers for Data Integrity

A common use of triggers is to protect, constrain, or add integrity to your data. To make this point more clearly, let's look at all the records from the Location table (Figure 2.21).

```
SELECT * FROM Location
```

	LocationID	Street	City	State	Latitude	Longitude	GeoLoc
1	1	111 First ST	Seattle	WA	47.455	-122.231	0xE6100000010C
2	2	222 Second AVE	Boston	MA	42.372	-71.0298	0xE6100000010C
3	3	333 Third PL	Chicago	IL	41.953	-87.643	0xE6100000010C
4	4	444 Ruby ST	Spokane	WA	47.668	-117.529	0xE6100000010C
5	5	1595 Main	Philadelphia	PA	39.888	-75.251	0xE6100000010C
6	6	915 Wallaby Dr...	Sydney	NU...	-33.876	151.315	0xE6100000010C

Figure 2.21 All of the records of the Location table (JProCo.dbo.Location).

Suppose that we are decommissioning Location 3 (the Chicago office). The record containing LocationID 3 needs to be deleted from the Location table. This DELETE statement should accomplish that task (Figure 2.22). However, take caution – if you inadvertently select and run only the first line of this DELETE statement, then you will delete every record in the Location table. If you see "6 rows affected", then you have accidentally deleted all of your records and your Location table is now unpopulated. Yikes!

```
DELETE FROM Location
WHERE LocationID = 3
```

```
(6 row(s) affected)
```

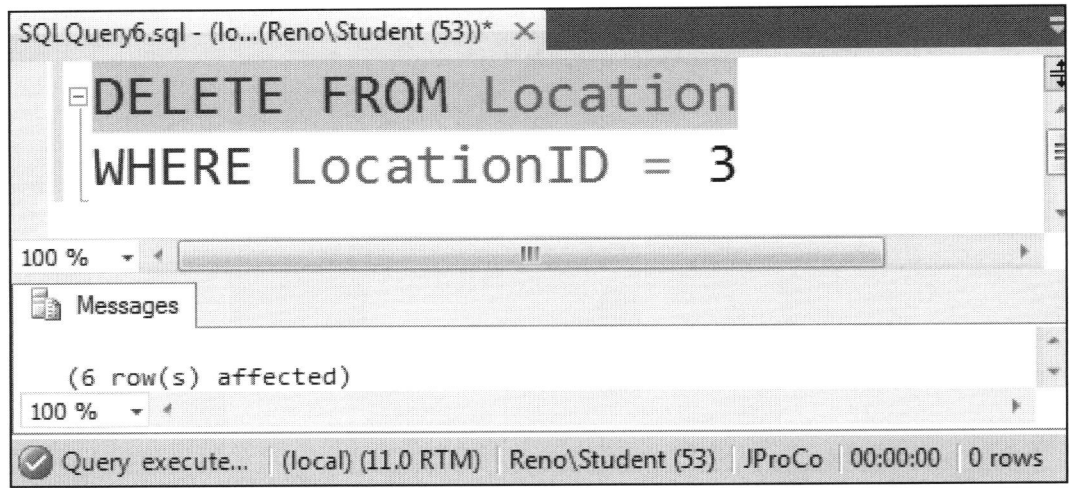

Figure 2.22 Be careful – by selecting only part of this code, you might accidently delete all of the records from your Location table.

[*Note:* If you delete all the records from your Location table, either accidentally or because you wanted to fully demo the worst-case scenario, then please run the reset script **SQLProgrammingExtraResetLocation.sql** in order to restore the original six records to your Location table.]

To prevent this type of mishap in the future, we can add a trigger which will allow you to DELETE just one record per DML statement run against the Location table. A good name for this trigger would be trg_DelLocation. This **(after) delete trigger** will fire with each delete that takes place on the Location table. The code which you want to run when a delete occurs against dbo.Location will appear between the BEGIN and END keywords:

```
CREATE TRIGGER trg_DelLocation ON dbo.Location
AFTER DELETE AS
BEGIN

--code here

END
GO
```

What code should we place between the BEGIN and END commands? We can use an IF statement to get the count of the number of records in the Deleted table. If more than 1 record is found in the Deleted table, then we should roll back the entire transaction. Knowing this trigger runs after the DELETE statement has been called, will it be too late to undo the DELETE operation? No, because all "After Triggers" fire after the change has been made to the intermediate state records but before the transaction has been committed to storage. This means that within the trigger, you have the ability to roll back the transaction:

```
CREATE TRIGGER trg_DelLocation ON dbo.Location
AFTER DELETE AS
BEGIN
IF((SELECT COUNT(*) FROM Deleted) > 1)
ROLLBACK TRAN
END
GO
```

Once you create the trigger, let's test our code. Attempt to delete all of the records from the Location table (DELETE From Location). If your trigger was created properly, then you will get the error shown in Figure 2.23.

```
DELETE FROM Location
```

```
Messages
Msg 3609, Level 16, State 1, Line 1
The transaction ended in the trigger. The batch has been aborted.
                                                                    0 rows
```

Figure 2.23 Deleting more than one location record at a time is rolled back by trg_DelLocation.

Now run the full DELETE statement, which removes only Location 3. The code in Figure 2.24 deletes one record. When you see the confirmation message "1 row(s) affected" you know that exactly one record was deleted. In order for the transaction to have completed – and therefore to have been allowed by the trigger – at most, one record could have been deleted.

```
DELETE FROM Location WHERE LocationID = 3
```

```
Messages
(1 row(s) affected)
                                                                    0 rows
```

Figure 2.24 The trg_DelLocation trigger allowed the deletion of exactly one record.

Run a SELECT query and confirm Chicago is no longer in the Location table.

```
SELECT * FROM Location
```

Results | Spatial results | Messages

	LocationID	Street	City	State	Latitude	Longitude	GeoLoc
1	1	111 First ST	Seattle	WA	47.455	-122.231	0xE6100000010C
2	2	222 Second AVE	Boston	MA	42.372	-71.0298	0xE6100000010C
3	4	444 Ruby ST	Spokane	WA	47.668	-117.529	0xE6100000010C
4	5	1595 Main	Philadelphia	PA	39.888	-75.251	0xE6100000010C
5	6	915 Wallaby Drive	Sydney	NULL	-33.876	151.315	0xE6100000010C

Query executed successfully. | RENO (11.0 RTM) | Reno\Student (51) | JProCo | 00:00:00 | 5 rows

Figure 2.25 LocationID 3 (Chicago) has been deleted from the Location table.

The deletion of all the Location records at once will fail because of the trigger. Because of the trigger, any DELETE statement without a WHERE clause will not run (i.e., assuming the Location table contains more than one record).

When we ran a DELETE statement for one record, it successfully ran and committed that transaction. Therefore, we see we have Locations 1 through 6 (minus Location 3) left in our Location table. The trg_DelLocation trigger protected our data from any multi-record DELETE statement.

Lab 2.2: Delete Triggers

Lab Prep: Each lab has one or more Skill Checks. Start with Skill Check 1 and proceed until reaching the Points to Ponder section.

Before beginning this lab, verify that SQL Server 2012 is properly installed and operating. Before running the lab setup script for resetting the database (SQLQueries2012Vol4Chapter2.2Setup.sql), please make sure to close all query windows within SSMS. An open query window pointing to a database context can lock that database preventing it from updating when the script is executing. A simple way to assure all query windows are closed, is to exit out of SSMS, then open a new instance of SSMS, and lastly run the setup script.

Skill Check 1: Create a trigger called trg_DeletePayRates that takes records deleted from the PayRates table and inserts them into the dbo.FormerPayRates table (Figure 2.26). Test your trigger by deleting the pay for Employee 1 (Figure 2.27).

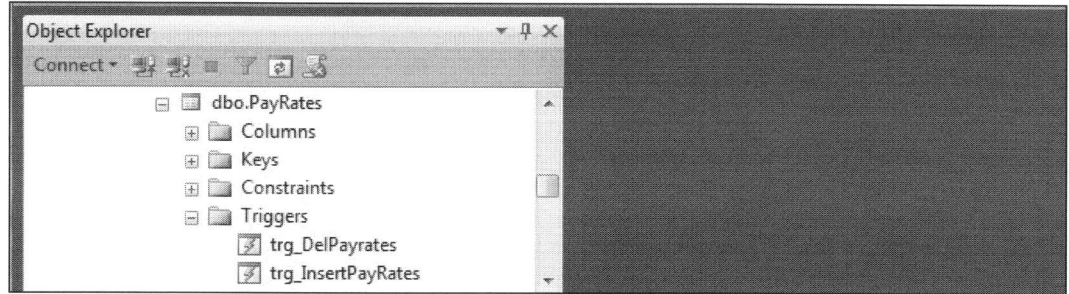

Figure 2.26 Shows trigger trg_DeletePayRates was created.

```
DELETE FROM dbo.PayRates WHERE EmpID = 1
```

```
Messages
(1 row(s) affected)

(1 row(s) affected)
                                                                    0 rows
```

Figure 2.27 Skill Check 1.

Skill Check 2: Create a trigger called trg_DelStateList that ensures you can never delete multiple records at once from the StateList table.

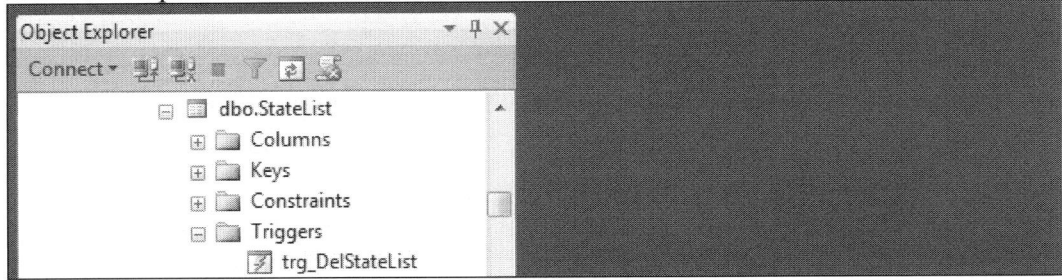

Figure 2.28 Shows trigger trg_DelStateList_DelStateList was created.

```
DELETE StateList
DELETE StateList WHERE StateID = 'ZU'
```

```
Messages
Msg 3609, Level 16, State 1, Line 1
The transaction ended in the trigger. The batch has been aborted.
                                                            0 rows
```

Figure 2.29 Skill Check 2.

Answer Code: The T-SQL code to this practice lab can be found in the downloadable files in a file named Lab2.2_DeleteTriggers.sql.

Points to Ponder - Delete Triggers

1. A DML trigger is a type of stored procedure that executes when the DML (Data Manipulation Language) statements UPDATE, INSERT, or DELETE run against a table or a view.
2. Much like constraints, it is possible to enforce data integrity through triggers. However, you should use constraints whenever possible.
3. A delete trigger is a stored procedure that executes whenever a DELETE statement deletes data from a table.
4. When a delete trigger is fired, deleted rows from the affected table are placed in a special Deleted table.
5. When a row is appended to a Deleted table, it no longer exists in the table that fired the trigger.
6. A TRUNCATE TABLE statement run against a table will empty that table. However, no DML triggers will be fired off since TRUNCATE is a DDL statement.
7. An "After Delete Trigger" fires after the change has been made to the intermediate state of the records. Records still in the intermediate state allow you the ability to roll back the transaction, if needed.

Update Triggers

We've learned that insert triggers create an Inserted table and delete triggers create a Deleted table. You can also create an **(after) update trigger,** which is more commonly referred to as an **update trigger.** This is the only trigger which creates both of these memory resident tables, since an update is really just a delete and an insert which occur in the same transaction.

Creating Update Triggers

The trg_InsertEmployee trigger does a fine job of keeping all the inserts to dbo.Employee in sync with dbo.EmployeeHistory. However, it won't work with an UPDATE statement run against the Employee table. *Insert triggers ignore updates.*

Let's look at one particular employee example. Employee 11 is "Sally Smith". She appears as EmpID 11 in the Employee table, as well as in the EmployeeHistory table. We have learned she will soon be married and her last name will become "Bowler". The JProCo database must be updated accordingly:

```
UPDATE dbo.Employee
SET LastName = 'Bowler' WHERE EmpID = 11
```

Her name now appears as "Bowler" in the Employee table. But her name is still "Smith" in the EmployeeHistory table (Figure 2.30).

```
SELECT * FROM dbo.Employee WHERE EmpID = 11
SELECT * FROM dbo.EmployeeHistory WHERE EmpID = 11
```

EmpID	LastName	FirstName	HireDate	LocationID	ManagerID	Status	HiredOffset
11	Bowler	Sally	1989-04-01 00:00:00.000	1	NULL	Active	1989-04-01 00:00:00.0000000

EmpID	LastName	FirstName	HireDate	LocationID	ManagerID	Status	HiredOffset
11	Smith	Sally	1989-04-01 00:00:00.000	1	NULL	Active	1989-04-01 00:00:00.0000000

Figure 2.30 The LastName "Bowler" was updated in dbo.Employee but not in EmployeeHistory.

This update to the Employee table was not reflected in the EmployeeHistory table because the insert trigger ignores UPDATE statements. We want to keep the Employee and EmployeeHistory tables in tandem. An update trigger on the Employee table can help us accomplish this.

The following code shows the new trg_UpdEmployee trigger will take the latest LastName from the Inserted table and write that LastName value to the EmployeeHistory table. The trg_UpdEmployee will generate two memory resident tables, each having the same number of records but different values. The Deleted table will have one record containing the data you just replaced (Smith). The Inserted table will have one record showing the new data introduced by the UPDATE statement (Bowler). Since we want the new record "Bowler" to be in the EmployeeHistory table, this data must come from the Inserted table. The following code creates the trg_UpdEmployee trigger:

```
CREATE TRIGGER trg_UpdEmployee ON dbo.Employee
AFTER UPDATE AS

BEGIN
UPDATE dbo.EmployeeHistory
SET LastName = em.LastName
FROM dbo.EmployeeHistory AS eh
INNER JOIN Inserted AS em
ON eh.EmpID = em.EmpID
END

GO
```

Running Update Triggers

After successfully creating trg_UpdEmployee, we will test it with another update to the Employee table. There was some confusion about Sally's name, which actually should have been changed to "Zander", not "Bowler" (Figure 2.31).

```
UPDATE dbo.Employee
SET LastName = 'Zander'
WHERE EmpID = 11
```

Messages
(1 row(s) affected)
(1 row(s) affected)

0 rows

Figure 2.31 An UPDATE to the Employee table will now also update the EmployeeHistory table.

Let's rerun our two SELECT statements to confirm that Sally's LastName value has been successfully updated to "Zander" in both tables (Figure 2.32).

```
SELECT * FROM dbo.Employee WHERE EmpID = 11
SELECT * FROM dbo.EmployeeHistory WHERE EmpID = 11
```

	EmpID	LastName	FirstName	HireDate	LocationID	ManagerID	Status	HiredOffs
1	11	Zander	Sally	1989-04-01...	1	NULL	Active	1989-04-

	EmpID	LastName	FirstName	HireDate	LocationID	ManagerID	Status	HiredOffs
1	11	Zander	Sally	1989-04-01...	1	NULL	Active	1989-04-

Query executed successfully. | RENO (11.0 RTM) | Reno\Student (51) | JProCo | 00:00:00 | 1 rows

Figure 2.32 The LastName value of "Zander" for EmpID 11 appears in both the Employee and EmployeeHistory tables.

Update Triggers and Data Integrity

You saw how an update trigger is useful for keeping two tables updated in tandem. You might be wondering just how an update trigger is useful for data integrity. Take the example of the StateList table. Changes to this table will be extremely rare – the U.S. hasn't added a new state since 1959, and LandMass changes would also be rare. Therefore, the data in the StateList table is very stable. Let's imagine the U.S. entered into a contract whereby Russia will sell us 50 square miles of an island which it is not using and which will be useful for our fishing business. This new island will be added to the Aleutian Island Chain in Alaska. As a result, Alaska will increase in size by 50 square miles.

```
SELECT * FROM StateList
```

	StateID	StateProvinceName	RegionID	LandMass
1	AB	Alberta	1	247999
2	AK	Alaska	2	656425
3	AL	Alabama	2	52423
4	AR	Arkansas	2	53182
5	AZ	Arizona	2	114006
6	BC	British Columbia	1	357216

62 rows

Figure 2.33 The StateList table.

The LandMass for Alaska will go from 656,425 to 656,475. The UPDATE statement (Figure 2.34) will make this change to our StateList table.

```
UPDATE StateList SET LandMass = LandMass +50
WHERE StateID ='AK'

SELECT * FROM StateList
WHERE StateID ='AK'
```

StateID	StateProvinceName	RegionID	LandMass
AK	Alaska	2	656475 = 656425 + 50

Query executed successfully.   RENO (11.0 RTM)   Reno\Student (51)   JProCo   00:00:00   1 rows

Figure 2.34 This UPDATE statement shows Alaska will gain 50 square miles of LandMass.

You could have easily and unintentionally run this UPDATE statement and forgotten your WHERE clause. Then all states would have increased by 50 square miles. Since changes to the StateList table are very uncommon, we're going to limit it so that only one state record may be updated at a time (Figure 2.35).

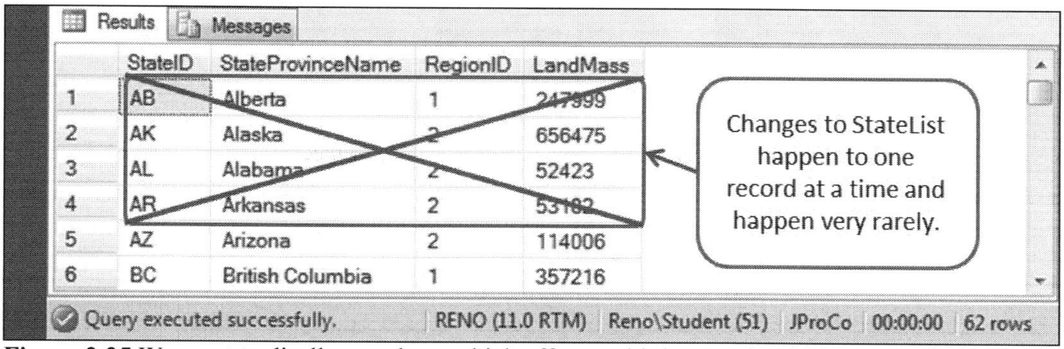

Chapter 2. After Triggers

Figure 2.35 We want to disallow updates which affect multiple records within one statement.

Some changes should never happen. For example, once a StateID is set, it should never be changed. For example, you would want an update changing the StateID 'AK' to 'AS' to fail (Figure 2.36).

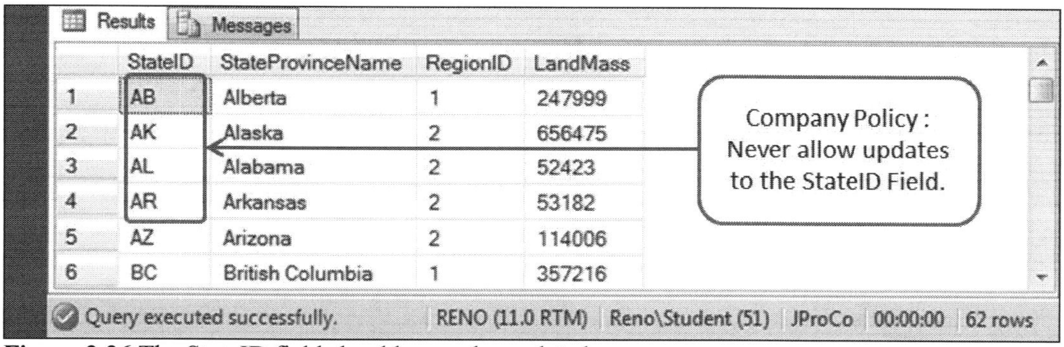

Figure 2.36 The StateID field should never be updated.

You might be tempted to create two delete triggers on the StateList table, one which prevents multiple deletes and another which prevents StateID changes. Like any other table, the StateList table can have only one delete trigger. We need to create a very complicated trigger that will accomplish two things for us: 1) ensure that you can't update more than one state at a time, and 2) never allow updates to the StateID field.

We will write the code to create the trg_UpdateStateList on the StateList table with the BEGIN and END ready to hold the code logic for our trigger. Remember, the "Update Trigger" is the only trigger which uses both the Inserted and Deleted tables (Figure 2.37).

```
CREATE TRIGGER trg_updStateList ON StateList
AFTER UPDATE AS
    BEGIN
    END
GO
```

The "Update trigger" exposes the inserted and deleted "Memory Resident" tables.

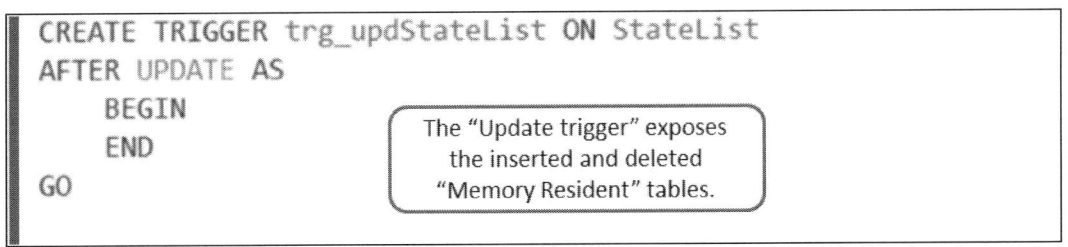

Figure 2.37 Update triggers will create two memory resident tables (Inserted and Deleted).

The following code checks for a count of more than one record that has been changed (If such a change is found, the transaction will be rolled back). To handle policy #2, we need another statement that says, "If we find a record where the Inserted and Deleted tables seem to have a different StateID value, then the transaction should be rolled back:

```
CREATE TRIGGER trg_updStateList ON StateList
AFTER UPDATE AS
BEGIN
IF((SELECT COUNT(*) FROM Inserted )> 1)
ROLLBACK TRAN
END
GO
```

We want this trigger to have more logic. To find out if two StateID fields don't match, simply run an unmatched query between the Inserted and Deleted tables. If you find NULL values in the StateID field of the Deleted table, then roll back the transaction:

```
DROP TRIGGER trg_updStateList
GO

CREATE TRIGGER trg_updStateList ON StateList
AFTER UPDATE AS
BEGIN
IF((SELECT COUNT(*) FROM Inserted )> 1)
ROLLBACK TRAN

IF EXISTS(SELECT * FROM Inserted LEFT OUTER JOIN Deleted
ON Inserted.StateID = Deleted.StateID
WHERE Deleted.StateID IS NULL)
ROLLBACK TRAN
END
GO
```

After the trg_updStateList has been successfully created, we will do some testing. Observe that the UPDATE statement shown in Figure 2.38 would attempt to run multiple updates. However, trg_UpdateStateList blocks these updates. Because the count in the IF block is greater than one, the ROLLBACK TRAN code is executed (Figure 2.38).

```
UPDATE StateList SET LandMass = LandMass +50
```

```
Messages
Msg 3609, Level 16, State 1, Line 1
The transaction ended in the trigger. The batch has been aborted.
                                                                 0 rows
```

Figure 2.38 An update to multiple records in one transaction is disallowed by the trigger.

The UPDATE statement in Figure 2.39 would try to change a StateID field. The IF EXISTS code inside of the trigger finds an unmatched record, and thus the trigger rolls back the transaction.

```
UPDATE StateList SET StateID = 'AS'
WHERE StateID ='AK'
```

```
Messages
Msg 3609, Level 16, State 1, Line 1
The transaction ended in the trigger. The batch has been aborted.
                                                                 0 rows
```

Figure 2.39 Updating a StateID is also not allowed.

Let's attempt a change which should be allowed. The UPDATE statement in only affects one record at a time and does not change the StateID:

```
UPDATE StateList SET LandMass = LandMass - 50
WHERE StateID = 'AK'
```

Lab 2.3: Update Triggers

Lab Prep: Lab Prep: Each lab has one or more Skill Checks. Start with Skill Check 1 and proceed until reaching the Points to Ponder section.

Before beginning this lab, verify that SQL Server 2012 is properly installed and operating. Before running the lab setup script for resetting the database (SQLQueries2012Vol4Chapter2.3Setup.sql), please make sure to close all query windows within SSMS. An open query window pointing to a database context can lock that database preventing it from updating when the script is executing. A simple way to assure all query windows are closed, is to exit out of SSMS, then open a new instance of SSMS, and lastly run the setup script.

Skill Check 1: Create a trigger called trg_UpdPayRates, which updates all fields of the PayRatesHistory table based on changes to the PayRates table. Test the trigger by updating the YearlySalary of EmpID 11 to 150,000.

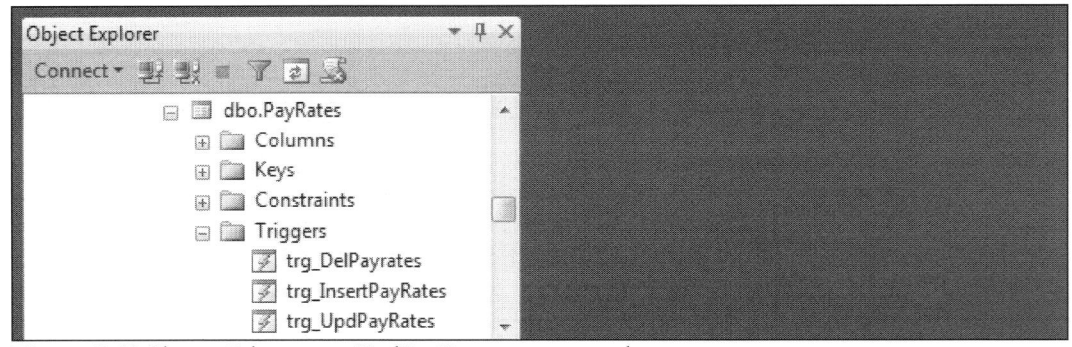

Figure 2.40 Shows Trigger trg_UpdPayRates was created.

```
UPDATE dbo.PayRates
SET YearlySalary = 150000
WHERE EmpID = 11
```

```
Messages
(0 row(s) affected)

(1 row(s) affected)
                                                        0 rows
```

Figure 2.41 Skill Check 1 Test results.

Chapter 2. After Triggers

Skill Check 2: Create a trigger called trg_updGrant, which will not allow you to make updates to the existing values of the GrantID field.

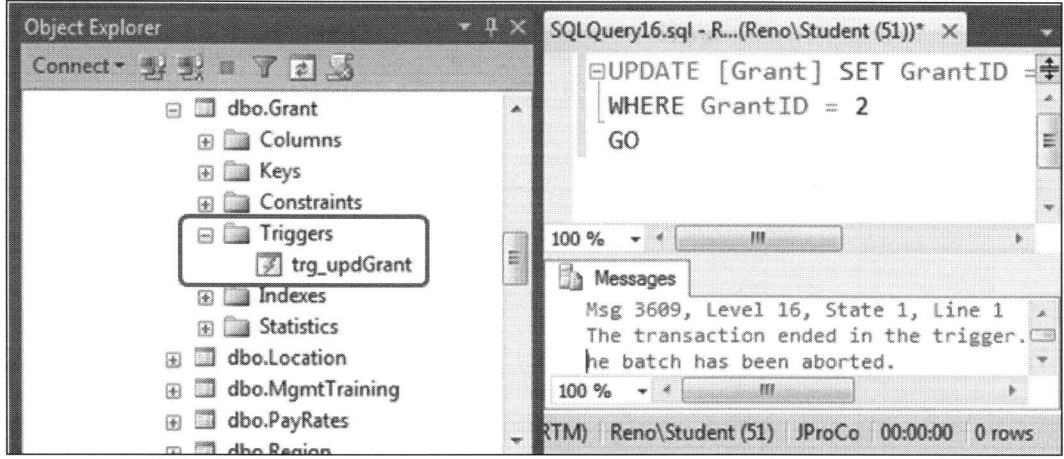

Figure 2.42 Skill Check 2 result.

Skill Check 3: Sometimes updates are made to the SalesInvoiceDetail table; these updates represent a new OrderDate for an existing SalesInvoice. After a change is made to the SalesInvoiceDetail table, you need to update the SalesInvoice.UpdatedDate field to reflect the current date and time. Write a trigger named trg_updSalesInvoiceDetail to achieve this goal. Test your trigger by updating InvoiceID 1 to have a 0.05 Unit Discount (Figure 2.43). Check to see that the SalesInvoice table has the newer timestamp (Figure 2.44).

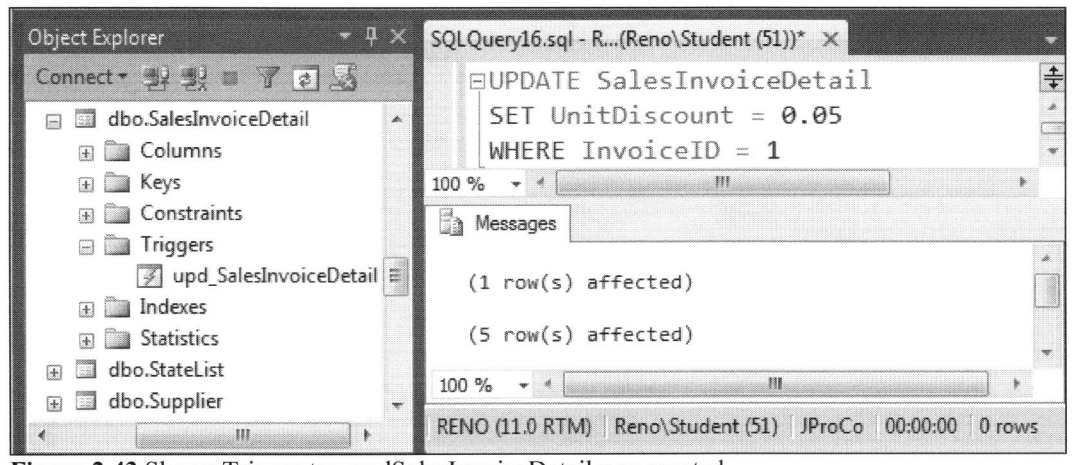

Figure 2.43 Shows Trigger trg_updSalesInvoiceDetail was created.

```
SQLQuery16.sql - R...(Reno\Student (51))* X
SELECT * FROM SalesInvoice
WHERE InvoiceID = 1
```

	InvoiceID	OrderDate	PaidDate	CustomerID	Comment	UpdatedDate
1	1	2009-01-03...	2009-01-11...	472	NULL	2012-10-01 22:48:38.8...

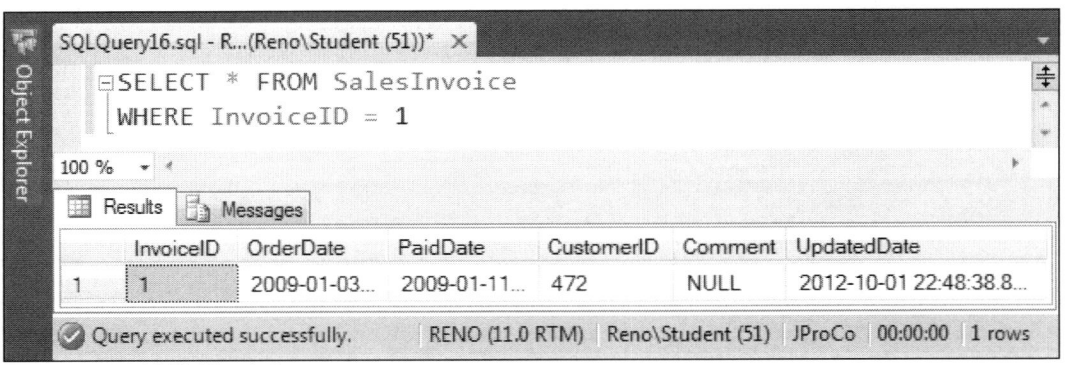

Figure 2.44 Skill Check 3.

Answer Code: The T-SQL code to this lab can be found in the downloadable files in a file named Lab2.3_UpdateTriggers.sql.

Points to Ponder - Update Triggers

1. An update trigger is a trigger that executes whenever an UPDATE statement changes data in a table or view on which the trigger is configured.
2. An update operation is really comprised of two steps: a delete and an insert.
3. The update trigger actually exposes two memory resident tables (Deleted and Inserted).
4. If you don't want a trigger to run, there are three ways to disable the trigger:
    - Right-click the trigger and select Disable.
    - Execute the DISABLE TRIGGER T-SQL command.
    - Execute the ALTER TABLE T-SQL command.
5. INTERVIEW QUESTION: What are the special memory resident tables available when dealing with triggers? Most people answer "Inserted, Updated, and Deleted". However, there are only two tables: Inserted and Deleted.

Chapter Glossary

AFTER trigger: A stored procedure that executes after the action specified has taken place.

CREATE *TriggerName*: The DDL statement used to create all types of triggers.

DDL: Data Definition Language. Statements that define data structures. The most common are CREATE, ALTER, and DROP.

DELETE *TableName*: A DML statement that removes records from your table and logs the action.

Delete trigger: Also called an "after delete trigger". A trigger that fires after a DELETE statement has taken place on the table containing the trigger.

DML: Data Manipulation Language. Statements which manipulate or retrieve data. The most common are SELECT, INSERT, UPDATE, and DELETE.

Insert trigger: A trigger that executes after, or instead of, an insert operation.

Magic tables: See *Memory resident tables.*

Memory resident tables: Conceptual tables (Inserted and Deleted) that have the same structure as the table containing the trigger. These work behind the scenes of every INSERT, UPDATE, and DELETE operation. Several techniques make use of DML statements run against these memory resident tables (e.g., triggers, the OUTPUT clause, the MERGE statement, Change Tracking). The Inserted and Deleted tables can only be accessed within the execution (trigger) context. As of this book's publication, there is no uniformly recognized term for the Inserted and Deleted tables; you may hear SQL pros refer to them as "magic tables", "special tables", or "pseudo tables".

SELECT INTO: Selects data from one table and inserts it into another table.

Special tables: See *Memory resident tables.*

Transaction: The process SQL performs to take a DML request to get committed to permanent storage.

Trigger: A stored procedure that automatically fires based on an event.

TRUNCATE TABLE: A DDL statement which removes all records from a table and does not perform any logging of the action.

Update trigger: A trigger that fires after an UPDATE statement has taken place on the table containing the trigger.

Review Quiz - Chapter Two

1.) What is the only DML statement that will never fire off an AFTER trigger?

- O a. **SELECT**
- O b. **INSERT**
- O c. **UPDATE**
- O d. **DELETE**

2.) Which of the following are memory resident tables are accessible because of an update trigger? (Choose two)

- ☐ a. **INSERTED**
- ☐ b. **UPDATED**
- ☐ c. **DELETED**

3.) You want to perform a test insert against your dbo.Employee table which has an insert trigger on it. You are not allowed to delete the trigger but want to perform this insert without the trigger firing. How can you do this?

- O a. You can't.
- O b. Downgrade the trigger before your test and then upgrade afterwards.
- O c. Move the trigger to a new table then move it back after your test.
- O d. Disable the trigger before the test and then enable it afterwards.
- O e. Enable the trigger before the test and then disable it afterwards.

4.) You have a trigger named trg_InsertEmployee which fires whenever a new employee is inserted into the Employee table. You are getting ready to test a new process to import employees from an external feed. As your first test, you are going to insert five fictitious employees named Dummy1 through Dummy5. If the test succeeds, then you will later delete these employees. You never want these employees to appear in the EmployeeHistory table. Your boss tells you she likes your existing triggers, so you can't delete them. To disable your trigger during testing, which two T-SQL statements could you run? (Choose two)

- ☐ a. **ALTER TABLE** Employee **DISABLE TRIGGER** trg_InsertEmployee
- ☐ b. **DROP TRIGGER** trg_InsertEmployee
- ☐ c. **DISABLE TRIGGER** trg_InsertEmployee **ON** Employee
- ☐ d. **ALTER TRIGGER** trg_InsertEmployee **ON** Employee **NOT FOR REPLICATION**
- ☐ e. **Sp_SetTrigger** @TriggerName = 'trg_InsertEmployee'. @Order = 'none'

5.) Sometimes an AFTER trigger will have no populated memory resident tables.

O a. True

O b. False

6.) The SalesInvoice and SalesInvoiceDetail tables relate to each other on the InvoiceID column. You require that the SalesInvoice.UpdatedDate column reflect the date when a change was made to the corresponding InvoiceID in the SalesInvoiceDetail table. You want to use a trigger to fulfill the requirement. What code should you use?

O a.
```
CREATE TRIGGER upd_SalesInvoiceDetail ON SalesInvoiceDetail
INSTEAD OF UPDATE
AS
UPDATE SalesInvoiceDetail SET UpdatedDate = GETDATE()
FROM Inserted INNER JOIN SalesInvoiceDetail
ON Inserted.InvoiceID = SalesInvoiceDetail.InvoiceID
```

O b.
```
CREATE TRIGGER upd_SalesInvoiceDetail ON SalesInvoiceDetail
INSTEAD OF UPDATE
AS
UPDATE SalesInvoice SET UpdatedDate = GETDATE()
FROM Inserted INNER JOIN SalesInvoice
ON Inserted.InvoiceID = SalesInvoice.InvoiceID
```

O c.
```
CREATE TRIGGER upd_SalesInvoiceDetail ON SalesInvoiceDetail
AFTER UPDATE
AS
UPDATE SalesInvoiceDetail SET UpdatedDate = GETDATE()
FROM Inserted INNER JOIN SalesInvoiceDetail
ON Inserted.InvoiceID = SalesInvoiceDetail.InvoiceID
```

O d.
```
CREATE TRIGGER upd_SalesInvoiceDetail ON SalesInvoiceDetail
AFTER UPDATE
AS
UPDATE SalesInvoice SET UpdatedDate = GETDATE()
FROM Inserted INNER JOIN SalesInvoice
ON Inserted.InvoiceID = SalesInvoice.InvoiceID
```

Answer Key

1.) The only DML statement that does not make any changes to a table is SELECT which makes (a) the correct answer.

2.) There is no such thing as an updated memory resident table, so (b) is incorrect. The insert event makes the inserted table and the delete event makes the deleted table. The update event is both an insert and delete event, making (a) and (c) correct.

3.) There are only two ways to stop a trigger from firing on its event. One way is to drop it and the other is to disable it. Therefore (a) is incorrect and (d) is the right answer.

4.) You are not supposed to drop this trigger, so (b) is incorrect. You can't alter a trigger, so (d) is wrong. There are two ways to disable a trigger. You can alter the table and disable the trigger or disable the trigger directly. This makes both (a) and (c) correct.

5.) AFTER triggers only fire if data was changed and those changes are always populated into the memory resident tables. This makes (b) the correct answer.

6.) Since you require the update to take place along with the date, it means you want the event to run. This means you don't want an "Instead Of" trigger, making (a) and (b) wrong. The update to the SalesInvoiceDetail is done by the event and the trigger should update the SalesInvoice table and not make another update to the SalesInvoiceDetail table. This means (c) is wrong. The update needs to be on the date field of the SalesInvoice table, making (d) correct.

Bug Catcher Game

To play the Bug Catcher game, run the file SQLQueries2012Vol4BugCatcher2.pps from the BugCatcher folder of the companion files found at www.Joes2Pros.com.

[THIS PAGE INTENTIONALLY LEFT BLANK.]

Chapter 3. Other Triggers

While growing up, I recall my mother asking whether I had homework to do over the weekend. She taught me well! After I would say, "Yeah, but I will do it on Sunday," she told me that instead of procrastinating, I should do it on Friday night and free my schedule for the rest of the weekend. Thus, my action of doing homework on Sunday didn't need to happen. That behavior (i.e., that old routine of Sunday homework) was superseded and replaced with a new action of doing the work on Friday night. My mom is a great teacher, and that paradigm shift has helped transform my lifelong study habits and approach to learning.

This relates to the **instead of triggers** we will see in this chapter. In the last chapter, we saw triggers which handled operations that sometimes we wanted to complete but under other conditions we wanted them halted and rolled back. AFTER triggers watch our tables – they allow good actions and disallow the bad. However, the activities **instead of triggers** watch for are ones which we never want to happen. If there's an activity you know you're never going to allow, why even let it begin to run? When AFTER triggers roll back disallowed transactions, that process consumes system resources. The DML statement runs, the trigger determines it must be disallowed, and then the transaction gets rolled back. **Instead of triggers** block the bad actions before they even begin.

In this chapter we will also look at nested triggers, DDL triggers, and some additional techniques for using triggers to control input and activity in our database.

READER NOTE: *Please run the script SQLQueries2012Vol4Chapter3.0Setup.sql in order to follow along with the examples in the first section of Chapter 3. All scripts mentioned in this chapter may be found at* **www.Joes2Pros.com**.

The "Instead Of" Trigger

The **instead of trigger** never allows the user action to run. When a statement which is disallowed by the system runs, the trigger runs and provides the user a message regarding the attempted action. This is perfect for historical tables, which shouldn't be updated. Rather than allowing the update to run, you want to display a friendly message (not an error), which will prompt your users not to update this table directly.

By way of contrast, let's review the structure and code syntax of an after delete trigger. In each example in Chapter 2, we saw the DML statement run. If a DML statement met a prohibited condition, the trigger was invoked and the transaction rolled back. The trigger trg_DelEmployeeHistory enforces the policy that historical records of the EmployeeHistory archive table may not be changed:

```
CREATE TRIGGER trg_DelEmployeeHistory
ON dbo.EmployeeHistory
AFTER DELETE AS
BEGIN
ROLLBACK TRAN
END
GO
```

If a user attempts to delete a record from the EmployeeHistory table, they will get an error message (Figure 3.1).

```
DELETE TOP(1) FROM EmployeeHistory
```

```
Messages
Msg 3609, Level 16, State 1, Line 1
The transaction ended in the trigger. The batch has been aborted.
                                                            0 rows
```

Figure 3.1 The trigger trg_DelEmployeeHistory is rolling back all EmployeeHistory deletes.

The DELETE statement actually ran, reached the intermediate state, and then we rolled it back before the transaction could be committed.

Since all DELETE statements from the EmployeeHistory table are prohibited by policy, it would be better to have the database disallow them entirely and give your users some specific message letting them know why their operation is not allowed. As well, it would be better to not waste system resources by allowing each attempted operation to run and then be rolled back.

Let's remove the existing trg_DelEmployeeHistory trigger so that we can re-create it as an instead of trigger:

```
DROP TRIGGER trg_DelEmployeeHistory
GO
```

Creating "Instead Of" Triggers

The trg_DelEmployeeHistory trigger was dropped so we can re-create it differently. Contrast this code with the AFTER trigger we built earlier. There is no ROLLBACK TRAN statement needed, since the trigger stops the DELETE statement from ever running. Observe that INSTEAD OF DELETE AS replaces AFTER DELETE AS.

The code we want to run instead will appear between the BEGIN and the END commands. This code builds the trg_DelEmployeeHistory instead of trigger:

```
CREATE TRIGGER trg_DelEmployeeHistory
ON dbo.EmployeeHistory
INSTEAD OF DELETE AS
BEGIN

--Place code here to run instead of the delete

END

GO
```

Put what you want to run between the BEGIN and END keywords. We will display a print message to the user, "Historical records are never to be deleted" with the following code:

```
CREATE TRIGGER trg_DelEmployeeHistory
ON dbo.EmployeeHistory
INSTEAD OF DELETE AS
BEGIN
PRINT 'Historical Records are never to be deleted'
END
GO
```

Running "Instead Of" Triggers

Let's test our new trigger by reattempting the record deletion from the EmployeeHistory table (Figure 3.2).

```
DELETE TOP(1) FROM EmployeeHistory
```

```
Messages
Historical Records are never to be deleted
(1 row(s) affected)
                                                    0 rows
```

Figure 3.2 Testing the trigger on the EmployeeHistory table displays the print message to the user.

This transaction never takes place. The user receives the *"Historical Records are never to be deleted"* message. Notice the "1 row(s) affected" message also appears (This will display unless NOCOUNT is set to ON). No row in the EmployeeHistory table is affected – this is simply a reference to the Deleted table. The memory resident tables (Inserted and Deleted) are always impacted by a delete or insert trigger, even in the case of instead of triggers.

After Trigger Abstraction Layer

In our next example, we'll see that this behavior can be useful and that our instead of triggers can utilize data from the memory resident tables. This example is best shown using a small dbo.Test table and a row of values to be inserted into it (Figure 3.3). We need to insert just two values; since TestID is an identity field (Identity fields are covered in Chapter 3 of *SQL Queries 2012 Joes 2 Pros Volume 2*). Suppose that the hardcoded date value represents data from a feed – in any case, our scenario will require us to update this field. Create the simple table named Test with three fields using the following code:

```
CREATE TABLE Test
(TestID INT IDENTITY(1,1), TestName VARCHAR(40),
CreationDate DATE)
GO

INSERT INTO Test
VALUES ('Field Test','1/1/2005')

SELECT * FROM Test
```

TestID	TestName	CreationDate
1	Field Test	2005-01-01

1 rows

Figure 3.3 One record has been inserted into the Test table.

We have been instructed to change any hardcoded date value to today's date. If we owned this data, we could simply include the GETDATE() function as part of our INSERT statement. However, in this scenario we aren't the data owners of this data feed. Someone else provided this data; we neither own the code, nor are we allowed to change it. That feed is coming from a C# (C-Sharp) calling application which we are not allowed to touch or change. Thus, whenever new data comes in, we run the UPDATE statement (Figure 3.4).

```
UPDATE Test
SET CreationDate = GETDATE()
WHERE TestName = 'Field Test'

SELECT * FROM Test
```

TestID	TestName	CreationDate
1	Field Test	2012-10-04

1 rows

Figure 3.4 CreationDate now reflects today's date.

If we could capture the calling INSERT statement and feed the current date instead of the hardcoded values, then we could turn this into a single step with no need to update the record later. The **trg_InsertTest** instead of trigger will help us accomplish this. Study the following code and notice that this trigger will halt each INSERT statement and prevent it from loading data directly into the Test table. Instead, the trigger retrieves the TestName data which has been captured by the (memory resident) Inserted table, uses GETDATE() as the CreationDate value, and then passes those data points into the Test table. The trigger will insert a new record with the current date into the dbo.Test table:

```sql
CREATE TRIGGER trg_InsertTest
ON dbo.Test
INSTEAD OF INSERT
AS
BEGIN
INSERT INTO dbo.Test
SELECT TestName, GETDATE() FROM Inserted
END
GO
```

Let's test our new trigger by running a second insert (Figure 3.5).

```sql
INSERT INTO Test
VALUES ('Row Test','1/1/2005')
```

Messages
(1 row(s) affected)
(1 row(s) affected)
0 rows

Figure 3.5 An insert into the Test table shows the 1 row(s) affected message twice.

The two "1 row(s) affected" confirmations represent the Inserted table transaction and the actual record added to the Test table. Run a SELECT query to look at all the data in the Test table (Figure 3.6). You'll notice the record was inserted as specified, except the CreationDate values reflect the current date. *READERNOTE:* When you run this example, your CreationDate will not match Figure 3.6. It will be the current date shown by your system when you run the inserts.

```
SELECT * FROM Test
```

TestID	TestName	CreationDate
1	Field Test	2012-10-04
2	Row Test	2012-10-04

2 rows

Figure 3.6 The CreationDate value for the newly inserted record is the current date.

Putting Multiple Events on One Trigger

We've learned that there are a lot of different activities that can fire off a trigger. An insert can fire off a trigger, an update can fire off a trigger and a delete can fire off a trigger. So, what if we wanted to prevent inserts, updates and deletes to the [StateList] table. Our goal is to make sure that we can't update the [StateList] table in any way with any DML statement directly. Suppose that no changes may be made directly to the StateList table for the next month. This means no inserts, updates, or deletions will be allowed to run.

In order to solve this, you could create three separate triggers on one table (trg_InsertStateList for the inserts, trg_UpdateStateList for the updates, and trg_DelStateList for the deletions).

One trigger can look for many events (inserts, updates, and deletes). Alternatively, you could create one instead of trigger to look for all three events. The following code demonstrates the syntax for this type of a trigger:

```
CREATE TRIGGER trg_InsteadStateList
ON dbo.StateList
INSTEAD OF INSERT, DELETE, UPDATE AS

BEGIN
Print 'No changes are to be made directly to the StateList
table'
END
GO
```

With this new trg_InsteadStateList trigger created, let's see what happens if we try to delete records from the [StateList] table. Can we delete any records? Test this trigger by attempting to delete records contained in the StateList table. Instead of allowing any DML change to be made to StateList, this instead of trigger prints a message ("No changes are to be made to the StateList table").

DELETE StateList

Messages
No changes are to be made directly to the StateList table
(62 row(s) affected)

0 rows

Figure 3.7 Any attempted DML change to StateList causes the trg_InsteadStateList trigger to run.

In Figure 3.7 we see that no such changes were made. If we were to run an update or INSERT Statement, that would fail too.

Lab 3.1: "Instead Of" Triggers

Lab Prep: Lab Prep: Each lab has one or more Skill Checks. Start with Skill Check 1 and proceed until reaching the Points to Ponder section.

Before beginning this lab, verify that SQL Server 2012 is properly installed and operating. Before running the lab setup script for resetting the database (SQLQueries2012Vol4Chapter3.1Setup.sql), please make sure to close all query windows within SSMS. An open query window pointing to a database context can lock that database preventing it from updating when the script is executing. A simple way to assure all query windows are closed, is to exit out of SSMS, then open a new instance of SSMS, and lastly run the setup script.

Skill Check 1: Create a trigger called trg_DelPayRatesHistory on the PayRatesHistory table that shows the message "Historical records are never to be deleted" instead of performing the delete action. Test the new trigger by attempting to delete all records from the PayRatesHistory table.

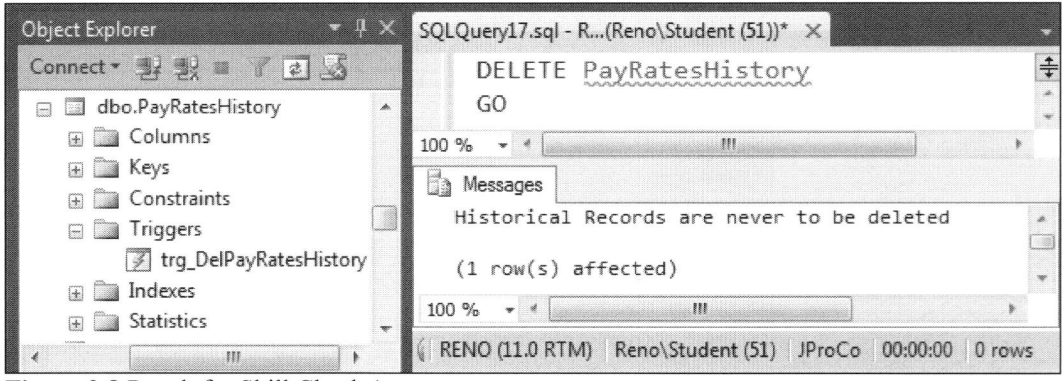

Figure 3.8 Result for Skill Check 1.

Skill Check 2: Create a trigger called trg_InsertEmployeeHistory on the EmployeeHistory table that shows the message "Insertion of new records to the EmployeeHistory table must take place by inserting to the Employee table."

```
INSERT INTO dbo.[EmployeeHistory]
VALUES (20, 'Winds', 'Gale', '3-25-2010', 1, 11,
DEFAULT, DEFAULT, DEFAULT)
```

```
Messages
Insertion of new records to the EmployeeHistory table must take place by
inserting to the Employee table

(1 row(s) affected)

                                                                      0 rows
```
Figure 3.9 Skill Check 2.

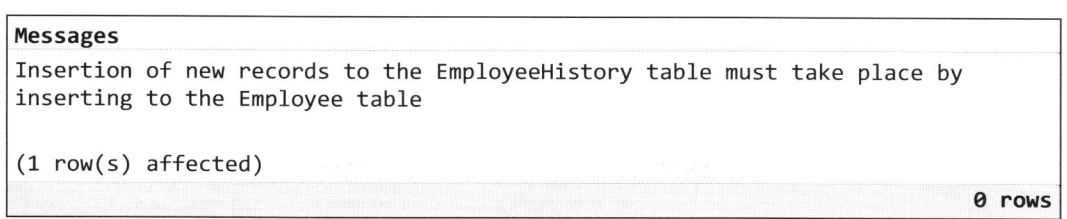

Skill Check 3: The MgmtTraining table has the CK_MgmtTraining_ApprovedDate constraint, which disallows dates prior to 2006. The calling application has been traced using the following code and is getting the error message you see in Figure 3.10.

```sql
INSERT INTO MgmtTraining (ClassName, ClassDurationHours,
ApprovedDate)
VALUES ('Passing Certifications', 13, 0)
```

```
Messages
The INSERT statement conflicted with the CHECK constraint
"CK_MgmtTraining_ApprovedDate". The conflict occurred in database "JProCo",
table "dbo.MgmtTraining", column 'ApprovedDate'.
The statement has been terminated.
                                                                      0 rows
```
Figure 3.10 The INSERT statement above is failing but you are not allowed to change it.

Without changing the INSERT statement, insert the current time in the ApprovedDate field. Create the trg_InsertManagmentTraining trigger to use GetDate instead of zero. Run the INSERT statement and query your MgmtTraining table. When complete, your result should resemble Figure 3.11. The ApprovedDate field of the last two records may differ on your system depending on when it is run.

```sql
SELECT * FROM MgmtTraining
```

	ClassID	ClassName	ClassDur…	ApprovedDate
1	1	Embracing Diversity	12	2007-01-01 00:00:00.000
2	2	Interviewing	6	2007-01-15 00:00:00.000
3	3	Difficult Negotiations	30	2008-02-12 00:00:00.000
4	4	Empowering Others	18	2012-10-01 22:59:28.747
5	8	Passing Certifications	13	2012-10-01 23:17:02.490

5 rows

Figure 3.11 Skill Check 3 result.

Answer Code: The T-SQL code to this lab can be found in the downloadable files in a file named Lab3.1_InsteadOfTriggers.sql.

Points to Ponder - "Instead Of" Triggers

1. Triggers can intercept INSERT, UPDATE, or DELETE statements which you don't want to run.

2. There are two categories of triggers.

3. After Triggers – executed after the INSERT, UPDATE, or DELETE is performed. You can only define these on tables. AFTER triggers can be specified for tables but not for views.

4. Instead of Triggers – are executed in place of the usual triggering action. Unlike AFTER triggers, INSTEAD OF triggers can be specified for both tables and views.

5. An instead of trigger executes in place of the triggering action.

6. When an INSERT or DELETE trigger is associated with a table, any data inserted or deleted from the table will be written to a corresponding temporary table (also known as memory resident tables, magic tables, or special tables).

7. Each table or view is limited to one instead of trigger for each DML action. This means you may have one for inserts, one for updates, and/or one for deletes.

8. You cannot create an instead of trigger on views that have the WITH CHECK OPTION defined.

9. If you are not using an instead of trigger, then multiple triggers can fire off from the same event. In other words, you can have two triggers on the same table.

Nesting Triggers

A trigger which fires another trigger is known as a **nested trigger**.

Earlier in this chapter we ensured that no direct inserts could be made to the EmployeeHistory table as we saw back in Figure 3.9. We see this rule enforced (Figure 3.12) where the attempted insert of EmpID 20 (Gale Winds) results in the message, "Insertion of new records to the EmployeeHistory table must take place by inserting to the Employee table". Thus, the trg_InsertEmployeeHistory trigger is still behaving as we expect it to – *we are not allowed to directly insert records into the EmployeeHistory table.*

Let's think back to the last chapter and recall the rules we established for the Employee table. Direct inserts are allowed to the Employee table, and each employee record must be copied into the EmployeeHistory table by the trg_InsertEmployeeHistory trigger. Only the trigger should be adding records to the EmployeeHistory table – humans should not be allowed to directly enter records into the EmployeeHistory table. Let's attempt to insert Gale's record into the Employee table and confirm our expected rules are in place (Figure 3.12).

```
INSERT INTO dbo.[Employee]VALUES
(20, 'Winds', 'Gale', '3-25-2010', 1, 11,
DEFAULT, DEFAULT, DEFAULT)
```

Message
Insertion of new records to the EmployeeHistory table must take place by inserting to the Employee table
(1 row(s) affected)
(1 row(s) affected)

0 rows

Figure 3.12 We can insert this record directly into the Employee table. However, the trigger on the EmployeeHistory table is disallowing the insert from the Employee table (trg_InsertEmployee).

We see two separate row transactions and the print message. Let's check the Employee table to see whether Gale's record was inserted successfully.

Chapter 3. Other Triggers

```
SELECT * FROM Employee
```

	EmpID	LastName	FirstName	HireDate	LocationID	ManagerID	Status	Hire
14	14	Smith	Janis	2009-10-18...	1	4	Active	200
15	15	Jones	Tess	2012-10-04...	1	11	Orientation	NUl
16	16	Biggs	Nancy	2012-10-04...	1	11	Orientation	NUl
17	17	Downs	Wendy	2012-10-04...	1	11	Orientation	201
18	18	Walker	Rainy	2010-01-01...	1	11	NULL	NUl
19	20	Winds	Gale	2010-03-25...	1	11	NULL	NUl

Query executed successfully. RENO (11.0 RTM) Reno\Student (51) JProCo 00:00:00 19 rows

Figure 3.13 Yes, the Employee table accepted our direct insertion of Gale's record.

Let's look back to the result displayed (Figure 3.12) when we attempted to insert Gale's record directly into the Employee table. Since we know the Employee table accepted our direct insertion of Gale's record as demonstrated by Figure 3.13, then one of the row transactions was our insert to the Employee table. Thus, it's clear the other row transaction ("1 row(s) affected") was the record temporarily captured by the Inserted table, and the printed message was produced by the EmployeeHistory tables' instead of trigger (trg_InsertEmployeeHistory).

We have a problem with trg_InsertEmployeeHistory's design, because it is currently blocking all types of inserts to the EmployeeHistory table. It should allow inserts by the trigger on the Employee table but continue to disallow attempts by users to insert records directly into the Employee table. *How do you forbid just the direct inserts but allow inserts from other triggers to run?*

```
INSERT INTO dbo.[Employee] VALUES
(20, 'Winds', 'Gale', '3-25-2010', 1, 11, DEFAULT, DEFAULT, DEFAULT)
```

```
INSERT INTO dbo.[Employee] VALUES
(20, 'Winds', 'Gale', '3-25-2010', 1, 11, DEFAULT, DEFAULT, DEFAULT)
```

trg.InsertEmployeeHistory ← dbo.Employee
dbo.EmployeeHistory   trg.InsertEmployee

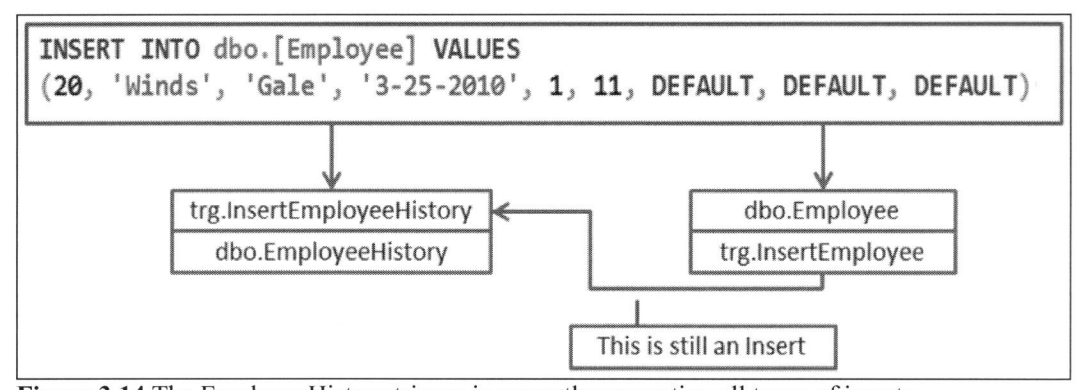

This is still an Insert

Figure 3.14 The EmployeeHistory trigger is currently preventing all types of inserts.

Using @@NESTLEVEL

Sometimes people think that nesting triggers are also recursive triggers. However, **recursion** occurs when an object runs an action which, in turn, causes the action to be repeated. If the trg_InsertEmployee inserted a record into the Employee table, this would cause the trg_InsertEmployee to fire again. Notice that this is not happening here. Instead, the insert is firing another trigger, which means that these two separate triggers are nested.

The EmployeeHistory table should accept inserts which come from the Employee tables' trigger (trg_InsertEmployee). We've learned that the trigger on the EmployeeHistory table (trg_InsertEmployeeHistory) is overly restrictive and is blocking inserts from other triggers. In order to correct this situation, we need to understand how to differentiate between inserts coming from other triggers and inserts made directly to the table.

When an insert comes from a trigger and fires off another trigger, this is a **nested trigger**. Inserts from nested triggers into the EmployeeHistory table should be allowed. If an insert is called directly, the trigger will have a @@NESTLEVEL of 1. If a trigger runs a DML statement which causes another trigger to run, then the second trigger would have a @@NESTLEVEL of 2.

```
INSERT INTO dbo.[Employee] VALUES
(20, 'Winds', 'Gale', '3-25-2010', 1, 11, DEFAULT, DEFAULT, DEFAULT)
```

@@NESTLEVEL = 1 → trg.InsertEmployeeHistory → dbo.EmployeeHistory

@@NESTLEVEL = 1 → dbo.Employee → trg.InsertEmployee

@@NESTLEVEL = 2

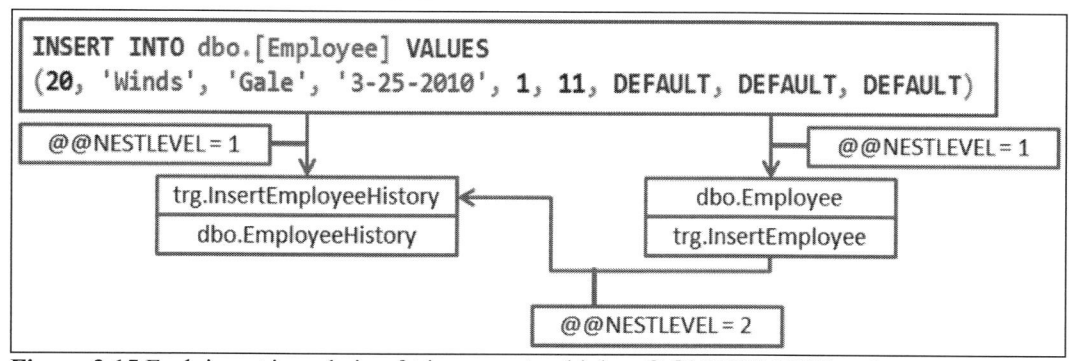

Figure 3.15 Each insert in a chain of triggers gets a higher @@NESTLEVEL value.

What we need is a more discriminating trigger, one that will deny inserts at the nest level 1, but will allow inserts from other triggers at a higher nest level.

Let's reset the Employee table by deleting our last insert of EmpID 20, Gale Winds (Figure 3.16).

```
DELETE FROM Employee WHERE EmpID = 20
```

```
Messages
(1 row(s) affected)
(1 row(s) affected)
                                                              0 rows
```

Figure 3.16 Reset the Employee table by removing our last inserted record (Gale Winds).

We must modify the trg_InsertEmployeeHistory trigger to check for the @@NESTLEVEL. Run the ALTER TRIGGER statement, which will block inserts where the @@NESTLEVEL is 1 and display a print message to the user. If a @@NESTLEVEL of 1 is not found, then the record will be inserted into the Employee Table:

```
ALTER TRIGGER dbo.trg_InsertEmployeeHistory
ON dbo.EmployeeHistory
INSTEAD OF INSERT AS
BEGIN
IF @@NESTLEVEL = 1
Print 'Do not insert to Employee History Directly'
ELSE
INSERT INTO EmployeeHistory
SELECT * FROM Inserted
END
GO
```

The insert is allowed if the @@NESTLEVEL is not equal to 1. The trg_InsertEmployeeHistory trigger intercepts all inserts to the EmployeeHistory table. Inserts coming from a @@NESTLEVEL of 1 (i.e., inserts attempted directly on the EmployeeHistory table) are disallowed. If the @@NESTLEVEL is not 1, then the record is retrieved from the Inserted table (i.e., the special memory resident table) and inserted into the EmployeeHistory table.

Let's test the revised trigger by reattempting to insert Gale's record into the Employee table (Figure 3.17).

```
INSERT INTO dbo.[Employee] VALUES
(20, 'Winds', 'Gale', '3-25-2010', 1, 11,
DEFAULT, DEFAULT, DEFAULT)
```

Messages
(1 row(s) affected)
(1 row(s) affected)
(1 row(s) affected)

0 rows

Figure 3.17 The trigger from the Employee table is able to insert into the EmployeeHistory table.

The lack of a print message, other than the three transaction confirmations ("1 row(s) affected"), is the result we expected to see. The Employee table, the Inserted table, and the EmployeeHistory table each received one record.

Let's confirm our successful result by querying the EmployeeHistory table and seeing that Gale's record (EmpID 20) has been inserted successfully by the nested trigger (Figure 3.18).

```
SELECT *
FROM EmployeeHistory
Where EmpID = 20
```

EmpID	LastName	FirstName	HireDate	LocationID	ManagerID	Status	HiredOffset
20	Winds	Gale	2010-03-25...	1	11	NULL	NULL

Query executed successfully. RENO (11.0 RTM) Reno\Student (51) JProCo 00:00:00 1 rows

Figure 3.18 Gale's record (EmpID 20) was successfully inserted into the EmployeeHistory table.

Lab 3.2: Nested Triggers

Lab Prep: Lab Prep: Each lab has one or more Skill Checks. Start with Skill Check 1 and proceed until reaching the Points to Ponder section.

Before beginning this lab, verify that SQL Server 2012 is properly installed and operating. Before running the lab setup script for resetting the database (SQLQueries2012Vol4Chapter3.2Setup.sql), please make sure to close all query windows within SSMS. An open query window pointing to a database context can lock that database preventing it from updating when the script is executing. A simple way to assure all query windows are closed, is to exit out of SSMS, then open a new instance of SSMS, and lastly run the setup script.

Skill Check 1: On the PayRatesHistory table, create an INSTEAD OF trigger called trg_InsertPayRatesHistory that will prevent direct inserts into the PayRatesHistory table but will not prevent inserts from other triggers. Test to see that direct inserts to PayRatesHistory fail (Figure 3.19) but inserts from other triggers succeed (Figure 3.20).

```
INSERT INTO PayRatesHistory
VALUES (20, 77000, NULL, NULL, 1, 1)
```

```
Messages
Do not insert to PayRates History directly
(1 row(s) affected)
                                                    0 rows
```

Figure 3.19 Skill Check 1 (part 1).

```
INSERT INTO PayRates
VALUES (20, 77000, NULL, NULL, 1, 1)
```

```
Messages
(1 row(s) affected)
(1 row(s) affected)
(1 row(s) affected)
                                                    0 rows
```

Figure 3.20 Skill Check 1 (part 2).

Skill Check 2: Disable all the triggers from the query in Figure 3.21. You can check your work by running the following code after the triggers are disabled and the is_disabled field will be one for all records where the trigger is disabled.

```sql
SELECT OBJECT_NAME(parent_id)
AS TableName , [name], is_disabled
FROM JProCo.sys.triggers
WHERE OBJECT_NAME(parent_id) IN
('Employee', 'PayRates', 'Grant', 'StateList')
ORDER BY TableName
```

	TableName	name	is_disabled
1	Employee	trg_InsertEmployee	1
2	Employee	trg_DelEmployee	1
3	Employee	trg_UpdEmployee	1
4	Grant	trg_updGrant	1
5	PayRates	trg_DelPayrates	1
6	PayRates	trg_InsertPayRates	1
7	PayRates	trg_UpdPayRates	1
8	StateList	trg_DelStateList	1
9	StateList	trg_InsteadStateList	1
10	StateList	trg_updStateList	1

10 rows

Figure 3.21 Results before Skill Check 2.

Answer Code: The T-SQL code to this lab can be found in the downloadable files in a file named Lab3.2_NestingTriggers.sql.

Points to Ponder - Nested Triggers

1. Nested triggers are triggers which are fired by another trigger's DML statement(s).

2. Triggers can be linked, if necessary, to perform a series of actions in a particular situation.

3. Triggers are reactive. In other words, the action has already taken place before the trigger fires.

4. When an INSERT or DELETE trigger is associated with a table, any data inserted or deleted from the table will be written to a corresponding memory resident table (i.e., the Inserted or Deleted table).

5. A nested trigger is a trigger which executes a statement that causes an AFTER trigger to fire again.

6. There are two types of recursion:

    a. Indirect recursion occurs when the execution of the trigger causes another trigger to fire, which causes the first trigger to fire again. For example, a trigger (trig_1) fires when a table (tbl_a) is updated. The trigger executes an UPDATE statement for a second table (tbl_b). A trigger (trig_2) in tbl_b fires a trigger that executes an UPDATE statement for tbl_a. This causes trig_1 to fire again.

    b. Direct recursion occurs when the execution of a trigger causes it to fire again. For example, trig_1 fires when tbl_a is updated and code inside trig_1 also updates tbl_a, causing trig_1 to fire again.

7. Use an ALTER TRIGGER statement to modify a trigger.

8. Use ENABLE and DISABLE TRIGGER to control whether a trigger fires without dropping the trigger. For DML triggers, you can also use ALTER TABLE to enable or disable a trigger.

9. Use DROP TRIGGER to delete a trigger.

10. You should not use a trigger on a system table.

11. Constraints are checked after an INSTEAD OF trigger(s) executes. If constraints are violated, the actions executed by the INSTEAD OF trigger(s) are rolled back.

12. You cannot use INSTEAD OF DELETE/UPDATE triggers when a table has a foreign key with a cascade on DELETE/UPDATE action defined.

DDL Triggers

Thus far, our examination of triggers has focused on DML statements run against tables. As the title "DDL Triggers" implies, there are also triggers which work with DDL statements (CREATE, ALTER, or DROP). These triggers monitor your database for the attempted creation, modification, or removal of objects according to your specifications.

For example, the following trigger (Figure 3.22) watches for any new CREATE TABLE statement appearing in your database.

```
CREATE TRIGGER trg_AuditNewTables
ON DATABASE FOR CREATE_TABLE
AS
  BEGIN
  END
GO
```

Note: This trigger will fire off any time a CREATE TABLE statement is run in the database.

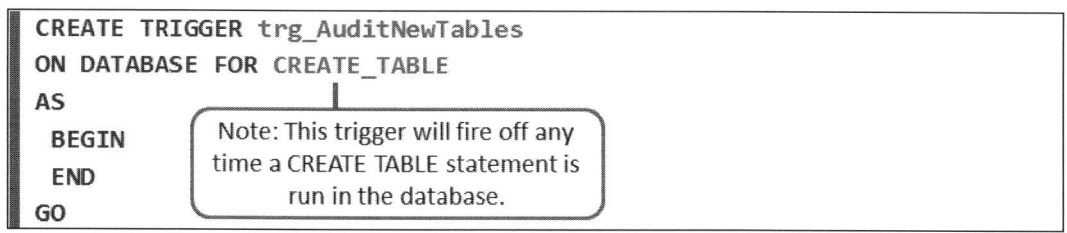

Figure 3.22 DDL triggers monitor events which take place in your database.

It's not difficult to imagine many reasons why extra scrutiny and support would be useful with respect to the creation, modification, or destruction of database objects in a production environment. Our premise for this section will be a harmless prankster who occasionally amuses himself by sneaking new tables into the database. While not a dangerous "black-hat" or a hacker, this individual's juvenile behavior actually provides a good opportunity to review and strengthen the way we enforce our database policies.

We can create DDL triggers to monitor and prompt users each time they attempt a DDL statement. We will also see examples of DDL triggers that will prohibit the creation of objects containing certain keywords.

Given our prankster's fondness for the keywords "Boss", "Slacker", and "Slax", a DDL trigger prohibiting those keywords would prevent him from creating tables whose names include those keywords.

His favorite trick is to stealthily create a dbo.BossSlax table. In fact, this gets termed the "Slax Attack". When the boss wants to know who created the BossSlax table, the chances of the anonymous prankster confessing are low.

```
CREATE TABLE BossSlax
(BossSlaxID INT PRIMARY KEY)
GO
```

Let's drop the BossSlax table using this code, so that we can later re-use it to test our DDL triggers. Use the following code to drop the BossSlax table so that we can re-create it later to test our DDL triggers:

```
DROP TABLE BossSlax
GO
```

Creating DDL Triggers

Let's begin by creating a DDL trigger on the entire database which will fire off each time a CREATE TABLE statement is attempted. Whenever a user creates a table, we want to display the message, "Are you sure you want to do that?".

Make sure your context is set to the JProCo database before running this code. One way to accomplish this is to precede your CREATE TRIGGER statement with USE JProCo with a GO on the next line.

```
USE JProCo
GO
CREATE TRIGGER trg_AuditNewTables
ON DATABASE FOR CREATE_TABLE
AS
BEGIN
PRINT 'Are you sure you want to do that?'
END
GO
```

The trg_AuditNewTables trigger will run whenever you create a new table in JProCo. Test this new trigger by executing a CREATE TABLE statement (Figure 3.23). The message "Are you sure you want to do that?" confirms that the trigger ran when the table was created.

```
CREATE TABLE BossSlax
(BossSlaxID INT PRIMARY KEY)
GO
```

```
Messages
Are you sure you want to do that?
                                                      0 rows
```

Figure 3.23 The CREATE TABLE statement caused the trigger trg_AuditNewTables to run.

Thus far, the only event we are monitoring the database for is a CREATE TABLE statement. The trg_AuditNewTables trigger only runs when you create a table in the database, but not when you alter or drop a table.

You can use DDL triggers on an entire database to look for certain CREATE, ALTER or DROP statements. Let's build a trigger which runs when you drop a table and displays a helpful message to your users:

```
CREATE TRIGGER trg_OutgoingTables
ON DATABASE FOR DROP_TABLE
AS

BEGIN
PRINT 'Table going away'
END
GO
```

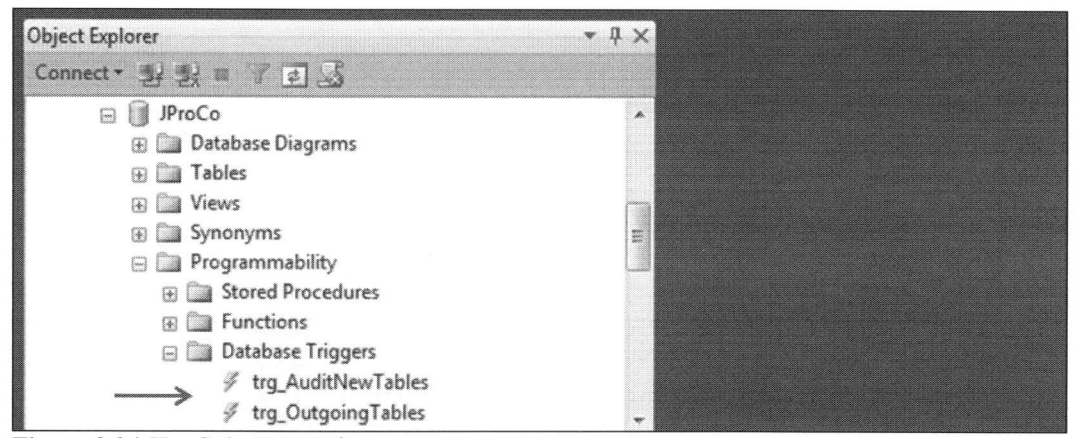

Figure 3.24 JProCo's DDL Triggers.

The trigger trg_OutgoingTables watches for the DROP_TABLE event. Let's test our DROP_TABLE trigger by dropping the BossSlax table (Figure 3.25). This is the same result we will see when any JProCo table is dropped. The trg_OutgoingTables trigger fires and we see the "Table going away" message.

```
DROP TABLE BossSlax
GO
```

Messages
Table going away
0 rows

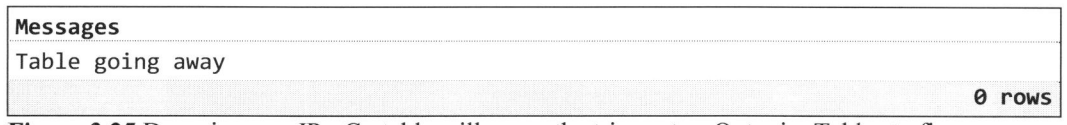

Figure 3.25 Dropping any JProCo table will cause the trigger trg_OutgoingTables to fire.

Trigger Event Details

DDL triggers give us the ability to see event details for DDL statements.

Let's modify our trg_AuditNewTables trigger to include the EVENTDATA() system-supplied function in place of our user message (*READERNOTE: EVENTDATA() does not work with DML triggers*). The EVENTDATA() function captures data from our trigger event, which we can then view using the PRINT command.

Since the output of the EVENTDATA() function is an XML data type, we will get an error if we attempt to build our trigger using just this code (Figure 3.26). We must first CAST the output using another character type, because data can't be printed from the XML data type. The PRINT statement works with all types of character data, so we can use a VARCHAR(max) data type.

(*Note*: The XML data type is explored in detail in Volume 5 of this series, *SQL Queries 2012 Joes 2 Pros Volume 5*, Chapters 1-7.)

```
ALTER TRIGGER trg_AuditNewTables
ON DATABASE FOR CREATE_TABLE
AS
BEGIN
PRINT EVENTDATA()
END
GO
```

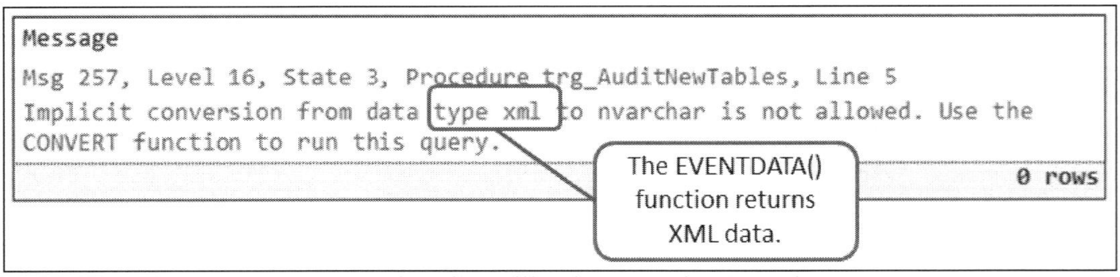

```
Message
Msg 257, Level 16, State 3, Procedure trg_AuditNewTables, Line 5
Implicit conversion from data type xml to nvarchar is not allowed. Use the
CONVERT function to run this query.

0 rows
```

The EVENTDATA() function returns XML data.

Figure 3.26 The EVENTDATA() function will only return the XML data type.

By casting the XML data into a VARCHAR(MAX), you can print the message as seen in the following code:

```
ALTER TRIGGER trg_AuditNewTables
ON DATABASE FOR CREATE_TABLE
AS
BEGIN
DECLARE @MessageAction VARCHAR(MAX)
SET @MessageAction = CAST(EVENTDATA() AS VARCHAR(MAX))
PRINT @MessageAction
END
GO
```

Let's test this trigger by creating the BossSlax table again. Thanks to the trigger (trg_AuditNewTables), we can see the details for this "event", namely the CREATE TABLE event (Figure 3.27).

```
CREATE TABLE BossSlax
(BossSlaxID INT PRIMARY KEY)
GO
```

Messages
<EVENT_INSTANCE><EventType>CREATE_TABLE</EventType>
0 rows

Figure 3.27 Creating a table ran the trigger that shows all the event data in your Messages tab.

Copy-Paste all of the data from the Messages tab into Notepad, so we can take a closer look at the event information. We can see the type of event (CREATE_TABLE), the time the event data was generated, the SPID (ServerProcessID), ServerName, LoginName, and UserName for the individual who ran the event. We can also see the database, schema, object name (JProCo.dbo.BossSlax table), and other details related to the event, including the full DDL statement which ran (CREATE TABLE BossSlax (BossSlaxID INT PRIMARY KEY)).

```
<EVENT_INSTANCE><EventType>CREATE_TABLE</EventType>
<PostTime>2012-10-04T23:50:46.200</PostTime>
<SPID>51</SPID>
<ServerName>RENO</ServerName>
<LoginName>Reno\Student</LoginName>
<UserName>dbo</UserName>
<DatabaseName>JProCo</DatabaseName>
<SchemaName>dbo</SchemaName>
<ObjectName>BossSlax</ObjectName>
<ObjectType>TABLE</ObjectType>
<TSQLCommand><SetOptions ANSI_NULLS="ON" ANSI_NULL_DEFAULT="ON"
   ANSI_PADDING="ON" QUOTED_IDENTIFIER="ON" ENCRYPTED="FALSE"/>
<CommandText>CREATE TABLE BossSlax &#x0D;
   (BossSlaxID int PRIMARY KEY) &#x0D;</CommandText>
</TSQLCommand></EVENT_INSTANCE>
```

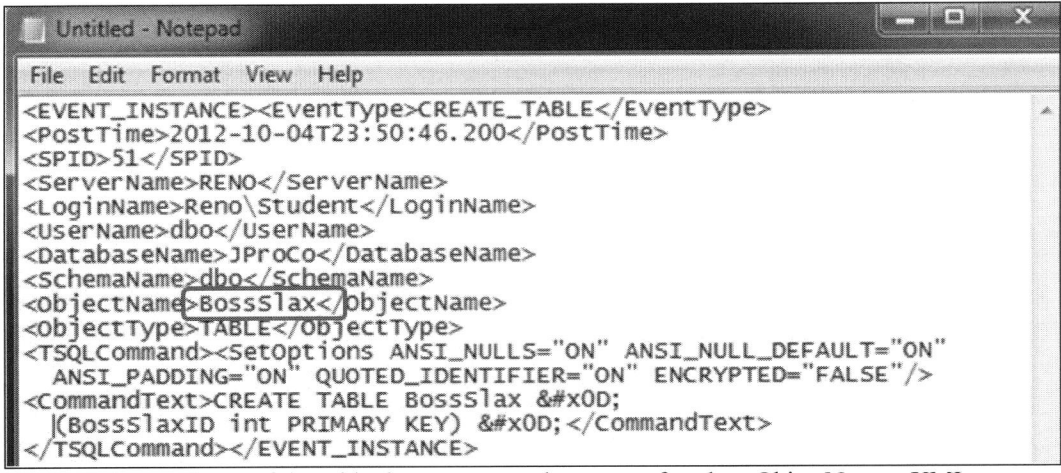

Figure 3.28 The name of the table that was created appears after the <ObjectName> XML tag.

Using Rollback

Whenever we see a table with "Slax" in the name, it's a red flag indicating that our juvenile prankster has been making trouble again. The boss gets upset, and we always have to remove the table from the database. A more efficient process would be to prevent the bogus table from being created in the first place. In other words, we would like a trigger to roll back any DDL statement with the word "Slax" in the object name.

Using what we just learned about the EVENTDATA() function, we can alter our trigger (trg_AuditNewTables) to search for the keyword "Slax" within the event details. In the following code, we see a variable @MessageAction which contains the event data. The CHARINDEX ("character index") function searches the contents of this variable for the word "Slax".

CHARINDEX returns a 1 or higher if a match is found and returns a 0 if nothing is found. If CHARINDEX finds 'Slax', it will return a 1 or higher. If CHARINDEX finds 'Slax', then the CREATE TABLE statement will be rolled back. If this word is found, the trigger will ROLLBACK the transaction, and the attempted CREATE_TABLE action will not be allowed to complete:

```
ALTER TRIGGER trg_AuditNewTables
ON DATABASE FOR CREATE_TABLE
AS
BEGIN
DECLARE @MessageAction VARCHAR(MAX)
SET @MessageAction = CAST(EVENTDATA() AS VARCHAR(MAX))
IF(CHARINDEX('Slax' ,@MessageAction, 0) >0 )
ROLLBACK
END
GO
```

Let's test our robust trigger by dropping the BossSlax table and then attempting to re-create it (Figure 3.29). We must first DROP the BossSlax table, so that we can attempt to re-create it:

```
DROP TABLE BossSlax
GO
```

```
CREATE TABLE BossSlax
(BossSlaxID INT PRIMARY KEY)
```

```
Messages
Msg 3609, Level 16, State 2, Line 1
The transaction ended in the trigger. The batch has been aborted.

                                                              0 rows
```

Figure 3.29 You can't create a table with the word "Slax" in it.

Our trigger is successful! Because it found the "Slax" in the event detail, it disallowed the CREATE TABLE statement.

You are still free to create other tables, as long as they don't have the word "Slax" in the name. In Figure 3.30 we see the creation of the BossIsCool table completed successfully.

```
CREATE TABLE BossIsCool
(BossID INT PRIMARY KEY)
GO
```

```
Messages
Command(s) completed successfully.

                                                              0 rows
```

Figure 3.30 DDL statements that don't have the word 'Slax' run successfully.

Such a DDL trigger could also help our business by giving us a way to prevent the creation of objects using prohibited names. *Examples:* You want to enforce the guideline that actual names of merger targets are prohibited. Similarly, in an R&D

environment where the code names of projects sometimes change, a DDL trigger could help ensure an old code name isn't accidentally used.

Lab 3.3: DDL Triggers

Lab Prep: Lab Prep: Each lab has one or more Skill Checks. Start with Skill Check 1 and proceed until reaching the Points to Ponder section.

Before beginning this lab, verify that SQL Server 2012 is properly installed and operating. Before running the lab setup script for resetting the database (SQLQueries2012Vol4Chapter3.3Setup.sql), please make sure to close all query windows within SSMS. An open query window pointing to a database context can lock that database preventing it from updating when the script is executing. A simple way to assure all query windows are closed, is to exit out of SSMS, then open a new instance of SSMS, and lastly run the setup script.

Skill Check 1: To do this Skill Check properly, the computer's system clock needs to be set to any date or time in January. Create a trigger called trg_NoViewsInJanuary that will not allow anyone to create views in the JProCo database during the month of January. *Hint*: To find out if it's January, use DATEPART(month, GETDATE()) = 1 somewhere in your trigger.

```
--Set system date/time to January before running this query.
CREATE VIEW vTest
AS
SELECT * FROM Employee
GO
```

```
Messages

Msg 3609, Level 16, State 2, Procedure vTest, Line 1

                                                        0 rows
```

Figure 3.31 Skill Check 1.

Note: The easiest way to test this is to set your system clock to any date in January. After you are done with this lab example, be sure to return your system clock to your current local time.

Answer Code: The T-SQL code to this lab can be found in the downloadable files in a file named Lab3.3_DDLTriggers.sql.

Points to Ponder - DDL Triggers

1. DML stands for Data Manipulation Language and includes SELECT, INSERT, UPDATE and DELETE statements. DDL stands for Data Definition Language which includes CREATE, ALTER, and DROP statements run against database objects.

2. A DDL trigger is a type of stored procedure programmed to execute when a Data Definition Language (DDL) event occurs in the database server.

3. DDL triggers allow you to perform administrative tasks on a database as well as protect against database schema changes.

4. You can use DDL triggers to intercept database schema changes and send an error message to the user executing the code. You can also use DDL triggers to record and audit DDL statements executed on a database or server.

5. DDL triggers can be executed against more than just the standard list of DDL statements. Examples include CREATE, ALTER, DROP, GRANT, DENY, REVOKE, and UPDATE STATISTICS statements.

6. Information about an event that fires a DDL trigger may be captured by using the EVENTDATA() function.

7. EVENTDATA() must be directly referenced inside the DDL trigger. You cannot call EVENTDATA() from a routine, even a routine called by a DDL trigger.

8. DML and DDL triggers are similar in the following ways:
    - DDL triggers are created, modified, and dropped using T-SQL syntax similar to that used to create DML triggers.
    - Like DML triggers, DDL triggers can run managed code.
    - A trigger and the statement that fires it are run within the same transaction.
    - Like DML triggers, DDL triggers can be nested.

9. DML and DDL triggers are different in the following ways:
    - DDL triggers run only after a T-SQL statement is completed.
    - DDL triggers cannot be used as INSTEAD OF triggers.
    - DDL triggers do not create temporary Inserted and Deleted tables.

Chapter Glossary

ADO.net: A set of software components that developers use to access data in a database.

@@NESTLEVEL: Returns the nesting level on the local server of the current stored procedure execution (if no nesting then the level is 0).

DDL: Data Definition Language. Statements which define data structures. The most common are CREATE, ALTER, and DROP.

DDL trigger: A trigger that executes based on a specified DDL event.

Direct recursion: This occurs when the execution of a trigger causes it to fire again.

DML trigger: A trigger that executes based on a specified DML event.

Identity field: A field that automatically generates its values in an incremental fashion.

Indirect recursion: This occurs when the execution of the trigger causes another trigger to fire, which causes the first trigger to fire again.

Nested trigger: A trigger that executes an event and fires another trigger.

Recursion: A programming concept where a named piece of code invokes itself.

Recursive trigger: A trigger which executes a statement that causes the same trigger to fire again.

Rollback: A process when new records in memory are discarded and never saved to permanent storage.

Transaction: The process SQL performs to take a DML request to get committed to permanent storage.

Trigger: A stored procedure that automatically fires based on an event.

Update trigger: A trigger that fires after an UPDATE statement has taken place on the table which the trigger is defined.

Review Quiz - Chapter Three

1.) What is the only DML event that does not fire off a trigger?

   O a. `SELECT`
   O b. `INSERT`
   O c. `UPDATE`
   O d. `DELETE`

2.) What are the main types of DML triggers? (Choose two)

   ☐ a. Before Trigger
   ☐ b. After Trigger
   ☐ c. Instead of Trigger
   ☐ d. In Addition to Trigger

3.) You have a trigger on the dbo.Action table that inserts records into the dbo.ActivityHistory table. The trigger in the dbo.ActivityHistory table checks for the @@NESTLEVEL. What is the value of the @@NESTLEVEL when the inserted records come from the trigger of the dbo.Action table?

   O a. 0
   O b. 1
   O c. 2
   O d. 3

4.) You have a trigger on the dbo.Action table that inserts records into the dbo.ActivityHistory table. The trigger in the dbo.ActivityHistory table does a check for the @@NESTLEVEL. What is the value of the @@NESTLEVEL when the inserted records are inserted directly by you from an INSERT INTO statement?

   O a. 0
   O b. 1
   O c. 2
   O d. 3

5.) You want a trigger to stop firing when you perform inserts. You don't want to drop and re-create the trigger. How can you temporarily stop the trigger from firing?

   O a. You can't.

   O b. You must disable the trigger.

6.) You have a foreign key which prevents the insertion of invalid LocationID values into the Employee table. You want to see the bad records which were attempted to be inserted into the Employee table. You create a table named dbo.BadEmployeeRecords. How do you insert records into this table?

   O a. Create a DML INSTEAD OF trigger which writes the failed records to your dbo.Employee table.

   O b. Create a DML AFTER trigger which writes the failed records to your dbo.Employee table.

   O c. Create a DML INSTEAD OF trigger which writes the failed records to your dbo.BadEmployeeRecords table.

   O d. Create a DML AFTER trigger which writes the failed records to your dbo.BadEmployeeRecords table.

7.) You have an ADO.net application that inserts data into your table. You alter the table and add two new fields to that table and make both fields non-nullable. The ADO application can no longer insert data into the table directly. You are not allowed to change the ADO code or the table. How do you insert records containing values for the new columns?

   O a. Create a DDL trigger to add the new fields.

   O b. Create an AFTER trigger to supply the new fields.

   O c. Create an INSTEAD OF trigger to supply the new fields.

8.) You have a table named dbo.Widgets with the following fields:
- WidgetID SMALLINT (primary key)
- WidgetName VARCHAR(100) NULL
- ToBeDeleted bit NULL

You do not want to allow any deletes to this table. If someone attempts to run a delete statement you want to set the ToBeDeleted flag to 1. You place the following code inside the BEGIN…END block of a trigger.

```
BEGIN
UPDATE p SET isDeleted = 1
FROM dbo.Widgets as P INNER JOIN DELETED as d
ON p.WidgetID = d.WidgetID
END
```

Which SQL code would you use above this BEGIN...END block?

- a. `CREATE TRIGGER del_Widget ON Widgets AFTER DELETE AS`
- b. `CREATE TRIGGER del_Widget ON Widgets INSTEAD OF DELETE AS`

9.) Which statement will never fire a DDL trigger?
- a. `CREATE TABLE`
- b. `ALTER TRIGGER`
- c. `DROP PROCEDURE`
- d. `DELETE TABLE`
- e. `GRANT CONTROL`

10.) You want to write a trigger which will fire when someone removes a table from your database. Which DDL statement will achieve this result?

- ○ a. `CREATE TRIGGER trg_DroppedTables`
  `ON DATABASE FOR CREATE_TABLE`
  `AS`

- ○ b. `CREATE TRIGGER trg_DroppedTables`
  `ON DATABASE FOR CREATE_TABLE, ALTER_TABLE`
  `AS`

- ○ c. `CREATE TRIGGER trg_DroppedTables`
  `ON DATABASE FOR DELETE_TABLE`
  `AS`

- ○ d. `CREATE TRIGGER trg_DroppedTables`
  `ON DATABASE FOR DROP_TABLE`
  `AS`

- ○ e. `CREATE TRIGGER trg_DroppedTables`
  `ON DATABASE FOR REMOVE_TABLE`
  `AS`

11.) Which system-supplied function captures and holds the details of the event that fired the DDL trigger?

- ○ a. `EVENTDATA()`
- ○ b. `EVENTLOG()`
- ○ c. `EVENTDETAILS()`
- ○ d. `EVENTXML()`
- ○ e. `OGXML()`
- ○ f. `SHOWXML()`

12.) You only allow DDL changes to be made to your database at the beginning of the month. Changes must take place before the 6th day of the month. You need to ensure that attempts to modify or create tables on the 6th day of any given month will get rolled back. Which SQL statement will achieve this result?

○ a. `CREATE TRIGGER` trg_TablesBeforeFifth
   `ON DATABASE FOR CREATE_TABLE`
   `AS`
   `IF DATEPART(day, GETDATE())>5`
   `BEGIN`
   `ROLLBACK`
   `END`
   `GO`

○ b. `CREATE TRIGGER` trg_TablesBeforeFifth
   `ON DATABASE FOR CREATE_TABLE, ALTER_TABLE`
   `AS`
   `IF DATEPART(day, GETDATE())>5`
   `BEGIN`
   `COMMIT`
   `END`
   `GO`

○ c. `CREATE TRIGGER` trg_TablesBeforeFifth
   `ON DATABASE FOR CREATE_TABLE, ALTER_TABLE`
   `AS`
   `IF DATEPART(day, GETDATE())>5`
   `BEGIN`
   `ROLLBACK`
   `END`
   `GO`

○ d. `CREATE TRIGGER` trg_TablesBeforeFifth
   `ON DATABASE FOR ALTER_TABLE`
   `AS`
   `IF DATEPART(day, GETDATE())>5`
   `BEGIN`
   `ROLLBACK`
   `END`
   `GO`

13.) You have a function named Verify that returns a 1 if true and a 0 if false. If a 0 is returned, then SQL should generate an error and the event should not be allowed to commit. Which SQL statement will achieve this result?

○ a.
```
CREATE TRIGGER trg_TEST
FOR CREATE_TABLE, ALTER_TABLE AS
IF Verify()=0
BEGIN
RAISERROR ('Must wait until next month.', 16, 5)
END
GO
```

○ b.
```
CREATE TRIGGER trg_TEST ON DATABASE
FOR CREATE_TABLE,ALTER_TABLE
AS
IF Verify()=0
BEGIN
ROLLBACK
RAISERROR ('Must wait until next month.', 16, 5)
END
GO
```

○ c.
```
CREATE TRIGGER trg_TEST
FOR CREATE_TABLE, ALTER_TABLE
AS
IF Verify()=1
BEGIN
RAISERROR ('Must wait until next month.', 16, 5)
END
GO
```

○ d.
```
CREATE TRIGGER trg_TEST ON DATABASE
FOR CREATE_TABLE, ALTER_TABLE
AS
IF Verify()=1
BEGIN
ROLLBACK
RAISERROR ('Must wait until next month.', 16, 5)
END
GO
```

14.) You have a Parent table and a Child table for a local school. Since the relationship between Parent and Child is a Many-to-Many relationship, you have created a ParentChild table. Your company got into legal trouble when a child's records were accidentally deleted from the Child table and the parent needed transcript records. You are not allowed to delete a child's record from the Child table if it has at least one corresponding active parent listed in the Parent table. If someone tries to delete a child, the record should remain in the table but the IsDeleted column for the child's row will be set to 1. You have proposed putting the following 2 DML statements in your trigger.

```
--Statement 1
UPDATE c SET IsDeleted = 1
FROM ParentChild pc INNER JOIN deleted d ON pc.ChildID =
d.ChildID INNER JOIN Child c ON pc.ChildID = c.ChildID
```

```
--Statement 2
DELETE p
FROM Child c INNER JOIN deleted d ON c.ChildID = d.ChildID
LEFT OUTER JOIN ParentChild pc ON c.ChildID = pc.ChildID
WHERE pc.ParentID IS NULL
```

You are not allowed to use any rollback statement in your trigger but want to prevent delete changes that would cause a child record to disappear. Which trigger syntax should you use?

- a. **CREATE TRIGGER** trg_Child_d
  ON Child **AFTER DELETE AS**
- b. **CREATE TRIGGER** trg_Child_d
  ON Child **INSTEAD OF DELETE AS**
- c. **CREATE TRIGGER** trg_ParentChild_d
  ON ParentChild **AFTER DELETE AS**
- d. **CREATE TRIGGER** trg_ParentChild_d
  ON ParentChild **INSTEAD OF DELETE AS**

15.) Your database contains two tables named Order and OrderDetails that store order information. They relate to each other using the OrderID column in each table. Your business requires that the LastModifiedDate column in the Order table must reflect the date and time when a change is made in the OrderDetails table for the related order. You need to create a trigger to implement this business requirement. Which T-SQL statement should you use?

- O a.
    ```
    CREATE TRIGGER [uModDate] ON [Order]
    INSTEAD OF UPDATE
    AS
    UPDATE [Order]
    SET [LastModifiedDate] = GETDATE()
    FROM Inserted
    WHERE Inserted.[OrderID] = [Order].[OrderID];
    GO
    ```
- O b.
    ```
    CREATE TRIGGER [uModDate] ON [OrderDetails]
    AFTER UPDATE
    AS
    UPDATE [Order]
    SET [LastModifiedDate] = GETDATE()
    FROM Inserted
    WHERE Inserted.[OrderID] = [Order].[OrderID];
    GO
    ```

16.) You need to ensure that tables are not dropped from your database. What should you do?

- O a.   Create a DDL trigger that contains COMMIT.
- O b.   Create a DML trigger that contains COMMIT.
- O c.   Create a DDL trigger that contains ROLLBACK.
- O d.   Create a DML trigger that contains ROLLBACK.
- O e.   GRANT CONTROL

Answer Key

1.) The only DML statement that does not make any changes to a table is SELECT which makes (a) the correct answer.

2.) DML triggers can either be "After" or "Instead of", making (b) and (c) correct.

3.) If you make an update to a table directly it gets a @@NESTLEVEL of 0. If a trigger makes the update then it has a @@NESTLEVEL of 1. If a trigger runs another trigger then that second trigger has a @@NESTLEVEL of 2. This means (c) is the correct answer.

4.) If you make an update to a table directly it gets a @@NESTLEVEL of 0. If a trigger makes the update then it has a @@NESTLEVEL of 1. This means (b) is the correct answer.

5.) You can stop a trigger from firing, so (a) is incorrect. The only way to stop a trigger without dropping it is by disabling it, so (b) is the correct answer.

6.) For records that are not to be inserted you don't use an "After" trigger, so (b) and (d) are wrong. You want to log the change to the BadEmployeeRecords table, making (a) wrong, therefore (c) is the correct answer.

7.) If the insert will not work directly then instead of inserting you can add your own fields. This means (c) is the correct answer.

8.) If you don't want to allow the event to take place then you need an "Instead of" trigger, so (b) is the correct answer.

9.) DDL triggers only fire on DDL statement. Since DELETE is a DML statement, that is the one event that will never fire a DDL trigger, making (d) the correct answer.

10.) When someone removes a table from the database that is a DROP_TABLE event. This means (d) is the correct answer.

11.) All the event details of a trigger are captured and exposed through the EVENTDATA() function which is why (a) is correct.

12.) DDL changes can come in the form of creating or altering. If you only check for one event then that is not enough, so (a) and (d) are wrong. We want to roll back the event if the date is before the 5th, so (c) is correct.

13.) You want to check for the zero to be the error, so (c) and (d) are incorrect. If you find a zero, you want an error and to make sure the record does not commit. To roll back and raise the error, (b) is the correct answer.

14.) You want to prevent the deletion of a record from the Child table so that is where the trigger should be. Since (c) and (d) are on the ParentChild table they are incorrect. The delete should never happen to the child table so you want an "Instead of" trigger, making (b) the correct answer.

15.) The order table must be updated after the OrderDetails gets an update event. Since you have to put the trigger on the OrderDetails table this means (b) is the correct answer.

16.) To prevent a table from being dropped you need a DDL trigger, so (b), (d) and (e) are wrong. You don't want the drop to work so you need to roll back the event, making (c) correct.

Bug Catcher Game

To play the Bug Catcher game, run the file SQLQueries2012Vol4BugCatcher3.pps from the BugCatcher folder of the companion files found at www.Joes2Pros.com.

Chapter 4.   Views

A great memory from my early teens is the time my science class visited a space telescope. The telescope had been preset for us to see the rings of Saturn. We all lined up and took turns looking into the telescope. That predefined view showed us the array of different orange, gold, and silver hues comprising the stunning rings around the sixth planet from our sun. If Saturn had blue and green rings, then that is what we would have seen that day. The telescope was preset to show our class precisely the information we wanted to see.

Views in SQL Server play a similar role. They provide a preset way to view data from one or more tables. They may also include aggregate fields (e.g., COUNT, SUM). Views allow your users to query a single object which behaves like a table and contains the needed joins and fields you have specified. In this way, a simple query (SELECT * FROM *ViewName*) can produce a more refined result which can serve as a report and answer business questions.

In addition to the benefit of reusable code, views offer the DBA a way to allow users to run queries without directly interacting with the production tables. We will see some **encryption** examples where users querying a view aren't even allowed to see the code which built the view.

READER NOTE: *Please run the script SQLQueries2012Vol4Chapter4.0Setup.sql in order to follow along with the examples in the first section of Chapter 4. All scripts mentioned in this chapter may be found at* ***www.Joes2Pros.com***.

Using Views

A **view** is a virtual table whose contents are defined by a query. Views can be based on one or more tables. In fact, a view can be comprised of any tabular data source, such as a function(s) or even another view(s). You might choose to create a view because you want to expose a limited set of fields from a table(s) to certain users. By giving users permissions to a view, you allow them to see the data they need without having to grant them access to the underlying table(s). At other times, you might use a view in order to see a complex report consisting of many tables and joins, but you want to be able to obtain or refresh your report using a single object (i.e., the view).

Since we will base our first view on the Employee table, let's look at a query showing all of the records and all nine fields of this table (Figure 4.1).

```
SELECT * FROM Employee
```

	EmpID	LastName	FirstName	HireDate	LocationID	ManagerID	Status	HiredOffset	TimeZone
1	1	Adams	Alex	2001-01-01...	1	11	Active	2001-01-01...	-08:00
2	2	Brown	Barry	2002-08-12...	1	11	Active	2002-08-12...	-08:00
3	3	Osako	Lee	1999-09-01...	2	11	Active	1999-09-01...	-05:00
4	4	Kennson	David	1996-03-16...	1	11	Has Tenure	1996-03-16...	-08:00
5	5	Bender	Eric	2007-05-17...	1	11	Active	2007-05-17...	-08:00
6	6	Kendall	Lisa	2001-11-15...	4	4	Active	2001-11-15...	-08:00

Figure 4.1 This SELECT query displays all nine fields of the Employee table.

Tables in a production environment typically contain more fields than you wish to see in a report. A simple query (SELECT * FROM *Table*) can return an unwieldy amount of information and make reviewing your table data a challenge.

Suppose the Employee table query we use most often contains just the first seven fields of this table. Let's itemize our field list accordingly (Figure 4.2).

```
SELECT EmpID, LastName, FirstName,
HireDate, LocationID, [Status]
FROM Employee
```

	EmpID	LastName	FirstName	HireDate	LocationID	Status
1	1	Adams	Alex	2001-01-01 ...	1	Active
2	2	Brown	Barry	2002-08-12 ...	1	Active
3	3	Osako	Lee	1999-09-01 ...	2	Active
4	4	Kennson	David	1996-03-16 ...	1	Has Tenure
5	5	Bender	Eric	2007-05-17 ...	1	Active
6	6	Kendall	Lisa	2001-11-15 ...	4	Active

Figure 4.2 This query shows every record but only a subset of fields from the Employee table.

Creating Views with Management Studio

We want to create a view named vEmployee based on our query (Figure 4.2).

We will use SQL Server Management Studio (SSMS) to create vEmployee. In the Databases folder of Object Explorer, expand the JProCo database, right-click on the Views folder, and click New View (Figure 4.3).

A view designer window appears behind a dialog listing the objects (tables, views, functions) we may use to build our view. Since we know our view will be based on the Employee table, click "Employee" and then click the "Add" button (Figure 4.4) then click the "Close" button to exit the dialog.

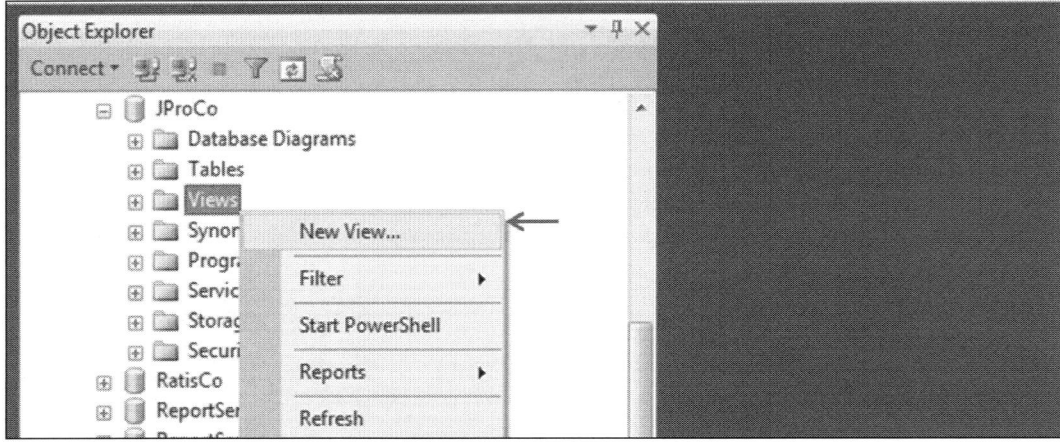

Figure 4.3 Right-click Views and select New View.

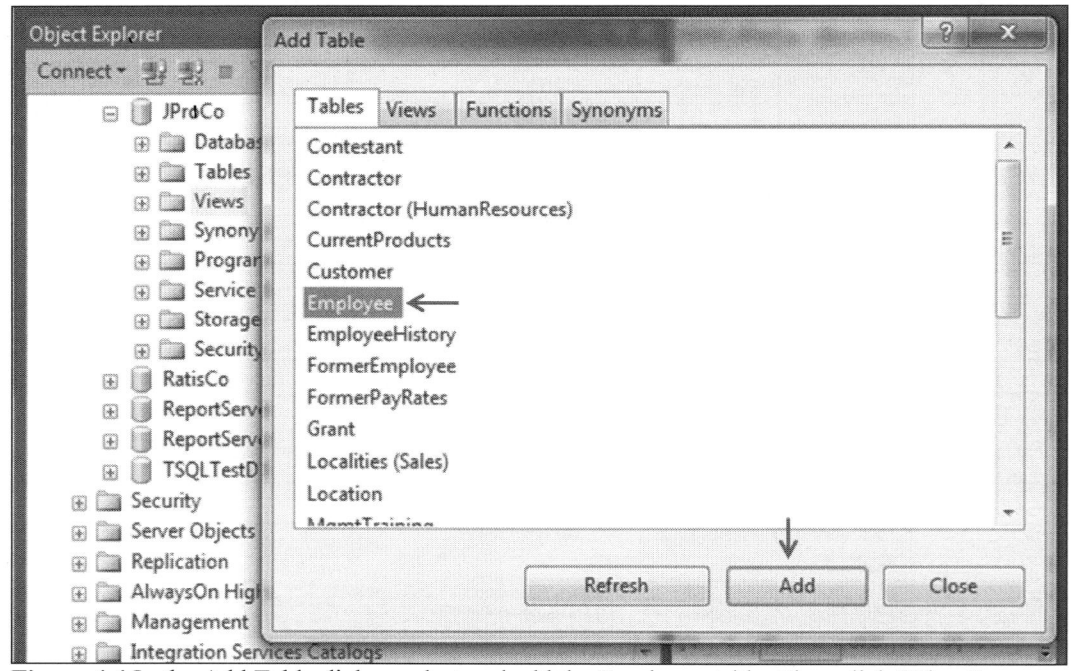

Figure 4.4 In the Add Table dialog, select and add the Employee table. Then click "Close".

Once the Add Table dialog box closes, your View Designer window opens a Diagram Pane displaying a list box for each table you selected. When you check each field you need, you will see it appear in the other panes (the Criteria and SQL Panes).

Chapter 4. Views

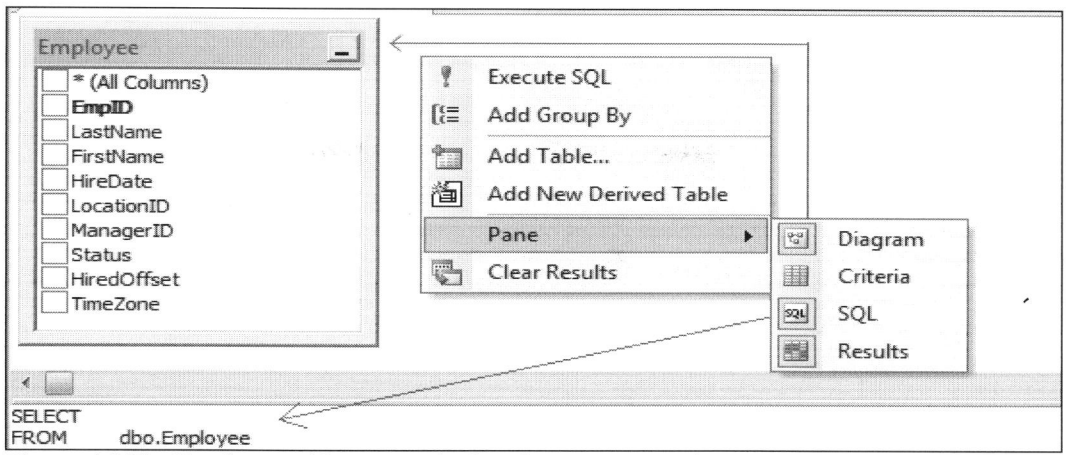

Figure 4.5 The Employee table appears in the Diagram Pane and SQL Pane of the View Designer. To see the Pane options (Diagram, Criteria, SQL, Results), right-click on Pane.

Let's check the boxes next to EmpID, FirstName, LastName, HireDate, LocationID, ManagerID, and Status *(Be certain to check FirstName before you check LastName.* As you check each box, you will see the selected field appear in the Criteria and SQL Panes). When you save the view (click the save icon or File > Save), the Choose Name dialog appears. Enter the name vEmployee and click OK to create this view (Figure 4.6).

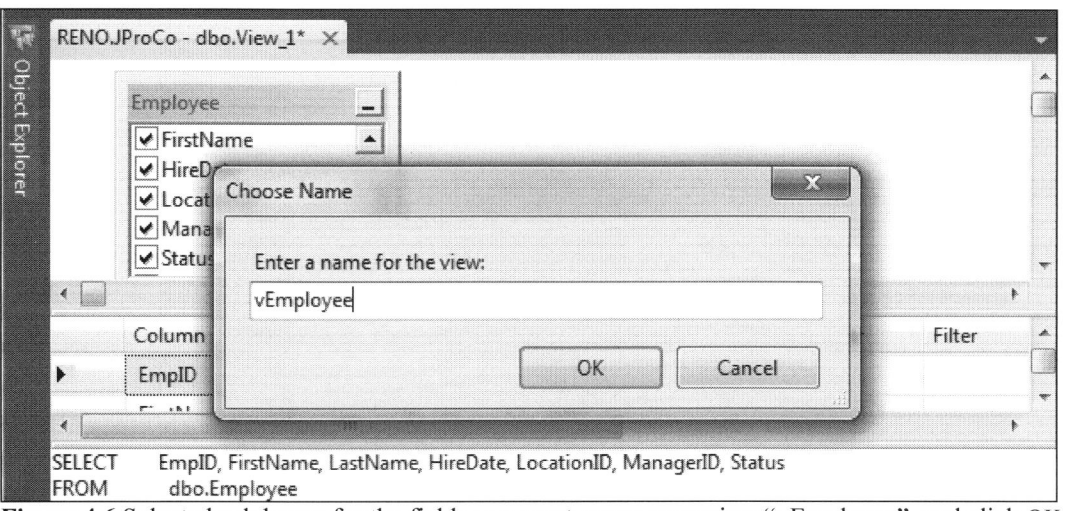

Figure 4.6 Select check boxes for the fields you want, name your view "vEmployee", and click OK.

If you get an error that says "The transaction ended in the trigger" then you must delete the trg_NoViewsInJanuary trigger you created in the last chapter. We have successfully built the vEmployee view and can now query it. This simplified query achieves nearly the same result produced in Figure 4.2. Our result set looks like the

Employee table, except it contains just the seven fields we specified – and in our specified order (Figure 4.7).

```
SELECT * FROM vEmployee
```

	EmpID	FirstName	LastName	HireDate	LocationID	ManagerID	Status
1	1	Alex	Adams	2001-01-01...	1	11	Active
2	2	Barry	Brown	2002-08-12...	1	11	Active
3	3	Lee	Osako	1999-09-01...	2	11	Active
4	4	David	Kennson	1996-03-16...	1	11	Has Tenure
5	5	Eric	Bender	2007-05-17...	1	11	Active

Query executed successfully. | RENO (11.0 RTM) | Reno\Student (51) | JProCo | 00:00:00 | 19 rows

Figure 4.7 A query of our new view, vEmployee.

Creating Views Using T-SQL Code

Our last example provided an overview of the toolset which SQL Server Management Studio (SSMS) offers for creating views. However, the most robust and repeatable way of creating and maintaining your views is with T-SQL code.

A view is a great solution for reports or queries you run frequently, because you write the join logic once and then use it many times. One of our common JProCo tasks is to build a query showing all of the JProCo employees and their locations. This means we often join the Employee table to the Location table on LocationID. Suppose the key fields we always want are FirstName, LastName, City, and State. The view we will build is vEmployeeLocations and it will be based on the query shown here (Figure 4.8). Note that we want to exclude any employee without a location. Therefore, this is an inner join query, which excludes John Marshbank.

```
SELECT em.FirstName, em.LastName, lo.City, lo.[State]
FROM Employee AS em
INNER JOIN Location AS lo
ON em.LocationID = lo.LocationID
```

	FirstName	LastName	City	State
1	Alex	Adams	Seattle	WA
2	Barry	Brown	Seattle	WA
3	Lee	Osako	Boston	MA
4	David	Kennson	Seattle	WA
5	Eric	Bender	Seattle	WA
6	Lisa	Kendall	Spokane	WA

18 rows

Figure 4.8 This join of the Employee and Location tables containing these 4 fields is the query we run most frequently.

Let's add the needed code to this statement in order to turn our employee location report query into a view. Notice we simply need to place a CREATE VIEW *ViewName* AS statement before our existing query. The query from our employee location report has been turned into a view by using the following code:

```
CREATE VIEW dbo.vEmployeeLocations
AS
SELECT em.FirstName, em.LastName, lo.City, lo.[State]
FROM Employee AS em INNER JOIN Location AS lo
ON em.LocationID = lo.LocationID
GO
```

Let's check Object Explorer and find our newly created object. Within the Databases folder, expand the Views folder inside of JProCo (Figure 4.9). Remember that you may need to refresh the folder (right-click Views > Refresh), if you don't immediately see vEmployeeLocations. The Object Explorer doesn't spend system resources dynamically refreshing itself in real time.

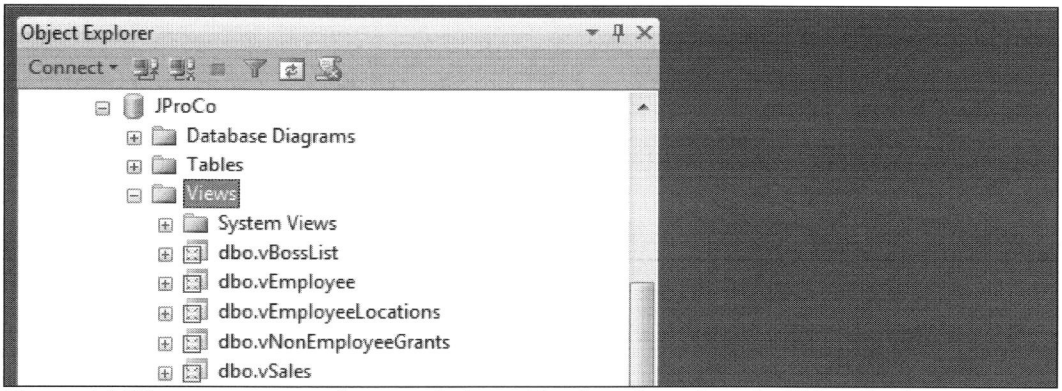

Figure 4.9 We can see our newly created view, vEmployeeLocations, in Object Explorer.

Let's query the view (Figure 4.10). Notice that our result is identical to that which was produced by the underlying query shown earlier in Figure 4.8.

```
SELECT * FROM vEmployeeLocations
```

	FirstName	LastName	City	State
1	Alex	Adams	Seattle	WA
2	Barry	Brown	Seattle	WA
3	Lee	Osako	Boston	MA
4	David	Kennson	Seattle	WA
5	Eric	Bender	Seattle	WA
6	Lisa	Kendall	Spokane	WA

18 rows

Figure 4.10 This view produces the same result that we saw when running the query (Figure 4.8).

Analyzing Existing Views

Suppose you have a view and you want to see its underlying code. We will look at a few techniques for accomplishing that.

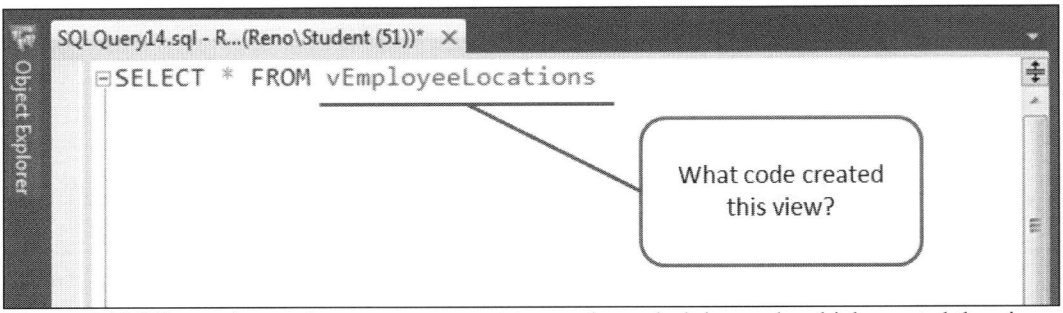

Figure 4.11 When using a view, you may want to see the underlying code which created the view.

One way of generating the underlying code for an object is to right-click it in Object Explorer and use the "Script View as" option (Figure 4.12).

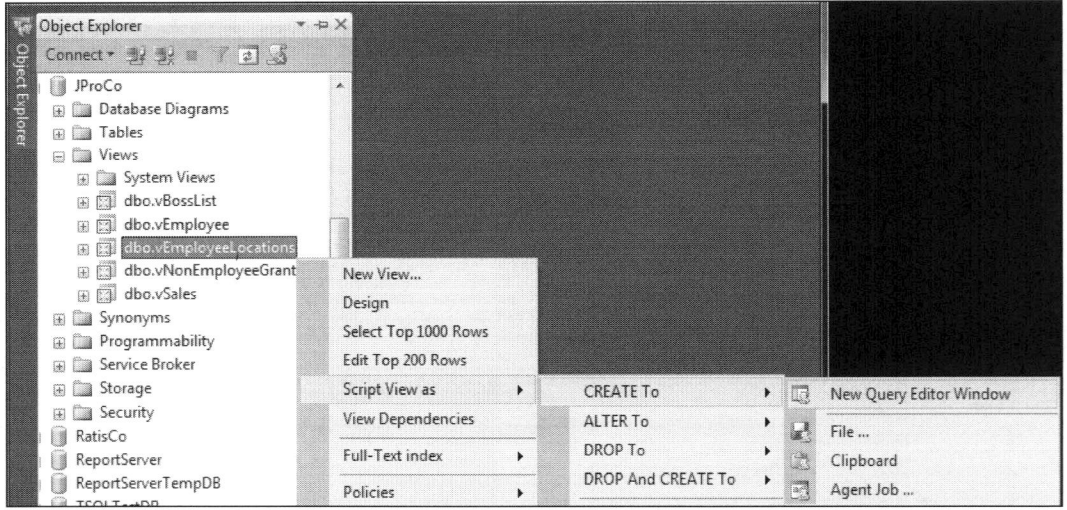

Figure 4.12 When using a view, you may want to see the underlying code which created the view.

Another handy way to see the code for any SQL Server object is to use the system stored procedure, sp_helptext (Figure 4.13).

```
sp_helptext 'dbo.vEmployeeLocations'
```

	Text
1	CREATE VIEW dbo.vEmployeeLocations
2	AS
3	SELECT em.FirstName, em.LastName,
4	lo.City, lo.[State]
5	FROM Employee AS em
6	INNER JOIN Location AS lo
7	ON em.LocationID = lo.LocationID

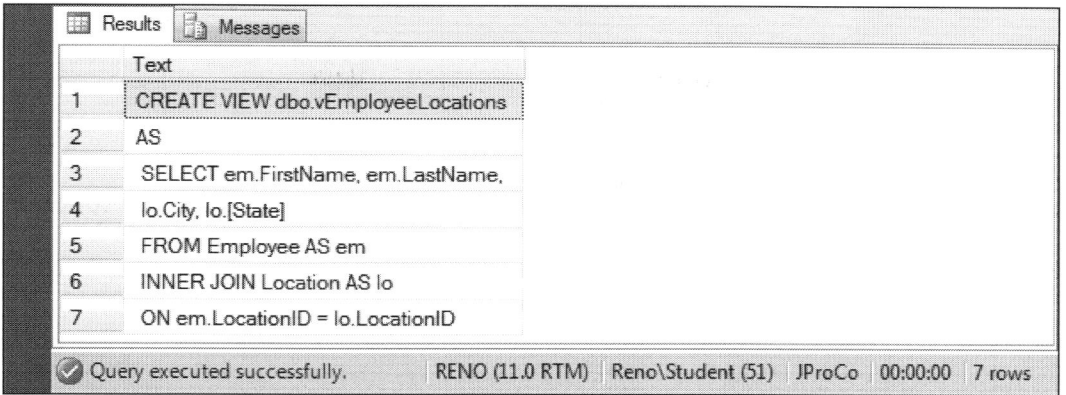

Figure 4.13 The sp_helptext system stored procedure can show the code that created an object.

Click the field header ("Text") to select all of the code. Then **ctrl+c** to copy (or right-click the field header and choose "Copy") and then **ctrl+v** to paste (or right click then select "Paste") the code into a new query window. The result of your sp_helptext query is shown in the following code:

```
CREATE VIEW [dbo].[vEmployeeLocations]
AS
SELECT em.FirstName, em.LastName, lo.City, lo.[State]
FROM Employee AS em INNER JOIN Location AS lo
ON em.LocationID = lo.LocationID
GO
```

Yet another way to get the code for the objects in a database is by querying the database's **sys.SysComments** catalog view (Figure 4.14).

```
USE JProCo
GO
SELECT * FROM sys.SysComments
```

	id	number	colid	status	ctext	texttype	language	encrypted	compressed	text
1	437576597	1	1	0	0x...	2	0	0	0	create procedure spGetEm
2	629577281	1	1	0	0x...	2	0	0	0	CREATE PROC GetCateg
3	645577338	1	1	0	0x...	2	0	0	0	CREATE PROC GetLocatic
4	661577395	1	1	0	0x...	2	0	0	0	CREATE PROC GetOrders
5	677577452	1	1	0	0x...	2	0	0	0	CREATE PROC GetCateg
6	693577509	0	1	0	0x...	2	0	0	0	CREATE VIEW vSales AS

Figure 4.14 The sys.SysComments catalog view shows metadata for your database objects.

The OBJECT_ID function (Figure 4.15) is one way of getting the object's ID, which you can use to filter your **sys.SysComments** query shown in Figure 4.14.

```
SELECT OBJECT_ID('dbo.vEmployeeLocations')
```

(No column name)
1925581898

1 rows

Figure 4.15 The OBJECT_ID function can be used to get an object's ID.

An alternate way to get the code for an object is to query the sys.SysComments catalog view and copy from the text field. Alternatively, you can use the OBJECT_ID function in your WHERE clause and thus filter your query for the object you want.

```
SELECT * FROM sys.SysComments
WHERE [id] = OBJECT_ID('dbo.vEmployeeLocations')
```

id	number	colid	status	ctext	texttype	language	encrypted	compressed	text
1925581898	0	1	0	0x430...	2	0	0	0	CREATE VIEW dbo.vEm

Query executed successfully.   RENO (11.0 RTM)   Reno\Student (51)   JProCo   00:00:00   1 rows

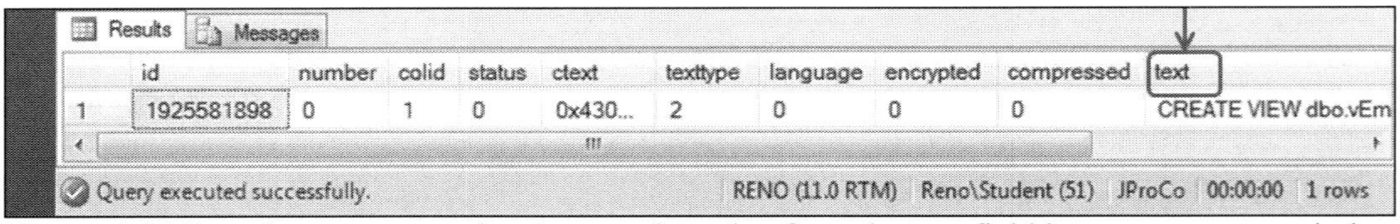

Figure 4.16 From here, you can simply copy the value from the text field into a new query window.

An alternate way to get the code for an object is to query the sys.SysComments catalog view and copy from the [text] field.

```
SELECT text FROM sys.SysComments
WHERE [id] = OBJECT_ID('dbo.vEmployeeLocations')
```

	text
1	CREATE VIEW dbo.vEmployeeLocations AS SELECT em.FirstName, em.LastName,...

1 rows

Figure 4.17 We've narrowed our SELECT list to display just the [text] field.

Lab 4.1: Creating Views

Lab Prep: Lab Prep: Each lab has one or more Skill Checks. Start with Skill Check 1 and proceed until reaching the Points to Ponder section.

Before beginning this lab, verify that SQL Server 2012 is properly installed and operating. Before running the lab setup script for resetting the database (SQLQueries2012Vol4Chapter4.1Setup.sql), please make sure to close all query windows within SSMS. An open query window pointing to a database context can lock that database preventing it from updating when the script is executing. A simple way to assure all query windows are closed, is to exit out of SSMS, then open a new instance of SSMS, and lastly run the setup script.

Skill Check 1: Create a view named vEmployeeGrants that shows the FirstName, LastName, GrantName, and Amount from an inner join of the Employee and Grant tables. Your result should match Figure 4.18.

```
SELECT * FROM vEmployeeGrants
```

	FirstName	LastName	GrantName	Amount
1	David	Lonning	92 Purr_Scents %% team	4750.00
2	Barry	Brown	K-Land fund trust	15750.00
3	David	Lonning	Robert@BigStarBank.com	18100.00
4	David	Kennson	BIG 6's Foundation%	21000.00
5	Lee	Osako	TALTA_Kishan International	18100.00
6	Terry	O'Haire	Ben@MoreTechnology.com	41000.00

11 rows

Figure 4.18 Skill Check 1.

Skill Check 2: Create a view named vEmployeePayRates which shows every employee's FirstName and LastName from the Employee table, along with all fields from the PayRates table. Be sure to show every employee, even ones who don't yet have a PayRate. The result should resemble Figure 4.19.

```
SELECT * FROM vEmployeePayRates
```

	FirstName	LastName	EmpID	YearlySalary	MonthlySalary	HourlyRate	Selector	Estimate
1	Alex	Adams	1	76000.00	NULL	NULL	1	1
2	Barry	Brown	2	79000.00	NULL	NULL	1	1
3	Lee	Osako	3	NULL	NULL	45.00	3	2080
4	David	Kennson	4	NULL	6500.00	NULL	2	12
5	Eric	Bender	5	NULL	5800.00	NULL	2	12
6	Lisa	Kendall	6	52000.00	NULL	NULL	1	1

Figure 4.19 Skill Check 2.

Skill Check 3: The vSales view shows JProCo's customers and the products they ordered. Show the code which was used to create this view of dbo.vSales (Figure 4.20).

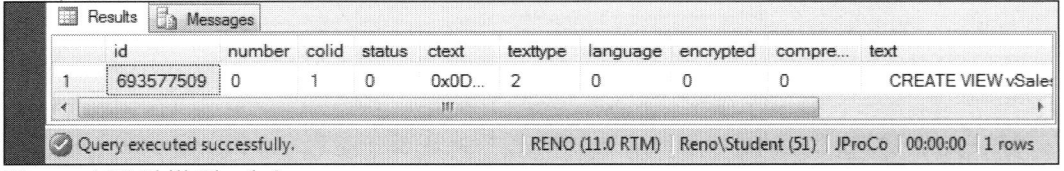

id	number	colid	status	ctext	texttype	language	encrypted	compre...	text
1	693577509	0	1	0	0x0D...	2	0	0	0	CREATE VIEW vSale

Figure 4.20 Skill Check 3.

Answer Code: The T-SQL code to this lab can be found in the downloadable files in a file named Lab4.1_CreatingViews.sql.

Points to Ponder - Creating Views

1. A view is a virtual table whose contents are defined by a query.
2. Views are database objects and are stored in your database, similar to tables, stored procedures, and functions.
3. A view is a stored SELECT statement that works like a virtual table.
4. Views are a convenient way to provide access to data through a predefined query.
5. To create a view using SQL Server Management Studio, expand your database, right-click the Views folder, and choose New View.
6. A view can contain up to 1024 columns.
7. You need to have SELECT permissions on the base tables before you can create the view.
8. Views can combine data from multiple tables, columns, or sources into what looks like a single table.
9. Views can aggregate data. For example, they can show the sum of a column rather than individual values in the column.
10. The code syntax to make a new view is CREATE VIEW *ViewName* AS.
11. The tables that make up a view are called "base tables".
12. The sys.SysComments catalog view contains the definitions for views and stored procedures.

Altering Views

Now that we know how to create views, we want to examine the steps for modifying an existing view. We will continue working with the view we created in the last section, vEmployeeLocations. The left panel of Figure 4.21 shows the four fields currently contained in vEmployeeLocations. The right pane shows our new goal, which will be to add the EmpID field.

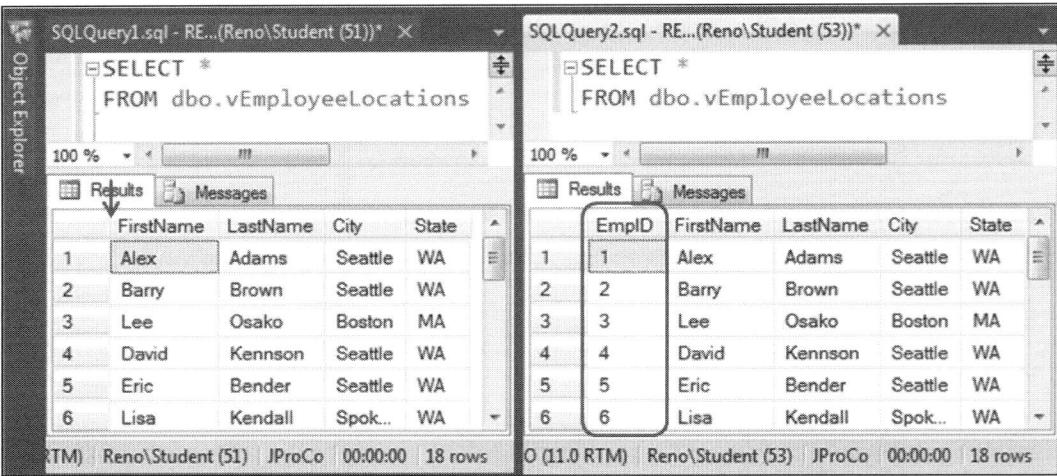

Figure 4.21 We need to add the EmpID field to the vEmployeeLocations view.

To obtain the code that created vEmployeeLocations, run sp_helptext and pass in the object name (Figure 4.22). Paste this code into a new query window.

```
sp_helptext 'dbo.vEmployeeLocations'
```

```
Text
1  CREATE VIEW dbo.vEmployeeLocations
2  AS
3  SELECT em.FirstName, em.LastName, lo.City, lo.[State]
4  FROM Employee AS em INNER JOIN Location AS lo
5  ON em.LocationID = lo.LocationID
```

Figure 4.22 The system stored procedure sp_helptext shows the source code which built the object.

As is the case with most other database objects we've encountered (tables, triggers, stored procedures, etc.), we can use an ALTER statement to modify our view.

We've pasted the code we obtained from sp_helptext (Figure 4.22) into a new window. Change the CREATE keyword to ALTER, and add the EmpID field to achieve our goal (Figure 4.23).

```
ALTER VIEW dbo.vEmployeeLocations
AS SELECT em.EmpID, em.FirstName,
em.LastName, lo.City, lo.[State]
FROM Employee AS em INNER JOIN Location AS lo
ON em.LocationID = lo.LocationID
GO
```

```
Messages
Command(s) completed successfully
                                                                    0 rows
```

Figure 4.23 The ALTER VIEW statement modifies an existing view.

Query the newly modified view. Notice that the result set (Figure 4.24) now contains the EmpID field and matches our goal data shown earlier in the right pane of Figure 4.21.

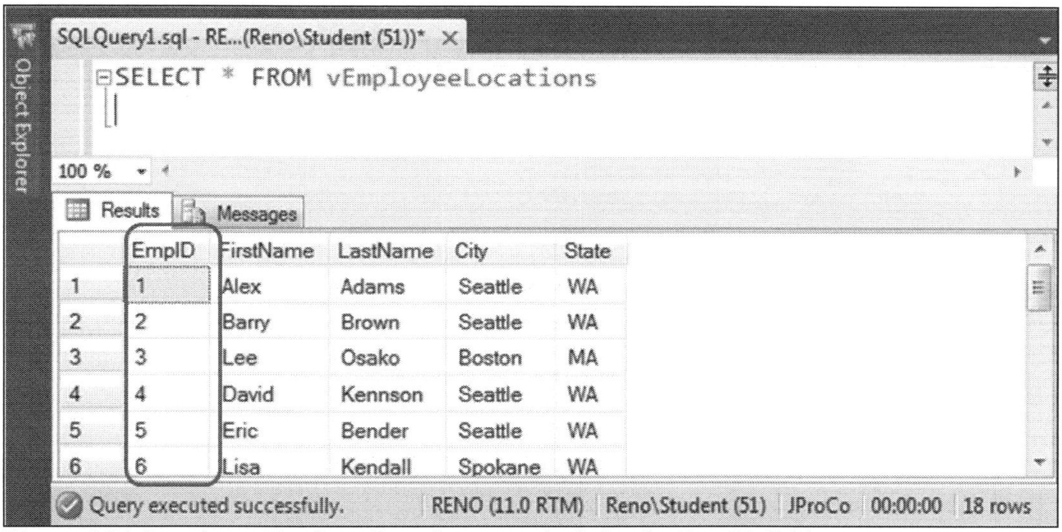

Figure 4.24 Our view, vEmployeeLocations, now includes the EmpID field.

Nesting Views

You will find that working with views is very similar to working with tables in your DML programming. Our next demonstration will illustrate joining a table to a view. Now that we have added EmpID to vEmployeeLocations, it will be easier to join this view to other objects.

The Grant table is one of the JProCo objects which contain the EmpID field. We would like to run a query which will add all fields of the Grant table to our employee locations report. The focus of this report will be JProCo's grants (currently there are

11, as shown in Figure 4.26). For each Grant, we want to see the associated employee information, including the employee's location.

```sql
SELECT * FROM vEmployeeLocations

sp_helptext 'dbo.vEmployeeLocations'

SELECT *
FROM [Grant] AS gr
INNER JOIN vEmployee
```

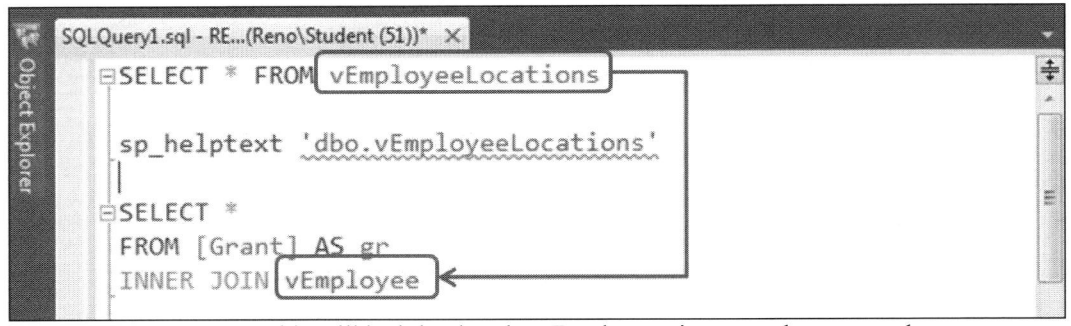

Figure 4.25 The Grant table will be joined to the vEmployee view to make one result set.

Since all 11 current Grant records contain an EmpID, we expect to see all 11 grants appear in the result. The one JProCo employee not appearing in the view (John Marshbank, EmpID 8) hasn't found any grants, so there's no problem with him being omitted from the dataset.

The syntax for joining the Grant table to the vEmployeeLocations view is precisely the same as the syntax we use to join two tables (Figure 4.27).

	GrantID	GrantName	EmpID	Amount
1	001	92 Purr_Scents %% team	7	4750.00
2	002	K-Land fund trust	2	15750.00
3	003	Robert@BigStarBank.com	7	18100.00
4	005	BIG 6's Foundation%	4	21000.00
5	006	TALTA_Kishan International	3	18100.00
6	007	Ben@MoreTechnology.com	10	41000.00
7	008	www.@-Last-U-Can-Help....	7	25000.00
8	009	Thank you @.com	11	21500.00
9	010	Just Mom	5	9900.00
10	011	Big Giver Tom	7	95900.00
11	012	Mega Mercy	9	55000.00

Figure 4.26 JProCo currently has 11 grants.

```
SELECT *
FROM [Grant] AS gr
INNER JOIN vEmployeeLocations AS vel
ON vel.EmpID = gr.EmpID
```

	GrantID	GrantName	EmpID	Amount	EmpID	FirstName	LastName	City	State
1	001	92 Purr_Scents %% t...	7	4750.00	7	David	Lonning	Seattle	WA
2	002	K-Land fund trust	2	15750.00	2	Barry	Brown	Seattle	WA
3	003	Robert@BigStarBan...	7	18100.00	7	David	Lonning	Seattle	WA
4	005	BIG 6's Foundation%	4	21000.00	4	David	Kennson	Seattle	WA
5	006	TALTA_Kishan Intern...	3	18100.00	3	Lee	Osako	Boston	MA
6	007	Ben@MoreTechnolo...	10	41000.00	10	Terry	O'Haire	Boston	MA

Figure 4.27 The result set from joining the Grant table to the vEmployeeLocations view.

Let's refine our report to omit the employee names and the extra instance of the EmpID field. We will narrow the field selection list to include all fields from the Grant table and only City and State from vEmployeeLocations (Figure 4.28).

```
SELECT gr.*, vel.City, vel.[State]
FROM [Grant] AS gr
INNER JOIN vEmployeeLocations AS vel
ON vel.EmpID = gr.EmpID
```

	GrantID	GrantName	EmpID	Amount	City	State
1	001	92 Purr_Scents %% team	7	4750.00	Seattle	WA
2	002	K-Land fund trust	2	15750.00	Seattle	WA
3	003	Robert@BigStarBank.com	7	18100.00	Seattle	WA
4	005	BIG 6's Foundation%	4	21000.00	Seattle	WA
5	006	TALTA_Kishan International	3	18100.00	Boston	MA
6	007	Ben@MoreTechnology.com	10	41000.00	Boston	MA

Figure 4.28 The field selection list has been limited to the Grant table fields plus City and State.

Suppose JProCo's Grant office says this report is perfect and they would like it in the form of a view, so they won't need to ask the IT team to re-write the code each time they want to run it.

Basing a view on another view is known as **nesting views**. The GrantLocations view is based on the grant table and the vEmployeeLocations view. From the following code you can see that one of the base tables of the GrantLocations view is itself a view (vEmployeeLocations):

```
CREATE VIEW dbo.GrantLocations
AS
SELECT gr.*, vel.City, vel.[State]
FROM [Grant] AS gr INNER JOIN vEmployeeLocations AS vel
ON vel.EmpID = gr.EmpID
GO
```

Notice that SQL Server allowed us to create the view using the name "GrantLocations". While a best practice is to prefix objects (e.g., v for views, trg for triggers) so that you can easily differentiate them from tables in your code, SQL Server doesn't enforce naming conventions for database objects.

Let's query our new view to confirm it gives us the expected result. If we created the GrantLocations view correctly, it should resemble the base query. Success! Both queries produce the same result set.

```
SELECT * FROM GrantLocations
```

	GrantID	GrantName	EmpID	Amount	City	State
1	001	92 Purr_Scents %% team	7	4750.00	Seattle	WA
2	002	K-Land fund trust	2	15750.00	Seattle	WA
3	003	Robert@BigStarBank.com	7	18100.00	Seattle	WA
4	005	BIG 6's Foundation%	4	21000.00	Seattle	WA
5	006	TALTA_Kishan International	3	18100.00	Boston	MA
6	007	Ben@MoreTechnology.com	10	41000.00	Boston	MA

Query executed successfully. RENO (11.0 RTM) | Reno\Student (51) | JProCo | 00:00:00 | 11 rows

Figure 4.29 Result set from querying the GrantLocations view.

Lab 4.2: Altering Views

Lab Prep: Lab Prep: Each lab has one or more Skill Checks. Start with Skill Check 1 and proceed until reaching the Points to Ponder section.

Before beginning this lab, verify that SQL Server 2012 is properly installed and operating. Before running the lab setup script for resetting the database (SQLQueries2012Vol4Chapter4.12Setup.sql), please make sure to close all query windows within SSMS. An open query window pointing to a database context can lock that database preventing it from updating when the script is executing. A simple way to assure all query windows are closed, is to exit out of SSMS, then open a new instance of SSMS, and lastly run the setup script.

Skill Check 1: Alter the vEmployeeGrants view to include EmpID as the first field of the view.

```
SELECT * FROM vEmployeeGrants
```

	EmpID	FirstName	LastName	GrantName	Amount
1	7	David	Lonning	92 Purr_Scents %% team	4750.00
2	2	Barry	Brown	K-Land fund trust	15750.00
3	7	David	Lonning	Robert@BigStarBank.com	18100.00
4	4	David	Kennson	BIG 6's Foundation%	21000.00
5	3	Lee	Osako	TALTA_Kishan International	18100.00
6	10	Terry	O'Haire	Ben@MoreTechnology.com	41000.00

11 rows

Figure 4.30 Skill Check 1.

Skill Check 2: Alter the vEmployeePayRates view to be based on a join of the vEmployeeLocations view and the PayRates table. Include City as a field in the SELECT list. Show all employees even if they do not have a PayRate.

```
SELECT * FROM vEmployeePayRates
```

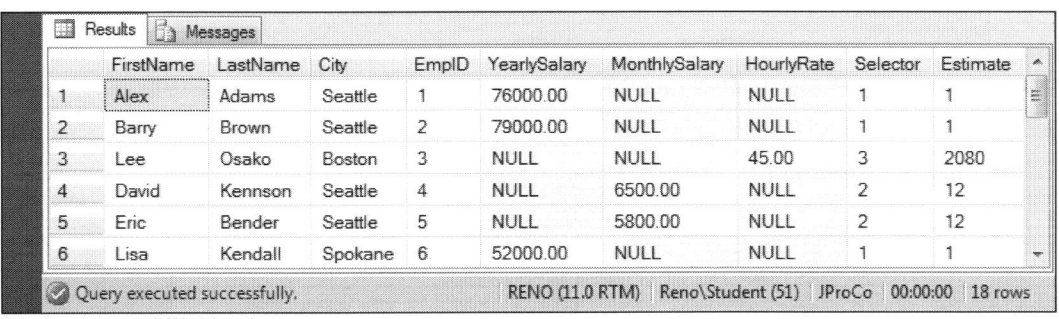

	FirstName	LastName	City	EmpID	YearlySalary	MonthlySalary	HourlyRate	Selector	Estimate
1	Alex	Adams	Seattle	1	76000.00	NULL	NULL	1	1
2	Barry	Brown	Seattle	2	79000.00	NULL	NULL	1	1
3	Lee	Osako	Boston	3	NULL	NULL	45.00	3	2080
4	David	Kennson	Seattle	4	NULL	6500.00	NULL	2	12
5	Eric	Bender	Seattle	5	NULL	5800.00	NULL	2	12
6	Lisa	Kendall	Spokane	6	52000.00	NULL	NULL	1	1

Query executed successfully. RENO (11.0 RTM) | Reno\Student (51) | JProCo | 00:00:00 | 18 rows

Figure 4.31 Skill Check 2.

Answer Code: The T-SQL code to this lab can be found in the downloadable files in a file named Lab4.2_AlteringViews.sql.

Points to Ponder - Altering Views

1. The tables that make up a view are called "base tables".
2. The data available through the view continues to reside in the base table or base tables.
3. You can't create a view from temporary tables.
4. Views can reference data in multiple tables and across multiple databases on the same or even remote servers. In addition, views can reference other views (*READERNOTE*: the topic of remote servers is outside the scope of this book).
5. The sys.SysComments catalog view contains the definitions for views and stored procedures.
6. You can build views on other views and nest them up to 32 levels.
7. You can see the definition of a view with the sp_helptext stored procedure, as long as the view is not encrypted (see next lab).

View Options

Not every query may be turned into a view. Not unlike tables, there are rules which must be followed before your queries may be turned into views.

For example, you must give each field in your table a name – you cannot create a table with a nameless field. This same rule applies to fields in your views. We are going to create a new view with a nameless field but first let's write it as a query as seen in Figure 4.32:

```
SELECT EmpID, SUM(Amount)
FROM [Grant]
GROUP BY EmpID
```

	EmpID	(No column name)
1	2	15750.00
2	3	18100.00
3	4	21000.00
4	5	9900.00
5	7	143750.00
6	9	55000.00

8 rows

Figure 4.32 A simple aggregation query.

In this section, we will also examine options for encrypting and schema binding your views.

View Rules

This query (Figure 4.33) includes a simple aggregation which totals the grant amounts according to EmpID. It's a handy report, but we can't turn it into a view. The following error message (Figure 4.33) displays when you attempt to run this code and create the view. Notice that it says "no column name was specified for column 2".

We must first make certain this expression field column has a name before we can create this view.

Chapter 4. Views

```sql
CREATE VIEW dbo.vEmpGrantTotals
AS
SELECT EmpID, SUM(Amount)
FROM [Grant]
GROUP BY EmpID
GO
```

Messages
Msg 4511, Level 16, State 1, Procedure vEmpGrantTotals, Line 3 Create View or Function failed because no column name was specified for column 2.
0 rows

Figure 4.33 A query with unnamed fields cannot become a view.

Alias the expression field as "TotalAmount" and then run this CREATE VIEW statement for vEmpGrantTotals (Figure 4.34).

```sql
CREATE VIEW dbo.vEmpGrantTotals
AS
SELECT EmpID, SUM(Amount) AS TotalAmount
FROM [Grant]
GROUP BY EmpID
GO
```

Messages
Command(s) completed successfully.
0 rows

Figure 4.34 Aliasing your expression field to have a name allows the view to be created.

Query the newly created view, vEmpGrantTotals, and look at its data (Figure 4.35). We see eight records, and the amounts are the same as we saw produced by the base query shown earlier in Figure 4.32.

```sql
SELECT * FROM dbo.vEmpGrantTotals
```

	EmpID	TotalAmount
1	2	15750.00
2	3	18100.00
3	4	21000.00
4	5	9900.00
5	7	143750.00
6	9	55000.00
		8 rows

Figure 4.35 The vEmpGrantTotals view shows eight records and both fields have their own name.

Encrypting Views

Suppose you want to make sure that people can utilize this view to run reports, but you don't want them to be capable of seeing or recreating the underlying code. As we saw earlier in this chapter, the sp_helptext system stored procedure reveals the code which created an object as illustrated in Figure 4.36.

```
sp_helptext 'dbo.vEmpGrantTotals'
```

	Text
1	CREATE VIEW dbo.vEmpGrantTotals
2	AS
3	SELECT EmpID, SUM(Amount) AS TotalAmount
4	FROM [Grant]
5	GROUP BY EmpID

5 rows

Figure 4.36 sp_helptext shows the code that created the vEmpGrantTotals view.

We want to alter this view so that the source code is encrypted. Two modifications to the code for vEmpGrantTotals (Figures 4.34 and the following code) will make this change:

- o Change CREATE VIEW to ALTER VIEW.
- o Add WITH ENCRYPTION before the AS keyword.

This code encrypts the vEmpGrantTotals view:

```sql
ALTER VIEW dbo.vEmpGrantTotals
WITH ENCRYPTION
AS
SELECT EmpID, SUM(Amount) AS TotalAmount
FROM [Grant]
GROUP BY EmpID
GO
```

The best practice after we create or alter an object is to run a SELECT statement to confirm that it produces the expected result. When we do this with our newly encrypted view, vEmpGrantTotals, we see that the data appears correctly. This matches the result we saw before we encrypted the view shown earlier in Figure 4.35. But look at Object Explorer and notice that a small padlock now appears on the icon for vEmpGrantTotals (Figure 4.37).

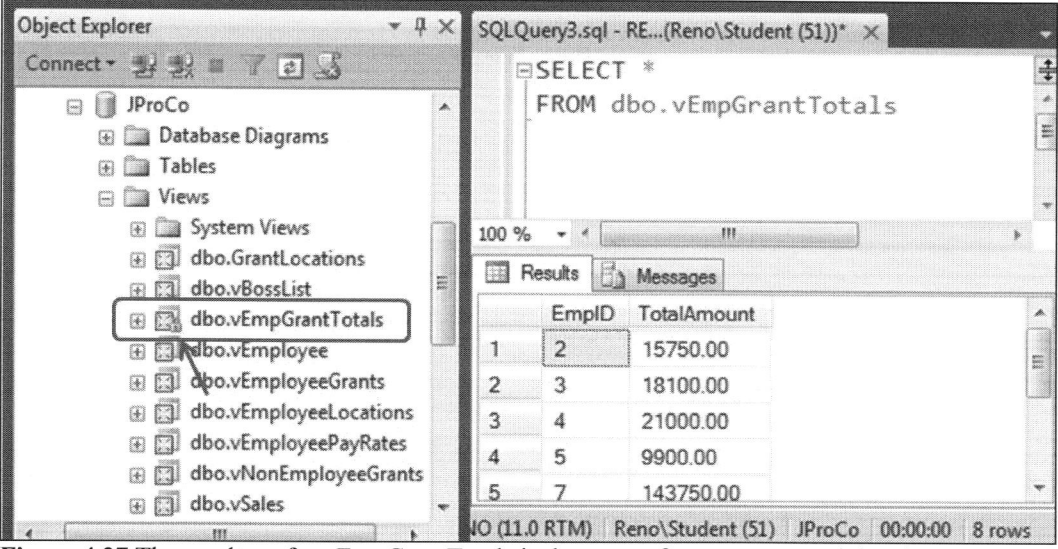

Figure 4.37 The result set for vEmpGrantTotals is the same after we encrypted the view.

Earlier in this chapter, we were able to right-click a view in Object Explorer and choose "Script View as" to see the code for the view shown earlier in Figure 4.13. Now when we attempt that maneuver for our encrypted view, SSMS gives us a message saying that the text is encrypted and we can't script this view.

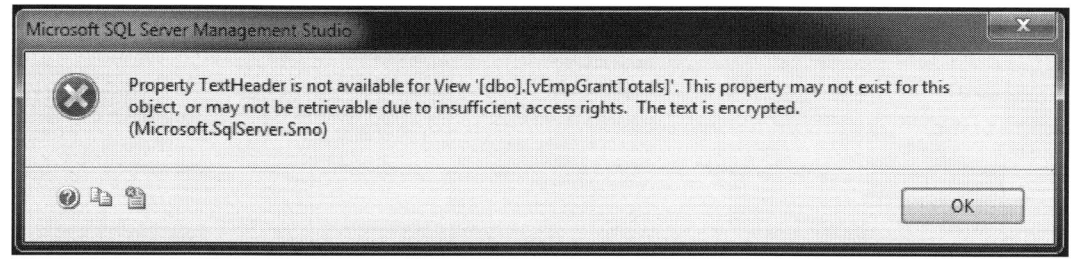

Figure 4.38 Management Studio (SSMS) will not allow us to generate code for the encrypted view.

The properties dialog for vEmpGrantTotals also tells us that the view is now encrypted (Figure 4.39, Encrypted = True).

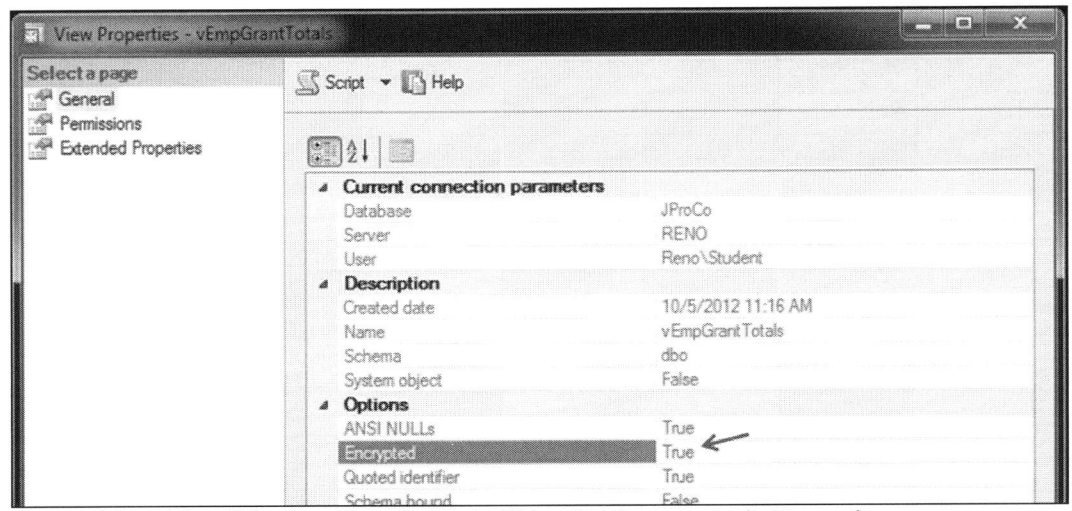

![View Properties - vEmpGrantTotals dialog showing Encrypted option set to True]

Figure 4.39 Right-click vEmpGrantTotals in Object Explorer to see its Properties.

Attempt to run the sp_helptext stored procedure and notice the message, "The text for object 'dbo.vEmpGrantTotals' is encrypted". (Figure 4.40)

```
sp_helptext 'dbo.vEmpGrantTotals'
```

```
Messages
The text for object 'dbo.vEmpGrantTotals' is encrypted.
                                                                    0 rows
```

Figure 4.40 You can't use sp_helptext to see the code for an encrypted view.

The catalog views also will not reveal source code for an encrypted object.

```
SELECT * FROM sys.SysComments
WHERE [id] = OBJECT_ID ('dbo.vEmpGrantTotals')
```

id	number	colid	status	ctext	texttype	language	encrypted	compressed	text
1989582126	0	1	1	NULL	6	0	1	0	NULL

Figure 4.41 sys.SysComments says vEmpGrantTotals is encrypted and won't reveal the code.

The WITH ENCRYPTION option allows the view to run properly with respect to running DML statements (e.g., returning data to a query). The difference is that the code which created the object cannot be seen. *Every utility we previously used to see the source code is now unavailable for vEmpGrantTotals.*

To remove encryption, simply rerun the ALTER VIEW statement without the "WITH ENCRYPTION" clause (Figure 4.42). Refresh JProCo's Views folder and notice the padlock icon disappears from the view.

Chapter 4. Views

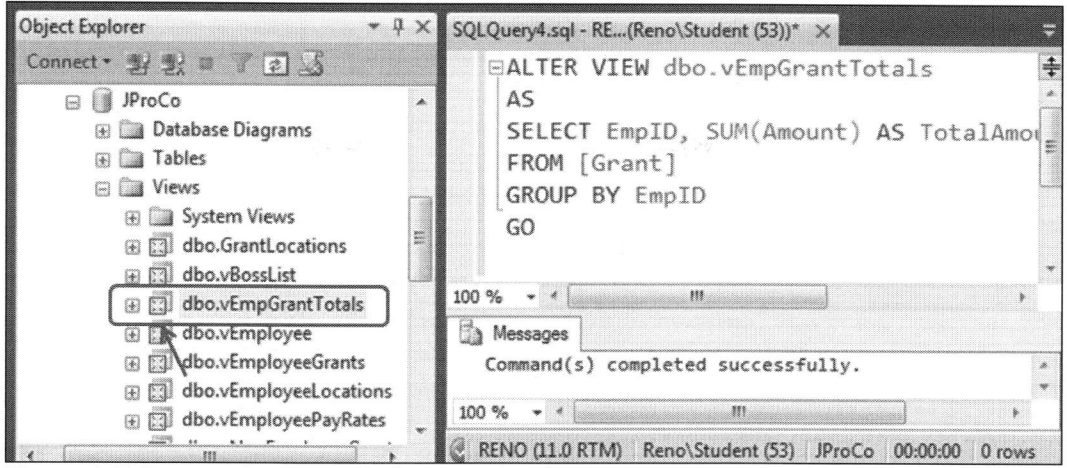

Figure 4.42 Remove the encryption by rerunning the ALTER VIEW statement without the "WITH ENCRYPTION" syntax.

Now that we have removed the encryption, the stored procedure sp_helptext again displays the source code for vEmpGrantTotals (Figure 4.43). The same is true for all of the other utilities (e.g., "Script View as" in Object Explorer, sys.views query).

```
sp_helptext 'dbo.vEmpGrantTotals'
```

	Text
1	CREATE VIEW dbo.vEmpGrantTotals
2	AS
3	SELECT EmpID, SUM(Amount) AS TotalAmount
4	FROM [Grant]
5	GROUP BY EmpID

5 rows

Figure 4.43 Since we removed the encryption on vEmpGrantTotals, sp_helptext now shows us the source code.

Schemabinding Views

Let's look at a view with multiple sources of data – in other words, a view which has two or more base tables. Run the sp_helptext stored procedure on vEmployeeGrants to obtain the code which created this view (Figure 4.44).

```
sp_helptext 'dbo.vEmployeeGrants'
```

	Text
1	CREATE VIEW vEmployeeGrants
2	AS
3	SELECT em.FirstName, em.LastName, gr.GrantName, gr.Amount
4	FROM Employee as em
5	INNER JOIN [Grant] as gr
6	ON em.EmpID = gr.EmpID

6 rows

Figure 4.44 Results after running the sp_helptext stored procedure.

The vEmployeeGrants view has two sources of data (i.e., two base tables): the Employee table and the Grant table. The two base tables of vEmployeeGrants are Employee and Grant as seen in the following code:

```
ALTER VIEW vEmployeeGrants
AS
SELECT em.EmpID, em.FirstName, em.LastName, gr.GrantName,
gr.Amount
FROM Employee AS em INNER JOIN [Grant] AS gr
ON em.EmpID = gr.EmpID
GO
```

Every view depends on its base table(s) in order to properly run and display its data. A change to the base table data can change what the view displays. Dropping a base table would break any view which depends on that table.

To learn more about specific views and their base tables (i.e., their sources of data), we will look at a few system catalog views. The **sys.views** catalog view shows us the names of all of the views in our database. The **Sys.Sql_Dependencies** catalog view keeps track of objects which depend on other objects in your database.

We will join both of these catalog views on object_id to show our list of views. Since we are only interested in the base tables of vEmployeeGrants, this query will filter on the [name] field (name = 'vEmployeeGrants', as shown in Figure 4.45).

```
SELECT * FROM sys.views AS sv
INNER JOIN Sys.Sql_Dependencies AS sd
ON sv.object_id = sd.object_id
WHERE sv.[name] = 'vEmployeeGrants'
```

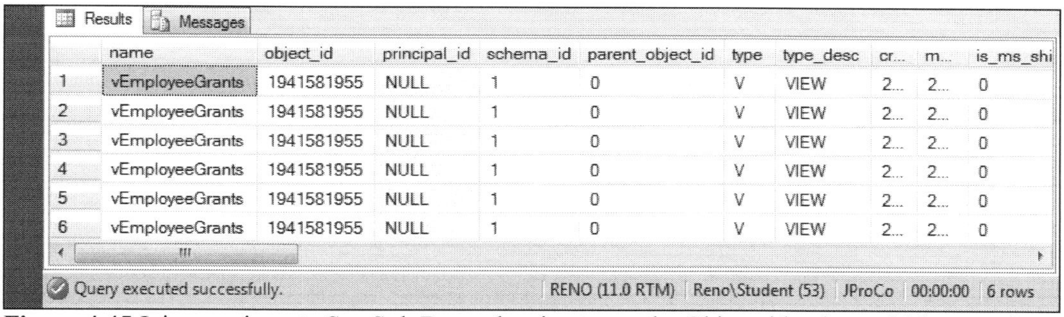

	name	object_id	principal_id	schema_id	parent_object_id	type	type_desc	cr...	m...	is_ms_shi
1	vEmployeeGrants	1941581955	NULL	1	0	V	VIEW	2...	2...	0
2	vEmployeeGrants	1941581955	NULL	1	0	V	VIEW	2...	2...	0
3	vEmployeeGrants	1941581955	NULL	1	0	V	VIEW	2...	2...	0
4	vEmployeeGrants	1941581955	NULL	1	0	V	VIEW	2...	2...	0
5	vEmployeeGrants	1941581955	NULL	1	0	V	VIEW	2...	2...	0
6	vEmployeeGrants	1941581955	NULL	1	0	V	VIEW	2...	2...	0

Query executed successfully. | RENO (11.0 RTM) | Reno\Student (53) | JProCo | 00:00:00 | 6 rows

Figure 4.45 Join sys.views to Sys.Sql_Dependencies to see the Object_id values which your view depends upon.

Our query joining sys.views and Sys.Sql_Dependencies (Figure 4.45) needs one improvement in order for us to see the actual names of the base tables. The Object_id for each base table appears in the field, referenced_major_id. In order to find the names of these objects, we will use the OBJECT_NAME() function and pass in the referenced_major_id values (see first line of code, Figure 4.46).

```
SELECT OBJECT_NAME(referenced_major_id) AS BaseTable, *
FROM sys.views sv
INNER JOIN Sys.Sql_Dependencies sd
ON sv.object_id = sd.object_id
WHERE [name] = 'vEmployeeGrants'
```

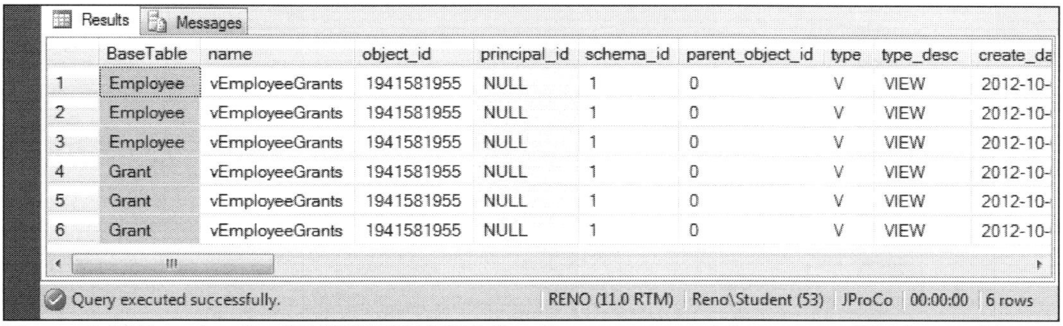

	BaseTable	name	object_id	principal_id	schema_id	parent_object_id	type	type_desc	create_da
1	Employee	vEmployeeGrants	1941581955	NULL	1	0	V	VIEW	2012-10-
2	Employee	vEmployeeGrants	1941581955	NULL	1	0	V	VIEW	2012-10-
3	Employee	vEmployeeGrants	1941581955	NULL	1	0	V	VIEW	2012-10-
4	Grant	vEmployeeGrants	1941581955	NULL	1	0	V	VIEW	2012-10-
5	Grant	vEmployeeGrants	1941581955	NULL	1	0	V	VIEW	2012-10-
6	Grant	vEmployeeGrants	1941581955	NULL	1	0	V	VIEW	2012-10-

Query executed successfully. | RENO (11.0 RTM) | Reno\Student (53) | JProCo | 00:00:00 | 6 rows

Figure 4.46 By using the OBJECT_NAME() function, you can get the names of the base tables.

We now see that vEmployeeGrants depends on the Employee table and the Grant table as its base tables. Next we will drop the Grant table. Notice that we are only dropping the Grant table - we are *not* dropping vEmployeeGrants using the following code:

```
DROP TABLE [Grant]
```

The Grant table has been dropped. Recognize that we have just dropped one of this view's (vEmployeeGrants) base tables. For the moment, we won't consider the many other JProCo views, functions, or stored procedures which rely upon the Grant table. We will restrict our focus to this dependent object, vEmployeeGrants, and its dependency, the Grant table.

Query the view and notice we get an "Invalid object name 'Grant'" error message (Figure 4.47). When you drop a dependency, you break all of the objects that depend on it.

```
SELECT * FROM dbo.vEmployeeGrants
```

```
Messages
Msg 208, Level 16, State 1, Procedure vEmployeeGrants, Line 15
Invalid object name 'Grant'.
Msg 4413, Level 16, State 1, Line 1
Could not use view or function 'dbo.vEmployeeGrants' because of binding
errors.
                                                                    0 rows
```

Figure 4.47 With the Grant table gone, the vEmployeeGrants view no longer works.

Note: If you just dropped your Grant table, please replace it by running the latest setup script (SQLProgrammingChapter4.2Setup.sql).

Finding Dependencies

We know that dropping the Grant table would cause serious problems for the view, vEmployeeGrants. Let's now think about the many JProCo objects which depend on the Grant table. In case the Grant table were ever accidentally dropped, or a design change was contemplated which would remove the Grant table, we would need a utility to show us all the objects which depend on the Grant table.

There is a system-supplied stored procedure, sp_depends, which will list all dependent objects for the object name you pass in. In this case, we want to find out every object that depends on the Grant table (Figure 4.48).

```
sp_depends 'dbo.[Grant]'
```

	name
1	dbo.GrantLocations
2	dbo.vEmpGrantTotals
3	dbo.vEmployeeGrants
4	dbo.vNonEmployeeGrants

4 rows

Figure 4.48 These six objects will break if the Grant table is dropped.

Knowing the objects which use the Grant table might be very useful. Perhaps company policy can be built around which tables will need extra care before you change them. You might even create a DDL trigger which will roll back if someone tries to drop the Grant table.

Losing the Grant table is just one way to break our vEmployeeGrants view. If the Employee table were dropped, that would also cripple vEmployeeGrants. Therefore, our next goal is to ensure that vEmployeeGrants never loses a dependency.

Add "ALTER VIEW" and "WITH SCHEMABINDING" to your code which creates vEmployeeGrants. The syntax WITH SCHEMABINDING will prevent dependencies of this view from being dropped. Notice that in order to use SCHEMABINDING, we must use two-part naming for our tables (dbo.Employee, dbo.[Grant]) as seen in Figure 4.49.

```
ALTER VIEW vEmployeeGrants
WITH SCHEMABINDING
AS
SELECT em.EmpID, em.FirstName, em.LastName,
    gr.GrantName, gr.Amount
FROM dbo.Employee AS em
INNER JOIN dbo.[Grant] AS gr
ON em.EmpID = gr.EmpID
```

Figure 4.49 To successfully add the SCHEMABINDING option, you must use at least two-part naming for the base tables. Run the code you see here in order to schema bind both of these tables.

To confirm that our schema binding is now protecting the base tables, let's try dropping one of them. Success! When we attempt to drop the Grant table, we get an error message informing us that we cannot drop the Grant table because it is being referenced by the object vEmployeeGrants (Figure 4.50).

```
DROP TABLE [Grant]
```

```
Messages
Msg 3729, Level 16, State 1, Line 1
Cannot DROP TABLE 'Grant' because it is being referenced by object
'vEmployeeGrants'.

                                                        0 rows
```

Figure 4.50 The Grant table can't be dropped as long as one of its dependencies is schema bound.

When you use the WITH SCHEMABINDING option on an object, it prevents any of the dependencies of the object from being deleted. If you wanted to drop the

Grant table, you would first need to either drop the vEmployeeGrants view or remove the schema binding.

If we wanted to add both schema binding and encryption to vEmployeeGrants, we would need to use this syntax. You must include both in the same WITH clause, because a DDL statement may have only one WITH clause.

After we run the following code, vEmployeeGrants is both schema bound and encrypted. This means that neither of the base tables (Grant, Employee) of vEmployeeGrants may be dropped, and no one will be able to see the code which created the view. The vEmployeeGrants view is now encrypted and schema bound using the following code:

```sql
ALTER VIEW vEmployeeGrants
WITH SCHEMABINDING, ENCRYPTION
AS
SELECT em.EmpID, em.FirstName, em.LastName, gr.GrantName,
gr.Amount
FROM dbo.Employee AS em INNER JOIN dbo.[Grant] AS gr
ON em.EmpID = gr.EmpID
GO
```

The process to remove SCHEMABINDING is the same process we used to remove encryption. Simply rerun the ALTER VIEW statement without the "WITH SCHEMABINDING" clause. This view has been modified to remove the encryption and schema bound base as shown in the following code:

```sql
ALTER VIEW vEmployeeGrants
AS
SELECT em.EmpID, em.FirstName, em.LastName, gr.GrantName,
gr.Amount
FROM dbo.Employee AS em INNER JOIN dbo.[Grant] AS gr
ON em.EmpID = gr.EmpID
```

With the schema binding protection removed, we again are able to make the blunder of dropping our Grant table.

```sql
DROP TABLE [Grant]
```

Messages
Command(s) completed successfully.
0 rows

Figure 4.51 The DROP TABLE now succeeds.

Lab 4.3: View Options

Lab Prep: Lab Prep: Each lab has one or more Skill Checks. Start with Skill Check 1 and proceed until reaching the Points to Ponder section.

Before beginning this lab, verify that SQL Server 2012 is properly installed and operating. Before running the lab setup script for resetting the database (SQLQueries2012Vol4Chapter4.3Setup.sql), please make sure to close all query windows within SSMS. An open query window pointing to a database context can lock that database preventing it from updating when the script is executing. A simple way to assure all query windows are closed, is to exit out of SSMS, then open a new instance of SSMS, and lastly run the setup script.

Skill Check 1: Create an aggregate view called vCustomerQuantity based on the vSales view that shows each CustomerID and the total quantity they have ordered. The expression field should be called TotalQty.

```
SELECT * FROM vCustomerQuantity
```

	CustomerID	TotalQty
1	593	10
2	261	4
3	0	6
4	355	40
5	238	122
6	570	34

712 rows

Figure 4.52 Skill Check 1.

Skill Check 2: Take the vCustomerQuantity view and encrypt it so that nobody can read the code used to create the view.

```
sp_helptext 'vCustomerQuantity'
```

Messages
The text for object 'vCustomerQuantity' is encrypted.

0 rows

Figure 4.53 Skill Check 2.

Skill Check 3: Find out how many objects depend on the dbo.Employee table. *READERNOTE:* If you don't run the current setup script, SQLQueries2012Vol4Chapter4.3Setup.sql, the query may return a seventh record.

	name	type
1	dbo.GetLocationCount	stored procedure
2	dbo.spGetEmployeeLastAndState	stored procedure
3	dbo.vBossList	view
4	dbo.vEmployee	view
5	dbo.vEmployeeGrants	view
6	dbo.vEmployeeLocations	view

6 rows

Figure 4.54 Skill Check 3.

Skill Check 4: Write a statement that ensures all dependencies of the vSales view cannot be deleted.

```
DROP TABLE SalesInvoiceDetail
```

```
messages
Msg 3729, Level 16, State 1, Line 1
Cannot DROP TABLE 'SalesInvoiceDetail' because it is being referenced by
object 'vSales'.
                                                                    0 rows
```

Figure 4.55 Skill Check 4.

Answer Code: The T-SQL code to this lab can be found in the downloadable files in a file named Lab4.3_ViewOptions.sql.

Points to Ponder - Altering Views

1. There are four main ways to obtain information about views.
   - SQL Server Management Studio (SSMS)
   - sys.views catalog view
   - sp_helptext stored procedure
   - Sys.Sql_Dependencies catalog view

2. Views can aggregate data. For example, they can show the sum of a column rather than individual values in the column.

3. In views, you must specify column names for:
   - Columns derived from mathematical expressions, functions, or constants.
   - Columns in the tables (usually from a join) that share the same name.

4. If you specify the WITH ENCRYPTION option, no one (including you) will be able to read your view's description in the sys.SysComments catalog view or the sp_helptext stored procedure.

5. To remove WITH ENCRYPTION from a view, simply remove the WITH ENCRYPTION syntax and run the ALTER VIEW statement.

6. Altering a view has an advantage over dropping and re-creating the view, since the original permissions are retained.

7. If you need to change a view, you can modify it by either using the UI or an ALTER VIEW statement.

8. Modifying a view does not change the permissions of the view. If you drop a view, however, the permissions must be reassigned.

9. Dropping a base table will cause the dependent view to break.

10. Before you drop any table or view, you should check to see if any view depends on it.

11. If you no longer need a view, you can remove its definition from the database by either using the UI or running a DROP VIEW statement.

12. The T-SQL syntax to drop a view is DROP VIEW *ViewName*.

13. Views cannot use ORDER BY unless a TOP *n* or a FOR XML, clause is included (The latter point is discussed in Volume 5, *SQL Interoperability*).

Chapter Glossary

ALTER VIEW: A DDL statement to change the definition of an existing view.

Catalog views: A predefined view you can query from to see your database metadata.

CREATE VIEW: DDL statement to create the definition of a new view.

Dependencies: Upon another object.

Dependent object: A database object (e.g., a view) which references – in other words, depends upon – another database object(s).

Encrypt(ion): A way to scramble data so it can't be read by others.

SCHEMABINDING: Objects that are schema-bound can have their definition changed, but objects that are referenced by schema bound objects cannot have their definition changed.

sp_helptext: System-supplied stored procedure that reports information about a database object.

Sys.Sql_Dependencies: A catalog view that contains a row for each dependency of a referencing object.

sys.SysComments: A catalog view which contains the code that created each SQL object created within a database.

sys.SysObjects: Contains one row for each object created in a database.

sys.views: Contains one row for each View created in a database.

Temporary table: A table prefixed with a # ("pound sign") and is only visible within one session of SQL Server.

TOP *n*: A row limiting clause that takes the top number of rows that you specify.

Two-part naming: A combination of schema and table name separated by a do (example: Sales.Campaigns, dbo.Employee).

Indexed view: A virtual table created when you place a clustered index on a view.

View Designer: A graphical design tool that will construct the create view statement for you.

WITH ENCRYPTION: The code option which will encrypt the definition of an object.

WITH SCHEMABINDING: The code option which will schema bind an object.

Review Quiz - Chapter Four

1.) You have a view that joins the Employee table to the Location table. These two tables in this view are called what?

   O a. View Table(s)
   O b. Base Table(s)
   O c. Dependent Table(s)
   O d. Source Table(s)

2.) You can base a view on another view (True/False).

   O a. True
   O b. False

3.) The following query cannot be made into a view

   ```
   CREATE VIEW Sales.vTravelTripsLocationRating
   AS
   SELECT LocationID, AVG(Rating)
   FROM Sales.TravelTrip
   GROUP BY LocationID
   ```

   What must you do in order for this view to be created?

   O a. Change the word CREATE to ALTER.
   O b. Add the words ORDER BY after GROUP BY.
   O c. Alias all expression fields with an identifier.
   O d. Remove the schema name from the base table.

4.) What are two ways to see the code that created a view? (Choose two)

   ☐ a. WITH SCHEMABINDING
   ☐ b. WITH ENCRYPTION
   ☐ c. Sp_helptext
   ☐ d. Sp_depends
   ☐ e. Sys.SysComments

5.) What does the WITH ENCRYPTION option achieve?

   O a. It prevents other users from seeing the code that created the view.
   O b. It prevents the deletion of base tables being used by the view.
   O c. It hides the information in the Sys.Sql_Dependencies.
   O d. It prevents the view from ever being altered again.

6.) What happens to a view if the underlying table is dropped?

- a. The view no longer works.
- b. The view uses the latest cached data until the table is restored.
- c. The view uses the default or fallback table.

7.) What is a requirement that must be in place in order for you to use WITH SCHEMABINDING?

- a. All base tables must be tables and can't be views.
- b. All base tables must be referenced by the schema name.
- c. The base tables must be deleted first.
- d. All tables must be temp tables.
- e. All views must be place in read only mode.

8.) What is one reason why **sp_helptext** won't allow you to see the code used to build a view?

- a. The view is set to read only.
- b. The table behind the view is set to read only.
- c. The view is set to encryption.
- d. The view is built with compression.

9.) You have a table named Sales.TravelTrip and a developer has given you some suggested code for building a view. The code for the view is as follows:

```
CREATE VIEW vTravelSelect AS SELECT * FROM TravelTrip
```

The code errors out. What must you do?

- a. Change the column type so there are no text fields.
- b. Include the Sales schema name with the table in the statement.
- c. Change the column count so it does not use the * notation.

Answer Key

1.) The tables that retrieve the data that makes up a view are called "Base Tables", making (b) the correct answer.

2.) Your base tables can either be a table or another view which makes (a) the correct answer.

3.) If you have an expression field in a view it must have an alias. The code shows AVG(Rating) with no alias. Therefore (c) is the correct answer.

4.) The WITH options are used when creating a view, not when looking at the code of an existing view, so (a) and (b) are wrong. Sp_depends does not show you the code but shows what objects depend on this object, so (d) is wrong. The two ways to see the code that created a SQL object are Sp_helptext or with Sys.SysComments, making both (c) and (e) correct.

5.) The WITH ENCRYPTION option prevents others from seeing the code that created this object, so (a) is correct.

6.) Views can't run if the base tables within them are dropped, so (a) is correct.

7.) The WITH SCHEMABINDING option will prevent any base tables of a view from being dropped. This means (b) is the correct answer.

8.) The sp_helptext can see the source code even if it's read only, so (a) and (c) are wrong. The only time it can't see the code is if it's encrypted, so (c) is the correct answer.

9.) View can't use text fields, so (a) is wrong. Views can use the SELECT * notation, so (c) is wrong. Since the base table is from the Sales schema and that is likely not the default schema, we should qualify the table which makes (b) the correct answer.

Bug Catcher Game

To play the Bug Catcher game, run the file SQLQueries2012Vol4BugCatcher4.pps from the BugCatcher folder of the companion files found at www.Joes2Pros.com.

[THIS PAGE INTENTIONALLY LEFT BLANK.]

Chapter 5. Updating and Maintaining Views

As we saw in the previous chapter, views are great tools for narrowing the focus of your data. Like a spotlight in a theatrical stage production, a view can provide a laser-like focus on just the portion of data that you need and can help reduce complexity by tuning out data which you don't need to see.

This chapter expands our work with views to include all of the DML statements (SELECT, INSERT, UPDATE, DELETE). Much the same way views allow DBAs and their users to see just the needed data, views also offer a more controlled and surgical approach to updating table data. DBAs can also use tools, such as CHECK OPTION, in combination with views to limit the updates that users are allowed to make to base tables. We will also see an example where a view with CHECK OPTION does a better job of controlling user input than would a trigger.

The strategy of utilizing views with data is similar to the mission and goal of the *Joes 2 Pros* method. For a beginner contemplating the journey to master a toolset as vast and powerful as SQL Server, the outlook can be daunting. By spotlighting one new tool at a time and scaling down examples to be manageable, *Joes 2 Pros* aims to let students wade into deeper waters at their own pace and gain proficiency without fear of drowning.

In this chapter we will also look at **indexed views**. These are a departure from "regular" views, because placing an index on a view causes the view to be materialized persistently – that is, not just at runtime – and it retains a copy of the data.

READER NOTE: *Please run the script SQLQueries2012Vol4Chapter5.0Setup.sql in order to follow along with the examples in the first section of Chapter 5. All scripts mentioned in this chapter may be found at **www.Joes2Pros.com**.*

Manipulating Data through Views

As we learned in the previous chapter, a view is a stored query against one or more database tables. Views are also known as "virtual tables". The data and query results made available by views are not stored physically. While the Object Explorer keeps track of the views you create, views don't occupy any permanent memory storage the way database tables do.

Views behave much like tables when it comes to writing SELECT statements against them. In this section, we will see how views work with other DML statements like INSERT, UPDATE, and DELETE.

Views do NOT contain data, but updates to views affect the data in the base tables. This portion of the chapter is called manipulating data "through views" to help emphasize that point. Views do not maintain separate copies of data. Instead, they give you another way to interact with the data residing in your base tables.

Selecting Data through Views

Selecting data through a view works and looks just the same as selecting data from a table. In the example we'll see here, the Employee table is the base table (19 records, 9 fields). If we look at the records from the vEmployee view, it appears to be nearly the same with 19 records and 7 fields (Figure 5.1).

```
SELECT * FROM Employee ORDER BY EmpID
SELECT * FROM vEmployee ORDER BY EmpID
```

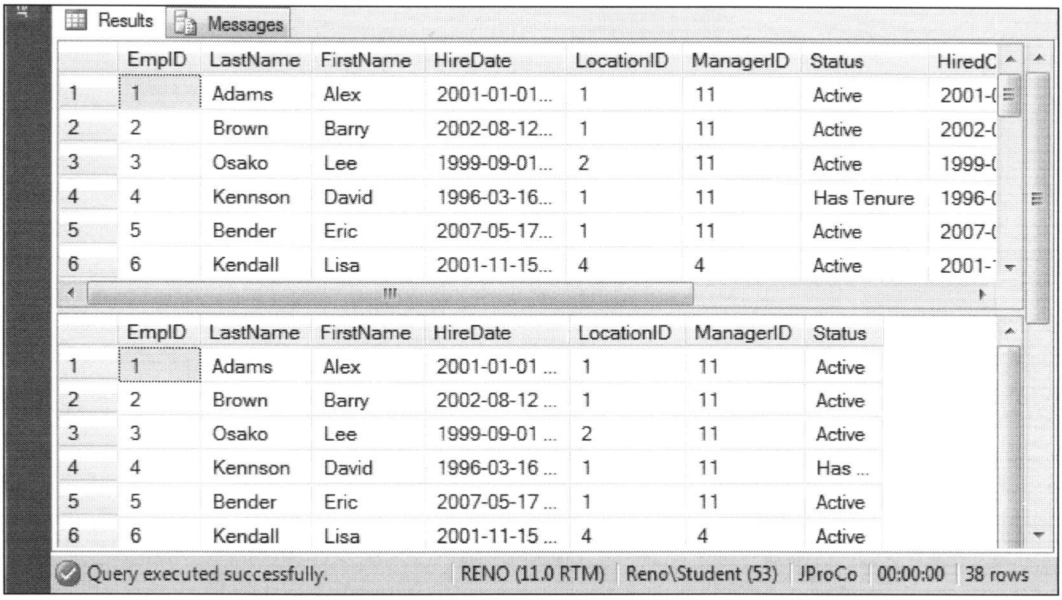

Chapter 5. Updating and Maintaining Views

Figure 5.1 The Employee table and the vEmployee view show the same 19 records.

Views are useful for showing just the relevant data. The vEmployee view contains the same records as the table, but most of our reports don't need the timezone data. This view has simply omitted a few fields and we've chosen to show just the key fields we need to see.

Updating Records through Views

Most of the time, DML statements (inserts, updates, and deletes) against views work the same as they do against tables. Let's take a look at Alex Adams who is EmpID 1 and currently works for ManagerID 11 (Sally Zander). If we were to make a change to Alex Adams in the Employee table, that change would also be reflected in the view. Let's change Alex to report to ManagerID 4 (David Kennson) with the following code:

```
UPDATE Employee SET ManagerID = 4
WHERE EmpID = 1
```

After you've successfully run the code, check the records of the Employee table. We can see Alex's new manager reflected in the Employee table. If you query the vEmployee view, you can see the new data there, too (Figure 5.2).

```
SELECT * FROM Employee ORDER BY EmpID
```

	EmpID	LastName	FirstName	HireDate	LocationID	ManagerID	Status	Hire
1	1	Adams	Alex	2001-01-01...	1	4	Active	200
2	2	Brown	Barry	2002-08-12...	1	11	Active	200
3	3	Osako	Lee	1999-09-01...	2	11	Active	199
4	4	Kennson	David	1996-03-16...	1	11	Has Tenure	199
5	5	Bender	Eric	2007-05-17...	1	11	Active	200
6	6	Kendall	Lisa	2001-11-15...	4	4	Active	200

Query executed successfully.   RENO (11.0 RTM)   Reno\Student (51)   JProCo   00:00:00   19 rows

Figure 5.2 The Employee table and the vEmployee view both reflect Alex's new manager.

Currently the Employee table shows us 19 records, and the vEmployee view based on the Employee table also shows us the same 19 records. Notice in Figure 5.3 that both result sets show Alex Adams' record with the new ManagerID of 4.

```
SELECT * FROM Employee WHERE EmpID = 1
SELECT * FROM vEmployee WHERE EmpID = 1
```

	EmpID	LastName	FirstName	HireDate	LocationID	ManagerID	Status	HiredOffse
1	1	Adams	Alex	2001-01-01...	1	4	Active	2001-01-0

	EmpID	LastName	FirstName	HireDate	LocationID	ManagerID	Status
1	1	Adams	Alex	2001-01-01...	1	4	Active

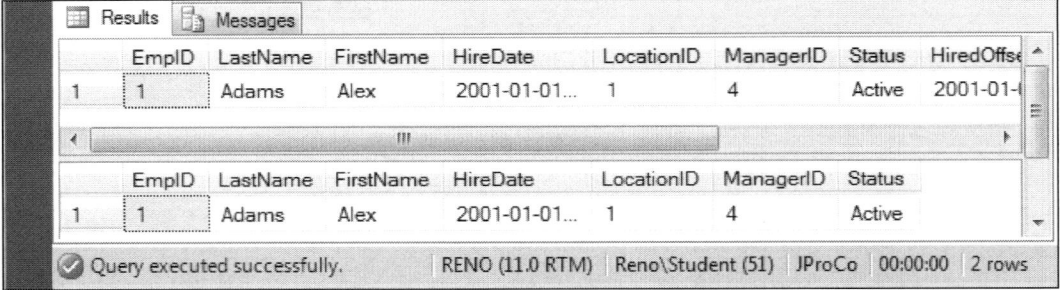

Query executed successfully.   RENO (11.0 RTM)   Reno\Student (51)   JProCo   00:00:00   2 rows

Figure 5.3 After the table update, the Employee table and the vEmployee view are still in sync and showing the same records.

Inserting Records through Views

Since the vEmployee view was built without criteria, it will always show the same number of records as the base table. This view contains a SELECT statement (Figure 5.4) whose purpose is simply to narrow the field list down to our seven key fields. Therefore, vEmployee will always be in sync with the Employee table.

Chapter 5. Updating and Maintaining Views

```
sp_helptext vEmployee
```

	Text
1	CREATE VIEW vEmployee
2	AS
3	SELECT EmpID, LastName, FirstName, HireDate, Loc...
4	FROM Employee

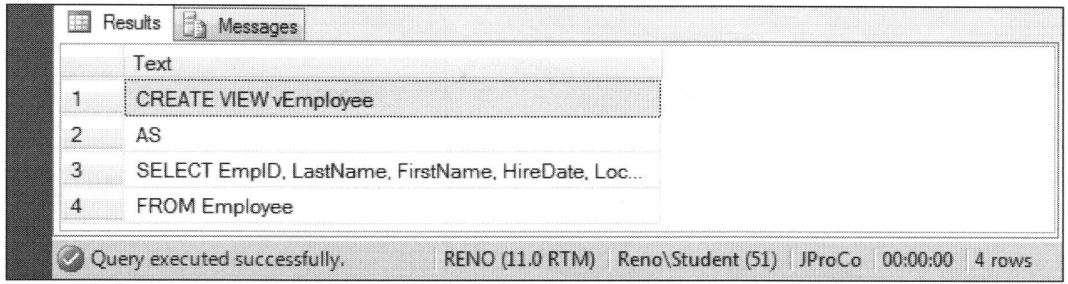

Query executed successfully. RENO (11.0 RTM) | Reno\Student (51) | JProCo | 00:00:00 | 4 rows

Figure 5.4 The vEmployee view was designed to constantly be in sync with the Employee table.

This means that if we insert a 21st record into the Employee table, then we will also see the 21st record in the view.

But what if we were to insert a record into the view – *would it also show up in the Employee table?* Let's test that out using the following code:

```
INSERT INTO vEmployee
VALUES (21, 'Fines', 'Sue', GETDATE(), 1, 4, DEFAULT)
```

The "1 row(s) affected" confirmation tells us that our insert of one record (Sue Fines) has impacted one object, namely the Employee table.

We now see 20 records in the Employee table, including the new record for Sue Fines (Figure 5.5). So the answer is yes – the record inserted through the view was successfully inserted into the Employee table.

```
SELECT * FROM Employee
```

	EmpID	LastName	FirstName	HireDate	LocationID	ManagerID	Status	Hire
18	18	Walker	Rainy	2010-01-01...	1	11	NULL	NUL
19	20	Winds	Gale	2010-03-25...	1	11	NULL	NUL
20	21	Fines	Sue	2012-10-05...	1	4	NULL	NUL

Query executed successfully. RENO (11.0 RTM) | Reno\Student (51) | JProCo | 00:00:00 | 20 rows

Figure 5.5 We are delighted to see 20 records showing in the Employee table.

Following the insert, we see all 20 records from the Employee table showing in the vEmployee view (Figure 5.6).

```
SELECT * FROM vEmployee
```

	EmpID	LastName	FirstName	HireDate	LocationID	ManagerID	Status
17	17	Downs	Wendy	2012-10-05...	1	11	Orientation
18	18	Walker	Rainy	2010-01-01...	1	11	NULL
19	20	Winds	Gale	2010-03-25...	1	11	NULL
20	21	Fines	Sue	2012-10-05...	1	4	NULL

Query executed successfully.   RENO (11.0 RTM)   Reno\Student (51)   JProCo   00:00:00   20 rows

Figure 5.6 As expected, all 20 records from the Employee table appear in the view, vEmployee.

You can run DML statements against base tables through views. *But let's recall that views don't actually contain data. Most views are dynamic, unmaterialized objects which do not contain data.* The exception case is an indexed view, since the index contains a copy of the data. So when we inserted the 20th record, the view simply passed the record into the Employee table.

In the last example we changed a single record through the view, which changed the same record in the base table. We're now going to update many records at once through a view. Before we get started, let's look at all of the records in the Grant table (Figure 5.7).

```
SELECT * FROM [Grant]
```

	GrantID	GrantName	EmpID	Amount
1	001	92 Purr_Scents %% team	7	4750.00
2	002	K-Land fund trust	2	15750.00
3	003	Robert@BigStarBank.com	7	18100.00
4	005	BIG 6's Foundation%	4	21000.00
5	006	TALTA_Kishan International	3	18100.00
6	007	Ben@MoreTechnology.com	10	41000.00

11 rows

Figure 5.7 In preparation for the next example, we look at the records and data in the Grant table.

We see 11 records in the Grant table, which includes some small grants and some larger ones. Let's call grants with an amount greater than $20,000 "large grants". We will use the following code to build a view showing just these large grants:

```
CREATE VIEW vHighValueGrants
AS
SELECT GrantName, EmpID, Amount
FROM [Grant]
WHERE Amount > 20000
GO
```

Let's run this code and then look at our newly created view. Recall this won't show us all the grants, just the ones with amounts exceeding 20,000 (Figure 5.8).

```
SELECT * FROM vHighValueGrants
```

	GrantName	EmpID	Amount
1	BIG 6's Foundation%	4	21000.00
2	Ben@MoreTechnology.com	10	41000.00
3	www.@-Last-U-Can-Help.com	7	25000.00
4	Thank you @.com	11	21500.00
5	Big Giver Tom	7	95900.00
6	Mega Mercy	9	55000.00

6 rows

Figure 5.8 Our newly created view, vHighValueGrants, shows that we have six large grants.

There are six large grants. Now let's make an update to all the large grants. Suppose the company plans to match an additional $1,000 for each grant over $20,000. In other words, the Amount of the $21,000 grant will become $22,000. The $41,000 grant will become $42,000, and so forth. The data changes we expect to see are penciled (Figure 5.9).

```
SELECT * FROM vHighValueGrants
```

	GrantName	EmpID	Amount	
1	BIG 6's Foundation%	4	21000.00	22,000
2	Ben@MoreTechnology.com	10	41000.00	42,000
3	www.@-Last-U-Can-Help.com	7	25000.00	26,000
4	Thank you @.com	11	21500.00	22,500
5	Big Giver Tom	7	95900.00	96,900
6	Mega Mercy	9	55000.00	56,000

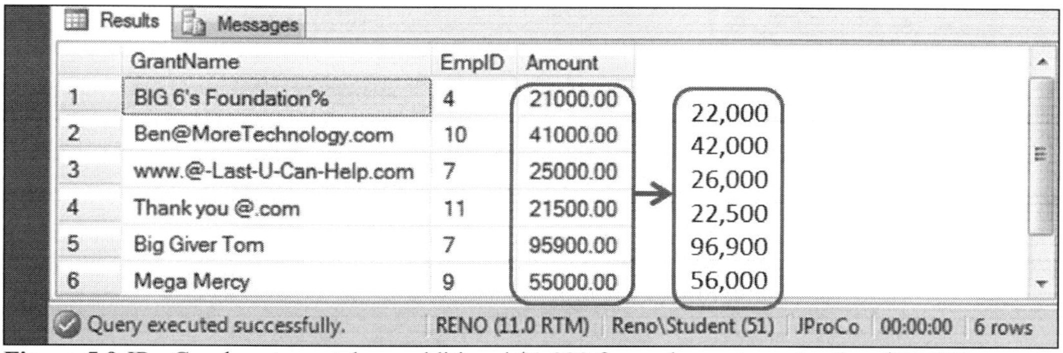

Query executed successfully. | RENO (11.0 RTM) | Reno\Student (51) | JProCo | 00:00:00 | 6 rows

Figure 5.9 JProCo plans to match an additional $1,000 for each grant greater than $20,000.

JProCo plans to match an additional $1,000 for each grant greater than $20,000. Let's write the UPDATE statement to implement this change and increment each record appearing in vHighValueGrants by 1,000. Notice that the UPDATE statement for a view uses the same syntax as we use when updating a table:

```
UPDATE vHighValueGrants
SET Amount = Amount + 1000
```

Let's query vHighValueGrants and see the effect of the UDPATE statement (Figure 5.10).

	GrantName	EmpID	Amount
1	BIG 6's Foundation%	4	22000.00
2	Ben@MoreTechnology.com	10	42000.00
3	www.@-Last-U-Can-Help.com	7	26000.00
4	Thank you @.com	11	22500.00
5	Big Giver Tom	7	96900.00
6	Mega Mercy	9	56000.00

6 rows

Figure 5.10 Our update statement increases each Amount, as expected.

Following the UPDATE statement, we see each Amount has increased by 1,000 and matches the values we expected to see. Now let's check the Grant table and confirm the view passed the six new amounts to the base table (Figure 5.11).

```
SELECT * FROM [Grant]
```

	GrantID	GrantName	EmpID	Amount
1	001	92 Purr_Scents %% team	7	4750.00
2	002	K-Land fund trust	2	15750.00
3	003	Robert@BigStarBank.com	7	18100.00
4	005	BIG 6's Foundation%	4	22000.00 ←
5	006	TALTA_Kishan International	3	18100.00
6	007	Ben@MoreTechnology.com	10	42000.00 ←
7	008	www.@-Last-U-Can-Help....	7	26000.00 ←
8	009	Thank you @.com	11	22500.00 ←
9	010	Just Mom	5	9900.00
10	011	Big Giver Tom	7	96900.00 ←
11	012	Mega Mercy	9	56000.00 ←

Query executed successfully.   RENO (11.0 RTM)   Reno\Student (51)   JProCo   00:00:00   11 rows

Figure 5.11 The vHighValueGrants view successfully passed the new amounts to the Grant table.

We see that the six records affected by the UPDATE statement were stored in the Grant table, and we can see the changes there. Keep in mind that not all grants were updated. For example, the amount of GrantID 001 was $4,750 before the update and remains the same afterward. **Only the records returned by a view may be updated through the view.**

Compare this rule and the vHighValueGrants scenario to the first example we saw in this chapter (Figures 5.1 thru 5.6). Since the vEmployee view was created without criteria, it is able to write to every record in the Employee table. However, we created the vHighValueGrants view with a scope of just the records having an amount >$20,000. It is only permitted to SELECT, INSERT, UPDATE, or DELETE records which are >$20,000 in the base table.

Lab 5.1: Manipulating Data through Views

Lab Prep: Lab Prep: Each lab has one or more Skill Checks. Start with Skill Check 1 and proceed until reaching the Points to Ponder section.

Before beginning this lab, verify that SQL Server 2012 is properly installed and operating. Before running the lab setup script for resetting the database (SQLQueries2012Vol4Chapter5.1Setup.sql), please make sure to close all query windows within SSMS. An open query window pointing to a database context can lock that database preventing it from updating when the script is executing. A simple way to assure all query windows are closed, is to exit out of SSMS, then open a new instance of SSMS, and lastly run the setup script.

Skill Check 1: Create a view called vSeattleEmployee which shows the 14 employees from LocationID 1. Show the EmpID, FirstName, LastName, LocationID, and Status fields.

```
SELECT * FROM vSeattleEmployee
```

	EmpID	FirstName	LastName	LocationID	Status
1	1	Alex	Adams	1	Active
2	2	Barry	Brown	1	Active
3	4	David	Kennson	1	Has Tenure
4	5	Eric	Bender	1	Active
5	7	David	Lonning	1	On Leave
6	11	Sally	Zander	1	Active

14 rows

Figure 5.12 Skill Check 1.

Chapter 5. Updating and Maintaining Views

Skill Check 2: Write an UPDATE statement against the vSeattleEmployee view to change employees currently showing a Status of 'Orientation' to a Status of 'Active'.

```
SELECT * FROM vSeattleEmployee
```

	EmpID	FirstName	LastName	LocationID	Status
1	1	Alex	Adams	1	Active
2	2	Barry	Brown	1	Active
3	4	David	Kennson	1	Has Tenure
4	5	Eric	Bender	1	Active
5	7	David	Lonning	1	On Leave
6	11	Sally	Zander	1	Active

14 rows

Figure 5.13 Skill Check 2.

Skill Check 3: Write an UPDATE statement against the vEmployee view to change James Newton (EmpID = 9) to work in Seattle (LocationID = 1). When that is done, check to confirm that James now appears in the vSeattleEmployee view. You should have 15 Seattle employee records in your view instead of 14.

```
SELECT * FROM vSeattleEmployee
```

	EmpID	FirstName	LastName	LocationID	Status
1	1	Alex	Adams	1	Active
2	2	Barry	Brown	1	Active
3	4	David	Kennson	1	Has Tenure
4	5	Eric	Bender	1	Active
5	7	David	Lonning	1	On Leave
6	9	James	Newton	1	Active

15 rows

Figure 5.14 Skill Check 3 results show James Newton.

Answer Code: The T-SQL code to this lab can be found in the downloadable files in a file named Lab5.1_DataManipulationThroughViews.sql.

Points to Ponder - Manipulating Data through Views

1. Views do not maintain separate copies of data. Therefore, when you are modifying records in a view, you are really modifying the records in the underlying base table.

2. Any DML changes made to a table through a view can SET columns to just one base table at a time.

View Modification Restrictions

In this section, we will learn a few restrictions and some pitfalls to avoid when using view to modify your data. After seeing some tricky scenarios involving INSERT, UPDATE, and DELETE statements against views, we will explore the use of CHECK OPTION to prevent unintended changes to our data.

Inserting Data through Views

When inserting records into a table, you must supply values for all required fields. *The same rule holds true for views.*

Our first example involves the Grant table and the vHighValueGrants view. Query the Grant table and notice that it currently has 4 fields and 11 records (Figure 5.15).

```
SELECT * FROM [Grant]
```

	GrantID	GrantName	EmpID	Amount
1	001	92 Purr_Scents %% team	7	4750.00
2	002	K-Land fund trust	2	15750.00
3	003	Robert@BigStarBank.com	7	18100.00
4	005	BIG 6's Foundation%	4	22000.00
5	006	TALTA_Kishan International	3	18100.00
6	007	Ben@MoreTechnology.com	10	42000.00

11 rows

Figure 5.15 The Grant table contains 4 fields and 11 records.

The vHighValueGrants view shows the large grants (defined as >$20k) from the Grant table. It currently includes three fields and six records.(Figure 5.16).

```
SELECT * FROM vHighValueGrants
```

	GrantName	EmpID	Amount
1	BIG 6's Foundation%	4	22000.00
2	Ben@MoreTechnology.com	10	42000.00
3	www.@-Last-U-Can-Help.com	7	26000.00
4	Thank you @.com	11	22500.00
5	Big Giver Tom	7	96900.00
6	Mega Mercy	9	56000.00

Query executed successfully.   RENO (11.0 RTM)   Reno\Student (51)   JProCo   00:00:00   6 rows

Figure 5.16 The vHighValueGrants view currently includes 3 fields and 6 records.

Let's attempt to add this new record (Figure 5.17) to the Grant table through the vHighValueGrants view. Note that the INSERT statement fails, and the error message indicates that we attempted to insert a NULL value into the GrantID column.

```
INSERT INTO vHighValueGrants
VALUES ('A Fighting Chance', 19, 31000)
```

Messages
Msg 515, Level 16, State 2, Line 1
Cannot insert the value NULL into column 'GrantID', table 'JProCo.dbo.Grant'; column does not allow nulls. INSERT fails.
The statement has been terminated.
0 rows

Figure 5.17 Our attempt to update the Grant table through vHighValueGrants is unsuccessful.

GrantID is a non-nullable, primary key field. This means that every record added to the Grant table must include a unique GrantID value.

The root problem is that the GrantID field isn't included in the view. Therefore, vHighValueGrants cannot "see" or manipulate the GrantID field. As long as vHighValueGrants doesn't include the GrantID field, you won't be able use this view to manipulate the Grant table as currently structured.

You can't place a NULL value in a non-nullable field. If a DML statement through a view would place a NULL value in a non-nullable field, then the change will be disallowed.

Deleting Data through Views

The syntax for deleting records through views is the same syntax used to delete records from tables. This DELETE statement against vHighValueGrants (Figure 5.18) will remove all of the large grants from the Grant table.

```
DELETE FROM vHighValueGrants
```

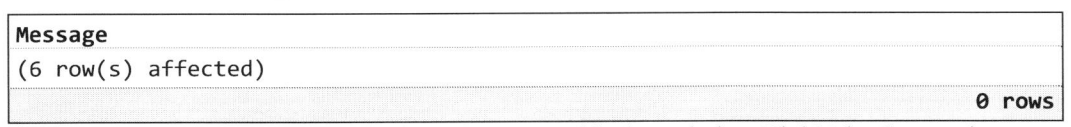

Message
(6 row(s) affected)
0 rows

Figure 5.18 You can delete records from the Grant table through the vHighValueGrants view.

Following the deletion, there are now five records remaining in the Grant table.

```
SELECT * FROM [Grant]
```

	GrantID	GrantName	EmpID	Amount
1	001	92 Purr_Scents %% team	7	4750.00
2	002	K-Land fund trust	2	15750.00
3	003	Robert@BigStarBank.com	7	18100.00
4	006	TALTA_Kishan International	3	18100.00
5	010	Just Mom	5	9900.00

5 rows

Figure 5.19 The Grant table now contains five records. It previously contained 11 (Figure 5.15).

You cannot use a view to run DELETE statements affecting more than one base table. The previous deletion (Figure 5.18) was successful because it involved a single base table. This DELETE statement against the GrantLocations view fails, because it would affect multiple base tables (Figure 5.20).

```
DELETE FROM GrantLocations
```

```
Messages
Msg 4405, Level 16, State 1, Line 1
View or function 'GrantLocations' is not updatable because the modification
affects multiple base tables.
                                                                    0 rows
```

Figure 5.20 The GrantLocations view may not be used to remove records, because this would affect multiple base tables. As mentioned in Chapter 4, SQL Server doesn't enforce naming conventions for views. SQL pros tend to prefix a view with "v" or "vw" (vGrantLocations versus GrantLocations), but this is simply a best practice and not a requirement.

Note: We've just performed some destructive examples impacting our Grant data. To continue our demonstration using the views which we've built, we must reset the Grant table and vHighValueGrants to again display the values shown in Figure 5.15 and Figure 5.16. Run the script SQLProgrammingExtraResetGrant.sql (Figure 5.21).

```
--SQLProgrammingExtraResetGrant.sql
USE JProCo
GO

IF NOT EXISTS(SELECT * FROM sys.tables WHERE [name] = 'Grant')
CREATE TABLE [Grant]
(
```

Figure 5.21 The script SQLProgrammingExtraResetGrant.sql may be found at *Joes2Pros.com*.

Updating Data through Views

In the last section, we used an UPDATE statement to increment a single field in a view having a single base table. Just like with DELETE statements against views,

Chapter 5. Updating and Maintaining Views

SQL Server will not allow an UPDATE statement to affect multiple base tables. However, we must be cautious when using a view to modify data.

sp_helptext vEmployeeLocations

Text
CREATE VIEW dbo.vEmployeeLocations
AS
SELECT em.EmpID, em.FirstName, em.LastName, lo.City, lo.[State]
FROM Employee as em INNER JOIN Location as lo
ON em.LocationID = lo.LocationID

8 rows

Figure 5.22 The source code for vEmployeeLocations.

Let's return to the vEmployeeLocations view. This view includes data from multiple base tables. Three of its fields (EmpID, FirstName, LastName) come from dbo.Employee, and the other two fields (City, State) come from dbo.Location.

SELECT * FROM vEmployeeLocations

	EmpID	FirstName	LastName	City	State
1	1	Alex	Adams	Seattle	WA
2	2	Barry	Brown	Seattle	WA
3	3	Lee	Osako	Boston	MA
4	4	David	Kennson	Seattle	WA
5	5	Eric	Bender	Seattle	WA
6	6	Lisa	Kendall	Spokane	WA

(3 fields from dbo.Employee / 2 fields from dbo.Location)

Query executed successfully. RENO (11.0 RTM) Reno\Student (51) JProCo 00:00:00 19 rows

Figure 5.23 The vEmployeeLocations view pulls data from multiple base tables.

A view can make an update to one or more fields in a single base table. The following two updates affect data in the Employee table. After you successfully run each UPDATE statement (and you see "1 row(s) affected" for each), run the SELECT statement against the view in order to see the changed data.

The first statement will change Employee 11's last name from Zander back to Smith. Apparently the record changes for JProCo's internal systems and her external professional associations were too numerous, so Sally is choosing to postpone her official name change for awhile (Figure 5.24).

```
UPDATE vEmployeeLocations
SET LastName = 'Smith' WHERE EmpID = 11

SELECT * FROM vEmployeeLocations
```

Chapter 5. Updating and Maintaining Views

	EmpID	FirstName	LastName	City	State
7	7	David	Lonning	Seattle	WA
8	9	James	Newton	Seattle	WA
9	10	Terry	O'Haire	Boston	MA
10	11	Sally	Smith	Seattle	WA
11	12	Barbara	O'Neil	Spokane	WA
12	13	Phil	Wilconkinski	Seattle	WA

19 rows

Figure 5.24 EmpID 11's LastName value is successfully changed from Zander to Smith.

Another change is needed for David Kennson, whose name is incorrect in the database. His name should appear as "Dave Kinnison". SQL Server will allow this change to multiple fields, because both fields are in the same base table. After we run the UPDATE statement, we see the change appears in the view (Figure 5.25).

```
UPDATE vEmployeeLocations
SET FirstName = 'Dave', LastName = 'Kinnison'
WHERE EmpID = 4
SELECT * FROM vEmployeeLocations
```

	EmpID	FirstName	LastName	City	State
1	1	Alex	Adams	Seattle	WA
2	2	Barry	Brown	Seattle	WA
3	3	Lee	Osako	Boston	MA
4	4	Dave	Kinnison	Seattle	WA
5	5	Eric	Bender	Seattle	WA
6	6	Lisa	Kendall	Spokane	WA

19 rows

Figure 5.25 With one UPDATE statement, we can change Dave's FirstName and LastName.

Now let's look at a change that may seem as straightforward as our last two updates but is actually problematic. We will run the UPDATE statement in order to demonstrate a pitfall to watch for when updating your table data through a view that has multiple base tables.

We need to make another update to Employee 4. He has been working in the Seattle office, but next week he will begin working in Tacoma. Notice that the UPDATE statement reflecting Dave's new City would change the value of a field in the Location table, yet it predicates on the Employee table (Figure 5.26). Our previous two UPDATE operations changed values in the Employee table and predicated on the Employee table as shown in Figure 5.24 and Figure 5.25.

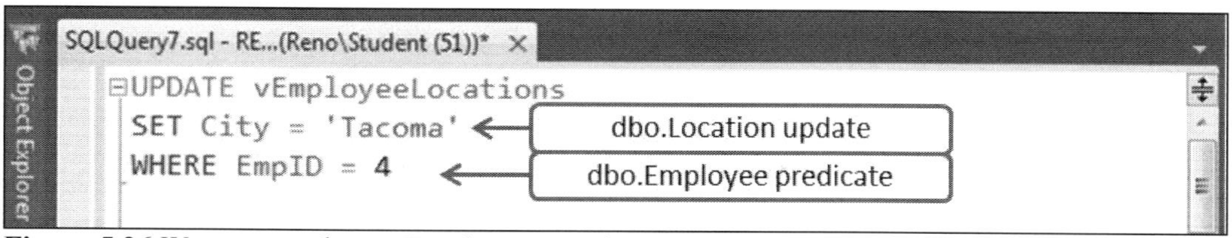

Chapter 5. Updating and Maintaining Views

```
UPDATE vEmployeeLocations
    SET City = 'Tacoma'      ← dbo.Location update
    WHERE EmpID = 4          ← dbo.Employee predicate
```

Figure 5.26 We want to change Employee 4's City value to Tacoma.

Let's see what happens when we run this query (Figure 5.27) .Then let's query the view and see the change reflected by the data (
Figure 5.28).

```
UPDATE vEmployeeLocations
SET City = 'Tacoma'
WHERE EmpID = 4
```

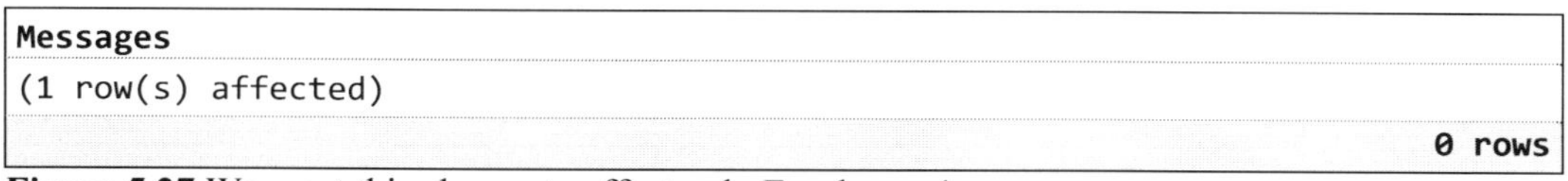

```
Messages
(1 row(s) affected)
                                                                         0 rows
```

Figure 5.27 We want this change to affect only Employee 4.

```
SELECT * FROM vEmployeeLocations
```

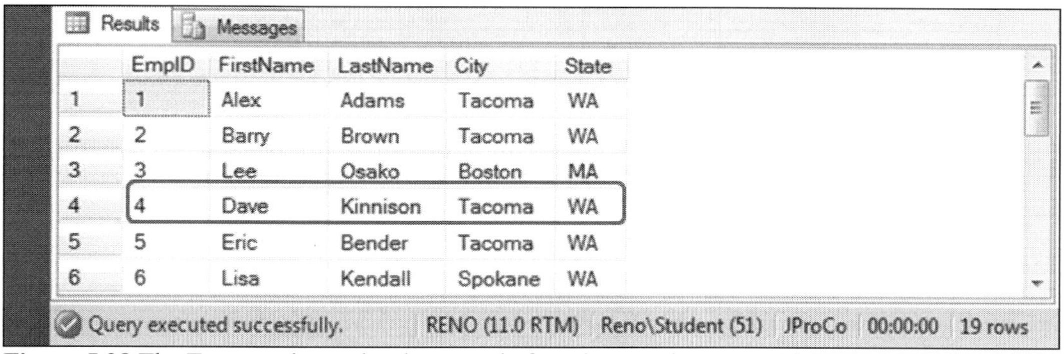

EmpID	FirstName	LastName	City	State
1	Alex	Adams	Tacoma	WA
2	Barry	Brown	Tacoma	WA
3	Lee	Osako	Boston	MA
4	Dave	Kinnison	Tacoma	WA
5	Eric	Bender	Tacoma	WA
6	Lisa	Kendall	Spokane	WA

Query executed successfully.   RENO (11.0 RTM)   Reno\Student (51)   JProCo   00:00:00   19 rows

Figure 5.28 The Tacoma change has been made for other employees, not just Dave Kinnison.

While the "1 row(s) affected" confirmation initially looks encouraging, our query of the view reveals that all employees working at the Seattle location now have a City value of "Tacoma" (Figure 5.28).

A query of the Location table will help clarify the issue. The UPDATE statement we ran (Figure 5.27) changed the City value for LocationID 1 to Tacoma (Figure 5.29). This is the change signified by the "1 row(s) affected" confirmation shown in Figure 5.27!! Dave's LocationID is 1. The UPDATE statement changed the City value for LocationID 1 to Tacoma. Our update was intended for Dave's record, but it affected all employees with a LocationID of 1.

```
SELECT * FROM Location
```

	LocationID	Street	City	State	Latitude	Longitude	GeoLoc
1	1	111 First ST	Tacoma	WA	47.455	-122.231	0xE61000000010C
2	2	222 Second AVE	Boston	MA	42.372	-71.0298	0xE61000000010C
3	3	333 Third PL	Chicago	IL	41.953	-87.643	0xE61000000010C
4	4	444 Ruby ST	Spokane	WA	47.668	-117.529	0xE61000000010C
5	5	1595 Main	Philadelphia	PA	39.888	-75.251	0xE61000000010C
6	6	915 Wallaby Drive	Sydney	NULL	-33.876	151.315	0xE61000000010C

Query executed successfully. | RENO (11.0 RTM) | Reno\Student (51) | JProCo | 00:00:00 | 6 rows

Figure 5.29 LocationID 1 now reflects the City of Tacoma.

To understand how this happened, let's take a look behind the scenes at the underlying tables and fields of vEmployeeLocations. The City and State fields are normalized data being supplied by the lookup table, Location. In other words, these values aren't part of a denormalized table where each employee record would contain its own City field (Had that been the case, then our UPDATE statement would have only changed Dave Kinnison's city to Tacoma, and the other employee records wouldn't have been impacted).

So this is one pitfall to be cautious of. ***When updating a base table, be careful – it might be representative of other records in related tables.*** We've just seen an example where SQL Server was overly permissive and allowed us to change many more records than we intended. If you have a doubt, it may be safest to run the UPDATE directly against the base table instead of against the view.

One way of correcting our mistake is to run another UPDATE statement through the view to revert Location 1 back to Seattle. This UPDATE statement corrects our mistake and changes Location 1 back to Seattle:

```
UPDATE vEmployeeLocations
SET City = 'Seattle'
WHERE EmpID = 4
```

When we re-query vEmployeeLocations, we see that all Seattle employees (including Dave Kinnison) again show Seattle as their City (Figure 5.30).

```
SELECT * FROM vEmployeeLocations
```

	EmpID	FirstName	LastName	City	State
1	1	Alex	Adams	Seattle	WA
2	2	Barry	Brown	Tacoma	WA
3	3	Lee	Osako	Boston	MA
4	4	Dave	Kinnison	Tacoma	WA
5	5	Eric	Bender	Tacoma	WA
6	6	Lisa	Kendall	Spokane	WA

19 rows

Figure 5.30 This update statement corrects our mistake and changes Location 1 back to Seattle.

Another way to change the LocationID 1 from Tacoma back to Seattle would be to directly update the Location table, as shown in the following code. Directly updating the Location table is another way of correcting LocationID 1's value as seen by the following code:

```
UPDATE Location
SET City = 'Seattle'
WHERE LocationID = 1
```

Finally, let's attempt a query to illustrate the rule that ***SQL Server will not allow an UPDATE statement to affect multiple base tables.***

The UPDATE statement here attempts to change a field in one base table (the LastName field in the Employee table) at the same time it changes a field in another base table (the City field in the Location table) as seen in Figure 5.31.

```
UPDATE vEmployeeLocations
SET LastName = 'Osaka', City = 'Cambridge'
WHERE EmpID = 3
```

```
Messages
Msg 4405, Level 16, State 1, Line 1
View or function 'vEmployeeLocations' is not updatable because the
modification affects multiple base tables.
```

0 rows

Figure 5.31 This UPDATE statement affecting LastName in the Employee table and City in the Location table is disallowed by SQL Server, since it would affect multiple base tables.

If the JProCo DBA needs to make these changes, he would need to accomplish them in another way. The City value change would need to be made directly to the Location table. The LastName value could be done either through the view or directly to the Employee table.

Using Check Option

CHECK OPTION is a very handy tool we can use with our views. Each time a DML statement is run against the view, CHECK OPTION validates that the resulting record set will be true to the SELECT statement which built the view. If a modification would remove a record defined by the view, then CHECK OPTION prevents the transaction from being committed.

Our demonstration of CHECK OPTION will utilize the vHighValueGrants view. If you have already run the Grant reset script SQLProgrammingExtraResetGrant.sql, then your vHighValueGrants view should be reset to the values shown in Figure 5.32. and identical to Figure 5.15, before we performed the destructive examples.

Recall that, in order to incentivize large grants, JProCo planned to offer a $1,000 match for each grant larger than $20,000. The $1,000 match is currently included in our vHighValueGrants amounts (Figure 5.32).

```
SELECT * FROM vHighValueGrants
```

	GrantName	EmpID	Amount
1	BIG 6's Foundation%	4	22000.00
2	Ben@MoreTechnology.com	10	42000.00
3	www.@-Last-U-Can-Help.com	7	26000.00
4	Thank you @.com	11	22500.00
5	Big Giver Tom	7	96900.00
6	Mega Mercy	9	56000.00

6 rows

Figure 5.32 Each large grant Amount value has been increased by $1,000.

We have just been informed that the campaign didn't receive the necessary approval from the business stakeholders. Therefore, we must remove all of the $1,000 matching amounts.

This UPDATE statement decrements each record in vHighValueGrants by $1000:

```
UPDATE vHighValueGrants
SET Amount = Amount - 1000
```

The $1000 increase has been removed. After we run the previous UPDATE statement, the grants will all be returned to their baseline values (shown in Figure 5.33).

```
SELECT * FROM vHighValueGrants
```

	GrantName	EmpID	Amount
1	BIG 6's Foundation%	4	21000.00
2	Ben@MoreTechnology.com	10	41000.00
3	www.@-Last-U-Can-Help.com	7	25000.00
4	Thank you @.com	11	21500.00
5	Big Giver Tom	7	95900.00
6	Mega Mercy	9	55000.00

6 rows

Figure 5.33 The large grants are decremented by $1,000 and thus returned to their baseline values.

Suppose you accidentally ran the decrement step twice. Before we "accidentally" run the UPDATE statement again in order to create this scenario, let's consider the amounts currently shown by the view (Figure 5.33).

The smallest grant in the vHighValueGrants view is $21,000. If we rerun the UPDATE statement, this grant will become $20,000. *Recall that each grant must be greater than $20,000 in order to appear in the view.*

Run the UPDATE statement again and then run a SELECT statement to see all of the records in the vHighValueGrants view (Figure 5.34). The $21,000 grant (contributed by Big 6's Foundation %) was reduced to $20,000 and thus has fallen out of the view. Now that this grant has fallen outside the criteria of vHighValueGrants, the view no longer has the ability to "see" or manipulate this record using DML statements.

```
UPDATE vHighValueGrants
SET Amount = Amount - 1000

SELECT * FROM vHighValueGrants
```

	GrantName	EmpID	Amount
1	Ben@MoreTechnology.com	10	40000.00
2	www.@-Last-U-Can-Help.com	7	24000.00
3	Thank you @.com	11	20500.00
4	Big Giver Tom	7	94900.00
5	Mega Mercy	9	54000.00

5 rows

Figure 5.34 There are only 5 large grants remaining in the view after the second $1000 decrement.

This action was clearly a mistake. We didn't intend to remove a record from the view, but as it is currently configured, vHighValueGrants isn't protected against these kinds of mistakes. In order to prevent data updates which would cause records to disappear from our view, we can either place a trigger on the Grant table, or we can use CHECK OPTION.

For the five remaining grants, you can correct their amounts and reverse the "accidental" run of the UPDATE statement by incrementing each grant by $1000. However, the only way to correct the amount of the missing grant is by running an UPDATE statement directly against the Grant table.

Before proceeding, let's reset the amounts for all of the large grants by running this UPDATE statement and then a SELECT statement to verify the amounts (Figure 5.35 – these amounts are the same as seen in Figure 5.33).

```
UPDATE [Grant]
SET Amount = Amount + 1000
WHERE Amount >= 20000

SELECT * FROM vHighValueGrants
```

	GrantName	EmpID	Amount
1	BIG 6's Foundation%	4	21000.00
2	Ben@MoreTechnology.com	10	41000.00
3	www.@-Last-U-Can-Help.com	7	25000.00
4	Thank you @.com	11	21500.00
5	Big Giver Tom	7	95900.00
6	Mega Mercy	9	55000.00

6 rows

Figure 5.35 This SELECT statement shows our large grant amounts have all been restored.

Let's examine the trigger approach. This trigger will prevent large grants (>$20,000) from falling to, or below, $20,000:

```
CREATE TRIGGER trg_UpdateGrant
ON dbo.[Grant]
AFTER UPDATE
AS
BEGIN
IF EXISTS( SELECT * FROM Inserted ins INNER JOIN Deleted del
ON ins.GrantName = del.GrantName
WHERE del.Amount > 20000
AND ins.Amount <= 20000)
ROLLBACK TRAN
END
```

If you create the trigger and then attempt to decrement the vHighValueGrants view, you'll find that the trigger will not allow the transaction. The decrement would cause a grant (the one contributed by Big 6's Foundation %) to fall to $20,000 and thus it won't meet the criteria of the vHighValueGrants view.

```
UPDATE vHighValueGrants
   SET Amount = Amount - 1000
```

Messages
Msg 3609, Level 16, State 1, Line 1
The transaction ended in the trigger. The batch has been aborted.

Figure 5.36 trg_UpdateGrant will not allow vHighValueGrants to fall to, or below, $20,000.

The trigger has protected our view. The transaction which attempted to reduce a large grant from $21,000 to $20,000 was forbidden and ended in the trigger (Figure 5.36).

But let's recognize that the trigger would also prevent any existing grant from ever being changed to an amount of $20,000, or lower. In other words, the trigger is so restrictive that even a DBA would be disallowed from directly updating the Grant table if the change would reduce an existing grant amount to become $20,000 or lower (Figure 5.37).

```
UPDATE vHighValueGrants
SET Amount = Amount - 1000
WHERE Amount >= 20000
```

Messages
Msg 3609, Level 16, State 1, Line 1
The transaction ended in the trigger. The batch has been aborted.
                                                                    0 rows

Figure 5.37 trg_UpdateGrant prevents certain updates made directly to the Grant table.

Chapter 5. Updating and Maintaining Views

The trigger is more restrictive than we intended. Our goal was simply to restrict users from making an accidental data change through the view which would result in a grant being removed from the view.

Let's reattempt our goal by using CHECK OPTION. First we will remove the trigger, since it is an "overkill" approach and constrains more activities than we intended.

In Object Explorer, right-click the trigger to delete it (Figure 5.38).

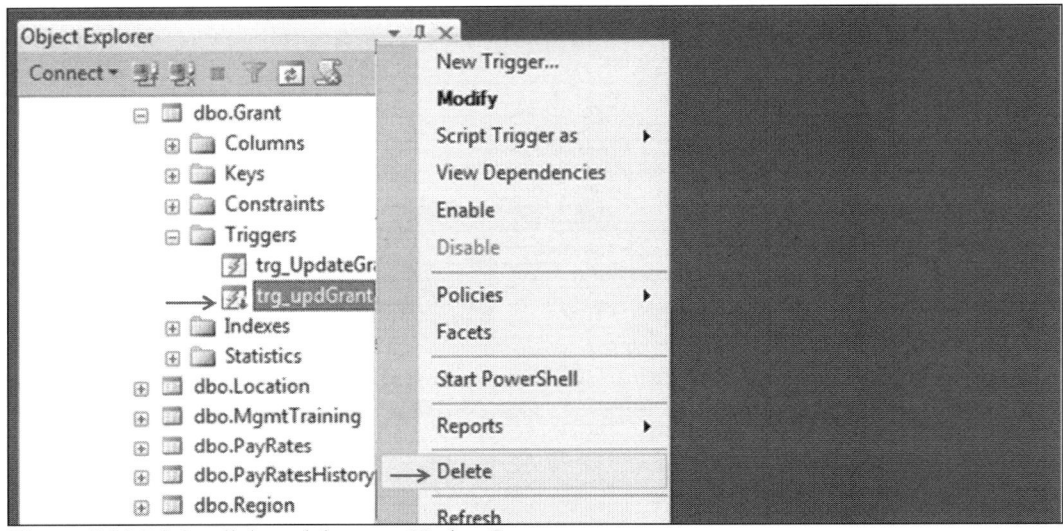

Figure 5.38 Right-click to delete trg_UpdateGrant.

Let's rebuild the vHighValueGrants view to include CHECK OPTION. This tells the view to disallow data changes through the view which would cause any record to fall outside of the criteria of the view (Figure 5.39).

```
ALTER VIEW vHighValueGrants
AS
SELECT GrantName, EmpID, Amount
FROM [Grant]
WHERE Amount > 20000
WITH CHECK OPTION
GO
```

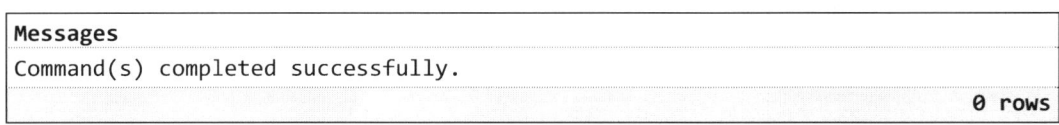

```
Messages
Command(s) completed successfully.
                                                              0 rows
```

Figure 5.39 The vHighValueGrants view is rebuilt to include WITH CHECK OPTION.

Let's test CHECK OPTION by reattempting the decrement step through the vHighValueGrants view (Figure 5.40). The error message shows that CHECK OPTION causes the UPDATE statement to fail, because it would cause a row (i.e., the Big 6's Foundation % grant) to fall out of the view.

```
UPDATE vHighValueGrants
SET Amount = Amount - 1000
```

```
Messages
Msg 550, Level 16, State 1, Line 1
The attempted insert or update failed because the target view either specifies
WITH CHECK OPTION or spans a view that specifies WITH CHECK OPTION and one or
more rows resulting from the operation did not qualify under the CHECK OPTION
constraint.
The statement has been terminated.
                                                                        0 rows
```

Figure 5.40 This decrement was prevented by the CHECK OPTION on the view.

While CHECK OPTION is protecting our grant data from unintended changes made through the view, it doesn't interfere with our ability to make changes directly against the Grant table.

To prove this point, let's run this decrement (Figure 5.41) which we know will bring a large grant amount down to $20,000 – a value which puts it outside the criteria underlying the vHighValueGrants view. CHECK OPTION does not stop us from making this change.

```
UPDATE [Grant]
SET Amount = Amount - 1000
WHERE Amount >= 20000
```

```
Messages
(6 row(s) affected)
                                                                        0 rows
```

Figure 5.41 This UPDATE statement to the Grant table is allowed. CHECK OPTION only serves to protect a view – it doesn't restrict your ability to directly update a base table.

Lab 5.2: View Modification Restrictions

Lab Prep: Lab Prep: Each lab has one or more Skill Checks. Start with Skill Check 1 and proceed until reaching the Points to Ponder section.

Before beginning this lab, verify that SQL Server 2012 is properly installed and operating. Before running the lab setup script for resetting the database (SQLQueries2012Vol4Chapter5.2Setup.sql), please make sure to close all query windows within SSMS. An open query window pointing to a database context can lock that database preventing it from updating when the script is executing. A simple way to assure all query windows are closed, is to exit out of SSMS, then open a new instance of SSMS, and lastly run the setup script.

Skill Check 1: Query the vBossList view. Attempt to update Sally's last name back to 'Zander' through the view. If you can't, then state the reason why.

Skill Check 2: Alter the vSeattleEmployee view so that any attempted change through the view will not allow updates which would cause records to disappear from the view.

```
Messages

Msg 550, Level 16, State 1, Line 2
The attempted insert or update failed because the target view either specifies
WITH CHECK OPTION or spans a view that specifies WITH CHECK OPTION and one or
more rows resulting from the operation did not qualify under the CHECK OPTION
constraint.
The statement has been terminated.
                                                                       0 rows
```
Figure 5.42 Skill Check 2.

Skill Check 3: Run an update statement against the GrantLocations view to change the amount of GrantID 011 to be exactly 19000.

```
SELECT * FROM GrantLocations
```

	GrantID	GrantName	EmpID	Amount	City	GrantID
6	007	Ben@MoreTechnology.com	10	42000.00	Boston	007
7	008	www.@-Last-U-Can-Help.com	7	26000.00	Seattle	008
8	009	Thank you @.com	11	22500.00	Seattle	009
9	010	Just Mom	5	9900.00	Seattle	010
10	011	Big Giver Tom	7	19000.00	Seattle	011
11	012	Mega Mercy	9	56000.00	Seattle	012

11 rows

Figure 5.43 Shows the records of the GrantLocations view with GrantID 11 changed to 19000.

Answer Code: The T-SQL code to this lab can be found in the downloadable files in a file named Lab5.2_ViewModificationRestrictions.sql.

Points to Ponder - View Modifications

1. The query defined by a view can include another view.
2. You cannot make updates to fields through a view, if they are part of an expression or aggregated field.
3. You cannot make updates through a view if the records were summarized with a SELECT DISTINCT clause.
4. Two ways to restrict users from being able to update through a view:
    - use WITH CHECK OPTION
    - use an INSTEAD OF trigger
5. If a view has an INSTEAD OF UPDATE trigger defined on it, then the view is considered to be not at all updatable.
6. A view's underlying data cannot be changed by an UPDATE statement which would affect more than one of the view's base tables.

Indexed Views Overview

In *SQL Queries 2012 Joes 2 Pros Volume 3* (Chapters 9-11), we learned how to create a covering index so the fields in your query's WHERE and ON clauses require less processing time. When you use the same optimally-tuned query to build a view, your view will benefit from the covering indexes on the base tables.

Suppose you have a view with three base tables, and you've done a good job setting up indexes on the tables. The view benefits from the table indexes and consequently your queries against the view will have good performance. For example, a query from the view producing one record will use three seeks rather than three scans. If you took the additional step of indexing the view, then that same query would instead run a single seek and thus return your result faster.

Creating an Index on a View

Let's create another view, and later we will observe how indexing can increase the performance of the view. The following query joins the SalesInvoice table to the Customer table (Figure 5.44). Since we don't want all fields, we will select InvoiceID and OrderDate from the SalesInvoice table. From the Customer table we will get the CustomerID, FirstName, and LastName fields. This query produces a good report of customers, their InvoiceIDs, and the dates they placed their orders (Figure 5.44).

```
SELECT si.InvoiceID, si.OrderDate, cu.CustomerID,
cu.FirstName, cu.LastName
FROM SalesInvoice AS si
INNER JOIN Customer AS cu
ON si.CustomerID = cu.CustomerID
```

	InvoiceID	OrderDate	CustomerID	FirstName	LastName
1	1027	2011-04-17 16:13:59.480	1	Mark	Williams
2	824	2010-11-09 11:23:51.043	1	Mark	Williams
3	1401	2012-01-31 07:21:03.997	1	Mark	Williams
4	1880	2012-08-25 16:05:38.280	2	Lee	Young
5	1881	2012-09-06 13:41:38.280	2	Lee	Young
6	943	2011-02-07 02:45:03.840	2	Lee	Young

Query executed successfully. | RENO (11.0 RTM) | Reno\Student (51) | JProCo | 00:00:00 | 1884 rows

Figure 5.44 This query shows sales invoices and the customers who placed these orders.

Our current query is used to create the vCustomerSales view. Let's turn this query into a view named vCustomerSales using the following code:

```sql
CREATE VIEW vCustomerSales
AS
SELECT si.InvoiceID, si.OrderDate, cu.CustomerID,
cu.FirstName, cu.LastName
FROM SalesInvoice AS si INNER JOIN Customer AS cu
ON si.CustomerID = cu.CustomerID
GO
```

Let's query our new view, vCustomerSales, and notice that the result set (from code above) is the same as the result produced by the query used to create the view (Figure 5.45).

```sql
SELECT * FROM vCustomerSales
```

	InvoiceID	OrderDate	CustomerID	FirstName	LastName
1	1027	2011-04-17 16:13:59.480	1	Mark	Williams
2	824	2010-11-09 11:23:51.043	1	Mark	Williams
3	1401	2012-01-31 07:21:03.997	1	Mark	Williams
4	1880	2012-08-25 16:05:38.280	2	Lee	Young
5	1881	2012-09-06 13:41:38.280	2	Lee	Young
6	943	2011-02-07 02:45:03.840	2	Lee	Young

Figure 5.45 A query of the vCustomerSales view.

Examining the Execution Plan for this query, it appears to perform two scans. It takes approximately a 0.007 IO cost to run (Figure 5.45).

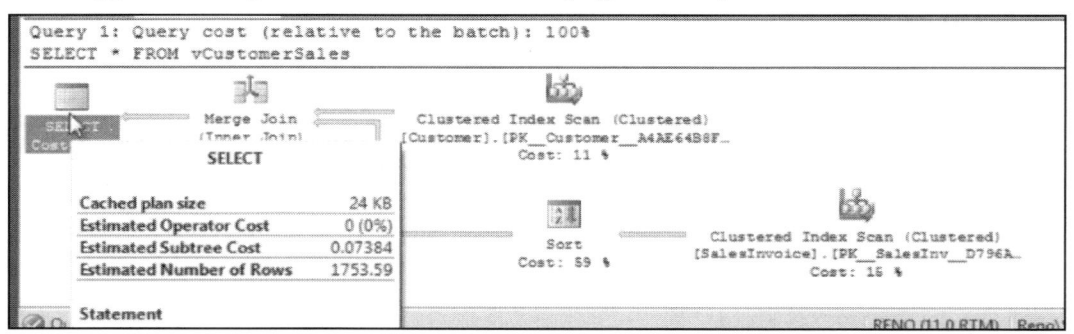

Figure 5.46 Our query of the vCustomerSales view is not very selective and runs in 0.07 seconds.

Now let's attempt a more selective query (Figure 5.46) and then examine its execution details (Figure 5.47).

```
SELECT * FROM vCustomerSales
WHERE InvoiceID = 950
```

InvoiceID	OrderDate	CustomerID	FirstName	LastName
1	950	2011-02-11...	370	Susan	Nelson

1 rows

Figure 5.47 This query is much more selective and returns just one record.

The query Execution Plan indicates that it ran two seeks – one for the clustered index on the primary key field of the SalesInvoice table and one for the clustered index on the primary key field of the Customer table (Figure 5.47). Because index seeks are performed for this query, we know there must be a covering index on the InvoiceID field.

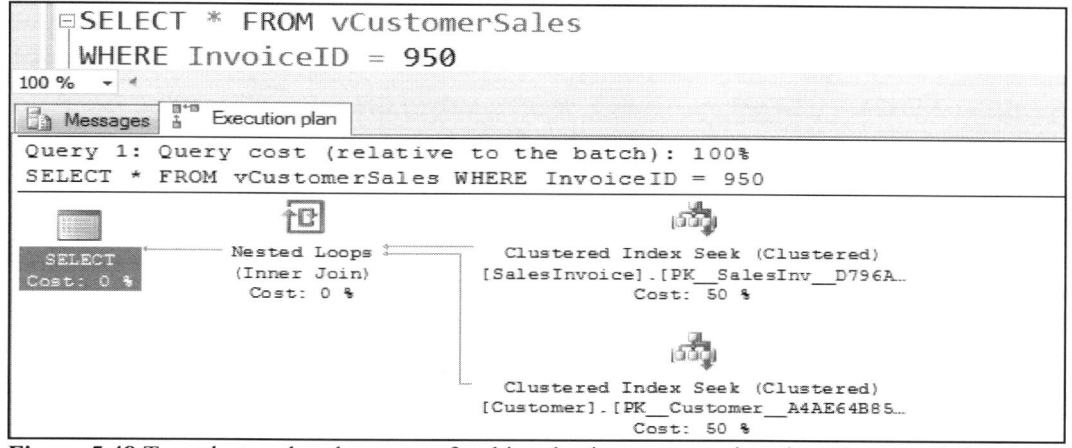

Figure 5.48 Two clustered seeks are run for this selective query against the vCustomerSales view.

The cost of this query is just over 0.006 (Figure 5.48).

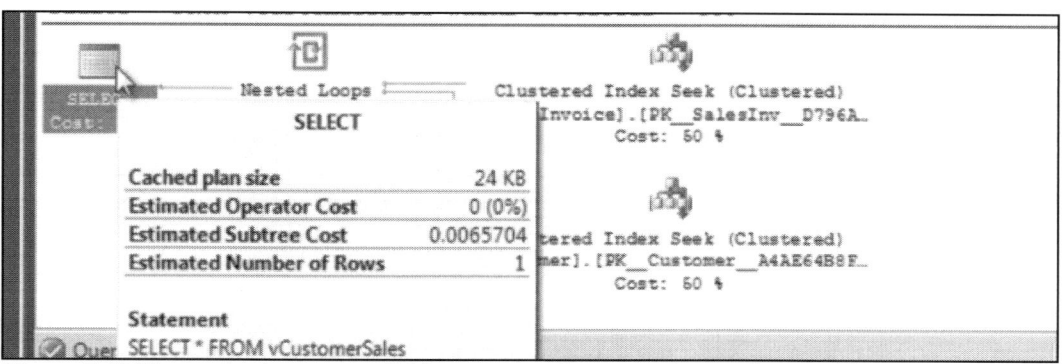

Figure 5.49 The total subtree cost of this query was just over six one-thousandths.

The performance of this query can be further enhanced if we add an index directly on the view. Our demonstration will focus on three key requirements for creating indexed views, all of which are enforced by SQL Server:

- o **The view must be schema bound.** Since you must ensure that no base table could be deleted from an indexed view, you must schema bind the view before SQL Server will allow you to add an index to it.
- o **An indexed view cannot be based upon another view.** In other words, nested views cannot be included in a view which you wish to index.
- o **All fields must be deterministic.** If any field included in the view produces non-deterministic values, SQL Server will disallow the index from being added to the view.

The first index you add to a view must be a unique clustered index. As shown in the following example, the code to create a clustered index on a view uses the same syntax as putting the index on a table. This code will place a unique clustered index on the InvoiceID field of the vCustomerSales view (Figure 5.50). If we fail to make the view schema bound, SQL Server will prompt us to schema bind the view.

```
CREATE UNIQUE CLUSTERED INDEX
UCI_vCustomerSales_InvoiceID
ON dbo.vCustomerSales(InvoiceID)
GO
```

```
Messages
Msg 1939, Level 16, State 1, Line 1
Cannot create index on view 'vCustomerSales' because the view is not schema
bound.
                                                                        0 rows
```

Figure 5.50 The index creation attempt on this view fails because the view is not schema bound.

Let's alter the vCustomerSales view and add the WITH SCHEMABINDING clause (Figure 5.51).

```
ALTER VIEW vCustomerSales
WITH SCHEMABINDING
AS
SELECT si.InvoiceID, si.OrderDate, cu.CustomerID,
cu.FirstName, cu.LastName
FROM SalesInvoice AS si
INNER JOIN Customer AS cu
ON si.CustomerID = cu.CustomerID
GO
```

```
Messages
Msg 4512, Level 16, State 3, Procedure vCustomerSales, Line 4
Cannot schema bind view 'vCustomerSales' because name 'SalesInvoice' is
invalid for schema binding. Names must be in two-part format and an object
cannot reference itself.
                                                                    0 rows
```

Figure 5.51 SQL Server requires us to use two-part naming when adding SCHEMABINDING.

Recall that SCHEMABINDING requires that we must use two-part naming for the base tables. In order to qualify the base table names, SalesInvoice becomes dbo.SalesInvoice, and Customer becomes dbo.Customer (The SQL Server error messaging appears in Figure 5.51). The corrected ALTER VIEW statement including the two-part table names appears in Figure 5.52.

```
ALTER VIEW vCustomerSales
WITH SCHEMABINDING
AS
SELECT si.InvoiceID,
si.OrderDate, cu.CustomerID,
cu.FirstName, Cu.LastName
FROM dbo.SalesInvoice AS si
INNER JOIN dbo.Customer AS cu
ON si.CustomerID = cu.CustomerID
```
```
Messages
Command(s) completed successfully.
```

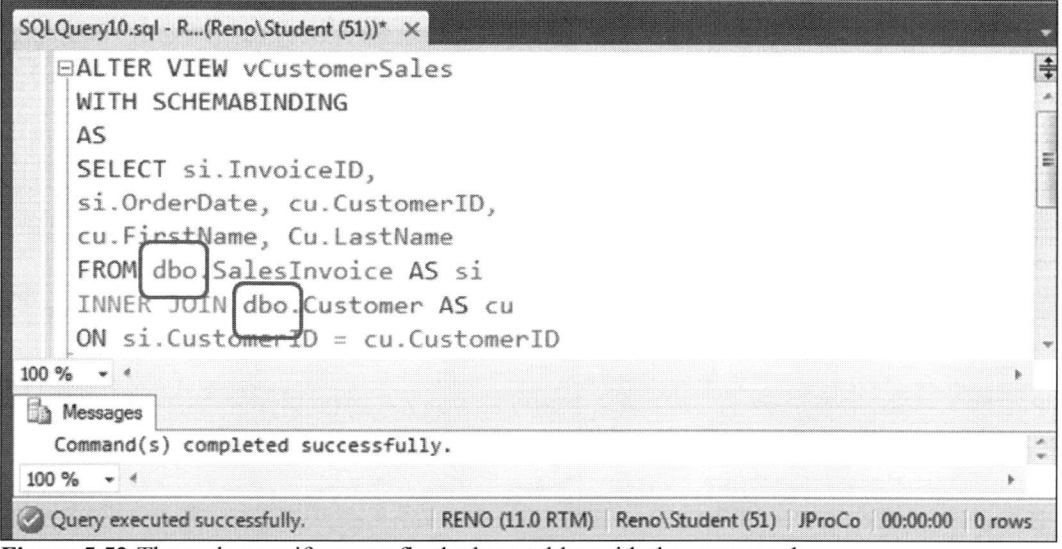

Figure 5.52 The code runs if you prefix the base tables with the correct schema name.

The ALTER VIEW statement completes successfully, so we know our view is now schema bound. We now may reattempt to create the index on the view.

```
CREATE UNIQUE CLUSTERED INDEX
UCI_vCustomerSales_InvoiceID
ON dbo.vCustomerSales(InvoiceID)
```

```
Messages
Command(s) completed successfully
                                                                    0 rows
```

Figure 5.53 Now that the view is schema bound, the index is successfully created.

With the unique clustered index successfully added to the vCustomerSales view, let's reattempt our selective query for InvoiceID 950 (Figure 5.53). The Execution

Plan tells us that the index we added to this view has improved performance considerably. The query now performs just one clustered index seek and runs in half the time or in roughly 0.003 (Figure 5.54) versus the original 0.006 cost shown in Figure 5.48.

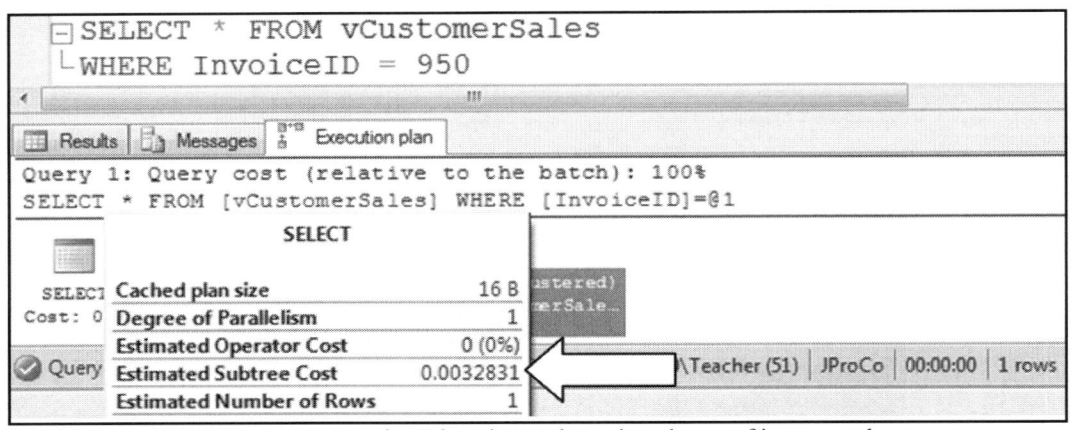

Figure 5.54 The new query Execution Plan shows the reduced cost of just over three one-thousandths of one second.

Materialized Views

In our extensive study of indexes in *SQL Queries 2012 Joes 2 Pros Volume 3*, we learned that a clustered index dictates the physical ordering of the data in a table. The same is true for indexed views. And since the first index you add to a view must be a unique clustered index, all indexed views have a clustered index to physically order the data contained in the view.

Indexing a view causes the view to be persistently **materialized** and stored in the database. In other words, the view contains a physical copy of the view data (including computations associated with joins, aggregate queries, etc.) for quicker retrieval. This is a departure from regular views (i.e., non-indexed views) which do not contain any data. Normally a view pulls data from its base table(s) and performs the needed computations at query runtime. However, queries against an indexed view run more rapidly because the view can leverage the pre-computed data and doesn't need to pull anything from the base tables – the materialized view already contains the latest data from the base tables.

Another benefit of indexed views is that their persistent data and computations are available for use by other processes or queries. In our study of SQL Server's Query Optimizer (Chapters 10-12, *SQL Queries 2012 Joes 2 Pros Volume 3*), we learned that it explores all available statistics in order to decide which objects will best accomplish a task. Therefore, all data from indexed views is available for Query Optimizer to utilize.

Other than the improved performance and visibility of the new clustered index in Object Explorer (Figure 5.54), there is no noticeable difference in the behavior of an indexed view versus a non-indexed view. There are no special steps you need to take to maintain a view once you have added an index to it.

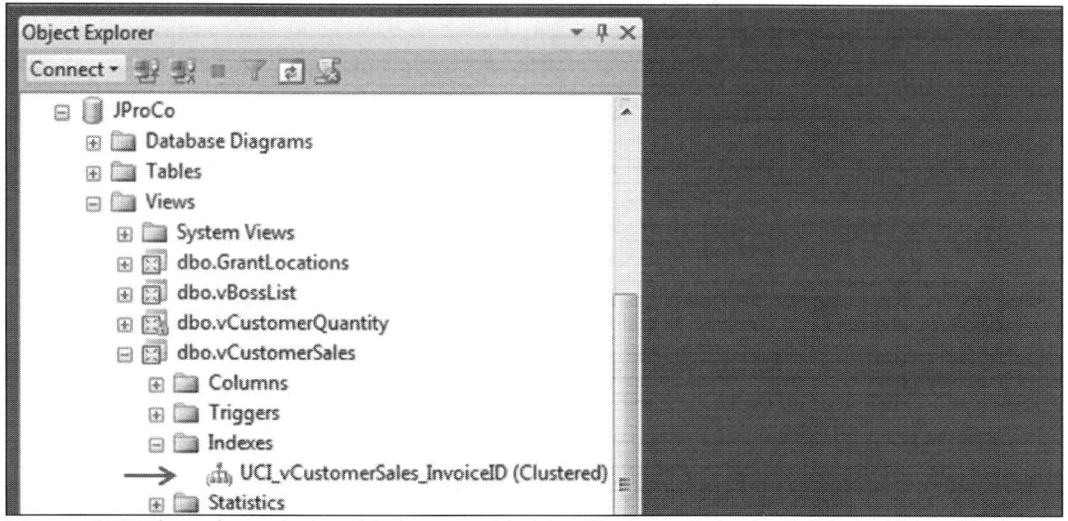

Figure 5.55 The unique clustered index we added to vCustomerSales is visible in Object Explorer.

Our next example involves the GrantLocations view, which shows the data for each grant, as well as the EmpID and location of the employee who obtained the grant (Figure 5.55). This view does not yet have an index.

```
SELECT * FROM dbo.GrantLocations
```

	GrantID	GrantName	EmpID	Amount	City	State
1	001	92 Purr_Scents %% team	7	4750.00	Seattle	WA
2	002	K-Land fund trust	2	15750.00	Seattle	WA
3	003	Robert@BigStarBank.com	7	18100.00	Seattle	WA
4	005	BIG 6's Foundation%	4	22000.00	Seattle	WA
5	006	TALTA_Kishan International	3	18100.00	Boston	MA
6	007	Ben@MoreTechnology.com	10	42000.00	Boston	MA

11 rows

Figure 5.56 The GrantLocations view does not yet have an index.

We can use sp_helptext to obtain the source code for the GrantLocations view.

```
sp_helptext 'GrantLocations'
```

Text
CREATE VIEW dbo.GrantLocations
WITH SCHEMABINDING
AS
SELECT gr.GrantID, gr.GrantName, gr.EmpID, gr.Amount,
vel.City, Vel.[State]
FROM dbo.[Grant] gr
INNER JOIN dbo.vEmployeeLocations vel
ON vel.EmpID = gr.EmpID

Figure 5.57 The source code for the GrantLocations view.

Suppose we want to enhance our GrantLocations report by adding a ReportTime field using the GETDATE() function. We are adding an expression field called ReportTime to the GrantLocations view. Run the following code to rebuild the view with this new field and then query the view:

```
ALTER VIEW dbo.GrantLocations
AS
SELECT gr.*, vel.City, Vel.[State], GETDATE() AS ReportTime
FROM [Grant] AS gr INNER JOIN vEmployeeLocations AS vel
ON vel.EmpID = gr.EmpID
GO
```

Observe that the ReportTime field shows us the time that the view was run. Run this query a few times and notice that you get a new ReportTime value each time.

```
SELECT * FROM dbo.GrantLocations
```

	GrantID	GrantName	EmpID	Amount	City	State	ReportTime
1	001	92 Purr_Scents %% team	7	4750.00	Seattle	WA	2012-10-05 ...
2	002	K-Land fund trust	2	15750.00	Seattle	WA	2012-10-05 ...
3	003	Robert@BigStarBank.com	7	18100.00	Seattle	WA	2012-10-05 ...
4	005	BIG 6's Foundation%	4	22000.00	Seattle	WA	2012-10-05 ...
5	006	TALTA_Kishan International	3	18100.00	Boston	MA	2012-10-05 ...
6	007	Ben@MoreTechnology.com	10	42000.00	Boston	MA	2012-10-05 ...

Figure 5.58 A query of the GrantLocations view shows the new ReportTime field.

Indexed View Requirements

Now that our GrantLocations view includes a seventh field (ReportTime), this gives us an opportunity to see all of the key requirements in action as we attempt to add an index to this view.

The first six fields of the GrantLocations view are **deterministic**. In other words, we can predict the result produced by a query of these fields. GrantID, GrantName, EmpID, Amount, City, and State will each produce the same values as they have in the base tables (The Grant table and the vEmployeeLocations view).

	GrantID	GrantName	EmpID	Amount	City	State	ReportTime
1	001	92 Purr_Scents %% team	7	4750.00	Seattle	WA	2012-10-05...
2	002	K-Land fund trust	2	15750.00	Seattle	WA	2012-10-05...
3	003	Robert@BigStarBank.com	7	18100.00	Seattle	WA	2012-10-05...
4	005	BIG 6's Foundation%	4	22000.00	Seattle	WA	2012-10-05...
5	006	TALTA_Kishan International	3	18100.00	Boston	MA	2012-10-05...
6	007	Ben@MoreTechnology.com	10	42000.00	Boston	MA	2012-10-05...

First six fields are deterministic

Figure 5.59 The first six fields of the GrantLocations view are deterministic.

As we saw earlier, the value of the ReportTime field cannot be determined prior to runtime. In other words, the ReportTime field is **non-deterministic**.

	GrantID	GrantName	EmpID	Amount	City	State	ReportTime
1	001	92 Purr_Scents %% team	7	4750.00	Seattle	WA	2012-10-05...
2	002	K-Land fund trust	2	15750.00	Seattle	WA	2012-10-05...
3	003	Robert@BigStarBank.com	7	18100.00	Seattle	WA	2012-10-05...
4	005	BIG 6's Foundation%	4	22000.00	Seattle	WA	2012-10-05...
5	006	TALTA_Kishan International	3	18100.00	Boston	MA	2012-10-05...
6	007	Ben@MoreTechnology.com	10	42000.00	Boston	MA	2012-10-05...

The last field is non deterministic

Figure 5.60 The last field of this view comes from the non-deterministic function called GETDATE().

We want to increase the performance of the GrantLocations view by adding an index. Since this is the first index being added to this view, we know it must be a unique clustered index (Figure 5.60).

We happen to know that the GrantLocations view doesn't already contain an index. One hint telling us this is that the source code we just saw doesn't include schema binding (Figure 5.55-Figure 5.56). Another way to confirm whether a view is already indexed is to check the view in Object Explorer as shown in Figure 5.54.

Since the GrantLocations view isn't yet schema bound, we know there is at least one factor preventing an index from being added to it. However, we will run this code to attempt the index creation and let SQL Server's messages guide us as we step through the process of adding a unique clustered index to this view.

```sql
CREATE UNIQUE CLUSTERED INDEX
UCI_GrantLocations_GrantID
ON dbo.GrantLocations(GrantID)
GO
```

```
Messages
Msg 1939, Level 16, State 1, Line 1
Cannot create index on view 'GrantLocations' because the view is not schema
bound.
                                                                    0 rows
```

Figure 5.61 An index cannot be created on a view if the view is not schema bound.

The first error message prompts us to schema bind the GrantLocations view. We will add the WITH SCHEMABINDING clause and make sure that all objects use two-part naming (Figure 5.61). SQL Server now tells us we can't use the * (asterisk) syntax. Therefore, we must itemize each field in the SELECT list.

```sql
ALTER VIEW dbo.GrantLocations
WITH SCHEMABINDING --Added this
AS
SELECT gr.*, vel.City, vel.[State],
GETDATE() AS ReportTime
FROM dbo.[Grant] AS gr
INNER JOIN dbo.vEmployeeLocations AS vel
ON vel.EmpID = gr.EmpID
GO
```

```
Messages
Msg 1054, Level 15, State 7, Procedure GrantLocations, Line 4
Syntax '*' is not allowed in schema-bound objects.
                                                                    0 rows
```

Figure 5.62 You can't create an index on a view that uses the * in its field SELECT list.

We have removed the asterisk (SELECT *) and have itemized all fields in the GrantLocations view and explicitly prefixed them according to which base table they come from (gr for the four fields coming from the Grant table, vel for the two fields coming from the vEmployeeLocations view - Figure 5.63). SQL Server now tells us that we must first schema bind the vEmployeeLocations view.

```sql
ALTER VIEW dbo.GrantLocations
WITH SCHEMABINDING
AS
SELECT gr.GrantID, gr.GrantName, gr.EmpID, gr.Amount
,vel.City, vel.[State],
GETDATE() AS ReportTime
FROM dbo.[Grant] AS gr
INNER JOIN dbo.vEmployeeLocations AS vel
ON vel.EmpID = gr.EmpID
GO
```

Messages
Msg 4513, Level 16, State 2, Procedure GrantLocations, Line 4 Cannot Schema bind view 'dbo.GrantLocations'. 'dbo.GrantLocations'. 'dbo.vEmployeeLocations' is not schema

0 rows

Figure 5.63 The gr.* has been replaced by an itemized field list.

Run sp_helptext to obtain the source code of the needed view (Figure 5.63). Then add the WITH SCHEMABINDING syntax and ensure all tables use two-part naming.

```sql
sp_helptext vEmployeeLocations
```

Text
CREATE VIEW vEmployeeLocations
WITH SCHEMABINDING
AS
SELECT em.EmpID, em.FirstName, em.LastName, lo.City, lo.[State]
FROM dbo.Employee AS em
INNER JOIN dbo.Location AS lo
ON em.LocationID = lo.LocationID

0 rows

Figure 5.64 The source code for vEmployeeLocations.

Run the following code to schema bind the vEmployeeLocations view:

```
ALTER VIEW vEmployeeLocations
WITH SCHEMABINDING
AS
SELECT em.EmpID, em.FirstName, em.LastName, lo.City,
lo.[State]
FROM dbo.Employee AS em INNER JOIN dbo.Location AS lo
ON em.LocationID = lo.LocationID
GO
```

The vEmployeeLocations view is now schema bound. With the vEmployeeLocations view schema bound, we have handled the most recent SQL Server error message (Which we saw in Figure 5.62). SQL Server now allows us to successfully schema bind the GrantLocations view (Figure 5.65).

```
ALTER VIEW dbo.GrantLocations
WITH SCHEMABINDING
AS
SELECT gr.GrantID, gr.GrantName, gr.EmpID, gr.Amount,
vel.City, Vel.[State],
GETDATE() AS ReportTime
FROM dbo.[Grant] AS gr
INNER JOIN dbo.vEmployeeLocations AS vel
ON vel.EmpID = gr.EmpID
GO
```

Messages
Command(s) completed successfully.
0 rows

Figure 5.65 The GrantLocations view is now schema bound.

Let's reattempt the code to create the unique clustered index (Figure 5.66). This error message from SQL Server reminds us that fields producing non-deterministic results cannot be included in an indexed view. Our use of the GETDATE() function in the ReportTime field is problematic.

```
CREATE UNIQUE CLUSTERED INDEX
UCI_GrantLocations_GrantID
ON dbo.GrantLocations(GrantID)
GO
```

```
Messages
Msg 1949, Level 16, State 1, Line 1
Cannot create index on view 'JProCo.dbo.GrantLocations'. The function
'GetDate' yields nondeterministic results. Use a deterministic system
function, or modify the user-defined function to return deterministic results.
                                                                    0 rows
```

Figure 5.66 You can't place an index on a view that uses a non-deterministic field.

Let's rerun the statement which builds the GrantLocations view and exclude the ReportTime field. Here we comment out the ReportTime field, so that it's not part of the view (Figure 5.67).

```
ALTER VIEW dbo.GrantLocations
WITH SCHEMABINDING
AS
SELECT gr.GrantID, gr.GrantName, gr.EmpID, gr.Amount,
vel.City, Vel.[State]--,GetDate() as ReportTime
FROM dbo.[Grant] AS gr
INNER JOIN dbo.vEmployeeLocations AS vel
ON vel.EmpID = gr.EmpID
GO
```

```
Messages
Command(s) completed successfully.
                                                                    0 rows
```

Figure 5.67 The non-deterministic field has been removed from the GrantLocations view.

Let's rerun the statement to create the index (Figure 5.67). SQL Server reminds us that an indexed view cannot be based upon another view. We will need to revise the GrantLocations view so that it pulls all needed fields directly from base tables, instead of from a view.

```
CREATE UNIQUE CLUSTERED INDEX
UCI_GrantLocations_GrantID
ON dbo.GrantLocations(GrantID)
```

```
Messages
Msg 1937, Level 16, State 1, Line 1
Cannot create index on view 'JProCo.dbo.GrantLocations' because it references
another view 'dbo.vEmployeeLocations'. Consider expanding referenced view's
definition by hand in indexed view definition.
                                                                    0 rows
```

Figure 5.68 An indexed view cannot be based upon another view.

The vEmployeeLocations view is based on two tables (Employee and Location). Let's run this code (Figure 5.69) to pull the City and State fields directly from a join of the Employee and Location tables instead of from the vEmployeeLocations view.

```
ALTER VIEW dbo.GrantLocations
WITH SCHEMABINDING
AS
SELECT gr.GrantID, gr.GrantName, gr.EmpID, gr.Amount,
vel.City, vel.[State]
FROM dbo.[Grant] gr INNER JOIN dbo.Employee em
ON gr.EmpID = em.EmpID
INNER JOIN dbo.Location vel
ON vel.LocationID = em.LocationID
```

```
Messages
Command(s) completed successfully.
                                                                    0 rows
```

Figure 5.69 The GrantLocations view is no longer using any views for any of its base tables.

We have met all of SQL Server's requirements and are finally able to add a unique clustered index to the GrantID field of the GrantLocations view (Figure 5.69). The index will create its own copy of the GrantLocations data and physically order the view's records according to GrantID.

Any query against the view which predicates on the GrantID field should see a marked improvement in performance.

```
CREATE UNIQUE CLUSTERED INDEX
UCI_GrantLocations_GrantID
ON dbo.GrantLocations(GrantID)
GO
```

```
Messages
Command(s) completed successfully.
                                                              0 rows
```

Figure 5.70 The GrantLocations view can now have indexes created on it.

We've successfully created the indexed view and have completed the main portion of our demonstration. But let's spend a moment considering SQL Server's error message which alerted us to the non-deterministic field we had to address before the index could be created (originally shown in Figure 5.66 and reproduced here as Figure 5.71).

```
Messages
Msg 1949, Level 16, State 1, Line 1
Cannot create index on view 'JProCo.dbo.GrantLocations'.
The function 'getdate' yields nondeterministic results.
Use a deterministic system function,
or modify the user-defined function to return deterministic results.
```

Figure 5.71 The GetDate() function is problematic, but some functions can produce deterministic results.

Notice that the error message points specifically to the GetDate() function as being problematic, because it produces non-deterministic values. However, SQL Server gives us the hint that we can use a deterministic system function, or we can use a user-defined function which returns deterministic results. Thus, it isn't simply that all functions will block your creation of indexed views, just the non-deterministic functions.

Let's briefly look at an example which includes a deterministic function. Here we take our current code (from Figure 5.68) which builds the GrantLocations view. Use the code shown here to rebuild the view with the L3Name field produced by the LEFT function. Rerun this code to alter the GrantLocations view (Figure 5.72).

Chapter 5. Updating and Maintaining Views

```
ALTER VIEW dbo.GrantLocations
WITH SCHEMABINDING
AS
SELECT gr.GrantID, gr.GrantName, gr.EmpID, gr.Amount,
vel.City, vel.[State], LEFT (GrantName,3)
as L3Name --This is deterministic
FROM dbo.[Grant] gr INNER JOIN dbo.Employee em
ON gr.EmpID = em.EmpID
INNER JOIN dbo.Location vel
ON vel.LocationID = em.LocationID
```

```
Messages
Command(s) completed successfully.
                                                              0 rows
```

Figure 5.72 The L3Name expression field is based on the LEFT() function, which is deterministic.

The L3Name field displays the first three letters of the GrantName field. In other words, the values of L3Name are determined by the values in the GrantName field. A SELECT query will always produce the GrantName values which currently appear in the base table. Therefore, the GrantName field is deterministic and will not be changed by a SELECT query. The same is true for the L3Name field. Therefore, L3Name is deterministic (Figure 5.73).

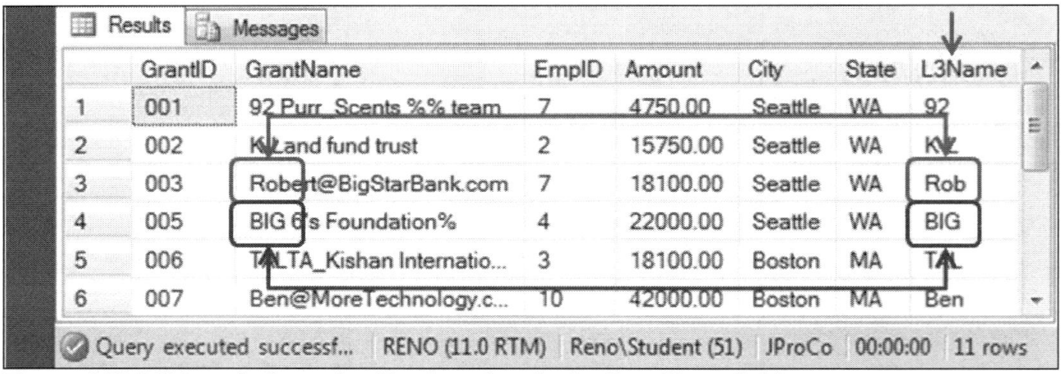

	GrantID	GrantName	EmpID	Amount	City	State	L3Name
1	001	92 Purr_Scents %% team	7	4750.00	Seattle	WA	92
2	002	K&L and fund trust	2	15750.00	Seattle	WA	K&L
3	003	Robert@BigStarBank.com	7	18100.00	Seattle	WA	Rob
4	005	BIG 6's Foundation%	4	22000.00	Seattle	WA	BIG
5	006	TALTA_Kishan Internatio...	3	18100.00	Boston	MA	TAL
6	007	Ben@MoreTechnology.c...	10	42000.00	Boston	MA	Ben

Query executed successf... RENO (11.0 RTM) Reno\Student (51) JProCo 00:00:00 11 rows

Figure 5.73 L3Name is determined by the values in the GrantName field.

Since the L3Name field is deterministic, SQL Server will allow you to successfully create a unique clustered index on the GrantLocations view. You can create an index on a view which includes a function(s), as long as the function(s) is deterministic.

Note: If you wish to test this yourself, be sure to first drop the existing index before running the code which will create it again. This code drops the index:

```
DROP INDEX UCI_GrantLocations_GrantID
ON dbo.GrantLocations
GO
CREATE UNIQUE CLUSTERED INDEX
UCI_GrantLocations_GrantID
ON dbo.GrantLocations(GrantID)
GO
```

Note: Deterministic functions will be further examined in Chapter 11.

Space Used by Indexed Views

So far we have accepted 'on faith' that views do not store their own data unless they are indexed. In this section, we will examine the data storage requirements of a view before and after an index is added to it:

Let's build a view based on the SalesInvoice and Customer tables:

```
CREATE VIEW vCustomerOrderDates
WITH SCHEMABINDING
AS
SELECT si.OrderDate, cu.FirstName, cu.LastName
FROM dbo.SalesInvoice AS si
INNER JOIN dbo.Customer AS cu
ON si.CustomerID = cu.CustomerID
GO
```

Messages
Command(s) completed successfully.
0 rows

Figure 5.74 We have built a new view based on the SalesInvoice and Customer tables.

When we query our new view, we see 1884 records displayed:

```
SELECT * FROM vCustomerOrderDates
```

	OrderDate	FirstName	LastName
1	2009-01-03 00:00:00.000	Mary	Robinson
2	2009-01-04 02:22:41.473	Karen	Hill
3	2009-01-04 05:33:01.150	Kevin	Campbell
4	2009-01-04 22:06:58.657	Betty	Campbell
5	2009-01-05 11:37:45.597	Michael	Moore
6	2009-01-06 23:53:14.320	Thomas	Wright
			1884 rows

Figure 5.75 Query the view and confirm that you see 1884 rows.

The sp_spaceused utility confirms that this view takes up no space:

```
sp_spaceused vCustomerOrderDates
```

name	rows	reserved	data	index_size	unused
vCustomerOrderDates	NULL	NULL	NULL	0 KB	0 KB

1 rows

Figure 5.76 This non-indexed view occupies no storage space.

Now let's create an index on the view:

```
CREATE UNIQUE CLUSTERED INDEX
UCI_vCustomerOrderDates_OrderDate
ON dbo.vCustomerOrderDates(OrderDate)
GO
```

Messages
Command(s) completed successfully.

0 rows

Figure 5.77 Add a unique clustered index on the OrderDate field of vCustomerOrderDates.

Once we add the index, which permanently materializes this view, we can see that the view now occupies space in the database. This view's data now occupies 88KB with another 16KB used by the index. SQL Server has reserved 136KB in JProCo for the view vCustomerOrderDates:

```
sp_spaceused vCustomerOrderDates
```

name	rows	reserved	data	index_size	unused
vCustomerOrderDates	1884	136 KB	88 KB	16 KB	32 KB

1 rows

Figure 5.78 After the view is indexed, a copy of the data is stored in the index and thus the view now occupies space in the JProCo database.

Chapter 5. Updating and Maintaining Views

Lab 5.3: Indexed Views

Lab Prep: Lab Prep: Each lab has one or more Skill Checks. Start with Skill Check 1 and proceed until reaching the Points to Ponder section.

Before beginning this lab, verify that SQL Server 2012 is properly installed and operating. Before running the lab setup script for resetting the database (SQLQueries2012Vol4Chapter5.3Setup.sql), please make sure to close all query windows within SSMS. An open query window pointing to a database context can lock that database preventing it from updating when the script is executing. A simple way to assure all query windows are closed, is to exit out of SSMS, then open a new instance of SSMS, and lastly run the setup script.

Skill Check 1: Alter the vSales view to include the InvoiceID and InvoiceDetailID right after the CustomerID. Make certain the view remains schema bound.

```
SELECT * FROM vSales
```

	CustomerID	InvoiceID	InvoiceDetailID	OrderDate	RetailPr...	Qu...	Prod...	ProductName
1	597	9	63	2009-01-08...	80.859	5	7	Underwater Tour 1 Day...
2	736	10	87	2009-01-09...	80.859	2	7	Underwater Tour 1 Day...
3	47	15	139	2009-01-13...	80.859	3	7	Underwater Tour 1 Day...
4	251	19	164	2009-01-16...	80.859	4	7	Underwater Tour 1 Day...
5	529	20	185	2009-01-17...	80.859	5	7	Underwater Tour 1 Day...
6	151	22	192	2009-01-17...	80.859	5	7	Underwater Tour 1 Day...

Query executed successfully.   RENO (11.0 RTM)   Reno\Student (53)   JProCo   00:00:00   6960 rows

Figure 5.79 Shows InvoiceID and InvoiceDetailID included in the vSales view.

Skill Check 2: Create the UCI_vSales_InvoiceDetailID unique clustered index on the vSales view's InvoiceDetailID field.

```
Object Explorer
Connect ▼
    dbo.vSales
        Columns
        Triggers
        Indexes
            UCI_vSales_InvoiceDetailID (Clustered)
        Statistics
```

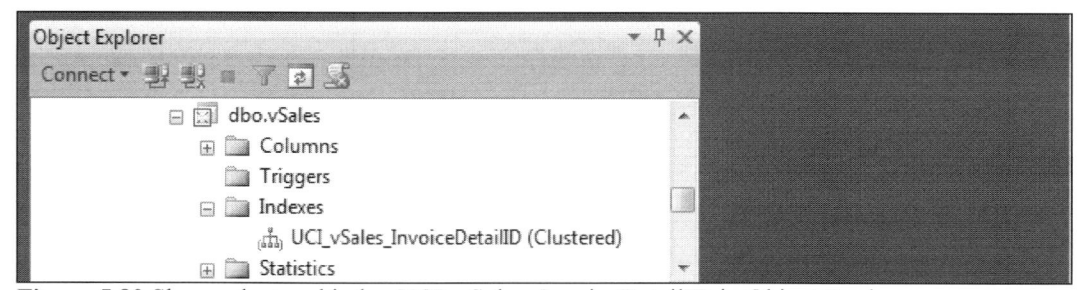

Figure 5.80 Shows clustered index UCI_vSales_InvoiceDetailID in Object Explorer.

Answer Code: The T-SQL code to this lab can be found in the downloadable files in a file named Lab5.3_IndexedViews.sql.

Points to Ponder - Indexed Views

1. Summary of rules for indexed views:
   - The first index must be a unique clustered index.
   - The view must be defined using the SCHEMABINDING option.
   - The view cannot have a nested view (it can only reference base tables).
   - All base tables must have the same schema as the view.
   - All base tables must be in the same database as the view.
   - All references must utilize two-part names.
   - Cannot use non-deterministic fields.
2. All indexed views contain a unique clustered index.
3. Use indexes for views which include many JOIN statements.
4. Indexed views are only supported by the Enterprise or Developer editions of SQL Server.
5. Indexed views store their own data instead of just being instructions for retrieving data from a base table(s).
6. In SQL Server there are three types of views:
   - Standard – Combines data from one or more base tables.
   - Indexed – A view with an index that has been computed and stored.
   - Partitioned – Has base tables from one or more servers.
7. You can create indexes on a view or calculated column only if you use deterministic functions. A deterministic function always returns the same result every time it is called. The result for a non-deterministic function may vary each time it is run.
8. For user-defined functions, SQL Server analyzes the functions and assesses whether they are deterministic or non-deterministic.
9. Views do not exist as a stored set of data values *unless* they are indexed.
10. Because of the system load imposed in maintaining indexes for views, you should limit their use to views that reference columns that change infrequently. Do not index views where the data receives many writes or updates (e.g., OLTP systems like CRM or order-processing systems).

Chapter Glossary

Deterministic function: A function which always returns the same result each time it is called.

Indexed view: A view with an index that has been computed and stored.

Materialized view: Indexing a view causes the view to be persistently materialized and stored in the database. In other words, the view contains a physical copy of the view data (including computations associated with joins, aggregate queries, etc.) for quicker retrieval.

Non-deterministic function: A function whose result can vary each time it is called.

Partitioned view: A view which has base tables from one or more servers.

sp_helptext: System-supplied stored procedure that reports information about a database object.

sp_spaceused: A system stored-procedure which obtains space statistics for a table.

Standard view: Combines data from one or more base tables.

Review Quiz - Chapter Five

1.) You are attempting to insert records into a table by performing these inserts through a view. You have verified you are updating only one base table and the insert syntax is correct. Your insert appears to run with no errors but the number of records in the table does not change. What are two possible reasons?

   ☐ a. The table is set to read only.
   ☐ b. The security context you are using does not have the proper permissions.
   ☐ c. The database is being backed up.
   ☐ d. The table has an instead of insert trigger.
   ☐ e. The table has an insert trigger with a rollback statement.

2.) Your SQL Server has a table named dbo.Employee. You need to create a view for each LocationID (named vSeattleEmployee, vBostonEmployee, vSpokaneEmployee and vChicagoEmployee). You are getting ready to create the vSeattleEmployee view for LocationID 1. You need to make sure that you can update, insert and delete against this view without changing the LocationID value for another location. Which code would you use?

   ○ a. `CREATE VIEW vSeattleEmployee AS`
         `SELECT * FROM dbo.Employee WHERE LocationID = 1`
         `WITH ENCRYPTION`
   ○ b. `CREATE VIEW vSeattleEmployee AS`
         `SELECT * FROM dbo.Employee WHERE LocationID = 1`
         `WITH SCHEMABINDING`
   ○ c. `CREATE VIEW WITH SCHEMABINDING, CHECK OPTION vSeattleEmployee`
         `AS SELECT * FROM dbo.Employee WHERE LocationID = 1`
   ○ d. `CREATE VIEW vSeattleEmployee AS`
         `SELECT * FROM dbo.Employee WHERE LocationID = 1`
         `WITH CHECK OPTION`

3.) Which is the only true statement about updating data through a view?

   ○ a. You can make updates to one base table while predicating on another.
   ○ b. You can make updates to two base tables if you only predicate on one.
   ○ c. You can make updates to two base tables if you don't use a predicate.

Chapter 5. Updating and Maintaining Views

4.) Your company uses SQL Server 2012. You are implementing a series of views that are used in ad hoc queries. Some of these views perform slowly. You create indexes on these views to increase performance, while still maintaining the company's security policy. One of the views returns the current date by using the GETDATE() function. This view does not allow you to create an index. You need to create an index on the view. Which two actions should you perform? (Choose two)

- ☐ a. Remove all deterministic calls from within the view.
- ☐ b. Remove all non-deterministic calls from within the view.
- ☐ c. Schema bind the view.
- ☐ d. Create the view and specify WITH CHECK OPTION.
- ☐ e. Base this view on another view instead of a base table.

5.) You are responsible for maintaining a SQL Server 2012 database. A business analyst in the company routinely uses a view named vCustomerSales, which joins the Customers and Sales tables in the database. You need to increase the performance of the view. What should you do?

- O a. Get the view to use an outer join between the Customers and Sales tables.
- O b. Create a clustered index on the vCustomerSales view.
- O c. Create two non-clustered indexes on the same field in the view.
- O d. Create two separate views that do not contain any joins – one view named vCustomer for the Customers table and another one names vSales for the Sales table.

6.) Which is the only untrue statement about indexed views?

- O a. The first index on a view must be a unique clustered index.
- O b. Indexed views store a copy of the data from the base tables.
- O c. Indexed views require all fields to be deterministic.
- O d. Indexed views require the view to be schema bound
- O e. Indexed views require the view to use Check Option.
- O f. Indexed views can't be based on other non-schema bound views.

Chapter 5. Updating and Maintaining Views

7.) You have a table named Employee and want to create several views from that table for various insert, update, and delete statements. One view will be called vSeattleEmployee and another will be called vBostonEmployee. Each regional office will use its own view. You want to make sure that updates made from Seattle do not change the other employees' locations. The same is true for Boston and all other views based on the Employee table. Seattle is LocationID 1. How do you create the vSeattleEmployee view?

- O a. **CREATE VIEW** dbo.vSeattleEmployee
  AS
  SELECT EmpID, FirstName, LastName, LocationID
  FROM dbo.Employee
  WHERE LocationID = **1**

- O b. **CREATE VIEW** dbo.vSeattleEmployee
  AS
  SELECT EmpID, FirstName, LastName, LocationID
  FROM dbo.Employee
  WHERE LocationID = **1**
  WITH CHECK OPTION

- O c. **CREATE VIEW** dbo.vSeattleEmployee
  AS
  SELECT EmpID, FirstName, LastName, LocationID
  FROM dbo.Employee
  WHERE LocationID = **1**
  WITH SCHEMABINDING

- O d. **CREATE VIEW** dbo.vSeattleEmployee
  WITH SCHEMABINDING
  AS
  SELECT EmpID, FirstName, LastName, LocationID
  FROM dbo.Employee
  WHERE LocationID = **1**

8.) You are creating a view that queries your Employee table. You need to prevent the Employee table from being dropped as long as your view exists. Which option should you use when you create the view?

- O a. WITH ENCRYPTION
- O b. WITH NOCHECK
- O c. WITH SCHEMABINDING
- O d. WITH OPENXML

9.) You have a table named dbo.Sales. You need to create three views from the sales table.

```
vSalesSeattle
vSalesBoston
vSalesSpokane
```

Each view will be used by each region to make changes to their rows. One day a Seattle sales manager updated his sales data to have a new LocationID and the record showed up on the vSalesBoston view. Changes made to the vSalesSeattle view must not be made in a way that the record falls outside of the scope of the view. Which view should you create for Region1?

- a.
  ```
  CREATE VIEW dbo.vSalesSeattle
  AS
  SELECT SalesID, OrderQty, SalesPersonID, RegionID
  FROM dbo.Sales
  WHERE RegionID = 1
  WITH DIFFERENTIAL
  ```

- b.
  ```
  CREATE VIEW dbo.vSalesSeattle
  AS
  SELECT SalesID, OrderQty, SalesPersonID, RegionID
  FROM dbo.Sales
  WHERE RegionID = 1
  WITH CHECK OPTION
  ```

- c.
  ```
  CREATE VIEW dbo.vSalesSeattle
  WITH SCHEMABINDING
  AS
  SELECT SalesID, OrderQty, SalesPersonID, RegionID
  FROM dbo.Sales
  WHERE RegionID = 1
  ```

- d.
  ```
  CREATE VIEW dbo.vSalesSeattle
  WITH NOCHECK
  AS
  SELECT SalesID, OrderQty, SalesPersonID, RegionID
  FROM dbo.Sales
  WHERE RegionID = 1
  ```

Answer Key

1.) If you are updating a view without getting an error then that means it's not a permission or read-only problem as that would generate an error. This means that (a) and (b) are wrong. A trigger should stop the event without an error if it is an "Instead of" trigger or an "After" trigger with a rollback. This makes (d) and (e) correct.

2.) WITH ENCRYPTION and WITH SHCEMABINDING do not put any restrictions on what records can be inserted though the view, so (a) and (b) are wrong. The WITH CHECK OPTION will prevent updated records from disappearing from the view but this option goes at the end of the statement, so (c) is wrong and (d) is correct.

3.) You can never update the data in two base tables at once, so (b) and (c) are wrong. You can update one base tables' data while predicating in any of the other base tables, making (a) the correct answer.

4.) You need all fields of a view to be deterministic, so (a) is incorrect. The CHECK OPTION only affects updates and not any indexing requirements, so (d) is wrong. You do need to make sure to schema bind the view too, so (b) and (c) are the correct answers.

5.) One way to increase the performance of a view is to put an index on the view. This means (b) is correct.

6.) Indexed views need to be schema bound and have deterministic fields but don't really care about CHECK OPTION since that is just to limit updates (not indexes) This means (e) is correct.

7.) Using SCHEMABIND will prevent base tables from being dropped but will not restrict updates to the view, so (c) and (d) are incorrect. The CHECK OPTION will prevent updates to a table that will cause records to disappear from the scope of the view, so (b) is the correct answer.

8.) Using SCHEMABIND will prevent base tables from being dropped, so (c) is correct.

9.) Using SCHEMABIND will prevent base tables from being dropped but will not restrict updates to the view, so (c) is incorrect. The NOCHECK applies to constraints, so (d) is wrong. WITH DIFFERNTIAL is for backing up SQL Server, so (a) is incorrect. The CHECK OPTION will prevent updates to table that will cause records to disappear from the scope of the view, so (b) is the correct answer.

Bug Catcher Game

To play the Bug Catcher game, run the file SQLQueries2012Vol4BugCatcher5.pps from the BugCatcher folder of the companion files found at www.Joes2Pros.com.

[THIS PAGE INTENTIONALLY LEFT BLANK.]

Chapter 6. Stored Procedures

When my brother found out that he and his wife were expecting the first addition to their family, he really got busy getting the house ready for the new baby. In addition to finding baby toys, baby furniture, and other needed items, he started remodeling the bathroom that was next to their bedroom. It was a bigger task than one person could do within the necessary timeframe, so help was needed from our dad, me, and many friends. My brother knew I had no plumbing or electrical skills, but when it came to drywall and paint, he could simply provide me the tools and materials and I would get the work done. My father loves woodwork and shelving, so when that stage of the job came my brother gave Dad a call. For tiling work, our friend, Rhonda came to help and as long as the materials were ready, she knew what to do and carried out the task.

Stored procedures are objects that do the work they are designed to do when you call upon them. You need to make sure they have what they need (the right values and parameters), and they will perform their important tasks. Stored procedures can act like views and select data, but they can also make updates, create objects, or even be set up to back up a database or perform other maintenance tasks.

This chapter will be a refresher from previous books and will also add a few new commonly used tricks, such as returning one or more values from a stored procedure. The next chapter will explore additional techniques using stored procedures.

READER NOTE: *Please run the script SQLQueries2012Vol4Chapter6.0Setup.sql in order to follow along with the examples in the first section of Chapter 6. All scripts mentioned in this chapter may be found at* **www.Joes2Pros.com**.

Stored Procedures Recap

Stored procedures may contain DML, DDL, TCL, or DCL statements. Our work in *SQL Queries 2012 Joes 2 Pros Volume 1* introduced us to stored procedures (commonly referred to as "sprocs"), as well as to the four T-SQL statement types.

Our subsequent performance tuning work in *SQL Queries 2012 Joes 2 Pros Volume 3* gave us an appreciation of stored procedures from a more sophisticated perspective. For example, a stored procedure has the advantage of caching its Execution Plan. In other words, SQL Server does not have to wait until runtime to evaluate a sproc's indexes, statistics, and query selectivity. For this reason, executing a sproc often runs faster than if you were to drop the code it contains into a new query window and run it.

Basic Stored Procedures

Let's begin with a query retrieving all the employees from Location 1.

```
SELECT * FROM Employee
WHERE LocationID = 1
```

Results | Messages

	EmpID	LastName	FirstName	HireDate	LocationID	ManagerID	Status	HiredOffset	TimeZone
1	1	Adams	Alex	2001-01-01...	1	4	Active	2001-01-01...	-08:00
2	2	Brown	Barry	2002-08-12...	1	11	Active	2002-08-12...	-08:00
3	4	Kinnison	Dave	1996-03-16...	1	11	Has Tenure	1996-03-16...	-08:00
4	5	Bender	Eric	2007-05-17...	1	11	Active	2007-05-17...	-08:00
5	7	Lonning	David	2000-01-01...	1	11	On Leave	2000-01-01...	-08:00
6	9	Newton	James	2003-09-30...	1	3	Active	2003-09-30...	-05:00

Query executed successfully. | RENO (11.0 RTM) | Reno\Student (51) | JProCo | 00:00:00 | 15 rows

Figure 6.1 Records for all the JProCo employees working in Location 1.

Suppose this is a query we run frequently, perhaps several times daily. It would be smarter for us to create a stored procedure rather than manually type out the query each time we need to retrieve the data. Not only will our query benefit from a cached Execution Plan and statistics, but the sproc will be a database object available for reuse by our team. For example, a fellow analyst or DBA can use this sproc to run this query that our team needs several times daily. Our dev team can also call upon the sproc from within another code routine or automated process they may be developing.

While in the JProCo database context, run the following code to include our query in a newly created sproc called GetSeattleEmployees. Notice that this code simply creates the object (i.e., the stored procedure). We need to write a separate statement to invoke the sproc. This code creates the stored procedure GetSeattleEmployees:

```
CREATE PROCEDURE dbo.GetSeattleEmployees
AS
SELECT *
FROM Employee
WHERE LocationID = 1
GO
```

An EXECUTE statement is what we need to actually run our newly created sproc. You can either choose to spell out the full keyword EXECUTE or use the shortened form EXEC, as shown here (Figure 6.2). Notice that the result set is identical to that produced by the original query (shown earlier in Figure 6.1).

```
EXEC GetSeattleEmployees
```

Figure 6.2 This code calls the stored procedure GetSeattleEmployees.

You may have noticed we were able to successfully call the sproc without including "dbo" in the EXEC statement. Specifying the schema name (e.g., dbo) is usually optional when creating or invoking an object (Chapter 13 will show performance related reasons for always using a two-part name with sprocs). In this case we could have created the sproc with the name "GetSeattleEmployees". Since dbo is the default schema for the JProCo database, SQL Server will implicitly read the object name "GetSeattleEmployees" as "dbo.GetSeattleEmployees". In most cases, you are safe using two-part naming. You are nearly as safe using just the object name. SQL Server's error messaging will prompt you whenever a different naming format is needed.

Stored Procedure Parameters

The EXEC(UTE) command runs the code contained within the stored procedure. Our result was what we expected to see – all the employees at LocationID 1. Suppose we want to see employees at the other locations (Boston, Spokane, etc.). Should we create a separate sproc for each office?

Stored procedures offer a more flexible option for achieving our goal. We can modify our stored procedure so that it will allow us to specify a location each time we execute the sproc. Readers of *SQL Queries 2012 Joes 2 Pros Volume 1* will likely recall a similar example we utilized (Chapter 8, Parameterized Stored Procedures). Rather than hardcoding the LocationID, we will let it be defined by a variable. Each time someone runs the sproc, they will need to supply a value for their desired LocationID. Values that you pass into a sproc at runtime are called *parameters*.

The code shown in Figure 6.5 will build the flexible sproc designed to show us the employee records for any JProCo location. Our current query will still be the basis of the sproc. While it may be easy to recognize the variable taking the place of the hardcoded value in our current query, let's examine all of the code syntax changes the new sproc will encompass (Figure 6.3 and Figure 6.4).

```
--This syntax declares the variable @LocationID, which is an integer.
--The variable is currently set to 1.
DECLARE @LocationID INT = 1

SELECT * FROM Employee       --Our current query with hardcoded LocationID.
WHERE LocationID = 1         --In order to make use of the declared variable,
                             --our query would need to call upon the variable.

--The variable now replaces the hardcoded value in our query.
--If you change the 1 to another LocationID (e.g., 2, 3, 4, etc.),
--then the query will return the records for your chosen location.
DECLARE @LocationID INT = 1
SELECT * FROM Employee
WHERE LocationID = @LocationID
```

Figure 6.3 The code syntax for declaring a variable and calling upon a variable are shown here.

When we substitute the variable @LocationID for the hardcoded value in our query, it will return the records for the location which we specify (Figure 6.4).

```
DECLARE @LocationID INT = 2
SELECT * FROM Employee
WHERE LocationID =@LocationID
```

	EmpID	LastName	FirstName	HireDate	LocationID	ManagerID	Status	HiredOffset	TimeZone
1	3	Osako	Lee	1999-09-01...	2	11	Active	1999-09-01...	-05:00
2	10	O'Haire	Terry	2004-10-04...	2	3	Active	2004-10-04...	-05:00

Figure 6.4 The location you specify populates the variable; our query now includes the variable.

Now let's turn to the code which creates GetEmployeeByLocationID, our new sproc (Figure 6.5). The base query is the same (compare the last 2 lines of code in Figure 6.4 and Figure 6.5). The CREATE PROCEDURE statement declares the variable. Since we want the flexibility to choose the location at runtime, our code doesn't include any LocationID value. Run this code to create the stored procedure.

```
CREATE PROCEDURE dbo.GetEmployeeByLocationID @LocationID INT
AS
SELECT * FROM Employee
WHERE LocationID = @LocationID
GO
```

```
Messages
Command(s) completed successfully.
                                                                    0 rows
```
Figure 6.5 The stored procedure GetEmployeeByLocationID.

We need to supply the LocationID value when we run the sproc. If we attempt to execute this sproc without telling it which location we want, we'll get an error message from SQL Server telling us that this procedure expects a parameter and that one wasn't supplie (Figure 6.6).

```
EXEC GetEmployeeByLocationID
```

```
Messages
Msg 201, Level 16, State 4, Procedure GetEmployeeByLocationID, Line 0
Procedure or function 'GetEmployeeByLocationID' expects parameter
'@LocationID', which was not supplied.
                                                                    0 rows
```
Figure 6.6 If no parameter is supplied, the GetEmployeeByLocationID sproc cannot run.

Let's reattempt to call on GetEmployeeByLocationID and request the records for Location 1. When we pass the value 1 to the variable, we see all the Seattle employee record (Figure 6.7).

```
EXEC GetEmployeeByLocationID 1
```

	EmpID	LastName	FirstName	HireDate	LocationID	ManagerID	Status	HiredOffset	TimeZone
1	1	Adams	Alex	2001-01-01	1	4	Active	2001-01-01	-08:00
2	2	Brown	Barry	2002-08-12	1	11	Active	2002-08-12	-08:00
3	4	Kinnison	Dave	1996-03-16	1	11	Has...	1996-03-16	-08:00
4	5	Bender	Eric	2007-05-17	1	11	Active	2007-05-17	-08:00
5	7	Lonning	David	2000-01-01	1	11	On...	2000-01-01	-08:00
6	9	Newton	James	2003-09-30	1	3	Active	2003-09-30	-05:00

Query executed successfully.   RENO (11.0 RTM)   Reno\Student (51)   JProCo   00:00:00   15 rows

Figure 6.7 This parameter specifies that we want the records for Location 1 (Seattle).

When we pass in a 2, the same sproc returns the records for Location 2, which is Boston (Figure 6.8). Notice that this result is identical to the query result shown in Figure 6.4.

```
EXEC GetEmployeeByLocationID 2
```

	EmpID	LastName	FirstName	HireDate	LocationID	ManagerID	Status	HiredOffset	TimeZone
1	3	Osako	Lee	1999-09-01...	2	11	Active	1999-09-01...	-05:00
2	10	O'Haire	Terry	2004-10-04...	2	3	Active	2004-10-04...	-05:00

Query executed successfully. | RENO (11.0 RTM) | Reno\Student (51) | JProCo | 00:00:00 | 2 rows

Figure 6.8 This parameter specifies that we want the records from Location 2 (Boston).

Let's create another stored procedure called GetBigGrants. This stored procedure should find grants at, or above, a specified amount. Run this code to create the stored procedure (Figure 6.9).

```
CREATE PROC GetBigGrants @Amount INT
AS
SELECT GrantName, Amount
FROM [Grant]
WHERE Amount >= @Amount
GO
```

Messages
Command(s) completed successfully.
0 rows

Figure 6.9 This code creates the GetBigGrants procedure that requires a parameter.

Let's call the GetBigGrants sproc and specify that we want to see all the grants at, or above, $40,000 (Figure 6.10) by passing in the value of 40000 for the parameter.

```
EXEC GetBigGrants 40000
```

	GrantName	Amount
1	Ben@MoreTechnology.com	42000.00
2	Mega Mercy	56000.00
		2 rows

Figure 6.10 Two grants have an amount greater than, or equal to, $40,000.

Let's change our code to pass in 25000 (Figure 6.11). There are three grants that are at or over the amount of $25,000 in our result set.

```
EXEC GetBigGrants 25000
```

	GrantName	Amount
1	Ben@MoreTechnology.com	42000.00
2	www.@-Last-U-Can-Help.com	26000.00
3	Mega Mercy	56000.00
		3 rows

Figure 6.11 Three grants have an amount greater than, or equal to, $25,000.

Scalar Result Sets

A scalar result consists of a single value. We need to be aware of scalar data, because we will encounter scenarios in SQL Server which require a scalar value as an input and objects (e.g., scalar functions) which only produce scalar results. Scalar values can be the result of simple expressions, such as the employee data expressions we will evaluate in this section. A scalar value can also result from a complex expression, such as the many calculations and inputs needed to produce a FICO score.

Here we see a query designed to produce a scalar result (Figure 6.12). Each time you run the query, exactly one value will be returned.

```sql
SELECT COUNT(*) AS PeopleCt
FROM Employee AS em
INNER JOIN Location AS lo
ON em.LocationID = lo.LocationID
WHERE City = 'Boston'
```

	PeopleCt
1	2

1 rows

Figure 6.12 This query returns the count of employees working in Boston.

When we change the criteria to get the Seattle employees, we get the scalar value 15 (Figure 6.13).

```sql
SELECT COUNT(*) AS PeopleCt
FROM Employee AS em
INNER JOIN Location AS lo
ON em.LocationID = lo.LocationID
WHERE City = 'Seattle'
```

	PeopleCt
1	15

← A Scalar Result produces 1 value.

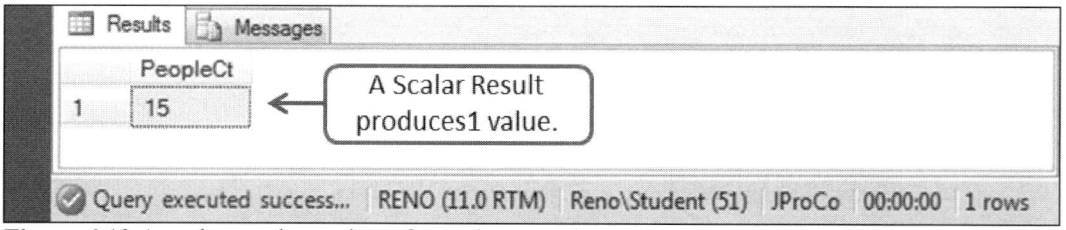

Query executed success... | RENO (11.0 RTM) | Reno\Student (51) | JProCo | 00:00:00 | 1 rows

Figure 6.13 A scalar result consists of exactly one value.

Let's create a scalar stored procedure GetCityCount, which will return a single value, no matter what parameter we pass in. This code creates the scalar stored procedure GetCityCount:

```sql
CREATE PROC dbo.GetCityCount @CityName VARCHAR(MAX)
AS
SELECT COUNT(*) AS PeopleCt
FROM Employee AS em
INNER JOIN Location AS lo
ON em.LocationID = lo.LocationID
WHERE City = @CityName
GO
```

Let's test our stored procedure and pass in Spokane for the parameter value.

```sql
EXEC GetCityCount 'Spokane'
```

PeopleCt
2

1 rows

Figure 6.14 This code calls the stored procedure GetCityCount for Spokane.

The same stored procedure shows us the total of 15 when we pass in Seattle.

```sql
EXEC GetCityCount 'Seattle'
```

PeopleCt
15

1 rows

Figure 6.15 This code calls the stored procedure GetCityCount for Seattle.

The scalar result 0 (i.e., zero employees) is returned for Chicago (Figure 6.16).

```sql
EXEC GetCityCount 'Chicago'
```

PeopleCt
0

1 rows

Figure 6.16 There are currently zero employees at the Chicago location.

Lab 6.1: Stored Procedures Recap

Lab Prep: Lab Prep: Each lab has one or more Skill Checks. Start with Skill Check 1 and proceed until reaching the Points to Ponder section.

Before beginning this lab, verify that SQL Server 2012 is properly installed and operating. Before running the lab setup script for resetting the database (SQLQueries2012Vol4Chapter6.1Setup.sql), please make sure to close all query windows within SSMS. An open query window pointing to a database context can lock that database preventing it from updating when the script is executing. A simple way to assure all query windows are closed, is to exit out of SSMS, then open a new instance of SSMS, and lastly run the setup script.

Skill Check 1: Create a Stored Procedure called GetLongClasses which takes an INT (integer) parameter and shows a result set of all MgmtTraining classes with a duration greater than or equal to the number of hours specified by the parameter. Show just the ClassName and the ClassDurationHours fields in the result. Run and test your stored procedure by passing in 18 hours (Figure 6.17).

```
EXEC GetLongClasses 18
```

	ClassName	ClassDurationHours
1	Difficult Negotiations	30
2	Empowering Others	18

2 rows

Figure 6.17 Skill Check 1 shows result with ClassDurationHours greater than or equal to 18.

Skill Check 2: Create a stored procedure that shows the number of products from the CurrentProducts table which are below a certain price. The variable should be called @Price and should have the data type of float. Call on the stored procedure by passing in the value of 35. When done, the result will resemble the figure shown here (Figure 6.18).

```
EXEC ShowProductsBelowPrice 35
```

	ProductName	RetailPrice
1	Ocean Cruise Tour 1 Day Mexico	32.601
2	Mountain Lodge 1 Day Scandinavia	32.574
3	Winter Tour 1 Day Scandinavia	34.506
4	Cherry Festival Tour 1 Day Mexico	31.909
5	Cherry Festival Tour 1 Day Canada	34.944

5 rows

Figure 6.18 Skill Check 2 Shows result with RetailPrice below 35.

Answer Code: The T-SQL code to this lab can be found in the downloadable files in a file named Lab6.1_StoredProcedureRecap.sql.

Points to Ponder - Stored Procedure Recap

1. A stored procedure is a named database object consisting of one or more T-SQL statements run together in a single execution.

2. A stored procedure is precompiled code that can be reused. You can also define your own custom stored procedures.

3. To run a stored procedure, use the EXECUTE PROCEDURE (or EXEC PROC) command.

4. With stored procedures, single Execution Plans are stored on the server and therefore run faster than the same statements run individually.

5. The syntax for creating a new stored procedure is CREATE PROCEDURE *sprocname* AS (The keyword PROCEDURE may be shortened to PROC).

6. Avoid naming your stored procedures with the "sp_" prefix, since you could confuse those with the built-in sprocs. Since SQL Server first searches for any sp_name in the master database, this initial search will slow down your execution of any sproc you misname as *sp_name*.

7. To modify an existing stored procedure, use the ALTER PROC statement.

8. If you want to alter an encrypted procedure, you must include the WITH ENCRYPTION statement when you run the ALTER PROC statement.

9. Use DROP PROCEDURE *sprocname* when dropping a stored proc.

10. Before you drop a stored procedure, run sp_depends to see if other objects depend on it.

11. To locate a stored procedure in Object Explorer, navigate to the "Programmability" folder of your database. You will find a "Stored Procedures" folder within the "Programmability" folder.

Stored Procedure Return Values

Up to this point in our programming journey, whenever we've performed an action, we've seen SQL Server return some form of output to one of the tabs in our query window (the data results tab, the message tab, or the spatial results tab).

After your stored procedure runs, oftentimes you will need to capture the output as a value or summary number to be supplied to your front-end application. Parameters returned by your procedure can drive application display elements (e.g., an update confirmation or a message produced by the PRINT command) and can even capture data for use by a web page.

Creating Return Values

Let's begin an example showing return values in action. Our SELECT statement shows that Alex Adams is EmpID 1 and works for ManagerID 3 (Figure 6.19).

```
SELECT *
FROM Employee
WHERE EmpID = 1
```

EmpID	LastName	FirstName	HireDate	LocationID	ManagerID	Status	HiredOffset	TimeZone
1	Adams	Alex	2001-01-01...	1	4	Active	2001-01-01...	-08:00

Figure 6.19 Alex Adams is EmpID 1 and he works for ManagerID 3.

Suppose that we want all management updates to be performed through a new stored procedure, UpdateEmployeeToNewManager. In order to update an existing employee record, this sproc requires two parameters (one for EmpID and one for ManagerID). Run this code to create the new sproc. The following code creates the UpdateEmployeeToNewManager stored procedure which updates an existing EmpID's ManagerID:

```
CREATE PROC UpdateEmployeeToNewManager @EmpID INT, @ManagerID INT
AS
UPDATE Employee SET ManagerID = @ManagerID
WHERE EmpID = @EmpID
GO
```

We want to update Alex Adams to work for ManagerID 4. We need to pass in a 1 to confirm his EmpID and a 4 to specify the new ManagerID 4. This call to the sproc should update Alex Adams to have a ManagerID of 4:

```
EXEC UpdateEmployeeToNewManager 1, 4
```

(*Note:* If you see more than one transaction confirmed ("1 row(s) affected") when you run UpdateEmployeeToNewManager, then you likely haven't run the latest setup script which disables the trigger trg_UpdEmployee.)

When we check to confirm the expected change was made, we see that yes, the Employee table now reflects Alex as working for ManagerID 4 (Figure 6.20).

```
SELECT *
FROM Employee
WHERE EmpID = 1
```

EmpID	LastName	FirstName	HireDate	LocationID	ManagerID	Status	HiredOffset	TimeZone
1	Adams	Alex	2001-01-01...	1	4	Active	2001-01-01...	-08:00

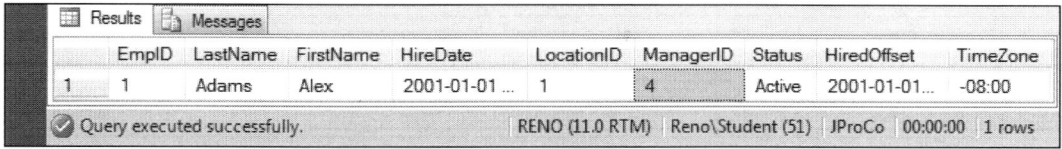

Figure 6.20 This SELECT statement confirms that Alex has a new manager.

We now want to modify our sproc to have it return the completion status with each run of the sproc. The additional code declares a new variable which is set to -1 unless a successful update occurs. The RETURN value will be -1 if no records are updated, and a 1 will indicate that at least one record is updated. This sproc returns -1 if no records are updated and 1 if at least one record is updated:

```
ALTER PROC UpdateEmployeeToNewManager @EmpID INT, @ManagerID INT
AS
DECLARE @Status INT
SET @Status = -1 --No Records Updated

UPDATE Employee SET ManagerID = @ManagerID
WHERE EmpID = @EmpID
IF(@@ROWCOUNT) > 0
SET @Status = 0
RETURN @Status
GO
```

Now we want to enhance our EXEC statement to capture the -1 or 1 value produced by the RETURN statement. The RETURN value produced by the sproc is captured and populated into the @Result variable. From there we can have our calling code take action based upon the value of @Result.

For example, this code (Figure 6.21) will print a message indicating that a change was successfully made (if the value of @Return is 1) or that no change was made (if the value of @Return is -1).

```
DECLARE @Result INT
EXEC @Result = UpdateEmployeeToNewManager 1, 3
IF @Result = -1
PRINT 'No Change was made'
ELSE
PRINT 'Update was made'
```

```
Messages
(1 row(s) affected)
Update was made
                                                    0 rows
```

Figure 6.21 Since EmpID 1 is changed back to Manager 3, the sproc returns a 1 to the calling code.

Let's test our sproc with an employee who doesn't exist (EmpID 99). The confirmation message confirms that "No change was made", so our sproc and calling code are working as expected (Figure 6.22).

```
DECLARE @Result INT
EXEC @Result = UpdateEmployeeToNewManager 99, 3
IF @Result = -1
PRINT 'No Change was made'
ELSE
PRINT 'Update was made'
```

```
Messages
(1 row(s) affected)
No Change was made
                                                    0 rows
```

Figure 6.22 There is no EmpID 99, so no records are updated and the sproc returns a -1.

Our next example uses this simple aggregate query (Figure 6.23) which returns a scalar result. The result shows us that it counts 15 employee records for LocationID 1.

```
SELECT COUNT(*)
FROM Employee
WHERE LocationID = 1
```

	(No column name)
1	15

1 rows

Figure 6.23 This simple aggregated query returns a scalar result.

Let's declare a variable called @Total to capture the output from this aggregate query. Set the variable equal to the count. For example, in this case the record count is 15, so the value of the variable here would be equal to 15.

```
DECLARE @Total INT
SELECT @Total = COUNT(*)
FROM Employee
WHERE LocationID = 1
```

Messages
Command(s) completed successfully.
0 rows

Figure 6.24 This code captures the value of 16 into the @Total variable.

The variable has been created and is capturing the amount from the aggregate query. However, in order to do something further with the result (e.g., print or display the result; provide the result as input to another function; etc.), we would need to add some more code.

Using Return Values

Let's put the code of our current query inside a new stored procedure, CountSeattleEmployees. This code adds a RETURN statement to our stored procedure, CountSeattleEmployees:

```
CREATE PROC CountSeattleEmployees
AS
DECLARE @Total INT
SELECT @Total = COUNT(*)
FROM Employee
WHERE LocationID = 1
RETURN @Total
GO
```

Let's also add a RETURN statement so our calling code can capture the value of the @Total variable (Figure 6.25). After creating the new sproc, let's execute it (Figure 6.26).

```
EXEC CountSeattleEmployees
```

Messages
Command(s) completed successfully.
0 rows

Figure 6.25 This code executes our new stored procedure, CountSeattleEmployees.

Recall that the RETURN statement simply returns the result of the stored procedure to the calling code behind the scenes. Here (Figure 6.26) it captures and returns the value of @Total, but we don't see any evidence of this because the calling code doesn't include any code which utilizes the handoff.

Let's modify our calling code to employ the information provided by the RETURN statement. We will declare a new variable called @SeattleCount and have it contain the return value from the sproc (CountSeattleEmployees). At this point, there are many things we can do with this value. Let's use a SELECT statement in order to display the value to the Results tab (Figure 6.26).

```
DECLARE @SeattleCount INT
EXEC @SeattleCount = CountSeattleEmployees
SELECT @SeattleCount
```

(No column name)
1   15

1 rows

Figure 6.26 This code shows us the scalar value 15, which is the count of Seattle employees.

Let's turn to the query currently contained in our sproc, CountSeattleEmployees. Let's change the LocationID value to 2, in order to see the count of Boston employees. We will capture the count into the variable (@Total) and then display the result to the Messages tab using a PRINT command (Figure 6.27).

```
DECLARE @Total INT
SELECT @Total = COUNT(*)
FROM Employee WHERE LocationID = 2
PRINT @Total
```

Messages
2

0 rows

Figure 6.27 This code shows us the scalar value 2, which is the count of Boston employees.

Notice that this query relies on a hardcoded value to determine which location's employee records to select. If we can modify this query to be more flexible, then we can parameterize our stored procedure and allow it to return records for any location we designate.

We will declare a new variable (@LocID) to store the LocationID value. By substituting the hardcoded value in the predicate with the variable, we can change the query output without having to alter the code inside the query. Observe that, since the variable @LocID is currently set to 2, identical results are seen in Figure 6.28 and Figure 6.29.

```
DECLARE @Total INT
SELECT @Total = COUNT(*)
FROM Employee WHERE LocationID = 2
PRINT @Total
```

Messages
2
0 rows

Figure 6.28 This query shows the number of employees from LocationID 2 by using a variable.

Now we're ready to build a parameterized stored procedure based on this query. Our query is able to work with all current and future JProCo locations, so we will name the sproc CountEmployeesByLocation. The variable @LocationID will receive the parameter passed in by the calling code. Rather than printing the value of @Total, we will use a RETURN statement to return the result to whomever is going to execute this sproc (i.e., the calling code) as seen in Figure 6.29.

```
CREATE PROC CountEmployeesByLocation @LocationID INT
AS
DECLARE @Total INT
SELECT @Total = COUNT(*)
FROM Employee WHERE LocationID = @LocationID
RETURN @Total
GO
```

Messages
Command(s) completed successfully.
0 rows

Figure 6.29 Instead of printing the output as a message, we'll return the output to the calling code.

Let's write our calling code and test it with our new parameterized sproc, CountEmployeesByLocation. We've designed our sproc to be flexible and location neutral. Let's write our calling code from the perspective of an analyst or DBA working in one of the regional offices. Rather than handling data for all of the locations, the Spokane analyst will be reporting only Spokane data. The same is true for Boston, and so forth. The calling code will pass in the value of the LocationID as a parameter, will capture the sproc result into a variable *@CityCount*, and will use a SELECT statement to show the output (Figure 6.30 and Figure 6.31).

```
DECLARE @CityCount INT
EXEC @CityCount = CountEmployeesByLocation 4
SELECT @CityCount
```

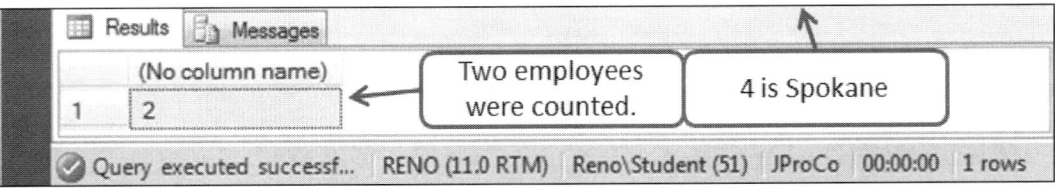

Figure 6.30 We are passing in the value 4, which is the LocationID for Spokane.

```
DECLARE @CityCount INT
EXEC @CityCount = CountEmployeesByLocation 3
SELECT @CityCount
```

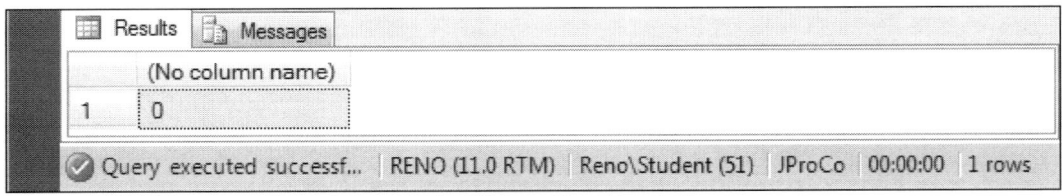

Figure 6.31 The count of employees at the Chicago location is 0.

Using Default Values

Calling this stored procedure and getting a return result works quite well, as long as we pass it the required parameter. Notice that we get an error message from SQL Server if we do not pass in a parameter (Figure 6.32).

```
DECLARE @CityCount INT
EXEC @CityCount = CountEmployeesByLocation
SELECT @CityCount
```

```
Messages
Msg 201, Level 16, State 4, Procedure CountEmployeesByLocation, Line 0
Procedure or function 'CountEmployeesByLocation' expects parameter
'@LocationID', which was not supplied.

0 rows
```

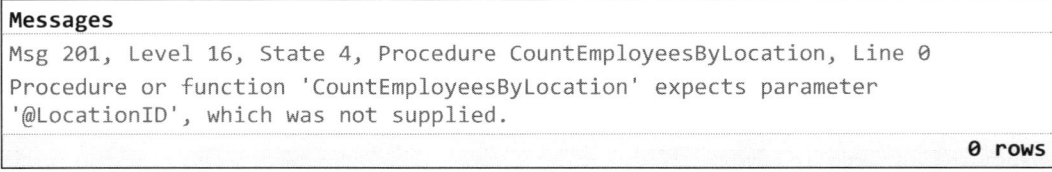

Figure 6.32 SQL Server returns an error message if no parameter is passed to the stored procedure.

Now let's return to a more typical scenario, where we assume the role of a JProCo DBA responsible for reporting data for the entire company. While we run reports for every JProCo location, most of the time we run reports involving data for just the Seattle office. Therefore, we would like the ability to have the CountEmployeesByLocation report assume the default location should be Seattle (LocationID 1), unless we specify otherwise.

The following code shows the slight adjustment to our current sproc which will supply 1 as the default value for LocationID. Compare this code with our current sproc (last seen in Figure 6.29) and notice that "=1" is the only additional code needed to specify the default value of 1. The following code uses the default LocationID of 1, which will be used if you don't pass in another parameter:

```
ALTER PROC CountEmployeesByLocation @LocationID INT = 1
AS
DECLARE @Total INT
SELECT @Total = COUNT(*)
FROM Employee WHERE LocationID = @LocationID
RETURN @Total
GO
```

Let's call on our newly revised sproc to see the default value in action. Our calling code is essentially the same as the statement which failed earlier (Figure 6.32), except that the city name has been genericized. When we run our calling code, we see the expected result of 15, since there are 15 employees in the default location (Seattle) as see n in Figure 6.33.

```
DECLARE @Count INT
EXEC @Count = CountEmployeesByLocation
SELECT @Count
```

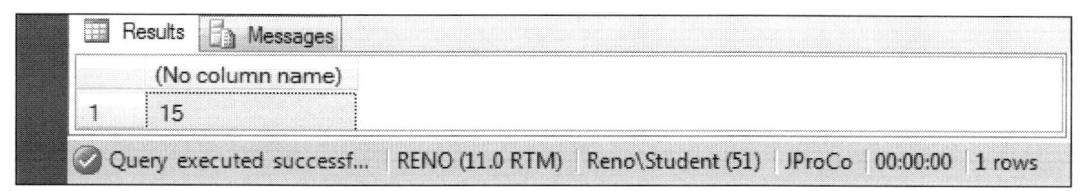

Figure 6.33 No parameter value was explicitly supplied so the default of 1 was used.

The default value is used when no parameter value is supplied. Providing a parameter value will override the default and run the sproc for the location you've designated. When we pass in a 4, the sproc returns the count of employees in the Spokane office (Figure 6.34).

```
DECLARE @Count INT
EXEC @Count = CountEmployeesByLocation 4
SELECT @Count
```

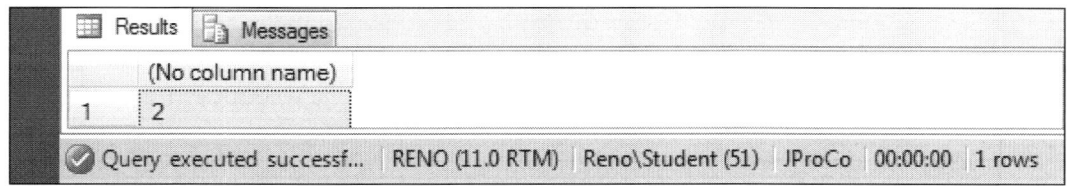

Figure 6.34 Supplying a parameter superseded the default value and caused it to not be used.

Omitting a parameter implicitly causes the sproc to use the default value. We may also choose to use the keyword DEFAULT in our calling code. It achieves the same result, yet explicitly supplying DEFAULT makes your code more readable (Figure 6.35).

```
DECLARE @Count INT
EXEC @Count = CountEmployeesByLocation DEFAULT
SELECT @Count
```

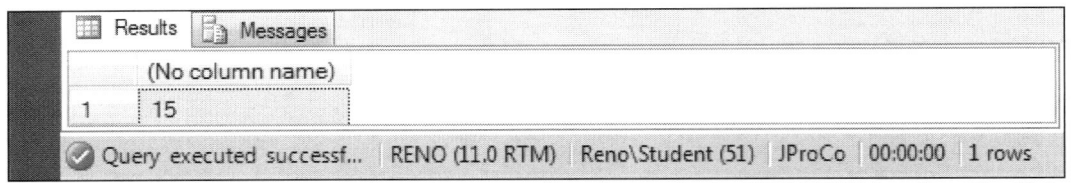

	(No column name)
1	15

Figure 6.35 An alternate way to show the count of employees in the DEFAULT location (Seattle).

Lab 6.2: Return Values

Lab Prep: Lab Prep: Each lab has one or more Skill Checks. Start with Skill Check 1 and proceed until reaching the Points to Ponder section.

Before beginning this lab, verify that SQL Server 2012 is properly installed and operating. Before running the lab setup script for resetting the database (SQLQueries2012Vol4Chapter6.2Setup.sql), please make sure to close all query windows within SSMS. An open query window pointing to a database context can lock that database preventing it from updating when the script is executing. A simple way to assure all query windows are closed, is to exit out of SSMS, then open a new instance of SSMS, and lastly run the setup script.

Skill Check 1: Create a scalar stored procedure named CountEmployeesByCityName which returns the total count of employees based on the city name. *Hint:* You will have to join two tables to get this done. Test your stored procedure by passing in the VARCHAR value of "Spokane".

```
DECLARE @SpokaneCount INT
EXEC @SpokaneCount = CountEmployeesByCityName 'Spokane'
SELECT @SpokaneCount
```

	(No column name)
1	2

1 rows

Figure 6.36 Skill Check 1.

Skill Check 2: Alter the stored procedure CountEmployeesByCityName from Skill Check 1 so that it defaults to Seattle. Test the stored procedure by using the DEFAULT keyword.

```
DECLARE @Count INT
EXEC @Count = CountEmployeesByCityName DEFAULT
SELECT @Count
```

	(No column name)
1	15

1 rows

Figure 6.37 Skill Check 2 result.

Answer Code: The T-SQL code to this lab can be found in the downloadable files in a file named Lab6.2_ReturnValues.sql.

Points to Ponder - Return Values

1. Stored procedures can run code, return a value, or do both.
2. Stored procedures can invoke all types of statements including data definition language (DDL), data manipulation language (DML) statements, and even data control language (DCL) and transaction control language (TCL) statements.
3. You may return a status value to a calling procedure or batch to indicate success or failure (and the reason for failure).
4. Stored procedures can display tables, but they can return only one value.
5. Return values are optional and you do not need to capture them during execution.
6. Return values are often used to indicate a status, such as 1 if successful and 0 if failed.
7. Once a return is executed, the stored procedure is done running.
8. To define a sproc which accepts input parameters, declare one or more variables as parameters in the CREATE PROC statement.
9. If you declare a default parameter value, then supplying a parameter becomes optiona. It is not required, but you are generally free to supply a parameter if you wish. A sproc having a default value will not prevent you from supplying a parameter.
10. There are two ways to utilize a default parameter:
    o No value is passed in.
    o The DEFAULT keyword is passed in.
11. To set a default value, include the syntax "= *value*" after the parameter declaration.

Output Parameters

RETURN statements are a great way to return data from a stored procedure to a single variable in your calling code. However, you will encounter programming situations where you need a sproc to simultaneously return data to multiple variables. In order to accomplish this, you will need to use **output parameters**.

Below is a query which returns the count of employees from Location 1, as well as the hire date for the employee who's been at Location 1 the longest. When we run this query, we see there are 16 employees, and the first Location 1 employee was hired April 1, 1989 (Figure 6.38).

```
SELECT COUNT(*), MIN(HireDate)
FROM Employee
WHERE LocationID = 1
GROUP BY LocationID
```

(No column name)	(No column name)
15	1989-04-01 00:00:00.000

1 rows

Figure 6.38 The count of Seattle employees (15) and the earliest employee's hire date (4/1/1989).

We want to build this query into a flexible stored procedure which returns data for any location you specify. We will declare a variable (@LocationID) to contain the LocationID you provide (as illustrated in Figure 6.39). You won't need to make changes to the sproc or the query – your location-specific data will be returned simply based upon the parameter value you pass into the sproc.

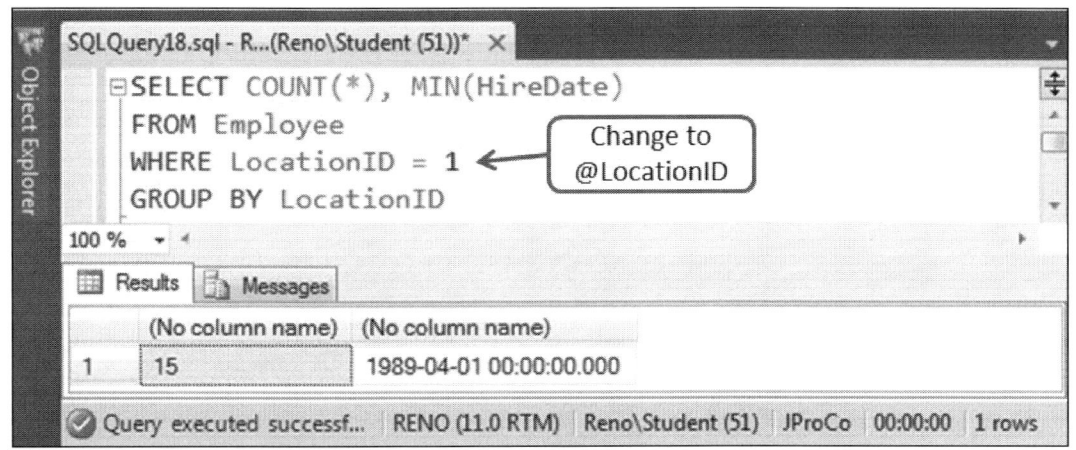

Figure 6.39 This query should accept any LocationID that you pass in.

The following statement (Figure 6.40) builds our new parameterized sproc named GetEmployeeCountAndFirstHire. We have swapped out the hardcoded value (1) for the new variable (@LocationID).

```
CREATE PROCEDURE GetEmployeeCountAndFirstHire @LocationID INT
AS
    SELECT COUNT(*), MIN(HireDate)
    FROM Employee
    WHERE LocationID = @LocationID
GO
```
Figure 6.40 Add CREATE PROCEDURE and GO statements to turn your query into this sproc.

Let's test our new sproc by passing in the value of 1. Notice that this result is identical to that shown in Figure 6.39. In other words, both the query and our new sproc return the correct data for Location 1, Seattle (Figure 6.41).

```
EXEC GetEmployeeCountAndFirstHire 1
```

	(No column name)	(No column name)
1	15	1989-04-01 00:00:00.000

1 rows

Figure 6.41 We invoke the sproc and pass in a value of 1, meaning the LocationID is 1.

Passing in a LocationID of 4 shows us there are two employees in the Spokane office, and the most senior employee was hired in 1995 (Figure 6.42).

```
EXEC GetEmployeeCountAndFirstHire 4
```

	(No column name)	(No column name)
1	2	1995-05-26 00:00:00.000

1 rows

Figure 6.42 This code executes the sproc GetEmployeeCountAndFirstHire for Location 4.

Our next goal is to re-work our sproc to include output parameters. While we haven't yet seen or worked with output parameters, we know we want multiple values to be returned to the calling code by the stored procedure.

Currently our calling code consists of just an EXEC statement (Figure 6.41-Figure 6.42). We know we will need to expand our calling code. We also need two variables to capture the results from the sproc execution: @Ct (integer) will contain the count of the employee records. @MinDate (datetime) will contain the earliest hiredate.

```
DECLARE @Ct INT
DECLARE @MinDate DATETIME
EXEC GetEmployeeCountAndFirstHire 4
    EXEC @ct = GetEmployeeCountAndFirstHire
    EXEC @MinDate = GetEmployeeCountAndFirstHire
```

Figure 6.43 A mockup of our goal: we want our calling code to receive two values from our sproc.

With a RETURN statement, we are restricted to getting back just one item at a time (either @Ct or @MinDate). But with output parameters, we can simultaneously retrieve as many values as we like.

Creating Output Parameters

With what we've learned so far, we know we can only use one return statement per stored procedure. To help illustrate this point, we've expanded our current sproc in an effort to make it produce our desired outcome. A variable has been declared for each of our required data points. However, as long as we utilize a RETURN statement, we will be limited to only capturing one value per execution of the sproc. It is not possible to use a RETURN statement within a single sproc to supply all of our needed data to our calling code.

This code cannot achieve our goal. It will get us the @LocCount but leaves us with no way to get the result of @MinDate. This stored procedure cannot achieve our goal since it is only capable of returning one of our two required values:

```
ALTER PROCEDURE GetEmployeeCountAndFirstHire @LocationID INT
AS
DECLARE @MinDate DATETIME
DECLARE @LocCount INT
SELECT @LocCount = COUNT(*), @MinDate = MIN(HireDate)
FROM Employee
WHERE LocationID = @LocationID
RETURN @LocCount
GO
```

With output parameters, you are allowed to return as many values as you need from the stored procedure. Below we have set up the calling code to capture two values from one execution of the sproc. The OUTPUT keyword is the hint that specifies that values populating these variables will come from the stored procedure. ***Don't***

run this code yet since our stored procedure is not yet ready for this syntax! This is our revised calling code. Output parameters allow you to return multiple values from a stored procedure:

```
DECLARE @Ct INT
DECLARE @MinDate DATETIME
EXEC GetEmployeeCountAndFirstHire 1,
@Ct OUTPUT, @MinDate OUTPUT
```

With our calling code perfected and ready to use (shown above – it also appears in Figure 6.45), our next task is to modify our sproc accordingly.

Notice that we have added the two parameters, their data types, and specified them as output (Figure 6.44).

```
ALTER PROCEDURE GetEmployeeCountAndFirstHire
@LocationID INT,
@CountEmp FLOAT OUTPUT,        Two output
@MinDate DATETIME OUTPUT       parameters
AS
BEGIN
    SELECT @CountEmp= COUNT(*), @MinDate = MIN(HireDate)
    FROM Employee
    WHERE LocationID = @LocationID
END
GO
```

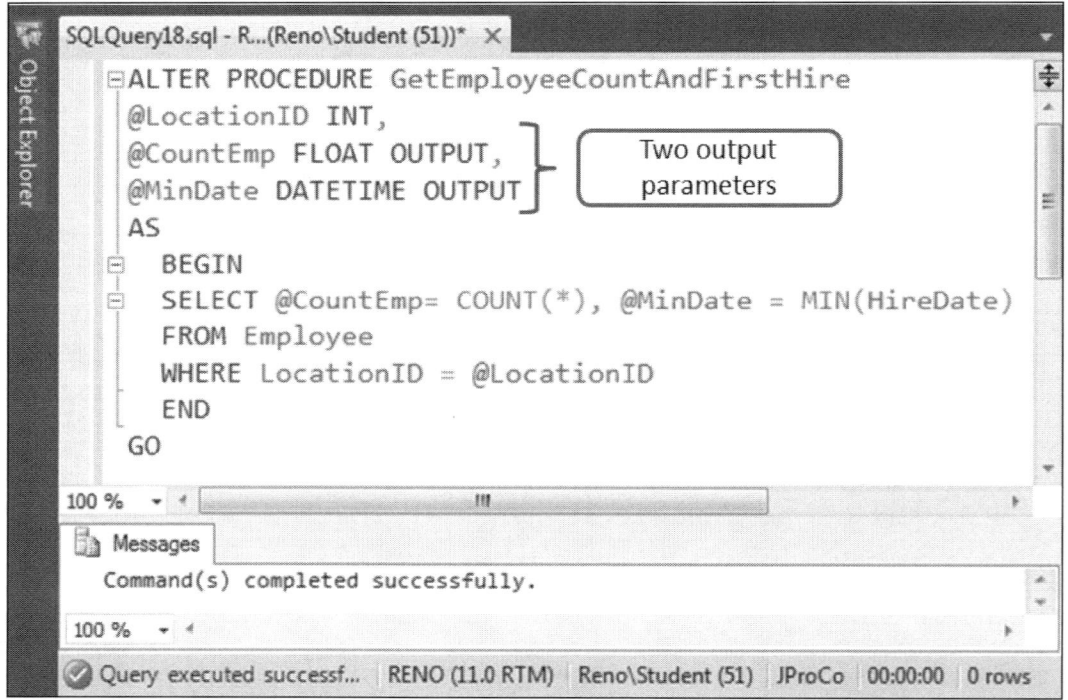

Figure 6.44 In order to modify our current sproc, run all of the code you see here.

Using Output Parameters

With output variables you can capture multiple values from one stored procedure.

Let's test our sproc to see whether our calling code can capture and use the expected values. Run all of the code you see here (Figure 6.45) to call the sproc and capture the output data.

```
DECLARE @Ct INT
DECLARE @MinDate DateTime
EXEC GetEmployeeCountAndFirstHire 1, @Ct OUTPUT, @MinDate OUTPUT

SELECT @Ct, @MinDate
```

(No column name)	(No column name)
15	1989-04-01 00:00:00.000

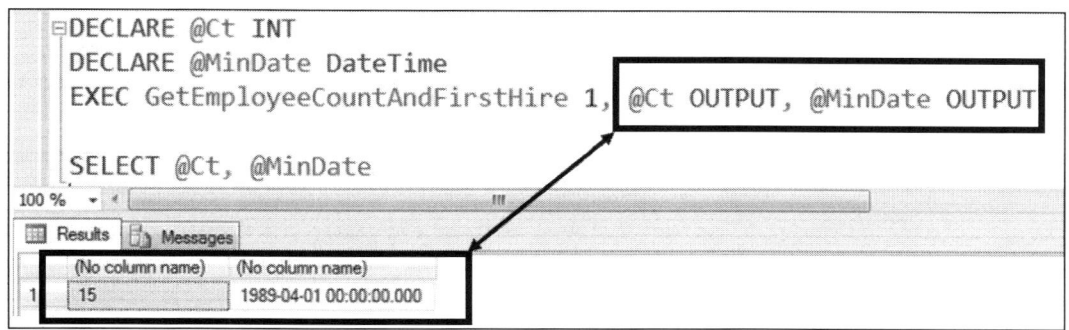

Figure 6.45 We have simultaneously captured two variables from our stored procedure.

The values supplied to our calling code may be used by other applications (e.g., a front-end application, a web page, etc.).

Let's modify our sproc again to add a third output parameter @MaxDate, which will capture the hire date of the newest employee. This code adds a third variable @MaxDate to capture data from our stored procedure:

```
ALTER PROCEDURE GetEmployeeCountAndFirstHire
@LocationID INT,
@CountEmp FLOAT OUTPUT,
@MinDate DATETIME OUTPUT,
@MaxDate DATETIME OUTPUT
AS

BEGIN
SELECT @CountEmp= COUNT(*), @MinDate = MIN(HireDate),
@MaxDate = MAX(HireDate)
FROM Employee
WHERE LocationID = @LocationID
END
GO
```

Our calling code runs the sproc for LocationID 4 (Spokane) There are currently two employees in the Spokane office. The employee who has been there the longest was hired in May 1995. The most recently hired person in the Spokane office was hired in November 2001 (Figure 6.46).

```
DECLARE @Ct INT
DECLARE @MinDate DATETIME
DECLARE @MaxDate DATETIME
EXEC GetEmployeeCountAndFirstHire 1, @Ct OUTPUT, @MinDate
OUTPUT, @MaxDate OUTPUT

SELECT @Ct, @MinDate, @MaxDate
```

	(No column name)	(No column name)	(No column name)
1	15	1989-04-01 00:00:00.000	2012-10-06 00:30:51.343

1 rows

Figure 6.46 Our calling code now gets three values from our stored procedure.

Lab 6.3: Output Parameters

Lab Prep: Lab Prep: Each lab has one or more Skill Checks. Start with Skill Check 1 and proceed until reaching the Points to Ponder section.

Before beginning this lab, verify that SQL Server 2012 is properly installed and operating. Before running the lab setup script for resetting the database (SQLQueries2012Vol4Chapter6.3Setup.sql), please make sure to close all query windows within SSMS. An open query window pointing to a database context can lock that database preventing it from updating when the script is executing. A simple way to assure all query windows are closed, is to exit out of SSMS, then open a new instance of SSMS, and lastly run the setup script.

Skill Check 1: Create a stored procedure called GetProductCountAndAvgPrice that takes a VARCHAR(100) input parameter called @CategoryID and two output parameters. One output parameter will return the count of the products. The other output parameter will return a value (Money data type) for the AveragePrice. Run and test the stored procedure with the SQL code shown in Figure 6.47.

```
DECLARE @prCt INT
DECLARE @AvgPrice MONEY
EXEC GetProductCountAndAvgPrice 'No-Stay',
@prCt OUTPUT, @AvgPrice OUTPUT
SELECT @prCt, @AvgPrice
```

(No column name)	(No column name)
1 80	78.449

1 rows

Figure 6.47 Skill Check 1 creates a stored procedure with multiple output parameters.

Answer Code: The T-SQL code to this lab can be found in the downloadable files in a file named Lab6.3_OutputParameters.sql.

Points to Ponder - Output Parameters

1. Stored procedures can use a mixture of RETURN statements and output parameters to provide data to the calling code.
2. Since they are always stored in variables, output parameters persist after procedure execution.
3. To use output parameters, you must specify the OUTPUT keyword in both the CREATE PROC and EXECUTE statements. If you don't specify a direction, then INPUT is used.
4. If the EXEC statement is missing the OUTPUT keyword, the sproc still runs but does not return the value.
5. A stored procedure may include up to 2100 parameters.
6. The RETURN statement can pass information from a sproc just like output parameters, but it is limited to one value per sproc. You can have many output parameters.
7. A stored procedure can accept parameters, produce a result set, return code, and send output parameters to the calling application.
8. SQL Server comes with many pre-defined stored procedures (called system stored procedures) for common tasks, system stored procedures begin with sp_.
9. Do not begin stored procedures that you create with "sp_". Use another unique prefix that will allow you to distinguish system stored procedures from the ones you create.
10. Common system stored procedures include:
    - sp_helpdb returns information about databases on the server.
    - sp_help returns a list of objects for the current database.
    - sp_helpindex ObjectName returns a list of indexes for the object.
11. You can only create a stored procedure in the current database context; therefore, you cannot include the USE *DatabaseName* statement inside a stored procedure.
12. If you execute a stored procedure that calls another stored procedure, the called stored procedure can access all objects created by the first (calling) stored procedure.
13. If you have permission to execute a stored procedure, you don't need permissions to the underlying tables that the stored procedure uses or modifies.

Chapter Glossary

Aggregate query: AVG(), COUNT(), MAX(), MIN(), SUM() are covered in *SQL Queries 2012 Joes 2 Pros Volume 2*.

ALTER PROC(EDURE): Statement used to revise an existing sproc.

CREATE PROC(EDURE): Statement used to create a new sproc.

DEFAULT: Optional keyword used when executing a parameterized sproc and you wish to explicitly specify that the default value will be used.

DROP PROC (EDURE): Statement used to remove a sproc from the database.

EXEC(UTE) PROC(EDURE): Command which runs the code contained within the stored procedure.

Materialized view: Indexing a view causes the view to be persistently materialized and stored in the database. In other words, the view contains a physical copy of the view data (including computations associated with joins, aggregate queries, etc.) for quicker retrieval.

OUTPUT: Keyword hint which specifies that values populating the variable(s) will come from the stored procedure.

Output parameters: Allow you to return multiple values from a stored procedure. Since they are always stored in variables, output parameters persist after procedure execution.

Parameters: Values which you pass into a sproc's variables at runtime.

Parameterized stored procedure: A stored procedure which requires values to be input into its' variable(s) at runtime.

PRINT: A statement used to print the result of a stored procedure's execution.

RETURN: A statement used to pass to the calling code the result of a stored procedure's execution.

Scalar result: Consists of a single value.

Scalar stored procedure: A sproc whose result consists of a single value.

sp_depends: A system-supplied stored procedure which returns all dependent objects for the database object specified.

sp_help: Returns a list of objects for the current database.

sp_helpdb: Returns information about databases on the server.

sp_helpindex *ObjectName*: Returns a list of indexes for the object.

Stored procedure: commonly referred to by the shorthand **sproc**. A reusable batch of code containing one or more statements (DML, DDL, TCL, or DCL). A sproc caches its' Execution Plan when it is compiled, thereby providing a performance advantage.

Review Quiz - Chapter Six

1.) Which one of the following is not a way to invoke the default parameter value?

   O a. `EXEC @Count = CountEmployeesByLocation NULL`
   O b. `EXEC @Count = CountEmployeesByLocation`
   O c. `EXEC @Count = CountEmployeesByLocation DEFAULT`

2.) You have permissions to execute a stored procedure called usp_A. Yesterday the SQL admin altered this stored procedure to call on usp_B. You do not have any permission on usp_B. The next time you call usp_A, what will the result be?

   O a. You can call usp_A but it will always fail.
   O b. You can no longer call usp_A.
   O c. You can call usp_A but will only get NULL values back from usp_B.
   O d. Usp_A will continue to work for you, just as it did before.

3.) Your stored procedure named GetEmployeeByCity has a default parameter of 'Seattle'. When you execute the stored procedure, you supply "Boston" as the parameter. What is the result of your execute statement.

   O a. Seattle will be used.
   O b. Boston will be used.
   O c. You will get an error message.

4.) You want to create all your user-defined stored procedures with the same prefix. You want to make sure your naming convention does not impose any unnecessary performance hit. Which prefix will achieve this?

   O a. `usp_SProcName`
   O b. `sp_SProcName`

5.) What is true about the type of SQL statements you can include in a stored procedure?

    O a. You can put only DML statement in a stored procedure.
    O b. You can put only DDL statement in a stored procedure.
    O c. You can put only TCL statement in a stored procedure.
    O d. You can put only DCL statement in a stored procedure.
    O e. You can put any type of SQL statement in a stored procedure.

Answer Key

1.) Using the DEFAULT keyword or leaving the value off will use the default values, so (b) and (c) are wrong. If you feed NULL in explicitly, it overrides the default. Since we are looking for the answer that does not use the default (a) is correct.

2.) If you have access to a stored procedure then you can run it even if you don't have access to the objects it is using. Therefore (d) is correct.

3.) You are allowed to override the default value with your own value without error, so (c) is incorrect. If you feed Boston in and Seattle is the default then you will get Boston, so (b) is correct.

4.) Since SQL thinks most sp_ names are system stored procedure it is better to give your user stored procedures another name. This makes (a) the correct answer.

5.) Functions can only take DML statements but stored procedures can use any type of statement. Therefore (e) is the correct answer.

Bug Catcher Game

To play the Bug Catcher game, run the file SQLQueries2012Vol4BugCatcher6.pps from the BugCatcher folder of the companion files found at www.Joes2Pros.com

[THIS PAGE INTENTIONALLY LEFT BLANK.]

Chapter 7.   Stored Procedure Techniques

As a child, the longest commute our family took was about 100 miles; it was to visit our grandparents in Skagit County. It seemed like a long drive and it took more preparation to get the family into the car than for a simple trip to the grocery store. As we would pull out of our driveway and onto Orchard Street, my father would point the car towards the nearest freeway entrance to start our long journey. My mother would diligently ask, "How are we doing on fuel?" My father would glance down at the fuel gauge to get an accurate answer and then reply.

Features like the steering wheel or brakes have a direct effect on the performance and handling of the car. The fuel gauge has no effect at all on how the car runs. Still it is very handy for knowing what is going on and making decisions on what to do next. There are some features in stored procedures that will have no effect on how they run but will be very handy to let you know what is happening or what has happened. This chapter will explore some of the most used options and techniques around stored procedures.

READER NOTE: *Please run the script SQLQueries2012Vol4Chapter7.0Setup.sql in order to follow along with the examples in the first section of Chapter 7. All scripts mentioned in this chapter may be found at **www.Joes2Pros.com**.*

Stored Procedure Execution Options

SQL Server offers several types of features and built-in options which can make your stored procedures more robust. Some of these items belong inside the stored procedure code, while others help the calling code which executes the stored procedure. This chapter will explore some built-in features you can use in conjunction with stored procedures.

Inserting Data with Stored Procedures

When using a stored procedure to insert a new record into a table, you may also need to have the sproc return a status or result to the calling code. For example, if your table contains a field with an identity counter, you may want to see what the next ID value will be. In this section, we will use the SCOPE_IDENTITY() function to accomplish these tasks.

One dictionary definition for **scope** is "range of operation". In computer programming, the term **scope** pertains to the accessibility of items (e.g., variables) within a batch of code (or module) from other other parts of the program. Think of a scope as all the things that happen within the running of a batch of code, such as a stored procedure or a function. If two different stored procedures run simultaneously, each will have its own scope. The same stored procedure run successively (i.e., run twice in a row) will have a separate scope for each run.

Let's create a sproc to add new records to the Supplier table of the JProCo database. We only need to provide two values (SupplierName, ContactFullName), since SupplierID is an identity field and automatically generates a SupplierID value for each new record (To learn more about setting the identity property for a field, see Volume 2 (*SQL Queries 2012 Joes 2 Pros Volume 2*, Chapter 3)).

```
SELECT * FROM Supplier
```

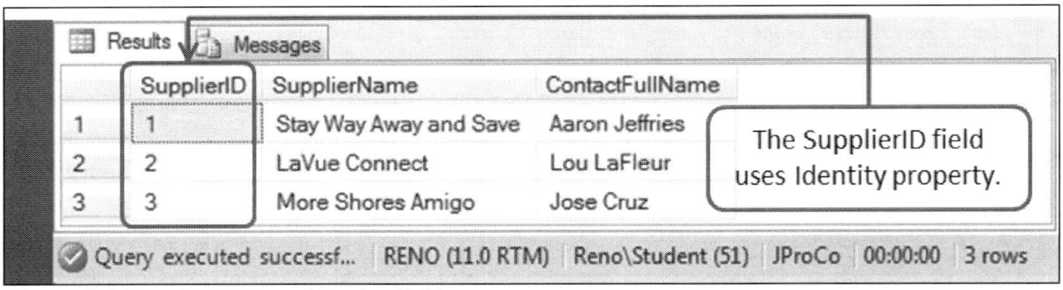

	SupplierID	SupplierName	ContactFullName
1	1	Stay Way Away and Save	Aaron Jeffries
2	2	LaVue Connect	Lou LaFleur
3	3	More Shores Amigo	Jose Cruz

The SupplierID field uses Identity property.

Figure 7.1 SupplierID is an identity field.

Thefollowing code creates the parameterized sproc, InsertOneSupplier. We will provide SupplierName and ContactFullName as parameter values to @sName and @sContact, respectively. This code creates the InsertOneSupplier stored procedure:

```
CREATE PROC InsertOneSupplier @sName VARCHAR(100), @sContact
VARCHAR(100)
AS
INSERT INTO dbo.Supplier VALUES (@sName, @sContact)
GO
```

Before executing our newly created sproc, let's look at our Supplier table (SELECT * FROM Supplier). It currently contains three records. When we run our sproc, we expect to create a fourth record for the supplier, White Elephant. We expect the next SupplierID value will be 4 (Figure 7.2).

	SupplierID	SupplierName	ContactFullName
1	1	Stay Way Away and Save	Aaron Jeffries
2	2	LaVue Connect	Lou LaFleur
3	3	More Shores Amigo	Jose Cruz
	4	White Elephant	Eric Gilman

Figure 7.2 We will insert "White Elephant" and expect the SupplierID value to be 4.

To insert a fourth record into this table, run the EXEC statement to call the stored procedure by using the following code:

```
EXEC InsertOneSupplier 'White Elephant', 'Eric Gilman'
```

```
Messages
(1 row(s) affected)
```

Figure 7.3 Calling the sproc affected 1 row and we are reasonably sure it was SupplierID 4.

Our sproc appears to have run successfully, but we can't know that for certain unless we check the table records (Figure 7.3).

Yes, our SELECT statement shows that SupplierID 4 was indeed created for our new supplier, White Elephant (Figure 7.4).

```
SELECT * FROM Supplier
```

	SupplierID	SupplierName	ContactFullName
1	1	Stay Way Away and Save	Aaron Jeffries
2	2	LaVue Connect	Lou LaFleur
3	3	More Shores Amigo	Jose Cruz
4	4	White Elephant	Eric Gilman

Figure 7.4 The "White Elephant" record has a SupplierID value of 4.

Capturing Stored Procedure Return Data

READER NOTE: The next figure is just to show you the end result but don't run it yet. We want to run this only after we have added more logic to the InsertOneSupplier stored procedure.

Our goal is to be able to see the SupplierID value at the time we insert our next supplier record (Fun and Far) by executing the sproc. We would like to capture this value into a variable, which we can use later in our program. *In other words, the goal is to have the sproc capture the value(s) from within its scope and return the value(s) to us.*

Before introducing SCOPE_IDENTITY() as a solution, let's first use what we've already learned in order to get this value to display at runtime.
We expect that Fun and Far's SupplierID will be 5 (Figure 7.5).

```
EXEC InsertOneSupplier 'Fun and Far', 'Cynthia Lee'
SELECT * FROM Supplier
```

	SupplierID	SupplierName	ContactFullName
1	1	Stay Way Away and Save	Aaron Jeffries
2	2	LaVue Connect	Lou LaFleur
3	3	More Shores Amigo	Jose Cruz
4	4	White Elephant	Eric Gilman
5	5	Fun and Far	Cynthia Lee

5 rows

Figure 7.5 When we add this supplier, we want the sproc to show us that it created SupplierID 5.

Hopefully you have not inserted Cynthia Lee into the table yet. To accomplish our goal, we will need to add a RETURN statement to the code block of our stored procedure. Our RETURN statement uses the MAX function in order to return the highest SupplierID found in the Supplier table. Use the following code to alter the InsertOneSupplier stored procedure to return the newest SupplierID:

```
ALTER PROC InsertOneSupplier @sName VARCHAR(100), @sContact
VARCHAR(100)
AS
INSERT INTO dbo.Supplier
VALUES (@sName, @sContact)
RETURN (SELECT MAX(SupplierID) FROM dbo.Supplier)
GO
```

After you run the ALTER PROC statement, let's run the calling code to execute InsertOneSupplier for Fun and Far (Figure 7.6).

We need to declare a variable (@SupplierID) to contain the value captured from the stored procedure and print that value to the screen. We expect to get "5" as the result for the newly created SupplierID.

Highlight and run the DECLARE, EXEC, and PRINT statements as one batch (as shown in Figure 7.6). Success! We see the value "5" printed along with the confirmation message (1 row(s) affected) for our inserted record.

```
DECLARE @SupplierID INT
EXEC @SupplierID = InsertOneSupplier
'Fun and Far', 'Cynthia Lee'
PRINT @SupplierID
```

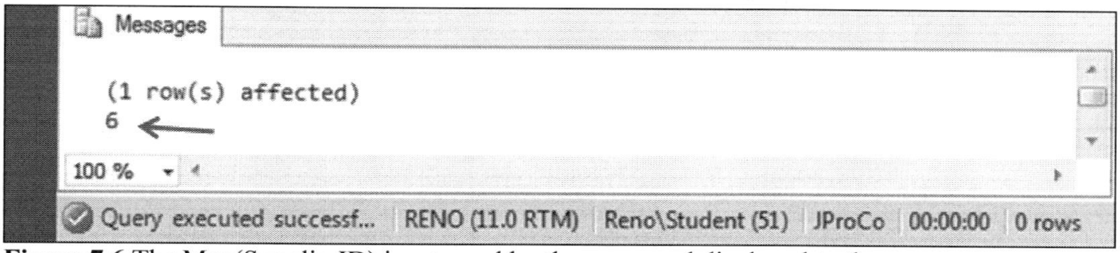

```
Messages
(1 row(s) affected)
6   ←
```

Figure 7.6 The Max(SupplierID) is returned by the sproc and displayed to the screen.

SCOPE_IDENTITY()

Let's now turn to the built-in function SCOPE_IDENTITY() and see how we can use it to accomplish our goal.

Run all of this code to change the RETURN statement to simply get the value generated by the SCOPE_IDENTITY() function:

```
ALTER PROC InsertOneSupplier @sName VARCHAR(100), @sContact VARCHAR(100)
AS
INSERT INTO dbo.Supplier
VALUES (@sName, @sContact)
RETURN
(SELECT MAX(SupplierID) FROM dbo.Supplier)
GO
```

The SCOPE_IDENTITY() function will return the value from InsertOneSupplier. Let's test our newly revised sproc, which now utilizes the SCOPE_IDENTITY() function. Using the same type of DECLARE, EXEC, and PRINT statements we used for "Fun and Far", let's add a sixth supplier record for "The World and Canada" (Run the highlighted code in Figure 7.7). Our new record is successfully inserted, and we see the new SupplierID value "6" displayed (Figure 7.8).

```
DECLARE @SupplierID INT
EXEC @SupplierID = InsertOneSupplier
'The World and Canada', 'Tim McGlade'
PRINT @SupplierID
```

```
Messages
(1 row(s) affected)
6
                                                    0 rows
```

Figure 7.7 Calling the InsertOneSupplier sproc shows the SupplierID which was generated during the scope of its execution.

Since our next example is going to accomplish our goal using a different SQL trick, let's be very clear that the SCOPE_IDENTITY() function is designed to work *inside the scope of a stored procedure*. Thus, the SCOPE_IDENTITY() function is included in the code which builds the stored procedure and captures the last identity generated during the scope of the sproc's execution. Not only is this coding easier but has a safety advantage. When you use the MAX function, you will get the highest number in the table. What if someone else is also inserting records at the same time as you, or even just a split second later? More numbers are coming into the table beyond what you have just inserted. If another insert took place after your insert but before the return result, you could get a higher number. However, SCOPE_IDENTITY() will capture just the number you inserted.

```
ALTER PROC InsertOneSupplier @sName
VARCHAR(100), @sContact VARCHAR(100)
AS
    INSERT INTO dbo.Supplier
    VALUES (@sName, @sContact)
    RETURN SCOPE_IDENTITY()
GO
DECLARE @SupplierID INT
EXEC @SupplierID = InsertOneSupplier
'The World and Canada', 'Tim McGlade'
PRINT @SupplierID
```

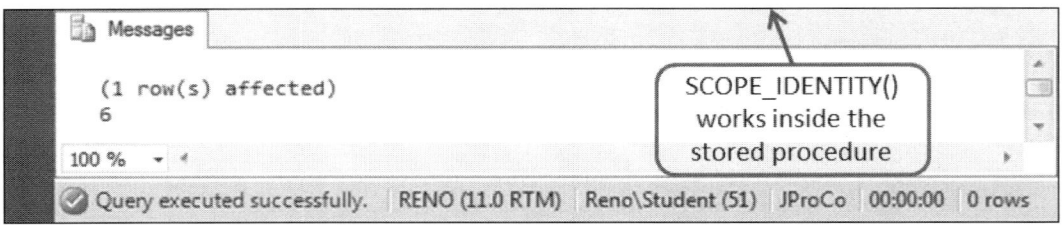

```
Messages
(1 row(s) affected)
6                                       SCOPE_IDENTITY()
                                        works inside the
100 %                                   stored procedure

Query executed successfully.  RENO (11.0 RTM)  Reno\Student (51)  JProCo  00:00:00  0 rows
```

Figure 7.8 The InsertOneSupplier stored procedure returns the value found by the SCOPE_IDENTITY() function.

@@IDENTITY

This is the IDENTITY feature developers used before the SCOPE_IDENTITY() function was introduced. Prior to SQL Server 2000, @@IDENTITY was the function available to developers for retrieving identity values.

A variable beginning with the two "at" signs (@@) is called a **global variable**. The @@IDENTITY global function works anywhere (including outside the stored proc) and tells you the most recently generated ID in your current session. In Figure 7.9, we insert a seventh supplier record and use **@@IDENTITY** to return the value of this record's SupplierID.

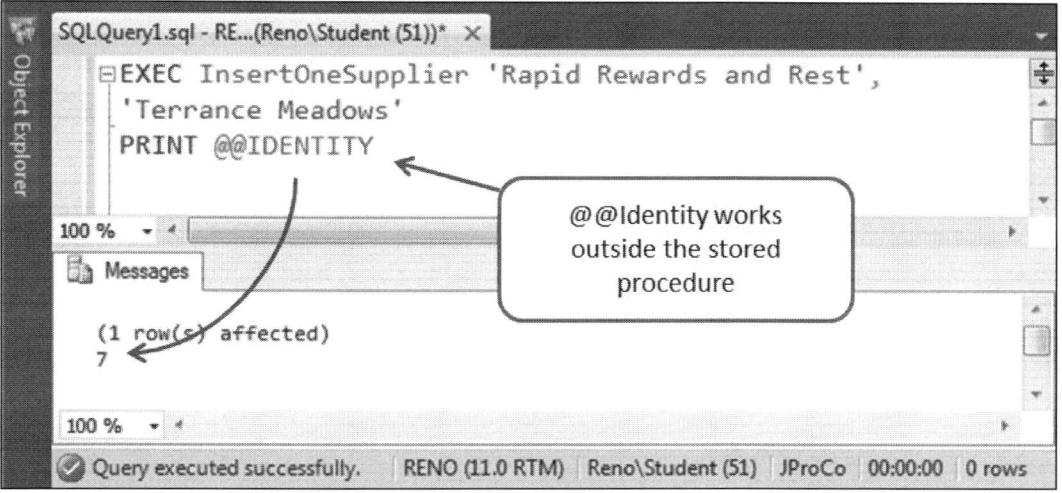

Figure 7.9 Calling on InsertOneSupplier and using @@IDENTITY to capture the return value.

The @@IDENTITY function contains the most recent value inserted into an IDENTITY column for our current connection. If there is no IDENTITY field in the current session, then our @@IDENTITY statement will return a null. If a statement inserts multiple rows, @@IDENTITY reflects the IDENTITY value for the last row inserted.

We can see that @@IDENTITY and SCOPE_IDENTITY() appear to do similar things for us. It is important to know when to use one of these functions versus the other. Keep in mind that these features have three points in common:

1) Both @@IDENTITY and SCOPE_IDENTITY() retrieve values generated within the current session. In other words, these will only work as long as IDENTITY values have been generated in the current session. If we open a new query window, neither of these features can retrieve a meaningful value.

2) We cannot specify a table with these features (Later in this section, we will look at IDENT_CURRENT which allows us to specify a table).

3) If we have a trigger that performs an insert on a table with an IDENTITY column, @@IDENTITY will return the IDENTITY column from the trigger insert, while SCOPE_IDENTITY() will return the IDENTITY column for the insert that fired the trigger.

Let's add an eighth supplier record and see what happens when we use the SCOPE_IDENTITY() function (see highlighted code in Figure 7.10). The row was affected, but the identity value didn't print out. There is no result from the function and therefore the print statement finds nothing to display.

```
EXEC InsertOneSupplier 'Water Lovers', 'Josh Walton'
PRINT SCOPE_IDENTITY()
```

Messages

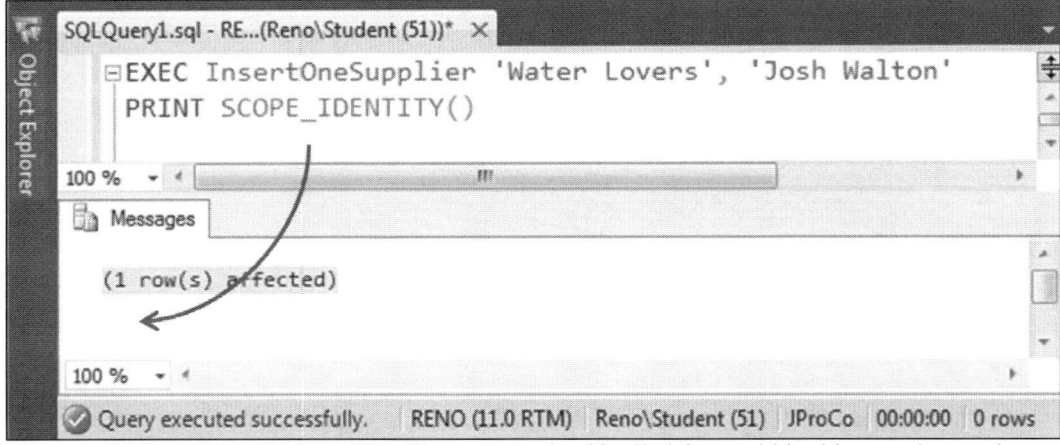

(1 row(s) affected)

Figure 7.10 SCOPE_IDENTITY() will return a value if called from within this stored procedure.

Because the scope of @@IDENTITY includes everything in the current session, it is able to display the most recently assigned IDENTITY value, which is 8.

PRINT @@IDENTITY

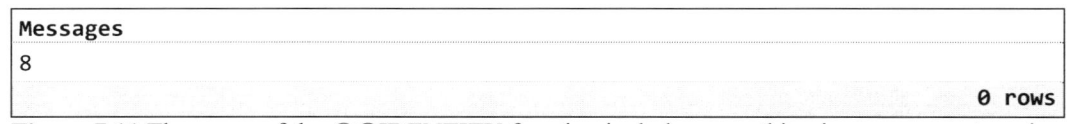

Messages
8
0 rows

Figure 7.11 The scope of the @@IDENTITY function includes everything in your current session.

```
SELECT * FROM Supplier
```

	SupplierID	SupplierName	ContactFullName
1	1	Stay Way Away and Save	Aaron Jeffries
2	2	LaVue Connect	Lou LaFleur
3	3	More Shores Amigo	Jose Cruz
4	4	White Elephant	Eric Gilman
5	5	Fun and Far	Cynthia Lee
6	6	Fun and Far	Cynthia Lee

10 rows

Figure 7.12 The eight records currently contained in the Supplier table.

IDENT_CURRENT()

Another IDENTITY function introduced in SQL Server 2000 is **IDENT_CURRENT**. This function will show the highest (i.e., most recently assigned) IDENTITY value for a table. IDENT_CURRENT() is not limited by session or scope. To demonstrate this, let's open a new query window and show the highest IDENTITY value of the two JProCo tables which contain IDENTITY fields (Figure 7.13 and Figure 7.14).

```
SELECT IDENT_CURRENT('CurrentProducts')
```

	(No column name)
1	485

1 rows

Figure 7.13 The most recently assigned ProductID value is 485. The next product inserted into the CurrentProducts table will have an IDENTITY value of 486.

```
PRINT IDENT_CURRENT('Supplier')
```

Messages
10

0 rows

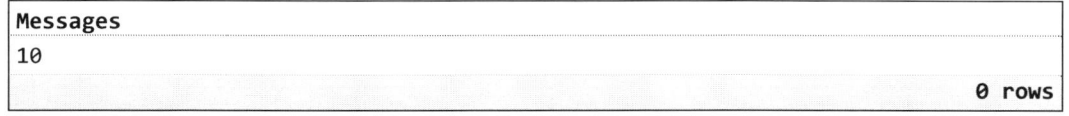

Figure 7.14 The most recently assigned SupplierID value is 9 The next supplier record inserted into this table will result in a SupplierID value of 10.

@@ROWCOUNT

What is the difference between the two similarly-named track and field events, the mile and the mile relay? They both end after 5280 feet (i.e., after one mile). In both cases, we cheer the final runner as he or she approaches the finish line. In the mile event, the person we are cheering has just run the entire mile all on his own. However, in the case of the relay race, the person we are cheering is the person on the relay team who is finishing the last part of the mile – they didn't run a whole mile. If the last record you affected was record 21, does that mean someone else did the first 20 records and you did just one more? Or did you manipulate all 21 records?

Sometimes you will want to know the last record you affected and sometimes you will want to return the count of records affected. The @@ROWCOUNT function will show you how many records were affected by the last DML statement. For example, this query will show 20 records in a result set:

```
SELECT * FROM Employee
```

You can't return 20 records from a stored procedure. Adding the @@ROWCOUNT will show you how many records the last run DML statement produced. In this case you get a scalar result of 20 from the code following code sample:

```
SELECT * FROM Employee
SELECT @@ROWCOUNT
```

Lab 7.1: Stored Procedure Options

Lab Prep: Lab Prep: Each lab has one or more Skill Checks. Start with Skill Check 1 and proceed until reaching the Points to Ponder section.

Before beginning this lab, verify that SQL Server 2012 is properly installed and operating. Before running the lab setup script for resetting the database (SQLQueries2012Vol4Chapter7.1Setup.sql), please make sure to close all query windows within SSMS. An open query window pointing to a database context can lock that database preventing it from updating when the script is executing. A simple way to assure all query windows are closed, is to exit out of SSMS, then open a new instance of SSMS, and lastly run the setup script.

Skill Check 1: Create a stored procedure called InsertOneProduct that takes 6 parameters of @ProductName NVARCHAR(MAX), @RetailPrice MONEY, @OrgDate DATETIME, @ToBeDeleted INT, @Category VARCHAR(20), @SupplierID INT and inserts these values into the CurrentProducts table. The stored procedure should return the Identity used. Test the stored procedure by using the following code. When done, the result should resemble Figure 7.15.
Note: for the OriginationOffset field, you should supply the default value.

```
DECLARE @ProdID INT
EXEC @ProdID = InsertOneProduct
'5 Day Idaho Waterpark', 1285.99,
'9/1/2011', 0,'Medium-Stay',8
PRINT @ProdID
```

```
Messages
(1 row(s) affected)
486
                                                            0 rows
```

Figure 7.15 Skill Check 1.

Skill Check 2: Create a stored procedure called UpdateEmployeeLocation that takes two integer parameters of @EmpID and @LocationID. The stored procedure(sproc) should update one record of the Employee table to the LocationID passed in to the stored procedure. The sproc UpdateEmployeeLocation should return the number of records affected. Test the code by moving EmpID 9 (James Newton) to Location #2 (Boston) and showing the return result of the sproc using the following code:

```
DECLARE @RecordCount INT
EXEC @RecordCount = UpdateEmployeeLocation 9, 2
SELECT @RecordCount
```

	(No column name)
1	1

1 rows

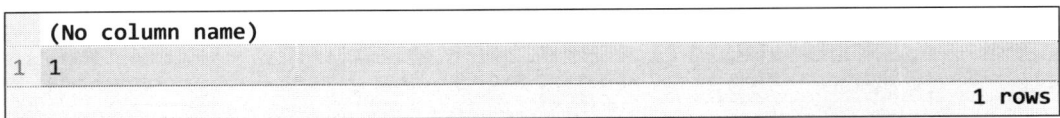

Figure 7.16 Shows result of the successful test of stored procedure @RecordCount 1 row affected.

Answer Code: The T-SQL code to this lab can be found in the downloadable files in a file named Lab7.1_StoredProcedureOptions.sql.

Points to Ponder - Stored Procedure Options

1. In computer programming, the term **scope** pertains to the accessibility of variables within a batch of code (or module) from other parts of the program.
2. SCOPE_IDENTITY and @@IDENTITY return the last identity value that is generated in any table in the current session.
3. @@IDENTITY is the older technique used by developers before the SCOPE_IDENTITY() function was created. SCOPE_IDENTITY() is much better for most programming situations, because it only handles values generated within the scope of a module or programming object (sproc, function, trigger, etc.). Global functions (e.g., @@IDENTITY) are trickier to handle.
4. IDENT_CURRENT() and SCOPE_IDENTITY() were introduced in SQL Server 2000.
5. IDENT_CURRENT() returns the last identity value generated by a specified table.
6. @@ROWCOUNT is useful for knowing how many rows were generated by the sproc.
7. The SET QUOTED_IDENTIFIER and SET ANSI_NULLS options of a sproc have the values that the database was set to at the time of the sproc creation. Those setting of the client sessions at runtime are ignored.

Table-Valued Stored procedure Parameters

Stored procedures can easily take a single parameter and use a variable to populate it. A stored procedure can readily handle two parameters in this same fashion. However, passing 1000 variables into a stored procedure would be unwieldy and would require the calling code to run 1000 times.

SQL Server offers a way to simply pass a table into a parameterized stored procedure. That's right – you can pass a table's worth of data into a single parameter and accomplish all the needed processing with just one call.

Declaring Table Types as Variables

Table type variables were introduced with SQL Server 2000 as an alternative to temp tables. A table can have as few as one and as many as 1024 fields. You can pick the field names and data types at the time you create the variable, or you can design the table before the variable is declared.

If we look at the MgmtTrainingNew table it has two records with two fields, at total of four values (Figure 7.17).

```
SELECT * FROM MgmtTrainingNew
```

	ClassName	ClassDurationHours
1	Effective Communications	35
2	Story Presentations	19

Figure 7.17 Shows the four values of the MgmtTrainingNew table.

The MgmtTrainingNew table holds a list of classes that are pending approval to be put into the MgmtTraining table. If we were to capture all this data into a variable or variables, how many would we need?

Chapter 7. Stored Procedures Techniques

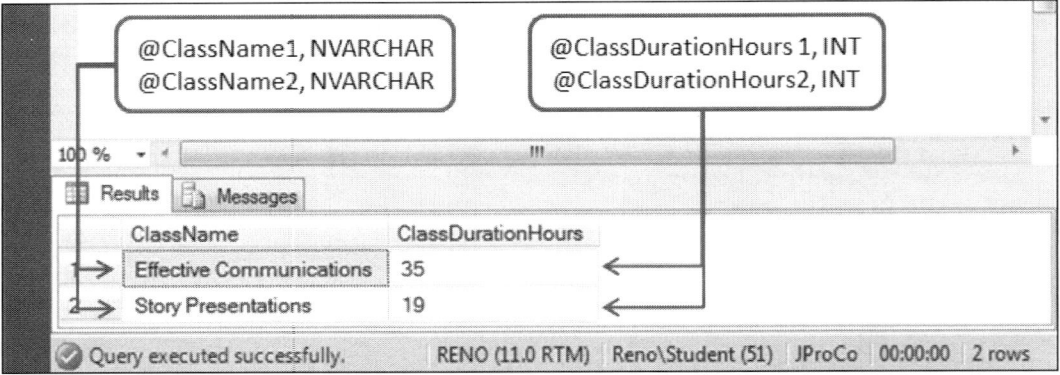

Figure 7.18 Shows the MgmtTrainingNew table has two NVARCHAR and two INT records.

It looks like we would need two NVARCHAR variables and two integer or decimal variables. There is another option. We can declare a table type as a variable that can hold all of this data and even more. Let's start by declaring the @MgmtTable as illustrated in the following code:

```
DECLARE @MgmtTable TABLE
  (ClassName VARCHAR(50) NOT NULL,
  ClassDurationHours INT NOT NULL,
  ApprovedDate DATETIME NOT NULL)
```

Notice we added a third field to hold the approved date which will be the time we run this script. The GETDATE() function will be used to populate this field. If we were to run the DECLARE statement now it would run successfully but not do much for us since it simply declares a variable. To make the DECLARE statement useful we need to set the variable. If the variable was only one value we would use the SET command. Our goal here is to put many records into the @MgmtTable variable which is a table type. The following code shows us what the records we want to pull in should look like.

```
SELECT ClassName, ClassDurationHours, GETDATE()
FROM MgmtTrainingNew
```

Figure 7.19 Shows all the data in the two records that will be put into the @MgmtTable variable.

Notice in Figure 7.19 the first two fields come from the MgmtTrainingNew table and the third expression field is to satisfy the third field we declared with the

294

www.Joes2Pros.com

variable. To set the @MgmtTable variable equal to the result in Figure 7.19 we will use the INSERT INTO command:

```
DECLARE @MgmtTable TABLE
  (ClassName VARCHAR(50) NOT NULL,
  ClassDurationHours INT NOT NULL,
  ApprovedDate DATETIME NOT NULL)

INSERT INTO @MgmtTable
SELECT ClassName, ClassDurationHours, GETDATE()
FROM MgmtTrainingNew
```

We have declared our variable @MgmtTable as a TABLE type with its fields to be congruent with the MgmtTrainingNew table. When we declared the fields of our table type we also added the ApprovedDate expression field. Using the INSERT command we set the variable equal to the MgmtTraining table with the GETDATE() date/time stamp expression field. The last step is to actually look at the variable with a SELECT statement (Figure 7.20).

```
DECLARE @MgmtTable TABLE
  (ClassName VARCHAR(50) NOT NULL,
  ClassDurationHours INT NOT NULL,
  ApprovedDate DATETIME NOT NULL)

INSERT INTO @MgmtTable
SELECT ClassName, ClassDurationHours, GETDATE()
FROM MgmtTrainingNew

SELECT * FROM @MgmtTable
```

	ClassName	ClassDurationHours	(No column name)
1	Effective Communications	35	2012-10-11 22:05:20.380
2	Story Presentations	19	2012-10-11 22:05:20.380

Figure 7.20 Shows the @MgmtTable table type variable with all the values inserted.

Declaring the table type variable and its fields is clear and easy to read. If you run this multiple times in different stored procedures, make sure the field names and field types are exactly the same. If you change one, then you need to change them all. If you use a table design many times you can save it and make all the variables using that design as a standard. The next example and explanation will show how this can be done.

Table Types

Most people today have a cell phone with a long list of contacts stored in a contact list. Do we store these numbers because we are unable to dial them manually? Many of the saved numbers in our contact list are there to save us time and to reduce the chance of a misdial. If you have a table design for a variable that is used by many stored procedures you can save your table design as a table type and really make the declare statement easy to use.

We are already familiar with data types like INT(eger), VARCHAR, and MONEY. We can also create our own user-defined types. With the new **table** data type available since SQL Server 2008, we can create a user-defined data type that is based upon a table.

Our first step in preparing our table-valued parameter demonstration is to create a **table** data type. We need to consider the fields to be included in the table which we want our stored procedure to accept, as well as the data types of these fields. Perhaps your table will look just like the Employee table. Perhaps the table this stored procedure will use is like no other table on your system. In the latter case, you don't have to create a new persistent table: you can define a table design without creating a table.

Using Table Types as Variables

After creating a new table type, our next step will be to declare a variable whose data type will be our new table type. In our previous examples, once we declare a variable, we can set it equal to a value or pass in a value. In the case of a **table** type, the value of that variable will be *a result set*.

Parameters will allow you to pass in any data type found in the database, including user-defined types. When you can create and declare a user-defined table type and pass that into a stored procedure, this is known as a **table-valued parameter**.

You can easily navigate Object Explorer to see the data types available for each of your databases. The Programmability folder of each database contains all of the system data types, as well as user-defined types. Within the System Data Types folder, you will find additional folders containing the numeric data types (exact and approximate), the character types, the date and time types, and so forth (Figure 7.21).

Chapter 7. Stored Procedures Techniques

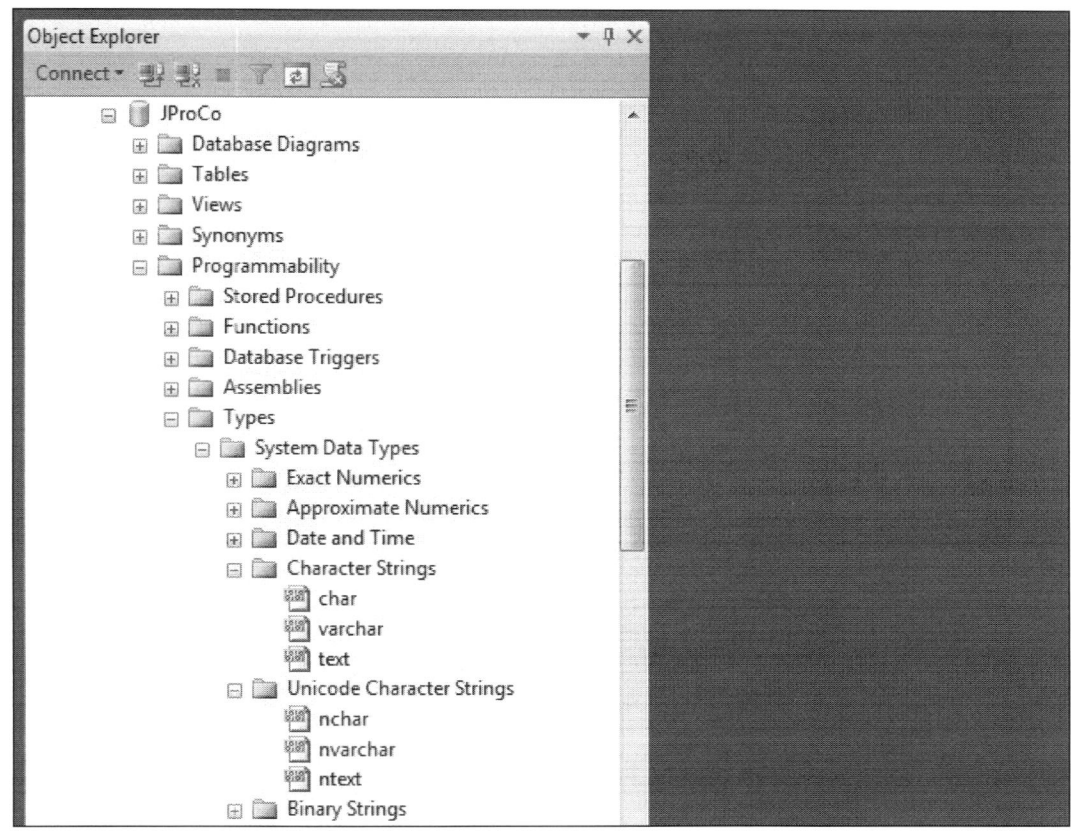

Figure 7.21 We can see all of our data types in the Object Explorer. The types we create in this section will be found in our User-Defined Table Types folder.

We will base our first example on the Grant table, which has four fields and eleven records (Figure 7.22).

```
SELECT * FROM [Grant]
```

	GrantID	GrantName	EmpID	Amount
1	001	92 Purr_Scents %% team	7	4750.00
2	002	K-Land fund trust	2	15750.00
3	003	Robert@BigStarBank.com	7	18100.00
4	005	BIG 6's Foundation%	4	22000.00
5	006	TALTA_Kishan International	3	18100.00
6	007	Ben@MoreTechnology.com	10	42000.00

11 rows

Figure 7.22 The Grant table has four fields.

The two fields from the Grant tabel we want are highled in the result set in Figure 7.23. The first table type we will define will be called GrantTableType. It will be based upon two fields of the Grant table, GrantName and Amount (Figure 7.23). The code to accomplish this is shown here.

```
CREATE TYPE GrantTableType AS TABLE
(GrantName VARCHAR(50) NOT NULL,
Amount SMALLMONEY NULL)
GO
```

	GrantID	GrantName	EmpID	Amount
1	001	92 Purr_Scents %% team	7	4750.00
2	002	K-Land fund trust	2	15750.00
3	003	Robert@BigStarBank.com	7	18100.00
4	005	BIG 6's Foundation%	4	22000.00
5	006	TALTA_Kishan International	3	18100.00
6	007	Ben@MoreTechnology.com	10	42000.00

11 rows

Figure 7.23 The GrantTableType is created with two fields.

After you run this code and create this new type, locate GrantTableType in Object Explorer (Figure 7.24). Traverse to JProCo > Programmability > Types > User-Defined Table Type > dbo.GrantTableType.

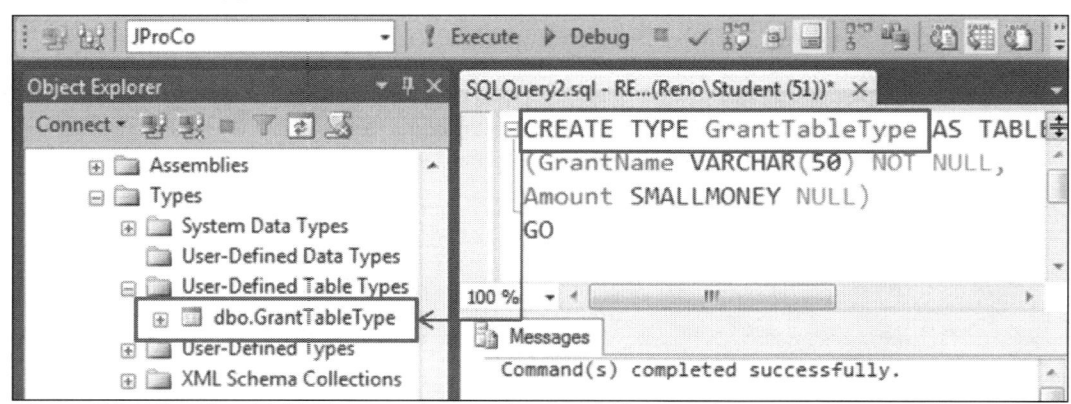

Figure 7.24 The GrantTableType can be seen in your Object Explorer.

Now let's declare a variable (@GrantTVP) whose data type is GrantTableType (i.e., our newly created table type). After we declare the variable, we will insert some data into it. Looking at the SELECT statement, we know this will bring in two fields and eleven records from the Grant table (Figure 7.25).

```
DECLARE @GrantTVP AS GrantTableType
INSERT INTO @GrantTVP
SELECT GrantName, Amount
FROM [Grant]
```

```
Messages
(11 row(s) affected)
```
0 rows

Figure 7.25 The GrantTableType variable @GrantTVP is declared and filled with 11 records from the Grant table.

The confirmation message tells us that our @GrantTVP variable has been populated with 11 rows (Figure 7.25). Notice that we get an error message if we attempt to query from @GrantTVP (Figure 7.26).

```sql
SELECT * FROM @GrantTVP
```

```
Messages
Msg 1087, Level 15, State 2, Line 1
Must declare the table variable "@GrantTVP".
```
0 rows

Figure 7.26 Trying to simply query from @GrantTVP throws an error message.

The error message we get from SQL Server hints that we need to declare the table variable (Figure 7.27). In order to see our intended data, we must declare our variable, fill it with data, and select from it all at once as shown in Figure 7.27.

```sql
DECLARE @GrantTVP AS GrantTableType
INSERT INTO @GrantTVP
SELECT GrantName, Amount
FROM [Grant]
SELECT * FROM @GrantTVP
```

	GrantName	Amount
1	92 Purr_Scents %% team	4750.00
2	K-Land fund trust	15750.00
3	Robert@BigStarBank.com	18100.00
4	BIG 6's Foundation%	22000.00
5	TALTA_Kishan International	18100.00
6	Ben@MoreTechnology.com	42000.00

11 rows

Figure 7.27 Run all of the code shown here in order to select from the table-valued parameter.

So what's the advantage of using a table type? To answer that question, let's first take a look at some familiar tables and their limitations. The MgmtTraining table, contains the approved list of classes for JProCo's managers (Figure 7.28).

```
SELECT * FROM MgmtTraining
```

	ClassID	ClassName	ClassDurationHours	ApprovedDate
1	1	Embracing Diversity	12	2007-01-01...
2	2	Interviewing	6	2007-01-15...
3	3	Difficult Negotiations	30	2008-02-12...
4	4	Empowering Others	18	2012-10-06...
5	8	Passing Certifications	13	2012-10-06...

5 rows

Figure 7.28 The MgmtTraining table contains the list of approved classes.

The MgmtTrainingNew table contains the list of classes we intend to approve soon. Currently there are only two fields and two records in the MgmtTrainingNew table (Figure 7.29).

```
SELECT * FROM MgmtTrainingNew
```

	ClassName	ClassDurationHours
1	Effective Communications	35
2	Story Presentations	19

2 rows

Figure 7.29 The MgmtTrainingNew table has two fields.

Table-Valued Parameters

Once a class from the MgmtTrainingNew table is approved, that class record must be placed in the MgmtTraining table. Now let's think about how we would add these two records using a stored procedure. Would we run the stored procedure twice (i.e., once for each record)? A better choice would be to pass the entire MgmtTrainingNew table into a stored procedure and have that stored procedure populate the MgmtTraining table.

We're going to pass in a value to our parameter @TableName and then use that parameter in the logic of our stored procedure. Notice that we get an error message when we attempt this (Figure 7.30). We cannot pass in a table, but one of the messages hints that we can pass in a type.

```
CREATE PROCEDURE AddNewTraining @TableName TABLE
AS
INSERT INTO dbo.MgmtTraining
(ClassName, ClassDurationHours, ApprovedDate)
SELECT mt.ClassName, mt.ClassDurationHours, GETDATE()
FROM @TableName AS mt
GO
```

```
Messages
Msg 156, Level 15, State 1, Procedure AddNewTraining, Line 1
Incorrect syntax near the keyword 'TABLE'.
Msg 1087, Level 15, State 2, Procedure AddNewTraining, Line 6
Must declare the table variable "@TableName".

                                                              0 rows
```

Figure 7.30 A table cannot be passed into a stored procedure but a type can.

Let's add a statement to create a type (MgmtTrainingType). Notice that we must add the type to the code of our sproc. When passing in a table type, you must set it to READONLY. The code to create the type and use it in the sproc follows:

```
CREATE TYPE MgmtTrainingType AS TABLE
(ClassName VARCHAR(50) NOT NULL,
ClassDurationHours INT NULL)
GO

CREATE PROCEDURE AddNewTraining @TableName MgmtTrainingType
READONLY
AS
INSERT INTO dbo.MgmtTraining (ClassName, ClassDurationHours,
ApprovedDate)
SELECT mt.ClassName, mt.ClassDurationHours, GETDATE()
FROM @TableName AS mt
GO
```

We will declare a variable named @ClassTVP using the table type (MgmtTrainingType) we created earlier. This table-type variable (@ClassTVP) is then populated with records from the MgmtTrainingNew table. We then can call upon the stored procedure AddNewTraining and pass this variable into the table-valued parameter (Figure 7.31).

```
DECLARE @ClassTVP AS MgmtTrainingType;
INSERT INTO @ClassTVP
SELECT ClassName, ClassDurationHours
FROM MgmtTrainingNew
EXEC AddNewTraining @ClassTVP
```

```
Messages
(2 row(s) affected)
(2 row(s) affected)
(2 row(s) affected)

                                                              0 rows
```

Figure 7.31 The @ClassTVP variable is populated and passed into the AddNewTraining stored procedure as a parameter.

Chapter 7. Stored Procedures Techniques

Let's run a query on the MgmtTraining table and check to see whether the new class records appear. Success! Both of the new records now show up in the MgmtTraining table (Figure 7.32).

```
SELECT * FROM MgmtTraining
```

	ClassID	ClassName	ClassDurationHours	ApprovedDate
2	2	Interviewing	6	2007-01-15...
3	3	Difficult Negotiations	30	2008-02-12...
4	4	Empowering Others	18	2012-10-06...
5	8	Passing Certifications	13	2012-10-06...
6	9	Effective Communications	35	2012-10-06...
7	10	Story Presentations	19	2012-10-06...

7 rows

Figure 7.32 Two records were successfully added to the MgmtTraining table.

Lab 7.2: Table-Valued Stored Procedure Parameters

Lab Prep: Lab Prep: Each lab has one or more Skill Checks. Start with Skill Check 1 and proceed until reaching the Points to Ponder section.

Before beginning this lab, verify that SQL Server 2012 is properly installed and operating. Before running the lab setup script for resetting the database (SQLQueries2012Vol4Chapter7.2Setup.sql), please make sure to close all query windows within SSMS. An open query window pointing to a database context can lock that database preventing it from updating when the script is executing. A simple way to assure all query windows are closed, is to exit out of SSMS, then open a new instance of SSMS, and lastly run the setup script.

Skill Check 1: Create a table type named GrantType which has an identical structure to the Grant table. When complete, verify the new type exists in SQL Server Management Studio Object Explorer. The Object Explorer tree should match that shown in Figure 7.33.

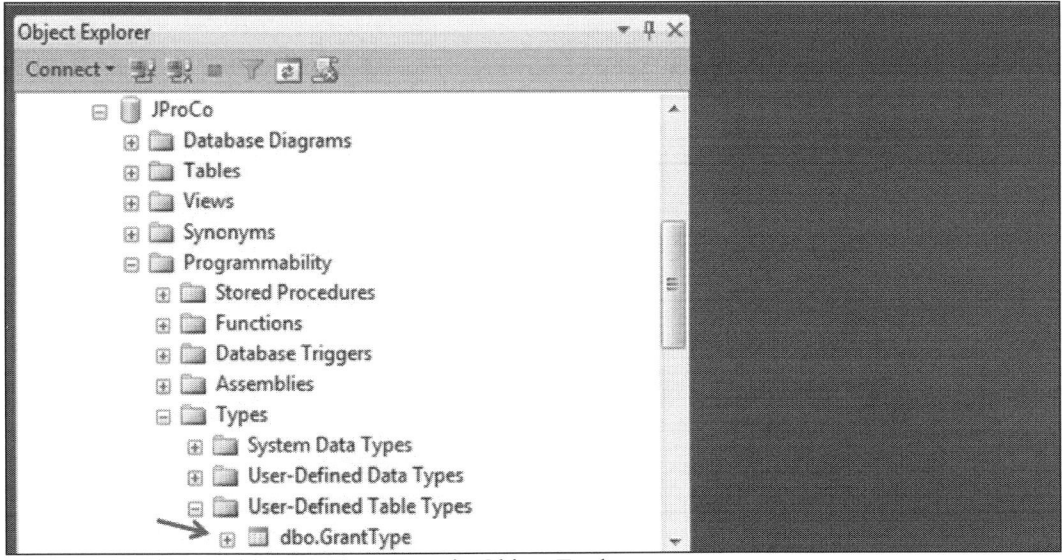

Figure 7.33 Shows table type GrantType in Object Explorer.

Skill Check 2: Create a sproc called AddNewGrants, which accepts a parameter called @TVP which is of the GrantType type created in the last Skill Check and populates all records in the grant table. Test the sproc by using the following code. Your result should resemble Figure 7.34.

```
DECLARE @GrantTVP as GrantType;
INSERT INTO @GrantTVP
VALUES
('013','Hope Reaches',7,29000),
('014','Everyone Wins',4,12500)
EXEC AddNewGrants @GrantTVP

SELECT * FROM @GrantTVP
```

	GrantID	GrantName	EmpID	Amount
1	013	Hope Reaches	7	29000.00
2	014	Everyone Wins	4	12500.00

2 rows

Figure 7.34 Skill Check 2.

Answer Code: The T-SQL code to this lab can be found in the downloadable files in a file named Lab7.2_TableValuedStoredProcedures.sql.

Points to Ponder - Table-Valued Stored Procedures

1. Table-valued parameters are new since SQL Server 2008.
2. Table-valued parameters are a great way to pass in multiple rows of data at once, instead of just one value at a time.
3. To declare table type variables, you must use user-defined table types.
4. You create a table as a data type and then you can create a parameter that refers to that type.
5. The type will exist in your database until you explicitly drop it.
6. After you create the table variable, you fill it with data by using an INSERT statement.
7. You must fill your table variable before passing it in as a parameter.
8. When used with stored procedures and other SQL routines, table-valued parameters must be passed in as READONLY.

9. Once the type is created, you can reuse the type with other DECLARE statements.

10. You create table-value variables as you do other local variables (i.e., create them using a DECLARE statement).

Chapter Glossary

@@IDENTITY: A global function which returns the last identity value generated within a session; used by developers prior to the inception of the newer function, SCOPE_IDENTITY().

@@ROWCOUNT: Returns the number of rows generated by a sproc.

Global variable: A variable whose scope is global and which begins with two "at" signs (@@).

IDENT_CURRENT(): Returns the last identity value generated by a specified table.

READONLY: Keyword used with stored procedures and other SQL routines; table-valued parameters must be passed in as READONLY.

Scope: "Range of operation"; think of a scope as all things that happen within the running of a batch of code, such as a stored procedure or a function.

SCOPE_IDENTITY(): Function which returns the last identity value generated within a batch.

Scalar stored procedure: A sproc whose result consists of a single value.

Table-valued parameter: A variable whose data type is table.

Review Quiz – Chapter Seven

1.) What does the SCOPE_IDENTITY() function do?

   O a. It gets the most recently generated identity value from inside the stored procedure.
   O b. It gets the most recently generated identity value from code calling the stored procedure.
   O c. It gets the next identity value from inside the stored procedure.
   O d. It gets the next identity value from code calling the stored procedure.

2.) What is the difference between SCOPE_IDENTITY() and @@IDENTITY?

   O a. SCOPE_IDENTITY() only works inside the stored procedure.
   O b. SCOPE_IDENTITY() only works with code which calls on the stored procedure.
   O c. SCOPE_IDENTITY() shows the most recent number, whereas @@Identity shows the next number.

3.) What are two advantages of running code inside a stored procedure versus running the same code in an ad hoc fashion? (Choose two)

   □ a. Cached plans can increase SQL performance.
   □ b. It's easier to call upon a stored procedure than to have to re-type or re-open a script.
   □ c. Stored procedures allow you to join more tables in a single query than ad hoc code.
   □ d. Running code explicitly does not allow you to mix DML and DDL statements within a single execution.

4.) Before you can create a table-valued stored procedure, what must you first do?

   O a. Execute the stored procedure.
   O b. Qualify the table with a schema.
   O c. Create a persistent table.
   O d. Create a table data type.
   O e. Create a view.

5.) You have the following code:

```
CREATE PROC AddNewGrants @TVP GrantType
AS
INSERT INTO dbo.[Grant]
(GrantID, GrantName, EmpID, Amount)
SELECT GrantID, GrantName, EmpID, Amount
FROM @TVP
GO
```

You have verified that the GrantType was created and the fields match. What do you need to do to make the code work?

O a. Add READONLY after the GO.

O b. Add READONLY after the type.

O c. Add READONLY after the grant table.

O d. Add READONLY after the FROM clause.

6.) You need to create a stored procedure which accepts a table-valued parameter named @Suppliers. What code will achieve this result?

O a. `CREATE PROCEDURE AddSuppliers`
   `@Suppliers FLOAT READONLY`

O b. `CREATE PROCEDURE AddSuppliers`
   `@Suppliers INT READONLY`

O c. `CREATE PROCEDURE AddSuppliers`
   `@Suppliers MONEY READONLY`

O d. `CREATE PROCEDURE AddSuppliers`
   `@Suppliers SupplierType READONLY`

O e. `CREATE PROCEDURE AddSuppliers`
   `@Suppliers Geography READONLY`

Answer Key

1.) SCOPE_IDENTITY() gets the most recent (not the next) id, so (c) and (d) are incorrect. SCOPE_IDENTITY() only works inside the stored procedure, so (a) is the correct answer.

2.) @@IDENTITY works at any scope level but SCOPE_IDENTITY() only works inside the stored procedure, so (a) is the correct answer.

3.) There is no limit to how many tables you can join inside of or outside of a stored procedure, so (c) is incorrect. Both a Script and a stored procedure can use a mixture of DML and DDL, so (d) is incorrect. Stored procedures are saved to SQL and easy to call on plus they remember Execution Plans, making (a) and (b) correct.

4.) You can't execute a stored procedure before you create it, so (a) is incorrect. Stored procedures take parameters and each parameter needs a data type. If you need to pass it a table, then you need a table type, making (d) the correct answer.

5.) You never specify an option for a stored procedure after the GO, so (a) is incorrect. Each parameter has its own name, type and optional specifier, so (b) is the correct answer.

6.) FLOAT, INT, and MONEY are value data types, so (a), (b), and (c) are incorrect. GEOGRPAHY holds a point or shape on the earth and not a table, making (e) incorrect. SupplierType is a possible name to give to a user supplies table type, making (d) is the only possible correct answer.

Bug Catcher Game

To play the Bug Catcher game, run the file SQLQueries2012Vol4BugCatcher7.pps from the BugCatcher folder of the companion files found at www.Joes2Pros.com.

[THIS PAGE INTENTIONALLY LEFT BLANK.]

Chapter 8.   String Functions

We first encountered string data in Volume 1 when we studied string patterns relating to the art of wildcard searching. When you work in the data world, you'll encounter some unusual things that you need a string function to accomplish. Your ability to use tricks like those shown in this chapter not only are timesavers but are skills which differentiate Joes from Pros – the ones who know about the power of SQL Server and have invested the time to become experts at harnessing that power in their database work. Joining the ranks of those who have prepared for – and passed – the SQL certification exam puts you in a special category and shows your serious intent to master SQL Server.

In this chapter we will also look at some of the system supplied functions included in SQL Server. I thought about these handy system supplied functions on a recent visit to the used bookstore. I asked what they would give me for a book I had just finished reading. This is an example where they could not return the information without some input from me. They were only able to tell me the value after I handed them the book, so they could look at its condition and what type of book it was. A few minutes earlier, I noticed a fellow shopper was wearing a watch and I asked him what time it was. He told me 3:15 p.m. without needing any information from me.

SQL Server's system supplied functions can provide you a fair amount of data. Some "time" functions can tell you what time it is without needing you to supply an input. Other system functions can provide metadata (e.g., which user created a table), but they first need you to supply some input.

READER NOTE: *Please run the script SQLQueries2012Vol4Chapter8.0Setup.sql in order to follow along with the examples in the first section of Chapter 8. All scripts mentioned in this chapter may be found at* ***www.Joes2Pros.com***.

Basic String Functions

Functions always do or return something. When you send data into a function, it does its work and then sends you back some information. In the case of string functions, they usually return a string and supply it to an expression or another function. There are also functions which tell you something about the string. Strings are made up of character data. The first function we will look at is LEN ( ), which counts the characters inside a string.

Using LEN()

Since we're focusing on string functions, let's begin with some string-related data like FirstName and LastName. In the Employee table, we can see there are varying lengths of data, e.g., the name "Alex" is 4 letters long, "Lee" is 3 letters long, "Barbara" is 7 letters long, and so forth.

```
SELECT FirstName, LastName
FROM Employee
```

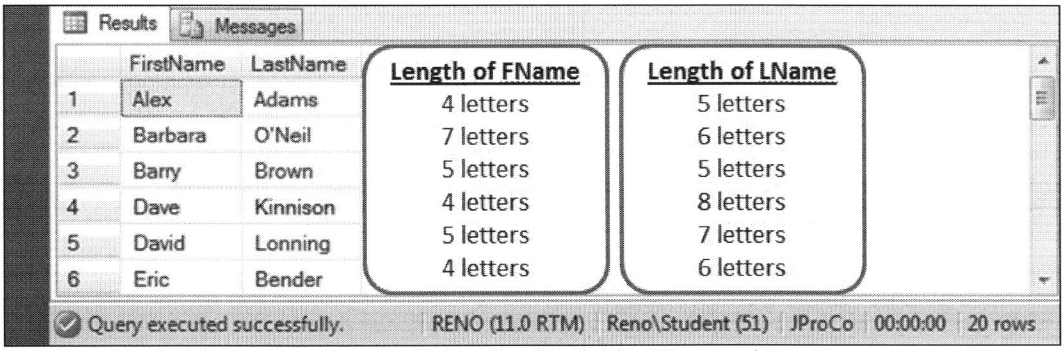

	FirstName	LastName	Length of FName	Length of LName
1	Alex	Adams	4 letters	5 letters
2	Barbara	O'Neil	7 letters	6 letters
3	Barry	Brown	5 letters	5 letters
4	Dave	Kinnison	4 letters	8 letters
5	David	Lonning	5 letters	7 letters
6	Eric	Bender	4 letters	6 letters

Query executed successfully. RENO (11.0 RTM) | Reno\Student (51) | JProCo | 00:00:00 | 20 rows

Figure 8.1 LEN() is used to measure the length of each FirstName and LastName.

But instead of counting letters manually, we can have SQL Server do it for us. Let's add the function LEN() to measure the length of each name (Alias the new expressions as FNameSize and LNameSize).

```
SELECT FirstName, LastName, LEN(FirstName) AS FNameSize,
LEN(LastName) AS LNameSize
FROM Employee
```

	FirstName	LastName	FNameSize	LNameSize
1	Alex	Adams	4	5
2	Barbara	O'Neil	7	6
3	Barry	Brown	5	5
4	Dave	Kinnison	4	8
5	David	Lonning	5	7
6	Eric	Bender	4	6

20 rows

Figure 8.2 The LEN() function measures the length of each name.

We can add AVG(), MAX(), and MIN() to see some summary information about JProCo's name data. For example, our shortest first name is three characters ("Lee"). Our last names range from five to 12 characters ("Smith" and "Wilconkinski", respectively) with an average of six characters.

```
SELECT
AVG (LEN (FirstName)) AS AvgFName,
AVG (LEN (LastName)) AS AvgLName,
MAX (LEN (FirstName)) AS LongestFName,
MAX (LEN (LastName)) AS LongestLName,
MIN (LEN (FirstName)) AS ShortestFName,
MIN (LEN (LastName)) AS ShortestLName
FROM Employee
```

	AvgFName	AvgLName	LongestFName	LongestLName	ShortestFName	ShortestLName
1	4	6	7	12	3	3

1 rows

Figure 8.3 The employee last names range from five ("Smith") to 12 letters ("Wilconkinski").

Returning Parts of Strings

Several functions can help you search within a string and return just part of the string. Examples of these are LEFT(), RIGHT(), and SUBSTRING().

```
-- go to the left edge of the string,
-- show just the first 3 characters found
SELECT LEFT ('Joes2Pros', 3)

-- go to the right edge of the string,
-- show just the last 5 characters found
SELECT RIGHT ('Joes2Pros', 5)
```

	(No column name)
1	Joe

	(No column name)
1	2Pros

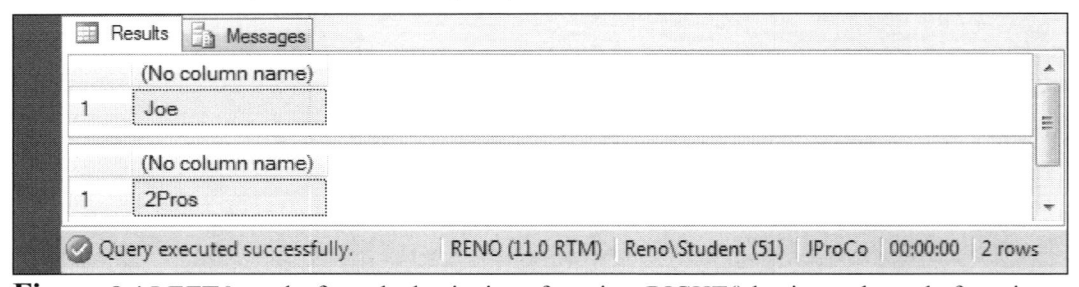

Query executed successfully.   RENO (11.0 RTM) Reno\Student (51) JProCo 00:00:00 2 rows

Figure 8.4 LEFT() works from the beginning of a string, RIGHT() begins at the end of a string.

Now let's look at the first employee, Alex. The first two letters of his name are "A-L". From what we've learned, we know LEFT(FirstName, 2) would return "Al" as a result. RIGHT(FirstName, 3) for Alex would return the result "lex".

Chapter 8. String Functions

```
SELECT FirstName, LastName,
LEFT(FirstName, 2), RIGHT(FirstName, 3)
FROM Employee
```

FirstName	LastName	(No col…	(No column name)
Alex	Adams	Al	lex
Barbara	O'Neil	Ba	ara
Barry	Brown	Ba	rry
Dave	Kinnison	Da	ave
David	Lonning	Da	vid
Eric	Bender	Er	ric

20 rows

Figure 8.5 The LEFT() and RIGHT() functions are demonstrated.

Lee's result may look a little odd, but the function RIGHT() returned just what we asked for…"L-e-e" are indeed the last three letters of his name.

You may be wondering why the string functions LEFT() and RIGHT() display in grey lettering, rather than the fuschia pink lettering of other functions we've studied. This is simply due to the fact that LEFT and RIGHT are reserved words SQL Server uses in other contexts (e.g., RIGHT and LEFT joins)

Ok, we've taken characters from the beginning and the end of a string. Now let's pull out letters from the middle of a string using the SUBSTRING() function. With SUBSTRING(), you have to specify where you want the function to start and how far to go. Let's tell SUBSTRING() to begin with the second letter of each first name (2) and retrieve three characters (3).

```
SELECT FirstName, SUBSTRING(FirstName, 2, 3)
FROM Employee
```

	FirstName	(No column name)
1	Alex	lex
2	Barbara	arb
3	Barry	arr
4	Dave	ave
5	David	avi
6	Eric	ric

20 rows

Figure 8.6 SUBSTRING (FirstName, 2, 3) begins at the second letter and returns 3 characters.

SUBSTRING() did the same for each name. It went to the second letter of each name, counted three characters, and returned those to us in our result. It performed the same task for each name. Note that SUBSTRING() returned just two letters for Lee.

Now let's have this function customize each result according to the length of each name. We will have SUBSTRING() return just the middle letters from each name – *we don't want to see the first letter or the last letter.* Let's think about how to accomplish this. Each name contains a different number of characters – Lee has three characters, and Barbara has seven – so we need our code to adjust to the varying length of each name.

Without the beginning and ending letters, the middle of Lee's name is "e", just one letter. Without her beginning and ending letters (B, a), the middle of Barbara's name is "arbar", five letters long. Mathematically, it appears if we subtract 2 (for two letters) from the total length of each name, we get the number of letters in the middle. Thus, SUBSTRING() needs to know what quantity is represented by LEN(FirstName), in order to subtract 2 from it. We then can have SUBSTRING() begin at the second letter of each name and count over [LEN(FirstName)-2] characters.

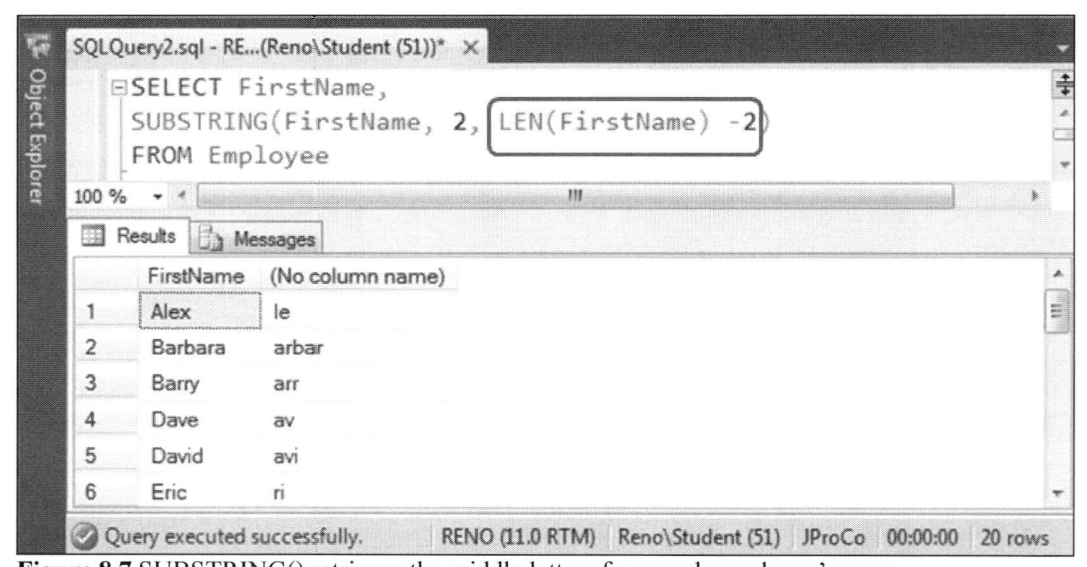

Figure 8.7 SUBSTRING() retrieves the middle letters from each employee's name.

And we see the expected result – we have the middle five letters of Barbara (arbar), Lee's single letter (e), and the middle of Barry shows as "arr".

Changing Strings

Some string functions will change the contents of a string. UPPER() and LOWER() change the case of alphabetical characters from upper to lower, and vice versa.

LTRIM( )and RTRIM() can help trim spaces from strings. REPLACE() is very handy and will substitute part or all of a string with character(s) which you specify. Recall the Employee list contains some last names with apostrophes.

```
SELECT LastName
FROM Employee
WHERE LastName LIKE '%''%'
```

	LastName
1	O'Neil
2	O'Haire

2 rows

Figure 8.8 Syntax to search for names containing an apostrophe.

We will have REPLACE() find every apostrophe in the Employee list and replace it with an empty string. In effect, this maneuver removes the apostrophes (Figure 8.9). This will come in handy later during a Skill Check using the Employee list to formulate email addresses, which should not contain any special characters (e.g., apostrophes, foreign language accents, etc.). We use 4 apostrophes because the two in the middle are a special sequence that means "look for 1 literal apostrophe" (See Chapter 2 of *SQL Queries 2012 Joes 2 Pros 2012 Volume 1*).

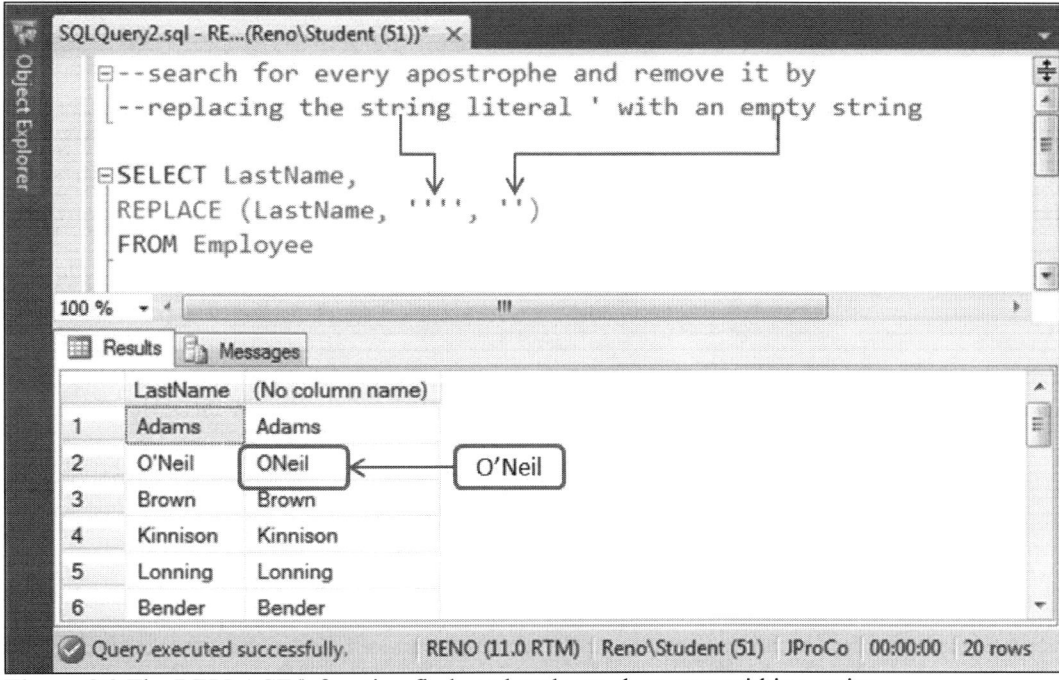

Figure 8.9 The REPLACE() function finds and replaces characters within a string.

Let's now work with UPPER() and LOWER(). If you wanted to force all letters to appear in caps or lowercase, you can use the UPPER or LOWER functions.

```
SELECT FirstName, LastName,
UPPER(FirstName) AS UpperFName,
LOWER(LastName) AS LowerLName
FROM Employee
```

	FirstName	LastName	UpperFName	LowerLName
1	Alex	Adams	ALEX	adams
2	Barbara	O'Neil	BARBARA	o'neil
3	Barry	Brown	BARRY	brown
4	Dave	Kinnison	DAVE	kinnison
5	David	Lonning	DAVID	lonning
6	Eric	Bender	ERIC	bender

20 rows

Figure 8.10 To force letters to appear in caps or lowercase, you can use UPPER or LOWER.

We can concatenate FirstName and LastName with a space in the middle to show the full name in upper case letters. You might use this format in a mailing list.

```
SELECT FirstName, LastName,
UPPER(FirstName + ' ' + LastName) AS LowerLName
FROM Employee
```

	FirstName	LastName	LowerLName
1	Alex	Adams	ALEX ADAMS
2	Barbara	O'Neil	BARBARA O'NEIL
3	Barry	Brown	BARRY BROWN
4	Dave	Kinnison	DAVE KINNISON
5	David	Lonning	DAVID LONNING
6	Eric	Bender	ERIC BENDER

20 rows

Figure 8.11 Upper case FirstName and LastName are concatenated with a space in the middle.

Casting to Strings

What is A + B? The answer is AB. So if someone asked what 5 + 5 is, would you say 55? The answer there is 10. We know adding works differently with numbers versus characters. So what should SQL do if you try the following expression in Figure 8.12?

```
SELECT 'A' + 5
```

Messages
Msg 245, Level 16, State 1, Line 1 Conversion failed when converting the varchar value 'A' to data type int.
0 rows

Figure 8.12 You can't add A to 5.

You get an error. The error says "Conversion failed when converting the varchar value 'A' to data type int". It tried to convert A into an int. We could have told it that A should remain a character and 5 should become a character 5, not a numeric 5.

Do you want the 5 to be treated like a string? If so the following results would not get an error but instead show A5. We can see that this CAST function allowed the A to be combined with the 5 as a VARCHAR. The result set says A5.

```
SELECT 'A' + CAST (5 AS VARCHAR(MAX))
```

(No column name)
A5
1 rows

Figure 8.13 When you CAST the 5 to a VARCHAR you can add it to A.

That was an example that converted numerical data into CHAR(acter) data in order to concatenate a needed character. Several years ago I worked with data applications which took a list of ID's (customer ID's or product ID's) as an input and then retrieved sales data for each ID from the data warehouse. In order to accept my list of ID's, the interface required that I include a delimiting semicolon after each ID. Otherwise, the application would have interpreted my list as one gigantic ID.

The list of ID's I needed to upload varied between 250 and 55000 ID's – far too many to manually type a semicolon after each ID. SQL Server made this task easy to accomplish.

So, how do we use this in a query? Let's go to the Sales Invoice table, and let's look at all records. Invoice 1 was ordered on January 3, 2009. Let's get these three values to say that in a single field. Our first attempt in doing so is seen in Figure 8.14.

```
SELECT InvoiceID + ' Was ordered on ' + OrderDate
FROM SalesInvoice
```

```
Messages
Msg 245, Level 16, State 1, Line 1
Conversion failed when converting the varchar value ' Was ordered on ' to data
type int.
                                                                        0 rows
```

Figure 8.14 You can't combine multiple different data types into one expression.

We have a conversion error. The first value of this expression is an integer, the second is a character data type and the third is a date. We're going to have to make them all consistent. In this case, let's turn this InvoiceID into a character and turn the OrderDate into a character. Some data types which aren't compatible with character data, such as DATETIME or numerical data must be converted to character strings before they can be concatenated with other string data. We're going to do some casting so that all three values are a character.

The second field is already a character type so we need to convert the InvoiceID and OrderDate to become character types. In Figure 8.15 we see this expression field work to combine all three values successfully.

```sql
SELECT
CAST(InvoiceID AS VARCHAR(MAX)) + ' Was ordered on ' +
CAST(OrderDate AS VARCHAR(MAX))
FROM SalesInvoice
```

(No column name)
1 Was ordered on Jan 3 2009 12:00AM
2 Was ordered on Jan 4 2009 2:22AM
3 Was ordered on Jan 4 2009 5:33AM
4 Was ordered on Jan 4 2009 10:06PM
5 Was ordered on Jan 5 2009 11:37AM
6 Was ordered on Jan 6 2009 11:53PM
1885 rows

Figure 8.15 Numerical data must convert to char data before it can concatenate with string data.

Let's just look for one record. Figure 8.16 shows us the results for InvoiceID 150 and when it was ordered.

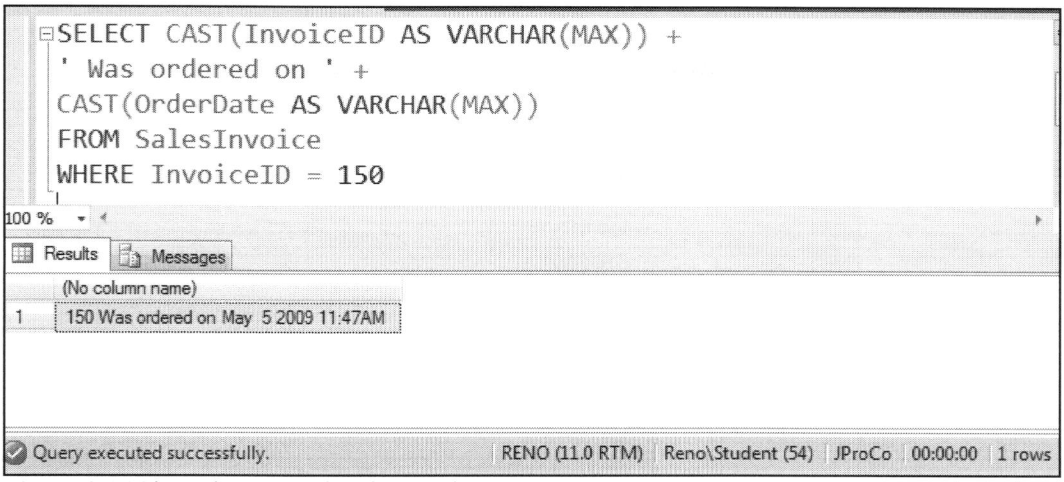

```sql
SELECT CAST(InvoiceID AS VARCHAR(MAX)) +
' Was ordered on ' +
CAST(OrderDate AS VARCHAR(MAX))
FROM SalesInvoice
WHERE InvoiceID = 150
```

(No column name)
150 Was ordered on May 5 2009 11:47AM

Figure 8.16 Show the expression for InvoiceID 150.

Let's clean up the wording to specify this is the invoice number. We will see where it says 150 was ordered on May 5, 2009, but 150 what? Let's make that a little more friendly. Let's say the OrderDate or Invoice by putting another value at the beginning of the concatenation.

```sql
SELECT 'The order date for Invoice ' +
CAST(InvoiceID AS VARCHAR(MAX)) + ' is ' +
CAST(OrderDate AS VARCHAR(MAX))
FROM SalesInvoice
WHERE InvoiceID = 150
```

(No column name)
The order date for Invoice 150 is May 5 2009 11:47AM

Figure 8.17 This combines 4 character fields into one expression.

Lab 8.1: Basic String Functions

Lab Prep: Lab Prep: Each lab has one or more Skill Checks. Start with Skill Check 1 and proceed until reaching the Points to Ponder section.

Before beginning this lab, verify that SQL Server 2012 is properly installed and operating. Before running the lab setup script for resetting the database (SQLQueries2012Vol4Chapter8.1-10Setup.sql), please make sure to close all query windows within SSMS. An open query window pointing to a database context can lock that database preventing it from updating when the script is executing. A simple way to assure all query windows are closed, is to exit out of SSMS, then open a new instance of SSMS, and lastly run the setup script.

Skill Check 1: Write a query that shows all records and all fields of the Location table. Be sure to show the City in all upper case characters. Alias the City field as Municipality. When done, your result should resemble Figure 8.18.

	LocationID	street	Municipality	state
1	1	111 First ST	SEATTLE	WA
2	2	222 Second AVE	BOSTON	MA
3	3	333 Third PL	CHICAGO	IL
4	4	444 Ruby ST	SPOKANE	WA
5	5	1595 Main	PHILADELPHIA	PA
6	6	915 Wallaby Drive	SYDNEY	NULL

6 rows

Figure 8.18 Skill Check 1

Skill Check 2: It's been said that Arnold Schwarzenegger is the biggest name in show business. Why? Because his first and last name contain a total of 21 letters. Write a query to show the name sizes of all the JProCo employees from the Employee table. Show just the FirstName and LastName fields and include a new expression field called NameSize which calculates the total number of characters in the employee's full name. When done, the query result should resemble Figure 8.19.

	FirstName	LastName	NameSize
1	Alex	Adams	9
2	Barbara	O'Neil	13
3	Barry	Brown	10
4	Dave	Kinnison	12
5	David	Lonning	12
6	Eric	Bender	10

20 rows

Figure 8.19 Skill Check 2.

Skill Check 3: All employees at JProCo will be assigned an email address. Management has decided that the first two letters of the employees FirstName plus all the letters of their LastName will be combined as the prefix to the @JProCo.com email path.

Write a query with an expression field called Email that contains each employees email address for JProCo.com. The result should show EmpID, FirstName, LastName, and Email expression field in one query. The Email addresses cannot contain special characters, such as apostrophes, foreign language accents or lettering. If special characters appear in the employee names, make sure those are not included in the email address.

	EmpID	FirstName	LastName	Email
1	1	Alex	Adams	AlAdams@JProCo.com
2	12	Barbara	O'Neil	BaONeil@JProCo.com
3	2	Barry	Brown	BaBrown@JProCo.com
4	4	Dave	Kinnison	DaKinnison@JProCo.com
5	7	David	Lonning	DaLonning@JProCo.com
6	5	Eric	Bender	ErBender@JProCo.com

20 rows

Figure 8.20 Skill Check 3 creates an email address for each JProCo employee.

Answer Code: The T-SQL code to this lab can be found in the downloadable files in a file named Lab8.1_BasicStringFunctions.sql

Points to Ponder – Basic String Functions

1. SUBSTRING() returns part of a character string starting from the specified start point and specified return length. SUBSTRING(*Column Name*, 2, 6) will begin with the second letter of data (2) and retrieve six characters (6).
2. LEN() returns the number of characters of the specified string expression, excluding trailing blanks.
3. UPPER() and LOWER() return a character expression in all upper or lower case letters.
4. LEFT() and RIGHT() return part of a character string with the specified number of characters from the left or the right.
5. The left trim function LTRIM() removes empty spaces preceding a string. Right trim RTRIM() begins at the end of a string to remove empty spaces.
6. Data types which aren't compatible with character data, such as DATETIME or numerical data, must be converted to character strings before they can be concatenated with other string data.

New 2012 String Functions

Each version of SQL Server adds new function and 2012 continues that tradition. Two new string related functions have been added to this version.

CONCAT

There is a new function to SQL 2012 called CONCAT(), which is short for concatenate. What this function does is shows data side-by-side. What is meant by that? Notice on the first record that we have Alex for the [FirstName] field and Adams for the [LastName] field. The full name would be Alex Adams. Figure 8.21 shows how we used the CONCAT() function to create this expression field.

```
SELECT EmpID, FirstName, LastName, LocationID, ManagerID,
CONCAT(FirstName, LastName)
FROM Employee
```

EmpID	FirstName	LastName	LocationID	ManagerID	(No column name)
1	Alex	Adams	1	4	AlexAdams
2	Barry	Brown	1	11	BarryBrown
3	Lee	Osako	2	11	LeeOsako
4	Dave	Kinnison	1	11	DaveKinnison
5	Eric	Bender	1	11	EricBender
6	Lisa	Kendall	4	4	LisaKendall

20 rows

Figure 8.21 The CONCAT() function is combining two fields into one expression field.

Notice in Figure 8.21 the text "AlexAdams" runs together. We really want to concatenate the [FirstName] and [LastName] fields with a space between the two values. So, we'll simply put another comma, and wrap a set of single quotes around a space as shown in Figure 8.22.

```
SELECT EmpID, FirstName, LastName, LocationID, ManagerID,
CONCAT(FirstName,' ', LastName)
FROM Employee
```

EmpID	FirstName	LastName	LocationID	ManagerID	(No column name)
1	Alex	Adams	1	4	Alex Adams
2	Barry	Brown	1	11	Barry Brown
3	Lee	Osako	2	11	Lee Osako
4	Dave	Kinnison	1	11	Dave Kinnison
5	Eric	Bender	1	11	Eric Bender
6	Lisa	Kendall	4	4	Lisa Kendall

20 rows

Figure 8.22 A space is now part of the concatenation for the expression field.

Now our expression field says "Alex Adams" with a space. To clarify this expression field we should add a column name. To name this field, type AS FullName to the end of the second line as seen in Figure 8.23.

```
SELECT EmpID, FirstName, LastName, LocationID, ManagerID,
CONCAT(FirstName,' ', LastName) AS FullName
FROM Employee
```

EmpID	FirstName	LastName	LocationID	ManagerID	FullName
1	Alex	Adams	1	4	Alex Adams
2	Barry	Brown	1	11	Barry Brown
3	Lee	Osako	2	11	Lee Osako
4	Dave	Kinnison	1	11	Dave Kinnison
5	Eric	Bender	1	11	Eric Bender
6	Lisa	Kendall	4	4	Lisa Kendall

20 rows

Figure 8.23 Our concatenated expression field has the [FullName] field alias.

FORMAT with Dates

Do you think January 5th 2013 should be shown as 1/5/2013 or 5/1/2013? The best answer is to each their own. The FORMAT function lets you pick the style, or better yet it can be relevant to the culture of the computer running the query.

SQL is notoriously good at saving and retrieving data in its original form. It also has a few formatting functions if you need them. One formatting function that's been around for a while is the CONVERT function. Why are we talking about CONVERT in the section about new SQL 2012 functions? So we can compare this old method with the new better option made available in SQL 2012. Figure 8.24 shows what happens if we convert the [HireDate] field to the NVARCHAR data type.

```
SELECT EmpID, FirstName, LastName, LocationID, ManagerID,
CONVERT(NVARCHAR, HireDate, 101) AS CharDate
FROM Employee
```

	EmpID	FirstName	LastName	LocationID	ManagerID	CharDate
1	1	Alex	Adams	1	4	01/01/2001
2	2	Barry	Brown	1	11	08/12/2002
3	3	Lee	Osako	2	11	09/01/1999
4	4	Dave	Kinnison	1	11	03/16/1996
5	5	Eric	Bender	1	11	05/17/2007
6	6	Lisa	Kendall	4	4	11/15/2001

20 rows

Figure 8.24 Using CONVERT() and style 101.

It looks like Barry Brown's hire date is August 12, 2002. That is because in the USA culture we specify month/day/year which makes 08/12/2002 as August 12th 2002. However, if we were in Europe (where it's day/month/year), 08/12/2002 would look a lot like December 8, 2002. Let's try a different formatting style using the CONVERT function. By changing the formatting style from 101 to 103 in the same query, notice we retrieve the date in the year, month, and then day format as seen in Figure 8.25.

```
SELECT EmpID, FirstName, LastName, LocationID, ManagerID,
CONVERT(NVARCHAR, HireDate, 103) AS CharDate
FROM Employee
```

	EmpID	FirstName	LastName	LocationID	ManagerID	CharDate
1	1	Alex	Adams	1	4	01/01/2001
2	2	Barry	Brown	1	11	12/08/2002
3	3	Lee	Osako	2	11	01/09/1999
4	4	Dave	Kinnison	1	11	16/03/1996
5	5	Eric	Bender	1	11	17/05/2007
6	6	Lisa	Kendall	4	4	15/11/2001

20 rows

Figure 8.25 Converting with style 102 shows year.month.day format.

Style 103 returns the European day/month/year, while style 109 returns 3 letter abbreviated month/integer day/ integer year as seen in the comparison in Figure 8.26.

```
SELECT EmpID, FirstName, LastName, LocationID, ManagerID,
CONVERT(NVARCHAR, HireDate, 103) AS CharDate
FROM Employee
WHERE EmpID = 2
```

```
SELECT EmpID, FirstName, LastName, LocationID, ManagerID,
CONVERT(NVARCHAR, HireDate, 109) AS CharDate
FROM Employee
WHERE EmpID = 2
```

Results | Messages

	EmpID	FirstName	LastName	LocationID	ManagerID	CharDate
1	2	Barry	Brown	1	11	12/08/2002

	EmpID	FirstName	LastName	LocationID	ManagerID	CharDate
1	2	Barry	Brown	1	11	Aug 12 2002 12:00:00:000AM

Query executed successfully. | RENO (11.0 RTM) | Reno\Student (51) | JProCo | 00:00:00 | 2 rows

Figure 8.26 Style 103 and 109 show the same date in different ways.

Now we will take the above code and utilize the new FORMAT function. Instead of going through the process of converting the field we will simply set the format we are looking for. In Figure 8.27 we replaced CONVERT with FORMAT and instead of naming it an NVARCHAR and picking a style, we simply (in parentheses) name the field, and in single quotes we set the parameter 'd' for day to achieve the same result.

```
SELECT EmpID, FirstName, LastName, LocationID, ManagerID,
CONVERT(NVARCHAR, HireDate, 101) AS CharDate
FROM Employee
WHERE EmpID = 4

SELECT EmpID, FirstName, LastName, LocationID, ManagerID,
FORMAT(HireDate, 'd') AS CharDate
FROM Employee
WHERE EmpID = 4
```

Results | Messages

	EmpID	FirstName	LastName	LocationID	ManagerID	CharDate
1	4	Dave	Kinnison	1	11	03/16/1996

	EmpID	FirstName	LastName	LocationID	ManagerID	CharDate
1	4	Dave	Kinnison	1	11	3/16/1996

Query executed successfully. | RENO (11.0 RTM) | Reno\Student (51) | JProCo | 00:00:00 | 2 rows

Figure 8.27 The new SQL 2012 FORMAT() function can be used for different date styles.

In that last example we choose d for day. You can also choose m (month) to return the month and day or y (year) as your parameters to return month and year. In all the examples so far the style is in the "en-us" culture because that's the culture set on the server we used. It is not normally necessary to set this function however; there is a third optional parameter. What if we had done 'en-gb' for Great Britain? You can see in Figure 8.28, the second record has a [HireDate] of 16/03/1996 and the numbers are separated with forward slashes '/' as would be customary in Great Britain.

```sql
SELECT EmpID, FirstName, LastName, LocationID, ManagerID,
FORMAT(HireDate, 'd', 'en-gb') AS CharDate
FROM Employee
WHERE EmpID = 4
```

	EmpID	FirstName	LastName	LocationID	ManagerID	CharDate
1	4	Dave	Kinnison	1	11	16/03/1996

1 rows

Figure 8.28 The FORMAT() function for 'en-gb' shows day/month/year format.

Let's change it up a bit more. Let's use the style format 'de-de', for German, Germany. What does that look like? We can see in Figure 8.29 that it gives us day, month and year, separated by dots as would be customary in Germany.

```sql
SELECT EmpID, FirstName, LastName, LocationID, ManagerID,
FORMAT(HireDate, 'd', 'de-de') AS CharDate
FROM Employee
WHERE EmpID = 4
```

	EmpID	FirstName	LastName	LocationID	ManagerID	CharDate
1	4	Dave	Kinnison	1	11	16.03.1996

1 rows

Figure 8.29 The FORMAT() function for 'de-de' shows day.month.year format.

What else can we do? Let's see what it looks like for the 'm'. The second record says 12 August, and if you look 2 spaces down, you see 01 Januar, 16 März, under that is 17 Mai. The 'm' month parameter returns month and day while the 'de-de' (German-Germany) style format sets how you will view the result set.

```sql
SELECT EmpID, FirstName, LastName, LocationID, ManagerID,
FORMAT(HireDate, 'm', 'de-de') AS CharDate
FROM Employee
```

Chapter 8. String Functions

EmpID	FirstName	LastName	LocationID	ManagerID	CharDate
1	Alex	Adams	1	4	01 Januar
2	Barry	Brown	1	11	12 August
3	Lee	Osako	2	11	01 September
4	Dave	Kinnison	1	11	16 März
5	Eric	Bender	1	11	17 Mai
6	Lisa	Kendall	4	4	15 November

20 rows

Figure 8.30 Using 'm' to show the previous example in German months.

FORMAT with Months

You have seen what happened to the [HireDate] field when we run it through the format using the 'd' and 'en-us'. This is great for days, but what if we put a series of "MMMM' in there? Let's put four M's for month and simplify the fields to show just the [HireDate] and formatted fields. What will the expression field look like? As you can see in Figure 8.31 this format will pull up just the month fully spelled out. In the first record it says "this is in January, and August, in the second record and so on.

```
SELECT HireDate,
FORMAT(HireDate, 'MMMM', 'en-us') AS CharDate
FROM Employee
```

	HireDate	CharDate
1	2001-01-01 00:00:00.000	January
2	2002-08-12 00:00:00.000	August
3	1999-09-01 00:00:00.000	September
4	1996-03-16 00:00:00.000	March
5	2007-05-17 00:00:00.000	May
6	2001-11-15 00:00:00.000	November

20 rows

Figure 8.31 Using 'MMMM' shows the entire month spelled out for the culture.

Let's try a few other combinations. What does three M's look like? It shows us a 3 letter month abbreviation, like Jan, Aug, Sep. Let's try two M's. This format returns a two digit numeric, like 01 for January and 08 for August. What does a single M return? This returns the whole month spelled out, with the day. For example, January 01 and August 12 and so forth as seen in Figure 8.32.

```sql
SELECT HireDate, FORMAT(HireDate, 'MMM', 'en-us') AS CharDate
FROM Employee
```

```sql
SELECT HireDate, FORMAT(HireDate, 'MM', 'en-us') AS CharDate
FROM Employee
```

```sql
SELECT HireDate, FORMAT(HireDate, 'M', 'en-us') AS CharDate
FROM Employee
```

	HireDate	CharDate
1	2001-01-01 00:00:00.000	Jan
2	2002-08-12 00:00:00.000	Aug
	HireDate	CharDate
1	2001-01-01 00:00:00.000	01
2	2002-08-12 00:00:00.000	08
	HireDate	CharDate
1	2001-01-01 00:00:00.000	January 01
2	2002-08-12 00:00:00.000	August 12

60 rows

Figure 8.32 Comparing 'M', 'MM' and 'MMM' for different month formats.

Up to this point the month, day and year formats all seem straight forward. There are a few things to be aware of that can get a little tricky. What happens if this 'M' is lower case? As you can see in Figure 8.33 there is no real change in the result. How about 'mm'? Now we are getting a different result. The lower case 'mm' calls for a return in minutes. Since the examples returned are all zeros it's really hard to tell exactly what this new field means because the hire dates don't go down to the minutes. To really see this example, let's utilize GETDATE() and we can see the formatted field returns 06 since this was run on July 18, 2012 at 16:06pm.

```sql
SELECT HireDate, FORMAT(HireDate, 'mm', 'en-us') AS CharDate
FROM Employee
```

```sql
SELECT GETDATE(), FORMAT(GETDATE(), 'mm', 'en-us')
```

HireDate	CharDate
2001-01-01 00:00:00.000	00
2002-08-12 00:00:00.000	00
(No column name)	(No column name)
2012-10-06 21:22:38.643	22

21 rows

Figure 8.33 Shows minutes instead of months with the lowercase 'mm' format.

FORMAT with Money

Format does more than dates, minutes, months and years. Format can also localize your currency. The grant table has an amount field that we know is a money data type. We may assume this is dollars, but you may be in another country and you've stored it natively. With this data you may want it to appear in your specified format. Let's look at a side-by-side comparison using the following code:

```
SELECT *, FORMAT(Amount, 'c', 'en-us') AS USA$
FROM [Grant]

SELECT *, FORMAT(Amount, 'c', 'en-gb') AS UK
FROM [Grant]

SELECT *, FORMAT(Amount, 'c', 'de-de') AS German
FROM [Grant]
```

In the previous code we pulled out the [Amount] field by typing and formatting it using 'c' which stands for currency. We set the first amount as English-United States with the alias of USA$. We set the second query as English-Great Britain and the third as German-Germany. In the first query we expect to see dollars and cents. What would you expect for the UK and German queries? As you can see in Figure 8.34, USA$ returned dollars and cents, the UK returned the British pound(£) and Germany the Euro(€).

```
SELECT *, FORMAT(Amount, 'c', 'en-us') AS USA$
FROM [Grant]

SELECT *, FORMAT(Amount, 'c', 'en-gb') AS UK
FROM [Grant]

SELECT *, FORMAT(Amount, 'c', 'de-de') AS German
FROM [Grant]
```

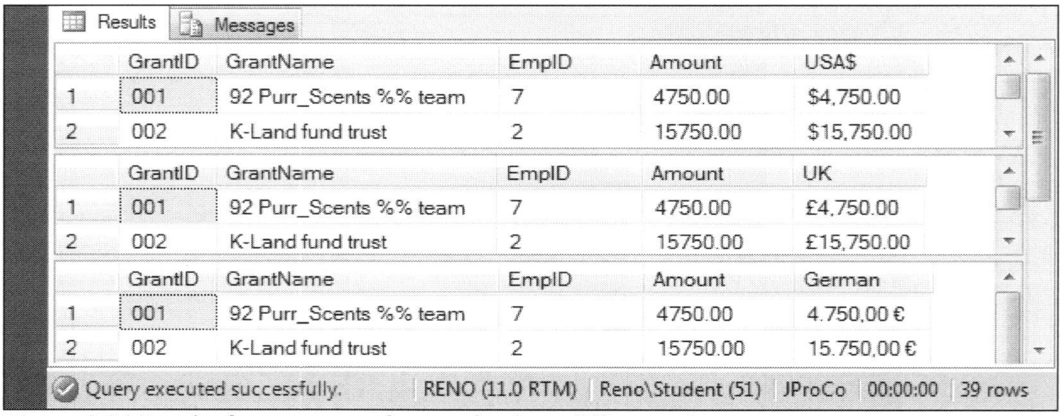

Figure 8.34 Results from currency formats for three different cultures.

Lab 8.2: New 2012 String Functions

Lab Prep: Lab Prep: Each lab has one or more Skill Checks. Start with Skill Check 1 and proceed until reaching the Points to Ponder section.

Before beginning this lab, verify that SQL Server 2012 is properly installed and operating. Before running the lab setup script for resetting the database (SQLQueries2012Vol4Chapter8.1-10Setup.sql), please make sure to close all query windows within SSMS. An open query window pointing to a database context can lock that database preventing it from updating when the script is executing. A simple way to assure all query windows are closed, is to exit out of SSMS, then open a new instance of SSMS, and lastly run the setup script.

Skill Check 1: From the JProCo database write a query that creates an expression field called Edition on the CurrentProducts table. The field should concatenate the ProductName and its category with a dash between the values. Show ProductID, ProductName, Category, and the expression field Edition.

	ProductID	ProductName	Category	Edition
1	1	Underwater Tour 1 Day West Coast	No-Stay	Underwater Tour 1 Day West Coast - No-Stay
2	2	Underwater Tour 2 Days West Coast	Overnight-Stay	Underwater Tour 2 Days West Coast - Overnight-Stay
3	3	Underwater Tour 3 Days West Coast	Medium-Stay	Underwater Tour 3 Days West Coast - Medium-Stay
4	4	Underwater Tour 5 Days West Coast	Medium-Stay	Underwater Tour 5 Days West Coast - Medium-Stay
5	5	Underwater Tour 1 Week West Coast	LongTerm-Stay	Underwater Tour 1 Week West Coast - LongTerm-Stay
6	6	Underwater Tour 2 Weeks West Coast	LongTerm-Stay	Underwater Tour 2 Weeks West Coast - LongTerm-Stay

Figure 8.35 Skill Check 1.

Skill Check 2: From the JProCo database write a query that creates an expression field called Description on the Grant table. The field should concatenate the GrantName and its Amount with a dash "space" dollar sign between the expression field values as shown in Figure 8.36

	GrantID	GrantName	EmpID	Amount	Description
1	001	92 Purr_Scents %% team	7	4750.00	92 Purr_Scents %% team - $4750.00
2	002	K-Land fund trust	2	15750.00	K-Land fund trust - $15750.00
3	003	Robert@BigStarBank.com	7	18100.00	Robert@BigStarBank.com - $18100.00
4	005	BIG 6's Foundation%	4	22000.00	BIG 6's Foundation% - $22000.00
5	006	TALTA_Kishan International	3	18100.00	TALTA_Kishan International - $18100.00
6	007	Ben@MoreTechnology.com	10	42000.00	Ben@MoreTechnology.com - $42000.00

Figure 8.36 Skill Check 2.

Skill Check 3: From the JProCo database write a query that creates an expression field called HireDay on the Employee table. The query should format the HireDay expression field as month day. Only show the EmpID, FirstName, LastName, HireDate, and HireDay expression fields.

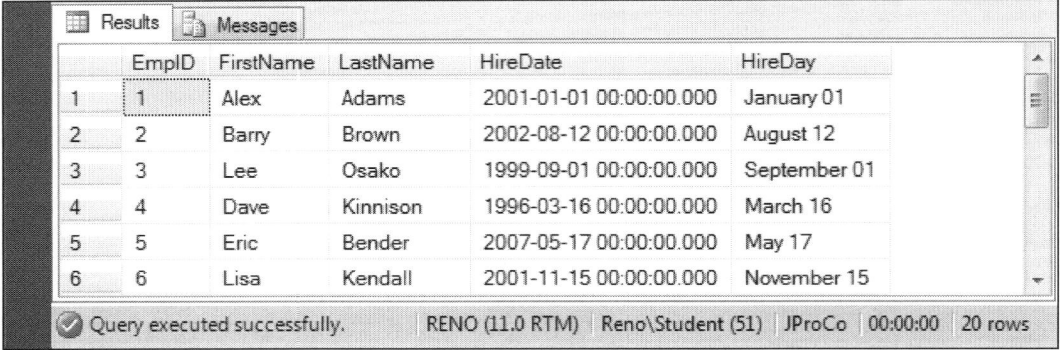

	EmpID	FirstName	LastName	HireDate	HireDay
1	1	Alex	Adams	2001-01-01 00:00:00.000	January 01
2	2	Barry	Brown	2002-08-12 00:00:00.000	August 12
3	3	Lee	Osako	1999-09-01 00:00:00.000	September 01
4	4	Dave	Kinnison	1996-03-16 00:00:00.000	March 16
5	5	Eric	Bender	2007-05-17 00:00:00.000	May 17
6	6	Lisa	Kendall	2001-11-15 00:00:00.000	November 15

Figure 8.37 Skill Check 3.

Skill Check 4: From the JProCo database write a query that creates an expression field called EuroDate on the CurrentProducts table. The field should format the OriginationDate down to the day and use the culture for Great Britain English. Only show ProductID, ProductName, OriginationDate and EuroDate expression fields.

	ProductID	ProductName	OriginationDate	EuroDate
1	1	Underwater Tour 1 Day West Coast	2009-05-07 13:33:09.957	07/05/2009
2	2	Underwater Tour 2 Days West Coast	2010-06-29 23:43:22.813	29/06/2010
3	3	Underwater Tour 3 Days West Coast	2012-02-03 16:07:49.900	03/02/2012
4	4	Underwater Tour 5 Days West Coast	2008-11-28 04:59:06.600	28/11/2008
5	5	Underwater Tour 1 Week West Coast	2004-04-13 19:20:11.400	13/04/2004
6	6	Underwater Tour 2 Weeks West Coast	2011-03-27 20:40:38.760	27/03/2011

Figure 8.38 Skill Check 4.

Answer Code: The T-SQL code to this lab can be found in the downloadable files in a file named Lab8.2_New2012StringFunctions.sql

Points to Ponder - New 2012 String Functions

1. The SQL CONCAT() function concatenates (or combine) multiple strings into one string.

2. The CONCAT() function takes a number of string arguments but it requires a minimum of two.

3. Null values are implicitly converted to an empty string unless, for example SELECT CONCAT('Cow','', 'boy') and SELECT CONCAT('Cow', NULL, 'boy') would both produce 'Cowboy'

4. CONCAT() and the + operator are mostly the same except for nulls. For example, SELECT 'Cow' + '' + 'boy' would produce Cowboy but 'Cow' + NULL + 'boy' would produce NULL.

5. The FORMAT() function is used to format how a date or value is displayed.

6. FORMAT converts the first argument to specified format and returns the string value.

7. This function is location aware and it can return the formatting of the date and time using the local specified string.

8. The arguments in the FORMAT() function can be case sensitive. For example 'MM' is months and 'mm' is minutes.

Viewing Table and Field Metadata

There will be times when you will need to locate metadata to learn something about SQL Server. For example, you may need to find out what version of SQL Server is running on a particular machine. Imagine you need to run some queries using a loaner machine, or perhaps you are assisting a colleague with a query and need to see what version of SQL Server they are using. At other times, you will need to find settings for certain objects in your database. This section will equip you with tools to help you find what you need.

You may be familiar with the term "metadata," which means data about data. Data and metadata are both pieces of information, so how do they differ? Data contains information like records. When you add a new employee record, you're adding new data. Metadata consists of data about that data. In other words, it describes the design of the table where you enter the employee data. It can also describe the settings and properties of your database or your instance of SQL Server.

So how do we begin looking for the metadata we need? There are several ways, but this chapter focuses on using functions to retrieve metadata. Let's begin by checking which version of SQL Server you are running. It's actually pretty easy to find out by looking at your Object Explorer.

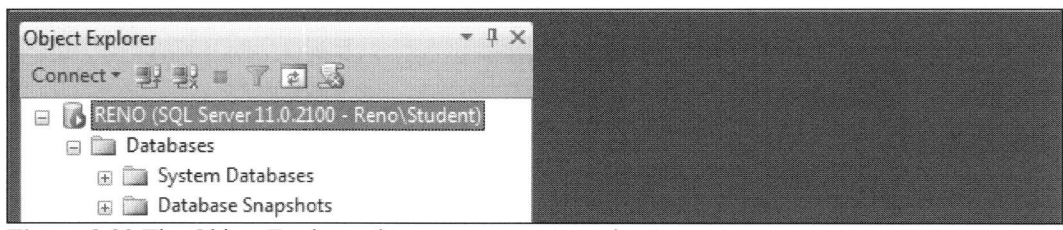

Figure 8.39 The Object Explorer shows your server version.

You most likely are running either the 2005, 2008, or 2012 version of SQL Server:

- o **2005** = SQL Version 9
- o **2008** = SQL Version 10
- o **2012** = SQL Version 11

But how do you use code to gather that information? One way is to use the SERVERPROPERTY() function, which can show a variety of properties for your server (e.g., ANSI NULL setting, language settings, etc.) We want to see ProductVersion. As you can see, I am running SQL Server 2012.

```
SELECT SERVERPROPERTY('ProductVersion')
```

(No column name)
11.0.2100.60

1 rows

Figure 8.40 The SERVERPROPERTY() function can show a variety of properties for your server.

We can use the SERVERPROPERTY() function to show the level of SQL Server running on a machine. SQL Server's product levels include Beta, RTM, Service Pack 1, Service Pack 2, and so on. Add the ProductLevel property to your query.

```
SELECT SERVERPROPERTY('ProductVersion')
SELECT SERVERPROPERTY('ProductLevel')
```

(No column name)
11.0.2100.60

(No column name)
RTM

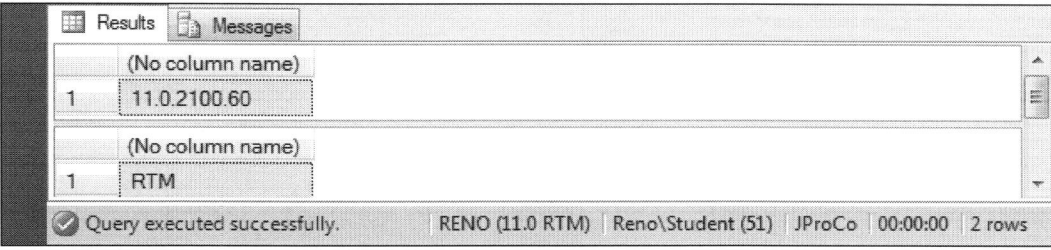

Figure 8.41 Add the ProductLevel property to your query.

We can see I'm running SQL Server Version 10 at the RTM (release to manufacturing) level – the one that became available when SQL Server 2012 was released to the world. Now let's look at which edition I'm running. SQL Server's editions include Developer, Enterprise Evaluation, Express, and Standard. Add the Edition property to our query and request all of this metadata using a single statement.

```
SELECT SERVERPROPERTY('ProductVersion'),
SERVERPROPERTY('ProductLevel'),
SERVERPROPERTY('Edition')
```

(No column name)	(No column name)	(No column name)
11.0.2100.60	RTM	Developer Edition (64-bit)

1 rows

Figure 8.42 Revise your query to be a single statement. Add the Edition property to your query.

As we've gotten further along in the *Joes2Pros* series, we've created many new objects in the JProCo database. When you open Object Explorer and navigate to the JProCo database, you see many tables, views, and other objects that we created. These objects were not included with the CD you used to install SQL Server on your machine. The software manufacturer (Microsoft) didn't create any of these objects. You created the JProCo database and all of its objects, whether you created them manually or whether you added them to the database by running a *Joes2Pros* setup script.

When we created the JProCo database and added objects (e.g., the Customer and Location tables, the UpsertMgmtTraining stored procedure, etc.), SQL Server created additional items in the background. Later we will look at metadata showing some of those additional items which SQL Server created behind the scenes.

Let's first look at a database which has nothing in it other than what is created behind the scenes when you initially create a new database. We will begin our demonstration by creating a brand new database called dbTest.

Open Object Explorer and navigate to "Databases". Right click on Databases, then right click New Database, which opens the New Databasedialog boxe (Figure 8.43). Enter the name as "dbTest" then click OK.

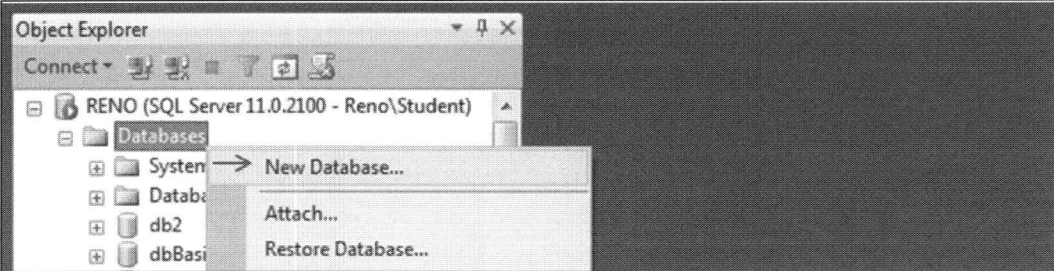

Figure 8.43 Right click on Databases, Click "New Database".

[Reader note: the followingdialog boxe will appear larger in your instance of SQL Server. For illustrative purposes, this screenshot has been altered in order to demonstrate quickly creating a new database by clicking the user interface. This method is useful for creating a database for a quick test or demonstration. However, creating your databases with reusable code remains the preferred "best practice" method.]

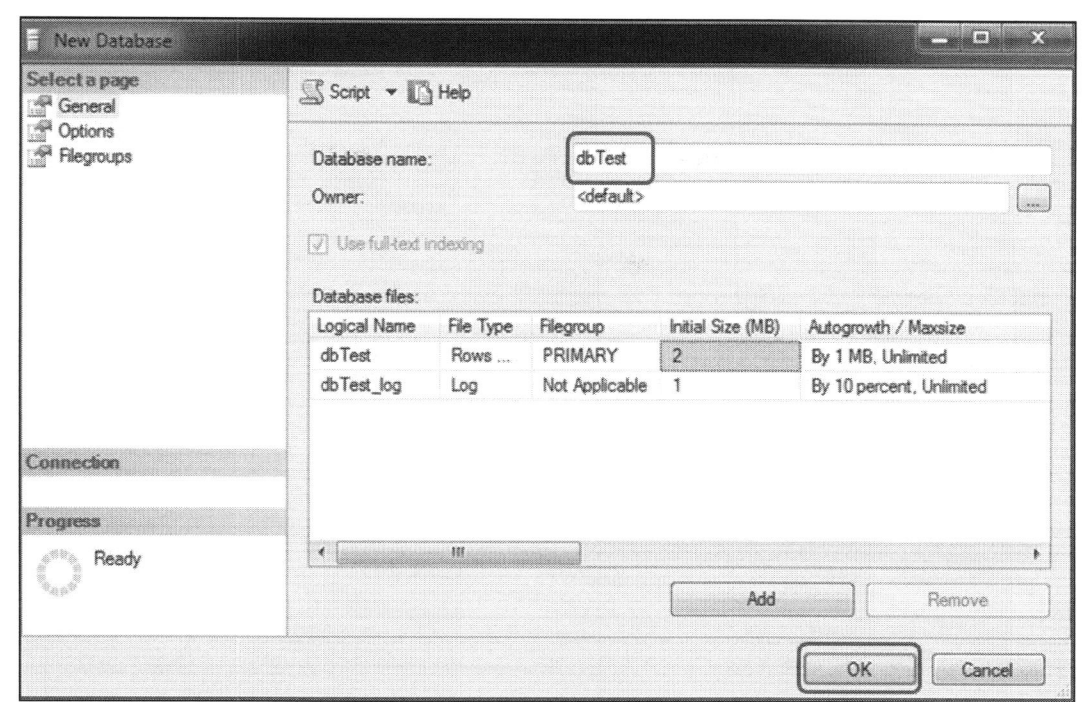

Figure 8.44 Creating a new database by clicking the UI is useful for quick tests and demonstrations.

Now return to your Object Explorer and locate dbTest. Notice it is an empty database – there are no user created objects, such as tables, views, or stored procedures. However, there are some System Views present, and we know we didn't create any of these items (Figure 8.45).

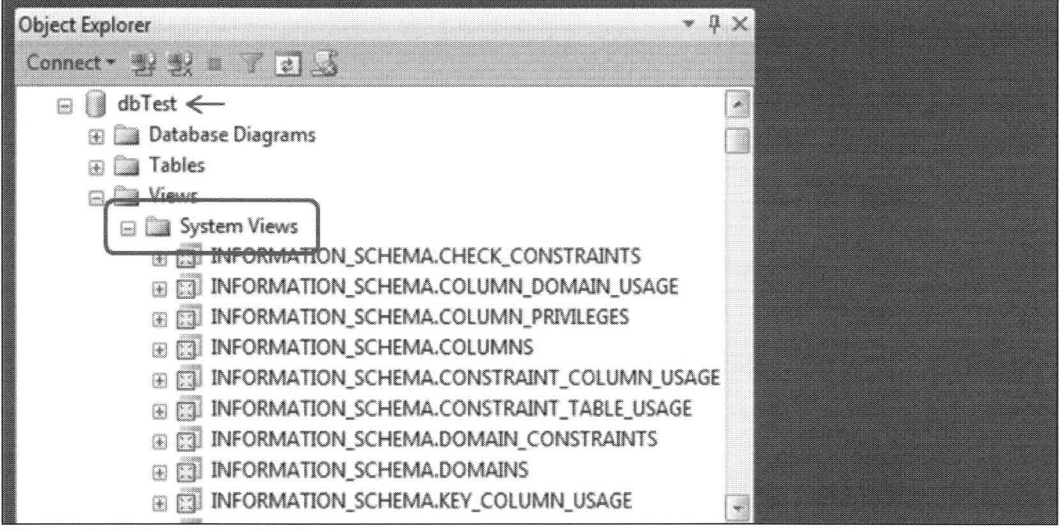

Figure 8.45 Contents of dbTest.

Thus, with each new database you create, you get infrastructure items which SQL Server automatically generates as part of the manufacturer's (Microsoft's) design. When a software manufacturer releases a program, a new version, or a service update pack, the design of all items contained in the release are considered "shipped" by the software provider. All items currently contained in dbTest were generated in that manner, so these items are all considered to have been shipped by Microsoft. However in JProCo we have roughly 100 objects, about half of which were user created (i.e., we created them ourselves) and the other half were auto-generated by SQL Server when we created the JProCo database.

There is a property in SQL Server which shows which items were created by Microsoft and which items were created by a user. Let's go to the JProCo database and look at the Sys.Objects list (Figure 8.46).

```
SELECT *
FROM Sys.Objects
```

	name	object...	principal...	schema...	parent...	type	type_desc	create_date	modify_date	is_ms_shipped
1	sysrscols	3	NULL	4	0	S	SYSTEM_TABLE	2012-02-10...	2012-02-10...	1
2	sysrowsets	5	NULL	4	0	S	SYSTEM_TABLE	2009-04-13...	2012-02-10...	1
3	sysclones	6	NULL	4	0	S	SYSTEM_TABLE	2012-02-10...	2012-02-10...	1
4	sysallocu...	7	NULL	4	0	S	SYSTEM_TABLE	2009-04-13...	2012-02-10...	1
5	sysfiles1	8	NULL	4	0	S	SYSTEM_TABLE	2003-04-08...	2003-04-08...	1
6	sysseobjv...	9	NULL	4	0	S	SYSTEM_TABLE	2012-02-10...	2012-02-10...	1

Figure 8.46 The Sys.Objects list tracks all system and user created items in your database context.

We see roughly 200+ objects. As you scroll through the list, you will see familiar object names, such as the Customer and Grant tables, the stored procedures and table functions we used in our exercises throughout this book.

Note the column header "is_ms_shipped" to the right of the Sys.Objects result (refer back to (Figure 8.46)), which indicates whether an object was created by a user or whether it was shipped by Microsoft. We would like to see a list containing just the objects we created.

We know we created the Customer table, so find it in the first column (name). Next to Customer is its Object_id, 357576312. *READERNOTE:* your particular Object_id may differ.

	name	object_id	principal_id	schema_id	parent_object_id	type	type_desc
95	UQ__Gra...	421576540	NULL	1	405576483	UQ	UNIQUE_CON
96	spGetEm...	437576597	NULL	1	0	P	SQL_STORED
97	Customer	453576654	NULL	1	0	U	USER_TABLE
98	PK__Cus...	469576711	NULL	1	453576654	PK	PRIMARY_KEY
99	SalesInv...	549576996	NULL	1	0	U	USER_TABLE
100	PK__Sal...	565577053	NULL	1	549576996	PK	PRIMARY_KEY

Query executed successfully. | RENO (11.0 RTM) | Reno\Student (51) | JProCo | 00:00:00 | 205 rows

Figure 8.47 Each object in Sys.Objects has a unique Object_id.

Many companies use SQL Server and all of them customize it by adding their own objects. Sometimes they will want to have a maintenance list of all their own objects and there is no need to perform this work on Microsoft Shipped objects. Let's take the Customer table's Object_id (453576654), drop it into our query window, and use OBJECTPROPERTY(), a system supplied function, to find out whether the manufacturer (Microsoft) shipped this object with SQL Server, or whether we created it during the course of this book.

```
SELECT OBJECTPROPERTY(453576654, 'ISMSShipped')
```

	(No column name)
1	0

1 rows

Figure 8.48 The 0 indicates the object was not shipped as part of SQL Server -- *we created it.*

The ISMSShipped property for the Customer table equals 0, which indicates it was not created by Microsoft. Now let's pick an object which was probably shipped by Microsoft. JProCo doesn't contain an object called "sysfiles1", so let's drop into our query the Object_id for sysfiles1 (which is 8).

```
SELECT OBJECTPROPERTY(8, 'ISMSShipped')
```

	(No column name)
1	1

1 rows

Figure 8.49 The 1 indicates the object was shipped as part of SQL Server - *we did not create it.*

The ISMSShipped property shows a "1" for sysfiles1, which indicates this object was provided as part of Microsoft's programmatic design – *we did not create sysfiles1.*

So let's use this function to see the list of all JProCo objects which we created. We can extend our earlier query of the JProCo.Sys.Objects list to include criteria which checks whether the object was created by us or by the manufacturer. Since we know items we created will have an ISMSShipped value of 0, we can look at the list of items where the ISMSShipped value is 0. Instead of passing in a single Object_id as an expression, we can have our query evaluate every item in the Object_id field with an ISMSShipped value of 0.

```sql
SELECT name, Object_id, is_ms_shipped
FROM Sys.Objects
WHERE OBJECTPROPERTY([Object_id],'ISMSShipped') = 0
```

	name	Object_id	is_ms_shipped
1	GetLongClasses	2099048	0
2	ShowProductsBelowPrice	18099105	0
3	CountSeattleEmployees	34099162	0
4	CountEmployeesByLocation	50099219	0
5	CountEmployeesByCityName	66099276	0
6	GetEmployeeCountAndFirstHire	82099333	0

126 rows

Figure 8.50 Roughly half the objects in JProCo show an ISMSShipped value of 0.

Of the 205 objects currently in JProCo, it appears that 126 of them were created by us during the last 8 chapters. *READERNOTE:* The total number of objects, system objects, and user created objects in your database may differ slightly from those shown.

Lab 8.3: Viewing Table and Field Metadata

Lab Prep: Lab Prep: Each lab has one or more Skill Checks. Start with Skill Check 1 and proceed until reaching the Points to Ponder section.

Before beginning this lab, verify that SQL Server 2012 is properly installed and operating. Before running the lab setup script for resetting the database (SQLQueries2012Vol4Chapter8.1-10Setup.sql), please make sure to close all query windows within SSMS. An open query window pointing to a database context can lock that database preventing it from updating when the script is executing. A simple way to assure all query windows are closed, is to exit out of SSMS, then open a new instance of SSMS, and lastly run the setup script.

Skill Check 1: Find all the objects in the dbBasics database which were not shipped by Microsoft. When complete, your result should contain about 15 rows and resemble Figure 8.51.

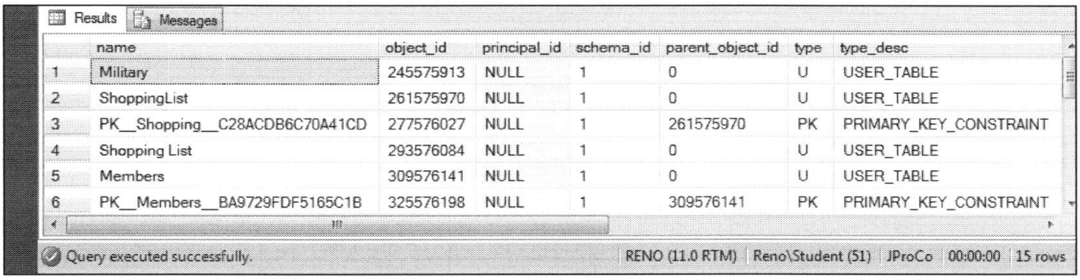

	name	object_id	principal_id	schema_id	parent_object_id	type	type_desc
1	Military	245575913	NULL	1	0	U	USER_TABLE
2	ShoppingList	261575970	NULL	1	0	U	USER_TABLE
3	PK__Shopping__C28ACDB6C70A41CD	277576027	NULL	1	261575970	PK	PRIMARY_KEY_CONSTRAINT
4	Shopping List	293576084	NULL	1	0	U	USER_TABLE
5	Members	309576141	NULL	1	0	U	USER_TABLE
6	PK__Members__BA9729FDF5165C1B	325576198	NULL	1	309576141	PK	PRIMARY_KEY_CONSTRAINT

Figure 8.51 Skill Check 1 finds all dbBasics objects which were not shipped by Microsoft.

Skill Check 2: From the Sys.Objects table, find all the primary key constraints in the JProCo database. When complete, the result should contain 19 rows and resemble Figure 8.52.

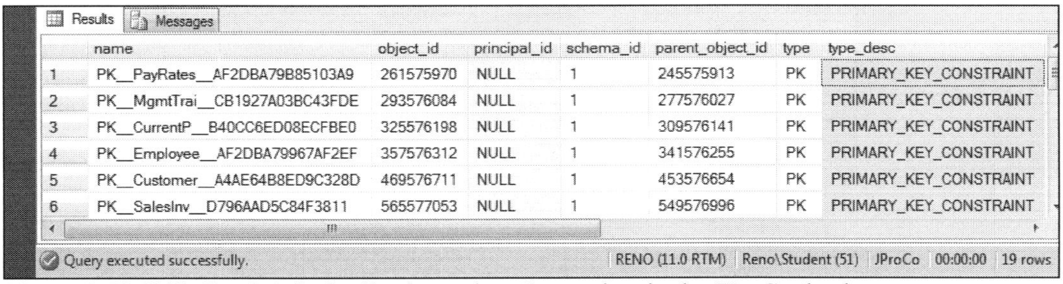

	name	object_id	principal_id	schema_id	parent_object_id	type	type_desc
1	PK__PayRates__AF2DBA79B85103A9	261575970	NULL	1	245575913	PK	PRIMARY_KEY_CONSTRAINT
2	PK__MgmtTrai__CB1927A03BC43FDE	293576084	NULL	1	277576027	PK	PRIMARY_KEY_CONSTRAINT
3	PK__CurrentP__B40CC6ED08ECFBE0	325576198	NULL	1	309576141	PK	PRIMARY_KEY_CONSTRAINT
4	PK__Employee__AF2DBA79967AF2EF	357576312	NULL	1	341576255	PK	PRIMARY_KEY_CONSTRAINT
5	PK__Customer__A4AE64B8ED9C328D	469576711	NULL	1	453576654	PK	PRIMARY_KEY_CONSTRAINT
6	PK__SalesInv__D796AAD5C84F3811	565577053	NULL	1	549576996	PK	PRIMARY_KEY_CONSTRAINT

Figure 8.52 Skill Check 2 finds all primary key Constraints in the JProCo database.

Answer Code: The T-SQL code to this lab can be found in the downloadable files in a file named Lab8.3_MetadataFunctions.sql

Points to Ponder - Table and Field Metadata

1. As your database design grows you will encounter more objects such as stored procedures and functions.
2. Every database is a combination of user defined and system supplied stored procedures.
3. OBJECTPROPERTY() returns information about objects in the current database.
4. If you are not sure which objects are system supplied in SQL Server, then the (ISMSShipped) property used with the OBJECTPROPERTY() function can tell you.
5. You can see the system supplied functions by navigating to Programmability --> Functions --> System Functions.

Chapter Glossary

Leading Space: Extra spaces before your data.

LEFT(): Returns part of a character string with the specified number of characters from the left.

LEN(): A string function that returns the number of characters of the specified string expression.

LOWER(): This function returns a character expression in all lower case letters.

LTRIM(): The left trim function removes empty spaces preceding a string.

RIGHT(): Returns part of a character string with the specified number of characters from the right.

RTRIM(): Right trim begins at the end of a string to remove empty spaces.

String functions: A function which returns a string that can then be used in an expression or another function.

SUBSTRING(): A function which returns part of a character string starting from the specified start point and specified return length.

UPPER(): Returns a character expression with all upper case letters.

ISMSSHIPPED: A SQL property that identifies which OBJECTS were shipped with SQL Server.

OBJECTPROPERTY(): Returns information about objects in the current database.

SERVERPROPERTY(): Used to show the level of SQL SERVER running on a machine.

Review Quiz - Chapter Eight

1.) What are two ways to find the first three letters for the FirstName field in the Employee table? (Choose two.)

   ☐ a. `SELECT LEFT(FirstName,3) FROM Employee`
   ☐ b. `SELECT RIGHT(FirstName,1,3) FROM Employee`
   ☐ c. `SELECT SUBSTRING (FirstName,1,3) FROM Employee`
   ☐ d. `SELECT SUBSTRING (FirstName,3,1) FROM Employee`

2.) You want to find the number of characters in a varchar field called ProductName. What function will achieve this result?

   O a. `LEFT()`
   O b. `RIGHT()`
   O c. `SUBSTRING()`
   O d. `LEN()`

3.) You must create e-mail addresses based off employee first and last names. You need to concatenate the first 2 letters of FirstName with all of the letters of the LastName and append @Joes2Pros.com. What expression in your SELECT list will achieve this result?

   O a. `LEFT(FirstName,2) + LEN(LastName) + '@Joes2Pros.com'`
   O b. `RIGHT(FirstName,2) + LEN(LastName) + '@Joes2Pros.com'`
   O c. `LEFT(FirstName,2) + LastName + '@Joes2Pros.com'`
   O d. `RIGHT(FirstName,2) + LastName + '@Joes2Pros.com'`

4.) You want to verify which service pack for SQL Server you are running. Which metadata function and parameter will achieve this result?

   O a. `SELECT SERVERPROPERTY('ProductVersion')`
   O b. `SELECT SERVERPROPERTY('ProductLevel')`
   O c. `SELECT SERVERPROPERTY('Edition')`

5.) What will the following predicate find?

   `OBJECTPROPERTY(Object_id, 'TableHasClustIndex') = 0?`

   O a. All Tables that have clustered indexes.
   O b. All Tables that do not have clustered indexes.

Chapter 8. String Functions

6.) Which answer will CONCAT and + , not return the same result ?

O a. `SELECT 'Air' + 'plane' | SELECT CONCAT('Air', 'plane')`

O b. `SELECT 'Air' + '' + 'plane' | SELECT CONCAT('Air', '', 'plane')`

O c. `SELECT 'Air' + '0' + 'plane' | SELECT CONCAT('Air', '0', 'plane')`

O d. `SELECT 'Air' + NULL + 'plane' | SELECT CONCAT('Air', NULL, 'plane')`

7.) Which function parameter signature will cause an error with the FORMAT function?

O a. `SELECT FORMAT(GETDATE())`

O b. `SELECT FORMAT(GETDATE(), 'd')`

O c. `SELECT FORMAT(GETDATE(), 'd', 'en-us')`

O d. `SELECT FORMAT(GETDATE(), 'd', 'de-de')`

O e. `SELECT FORMAT(GETDATE(), 'd', 'en-gb')`

O f. `SELECT FORMAT(GETDATE(), 'd', 'fr-fr')`

8.) Which query will always show the value as EUROs?

O a. `SELECT FORMAT(RetailPrice, 'c') FROM CurrentProducts`

O b. `SELECT FORMAT(RetailPrice, 'c', 'en-us') FROM CurrentProducts`

O c. `SELECT FORMAT(RetailPrice, 'c', 'en-gb') FROM CurrentProducts`

O d. `SELECT FORMAT(RetailPrice, 'c', 'de-de') FROM CurrentProducts`

Answer Key

1.) Because the RIGHT function requires only 2 arguments and starts counting characters from the end of the string, (b) will be an incorrect answer. SUBSTRING (FirstName, 3, 1) will return the first character starting at the third position in the FirstName field, so (d) is not correct either. Since LEFT (FirstName, 3) and SUBSTRING (FirstName, 1, 3) each return the first 3 characters of the FirstName field, (a) and (c) are both correct answers.

2.) Since LEFT(), RIGHT() and SUBSTRING() all return parts of a string but no information about its length (a), (b) and (c) are all wrong. LEN() will return the number of characters that make up a string expression excluding any trailing spaces, so (d) is the right answer.

3.) Since '+ LEN (FullName)' will concatenate the length of the last name instead of the letters in the last name both (a) and (b) are incorrect answers. 'RIGHT (FirstName, 2)' will return the last two characters of the first name instead of the first two, making (d) another wrong choice. Since 'LEFT (FirstName, 2) + LastName is the proper way to concatenate the first 2 letter of the first name with all of the letters of the last name (c) is the correct answer.

4.) The SERVERPROPERTY function used with the 'ProductVersion' parameter will display which version (i.e. 9 for SQL Server 2005, 10 for 2008, 11 for 2012, etc.) is being used, so (a) is incorrect. Using the 'Edition' parameter will display which edition (i.e. Developer, Enterprise, Evaluation, Express or Standard) is installed, so (c) is not correct either. The SERVERPROPERTY function used with the 'ProductLevel' parameter will return which product level (i.e. Beta, RTM, Service Pack 1, etc.) is running on the machine, making (b) the correct choice.

5.) A false reading is 0, so (a) is wrong, which means (b) is the correct answer.

6.) Since CONCAT and + work the same in all situations this makes (a) (b) and (c) incorrect answers. CONTACT turns NULL values into empty strings whereas + keeps them as nulls, making (d) is the correct answer.

7.) Since FORMAT uses the local culture if you don't provide one (b) has no error. You can override the local culture if you want, so (c) and (d) also work. Since we are looking for the answer that errors out and the FORMAT() function requires 2 to 3 arguments, (a) is the correct answer.

8.) 'en-us' shows as dollars, so (b) is wrong. 'en-gb' shows as pounds, so (c) is wrong. Not specifying a culture will only show euros if the local server is running in a euro culture region, so (a) is incorrect. 'de-de' is Germany which uses euros, so (d) is the correct answer.

Bug Catcher Game

To play the Bug Catcher game, run the file SQLQueries2012Vol4BugCatcher8.pps from the BugCatcher folder of the companion files found at www.Joes2Pros.com.

[THIS PAGE INTENTIONALLY LEFT BLANK.]

Chapter 9. Time Functions

A common question I get relating to time is "When will your next book be out". Well if it takes me two months to write a book, then 3 months in editing and testing then about 5 months from now the book should be released to publishing. If I started on April 15th then the projected release date would be September 15th. As of this writing that has not happened yet but the number is still real to me and many readers. If I miss that date, a few low grade amazon reviews have been known to pop up siting a missed timeline as the reason.

In my logged data of hours and work performed on these books, nowhere have I stored the date September 15th. That is a time function that came up with that number. It may not be stored as data but is very business information. There are many time functions in SQL Server that are very useful to businesses.

READER NOTE: *Please run the script SQLQueries2012Vol4Chapter8.1-10Setup.sql in order to follow along with the examples in the first section of Chapter 9. All scripts mentioned in this chapter may be found at* ***www.Joes2Pros.com****.*

System Time Functions

Time functions come in lots of flavors. For example, I could ask what is the time now or what will the date be next Thursday. The answer will be a date and time data type. You could also ask how many days have gone by since the first of the year. In that case you would use a time function, which returns an integer. Sometimes functions return points in time and others return numeric evaluations of time.

Returning DateTime from Time Functions

At the beginning of this book, we covered the GETDATE() function, which goes to the system you're running and finds the current time.

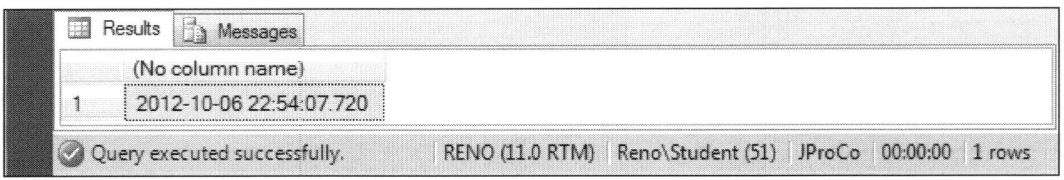

```sql
SELECT GETDATE()
```

(No column name)
2012-10-06 22:54:07.720

Figure 9.1 The GETDATE() function returns the date and time according to your system.

Using +1 with the function will increment one day into the future. To specify yesterday (at today's exact time), use -1.

```sql
SELECT GETDATE()
SELECT GETDATE() + 1  --Tomorrow
SELECT GETDATE() - 1  --Yesterday
```

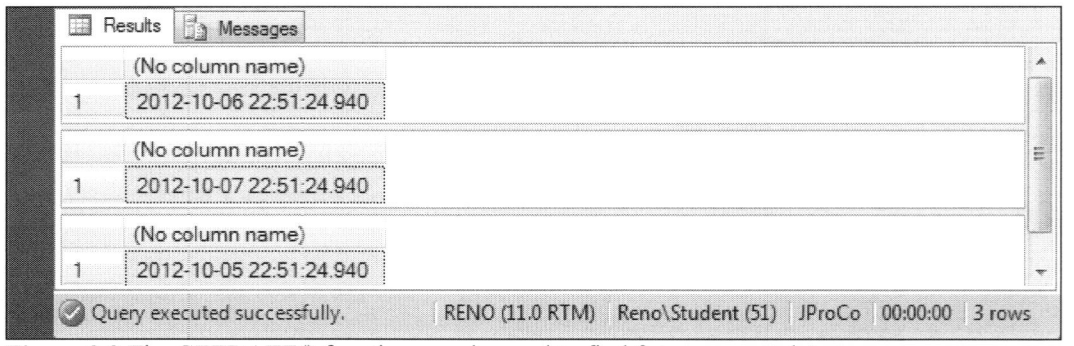

(No column name)
2012-10-06 22:51:24.940

(No column name)
2012-10-07 22:51:24.940

(No column name)
2012-10-05 22:51:24.940

Figure 9.2 The GETDATE() function may be used to find future or past dates.

Let's look at the two records contained in the Contractor table. We're going to work with the HireDate field values using an UPDATE statement.

```
SELECT * FROM Contractor
```

	ctrID	lastname	firstname	hiredate	LocationID
1	1	Barker	Bill	2006-01-07 00:00:00.000	1
2	2	Ogburn	Maurice	2006-10-27 00:00:00.000	1
3	3	Fortner	Linda	2009-11-22 00:00:00.000	2
4	4	Johnson	Davey	2009-03-07 00:00:00.000	1

Figure 9.3 We will work with the HireDate values in the Contractor table.

JProCo officially hired Bill yesterday, so we need to set his HireDate to show yesterday's date. Tomorrow they're going to hire Maurice (Figure 9.3). Keep in mind, when I ran this, the date was August 29th 2009. Based on when you run it, your current date will be different. We can use an UPDATE statement to change the hiredate values with the following code:

```
UPDATE Contractor SET HireDate = GETDATE() - 1
WHERE CtrID = 1

UPDATE Contractor SET HireDate = GETDATE() + 1
WHERE CtrID = 2
```

The official hire date for Bill now shows as yesterday (GETDATE -1). The official hire date for Maurice shows as tomorrow (GETDATE + 1).

```
SELECT * FROM Contractor
```

	CtrID	LastName	FirstName	HireDate	LocationID
1	1	Barker	Bill	2006-01-07 00:00:00.000	1
2	2	Ogburn	Maurice	2006-10-27 00:00:00.000	1

Figure 9.4 Bill was hired yesterday (GETDATE-1) and Maurice will be hired tomorrow (GETDATE+1).

We can combine GETDATE() with a comparison operator to find the contractors who were hired before today.

```
SELECT *
FROM Contractor
WHERE HireDate < GETDATE()
```

	CtrID	LastName	FirstName	HireDate	LocationID
1	1	Barker	Bill	2006-01-07 00:00:00.000	1
2	2	Ogburn	Maurice	2006-10-27 00:00:00.000	1
3	3	Fortner	Linda	2009-11-22 00:00:00.000	2
4	4	Johnson	Davey	2009-03-07 00:00:00.000	1

4 rows

Figure 9.5 We can combine a comparison operator with the GETDATE() function.

To see all the contractors who have been with us for at least 30 days, include "+ 30" to the query.

```
SELECT *
FROM Contractor
WHERE HireDate < GETDATE() + 30
```

	CtrID	LastName	FirstName	HireDate	LocationID
1	1	Barker	Bill	2006-01-07 00:00:00.000	1
2	2	Ogburn	Maurice	2006-10-27 00:00:00.000	1
3	3	Fortner	Linda	2009-11-22 00:00:00.000	2
4	4	Johnson	Davey	2009-03-07 00:00:00.000	1

4 rows

Figure 9.6 This code will find the contractors who have been with us for at least 30 days.

As we read in Chapter 3, CURRENT_TIMESTAMP is a property whose value is the current time in your time zone and produces a result identical to the GETDATE() function.

GETDATE() was invented by Microsoft, and CURRENT_TIMESTAMP is the ANSI (American National Standards Institute) equivalent for displaying the current date and time.

Lab 9.1: System Time Functions

Lab Prep: Lab Prep: Each lab has one or more Skill Checks. Start with Skill Check 1 and proceed until reaching the Points to Ponder section.

Before beginning this lab, verify that SQL Server 2012 is properly installed and operating. Before running the lab setup script for resetting the database (SQLQueries2012Vol4Chapter8.1-10Setup.sql), please make sure to close all query windows within SSMS. An open query window pointing to a database context can lock that database preventing it from updating when the script is executing. A simple way to assure all query windows are closed, is to exit out of SSMS, then open a new instance of SSMS, and lastly run the setup script.

Skill Check 1: Write a query to show all records from the SalesInvoice table that were paid in the last 30 days.

(Note: results will vary based on the current date. The results in the following figure are based on the date 10/02/2012)

Order your result to show most recent PaidDate first.

	InvoiceID	OrderDate	PaidDate	CustomerID	Comment	UpdatedDate
1	1614	2012-07-18 17:30:03.463	2012-09-04 06:05:39.763	87	NULL	NULL
2	1629	2012-08-01 01:10:33.300	2012-09-03 19:12:02.060	149	NULL	NULL
3	1631	2012-08-02 17:03:40.597	2012-09-10 12:18:32.893	544	NULL	NULL
4	1632	2012-08-03 10:53:31.373	2012-09-16 11:14:34.240	584	NULL	NULL
5	1634	2012-08-04 17:19:17.950	2012-09-10 18:23:29.280	342	NULL	NULL
6	1635	2012-08-05 07:10:43.577	2012-09-17 17:06:06.027	139	NULL	NULL

Figure 9.7 Skill Check 3 shows all invoices paid in the last 30 days.

Answer Code: The T-SQL code to this lab can be found in the downloadable files in a file named Lab9.1_TimeFunctions.sql

Points to Ponder – System Time Functions

1. GETDATE() displays the current date and time of the system you're running.
2. GETDATE() was invented by Microsoft, and CURRENT_TIMESTAMP is the ANSI (American National Standards Institute) equivalent for displaying the current date and time.

Time Calculation Functions

There's another useful time function known as DatePart(), which you can use to extract specific components from date-time values. Like parsing values from string data, or concatenating data to a string, there will be times your data work will require you to separate a date-time field into its individual components (e.g., month, day, year, time).

Using DatePart

Look at all the records in the MgmtTraining table and the approval dates for the five classes. We can see that two classes were approved in 2007, one in 2008, and several more have a more current time for the approval date.

```
SELECT * FROM MgmtTraining
```

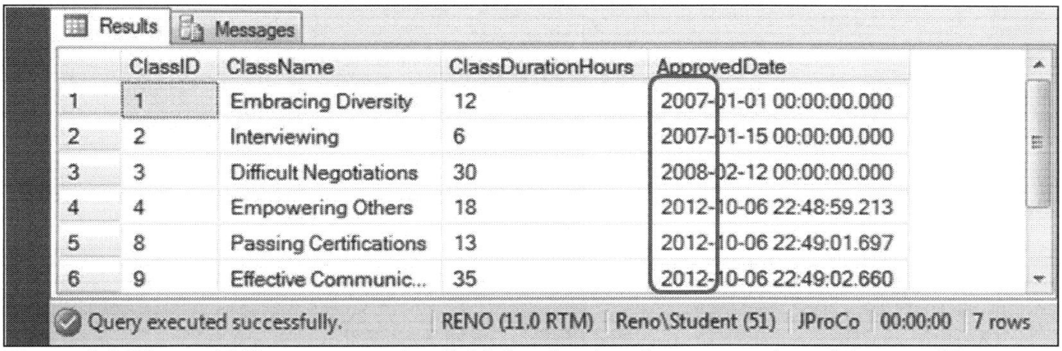

	ClassID	ClassName	ClassDurationHours	ApprovedDate
1	1	Embracing Diversity	12	2007-01-01 00:00:00.000
2	2	Interviewing	6	2007-01-15 00:00:00.000
3	3	Difficult Negotiations	30	2008-02-12 00:00:00.000
4	4	Empowering Others	18	2012-10-06 22:48:59.213
5	8	Passing Certifications	13	2012-10-06 22:49:01.697
6	9	Effective Communic...	35	2012-10-06 22:49:02.660

Figure 9.8 We would like an expression field showing just the year portion of ApprovedDate.

We would like to add an expression field to this query to show just the year portion of the approval date (e.g., 2007, 2008, and beyond). An easy way to do this is to use the DATEPART() function (Figure 9.9).

```sql
SELECT *, DATEPART(yy, ApprovedDate)
FROM MgmtTraining
```

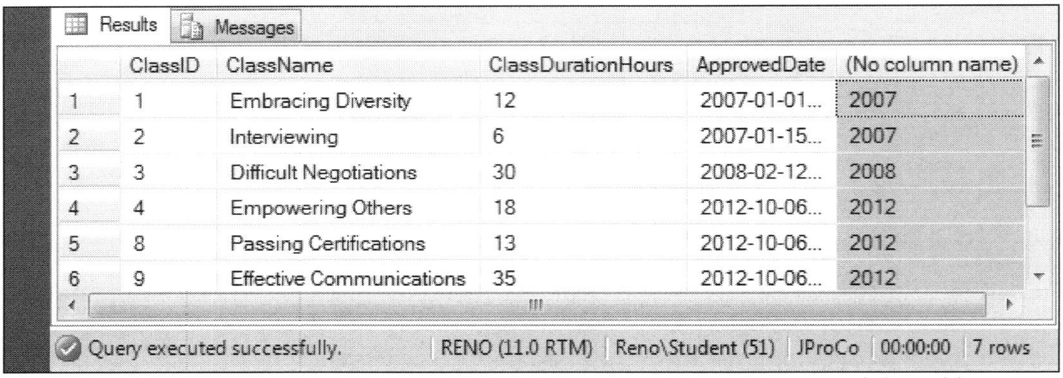

Figure 9.9 We will apply the DATEPART() function to records in the MgmtTraining table.

Now let's add another expression field showing the approval month. It looks like the first two classes were approved in January. The third class was approved in February, and the last class was approved in August.

```sql
SELECT *, DATEPART(yy, ApprovedDate),
DATEPART(mm, ApprovedDate)
FROM MgmtTraining
```

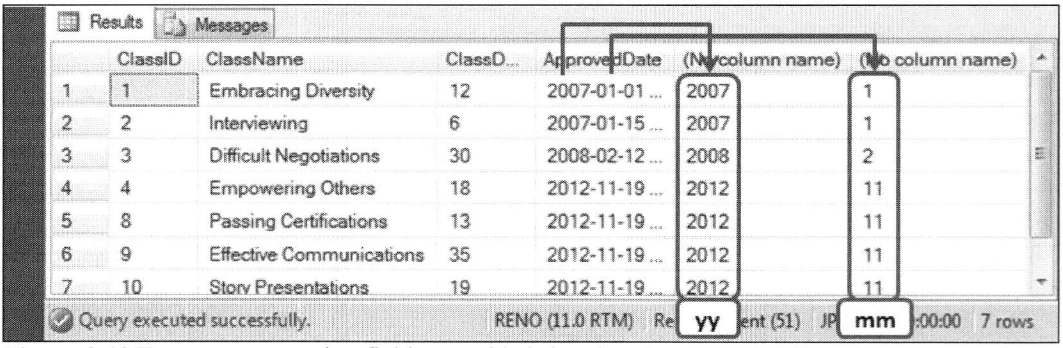

Figure 9.10 Two new expression fields are added showing the Approved Date's year and month.

You can do this for all components of the date – the quarter (based on calendar year), year, month, day, minute, hour, seconds, etc.

```
SELECT ApprovedDate,
DATEPART(QQ, ApprovedDate) AS [Quarter],
DATEPART(YY, ApprovedDate) AS [Year],
DATEPART(MM, ApprovedDate) AS [Month],
DATEPART(DD, ApprovedDate) AS [Day],
DATEPART(HH, ApprovedDate) AS [Hour],
DATEPART(MI, ApprovedDate) AS [Minute],
DATEPART(SS, ApprovedDate) AS [Second],
DATEPART(MS, ApprovedDate) AS [Millisecond],
DATEPART(NS, ApprovedDate) AS [Nanosecond]
FROM MgmtTraining
```

	ApprovedDate	Quarter	Year	Month	Day	Hour	Minute	Second	Millisecond	Nanosecond
1	2007-01-01 00:00:00.000	1	2007	1	1	0	0	0	0	0
2	2007-01-15 00:00:00.000	1	2007	1	15	0	0	0	0	0
3	2008-02-12 00:00:00.000	1	2008	2	12	0	0	0	0	0
4	2012-10-06 22:48:59.213	4	2012	10	6	22	48	59	213	213000000
5	2012-10-06 22:49:01.697	4	2012	10	6	22	49	1	697	697000000
6	2012-10-06 22:49:02.660	4	2012	10	6	22	49	2	660	660000000

Figure 9.11 You can use DATEPART() to parse all parts of a date-time field.

You can either pass in the interval's abbreviation to DATEPART() as shown in Figure 9.11, or you can spell out the full word as shown in Figure 9.12 for quarter, year, month, etc.

```
SELECT ApprovedDate,
DATEPART([Quarter], ApprovedDate) AS [QQ],
DATEPART([Year], ApprovedDate) AS [YY],
DATEPART([Month], ApprovedDate) AS [MM],
DATEPART([Day], ApprovedDate) AS [DD],
DATEPART([Hour], ApprovedDate) AS [HH],
DATEPART([Minute], ApprovedDate) AS [MI],
DATEPART([Second], ApprovedDate) AS [SS],
DATEPART([Millisecond], ApprovedDate) AS [MS],
DATEPART([Nanosecond], ApprovedDate) AS [NS]
FROM MgmtTraining
```

Chapter 9. Time Functions

	ApprovedDate	QQ	YY	MM	DD	HH	MI	SS	MS	NS
1	2007-01-01 00:00:00.000	1	2007	1	1	0	0	0	0	0
2	2007-01-15 00:00:00.000	1	2007	1	15	0	0	0	0	0
3	2008-02-12 00:00:00.000	1	2008	2	12	0	0	0	0	0
4	2012-10-06 22:48:59.213	4	2012	10	6	22	48	59	213	213000000
5	2012-10-06 22:49:01.697	4	2012	10	6	22	49	1	697	697000000
6	2012-10-06 22:49:02.660	4	2012	10	6	22	49	2	660	660000000

Figure 9.12 You can either pass in the interval's abbreviation or name to DATEPART().

Note that the Millisecond DATEPART() value shows the fractional seconds expressed in milliseconds. Likewise, Nanosecond shows this same value expressed in nanoseconds.

Another date measurement available in SQL Server is DayOfYear, which tells you which day of the year a date represents. For example, today (8/28/2012) is the 241st day of calendar year 2012 (Figure 9.13).

```
-- August 28th 2012 is the 241st day of the year
SELECT DATEPART(DAYOFYEAR,'8/28/2012')

--Show the day of the year for each approval date
SELECT ApprovedDate,
DATEPART(DAYOFYEAR, ApprovedDate) AS DayYr
FROM MgmtTraining
```

	(No column name)
1	241

	ApprovedDate	DayYr
1	2007-01-01 00:00:00.000	1
2	2007-01-15 00:00:00.000	15
3	2008-02-12 00:00:00.000	43
4	2012-10-06 22:48:59.213	280
5	2012-10-06 22:49:01.697	280

Figure 9.13 Examples combining DAYOFYEAR with DATEPART().

Earlier we saw GETDATE() +1 returns tomorrow's date. But what if we need to show the date exactly one month into the future?

```
SELECT GETDATE() AS [Today]
SELECT GETDATE() + 30 AS NextMonth
```

	Today
1	2012-10-06 23:46:28.990

	NextMonth
1	2012-11-05 23:46:28.990

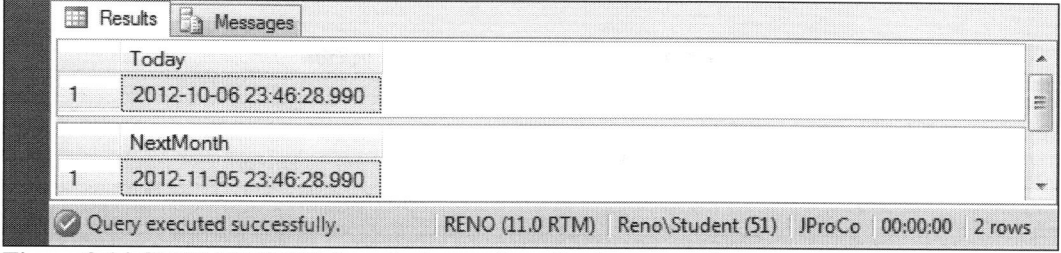

Figure 9.14 GETDATE()+30 doesn't always show the date a month away.

GETDATE() + 30 simply counts out 30 days – it doesn't take into consideration that a month can have a variable length (i.e., it can be 28, 29, 30, or 31 days long).

Using DateAdd

What we need here is the DATEADD() function, which is able to factor into its calculation the actual length of the month(s) in question.

```
SELECT GETDATE() AS [Today]
SELECT DATEADD(M, 1, GETDATE()) AS NextMonth
```

	Today
1	2012-10-06 23:52:21.713

	NextMonth
1	2012-11-06 23:52:21.713

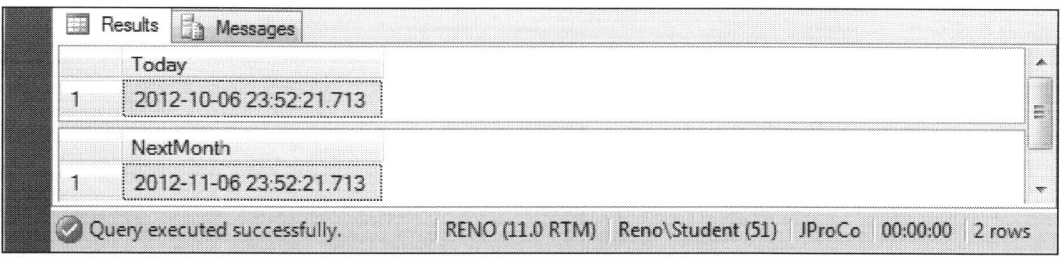

Figure 9.15 The DATEADD() function provides our expected date to next month.

Have DATEADD() show the date two months from now (2 months in the future).

```
SELECT DATEADD(M, 2, GETDATE())
```

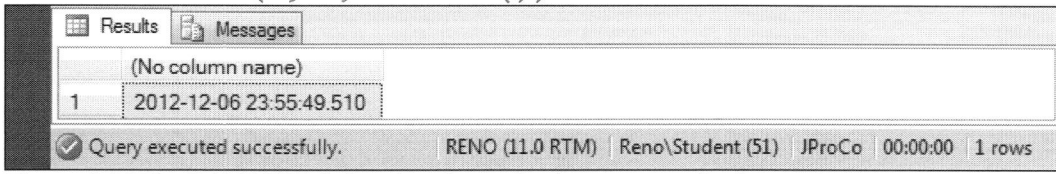

	(No column name)
1	2012-12-06 23:55:49.510

Figure 9.16 The DATEADD() function shows the date two months from today.

DATEADD() takes an interval, an increment, and an expression.

```
SELECT ApprovedDate,
  DATEADD(M, 1, ApprovedDate) AS [Date + 1 Month],
  DATEADD(M, 2, ApprovedDate) AS [Date + 2 Months]
FROM MgmtTraining
```

	ApprovedDate	Date + 1 Month	Date + 2 Months
1	2007-01-01 00:00:00.000	2007-02-01 00:00:00.000	2007-03-01 00:00:00.000
2	2007-01-15 00:00:00.000	2007-02-15 00:00:00.000	2007-03-15 00:00:00.000
3	2008-02-12 00:00:00.000	2008-03-12 00:00:00.000	2008-04-12 00:00:00.000
4	2012-10-06 22:48:59.213	2012-11-06 22:48:59.213	2012-12-06 22:48:59.213
5	2012-10-06 22:49:01.697	2012-11-06 22:49:01.697	2012-12-06 22:49:01.697
6	2012-10-06 22:49:02.660	2012-11-06 22:49:02.660	2012-12-06 22:49:02.660

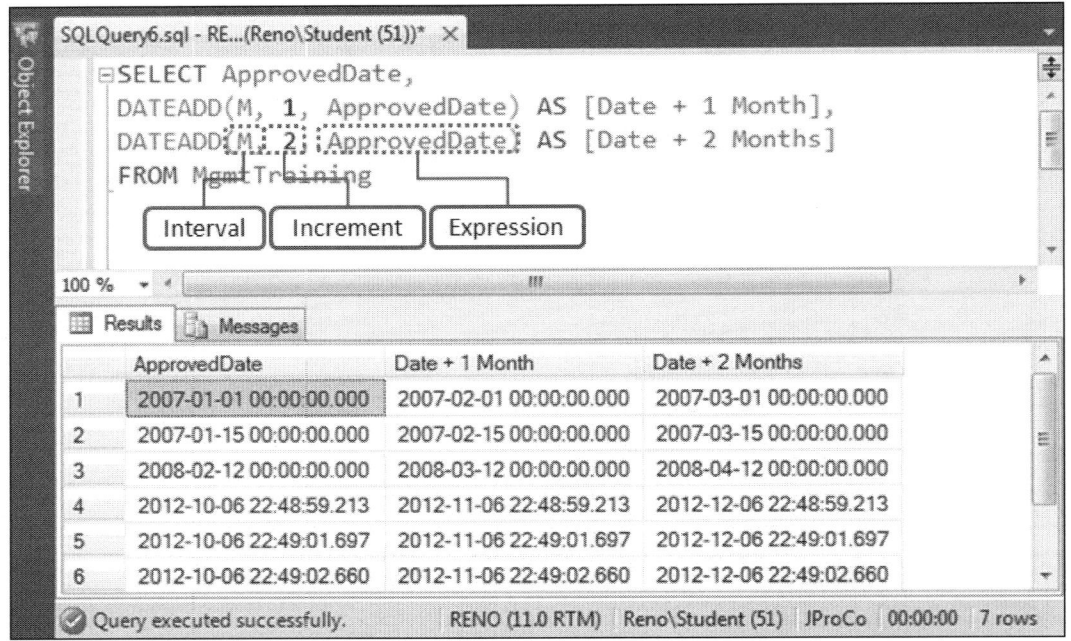

Figure 9.17 The DATEADD() function takes an interval, an increment, and an expression.

Now let's change the interval to "D" for days (instead of months) and show the date exactly 30 days from now, as well as the date from exactly 30 days ago.

```
SELECT DATEADD(D, 30, GETDATE()) AS [30DaysFromNow]
SELECT DATEADD(D, -30, GETDATE()) AS [30DaysFromAgo]
```

	30DaysFromNow
1	2012-06-28 12:18:22.013

	30DaysFromAgo
1	2012-04-29 12:18:22.013

Figure 9.18 We've changed the DATEADD() interval to "D" for days.

Let's now turn to the datetime data in the SalesInvoice table, where we have data from 2009, 2010, 2011, 2012 and even a few advance orders for 2013.

```
SELECT * FROM SalesInvoice
```

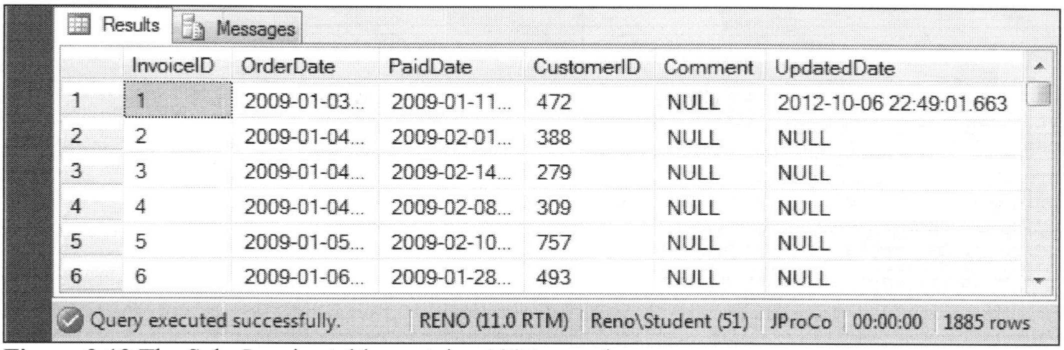

	InvoiceID	OrderDate	PaidDate	CustomerID	Comment	UpdatedDate
1	1	2009-01-03...	2009-01-11...	472	NULL	2012-10-06 22:49:01.663
2	2	2009-01-04...	2009-02-01...	388	NULL	NULL
3	3	2009-01-04...	2009-02-14...	279	NULL	NULL
4	4	2009-01-04...	2009-02-08...	309	NULL	NULL
5	5	2009-01-05...	2009-02-10...	757	NULL	NULL
6	6	2009-01-06...	2009-01-28...	493	NULL	NULL

Query executed successfully. RENO (11.0 RTM) | Reno\Student (51) | JProCo | 00:00:00 | 1885 rows

Figure 9.19 The SalesInvoice table contains 1885 records.

```
SELECT COUNT(*) AS OrderCount,
DATEPART(YY, ORDERDATE) AS ORDERYEAR
FROM SalesInvoice
GROUP BY DATEPART(YY, OrderDate)
ORDER BY DATEPART(YY, OrderDate)
```

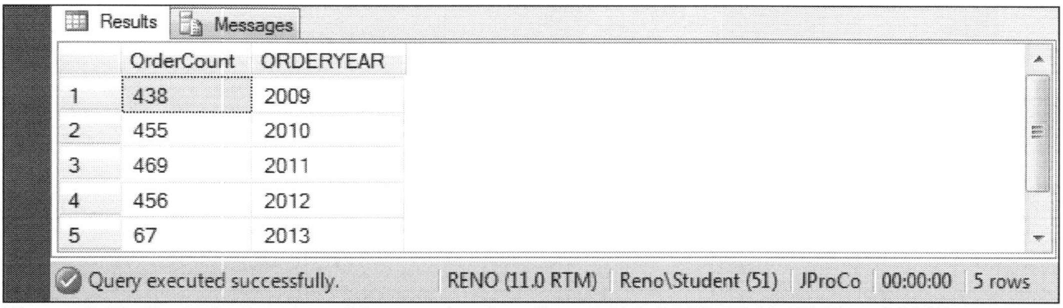

	OrderCount	ORDERYEAR
1	438	2009
2	455	2010
3	469	2011
4	456	2012
5	67	2013

Query executed successfully. RENO (11.0 RTM) | Reno\Student (51) | JProCo | 00:00:00 | 5 rows

Figure 9.20 The SalesInvoice table contains data from 2009, 2010, 2011, 2012 and 2013.

Suppose we want to find all orders which were paid at least 30 days ago. Assume today is 8/29/2009, we want to find records with a paid date of 7/29/2009, or earlier, to show in the result set. We will use the DATEADD() function and look for records having a PaidDate <30 days ago (Figure 9.21).

```
SELECT *
FROM SalesInvoice
WHERE PaidDate < DATEADD(D, -30, GETDATE())
ORDER BY PaidDate
```

	InvoiceID	OrderDate	PaidDate	CustomerID	Comment	UpdatedDate
1	1	2009-01-03...	2009-01-11...	472	NULL	2012-10-06 22:49:01.663
2	11	2009-01-10...	2009-01-18...	329	NULL	NULL
3	17	2009-01-16...	2009-01-20...	394	NULL	NULL
4	12	2009-01-11...	2009-01-22...	52	NULL	NULL
5	26	2009-01-19...	2009-01-22...	696	NULL	NULL
6	19	2009-01-16...	2009-01-24...	251	NULL	NULL

Query executed successfully. | RENO (11.0 RTM) | Reno\Student (51) | JProCo | 00:00:00 | 1650 rows

Figure 9.21 There are 1603 records in the SalesInvoice table which were paid ≥30 days ago.

Finally, we will incorporate the DATEPART() function in one of our string examples from the last section (Figure 9.22). You might imagine this result returning to a user app where someone in JProCo's billing department might be able to enter an invoice number and learn in what year the invoice was paid.

```
SELECT 'Invoice' +
CAST(InvoiceID AS VARCHAR(MAX)) +' was paid in ' +
CAST(DATEPART(YY, PaidDate) AS VARCHAR(4))
FROM SalesInvoice
WHERE InvoiceID = 975
```

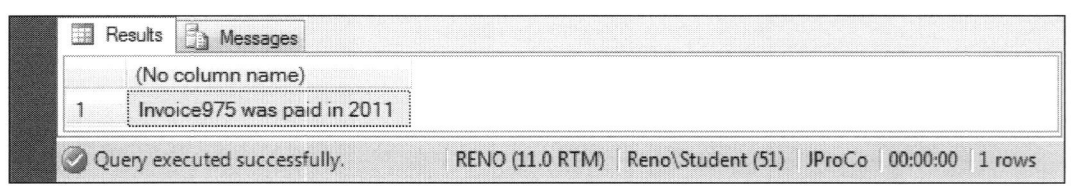

	(No column name)
1	Invoice975 was paid in 2011

Query executed successfully. | RENO (11.0 RTM) | Reno\Student (51) | JProCo | 00:00:00 | 1 rows

Figure 9.22 DATEPART() is shown combined in an earlier string example (Figure 9.21).

Chapter 9. Time Functions

Lab 9.2: Time Calculation Functions

Lab Prep: Lab Prep: Each lab has one or more Skill Checks. Start with Skill Check 1 and proceed until reaching the Points to Ponder section.

Before beginning this lab, verify that SQL Server 2012 is properly installed and operating. Before running the lab setup script for resetting the database (SQLQueries2012Vol4Chapter8.1-10Setup.sql), please make sure to close all query windows within SSMS. An open query window pointing to a database context can lock that database preventing it from updating when the script is executing. A simple way to assure all query windows are closed, is to exit out of SSMS, then open a new instance of SSMS, and lastly run the setup script.

Skill Check 1: Write a query to show all records from the CurrentProducts table which were originated in December, the 12th month of the year. Show the fields ProductName and OriginationDate and an expression field named OrigMonth. The expression field should pull out the month portion of OriginationDate and show it as an integer. When done, the query will contain at least 31 rows and should resemble Figure 9.23.

	ProductName	OriginationDate	OrigMonth
1	Underwater Tour 3 Days East Coast	2005-12-26 04:59:05.850	12
2	Underwater Tour 1 Week Mexico	2011-12-28 20:56:26.560	12
3	Underwater Tour 2 Weeks Mexico	2004-12-20 14:17:02.213	12
4	Underwater Tour 1 Week Canada	2006-12-05 07:21:53.690	12
5	Underwater Tour 1 Week Scandinavia	2006-12-03 01:03:05.267	12
6	Underwater Tour 2 Weeks Scandinavia	2011-12-24 14:10:22.090	12

Figure 9.23 Skill Check 1 adds an expression field pulling out the month from OriginationDate.

Skill Check 2: Assuming the date is 11/29/2009. Use DATEADD() to write a query showing records from the Employee table who were hired in the last two months.

EmpID	LastName	FirstName	HireDate	LocationID	ManagerID	Status	HiredOffset
14	Smith	Janis	2009-10-18 00:00:00.000	1	4	Active	2009-10-18 00:0(

Figure 9.24 Skill Check 2 shows all employees hired in the two months prior 11/29/2009.

Answer Code: The T-SQL code to this lab can be found in the downloadable files in a file named Lab9.2_TimeCalculationFunctions.sql.

Points to Ponder - Time Calculation Functions

1. DATEPART() extracts specific components from date-time values (e.g., year (YY), month (MM), and day (DD)).

2. The DATEADD() function is able to factor into its calculation the actual length of a particular time unit. Example: where GETDATE() + 60 will count ahead 60 days, the DATEADD(month,) function will detect the length of the interval months (e.g., whether 28, 29, 30, or 31 days) and can return what the precise date will be in two months. DATEADD() can handle the following time units: year, quarter, month, day-of-year, day, week, hour, minute, second, and millisecond.

New SQL 2012 Time Functions

The last several versions of SQL Server have added many new time function capabilities. This was true in SQL Server 2008 and SQL Server 2012 is no exception. We know that GETDATE() and CURRENT_TIMESTAMP create a date. If you don't want the current time than what are other ways to generate dates from input sources?

DATEFROMPARTS

Sometimes you need to create a date or time based on a calculation from another date. A date is really made up of many pieces, a day, a month and a year. Who decides what day it is or what year; it's not always one person or one source. We might have a source saying what year to use and another source to say what month and day to use (i.e.; 7 and 25). We can see 7-25-2013 is July 25th 2013 if we state these three values as one date value. All these values can now be combined into one date value based on the recognizable inputs from many values. Let's start with a simple statement that looks at a new function called DATEFROMPARTS().

```sql
SELECT DATEFROMPARTS(2013, 5, 2) AS DParts
```

	DParts
1	2013-05-02

1 rows

Figure 9.25 A date was returned from passing in three parameters to DATEFROMPARTS.

In Figure 9.25 the date is 2013-05-02. What happens if we run this and leave off the day and only pass in two of the three parameters? Figure 9.26 shows without the day parameter we get an error. The DATEFROMPARTS() function needs three arguments, a year, a month and day to run properly.

```sql
SELECT DATEFROMPARTS(2013, 5) AS DParts
```

Messages
Msg 174, Level 15, State 1, Line 1
The datefromparts function requires 3 argument(s).

0 rows

Figure 9.26 An error was returned since the 3rd parameter was missing.

In order to follow along through the next examples, we're going to have to run a special reset script. Run the SQLQueries2012Vol4Chapter9SpecialSetup.sql file. This will place everything needed for this chapter in the dbBasics database.

```
USE dbBasics
GO

SELECT *
FROM vSales
```

InvoiceID	OrdYear	OrdMo	OrdDay	OrdHour	OrdMin	OrdSec	OrdMil
1	2009	1	3	0	0	0	0
2	2009	1	4	2	22	41	473
3	2009	1	4	5	33	1	150
4	2009	1	4	22	6	58	657
5	2009	1	5	11	37	45	597
6	2009	1	6	23	53	14	320
7	2009	1	8	8	6	33	210

1885 rows

Figure 9.27 Results from querying vSales.

We can see in Figure 9.27 that the VSales table contains invoices, but the dates are not in a reader friendly format. They are spread over a bunch of fields. In the first record we see a value of 2009 for the OrdYear field. We also see OrdMo, OrdDay, OrdHour, OrdMin, OrdSec and OrdMil all containing values related to a specific date and time. We want to turn all of these individual parts into an exact date or an exact time or an exact date and time composite. Let's start with the one we know, DATEFROMPARTS(). Instead of using explicit values let's simply name the field we want each particular value to come from. To keep it neat we will alias the derived field AS OrderDate as seen in the following code:

```
USE dbBasics
GO

SELECT *, DATEFROMPARTS(OrdYear, OrdMo, OrdDay) AS OrderDate
FROM vSales
```

InvoiceID	OrdYear	OrdMo	OrdDay	OrdHour	OrdMin	OrdSec	OrdMil	OrderDate
1	2009	1	3	0	0	0	0	2009-01-03
2	2009	1	4	2	22	41	473	2009-01-04
3	2009	1	4	5	33	1	150	2009-01-04
4	2009	1	4	22	6	58	657	2009-01-04
5	2009	1	5	11	37	45	597	2009-01-05
6	2009	1	6	23	53	14	320	2009-01-06
7	2009	1	8	8	6	33	210	2009-01-08

1885 rows

Figure 9.28 Query shows date in reader friendly format.

Figure 9.28 shows the DATEFROMPARTS() function has taken the individual fields and combined them into a date formatted field, aliased as OrderDate.

TIMEFROMPARTS

The DATEFROMPARTS() function took the year, month, and day to satisfy the three arguments to make an exact date. What if we want to include time? We could have hours, minutes, seconds and fractions of seconds. The function would take a few more arguments. Let's explore how this works using the following code:

```
SELECT DATEFROMPARTS(2013, 5, 2) AS DParts
```

	DParts
1	2013-05-02

1 rows

Figure 9.29 Results from explicit DATEFROMPARTS query.

```
SELECT TIMEFROMPARTS(8, 32, 45, 5, 1) AS TMParts
```

	TMParts
1	08:32:45.5

1 rows

Figure 9.30 Results from explicit TIMEFROMPARTS query.

In Figure 9.30 we see the TIMEFROMPARTS() function gave us a result of 08:32:45.5. This is 8 hours, 32 minutes, 45 seconds, and 5 tenths of a second. Notice the final argument has a value of one but does not appear in the final result. What argument does the "1" answer in this function?

You may have noticed that the DATEFROMPARTS() function has three parameters and the date it returns has 3 parts. In Contrast, the TIMEFROMPARTS() function has 5 parameters and only returns 4 parts. To discover the purpose of the fifth parameter let's copy the exact same code and paste it a couple of times and then replace the "1" with a "2" and "4" in the fifth parameter like you see in the following code steps:

```
SELECT TIMEFROMPARTS(8, 32, 45, 5, 1) AS TMParts
```

	TMParts
1	08:32:45.5

1 rows

Figure 9.31 Query returns one decimal place.

Chapter 9. Time Functions

```sql
SELECT TIMEFROMPARTS(8, 32, 45, 5, 2) AS TMParts
```

	TMParts
1	08:32:45.05

1 rows

Figure 9.32 Query returns two decimal places.

```sql
SELECT TIMEFROMPARTS(8, 32, 45, 5, 4) AS TMParts
```

	TMParts
1	08:32:45.0005

1 rows

Figure 9.33 Query returns four decimal places.

We notice that the fifth parameter sets the number of decimal places for fractions of seconds in the fourth part of the time stamp. In Figure 9.31 the "1" gave us one decimal place. In Figure 9.32 the "2" gave us two and so forth. What if we don't want seconds at all? Let's put a "0" in the fifth parameter and see what happens.

```sql
SELECT TIMEFROMPARTS(8, 32, 45, 5, 0) AS TMParts
```

```
Messages
Msg 289, Level 16, State 2, Line 1
Cannot construct data type time, some of the arguments have values which are
not valid.
```

0 rows

Figure 9.34 A "0" decimals with seconds present returned an error.

It returns an error message. If you put a 5 into one decimal place you get .5, if you put a 5 into two decimal places you get .05. You cannot fit a 5 in zero decimal places. In Figure 9.34 we are trying to give precision and we haven't allowed enough room. Does that mean we have to use fractions of seconds? No. If we don't have a fraction of a second and don't want decimals then the "0" in the fifth parameter works just fine. As seen in Figure 9.35 where our time is shown as 8:32:45.

```sql
SELECT TIMEFROMPARTS(8, 32, 45, 0, 0) AS TMParts
```

	TMParts
1	08:32:45

1 rows

Figure 9.35 Query returns zero decimal places.

Now that we know how the TIMEFROMPARTS() function works, how do we use this with the vSales table the we worked with earlier.

	InvoiceID	OrdYear	OrdMo	OrdDay	OrdHour	OrdMin	OrdSec	OrdMil
1	1	2009	1	3	0	0	0	0
2	2	2009	1	4	2	22	41	473
3	3	2009	1	4	5	33	1	150
4	4	2009	1	4	22	6	58	657
5	5	2009	1	5	11	37	45	597
6	6	2009	1	6	23	53	14	320
7	7	2009	1	8	8	6	33	210

1885 rows

Figure 9.36 Simple query of the vSales table.

In order to get the time of an Invoice from the VSales table seen in Figure 9.36 we need to replace the explicit values with fields from the table. What would you expect if we set the query to return one decimal place as seen in the following code?

```sql
SELECT TIMEFROMPARTS(OrdHour, OrdMin, OrdSec, OrdMil, 1) AS TMParts
FROM vSales
```

```
Messages
Msg 289, Level 16, State 2, Line 1
Cannot construct data type time, some of the arguments have values which are
not valid.
                                                                        0 rows
```

Figure 9.37 One decimal place returned an error message.

As seen in Figure 9.36 record 2, there are 3 decimal places in .473 seconds. There needs to be 3 decimal places set in the fifth parameter. Just like "0" did not work when there was .5 seconds, "1" does not work in Figure 9.37 when there is .473 seconds in record two. In Figure 9.38 we see it runs just fine with the decimal place set at "3". We now see record two has a time stamp of 02:22:41.473.

```
SELECT *, TIMEFROMPARTS(OrdHour, OrdMin, OrdSec, OrdMil, 3)
AS TMParts
FROM vSales
```

InvoiceID	OrdYear	OrdMo	OrdDay	OrdHour	OrdMin	OrdSec	OrdMil	TMParts
1	2009	1	3	0	0	0	0	00:00:00.000
2	2009	1	4	2	22	41	473	02:22:41.473
3	2009	1	4	5	33	1	150	05:33:01.150
4	2009	1	4	22	6	58	657	22:06:58.657
5	2009	1	5	11	37	45	597	11:37:45.597
6	2009	1	6	23	53	14	320	23:53:14.320

1885 rows

Figure 9.38 Query of the vSales table TIMEFROMPARTS with 3 decimals.

DATETIMEFROMPARTS

DATEFROMPARTS() took the year, month and day and turned it into a date. TIMEFROMPARTS() took hours, minutes, seconds and fractions of seconds and turned it into a time. What if we wanted to return both? SQL Server 2012 has a cool new way to do this called DATETIMEFROMPARTS(). Let's create a date of May 2nd, 2013 at 8:32:45.005 using the following code:

```
SELECT DATETIMEFROMPARTS(2013, 5, 2, 8, 32, 45, 5) AS
DTmParts
```

	DTmParts
1	2013-05-02 08:32:45.007

1 rows

Figure 9.39 Results from DATETIMEFROMPARTS for May 2, 2013 at 8:32:45.005.

Notice we did not specify the fraction of a second because the DATETIMEFROMPARTS() functions nearest precision returns data rounded to the nearest 3 milliseconds. In Figure 9.39 the "5" in the seventh parameter is rounded to .007 seconds or 7 milliseconds.

Why did DATETIMEFROMPARTS() fail to return .005? It actually did return .005 but the data type does not support that much precision. The nearest number it could support is either .003 or .007. If we change the 5 milliseconds to 500 milliseconds then it rounds evenly. 650 milliseconds will return .650 but 651 will also return .650, rounding it to the nearest 3 millisecond increment. What do you predict DATETIMEFROMPARTS() will return for 659 milliseconds? You can see this in Figure 9.40.

```
SELECT DATETIMEFROMPARTS(2013, 5, 2, 8, 32, 45, 5)
SELECT DATETIMEFROMPARTS(2013, 5, 2, 8, 32, 45, 500)
SELECT DATETIMEFROMPARTS(2013, 5, 2, 8, 32, 45, 650)
SELECT DATETIMEFROMPARTS(2013, 5, 2, 8, 32, 45, 651)
SELECT DATETIMEFROMPARTS(2013, 5, 2, 8, 32, 45, 659)
```

	(No column name)
1	2013-05-02 08:32:45.007

	(No column name)
1	2013-05-02 08:32:45.500

	(No column name)
1	2013-05-02 08:32:45.650

	(No column name)
1	2013-05-02 08:32:45.650

	(No column name)
1	2013-05-02 08:32:45.660

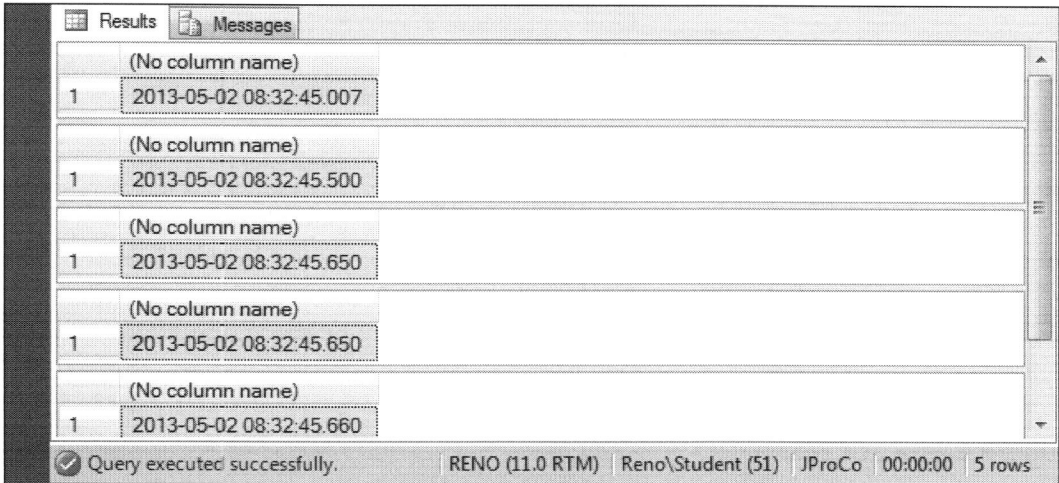

Figure 9.40 Examples of DATETIMEFROMPARTS rounding milliseconds.

EOMONTH

What if the boss says we have until the end of the month to finish the project we are working on? We are probably hoping there are 31 days in the month so we have extra time. Look at these two SELECT statements and think what might be the same and different between them:

```
SELECT '2/5/2012'
SELECT '2/5/2013'
```

They both read, February and both the 5th day of the month, but one is the year 2012 and the other is 2013. Both are 5 days into February, so 5 days ago, it was the end of January. How far are they from March? Maybe it's 23 days, or maybe 24 if it happens to be leap year. In other words, how can we find the end of the month for 2/5/2012 and 2/5/2013? Let's find that out using the following code:

```
SELECT EOMONTH('2/5/2012') AS EndMonth
```

	EndMonth
1	2012-02-29

Figure 9.41 EOMONTH for February leap year.

```
SELECT EOMONTH('2/5/2013') AS EndMonth
```

	EndMonth
1	2013-02-28

1 rows

Figure 9.42 EOMONTH for February non-leap year.

New for SQL 2012, the EOMONTH(), or "End of Month" function will tell us the last day of any given month. Notice in Figure 9.41 the last day of the month in February 2012 is the 29th because it's a leap year. In Figure 9.42 there are only 28 days in 2013 since leap year only happens once every 4 years. Although they are the same date in February, they don't have the same number of days left until the end of the month.

Let's start setting up an example that will use this function. In the JProCo database is the SalesInvoice table containing a bunch of invoice data, including OrderDate and PaidDate. The SalesInvoice table contains 1885 records. Using what we've learned let's get just the invoices that were paid in March of 2012 using the following code:

```
SELECT InvoiceID, PaidDate
FROM SalesInvoice
WHERE DATEPART(YY, PaidDate) = 2012
AND DATEPART(MM, PaidDate) = 3
```

	InvoiceID	PaidDate
1	1389	2012-03-02 12:44:38.660
2	1393	2012-03-01 12:39:51.977
3	1396	2012-03-09 08:38:17.213
4	1397	2012-03-11 05:58:55.400
5	1403	2012-03-14 23:53:13.210
6	1404	2012-03-12 19:33:34.880

Query executed successfully. RENO (11.0 RTM) | Reno\Student (51) | JProCo | 00:00:00 | 44 rows

Figure 9.43 The SalesInvoice table for March, 2012.

Figure 9.43 now shows 44 records where sales were made in March of 2012. Let's say there was a special offer that month. If someone paid X number of days before the end of the month, then they get a special credit on their next purchase. It looks like invoice 1389 has a customer who paid well before the end of the month. The third record shows another person that paid pretty far before the end of the month. The 15th record which is invoice 1414 shows payment 6 days before the end of the month.

Let's find out exactly how far before the end of the month everyone paid. By adding the EOMONTH() function to the SELECT Statement we will see the last day of the month in a third field expressed like 2012-03-31.

```sql
SELECT InvoiceID, PaidDate, EOMONTH(PaidDate) AS EndMarch
FROM SalesInvoice
WHERE DATEPART(YY, PaidDate) = 2012
AND DATEPART(MM, PaidDate) = 3
```

How would we query the number of days from the PaidDate to the last day of the month? Take the end of March value and subtract the pay date value to see the difference between the dates. This is done with one more new date function found in SQL Server 2012 called DATEDIFF(). On the third line of the upcoming query, notice we are using the DATEDIFF() function. We set the first parameters as day with d to let the function know we are looking for the difference in days. The second parameter with the PaidDate field is to set the start point of the equation. The final parameter is EOMONTH(PaidDate). The DATEDIFF will subtract these two values as seen in the following code steps:

```sql
SELECT InvoiceID, PaidDate,
EOMONTH(PaidDate) AS EndMarch,
DATEDIFF(d, PaidDate, EOMONTH(PaidDate)) AS DaysLeft
FROM SalesInvoice
WHERE DATEPART(YY, PaidDate) = 2012
AND DATEPART(MM, PaidDate) = 3 --March
```

You can see in Figure 9.44 we have the EndMarch field which contains the last day of the month and then the DATEDIFF() function returned the last field which shows us how many days there are left between the PaidDate and the last day of the Month.

	InvoiceID	PaidDate	EndMarch	DaysLeft
1	1389	2012-03-02 12:44:38.660	2012-03-31	29
2	1393	2012-03-01 12:39:51.977	2012-03-31	30
3	1396	2012-03-09 08:38:17.213	2012-03-31	22
4	1397	2012-03-11 05:58:55.400	2012-03-31	20
5	1403	2012-03-14 23:53:13.210	2012-03-31	17
6	1404	2012-03-12 19:33:34.880	2012-03-31	19

44 rows

Figure 9.44 SalesInvoice table query shows days between PaidDate and the end of the month.

Lab 9.3: New SQL 2012 Time Functions

Lab Prep: Lab Prep: Each lab has one or more Skill Checks. Start with Skill Check 1 and proceed until reaching the Points to Ponder section.

Before beginning this lab, verify that SQL Server 2012 is properly installed and operating. Before running the lab setup scripts for resetting the database (SQLQueries2012Vol4Chapter8.1-10Setup.sql and SQLQueries2012Vol4Chapter9SpecialSetup.sql), please make sure to close all query windows within SSMS. An open query window pointing to a database context can lock that database preventing it from updating when the script is executing. A simple way to assure all query windows are closed, is to exit out of SSMS, then open a new instance of SSMS, and lastly run the setup script.

Skill Check 1: From the dbBasics database, query the VSales table. Using DATEFROMPARTS(), create an expression field called CompletionDate that passes in the appropriate fields as parameters.

InvoiceID	OrdYear	OrdMo	OrdDay	OrdHour	OrdMin	OrdSec	OrdMil	CompletionDate
1	2009	1	3	0	0	0	0	2009-01-03
2	2009	1	4	2	22	41	473	2009-01-04
3	2009	1	4	5	33	1	150	2009-01-04
4	2009	1	4	22	6	58	657	2009-01-04
5	2009	1	5	11	37	45	597	2009-01-05
6	2009	1	6	23	53	14	320	2009-01-06

1885 rows

Figure 9.45 Results of Skill Check 1.

Skill Check 2: From the dbBasics database, query the Contestant table and include an expression field called CompletionDate. The expression field should use the DATETIMEFROMPARTS() function and pull in the CompletionYear, CompletionMonth and CompletionDay fields. When done, the result should resemble Figure 9.46

ContestType	ContestName	CompletionYear	CompletionMonth	CompletionDate
1 Inter	Ivan Drago	2010	5	2010-05-01
2 Inter	Piere LaFluer	2011	2	2011-02-22
3 Domestic	Bill Parker	2009	5	2009-05-16
4 Domestic	James McBrown	2012	8	2012-08-18
5 Inter	Newton Kommer	2013	9	2013-09-15

5 rows

Figure 9.46 Results of Skill Check 2.

Skill Check 3: From the dbBasics database, query the Contestant table to show all the contestants as an expression field called [CompletionDateTime]. This field should use the CompletionYear, CompletionMonth, CompletionDay, CompletionHour, CompletionMin, CompletionSec and CompletionMil fields with the DATETIMEFROMPARTS() function.

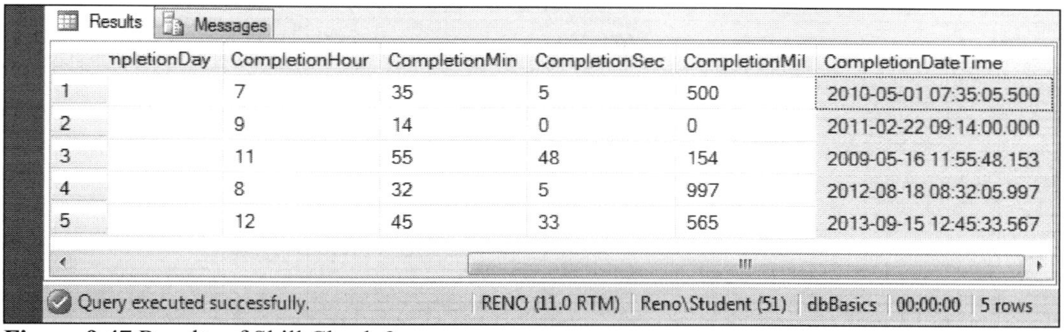

	npletionDay	CompletionHour	CompletionMin	CompletionSec	CompletionMil	CompletionDateTime
1		7	35	5	500	2010-05-01 07:35:05.500
2		9	14	0	0	2011-02-22 09:14:00.000
3		11	55	48	154	2009-05-16 11:55:48.153
4		8	32	5	997	2012-08-18 08:32:05.997
5		12	45	33	565	2013-09-15 12:45:33.567

Query executed successfully. RENO (11.0 RTM) | Reno\Student (51) | dbBasics | 00:00:00 | 5 rows

Figure 9.47 Results of Skill Check 3.

Answer Code: The T-SQL code to this lab can be found in the downloadable files in a file named Lab9.3_New2012TimeFunctions.sql.

Points to Ponder - New SQL 2012 Time Functions

1. DATEFROMPARTS() returns a DATE value based on the year, month and day you pass in as a part.
2. DATETIMEFROMPARTS() returns a DATETIME data type value based on the year, month, day and time you pass in a part.
3. TIMEFROMPARTS() returns a time value based on the hour, minute, second, fraction and precision.
4. In the TIMEFROMPARTS() function, the last parameter is the precision of DATETIME; it represents the fraction of the second.
5. If any of the required parameters for DATEFROMPARTS(), DATETIMEFROMPARTS() or TIMEFROMPARTS() is null, then the returned value will be null.
6. EOMONTH() returns the last day of the month you passed in.
7. Since March always has 31 days in it, this result will show March 31st of 2012.
    - SELECT EOMONTH('3/5/2012')
8. If you wanted to see the last date of the next month, you can use an optional 2nd parameter and specify the number of months to go into the future. This will show the last date in April 2012.
    - SELECT EOMONTH('3/5/2012', 1)
9. Since April always has 30 days in it, this result will show April 30th of 2012.
    - SELECT EOMONTH('4/5/2012')
    - SELECT EOMONTH('3/5/2012' , 1)
    - SELECT EOMONTH('5/5/2012' , -1)

Chapter Glossary

DATEADD(): A SQL function that takes an interval, an increment and an expression and is able to factor into its calculation the actual length of a particular time unit.

DATEPART(): A SQL function that extracts specific components from date-time values.

GETDATE(): A SQL function that returns the current date and time from the local system

DATEFROMPARTS(): A SQL function that returns a date value from specified date parts (Year, Month, Day). An error message is raised if all three arguments are not satisfied.

TIMEFROMPARTS(): A SQL function that returns a time value from specified time parts (Hour, Minute, Second, Fractions, Precision). The Precision argument determines the number of decimal places for the fractions. A three for precision sets each fraction to represent a millisecond. When the precision value is zero the fraction value must also be zero.

DATETIMEFROMPARTS(): A SQL function that returns a date and time value from specified date and time parts (Year, Month, Day, Hour, Minute, Seconds, Milliseconds). An error message is raised if all seven arguments are not satisfied. A NULL is returned when any of the seven arguments are NULL.

EOMONTH(): A SQL function that returns the last day of the specified month with an optional offset argument. The EOMONTH offset argument adds or subtracts whole numbers of months from the specified date. The EOMONTH() function will calculate the last day of the month for the resultant date.

Review Quiz - Chapter Nine

1.) You want to pull out just the year from all values in the PaidDate column of the SalesInvoice table. Which code will achieve this result?

   ○ a. `SELECT SalesOrderID, PaidDate AS Year FROM SalesInvoice`
   ○ b. `SELECT SalesOrderID, DATEDIFF(YY, PaidDate) AS Year FROM SalesInvoice`
   ○ c. `SELECT SalesOrderID, DATEPART (YY, PaidDate) AS Year FROM SalesInvoice`
   ○ d. `SELECT SalesOrderID, DATEADD (YY, PaidDate) AS Year FROM SalesInvoice`

2.) You need to find records for orders placed within the last 180 days. You must add a WHERE clause with the proper predicate to achieve this result. Which code would you append to this query?

   ```
   SELECT CustomerName, OrderDate
   FROM SalesInvoice
   ```

   ○ a. `WHERE OrderDate > DATEADD (D,180, GETDATE())`
   ○ b. `WHERE OrderDate > DATEADD (D,-180, GETDATE())`
   ○ c. `WHERE OrderDate > DATEADD (M,6, GETDATE())`
   ○ d. `WHERE OrderDate > DATEADD (M,-6, GETDATE())`

3.) You need to find all records with an order date within the last 12 hours. You need to add a WHERE clause with the proper predicate to achieve this result. Which code would you append to this query?

   ```
   SELECT CustomerName, OrderDate
   FROM SalesInvoice
   ```

   ○ a. `WHERE OrderDate > DATEPART (HH,12, GETDATE() )`
   ○ b. `WHERE OrderDate > DATEPART (HH,-12, GETDATE() )`
   ○ c. `WHERE OrderDate > DATEADD (HH,12, GETDATE() )`
   ○ d. `WHERE OrderDate > DATEADD (HH,-12, GETDATE() )`

4.) You want to pull out the day of the month from the HireDate field of the Employee table. Which code would you use?

○ a. `SELECT *, HireDate AS Day FROM Employee`
○ b. `SELECT *, DATEDIFF(DD, HireDate) AS Day FROM Employee`
○ c. `SELECT *, DATEPART (DD, HireDate) AS Day FROM Employee`
○ d. `SELECT *, DATEADD (D, HireDate) AS Day FROM Employee`

5.) You have two tables named Products and OldProducts. You need to copy data older than 30 days from Products into OldProducts. Which code segment should you use?

○ a. ```
DELETE FROM Products
OUTPUT DELETED.* INTO OldProducts
WHERE RecordDate < DATEADD(D,30,GETDATE())
```

○ b. ```
INSERT INTO OldProducts
SELECT *
FROM Products
WHERE RecordDate < DATEADD(D,30,GETDATE())
```

○ c. ```
DELETE FROM Products
OUTPUT DELETED.* INTO OldProducts
WHERE RecordDate < DATEADD(D,-30,GETDATE())
```

○ d. ```
INSERT INTO OldProducts
SELECT *
FROM Products
WHERE RecordDate < DATEADD(D,-30,GETDATE())
DELETE FROM Products
```

6.) Which one of the following will ALWAYS show you the first date of the next month?

○ a. `SELECT DATEADD(d, 1 ,GETDATE() )`
○ b. `SELECT DATEADD(d, -1 ,GETDATE() )`
○ c. `SELECT DATEADD(d, 1, EOMONTH(GETDATE() ) )`
○ d. `SELECT DATEADD(d, 1, EOMONTH(GETDATE() + 1) )`
○ e. `SELECT DATEADD(d, -1, EOMONTH(GETDATE() ) )`
○ f. `SELECT DATEADD(d, -1, EOMONTH(GETDATE() - 1) )`

7.) Which one of the following will NOT show you the last day of July 2013?

○ a. `SELECT EOMONTH('7/5/2013')`

○ b. `SELECT EOMONTH('6/5/2013', 1)`

○ c. `SELECT EOMONTH('8/5/2013', -1)`

○ d. `SELECT EOMONTH('9/5/2013', 2)`

8.) Which one of the following statements will throw an error message?

○ a. `SELECT DATEFROMPARTS(2013, 5, 2)`

○ b. `SELECT DATEFROMPARTS(2013, 5, NULL)`

○ c. `SELECT DATEFROMPARTS(NULL, NULL, NULL)`

○ d. `SELECT DATEFROMPARTS(2013, 5, 0)`

9.) Which one of the following statements produces the newest date?

○ a. `DECLARE @Date DATETIME`
`SET @Date = '3/5/2013'`
`SELECT EOMONTH(@Date)`

○ b. `DECLARE @Date DATETIME`
`SET @Date = '3/5/2013'`
`SELECT DATEADD(d, 30, @Date)`

○ c. `DECLARE @Date DATETIME`
`SET @Date = '3/5/2013'`
`SELECT DATEADD(d, -30, @Date)`

Answer Key

1.) 'PaidDate AS Year' will only alias the PaidDate column and still display the whole value in the field, so (a) is wrong. DATEDIFF is used to find out how much time has passed between two dates and requires 3 arguments, so (b) is wrong too. DATEADD is used to return a new DATETIME value by adding an interval of time to the specified date, so (d) is also wrong. DATEPART is used to return just a part of the DATETIME value stored in the specified date which means (c) is the correct answer.

2.) 'OrderDate > DATEADD (D, 180, GETDATE())' will return TRUE only if the OrderDate is in the future compared to a date 180 days in the future, so (a) is incorrect. Because months have varying lengths, using the interval of 'M' with an increment of 6 in the DATEADD function does not guarantee a day exactly 180 days in the future, so (c) and (d) are both wrong too. 'OrderDate > DATEADD (D, -180, GETDATE())' will return TRUE only if the OrderDate is in the future compared to a date 180 days before today's date, making (b) the right answer.

3.) The DATEPART function requires only 2 arguments and it would not return the correct value to compare to OrderDate for determining which came first anyway, so (a) and (b) are both wrong. Since adding 12 hours to the current time and checking if the OrderDate is greater than that would tell us if the OrderDate is more than 12 hours in the future it makes (c) an incorrect answer too. To find the orders that have occurred within the last 12 hours just use DATEADD to add minus 12 hours to (another way of saying subtract 12 hours from) the current time and select the records WHERE OrderDate is greater, making (d) the correct answer.

4.) 'HireDate AS Day' only alias's the HireDate column and still displays the whole value in the field, so (a) is wrong. DATEDIFF is used to find out how much time has passed between two dates and requires 3 arguments, so (b) is wrong too. DATEADD is used to return a new DATETIME value by adding an interval of time to the specified date, so (d) is also wrong. DATEPART is used to return just a part of the DATETIME value stored in the specified date which means (c) is the correct answer.

5.) Doing a DATEADD with 30 goes 30 days into the future (not the last 30 days), so (a) and (b) are wrong. Since (d) is two separate statements, one inserting the correct records and one deleting all records, it is also wrong. DATEADD with -30 is 30 days ago, and since you are using <, this means you will get products older than 30 days. It is also using OUTPUT to insert the deleted records into the OldProducts table, so (c) is the correct answer.

6.) Answer (a) will return next day's date, so (a) is incorrect. (b) will return the previous days date, so (b) is incorrect. Answer (d) will work until the last day of the month then the GETDATE() + 1 will push it to the following month, so (d) is incorrect. Answer (e) will return the second to the last day or the last day minus one, so (e) is incorrect. Choice (f) will return the second to the last day of the same month except for the first day of the next month will return the second the last day of the previous month, so (f) is incorrect. Answer (c) will always return the last day of the next month, so (c) is the correct answer.

7.) The key to question seven is the start month. Answer (a) is looking for the last day of the month in July 2013 with no offset value, so (a) is incorrect. Answer (b) is looking for the last day of June with a one month offset to July 2013, so (b) is incorrect. Answer (c) is looking for the last day of August with a minus one month offset to July 2013, so (c) is incorrect. Answer (d) is looking for the last day of September with a 2 month offset to November, so (d) is the correct answer.

8.) Choice (a) will return a valid date of 2013-05-02, so (a) is incorrect. If any argument is NULL the NULL is returned, so (b) and (c) are incorrect. Zero is an invalid value and will throw an error, so (d) is correct.

9.) Choice (a) will return the last day in March, so (a) is incorrect. Choice (c) will return the specified date minus 30 days which ends up being 2013-02-03, so (c) is incorrect. Choice (b) will return the specified date plus 30 days which ends up being 2013-04-04 and is the newest date, so (b) is the correct answer.

Bug Catcher Game

To play the Bug Catcher game, run the file SQLQueries2012Vol4BugCatcher9.pps from the BugCatcher folder of the companion files found at www.Joes2Pros.com.

[THIS PAGE INTENTIONALLY LEFT BLANK.]

Chapter 10. Logical and Analytical Functions

The other day I asked my self-employed friend how life was going. She said things were good since its Wednesday and she has completed over 90% of what needed to be done for the week. She then joked that it would either be a 3 or 4 day weekend coming up for her. We pretty much know what she is talking about because she performed a logical function and concluded the outcome. She made a sound judgment based on how things would turn out based on what has happened so far.

In databases there are many conclusions that point to only logical outcomes. If this logic is hard and fast, you no longer need that tedious work to be filled in by the human. You can let SQL Server do the hard work and report these values for you.

READER NOTE: *Please run the script SQLQueries2012Vol4Chapter8.1-10Setup.sql in order to follow along with the examples in the first section of Chapter 10. All scripts mentioned in this chapter may be found at **www.Joes2Pros.com**.*

Logical Functions

Let me admit that once in while I do like to go to Vegas and I don't let my emotional dreams and hopes of being the next James Bond let me do foolish things at the table. The $5 table has plenty of good fun and conversation for my liking.

The reason I am so conservative is because they want you to make a decision without knowing what is on the table. For example, if I have 12 points showing, the next card could be a 10 and then I bust. However it's unlikely that I will win with a 12. If I knew what the next card was then I would never bust and always get the best hand possible with what the table has presented me.

It's simple, if the next card does not put me over 21 then I would hit. If it does, then I stand. 21 is as high as I can get without going over. Logical functions will adhere to the goals you set forth if you know how to set them up.

Using ISNULL

Imagine you are supervising a street fair with many booths and each plot owner needs to sign a clipboard next to their corresponding number. The boss says no box shall be empty and put N/A in the box of any owner that does not show. In real life N/A is the ultimate ISNULL function since it shows you did not forget, but have a value to put in place where data could not be found.

```
DECLARE @Qty INT
SET @Qty = 5
SELECT @Qty
```

	(No column name)
1	5

1 rows

Figure 10.1 Shows @Qty when set equal to five.

It is not a surprise that this result in Figure 10.1 shows a five. If we change the variable value to 1 this query would return a one. What happens if we comment the second line out and query the variable without setting a value?

```
DECLARE @Qty INT
--SET @Qty = 5
SELECT @Qty
```

	(No column name)
1	NULL

1 rows

Figure 10.2 Shows a query of @Qty without a set value.

Just like the supervisor of the street fair would put N/A with an absent owner, SQL places a NULL in the absence of a set value. What if we want the query to return a zero any time there is a Null value? The ISNULL() function looks at the first parameter in the parenthesis and if it is NULL the function returns the second parameter to the result set.(Figure 10.3)

```
DECLARE @Qty INT
--SET @Qty = 5
SELECT ISNULL(@Qty ,0)
```

	(No column name)
1	0

1 rows

Figure 10.3 Shows the NULL value returned as a zero using the ISNULL function.

Let's uncomment the second line and run the query again with variable value set equal to five.

```
DECLARE @Qty INT
SET @Qty = 5
SELECT ISNULL(@Qty ,0)
```

	(No column name)
1	5

1 rows

Figure 10.4 Shows the five value returned using the ISNULL function where the value is not NULL.

ISNULL checks to see if @Qty is Null, and if it is, the 0 zero is the replacement value. If the value is not NULL, it shows the original value. Since the variable value is five and not NULL, it returned the actual variable value of five (Figure 10.4).

Let's use this in a table example. Take a look at all the records and all the fields in the PayRates table.

Chapter 10. Logical and Analytical Functions

```
SELECT *
FROM PayRates
```

	EmpID	YearlySalary	MonthlySalary	HourlyRate	Selector	Estimate
1	1	76000.00	NULL	NULL	1	1
2	2	79000.00	NULL	NULL	1	1
3	3	NULL	NULL	45.00	3	2080
4	4	NULL	6500.00	NULL	2	12
5	5	NULL	5800.00	NULL	2	12
6	6	52000.00	NULL	NULL	1	1

14 rows

Figure 10.5 Shows the PayRates table.

Let's use a WHERE clause to return only the records where HourlyRate is NULL (Figure 10.6).

```
SELECT *
FROM PayRates
WHERE HourlyRate IS NULL
```

	EmpID	YearlySalary	MonthlySalary	HourlyRate	Selector	Estimate
1	1	76000.00	NULL	NULL	1	1
2	2	79000.00	NULL	NULL	1	1
3	4	NULL	6500.00	NULL	2	12
4	5	NULL	5800.00	NULL	2	12
5	6	52000.00	NULL	NULL	1	1
6	7	NULL	6100.00	NULL	2	12

9 rows

Figure 10.6 Shows all the records of the PayRates table where the HourlyRate is NULL.

Figure 10.6 shows all the employees that do not have an hourly rate. They are either paid with a MonthlySalary or YearlySalary. If we use the ISNULL function we can return the YearlySalary for every employee in this query and if the YearlySalary is NULL then return the MonthlySalary.

```sql
SELECT *,
ISNULL(YearlySalary, MonthlySalary)
FROM PayRates
WHERE HourlyRate IS NULL
```

	EmpID	YearlySalary	MonthlySalary	HourlyRate	Selector	Estimate	(No column name)
1	1	76000.00 →	NULL	NULL	1	1	76000.00
2	2	79000.00 →	NULL	NULL	1	1	79000.00
3	4	NULL	6500.00 →	NULL	2	12	6500.00
4	5	NULL	5800.00 →	NULL	2	12	5800.00
5	6	52000.00 →	NULL	NULL	1	1	52000.00
6	7	NULL	6100.00 →	NULL	2	12	6100.00

Query executed successfully.   RENO (11.0 RTM)   Reno\Student (51)   JProCo   00:00:00   9 rows

Figure 10.7 Shows either the monthly or yearly salary of each EmpID of the PayRates table.

Figure 10.7 shows us exactly which values the ISNULL used. Since EmpID numbers four, five and seven do not have a YearlySalary and a NULL value is present, the MonthlySalary appeared. We want all the values in the ISNULL expression field to show a yearly pay amount. The Estimate field shows how many times each salary is paid per year. If the MonthlySalary, is multiplied by the Estimate field we will have the yearly pay amount for that EmpID. So, let's put a star and multiply it by the Estimate. The last step is to neaten up the fields and alias the ISNULL expression field AS EffectivePay.

```sql
SELECT *,
ISNULL(YearlySalary, MonthlySalary * Estimate)
   AS EffectivePay
FROM PayRates
WHERE HourlyRate IS NULL
```

	EmpID	YearlySalary	MonthlySalary	HourlyRate	Selector	Estimate	EffectivePay
1	1	76000.00	NULL	NULL	1	1	76000.00
2	2	79000.00	NULL	NULL	1	1	79000.00
3	4	NULL	6500.00	NULL	2	12	78000.00
4	5	NULL	5800.00	NULL	2	12	69600.00
5	6	52000.00	NULL	NULL	1	1	52000.00
6	7	NULL	6100.00	NULL	2	12	73200.00

Query executed successfully.   RENO (11.0 RTM)   Reno\Student (51)   JProCo   00:00:00   9 rows

Figure 10.8 Shows the annualized pay for each salaried employee in the EffectivePay field.

In Figure 10.8 we see the ISNULL function returned the YearlySalary for each employee and the yearly amount (MonthlySalary * Estimate) for all the employees that have a NULL value for YearlySalary.

Using CASE

Case is great for when there are several choices to make. For example; in case of winter I like to snow ski, in case of summer I like the beach. An IF statement works really well when you have two choices like winter and summer. If spring and fall are added, there are now four different actions based on four different cases and the IF statement breaks down. The CASE statement can use all the choices that are needed for the different possible results.

How do we use logic to cover three fields? Let's look at the PayRates table again.

```
SELECT *
FROM PayRates
```

	EmpID	YearlySalary	MonthlySalary	HourlyRate	Selector	Estimate
1	1	76000.00	NULL	NULL	1	1
2	2	79000.00	NULL	NULL	1	1
3	3	NULL	NULL	45.00	3	2080
4	4	NULL	6500.00	NULL	2	12
5	5	NULL	5800.00	NULL	2	12
6	6	52000.00	NULL	NULL	1	1

14 rows

Figure 10.9 Each EmpID has either a YearlySalary, MonthlySalary or HourlyRate.

Figure 10.9 shows for every record, two of the three pay fields are NULL. Every employee has a YearlySalary, MonthlySalary or an HourlyRate. Based on the Selector field, we can tell what type of pay each employee has. If the employee has a YearlySalary, the Selector is a pay type 1, a MonthlySalary is a pay type 2 and HourlyRate is a pay type 3. To demonstrate how the CASE function works, let's use it with the Selector field to specify each employees pay type.

```
SELECT *,
CASE Selector
  WHEN 1 THEN 'Yearly'
  WHEN 2 THEN 'Monthly'
  WHEN 3 THEN 'Hourly'
END
FROM PayRates
```

	EmpID	YearlySalary	MonthlySalary	HourlyRate	Selector	Estimate	(No column name)
1	1	76000.00	NULL	NULL	1	1	Yearly
2	2	79000.00	NULL	NULL	1	1	Yearly
3	3	NULL	NULL	45.00	3	2080	Hourly
4	4	NULL	6500.00	NULL	2	12	Monthly
5	5	NULL	5800.00	NULL	2	12	Monthly
6	6	52000.00	NULL	NULL	1	1	Yearly

Query executed successfully. | RENO (11.0 RTM) | Reno\Student (51) | JProCo | 00:00:00 | 14 rows

Figure 10.10 Shows CASE Selector returned each employees pay type.

Figure 10.10 shows all YearlySalary employees as Yearly, all HourlyRate employees as Hourly and all MonthlySalary employees as Monthly. Let's use the CASE function to show the actual yearly pay for all employees regardless of their pay type. Instead of returning the hard coded Yearly, Monthly, Hourly shown in Figure 10.10, let's take the actual field from the PayRates table.

```
SELECT *,
CASE Selector
  WHEN 1 THEN YearlySalary
  WHEN 2 THEN MonthlySalary
  WHEN 3 THEN HourlyRate
END
FROM PayRates
```

	EmpID	YearlySalary	MonthlySalary	HourlyRate	Selector	Estimate	(No column name)
1	1	76000.00	NULL	NULL	1	1	76000.00
2	2	79000.00	NULL	NULL	1	1	79000.00
3	3	NULL	NULL	45.00	3	2080	45.00
4	4	NULL	6500.00	NULL	2	12	6500.00
5	5	NULL	5800.00	NULL	2	12	5800.00
6	6	52000.00	NULL	NULL	1	1	52000.00

Query executed successfully. | RENO (11.0 RTM) | Reno\Student (51) | JProCo | 00:00:00 | 14 rows

Figure 10.11 Shows the CASE Selector field returned the actual pay amount from the PayRates table.

Not all the values in the expression field of Figure 10.11 represent the same type of value. EmpID one, two and six are YearlySalary. EmpID records 4 and 5 are MonthlySalary while EmpID three is HourlyRate. EmpID 3 will make more than $45.00 in a year's time. The average full time employee works 2080 hours in a year. Like in Figure 10.8, for each value to represent the employees yearly pay amount we need to multiply each employees pay type by the Estimate. For neatness and clarity we will also alias the CASE Selector field as EffectivePay.

```
SELECT *,
CASE Selector
  WHEN 1 THEN YearlySalary * Estimate
  WHEN 2 THEN MonthlySalary * Estimate
  WHEN 3 THEN HourlyRate * Estimate
END AS EffectivePay
FROM PayRates
```

	EmpID	YearlySalary	MonthlySalary	HourlyRate	Selector	Estimate	EffectivePay
1	1	76000.00	NULL	NULL	1	1	76000
2	2	79000.00	NULL	NULL	1	1	79000
3	3	NULL	NULL	45.00	3	2080	93600
4	4	NULL	6500.00	NULL	2	12	78000
5	5	NULL	5800.00	NULL	2	12	69600
6	6	52000.00	NULL	NULL	1	1	52000

Figure 10.12 Shows the EffectivePay field returned each employees yearly pay amount.

Figure 10.12 uses logic that takes care of all three pay types in their respective fields.

COALESCE

A few days ago I could not find my keys and was worried that I had locked them in the car. The driver door was indeed locked but I had many passengers who just got out. If any one of them did not lock the door then the day would be saved. I went around to the rear driver side door and it too was locked. The first unlocked door I found was the rear passenger door. I got in and got the keys. If all 4 doors were locked, then I would have come up empty. In SQL speak I ran a COALESCE look for the first non-NULL value and when I found it my search was over. Even though the front passenger door was also unlocked I did not need to try any more than the first unlocked door.

Coalesce can be really handy. Let's take a look at this simple SELECT Statement calling on COALESCE (1, 2, 3).

```sql
SELECT COALESCE(1, 2, 3)
```

(No column name)
1

1 rows

Figure 10.13 Shows the first non-NULL value the COALESCE function count was 1.

COALESCE looks for the first value that is not NULL and then shows it in the result. In Figure 10.13 the value of one was the first non-NULL value so that is what the function returned. What can we predict in the following two queries?

```sql
SELECT COALESCE(NULL, 2, 3)
SELECT COALESCE(NULL, NULL, 3)
```

The first query has a NULL for the first value and a two for the second value. Since the first non-NULL value is 2 the COALESCE function will return 2 in the result. For the same reason the second query will return three. Let's take a look at two more SELECT statements.

```sql
SELECT COALESCE(1,2,NULL)
SELECT COALESCE(1,NULL,NULL)
```

(No column name)
1

(No column name)
1

1 rows

Figure 10.14 Shows both queries returned the value of one.

Since 1 is the first non-NULL value in both queries of Figure 10.14 that is what was returned in both cases.

Look at the following query and predict what the result will be.

```sql
SELECT COALESCE(NULL,NULL,NULL)
```

The COALESCE function will continue to look until it finds a non-NULL value. If a non-NULL value does not exist, it will report an error message (Figure 10.15).

```
Messages
Msg 4127, Level 16, State 1, Line 1
At least one of the arguments to COALESCE must be an expression that is not
the NULL constant.
```
0 rows

Figure 10.15 If a non-NULL value does not exist then the COALESCE function will error out.

Chapter 10. Logical and Analytical Functions

Now that we understand what the COALESCE function does, let's explore a practical use. Start by looking at the PayRates table.

```
SELECT *
FROM PayRates
```

	EmpID	YearlySalary	MonthlySalary	HourlyRate	Selector	Estimate
1	1	76000.00	NULL	NULL	1	1
2	2	79000.00	NULL	NULL	1	1
3	3	NULL	NULL	45.00	3	2080
4	4	NULL	6500.00	NULL	2	12
5	5	NULL	5800.00	NULL	2	12
6	6	52000.00	NULL	NULL	1	1

14 rows

Figure 10.16 shows the PayRates table.

The COALESCE function is very useful at finding the first non-NULL value. For EmpID 1, the first non-NULL value is 76000.00. For EmpID 3, 45.00 is the first non-NULL value. The code for Figure 10.17 is looking for the first pay type for each EmpID that is not null.

```
SELECT *,
COALESCE(YearlySalary, MonthlySalary, HourlyRate)
FROM PayRates
```

EmpID	YearlySalary	MonthlySalary	HourlyRate	Selector	Estimate	(No column name)
1	76000.00	NULL	NULL	1	1	76000.00
2	79000.00	NULL	NULL	1	1	79000.00
3	NULL	NULL	45.00	3	2080	45.00
4	NULL	6500.00	NULL	2	12	6500.00
5	NULL	5800.00	NULL	2	12	5800.00
6	52000.00	NULL	NULL	1	1	52000.00

Query executed successfully. | RENO (11.0 RTM) | Reno\Student (51) | JProCo | 00:00:00 | 14 rows

Figure 10.17 COALESE isolated each employees pay type value into a single expression field.

The first non-NULL value for EmpID 1 is 76000.00. For EmpID 2, the first non-NULL value is 79000.00. For EmpID 3, it is 45.00 (Figure 10.17). All we need to do is multiply the COALESCE value by the estimate and alias the COALESCE AS EffectivePay. Figure 10.18 shows each employees yearly estimated pay for one year as EffectivePay.

```sql
SELECT *, COALESCE
    (YearlySalary*Estimate, MonthlySalary*Estimate,
    HourlyRate*Estimate) AS EffectivePay
FROM PayRates
```

EmpID	YearlySalary	MonthlySalary	HourlyRate	Selector	Estimate	EffectivePay
1	76000.00	NULL	NULL	1	1	76000
2	79000.00	NULL	NULL	1	1	79000
3	NULL	NULL	45.00	3	2080	93600
4	NULL	6500.00	NULL	2	12	78000
5	NULL	5800.00	NULL	2	12	69600
6	52000.00	NULL	NULL	1	1	52000

Figure 10.18 Shows the EffectivePay for each employee for a year.

Using IIF

Since I live in the Pacific Northwest it's hard to predict if the weather will be sunny or rainy on the weekend. If it's sunny outside I plan to go work outside in the sun with my family. If the weather turns to rain, I will stay indoors and clean my room. In SQL speak if the statement, " weather equals sunny" is true, I will rake leaves. If the statement is false I will clean my room. The IIF function works the same way. Regardless if either action happens there is still an action. Let's demonstrate this using the IIF function. Assume someone has to guess your age. Your actual age is 33 and we want a query that has a choice if the statement "guess equals age" is true then we want a "Correct" response. If "guess equals age" is false then we want a "Wrong" response.

```sql
DECLARE @Age INT = 33
DECLARE @GuessAge INT = 30
SELECT IIF(@Age=@GuessAge, 'Correct', 'Wrong')
```

(No column name)
Wrong

Figure 10.19 Since 33 = 30 is false, the IIF command returned Wrong to the result.

In Figure 10.19 the IIF() command is saying that if @Age = @GuessAge is true then return "Correct" and if @Age = @GuessAge is false then return "Wrong". Since 33 = 30 is false, the IIF command returned Wrong.

To use this in an in-line example let's take a look at the CurrentProducts table.

```
SELECT ProductID, ProductName, RetailPrice, Category
FROM CurrentProducts
```

	ProductID	ProductName	RetailPrice	Category
1	1	Underwater Tour 1 Day West Coast	61.483	No-Stay
2	2	Underwater Tour 2 Days West Coast	110.6694	Overnight-Stay
3	3	Underwater Tour 3 Days West Coast	184.449	Medium-Stay
4	4	Underwater Tour 5 Days West Coast	245.932	Medium-Stay
5	5	Underwater Tour 1 Week West Coast	307.415	LongTerm-Stay
6	6	Underwater Tour 2 Weeks West Coast	553.347	LongTerm-Stay

Query executed successfully. RENO (11.0 RTM) Reno\Student (51) JProCo 00:00:00 486 rows

Figure 10.20 Shows four fields of the CurrentProducts table.

The CurrentProducts table has 486 products that are divided into categories. There are some trips that are "come as you are" called No-Stay. The No-Stay customer will arrive at the at the registration office around noon and take part in an activity until 3:00 or 4:00pm. They will then be on their way home. There is no need for overnight gear such as a sleeping bag or toothbrush with the No-Stay products. For categories Overnight-Stay, Medium-Stay and LongTerm-Stay, where the customer is will be staying overnight, there are additional requirements. These customers will need to bring overnight gear.

```
SELECT ProductName, Category
FROM CurrentProducts
```

	ProductName	Category
1	Underwater Tour 1 Day West Coast	No-Stay
2	Underwater Tour 2 Days West Coast	Overnight-Stay
3	Underwater Tour 3 Days West Coast	Medium-Stay
4	Underwater Tour 5 Days West Coast	Medium-Stay
5	Underwater Tour 1 Week West Coast	LongTerm-Stay
6	Underwater Tour 2 Weeks West Coast	LongTerm-Stay

486 rows

Figure 10.21 Shows the ProductName and Category fields of the CurrentProducts table.

Figure 10.21 shows the first record is a No Stay. The second record is an Overnight-Stay and the third and fourth are Medium-Stay. The fifth and sixth records are LongTerm-Stay products.

Using the inquisitive IIF based on the Category field, let's create some action choices. First we need a statement such as "Category = No-Stay". Next we need a couple choices. If "Category = No-Stay is true then "Come as you are". If it is false then "Bring a tooth brush". Using the same process from Figure 10.19 we can create our query, and to tidy up our results let's alias the expression field as Prepare.

```
SELECT ProductName, Category,
IIF
(Category='No-Stay', 'Come as you are', 'Bring a toothbrush')
AS Prepare
FROM CurrentProducts
```

	ProductName	Category	Prepare
1	Underwater Tour 1 Day West Coast	No-Stay	Come as you are
2	Underwater Tour 2 Days West Coast	Overnight-Stay	Bring a toothbrush
3	Underwater Tour 3 Days West Coast	Medium-Stay	Bring a toothbrush
4	Underwater Tour 5 Days West Coast	Medium-Stay	Bring a toothbrush
5	Underwater Tour 1 Week West Coast	LongTerm-Stay	Bring a toothbrush
6	Underwater Tour 2 Weeks West Coast	LongTerm-Stay	Bring a toothbrush

Query executed successfully. RENO (11.0 RTM) Reno\Student (51) JProCo 00:00:00 486 rows

Figure 10.22 Shows the IIF command is an action based on the value of the Category field.

Lab 10.1: Logical Functions

Lab Prep: Lab Prep: Each lab has one or more Skill Checks. Start with Skill Check 1 and proceed until reaching the Points to Ponder section.

Before beginning this lab, verify that SQL Server 2012 is properly installed and operating. Before running the lab setup script for resetting the database (SQLQueries2012Vol4Chapter8.1-10Setup), please make sure to close all query windows within SSMS. An open query window pointing to a database context can lock that database preventing it from updating when the script is executing. A simple way to assure all query windows are closed, is to exit out of SSMS, then open a new instance of SSMS, and lastly run the setup script.

Skill Check 1: Write a query that returns the EmpID, FirstName, LastName and LocationID from the Employee table of JProCo. The LocationID field should be an expression field called LocID. The expression field should use the ISNULL function to return a zero for each record where the LocationID is NULL.

	EmpID	FirstName	LastName	LocID
1	5	Eric	Bender	1
2	6	Lisa	Kendall	4
3	7	David	Lonning	1
4	8	John	Marshbank	0
5	9	James	Newton	2
6	10	Terry	O'Haire	2

20 rows

Figure 10.23 Skill Check 1.

Skill Check 2: Run the SQLQueries2012Vol4Chapter10SpecialSetup.sql script and change your context to the dbBasics database. Notice States and Provinces are listed as separate fields.
```
SELECT * FROM StateList
```

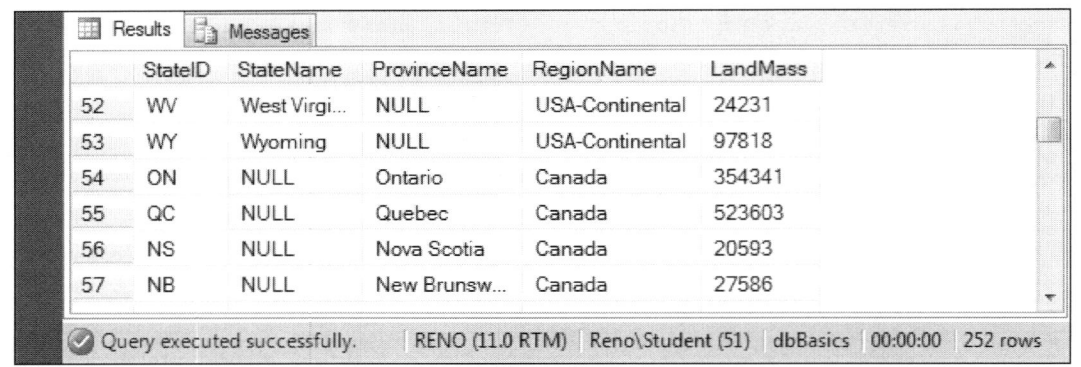

StateID	StateName	ProvinceName	RegionName	LandMass
52	WV	West Virgi...	NULL	USA-Continental	24231
53	WY	Wyoming	NULL	USA-Continental	97818
54	ON	NULL	Ontario	Canada	354341
55	QC	NULL	Quebec	Canada	523603
56	NS	NULL	Nova Scotia	Canada	20593
57	NB	NULL	New Brunsw...	Canada	27586

Figure 10.24 Skill Check 2.

COALLESE the StateName and ProvinceName fields into one expression field called StateProvinceName.

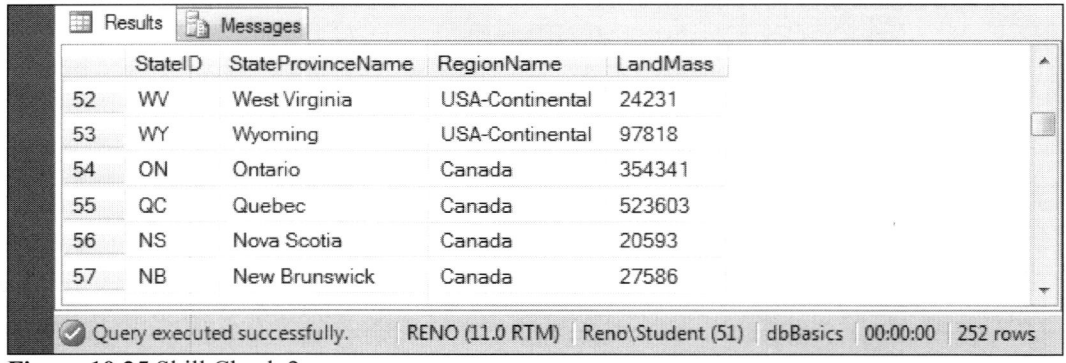

StateID	StateProvinceName	RegionName	LandMass
52	WV	West Virginia	USA-Continental	24231
53	WY	Wyoming	USA-Continental	97818
54	ON	Ontario	Canada	354341
55	QC	Quebec	Canada	523603
56	NS	Nova Scotia	Canada	20593
57	NB	New Brunswick	Canada	27586

Figure 10.25 Skill Check 2.

Chapter 10. Logical and Analytical Functions

Skill Check 3: In the JProCo Database, query the CurrentProducts table. Our preferred SupplierID is 1. SupplierID 0 is our own fulfilled products. Any other supplier is a 3rd party. Add an expression field SupplierType that shows 'US' for 0, 'Preferred' for 1, and '3rd Party' for any other number.

Deleted	Category	SupplierID	OriginationOffset	SupplierType
5	LongTerm-Stay	0	2004-04-13 19:20:11.4000000 -08:00	US
6	LongTerm-Stay	0	2011-03-27 20:40:38.7600000 -08:00	US
7	No-Stay	1	2010-01-01 08:25:43.2330000 -08:00	Prefered
8	Overnight-Stay	1	2008-03-07 09:52:12.9100000 -08:00	Prefered
9	Medium-Stay	1	2005-12-26 04:59:05.8500000 -08:00	Prefered
10	Medium-Stay	1	2008-01-08 04:34:35.0270000 -08:00	Prefered
11	LongTerm-Stay	1	2007-06-06 13:15:33.1830000 -08:00	Prefered
12	LongTerm-Stay	1	2011-08-22 19:59:47.4070000 -08:00	Prefered
13	No-Stay	3	2004-11-27 01:42:22.7470000 -08:00	3rd Party

Query executed successfully. RENO (11.0 RTM) Reno\Student (51) JProCo 00:00:00 486 rows

Figure 10.26 Skill Check 3.

Answer Code: The T-SQL code to this lab can be found in the downloadable files in a file named Lab10.1_LogicalFunctions.sql.

Points to Ponder - Logical Functions

1. ISNULL looks at the value of the first parameter and replaces any NULL values with the specified replacement value in the second parameter.
2. The ISNULL returns the same data type as the checked expression. In other words if the first Parameter is an INT then it returns in INT.
3. If the first parameter is not NULL then that value is returned.
4. The simple CASE expression returns one of multiple possible results.
5. The simple CASE expression allows only an equality check of exact matches.
6. COALESCE returns the first non-NULL value it finds among all its arguments in the order you passed them in.
7. If all of the values passed into COALESCE are NULL then NULL is returned.
8. If none of the values passed into COALESCE are NULL then the first value passed in will be returned.

New SQL 2012 Analytical Functions

There was a test in elementary school that the 2nd grade teacher warned was so difficult that nobody would pass. They wanted to see how we ranked as compared to other schools.

We've all seen spreadsheets like this. Figure 10.27 shows a spreadsheet that keeps track of company revenue.

	A	B	C	D	E
1					
2	Department	Amount	Running Total	Cume_Dist	
3	Hardware	$ 784,950	$ 784,950	23%	
4	Software	$ 97,500	$ 882,450	26%	
5	Service	$ 2,185,948	$ 3,068,398	89%	
6	Licenses	$ 375,000	$ 3,443,398	100%	
7			$ 3,443,398		

Figure 10.27 Shows a spreadsheet that keeps track of company revenue.

In the example in Figure 10.27, revenue comes from hardware, software, service and licenses. It looks like service makes the most money. The spreadsheet shows service making 2.1 of the 3.4 million company gross income. It's not uncommon to add another column to keep track of the running total. Hardware is the first line item and it produced $784,950. There's an additional $97,500 if we count the software. These combined give us a running total of $882,450. The Running Total gets bigger as we add in each department. The Running Total for the last line item is the total of all the revenue.

Running Total is not the only way to track revenue. Percentage running total or accumulative distribution is another option. Looking again at Figure 10.27 we see that hardware produces 23% of the 3.4 million in total Revenue. Hardware plus software makes up 26% of the total. Once service and licenses are added, we arrive at 100% of the total revenue. SQL 2012 has a number of analytical functions, where the function uses values from the records to get its answers.

Using CUME_DIST and PERCENT_RANK

You have a 5 day work week and the expectation is that your job will be finished at the end of the week. How much of the job should be done by the end of the day on

Wednesday? With 3 days down and 2 to go you should be .6 (or 60%) done to consider yourself on pace to finish. Considering that every Monday is a planning day you only have 4 days of front line work. With the planning day you would expect to be .5 (or 50%) done at the end of the day on Wednesday. In SQL, the relative position ratio of a specified record size sometimes starts with the first record and sometimes omits the first record.

Let's start off with an easy example by taking a look at the Location table.

```sql
SELECT *
FROM Location
ORDER BY LocationID
```

	LocationID	Street	City	State	Latitude	Longitude	GeoLoc
1	1	111 First ST	Seattle	WA	47.455	-122.231	0xE610...
2	2	222 Second AVE	Boston	MA	42.372	-71.0298	0xE610...
3	3	333 Third PL	Chicago	IL	41.953	-87.643	0xE610...
4	4	444 Ruby ST	Spokane	WA	47.668	-117.529	0xE610...
5	5	1595 Main	Philadelphia	PA	39.888	-75.251	0xE610...
6	6	915 Wallaby Drive	Sydney	NULL	-33.876	151.315	0xE610...

Figure 10.28 Shows the location table.

Figure 10.28 shows all the locations in order by LocationID. There are six locations so each location represents about 16% of the total number of locations. Let's use the CUME_DIST() function to perform an accumulative distribution of the Location table. We're going to put CUME_DIST() as an expression field with an OVER clause which will contain the ORDER BY LocationID from our original query.

```sql
SELECT LocationID, City, [State],
  CUME_DIST() OVER(ORDER BY LocationID)
FROM Location
```

	LocationID	City	State	(No column name)
1	1	Seattle	WA	0.166666666666667
2	2	Boston	MA	0.333333333333333
3	3	Chicago	IL	0.5
4	4	Spokane	WA	0.666666666666667
5	5	Philadelphia	PA	0.833333333333333
6	6	Sydney	NULL	1

Figure 10.29 Shows an expression field with the running percent of total locations.

Chapter 10. Logical and Analytical Functions

Each location represents 16% of the locations. Figure 10.29 shows Seattle as the first location and represents 16% of all the locations. Seattle and Boston make up 33% of the locations. Seattle, Boston and Chicago together are 50% of all the locations and so forth until all the locations make up 100% of the locations. Cumulative distribution is very similar to another analytical function called PERCENT_RANK().

```
SELECT *, PERCENT_RANK() OVER(ORDER BY LocationID)
FROM Location
```

	LocationID	Street	City	State	Latitude	Longitude	GeoLoc	(No column name)
1	1	111 First ST	Seattle	WA	47.455	-122.231	0xE6100000010C0A...	0
2	2	222 Second AVE	Boston	MA	42.372	-71.0298	0xE6100000010C56...	0.2
3	3	333 Third PL	Chicago	IL	41.953	-87.643	0xE6100000010C44...	0.4
4	4	444 Ruby ST	Spokane	WA	47.668	-117.529	0xE6100000010C2F...	0.6
5	5	1595 Main	Philadelphia	PA	39.888	-75.251	0xE6100000010C8B...	0.8
6	6	915 Wallaby Drive	Sydney	NULL	-33.876	151.315	0xE6100000010CE3...	1

Figure 10.30 Shows the PERCENT_RANK() of the location table by LocationID.

With PERCENT_RANK() the first record begins with zero. With a total of 6 records there are 5 records after the first. Each of the 5 remaining records represents 20% of the total records remaining. The running total starts with Boston at 20% then 40% with Seattle, Boston and Chicago all the way to 100% at Sydney.

Using FIRST_VALUE and LAST_VALUE

If we look at all of the records of the employee table we find there are many different HireDate values. Let's find out who was hired first with an ORDER BY clause.

```
SELECT EmpID, FirstName, LastName, HireDate, ManagerID
FROM Employee
ORDER BY HireDate
```

	EmpID	FirstName	LastName	HireDate	ManagerID
1	11	Sally	Smith	1989-04-01 00:00:00.000	NULL
2	12	Barbara	O'Neil	1995-05-26 00:00:00.000	4
3	4	Dave	Kinnison	1996-03-16 00:00:00.000	11
4	3	Lee	Osako	1999-09-01 00:00:00.000	11
5	7	David	Lonning	2000-01-01 00:00:00.000	11
6	1	Alex	Adams	2001-01-01 00:00:00.000	4

Figure 10.31 Shows select fields from the Employee table ordered by HireDate.

Figure 10.31 shows Sally Smith was hired first on April 1, 1989. The figure shows employees hired in the 90's. David Lonning was hired in 2000. If we scroll down we find that Sue Fines is our most recent hire (Figure 10.32).

	EmpID	FirstName	LastName	HireDate	ManagerID
15	18	Rainy	Walker	2010-01-01 00:00:00.000	11
16	20	Gale	Winds	2010-03-25 00:00:00.000	11
17	15	Tess	Jones	2012-10-12 11:59:40.640	11
18	16	Nancy	Biggs	2012-10-12 11:59:40.647	11
19	17	Wendy	Downs	2012-10-12 11:59:40.650	11
20	21	Fines	Sue	2012-10-12 11:59:41.113	4

Figure 10.32 Shows the most recent HireDate of the Employee table.

There is another way to find the first hire. Let's add FIRST_VALUE() to the fields list and move the ORDER BY into an OVER clause.

```
SELECT EmpID, FirstName, LastName, HireDate, ManagerID,
    FIRST_VALUE(HireDate) OVER(ORDER BY HireDate)
FROM Employee
```

	EmpID	FirstName	LastName	HireDate	ManagerID	(No column name)
1	11	Sally	Smith	1989-04-01 00:00:00.000	NULL	1989-04-01 00:00:00.000
2	12	Barbara	O'Neil	1995-05-26 00:00:00.000	4	1989-04-01 00:00:00.000
3	4	Dave	Kinnison	1996-03-16 00:00:00.000	11	1989-04-01 00:00:00.000
4	3	Lee	Osako	1999-09-01 00:00:00.000	11	1989-04-01 00:00:00.000
5	7	David	Lonning	2000-01-01 00:00:00.000	11	1989-04-01 00:00:00.000
6	1	Alex	Adams	2001-01-01 00:00:00.000	4	1989-04-01 00:00:00.000

Figure 10.33 Uses the FIRST_VALUE() function to return the first HireDate.

We learned in Figure 10.31 that Sally Smith was the first person hired to the company. Figure 10.33 shows the FIRST_VALUE() function listed Sally Smith's HireDate next to each person's record.

By adding PARTITION BY into the OVER clause we can find the most recently hired person for each location (Figure 10.34).

```
SELECT EmpID, FirstName, LastName, HireDate, LocationID,
    FIRST_VALUE(HireDate)
    OVER(PARTITION BY LocationID ORDER BY HireDate)
FROM Employee
```

Chapter 10. Logical and Analytical Functions

	EmpID	FirstName	LastName	HireDate	LocationID	(No column name)
14	17	Wendy	Downs	2012-10-12 11:59:40.650	1	1989-04-01 00:00:00.000
15	21	Fines	Sue	2012-10-12 11:59:41.113	1	1989-04-01 00:00:00.000
16	3	Lee	Osako	1999-09-01 00:00:00.000	2	1999-09-01 00:00:00.000
17	9	James	Newton	2003-09-30 00:00:00.000	2	1999-09-01 00:00:00.000
18	10	Terry	O'Haire	2004-10-04 00:00:00.000	2	1999-09-01 00:00:00.000
19	12	Barbara	O'Neil	1995-05-26 00:00:00.000	4	1995-05-26 00:00:00.000

Figure 10.34 Shows the date of the first employee hired from each LocationID.

Using LEAD

When you hear about economic news such as home sales or car sales, the report always compares the current number to the same number from the previous year. If you are a golf fan you might hear that at the Masters Tournament, Horton Smith has a 3 stroke lead over the next player. With SQL you may need to know what the difference is between your record and a value from a subsequent row in the same result set. Using LEAD() or LAG() to compare values against other values in the same result set can be accomplished without using a join.

Let's look at our StateList ordered by LandMass.

```
SELECT *
FROM StateList
ORDER BY LandMass DESC
```

	StateID	StateProvinceName	RegionID	LandMass
1	AK	Alaska	2	656425
2	QC	Quebec	1	523603
3	BC	British Columbia	1	357216
4	ON	Ontario	1	354341
5	TX	Texas	2	268601
6	AB	Alberta	1	247999

Figure 10.35 Shows the StateList table in descending order by LandMass

The table in Figure 10.35 contains a list of states and provinces that are sorted largest to smallest according to their LandMass. Alaska appears first because it has the largest LandMass followed by Québec, British Columbia and so on. Is there a way that we can list leading states next to the trailing state, and have at least two comparisons side-by-side?

Chapter 10. Logical and Analytical Functions

	StateID	StateProvinceName	RegionID	LandMass
1	AK	Alaska	2	656425
2	QC	Quebec	1	523603
3	BC	British Columbia	1	357216
4	ON	Ontario	1	354341
5	TX	Texas	2	268601
6	AB	Alberta	1	247999

```
   656425
  -523603
  -------
   132822
```

Figure 10.36 Shows the difference in LandMass between Alaska and Quebec is 132822.

Let's add an expression field that uses the LEAD() function to list the LandMass of the next largest State or Province next to each record. If you look at the following code, LEAD() has two arguments, the first answers what field will be used for the comparison and the second sets the skip sequence. Notice in Figure 10.36 the LEAD() function compares LandMass and uses a skip sequence of one. So the next largest LandMass will be listed at the end of the record. If we used a two for the skip sequence then British Columbia's LandMass would be next to Alaska.

```sql
SELECT *, LEAD(LandMass,1) OVER(ORDER BY LandMass DESC)
  AS NextLandMass
FROM StateList
ORDER BY LandMass DESC
```

	StateID	StateProvinceName	RegionID	LandMass	NextLandMass
1	AK	Alaska	2	656425	523603
2	QC	Quebec	1	523603	357216
3	BC	British Columbia	1	357216	354341
4	ON	Ontario	1	354341	268601
5	TX	Texas	2	268601	247999
6	AB	Alberta	1	247999	228445

Figure 10.37 Shows the LEAD() function created an expression field for the next largest LandMass.

The difference in LandMass can be easily calculated by subtracting NextLandMass from LandMass. Since NextLandMass is an expression field, we will have to subtract the entire LEAD() function in the query. Let's create a new expression field for this equation and alias it as SizeDiff.

Chapter 10. Logical and Analytical Functions

```
SELECT *,
  LEAD(LandMass,1) OVER(ORDER BY LandMass DESC)
    AS NextLandMass,
  LandMass - LEAD(LandMass,1) OVER(ORDER BY LandMass DESC)
    AS SizeDiff
FROM StateList
ORDER BY LandMass DESC
```

	StateID	StateProvinceName	RegionID	LandMass	NextLandMass	SizeDiff
1	AK	Alaska	2	656425	523603	132822
2	QC	Quebec	1	523603	357216	166387
3	BC	British Columbia	1	357216	354341	2875
4	ON	Ontario	1	354341	268601	85740
5	TX	Texas	2	268601	247999	20602
6	AB	Alberta	1	247999	228445	19554

Figure 10.38 Shows the difference in LandMass from each State or Province and the next largest.

Figure 10.36 showed us that Alaska is 132822 square miles larger than Quebec. Using the LEAD() function, Figure 10.38 lists the difference of each LandMass and the NextLandMass next to each record as SizeDiff.

Using LAG

LAG() searches in the opposite direction of LEAD() but works the same way. Take a look at the customer table in Figure 10.39. The first thing to notice is that it is ordered by CustomerID. Lee Young is customer number two. Who is the previous customer or who is the customer that LAGs by one? The customer that's previous to Lee is Patricia.

```
SELECT *
FROM Customer
ORDER BY CustomerID
```

	CustomerID	CustomerType	FirstName	LastName	CompanyName
1	1	Consumer	Mark	Williams	NULL
2	2	Consumer	Lee	Young	NULL
3	3	Consumer	Patricia	Martin	NULL
4	4	Consumer	Mary	Lopez	NULL
5	5	Business	NULL	NULL	MoreTechnology.com
6	6	Consumer	Ruth	Clark	NULL

Figure 10.39 Shows the Customer table in order by CustomerID.

We can say that Mark LAGs Lee by one. Let's write a query using the LAG() function that puts the first name of the previous customer next to each record. We will limit the fields to just the Customer ID, FirstName, LastName and the LAG() expression field.

```
SELECT CustomerID, FirstName, LastName,
  LAG(FirstName,1) OVER(ORDER BY CustomerID)
FROM Customer
```

	CustomerID	FirstName	LastName	(No column name)
1	1	Mark	Williams	NULL
2	2	Lee	Young	Mark
3	3	Patricia	Martin	Lee
4	4	Mary	Lopez	Patricia
5	5	NULL	NULL	Mary
6	6	Ruth	Clark	NULL

Figure 10.40 Shows the LAG() function putting the previous first name next to each record.

In Figure 10.40 the LAG() function listed the previous first name next to each record. Mark LAGs Lee by one, Lee LAGs Patricia by one, Patricia LAGs Mary by one and so on with all 775 records of the Customer table.

Using PERCENTILE_CONT

So the median price of a home in the town where I grew up is $175,000. This means that half the homes in the city cost more than $175K and the other half cost less. $175,000 is right in the middle. Keep in mind this in not the average number because all it would take is for one billionaire to build a 500 million dollar home and send the average home price all askew. The median price is the price right in the middle of all the homes. In SQL the middle is 0.5 (50%) and is used with PERCENTILE_CONT which can get you the median of any result set.

Let's take a look at the Grant table with the records in order by Amount smallest to biggest.

```
SELECT *
FROM [Grant]
ORDER BY Amount
```

	GrantID	GrantName	EmpID	Amount
1	001	92 Purr_Scents %% team	7	4750.00
2	010	Just Mom	5	9900.00
3	014	Everyone Wins	4	12500.00
4	002	K-Land fund trust	2	15750.00
5	003	Robert@BigStarBank.com	7	18100.00
6	006	TALTA_Kishan International	3	18100.00
7	011	Big Giver Tom	7	19000.00
8	005	BIG 6's Foundation%	4	22000.00
9	009	Thank you @.com	11	22500.00
10	008	www.@-Last-U-Can-Help....	7	26000.00
11	013	Hope Reaches	7	29000.00
12	007	Ben@MoreTechnology.co...	10	42000.00
13	012	Mega Mercy	9	56000.00

Figure 10.41 Shows all the records from the Grant table.

In Figure 10.41 the largest and smallest grant are easily seen since the query has been ordered by Amount. What is the median grant, the one in the middle? Big Giver Tom has an Amount of $19,000.00. There are six grants that have a larger Amount and six grants with a lesser Amount. We can conclude then that record seven, Big Giver Tom is the median grant. Using PERCENTILE_CONT() let's add an expression field to our query of the Grant table that pulls out the median Amount and lists it as an expression field at the end of each record.

```
SELECT *,
  PERCENTILE_CONT(0.5) WITHIN GROUP(ORDER BY Amount) OVER()
FROM [Grant]
```

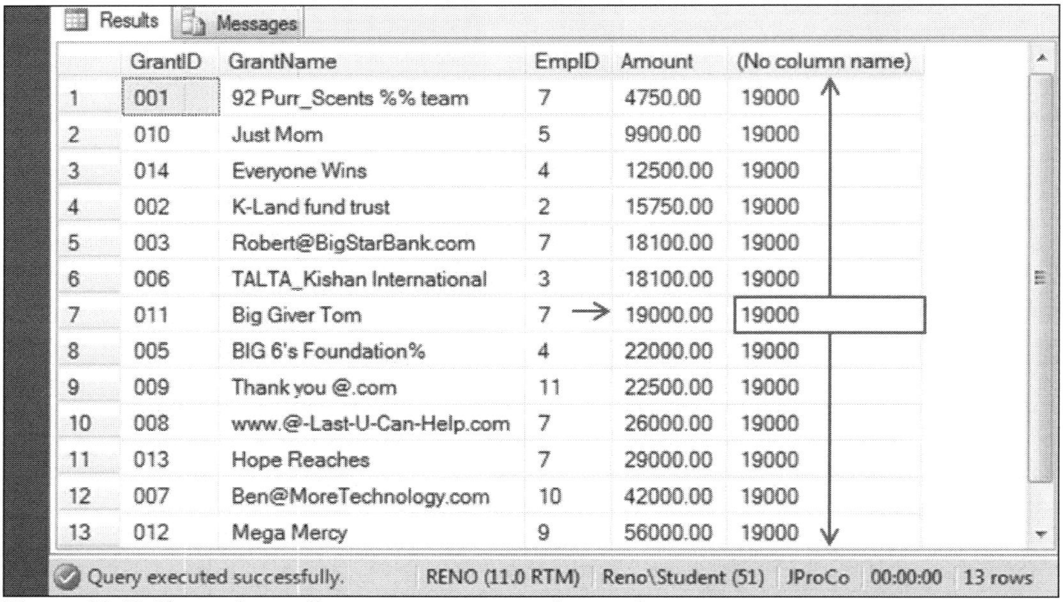

	GrantID	GrantName	EmpID	Amount	(No column name)
1	001	92 Purr_Scents %% team	7	4750.00	19000
2	010	Just Mom	5	9900.00	19000
3	014	Everyone Wins	4	12500.00	19000
4	002	K-Land fund trust	2	15750.00	19000
5	003	Robert@BigStarBank.com	7	18100.00	19000
6	006	TALTA_Kishan International	3	18100.00	19000
7	011	Big Giver Tom	7	19000.00	19000
8	005	BIG 6's Foundation%	4	22000.00	19000
9	009	Thank you @.com	11	22500.00	19000
10	008	www.@-Last-U-Can-Help.com	7	26000.00	19000
11	013	Hope Reaches	7	29000.00	19000
12	007	Ben@MoreTechnology.com	10	42000.00	19000
13	012	Mega Mercy	9	56000.00	19000

Figure 10.42 Shows the median amount next to each record.

Figure 10.42 clearly shows record 7 is the median grant with an Amount of $19,000. What if we want to pull out the median plus 10%, or 0.6?

```
SELECT *,
  PERCENTILE_CONT(0.6) WITHIN GROUP(ORDER BY Amount) OVER()
FROM [Grant]
```

	GrantID	GrantName	EmpID	Amount	(No column name)
1	001	92 Purr_Scents %% team	7	4750.00	22100
2	010	Just Mom	5	9900.00	22100
3	014	Everyone Wins	4	12500.00	22100
4	002	K-Land fund trust	2	15750.00	22100
5	003	Robert@BigStarBank.com	7	18100.00	22100
6	006	TALTA_Kishan International	3	18100.00	22100
7	011	Big Giver Tom	7	19000.00	22100
8	005	BIG 6's Foundation%	4	22000.00	22100
9	009	Thank you @.com	11	22500.00	22100
10	008	www.@-Last-U-Can-Help.com	7	26000.00	22100
11	013	Hope Reaches	7	29000.00	22100
12	007	Ben@MoreTechnology.com	10	42000.00	22100
13	012	Mega Mercy	9	56000.00	22100

Figure 10.43 Shows the PERCENT_CONT found record 8 to be the median offset by .06.

Record 8, Big 6's Foundation% with the Amount of $22,000 is found to be the median offset by 0.6

Using PERCENTILE_CONT with PARTITION

Let's get back to the test we took in 2nd Grade where our scores were going to be compared with other schools across the country. In fact, every grade was taking this test. I thought we would do pretty well, but if our 2nd grade class is compared to the 5th grade class in other states, we might look pretty bad. Well that was not the plan. The scores were going to be partitioned by grade so the aggregate scores for the 2nd grade would show up next to my score and my brother in 5th grade would be compared to the median score of all the 5th grade classes.

Let's take a look at the CurrentProducts table.

```
SELECT ProductID, ProductName, Category, RetailPrice
FROM CurrentProducts
ORDER BY Category, RetailPrice DESC
```

Chapter 10. Logical and Analytical Functions

	ProductID	ProductName	Category	RetailPrice
1	483	Yoga Mtn Getaway 2 Weeks	LongTerm-Stay	1695.00
2	336	Lakes Tour 2 Weeks West Coast	LongTerm-Stay	1161.099
3	342	Lakes Tour 2 Weeks East Coast	LongTerm-Stay	1147.986
4	372	Rain Forest Tour 2 Weeks East Coast	LongTerm-Stay	1144.773
5	402	River Rapids Tour 2 Weeks East Coast	LongTerm-Stay	1116.108
6	456	Wine Tasting Tour 2 Weeks West Coast	LongTerm-Stay	1101.969

Query executed successfully.   RENO (11.0 RTM)   Reno\Student (51)   JProCo   00:00:00   486 rows

Figure 10.44 Shows the records of the CurrentProducts table in order by RetailPrice.

In Figure 10.44 we see the Current products table. There are 486 products divided into four categories. What if we wanted a double level sort. Each Product should be sorted by Category and RetailPrice from highest to lowest. Our next goal is to find the median priced product for each category and return its RetailPrice as an expression field over the entire category.

```sql
SELECT ProductID, ProductName, Category, RetailPrice,
    PERCENTILE_CONT(0.5) WITHIN GROUP
    (ORDER BY RetailPrice DESC)
    OVER(PARTITION BY Category) AS MedianPrice
FROM CurrentProducts
```

	ProductID	ProductName	Category	RetailPrice	MedianPrice
160	77	Ocean Cruise Tour 1 Week Mexico	LongTerm-Stay	163.005	499.15
161	149	Mountain Lodge 1 Week Scandinavia	LongTerm-Stay	162.87	499.15
162	317	Cherry Festival Tour 1 Week Mexico	LongTerm-Stay	159.545	499.15
163	486	5 Day Idaho WaterPark	Medium-Stay	1285.99	273.638
164	481	Yoga Mtn Getaway 5 Days	Medium-Stay	875.00	273.638
165	485	Baja 5 Day	Medium-Stay	795.00	273.638

Query executed successfully.   RENO (11.0 RTM)   Reno\Student (51)   JProCo   00:00:00   486 rows

Figure 10.45 Shows the CurrentProducts table sorted by Category and Retail price with the median price of each Category listed next to every record.

When we look at Figure 10.45 we discover that the result of our query found the median price for long term to be $499.15 and the median price for medium stays to be $273.64. If we were to scroll down this result set the median score would be listed for Overnight-Stay and No-Stay products as well.

Chapter 10. Logical and Analytical Functions

Lab 10.2: New SQL 2012 Analytical Functions

Lab Prep: Lab Prep: Each lab has one or more Skill Checks. Start with Skill Check 1 and proceed until reaching the Points to Ponder section.

Before beginning this lab, verify that SQL Server 2012 is properly installed and operating. Before running the lab setup script for resetting the database (SQLQueries2012Vol4Chapter8.1-10Setup), please make sure to close all query windows within SSMS. An open query window pointing to a database context can lock that database preventing it from updating when the script is executing. A simple way to assure all query windows are closed, is to exit out of SSMS, then open a new instance of SSMS, and lastly run the setup script.

Skill Check 1: From the JProCo database, query the Grant table. Show all fields, in order from greatest Amount to least Amount plus an expression field called AmountMore. The expression field should show the amount of each grant's lead over the next largest Amount. The AmountMore field should show the difference in value from itself to the value of the next lowest grant.

	GrantID	GrantName	EmpID	Amount	AmountMore
1	012	Mega Mercy	9	56000.00	14000.00
2	007	Ben@MoreTechnology.com	10	42000.00	13000.00
3	013	Hope Reaches	7	29000.00	3000.00
4	008	www.@-Last-U-Can-Help.com	7	26000.00	3500.00
5	009	Thank you @.com	11	22500.00	500.00
6	005	BIG 6's Foundation%	4	22000.00	3000.00

```
 56000.00
-14000.00
 42000.00
```

Figure 10.46 Skill Check 1.

Skill Check 2: Skill Check 1 returned a NULL value for AmountMore on record 13 since there are no grants with a lesser Amount. Use the ISNULL function on the AmountMore expression field so that the last value is not NULL but uses its own total value from the Amount field as shown in Figure 10.47

Chapter 10. Logical and Analytical Functions

	GrantID	GrantName	EmpID	Amount	AmountMore
8	003	Robert@BigStarBank.com	7	18100.00	0.00
9	006	TALTA_Kishan International	3	18100.00	2350.00
10	002	K-Land fund trust	2	15750.00	3250.00
11	014	Everyone Wins	4	12500.00	2600.00
12	010	Just Mom	5	9900.00	5150.00
13	001	92 Purr_Scents %% team	7	4750.00	4750.00

Query executed successfully. | RENO (11.0 RTM) | Reno\Student (51) | JProCo | 00:00:00 | 13 rows

Figure 10.47 Skill Check 2.

Skill Check 3: From the JProCo database write a query that uses the PERCENTILE_CONT function to show the median number of hours of all the classes in the MgmtTraining table. This expression field should be called MedianHours and appear as the last field in each record.

	ClassID	ClassName	ClassDurationHours	ApprovedDate	MedianHours
1	2	Interviewing	6	2007-01-15 00:00:00.000	18
2	1	Embracing Diversity	12	2007-01-01 00:00:00.000	18
3	8	Passing Certifications	13	2013-01-02 12:26:20.177	18
4	4	Empowering Others	18	2013-01-02 12:26:18.293	18
5	10	Story Presentations	19	2013-01-02 12:26:21.953	18
6	3	Difficult Negotiations	30	2008-02-12 00:00:00.000	18

Query executed successfully. | RENO (11.0 RTM) | Reno\Student (51) | JProCo | 00:00:00 | 7 rows

Figure 10.48 Skill Check 3.

Skill Check 4: Use the query from Skill Check 3 and add an additional expression field called ExtraTime. ExtraTime should show how many hours over or under the median value each class is. Sort the results from highest to lowest ExtraTime.

	ClassID	ClassName	ClassDu...	ApprovedDate	MedianHours	ExtraTime
1	9	Effective Communications	35	2013-01-02 12:26:21.953	18	17
2	3	Difficult Negotiations	30	2008-02-12 00:00:00.000	18	12
3	10	Story Presentations	19	2013-01-02 12:26:21.953	18	1
4	4	Empowering Others	18	2013-01-02 12:26:18.293	18	0
5	8	Passing Certifications	13	2013-01-02 12:26:20.177	18	-5
6	1	Embracing Diversity	12	2007-01-01 00:00:00.000	18	-6

Query executed successfully. | RENO (11.0 RTM) | Reno\Student (51) | JProCo | 00:00:00 | 7 rows

Figure 10.49 Skill Check 4.

Answer Code: The T-SQL code to this lab can be found in the downloadable files in a file named Lab10.2_AnalyticalFunctions.sql.

Points to Ponder - New SQL 2012 Analytical Functions

1. Analytic functions compute a value based on a set of rows and are different from aggregate functions because they can return the aggregated results back to the detailed rows of the table. For example, an AVERAGE() aggregate will summarize the whole table and show the result once. The Analytic function can show that average listed over each row for a comparison.

2. Both CUME_DIST and PERCENT_RANK compute the relative position of a specified record in a group of records.

3. The first record in the set for PERCENT_RANK gets the value of zero and the first value for CUME_DIST gets its relative position which is 1 divided by the number of records in the set.

4. FIRST_VALUE returns the first value in an ordered set of records.

5. LAST_VALUE returns the last value in an ordered set of records.

6. LEAD gets a value from a subsequent row in your result set.

7. LAG gets a value from a previous row in your result set.

8. PERCENTILE_CONT is great for getting an exact median value if you use the value of 0.5 for the numeric literal.

9. If you use a number higher than 0.5 then the median offset is higher than the median. In other words if you used 0.75 then you would find the 75% highest number.

10. Using a lower number than 0.5 for the numeric literal of PERCENTILE_CONT will get a number lower than the true median.

Chapter Glossary

ISNULL(): A SQL function that if given a specified parameter that is NULL then the NULL will be replaced with a given replacement value.

CASE: A SQL function that compares a given value with a set of values to determine the result.

COALESCE(): A SQL function that will return the first non-NULL value from the specified values.

IIF: A SQL function that will return one of two possible values depending on whether the Boolean expression assesses true or false.

CUME_DIST(): A SQL function which stands for Cumulative Distribution. This function calculates the relative rank or position of a value in a set of values.

PERCENT_RANK(): A SQL function that calculates the relative rank of a row within a group of rows.

FIRST_VALUE(): A SQL function that returns the first value in an ordered set of values.

LAST_VALUE(): A SQL function that returns the last value in an ordered set of values.

LEAD(): A SQL function that accesses data from a subsequent row in the same result set without using a JOIN.

LAG(): A SQL function that accesses data from a preceding row in the same result set without using a JOIN

PERCENTILE_CONT(): A SQL function that calculates a percentage based on the continuous distribution of the column value.

Review Quiz - Chapter Ten

1.) You have the following query:

```
SELECT *,
ISNULL(YearlySalary * Estimate, MonthlySalary * Estimate)
FROM PayRates
```

What will the result be if there are no NULL values for any record?

O a. You will get the YearlySalary * Estimate expression value.
O b. You will get the MonthlySalary * Estimate expression value.
O c. You will get a null.
O d. You will get an error.

2.) You have the following query:

```
SELECT *,
CASE Selector
WHEN 1 THEN 'Yearly'
WHEN 2 THEN 'Monthly'
END AS [PayType]
FROM PayRates
```

You notice your selector field has the values of 1 and 2 for 99% of the records. You have few records where the selector field is 0. What will be the value of [PayType] expression field for all records that have a value of 0?

O a. 'Monthly'
O b. 0
O c. Null

3.) You have the following query:

```
SELECT COALESCE(NULL, 'I', NULL, 'Love', NULL, 'Cake', NULL)
```

What will be the output?

O a. NULL,
O b. 'I',
O c. 'Love',
O d. 'Cake'
O e. ,

4.) You have the following query:

```
SELECT EmpID, FirstName, LastName, LocationID
FROM Employee
```

Sometimes the LocationID is null. When this happens, the ADO application that consumes this query breaks from the NULL values. You are told to replace all NULL values with a zero. All of the following queries (except for one) will do this. Which query will not meet your company objectives?

○ a.
```
SELECT EmpID, FirstName, LastName,
   ISNULL(LocationID,0) AS LocationID
FROM Employee
```

○ b.
```
SELECT EmpID, FirstName, LastName,
   IIF(LocationID IS NULL,0,LocationID) AS LocationID
FROM Employee
```

○ c.
```
SELECT EmpID, FirstName, LastName,
   CASE LocationID
   WHEN NULL THEN 0 ELSE LocationID
   END AS LocationID
FROM Employee
```

○ d.
```
SELECT EmpID, FirstName, LastName,
   COALESCE (LocationID, 0) AS LocationID
FROM Employee
```

○ e.
```
SELECT EmpID, FirstName, LastName,
   COALESCE (LocationID, NULL) AS LocationID
FROM Employee
```

Answer Key

1.) The IS NULL will never give you an error from feeding NULLs or values into it, so (d) is incorrect. If all arguments are populated then you get the first value, so (b) is wrong and therefore (a) is the correct answer.

2.) If none of the values match in the CASE then you get a NULL, so (c) is correct.

3.) In COALESCE you get the first non-NULL value in order from left to right. It will never return a NULL, so (a) is wrong. The first value is the second value of 'I' which makes (b) the correct answer.

4.) Both ISNULL and COLASCE with using the first expression followed by a zero will give you a zero if the first expression is null. This makes (a) and (d) incorrect. Putting the NULL as the second expression does not give you zero, making (e) the correct answer.

Bug Catcher Game

To play the Bug Catcher game, run the file SQLQueries2012Vol4BugCatcher10.pps from the BugCatcher folder of the companion files found at www.Joes2Pros.com.

Chapter 11.   User-Defined Functions

The other day someone asked me for the time. I pulled out my cell phone and pressed the button to light up my screen and said, "It's 2:35 p.m". Without realizing it, I was acting much like a function in SQL Server does.

A function is a routine which performs a task and returns a result set. In this case, my result set was comprised of the single value returned after looking at my clock. Later that same day at Jack in the Box, I ordered a Jumbo Jack which was priced at $1.29. The register ran a function on my order total and displayed $1.39 for the price after sales tax. Again, a result was returned after some calculation and lookup activity.

Functions make our lives easier by performing predictable, repetitive tasks for use over and over again and providing us the end result. In *SQL Queries 2012 Joes 2 Pros 2012 Volume 2*, we examined system-supplied functions, including string functions (e.g., SUBSTRING(), LEFT(), RIGHT(), UPPER(), LOWER()). We also examined time functions (e.g., GETDATE(), DATEPART()). We passed in the requisite inputs which these functions processed and then returned an output. In this chapter, we will examine a variety of functions and create our own user-defined functions in SQL Server. The final section of this chapter includes a callback to Chapter 5, where we introduced deterministic and non-deterministic fields and their use in indexed views. Once we understand how to use and build our own functions, we will explore how to include them in views and indexed views.

READER NOTE: *Please run the script SQLQueries2012Vol4Chapter11.0Setup.sql in order to follow along with the examples in the first section of Chapter 11. All scripts mentioned in this chapter may be found at **www.Joes2Pros.com**.*

Functions versus Stored Procedures

As you might guess, my classroom students study topics in the same order they appear in this book series. When my classes reach this chapter on user-defined functions, I invariably have students ask me what differences exist between stored procedures and functions. We use similar T-SQL code to build both of these objects, and our work with parameterized stored procedures resembles passing an argument in to a function and receiving a result.

A detailed list comparing stored procedures and functions appears at the end of this section (See "Scalar Functions – Points to Ponder"). In this list, you will find several noteworthy points, including the following:

- o Everything you can accomplish with a user-defined function may also be accomplished using a stored procedure.
- o DML statements are the only type of statement you can run within a function (i.e., no DDL, DCL, or TCL statements allowed in functions but they are allowed in stored procedures).
- o User-defined functions are called by a SQL statement (e.g., a SELECT statement), whereas stored procedures must be invoked by an EXECUTE (or EXEC) statement.

Scalar Functions

From our earlier work with scalar data results (Chapter 6), you can likely guess that a **scalar function** is one where each time you run it, you get exactly one answer. For example, everyone would have one answer to the question, "How much did you pay in taxes last year?" The answer is a number, and for some folks that number may be zero. Warren Buffett's answer to that question would be larger than most but it would still be a single value. Scalar functions return a single value no matter how many calculations and how much input go into them. Up to this point in our study, we have seen many scalar functions, like GETDATE() which returns the current date and time according to your computer's clock.

Creating and Implementing Scalar Functions

You create scalar functions with a CREATE FUNCTION statement. You call upon a scalar function with a SELECT statement. Oftentimes functions are just calculations (like Sales Tax * Price). Our first example (Figure 11.1) sets the variable @MyFavNum to 4 and then performs a calculation to double that amount. Notice that the doubling calculation is done *ad hoc* – in other words, it's a one-time calculation and is not part of a repeatable code module. Another variable captures the doubled amount (@MyFavNum * 2), and a SELECT statement calls and displays this amount (Figure 11.1).

```
DECLARE @MyFavNum INT = 4
DECLARE @Dbl INT
SET @Dbl = @MyFavNum * 2
SELECT @Dbl
```

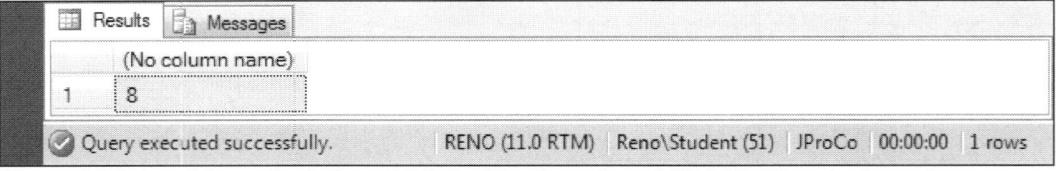

Figure 11.1 An ad hoc calculation which doubles the value of @MyFavNum is shown here.

If doubling numbers is a task you perform frequently, you can build a function to do this for you. Let's create a function called ReturnDouble that takes an integer parameter (@Num), runs a double calculation, and stores the result in the @Dbl variable. Finally, the value of @Dbl is returned to the calling code. The following code creates the ReturnDouble function:

```sql
CREATE FUNCTION dbo.ReturnDouble(@Num INT)
RETURNS INT
AS
BEGIN
DECLARE @Dbl INT
SELECT @Dbl = @Num * 2
RETURN @Dbl
END
GO
```

The ReturnDouble function will take a parameter and return twice that value. The most common way to call upon an existing function is via a SELECT statement. In Figure 11.2, we query the value of this function by passing in 14 and the result set is a scalar value of 28. *Note:* The schema name ("dbo") is optional in the CREATE FUNCTION statement; however, you must use the two-part name when calling upon your scalar functions. If you attempt to run this SELECT statement without the schema name (SELECT ReturnDouble(14)), it will not work.

```sql
SELECT dbo.ReturnDouble(14)
```

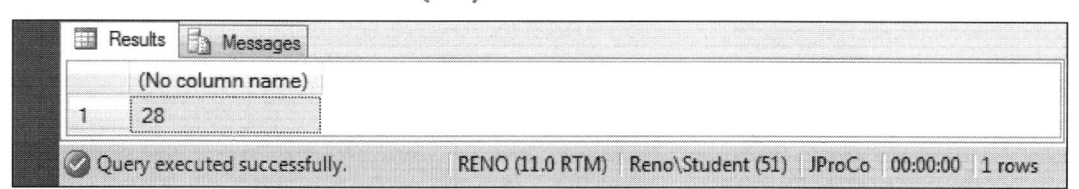

	(No column name)
1	28

Query executed successfully. | RENO (11.0 RTM) | Reno\Student (51) | JProCo | 00:00:00 | 1 rows

Figure 11.2 The ReturnDouble function is used in a SELECT Statement and the scalar result is shown.

You can create as many functions in your database as you need. Suppose you are taking over a database project from someone else and you want to see what functions exist on the system. All functions can be browsed as you would any other object created in SQL Server. In Figure 11.3 we can see our new function in the Object Explorer by traversing the following path:
OE > Databases > JProCo > Programmability > Functions > Scalar-valued Functions > dbo.ReturnDouble

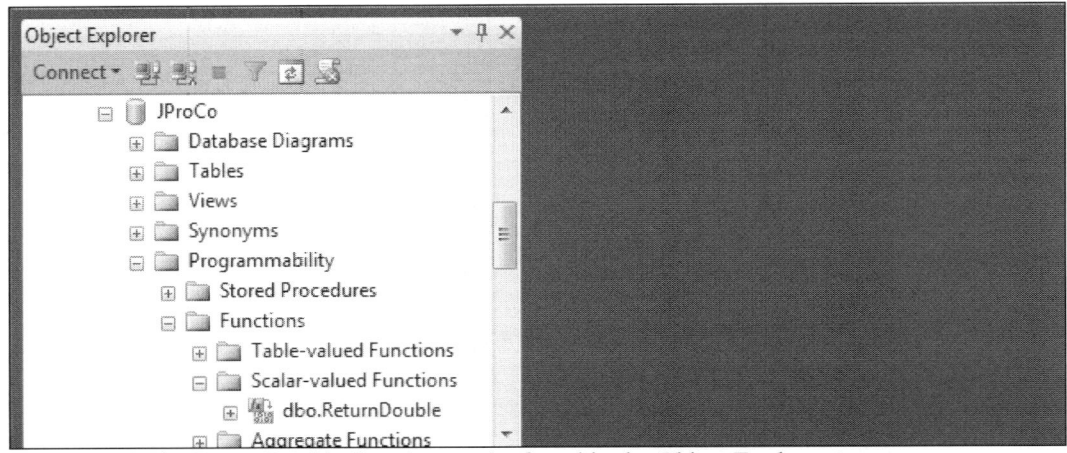

Figure 11.3 The ReturnDouble function can be found in the Object Explorer tree.

Using Functions with Queries

We just created a function containing a query in order to return data in a repeatable way. You can also include a function as an expression field within a SELECT list. For example, we know the retail price of the first product in the CurrentProducts table is roughly $61. If you were to double that amount, it would be roughly $122. In Figure 11.4 we have two queries. The first query shows all records but just two fields of the CurrentProducts table. The second query is the same but it also includes an expression field which uses the ReturnDouble function by passing in the Retail Price. The expression field values should be double the values of the RetailPrice field (Since the function uses integers, and the result is rounded to the nearest dollar, we don't see the pennies). The ReturnDouble function is used with this query to make a calculation on each record. This function ran 486 times within the query and produced 486 scalar results. *Note*: You must use the two-part name when calling upon ReturnDouble, since it's a user-defined function.

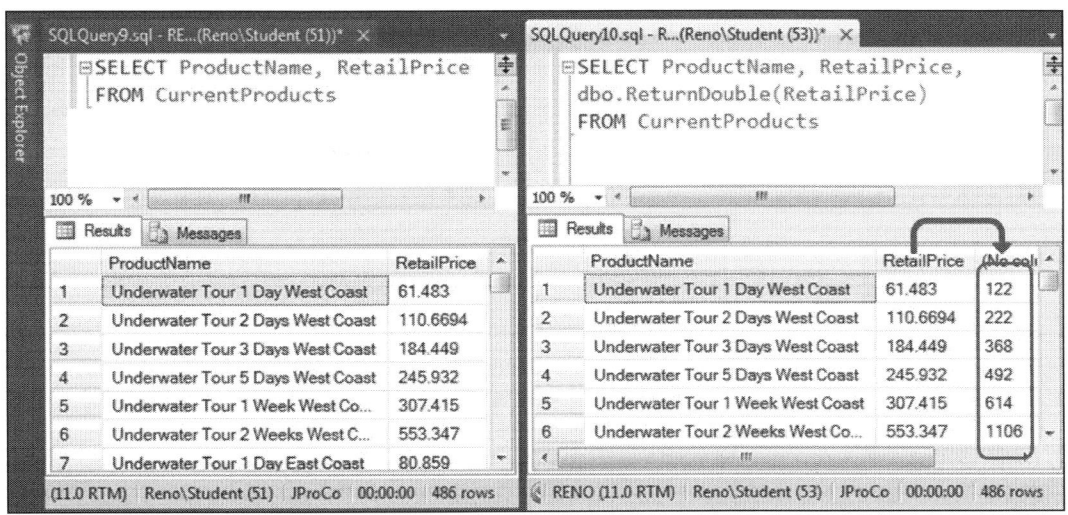

Figure 11.4 ReturnDouble function is used with a query to perform a calculation on each record.

Functions with Multiple Parameters

As you know, functions are SQL Server objects which are built using T-SQL code. Functions can accept one or more parameters and return a scalar or a table-like result set. The following code will build the AddTwoNumbers function which takes two integer parameters and returns the sum of the parameters:

```
CREATE FUNCTION dbo.AddTwoNumbers(@Num1 INT, @Num2 INT)
RETURNS INT
AS
BEGIN
DECLARE @ttl INT
SELECT @ttl = @Num1 + @Num2
RETURN @ttl
END
GO
```

The AddTwoNumbers function takes two parameters and returns a scalar result. Recall that scalar functions will always return just a single value, regardless of how many inputs are included in the function. When we pass two integers into the AddTwoNumbers function, we get just one number in our result (Figure 11.5).

```
SELECT dbo.AddTwoNumbers(8, 3)
```

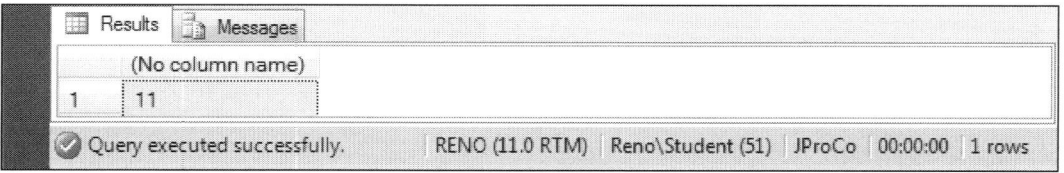

	(No column name)
1	11

Figure 11.5 Passing in 8 and 3 to the AddTwoNumbers function gives us a result of 11.

Aggregate Functions Recap

Scalar functions can be used to tell a significant story in business. The quantity that your customers tend to order of a certain product is an interesting number, and one you must know in order to formulate compelling sales offerings. For example, when shopping for paint brushes online, I frequently order 10-15 brushes at a time. When using an online travel site to book a vacation, I generally order two tickets. A volume discount for 20 paint brushes would get my attention – I would definitely increase my order to 20 brushes. However, a volume discount for 20 trips to Mexico would be unlikely to alter my purchasing behavior. I'm going to purchase two tickets for my Mexican vacation no matter how attractive the 20-ticket price is.

The query in Figure 11.6 shows us the average quantity that was ordered for a given ProductID. For example, when ProductID 7 is ordered, the customer (on average) puts three of them on one invoice.

```
SELECT AVG (Quantity)
FROM CurrentProducts AS cp
INNER JOIN SalesInvoiceDetail AS sdd
ON cp.ProductID = sdd.ProductID
WHERE cp.ProductID = 7
```

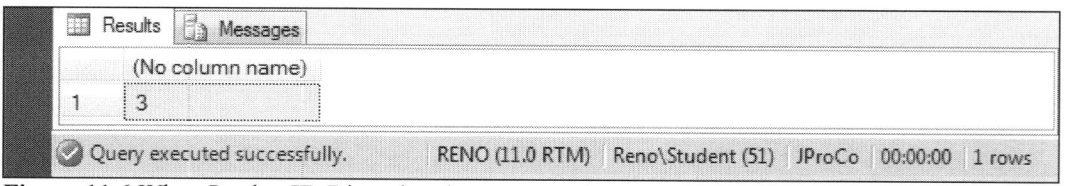

	(No column name)
1	3

Figure 11.6 When ProductID 7 is ordered, customers (on average) put 3 of them on one invoice.

Notice that this query does not give us the true average. The average is really 3.63 and not 3. That rounding error occurs because Quantity is an integer. In order to see the true average for ProductID 7, we can CAST Quantity as a float (Figure 11.7).

```
SELECT AVG (CAST(Quantity AS FLOAT))
FROM CurrentProducts AS cp
INNER JOIN SalesInvoiceDetail AS sdd
ON cp.ProductID = sdd.ProductID
WHERE cp.ProductID = 7
```

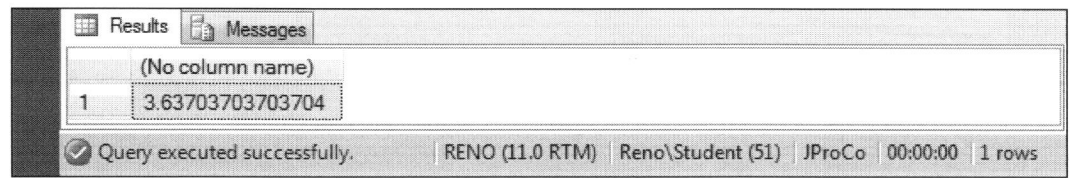

	(No column name)
1	3.637037037037037

Figure 11.7 By treating Quantity as a float instead of an INT, we see a more precise average.

If a product has never been ordered, then there is no way to determine an average quantity per order. In Figure 11.8 we see that, since ProductID 1 has never been ordered, the scalar result is null.

```
SELECT AVG (CAST(Quantity AS FLOAT))
FROM CurrentProducts AS cp
INNER JOIN SalesInvoiceDetail AS sdd
ON cp.ProductID = sdd.ProductID
WHERE cp.ProductID = 1
```

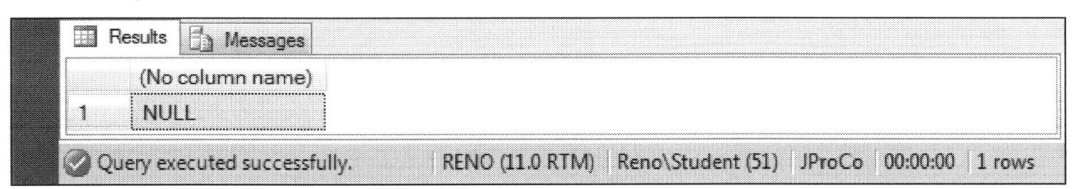

	(No column name)
1	NULL

Figure 11.8 If there are no records then the AVG() aggregate function returns a NULL result.

If we plan to use this query often, we can turn it into a scalar function. Each time we run it, the function will need to have the ProductID passed in.

Let's create the function GetAverageSalesByProduct, which will accept a ProductID parameter and predicate on all invoices matching that value. The result will be aggregated to find the average quantity. The following code creates the GetAverageSalesByProduct function:

```
CREATE FUNCTION GetAverageSalesByProduct(@ProductID INT)
RETURNS FLOAT
AS
BEGIN
DECLARE @Average FLOAT

SELECT @Average = AVG(CAST(Quantity AS FLOAT))
FROM CurrentProducts AS cp INNER JOIN SalesInvoiceDetail AS sdd
ON cp.ProductID = sdd.ProductID
WHERE cp.ProductID = @ProductID

RETURN @Average
END
GO
```

GetAverageSalesByProduct requires an integer to be passed in to @ProductID. Let's run our new function for ProductID 7 (Figure 11.9).

```
SELECT dbo.GetAverageSalesByProduct(7)
```

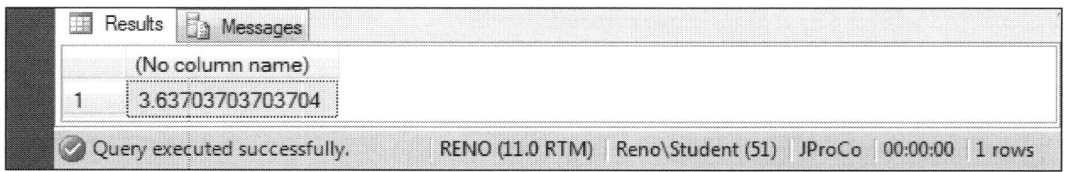

(No column name)
3.63703703703704

Figure 11.9 Calling on GetAverageSalesByProduct and passing in a 7 gets you the average scalar result.

Notice that this function we've created may not always produce the type of scalar result we want. For example, if we've never sold any units of ProductID 1, then the average should be zero. However, here we see our function returns a NULL for ProductID 1 (Figure 11.10). If the calling code will not accept nulls, then this function would break the calling code.

```
SELECT dbo.GetAverageSalesByProduct(1)
```

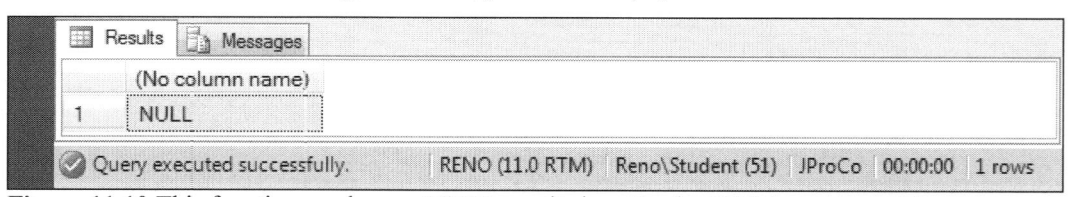

(No column name)
NULL

Figure 11.10 This function produces a NULL result since ProductID 1 has never sold.

Because NULLs and zeros (0) are NOT the same thing, we need to add a little extra logic to our code. Since we were told not to return any NULL values, we will change those to a value of zero before the final statement runs and returns the value of the variable (@Average) to the calling code. In the following code we alter the function to check the value of the @Average variable after the aggregation:

```sql
ALTER FUNCTION GetAverageSalesByProduct(@ProductID INT)
RETURNS FLOAT
AS
BEGIN
DECLARE @Average FLOAT

SELECT @Average = AVG(CAST(Quantity AS FLOAT))
FROM CurrentProducts AS cp INNER JOIN SalesInvoiceDetail AS sdd
ON cp.ProductID = sdd.ProductID
WHERE cp.ProductID = @ProductID

SET @Average = ISNULL(@Average, 0)
RETURN @Average
END
GO
```

Null values are changed to zero before the result is returned.

```sql
SELECT dbo.GetAverageSalesByProduct(1)
```

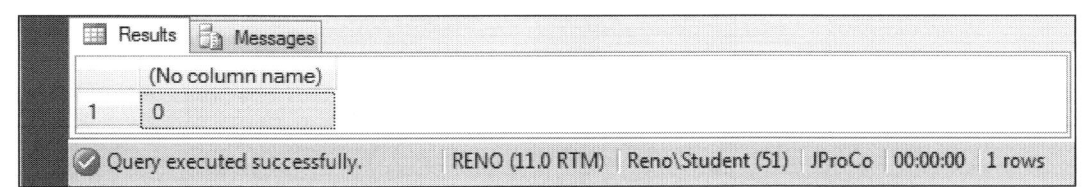

Figure 11.11 This ISNULL replaced any NULL value with a zero so this function never returns a NULL.

GetAverageSalesByProduct is the user-defined function we just created. It is not a built-in function. The Object Explorer tree shows the three scalar functions we have created thus far in this chapter (Figure 11.12).

Chapter 11. User-Defined Functions

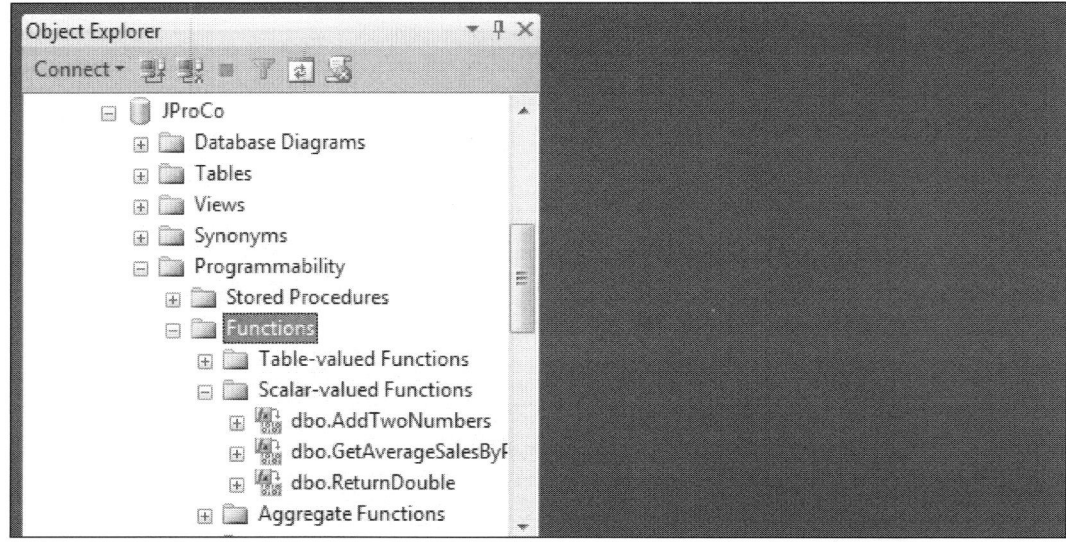

Figure 11.12 Object Explorer shows the three scalar functions we have created thus far.

With our robust scalar function, GetAverageSalesByProduct, we can query all the records of the CurrentProducts table and see the average quantity per invoice for each product. If a product has never been sold, then the average will be zero.

Let's write a statement to call upon GetAverageSalesByProduct and sort our result by ProductID. Here we've intentionally used the simple name (i.e., instead of the two-part name) in order to examine the error message that SQL Server returns (Figure 11.13).

```
SELECT ProductID, ProductName,
GetAverageSalesByProduct(ProductID) AS Rating
FROM CurrentProducts
ORDER BY ProductID
GO
```

```
Messages
Msg 195, Level 15, State 10, Line 2
'GetAverageSalesByProduct' is not a recognized built-in function name.

0 rows
```

Figure 11.13 To call upon a user-defined function, you cannot use the simple name.

The error message reads, "GetAverageSalesByProduct is not a recognized built-in function name". It may seem surprising to see this message, since we know GetAverageSalesByProduct is not a built-in function (i.e., it is one of the user-defined functions we've created). *SQL Server assumes that any function called by its simple name is a system-supplied function.*

Let's modify our code to prefix the function name with the schema name (dbo) and then re-attempt our code. By specifying dbo.GetAverageSalesByProduct, our query now runs successfully (Figure 11.14). Since we've passed the ProductID argument into the function, it will return one record for each of the 486 products found in the CurrentProducts table.

```
SELECT ProductID, ProductName,
dbo.GetAverageSalesByProduct(ProductID) AS Rating
FROM CurrentProducts
ORDER BY ProductID
GO
```

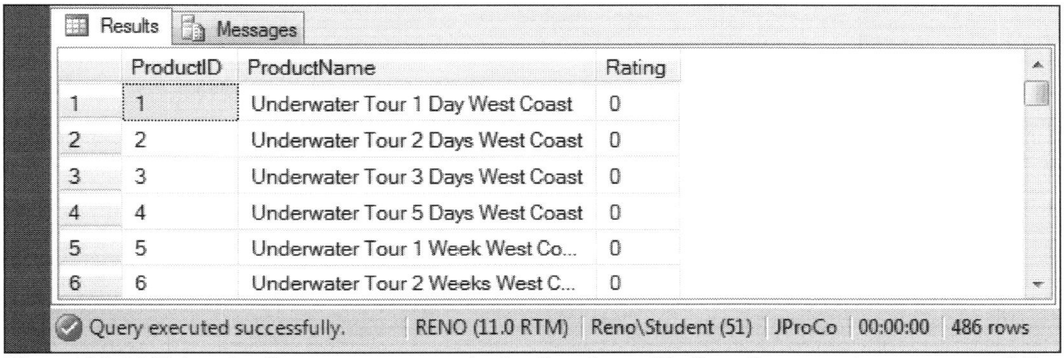

	ProductID	ProductName	Rating
1	1	Underwater Tour 1 Day West Coast	0
2	2	Underwater Tour 2 Days West Coast	0
3	3	Underwater Tour 3 Days West Coast	0
4	4	Underwater Tour 5 Days West Coast	0
5	5	Underwater Tour 1 Week West Co...	0
6	6	Underwater Tour 2 Weeks West C...	0

Query executed successfully. RENO (11.0 RTM) Reno\Student (51) JProCo 00:00:00 486 rows

Figure 11.14 Using the dbo two-part name in the function will allow the query to run successfully.

Lab 11.1: Scalar Functions

Lab Prep: Lab Prep: Each lab has one or more Skill Checks. Start with Skill Check 1 and proceed until reaching the Points to Ponder section.

Before beginning this lab, verify that SQL Server 2012 is properly installed and operating. Before running the lab setup script for resetting the database (SQLQueries2012Vol4Chapter11.1Setup.sql), please make sure to close all query windows within SSMS. An open query window pointing to a database context can lock that database preventing it from updating when the script is executing. A simple way to assure all query windows are closed, is to exit out of SSMS, then open a new instance of SSMS, and lastly run the setup script.

Skill Check 1: Using the CurrentProducts and InvoiceDetail tables, create a function called GetTotalSalesByProductID. The function will take in the ProductID and return an expression field that multiplies the Quantity from each ProductID by the RetailPrice to find total sales for each ProductID.

Test your function by using the code seen in the figure here.

```
SELECT ProductID, ProductName,
dbo.GetTotalSalesByProductID (ProductID) AS TotalSales
FROM CurrentProducts
ORDER BY ProductID
```

	ProductID	ProductName	TotalSales
5	5	Underwater Tour 1 Week West Coast	0.00
6	6	Underwater Tour 2 Weeks West Coast	0.00
7	7	Underwater Tour 1 Day East Coast	39702.00
8	8	Underwater Tour 2 Days East Coast	73501.00
9	9	Underwater Tour 3 Days East Coast	111585.00
10	10	Underwater Tour 5 Days East Coast	36548.00

486 rows

Figure 11.15 Skill Check 1 result.

Answer Code: The T-SQL code to this lab can be found in the downloadable files in a file named Lab11.1_ScalarFunctions.sql.

Points to Ponder - Scalar Functions

1. A function is a SQL object stored in a database and consisting of T-SQL code that accepts parameters.

2. A user-defined function is a routine that you can create to accept parameters, perform a task, and return a result set.

3. Functions are routines consisting of one or more T-SQL statements encapsulated for re-use.

4. The body of a function is defined within a BEGIN…END block.

5. There are many types of functions; scalar is just one of them. Some functions return a single value and others return a list of values.

6. A scalar function returns a single value of the type defined in the RETURNS clause.

7. If you are asked to create a function that returns a single value then always choose a scalar function.

8. Above the body the T-SQL syntax is CREATE FUNCTION *FunctionName* RETURNS *data-type* AS.

9. To alter a function you would use the ALTER FUNCTION command, to drop it you would use the DROP FUNCTION command.

10. Both User-Defined Functions (UDFs) and stored procedures allow you to combine and save SQL statements for future use.

11. You can use functions as part of an expression field in a SELECT statement. Stored procedures can't be part of a query.

12. Everything you can do in a UDF can be done with a stored procedure.

13. Not every SQL statement or operation is valid within a function. The following are not allowed in a UDF:
    - Calling on other non-deterministic functions like GetDate().
    - UPDATE, INSERT, or DELETE statements to a view or table. You can, however, update a variable (UPDATE @Num = @Num + 1).
    - No DDL, DCL, or TCL statements allowed in a function.
    - Functions do not support error handling (See Chapters 10 and 11).

14. UDF's have some limitations that stored procedures do not have, such as:
    o   Stored procedures are called independently with an EXEC command, whereas functions must be called by a SQL statement.
    o   Functions must always return a value, whereas stored procedures do not have this requirement.

Table-Valued Functions

In the last section, we learned that scalar-valued functions return a single value. **Table-valued functions** return tabular result sets ("tabular" meaning like a table). Table-valued functions look a lot like views because they both show us a tabular result set. Table-valued functions can be based on one or more base tables.

Creating and Implementing Table-Valued Functions

The body of a table-valued function will essentially contain a query. Let's begin with a query containing four fields and all of the records from the CurrentProducts table (Figure 11.16).

```
SELECT ProductID, ProductName, RetailPrice, Category
FROM CurrentProducts
```

	ProductID	ProductName	RetailPrice	Category
1	1	Underwater Tour 1 Day West Coast	61.483	No-Stay
2	2	Underwater Tour 2 Days West Coast	110.6694	Overnight-Stay
3	3	Underwater Tour 3 Days West Coast	184.449	Medium-Stay
4	4	Underwater Tour 5 Days West Coast	245.932	Medium-Stay
5	5	Underwater Tour 1 Week West Coast	307.415	LongTerm-Stay
6	6	Underwater Tour 2 Weeks West Coast	553.347	LongTerm-Stay

486 rows

Figure 11.16 This query contains four fields and all records of the CurrentProducts table.

This query will become the heart of a new table-valued function, GetAllProducts. By placing the query within a set of parentheses, and after the keyword RETURN, we have the body of the function. The RETURNS TABLE keyword specifies that the table-valued function GetAllProducts must return the result in the form of a table. The following code creates the GetAllProducts table valued function.

```
CREATE FUNCTION GetAllProducts()
RETURNS TABLE
AS
RETURN
(SELECT ProductID, ProductName, RetailPrice, Category
FROM CurrentProducts)
GO
```

The GetAllProducts table-valued function is created and returns a tabular result set. Just how do you query a table-valued function? The syntax is somewhat similar to how you would run a SELECT statement against a table or a view. Compare Figure 11.17 and Figure 11.18 and notice that SQL Server requires that a set of parentheses following the name of a table-valued function in a query.

```
SELECT * FROM GetAllProducts
```

```
Messages
Msg 216, Level 16, State 1, Line 1
Parameters were not supplied for the function 'GetAllProducts'.
                                                          0 rows
```

Figure 11.17 Querying a table-valued function without its parentheses results in an error message.

All functions need to be called by using a set of parentheses with all required parameters inside them. If the function has no parameters (which is currently the case with GetAllProducts), then you will simply include an empty set of parentheses (Figure 11.18).

```
SELECT * FROM GetAllProducts()
```

	ProductID	ProductName	RetailPrice	Category
1	1	Underwater Tour 1 Day West Coast	61.483	No-Stay
2	2	Underwater Tour 2 Days West Coast	110.6694	Overnight-Stay
3	3	Underwater Tour 3 Days West Coast	184.449	Medium-Stay
4	4	Underwater Tour 5 Days West Coast	245.932	Medium-Stay
5	5	Underwater Tour 1 Week West Coast	307.415	LongTerm-Stay
6	6	Underwater Tour 2 Weeks West Coast	553.347	LongTerm-Stay

486 rows

Figure 11.18 You must include parentheses when calling upon any type of function.

To view all of the table-valued functions contained in the JProCo database from within the Object Explorer tree, traverse this path:
OE > Databases > JProCo > Programmability > Functions > Table-valued Functions
In Figure 11.19, we see JProCo currently contains five table-valued functions. Notice that the GetAllProducts table-valued function which we just created is present.

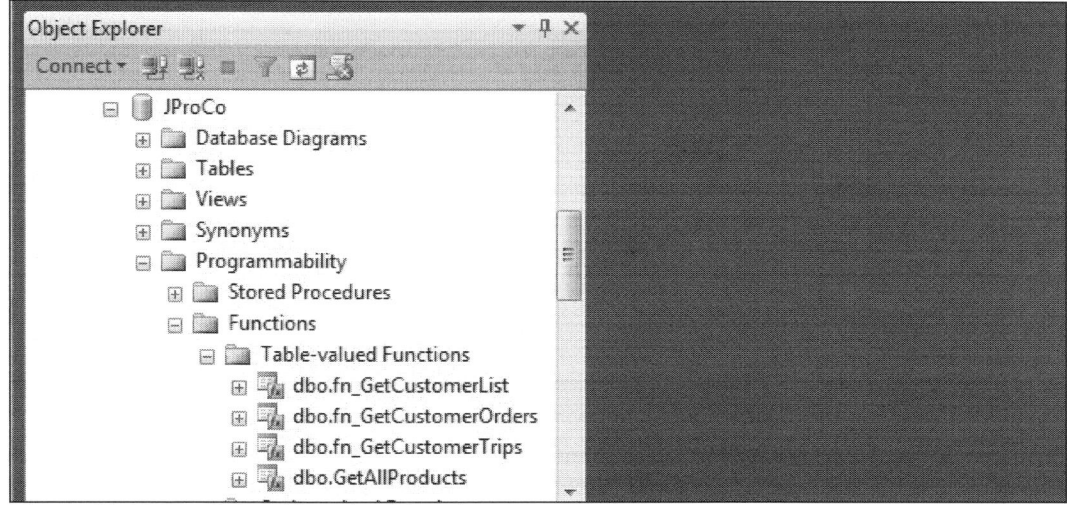

Figure 11.19 JProCo's table-valued functions.

Views versus Parameterized Table-Valued Functions

Views and table-valued functions are both useful ways to see the result set for a pre-defined query. There is no way to pass a variable into a view and change the way it runs. Views are hard-coded and their criteria do not change. A table-valued function can display different results by passing values into its parameter (s) at runtime. Let's begin by selecting all 'No-Stay' records from the CurrentProducts table (Figure 11.20). We want to turn this query into a function and allow that function to pick the category.

```sql
SELECT ProductID, ProductName, RetailPrice, Category
FROM CurrentProducts
WHERE Category = 'No-Stay'
```

	ProductID	ProductName	RetailPrice	Category
1	1	Underwater Tour 1 Day West Coast	61.483	No-Stay
2	7	Underwater Tour 1 Day East Coast	80.859	No-Stay
3	13	Underwater Tour 1 Day Mexico	105.059	No-Stay
4	19	Underwater Tour 1 Day Canada	85.585	No-Stay
5	25	Underwater Tour 1 Day Scandina…	116.118	No-Stay
6	31	History Tour 1 Day West Coast	74.622	No-Stay

Figure 11.20 This query shows all 'No-Stay' products from the CurrentProducts table.

We're going to enclose our query in parentheses, indent it, and then add some code to create a function. We will create the GetCategoryProducts function which takes a

@Category parameter (Figure 11.21). The query within the table-valued function will predicate on the value passed in when the function is called.

```
CREATE FUNCTION GetCategoryProducts (@Category NVARCHAR(25))
RETURNS TABLE
AS
RETURN
    (SELECT ProductID, ProductName, RetailPrice, Category
    FROM CurrentProducts
    WHERE Category = @Category)
GO
```

Figure 11.21 The GetCategoryProducts will return a result set predicating on the parameter value.

Now let's call upon our newly created table-valued function and specify 'No-stay' as the category. Running this query (Figure 11.22) against GetCategoryProducts while passing in the parameter value of 'No-stay' will return a result set consisting of 80 records.

```
SELECT * FROM GetCategoryProducts('No-stay')
```

	ProductID	ProductName	RetailPrice	Category
1	1	Underwater Tour 1 Day West Coast	61.483	No-Stay
2	7	Underwater Tour 1 Day East Coast	80.859	No-Stay
3	13	Underwater Tour 1 Day Mexico	105.059	No-Stay
4	19	Underwater Tour 1 Day Canada	85.585	No-Stay
5	25	Underwater Tour 1 Day Scandina...	116.118	No-Stay
6	31	History Tour 1 Day West Coast	74.622	No-Stay

Query executed successfully.   RENO (11.0 RTM)   Reno\Student (51)   JProCo   00:00:00   80 rows

Figure 11.22 Calling on GetCategoryProducts with the 'No-Stay' Category produces 80 rows.

Change the parameter value to 'Medium-stay' and run this query. The GetCategoryProducts function now returns 164 records (Figure 11.23).

```
SELECT * FROM GetCategoryProducts('Medium-Stay')
```

	ProductID	ProductName	RetailPrice	Category
1	3	Underwater Tour 3 Days West Coast	184.449	Medium-Stay
2	4	Underwater Tour 5 Days West Coast	245.932	Medium-Stay
3	9	Underwater Tour 3 Days East Coast	242.577	Medium-Stay
4	10	Underwater Tour 5 Days East Coast	323.436	Medium-Stay
5	15	Underwater Tour 3 Days Mexico	315.177	Medium-Stay
6	16	Underwater Tour 5 Days Mexico	420.236	Medium-Stay

164 rows

Figure 11.23 Changing the parameter value to 'Medium-stay' returns 164 rows.

Chapter 11. User-Defined Functions

Whenever you call a function, you must remember to use a set of parentheses and include the parameter (s) which the function expects. Earlier in this section, we demonstrated this by running our queries without parentheses. In the next figure (Figure 11.24), let's demonstrate the error message which results from forgetting to include the needed parameter within the parentheses. SQL Server's error message tells us that our code doesn't match the function's parameter signature. In other words, it reminds us that we need to specify a Category.

```
SELECT * FROM GetCategoryProducts()
```

Messages
Msg 313, Level 16, State 3, Line 1
An insufficient number of arguments were supplied for the procedure or function GetCategoryProducts.
0 rows

Figure 11.24 Not supplying the right parameters to your function will generate an error message.

Lab 11.2: Table-Valued Functions

Lab Prep: Lab Prep: Each lab has one or more Skill Checks. Start with Skill Check 1 and proceed until reaching the Points to Ponder section.

Before beginning this lab, verify that SQL Server 2012 is properly installed and operating. Before running the lab setup script for resetting the database (SQLQueries2012Vol4Chapter11.2Setup.sql), please make sure to close all query windows within SSMS. An open query window pointing to a database context can lock that database preventing it from updating when the script is executing. A simple way to assure all query windows are closed, is to exit out of SSMS, then open a new instance of SSMS, and lastly run the setup script.

Skill Check 1: Create a function named GetGrants() that returns the GrantID, GrantName, EmpID and Amount fields from all records of the Grant table. Call on this function with a SELECT Statement. The SELECT statement should resemble Figure 11.25.

```
SELECT * FROM GetGrants()
```

	GrantID	GrantName	EmpID	Amount
1	001	92 Purr_Scents %% team	7	4750.00
2	002	K-Land fund trust	2	15750.00
3	003	Robert@BigStarBank.com	7	18100.00
4	005	BIG 6's Foundation%	4	22000.00
5	006	TALTA_Kishan International	3	18100.00
6	007	Ben@MoreTechnology.com	10	42000.00

13 rows

Figure 11.25 Skill Check 1.

Chapter 11. User-Defined Functions

Skill Check 2: Create a Function named GetGrantsByCity that takes the variable @city with a VARCHAR(25) parameter and returns all the grants procured by employees of that city. Call on this function with a SELECT Statement and pass in 'Seattle' to your parameter. When done, the result should resemble Figure 11.26.

```
SELECT * FROM GetGrantsByCity('Seattle')
```

	GrantID	GrantName	EmpID	Amount
1	001	92 Purr_Scents %% team	7	4750.00
2	002	K-Land fund trust	2	15750.00
3	003	Robert@BigStarBank.com	7	18100.00
4	005	BIG 6's Foundation%	4	22000.00
5	008	www.@-Last-U-Can-Help.com	7	26000.00
6	009	Thank you @.com	11	22500.00

10 rows

Figure 11.26 Skill Check 2 result.

Answer Code: The T-SQL code to this lab can be found in the downloadable files in a file named Lab11.2_TableValuedFunctions.sql.

Points to Ponder - Table-Valued Functions

1. Functions are similar to stored procedures in the way they work, but you must call a function using a SELECT statement or a WHERE clause within a SELECT statement.
2. When functions are executed, they can return results in the form of a value or a table.
3. You can reference a table-valued function in the FROM clause of a SELECT statement just like you do when querying a view or a table.
4. User-defined functions accept values through parameters, and they return a result set based on the calculations performed on them.
5. User-defined functions allow you to create code once and invoke it (i.e., call upon it) multiple times.
6. There are three types of functions:
a. Scalar function – returns a single value like Count() or Max().
b. Table-valued function – returns a table that is the result of a single SELECT statement, similar to a view but it can take parameters.
c. Multi-statement table-valued function – returns a table built with one or more T-SQL statements.
7. Table functions specify TABLE as the return type (RETURNS TABLE).
8. Table functions have a great advantage over views: they allow a parameterized look at your table data.
9. The SELECT statement in the RETURN clause of a table-valued function must be enclosed in parentheses: RETURN SELECT().
10. When calling functions, a set of parentheses must follow the function name. Inside of these, you will include any values to be passed into the parameters of the function. If there are no parameters, leave the parentheses empty.
11. Use a table-valued function anywhere you would normally use a view. *Example:* SELECT * FROM dbo.GetEmployee(3).
12. SQL Server comes with pre-defined functions (called system functions), or you can define your own functions (user-defined functions or UDFs).

Function Determinability

Some questions always have the same answer. For example, if you ask for my initials, I will say "R.A.M". If you ask me that same question tomorrow you would get the same answer. Unless I actually change the source of the data (i.e., change my name), this answer will always be the same. This is an example of a **deterministic** operation.

If you were to ask what I am doing today, you might get an answer like "Work" on a Monday, or "Church" on a Sunday. This type of a question is a **non-deterministic** operation, because the answer is not always the same. In other words, the answer will vary depending upon conditions, such as when the question is asked, and thus cannot be answered prior to runtime. This section will explore both deterministic and non-deterministic functions.

Using Deterministic Functions

Let's begin with a query selecting four fields from the MgmtTraining table.

```
SELECT ClassID, ClassName, ClassDurationHours, ApprovedDate
FROM dbo.MgmtTraining
```

	ClassID	ClassName	ClassDurationHours	ApprovedDate
1	1	Embracing Diversity	12	2007-01-01 00:00:00.000
2	2	Interviewing	6	2007-01-15 00:00:00.000
3	3	Difficult Negotiations	30	2008-02-12 00:00:00.000
4	4	Empowering Others	18	2012-10-07 12:11:33.400
5	8	Passing Certifications	13	2012-10-07 12:11:35.110
6	9	Effective Communications	35	2012-10-07 12:11:36.527

Figure 11.27 A simple query returning four fields from the MgmtTraining table.

Let's create a fifth field (ShortName) that pulls the first five letters from the ClassName field. The ShortName value for the first record would be "Embra," which are the first five letters of "Embracing Diversity".

```sql
SELECT ClassID, ClassName, ClassDurationHours, ApprovedDate,
LEFT(ClassName,5) AS ShortName
FROM dbo.MgmtTraining
```

	ClassID	ClassName	ClassDurationHours	ApprovedDate	ShortName
1	1	Embracing Diversity	12	2007-01-01...	Embra
2	2	Interviewing	6	2007-01-15...	Inter
3	3	Difficult Negotiations	30	2008-02-12...	Diffi
4	4	Empowering Others	18	2012-10-07...	Empow
5	8	Passing Certifications	13	2012-10-07...	Passi
6	9	Effective Communications	35	2012-10-07...	Effec

Figure 11.28 The LEFT() deterministic function is being used as an expression field in the query.

Before we even run this query (Figure 11.28), we know what the results will be because they come directly from the ClassName field. No change to the ShortName field is possible unless a change first happens in the ClassName field. Deterministic fields will never change their values without their source fields changing first.

Deterministic Functions in Views

You can put all types of system-supplied functions into views. The following code shows a query using the LEFT() function to create the ShortName expression field for the vTraining view. The view is created with SCHEMABINDING to prevent someone from deleting the dbo.MgmtTraining base table. A query using the LEFT() function is created inside the vTraining view with the following code:

```sql
CREATE VIEW vTraining
WITH SCHEMABINDING
AS
SELECT ClassID, ClassName,
ClassDurationHours, ApprovedDate,
LEFT(ClassName,5) AS ShortName
FROM dbo.MgmtTraining
GO
```

We are able to predicate on any field contained in the vTraining view. In Figure 11.29, our query predicates on the ShortName field, which is the expression field that uses the LEFT function.

```
SELECT * FROM vTraining
WHERE ShortName = 'Embra'
```

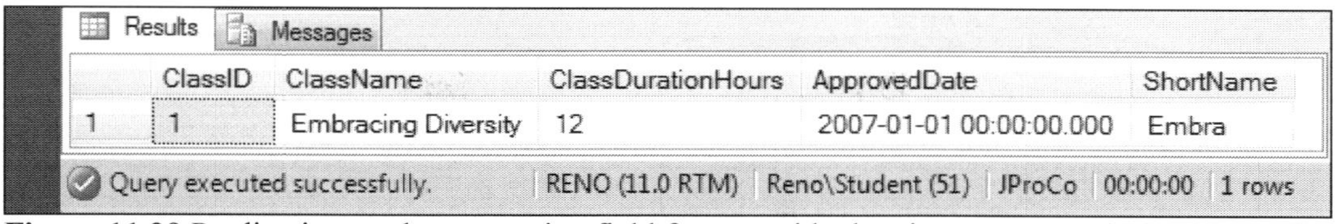
Results
Messages
ClassID
ClassName
ClassDurationHours
ApprovedDate
ShortName
1
1
Embracing Diversity
12
2007-01-01 00:00:00.000
Embra
Query executed successfully.
RENO (11.0 RTM)
Reno\Student (51)
JProCo
00:00:00
1 rows

Figure 11.29 Predicating on the expression field from outside the view gets your desired result set.

Suppose your company states that this query in Figure 11.29 needs to run as fast as possible. We know we'll get better performance if we predicate on an indexed field when we query the view. We can create an index on vTraining since all of its functions are deterministic. It runs successfully because all functions present (in this case we have just one) are deterministic. Let's create an index on this view by using the following code:

```
CREATE UNIQUE CLUSTERED INDEX
UCI_vTraining_ShortName
ON dbo.vTraining(ShortName)
GO
```

Non-Deterministic Functions in Views

You can index a view containing an expression field that is created with a function if all the fields are deterministic. If even one non-deterministic field is present, then the view cannot be indexed.

Our next example will use the Customer table in the JProCo database. Let's create an expression field from the GETDATE() function (Figure 11.30).

```
SELECT CustomerID, CustomerType,
FirstName, LastName, GETDATE() AS RunTime
FROM dbo.Customer
WHERE CustomerType = 'Consumer'
```

	CustomerID	CustomerType	FirstName	LastName	RunTime
1	1	Consumer	Mark	Williams	2012-10-07 12:24:16.840
2	2	Consumer	Lee	Young	2012-10-07 12:24:16.840
3	3	Consumer	Patricia	Martin	2012-10-07 12:24:16.840
4	4	Consumer	Mary	Lopez	2012-10-07 12:24:16.840
5	6	Consumer	Ruth	Clark	2012-10-07 12:24:16.840
6	7	Consumer	Tessa	Wright	2012-10-07 12:24:16.840

Query executed successfully. RENO (11.0 RTM) | Reno\Student (51) | JProCo | 00:00:00 | 773 rows

Figure 11.30 The query includes an expression field based upon a non-deterministic function.

Notice that Mark Williams appears here as Customer 1 because he's CustomerID 1 in the Customer table. CustomerID = 1 will always be Mark Williams (i.e., deterministic). However, each Runtime value returned by the GETDATE field will be different every time we run this query (i.e., non-deterministic).

We are able to successfully create a view (vCustomer), which includes the non-deterministic function, GETDATE(). The following code creates the vCustomer view and uses the GETDATE non-deterministic function:

```sql
CREATE VIEW vCustomer
WITH SCHEMABINDING
AS
SELECT CustomerID, CustomerType,
FirstName, LastName, GETDATE() AS Runtime
FROM dbo.Customer
WHERE CustomerType = 'Consumer'
GO
```

The vCustomer view is created from a query using a non-deterministic function. We are able to successfully query the vCustomer view and predicate on the CustomerID field (Figure 11.31).

```sql
SELECT * FROM vCustomer
WHERE CustomerID = 7
```

	CustomerID	CustomerType	FirstName	LastName	Runtime
1	7	Consumer	Tessa	Wright	2012-10-07 12:26:25.773

Query executed successfully. RENO (11.0 RTM) | Reno\Student (51) | JProCo | 00:00:00 | 1 rows

Figure 11.31 This vCustomer view is predicating on CustomerID.

Management has asked if you can get this query from Figure 11.31 to run any faster. You attempt to create an index on this view but it fails (Figure 11.32). The error message says you can't use non-deterministic fields.

```
CREATE UNIQUE CLUSTERED INDEX CI_vCustomer_CustomerID
ON dbo.vCustomer(CustomerID)
GO
```

```
Messages
Msg 1949, Level 16, State 1, Line 1
Cannot create index on view 'JProCo.dbo.vCustomer'. The function 'GetDate'
yields nondeterministic results. Use a deterministic system function, or
modify the user-defined function to return deterministic results.
                                                                    0 rows
```

Figure 11.32 An index can't be created on a view which includes a non-deterministic function.

User-Defined Function Determinability

SQL already knows that LEFT is a deterministic function and GETDATE is non-deterministic. When you create a user-defined function, you can create either type of function. The choices you make in constructing your function affect whether the function is deterministic or non-deterministic. Since deterministic functions always return the same result for each input value(s), this function is deterministic. For example, if we pass in $100 to the @Price parameter, the value returned will always be $109.50. The following code creates the CalculatePriceWithTax function:

```
CREATE FUNCTION dbo.CalculatePriceWithTax(@Price Money)
RETURNS Money
AS
BEGIN
DECLARE @Total Money
SET @Total = @Price * 1.095
RETURN @Total
END
GO
```

The CalculatePriceWithTax function is created. If we try to include our new function (CalculatePriceWithTax) in a new schema bound view (vProductPrices), we will get this error message (Figure 11.33). In order to schema bind this view, the function must first be schema bound.

```sql
CREATE VIEW vProductPrices
WITH SCHEMABINDING
AS
SELECT ProductID, ProductName, RetailPrice,
dbo.CalculatePriceWithTax(RetailPrice) AS TotalPrice
FROM dbo.CurrentProducts
GO
```

```
Messages
Msg 4513, Level 16, State 2, Procedure vProductPrices, Line 4
Cannot schema bind view 'vProductPrices'. 'dbo.CalculatePriceWithTax' is not
schema bound.
                                                                    0 rows
```

Figure 11.33 You can only use schema bound user-defined functions in schema bound views.

Let's ALTER the function to make it schema bound. SQL Server now allows us to include this user-defined function within a schema bound view. The following code will alter the CalculatePriceWithTax function to use schema binding:

```sql
ALTER FUNCTION dbo.CalculatePriceWithTax(@Price MONEY)
RETURNS MONEY
WITH SCHEMABINDING
AS
BEGIN
DECLARE @Total Money
SET @Total = @Price * 1.095
RETURN @Total
END
GO
```

The CalculatePriceWithTax function was altered to use SCHEMABINDING. We can now reattempt our code which failed earlier. It now runs successfully (Figure 11.34). The view is now schema bound and uses the dbo.CalculatePriceWithTax user-defined scalar function.

```sql
CREATE VIEW vProductPrices
WITH SCHEMABINDING
AS
SELECT ProductID, ProductName, RetailPrice,
dbo.CalculatePriceWithTax(RetailPrice) AS TotalPrice
FROM dbo.CurrentProducts
GO
```

```
Messages
Command(s) completed successfully.
                                                                    0 rows
```

Figure 11.34 The vProductPrices view is created successfully and is schema bound.

Any function that is schema bound is considered by SQL Server to be deterministic. Since this view (vProductPrices) is schema bound, we know it includes only deterministic function(s). Thus, we should now be able to add an index to this view. Let's add a unique clustered index to the ProductID field of the vProductPrices view (Figure 11.35).

```
CREATE UNIQUE CLUSTERED INDEX UCI_vProductPrices_ProductID
ON dbo.vProductPrices(ProductID)
GO
```

```
Messages
Command(s) completed successfully.
                                                                    0 rows
```

Figure 11.35 An index is added to vProductPrices.

Lab 11.3: Function Determinability

Lab Prep: Lab Prep: Each lab has one or more Skill Checks. Start with Skill Check 1 and proceed until reaching the Points to Ponder section.

Before beginning this lab, verify that SQL Server 2012 is properly installed and operating. Before running the lab setup script for resetting the database (SQLQueries2012Vol4Chapter11.3Setup.sql), please make sure to close all query windows within SSMS. An open query window pointing to a database context can lock that database preventing it from updating when the script is executing. A simple way to assure all query windows are closed, is to exit out of SSMS, then open a new instance of SSMS, and lastly run the setup script.

Skill Check 1: Create a view called vLocations which selects the LocationID, Street and City fields from the Location table. Include an expression field called BigCity which uses the UPPER() function to capitalize every city name found in the Location table. When done the vLocations table should resemble Figure 11.36

```
SELECT * FROM vLocations
```

	LocationID	street	city	BigCity
1	1	111 First ST	Seattle	SEATTLE
2	2	222 Second AVE	Boston	BOSTON
3	3	333 Third PL	Chicago	CHICAGO
4	4	444 Ruby ST	Spokane	SPOKANE
5	5	1595 Main	Philadelphia	PHILADELPHIA
6	6	915 Wallaby Drive	Sydney	SYDNEY

6 rows

Figure 11.36 Skill Check 1 result.

Chapter 11. User-Defined Functions

Skill Check 2: Create a Unique Clustered Index called UCI_vLocations_LocationID on the LocationID field of the vLocations view.

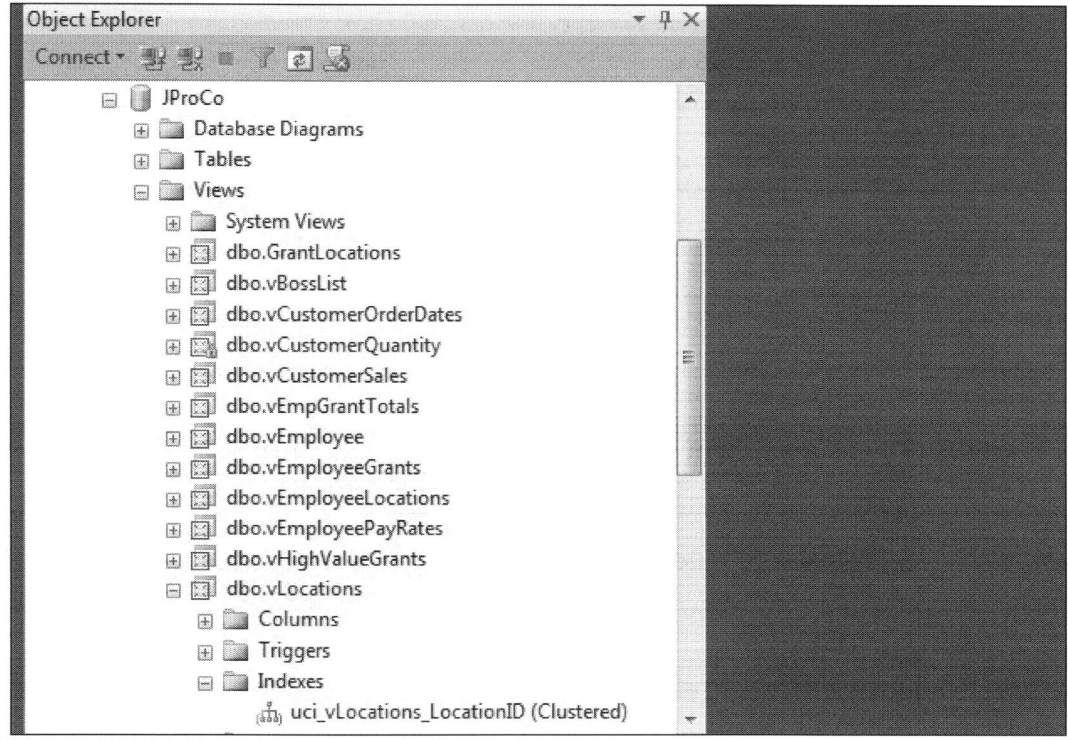

Figure 11.37 Add a unique clustered index to vLocations

Answer Code: The T-SQL code to this lab can be found in the downloadable files in a file named Lab11.3_DeterministicFunctions.sql.

Points to Ponder - Function Determinability

1. All functions are either deterministic or non-deterministic.
2. Deterministic functions are ones that don't change their value unless the underlying data in the table changes.
3. Non-deterministic functions can return different values even when the data in the database does not change.
4. You can place both deterministic and non-deterministic functions inside of a view.
5. You can only index a view containing functions if all the functions are deterministic.
6. User-defined functions are deterministic when:
   - The function is schema-bound.
   - All functions it calls upon are deterministic.

Chapter Glossary

BEGIN END block: used to enclose the body of a function.

Deterministic function: a function whose result doesn't change unless the underlying data in the table changes.

Function: a SQL object stored in a database and consisting of prewritten code that accepts parameters.

Multi-statement table-valued function: returns a table built by one or more T-SQL statements.

Non-deterministic function: a function whose result can return different values even when the data in the database does not change.

Scalar function: a function whose result consists of a single value; Count() and Max() are examples of scalar functions.

Table-valued function: a function which takes a table as an input and whose output is a result set; similar to a view but it can take parameters.

User-defined function (UDF): a routine that you can create to accept parameter values, perform a task, and return a result set.

Review Quiz - Chapter Eleven

1.) You are told to create a scalar function. This means your function should:

   O a. Return no values.
   O b. Return a single value.
   O c. Return a list of values.
   O d. Return a table of values.

2.) You need to create two functions that will each return a scalar result of the number of hours each user has logged for: 1) the current day, and 2) month to date. You will pass in the user ID as a parameter value. What must you do (choose two)?

   ☐ a. Create a function that returns a list of values representing the login times for a given user.
   ☐ b. Create a function that returns a list of values representing the people who have logged more hours than the current user has logged.
   ☐ c. Create a function that returns a numeric value representing the number of hours that a user has logged for the current day.
   ☐ d. Create a function that returns a number value representing the number of hours that a user has logged for the current month.

3.) You are responsible for managing a SQL Server 2012 database that stores sales information. Many values in NCHAR columns in the database tables contain preceding or trailing spaces. You need to implement a mechanism that selects the data from the tables but without the leading and trailing spaces. Your solution must be available for reuse in T-SQL statements and views. What should you do?

   O a. Create DML triggers that query the Inserted and Deleted tables.
   O b. Create a stored procedure that calls the LTRIM and RTRIM built-in functions.
   O c. Create a T-SQL function that calls the LTRIM and RTRIM built-in functions.
   O d. Call the TRIM built-in functions.

4.) You want to return a Boolean result that examines a date and determines whether it occurs in a leap year. What type of function will do this?

   O a. Table-valued.
   O b. Scalar-valued.

5.) You have a view that uses an expression field which comes from a function. You want to index this column but get the following error message:

```
Msg 1949, Level 16, State 1, Line 2
Cannot create index on view 'JProCo.dbo.vCustomer'
The function 'GetDate' yields nondeterministic results. Use a
deterministic system function, or modify the user-defined
function to return deterministic results.
```

You create another view using the LEFT() function as an expression field, and this view indexes just fine. Which object property is allowing the LEFT() function to be part of an indexed view?

O a. IsDeterministic is set to true.

O b. IsDeterministic is set to false.

6.) The following query finds all reports for leap year months since 1950:

```
SELECT *
FROM Reports
WHERE /*Code here*/ (rMonth, rYear) = 29
AND rYear > 1950
```

If, for a specified year, the month of February will contain 29 days, you want the query to include the record in your query. Which object should you use in your query predicate?

O a. DML trigger

O b. Stored procedure

O c. Table-valued function

O d. Scalar function

Answer Key

1.) All functions return value(s), so (a) is incorrect. Table valued functions return tabular values but scalar function only return a single value, so (d) is wrong but (b) is the correct answer.

2.) If you want to return two values from scalar functions that have one value per function then you need a table valued function. Scalar functions can only return single values (not a list of values), so (a) and (b) are wrong. The correct answers are (c) and (d).

3.) Triggers and Stored Procedures can't be used in line with a field in a query, so (a) and (b) are wrong. If you want to create your own mechanism then (c) is the correct answer.

4.) If you want to return a single value, use a scalar function. This means (b) is the correct answer.

5.) The only way to use a function in an indexed column is to make sure it is deterministic. This means (a) is the correct answer.

6.) Triggers and Stored Procedures can't be used in line with a field in a query, so (a) and (b) are wrong. The WHERE clause is checking to see if your single value is equal to 29 and must compare that with a scalar result. Therefore you need a scalar function, making (d) the correct answer.

Bug Catcher Game

To play the Bug Catcher game, run the file SQLQueries2012Vol4BugCatcher11.pps from the BugCatcher folder of the companion files found at www.Joes2Pros.com.

Chapter 12. SQL Error Messages

Have you ever heard a team member or co-worker say "That's not my problem" or "That's not my job"? Often when we hear this sentiment, it's associated with someone not willing to lend a hand to solve an issue but rather presumes someone else will do the work. Until SQL Server 2005, the "that's-not-my-problem" poster pretty well described SQL Server's approach toward error handling. It would tell you when an error occurred, but it was entirely up to the calling code to deal with the error. A custom application written in another language (e.g., C#) was needed to actually handle the error.

SQL Server has improved greatly since SQL Server 2000. It still has the same ability to point out errors, but has significantly enhanced its capabilities and options for handling errors. In this chapter, we will explore the ways SQL Server raises errors and the options for having SQL handle those errors for you.

READER NOTE: *Please run the script SQLQueries2012Vol4Chapter12.0Setup.sql in order to follow along with the examples in the first section of Chapter 12. All scripts mentioned in this chapter may be found at* **www.Joes2Pros.com**.

SQL Server Error Messages

By now, most readers have likely learned that it is better to deal with problems early on while they are small. SQL Server detects and helps you identify most errors before you are even allowed to run the code. For example, if you try to run a query against a table which does not exist, SQL Server informs you via IntelliSense while you're coding the query or via an error message when you attempt to run the query. You also will get an error message if you try to insert a NULL value into a non-nullable field. This section will cover how SQL Server raises error messages.

Errors in SQL Statements

SQL Server will raise errors when the code you have written cannot or should not execute. For example, a table should not be created if one with the same name already exists. Also, you can't run a stored procedure if the name you are calling does not exist. Attempting to run such code will cause SQL to raise an error.

SQL Server raises an error whenever a statement cannot, or should not, complete its execution. For example, we know there is already an Employee table in the JProCo database. In Figure 12.1 we see code to create another Employee table. *If we attempt* to run the following code, should SQL Server permit our longstanding Employee table to be overwritten?

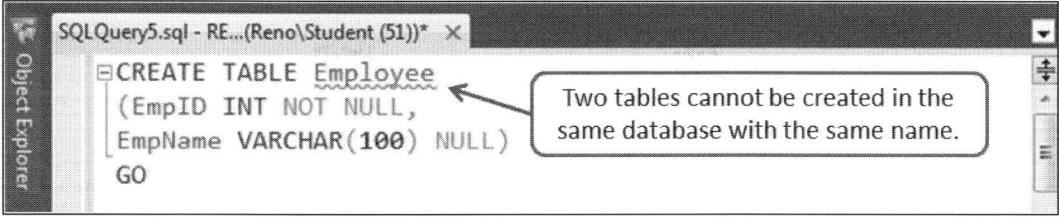

```
CREATE TABLE Employee
    (EmpID INT NOT NULL,
    EmpName VARCHAR(100) NULL)
GO
```

Two tables cannot be created in the same database with the same name.

Figure 12.1 There is already an Employee table in the database, which we don't want to be overwritten.

Having a new, empty Employee table overwrite the one we are using would *not* be a good idea. In Figure 12.2 we see SQL Server prevent the accidental loss of the valuable data in the existing Employee table. When we run this, SQL Server alerts us that our code cannot be run and displays the reason in an error message.

```
Msg 2714, Level 16, State 6, Line 1
There is already an object named 'Employee' in the database.
```

Error Message (Error Text)

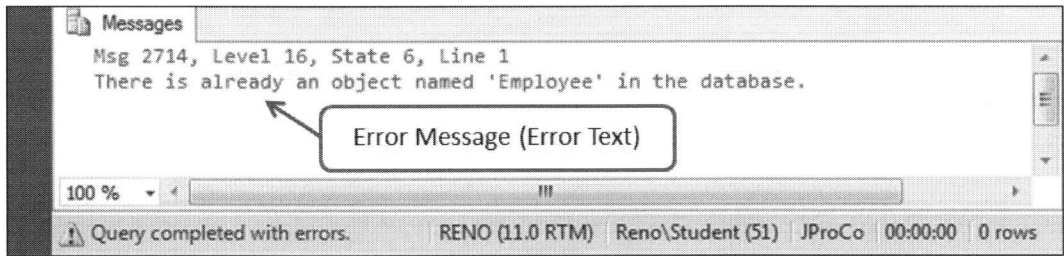

Figure 12.2 SQL Server alerts us that there is already an Employee table in our database.

Notice that this is error message 2714 (Figure 12.2 and Figure 12.3). Error severity levels range from a low of 0 to a maximum of 25, and the error severity level here is 16. We will discuss error severity later in this chapter.

```
Msg 2714, Level 16, State 6, Line 1
There is already an object named 'Employee' in the database.
```

Error Number = 2714   *Error Severity = 16*

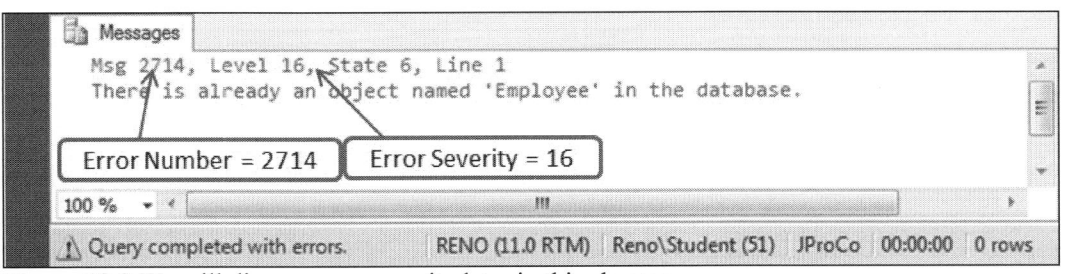

Figure 12.3 We will discuss error severity later in this chapter.

Now let's try a very similar statement, except we'll use a different name to create the table. Here is a table creation statement which will run without an error (Figure 12.4). *This is because there is no object named TempStaff in the JProCo database.*

Chapter 12. SQL Errors Messages

```
CREATE TABLE TempStaff
(TStaffID INT NOT NULL,
TStaffName VARCHAR(100) NULL)
GO
```

This will work since the TempStaff table does not already exist.

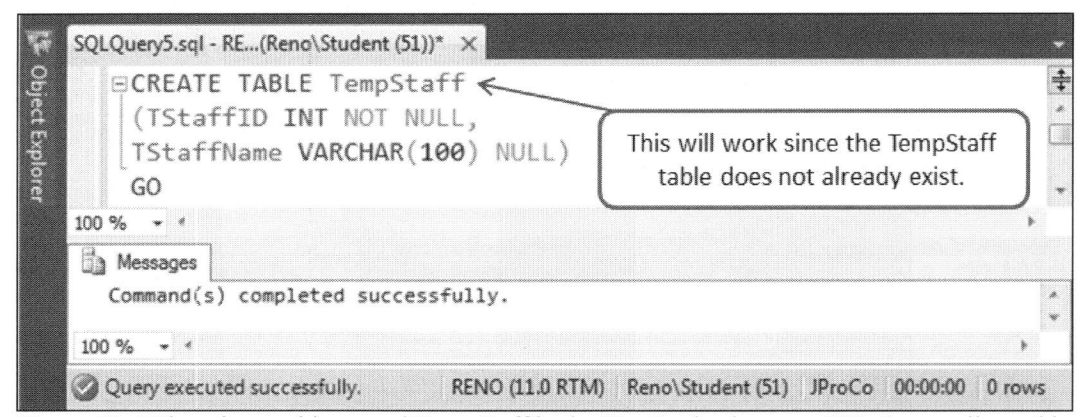

Messages
Command(s) completed successfully.

Figure 12.4 There is no table named TempStaff in the JProCo database, so SQL Server allows this code to run and the TempStaff table to be created.

As you can see, a perfectly written table creation statement sometimes will work and under other conditions it may error out. Next we want to create a statement which will never work; it will always return an error message.

In Figure 12.5, the SometimesBad stored procedure will sometimes throw an error message. Don't run this code yet – let's first examine what it does. If SQL finds the TempStaff table, then it will attempt to run the table creation statement. Imagine the TempStaff table didn't exist. In that case, nothing would happen. The IF EXISTS condition would be false so the CREATE TABLE statement would not be attempted.

```
CREATE PROC SometimesBad
AS
BEGIN
    IF EXISTS(SELECT * FROM sys.tables WHERE [name] = 'TempStaff')
    CREATE TABLE TempStaff
    (TStaffID INT NOT NULL,  TStaffName VARCHAR(100) NULL)
END
GO
```

This will throw an error only if the table exists

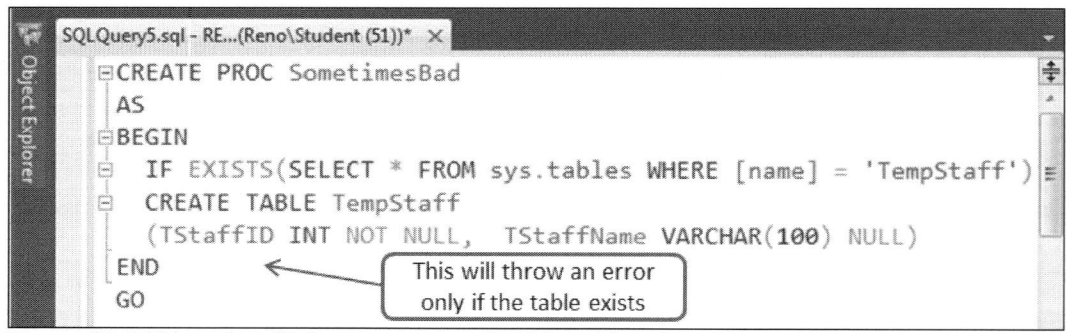

Figure 12.5 This code will throw an error only if the table exists.

We know one way to generate an error is to try creating a table which already exists. Another way is to try dropping a table which doesn't exist. If you run the SometimesBad stored procedure, it will only throw an error if the TempStaff table already exists. For testing purposes, we want a stored procedure like SometimesBad to always throw an error message. Our next step will be to add an ELSE statement which says that we want to drop the table if it is not found (Figure 12.6).

Look closely at this code and recognize that it will always throw an error (Figure 12.6). If the TempStaff table exists, then trying to execute a statement to create this table generates an error. And if the TempStaff table doesn't exist, then executing a statement which attempts to drop this table will similarly generate an error.

```
CREATE PROC AlwaysBad
AS                              This PROC will throw an error
BEGIN                           regardless if the table exists
    IF EXISTS(SELECT * FROM sys.tables WHERE [name] = 'TempStaff')
    CREATE TABLE TempStaff
    (TStaffID INT NOT NULL, TStaffName VARCHAR(100) NULL)
    ELSE
    DROP TABLE TempStaff
END
GO
```

Figure 12.6 This stored procedure will throw an error regardless of whether the table exists.

If you were to create and run the AlwaysBad sproc, you would see that attempting to execute it will <u>always</u> result in an error message (Figure 12.7-Figure 12.8). During the sproc execution, SQL tried to create the TempStaff table which already existed.

```
EXEC SometimesBad
```

Messages
Msg 2714, Level 16, State 6, Procedure SometimesBad, Line 5
There is already an object named 'TempStaff' in the database.
0 rows

Figure 12.7 The SometimesBad stored procedure throws an error message if the TempStaff table exists.

If the table is not present, then the same stored procedure would still throw an error. Message 3701 indicates that you can't drop the table because it does not exist (Figure 12.8).

```
EXEC AlwaysBad
```

Messages
Msg 3701, Level 11, State 5, Procedure AlwaysBad, Line 7
Cannot drop the table 'TempStaff', because it does not exist or you do not have permission
0 rows

Figure 12.8 The AlwaysBad sproc will also throw an error message if the table does not exist.

Again, we know that SQL Server will raise an error whenever a statement cannot, or should not, complete its execution. It's also possible to define your own conditions where SQL Server does not encounter an error but nonetheless doesn't run due to a situation which goes against company policy. For example, updating an employee's PayRate value to below minimum wage is not a SQL error. However, in such a situation you would prefer that SQL Server generate an error message rather than allowing the bad code to execute.

Custom Error Messages

Suppose you have a stored procedure named UpdateOneEmployee which changes one employee record at a time. The logic of this stored procedure will allow you to potentially update two employees with the same info. Since it is against company policy to update more than one employee record a time, it's extremely unlikely that anyone would ever attempt to update multiple records at once. However, because SQL Server has no restriction against inserting or updating many records in one transaction, you want to add a layer of protection to help enforce company policy. This is a case where you don't want SQL Server to allow this update, even though SQL Server doesn't define it as an error. To accomplish the goal, you can raise your own error message based on conditions which you define.

Let's begin this example by looking at all of the fields and records of the Employee table. We see 20 records and EmpID values ranging from 1 to 21 (Figure 12.9).

```
SELECT * FROM Employee
```

	EmpID	LastName	FirstName	HireDate	LocationID	ManagerID	Status	HiredOffset
1	1	Adams	Alex	2001-01-01...	1	4	Active	2001-01-01...
2	2	Brown	Barry	2002-08-12...	1	11	Active	2002-08-12...
3	3	Osako	Lee	1999-09-01...	2	11	Active	1999-09-01...
4	4	Kinnison	Dave	1996-03-16...	1	11	Has Tenure	1996-03-16...
5	5	Bender	Eric	2007-05-17...	1	11	Active	2007-05-17...
6	6	Kendall	Lisa	2001-11-15...	4	4	Active	2001-11-15...

Query executed successfully.   RENO (11.0 RTM) Reno\Student (51) JProCo 00:00:00 20 rows

Figure 12.9 Prepare for the next example by looking at the records and fields of the Employee table.

What we would like to do is create a stored procedure which changes the employee's status based on the EmpID. The update will change the value of the status field (Figure 12.10). Below we have a partially written stored procedure that uses the @Status parameter to set the value of the Status field in the Employee table. ***Don't run this code yet.*** Since it doesn't use criteria to filter the Employee records, this sproc would change ALL employees to the same status – *very bad!*

```
CREATE PROC SetEmployeeStatus @EmpID INT, @Status VARCHAR(20)
AS
BEGIN
      UPDATE Employee SET [Status] = @Status
      WHERE EmpID = @EmpID
END
GO
```

Figure 12.10 This stored procedure will change each employee's status but does not use the EmpID parameter yet.

Let's complete the code by using the @EmpID parameter (Figure 12.11). This stored procedure will change an individual employee's status based on the EmpID.

```
CREATE PROC SetEmployeeStatus @EmpID INT, @Status VARCHAR(20)
AS
BEGIN
      UPDATE Employee SET [Status] = @Status
      WHERE EmpID = @EmpID
END
GO
```

Figure 12.11 This stored procedure will change each employee's status based on the EmpID.

With the sproc created, we can test this procedure by executing it to set the record of Employee 1's status to "on leave":

EXEC SetEmployeeStatus 1, 'On Leave'

We can confirm the status change by querying the Employee table. Recall that Employee 1's status was Active in the previous figure. Passing the values 1 and 'On Leave' into SetEmployeeStatus changes the Status field for Employee 1 to 'On Leave.'

Chapter 12. SQL Errors Messages

```
SELECT * FROM Employee
```

[Screenshot of SQL Query window showing:
```
EXEC SetEmployeeStatus 1, 'On Leave'
SELECT * FROM Employee
```
Results table with columns EmpID, LastName, FirstName, HireDate, LocationID, ManagerID, Status, HiredC:
EmpID	LastName	FirstName	HireDate	LocationID	ManagerID	Status	HiredC
1	Adams	Alex	2001-01-01...	1	4	On Leave	2001-
2	Brown	Barry	2002-08-12...	1	11	Active	2002-
3	Osako	Lee	1999-09-01...	2	11	Active	1999-
4	Kinnison	Dave	1996-03-16...	1	11	Has Tenure	1996-
5	Bender	Eric	2007-05-17...	1	11	Active	2007-
6	Kendall	Lisa	2001-11-15...	4	4	Active	2001-
]

Figure 12.12 Passing in 1 and 'On Leave' into SetEmployeeStatus changes the status field for Employee 1 to 'On Leave.'

Let's execute this statement for an employee which doesn't exist (Figure 12.13). Notice that our result is not actually an error. The statement runs alright, but no rows are affected because no records in JProCo's Employee table meet the criteria.

[Screenshot showing:
```
EXEC SetEmployeeStatus 51, 'On Leave'
```
Messages: (0 row(s) affected)
Callout: "There is no EmpID 51 in the Employee table. Zero rows were affected."]

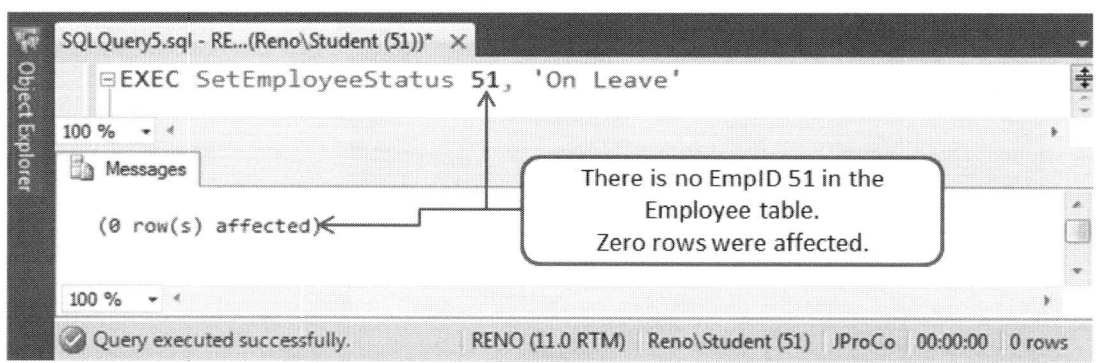

Figure 12.13 There is no EmpID 51, so no rows are affected.

This is not a SQL Server error. But what if the 51 was a typo? What if the intent was to update the status for Employee 11 or Employee 21? In that case, it would be helpful to program your code to alert you if you accidentally attempted to run a statement for a non-existent EmpID.

Let's alter the stored procedure by adding two more statements. If we see that no rows are affected then we will raise a level 16 error that alerts us, "Nothing was done!" The follow code alters the SetEmployeeStatus sproc to raise an error if no records are affected:

```
ALTER PROC SetEmployeeStatus @EmpID INT, @Status VARCHAR(20)
AS
BEGIN
UPDATE Employee SET [Status] = @Status
WHERE EmpID = @EmpID
IF @@ROWCOUNT = 0
RAISERROR('Nothing was done!', 16, 1)
END
GO
```

The SetEmployeeStatus sproc was altered to raise an error if no records are affected. With the sproc updated, let's run our prior EXEC statements for EmpID 1 and EmpID 51. EmpID 1 runs the same as it did previously. Here you can see that calling on the stored procedure and passing in 51 for the EmpID returns our user-defined error message (Figure 12.14). The severity is level 16 and the message says "Nothing was done!"

```
EXEC SetEmployeeStatus 51, 'On Leave'
```

```
Messages
(0 row(s) affected)
Msg 50000, Level 16, State 1, Procedure SetEmployeeStatus, Line 7
Nothing was done!
                                                                    0 rows
```

Figure 12.14 An error is thrown when you test the stored procedure with no affected records.

Error Severity

Most errors you will see have a severity of between 11 and 16. These are known as **user errors** and come with many options for how to deal with them. Did your error cause a simple rollback, or did it crash your system and break all connections? SQL has error severity levels ranging between 0 and 25. Anything over 20 is so bad that it will terminate your connection to the database. In fact, in order to raise errors that high, you must be a sysadmin.

Errors of severity 10 and below are not even errors but simply informational notifications of events which have taken place. Any code looking for errors will ignore those with severity levels less than or equal to 10.

An error severity level of 16 seems a bit too severe for just having zero records updated. Let's alter the stored procedure to throw a severity of 11 when no records are updated. The following code will alter the stored procedure to throw a severity 11 error message when no records are affected:

```
ALTER PROC SetEmployeeStatus @EmpID INT, @Status VARCHAR(20)
AS
BEGIN
UPDATE Employee SET [Status] = @Status
WHERE EmpID = @EmpID
IF @@ROWCOUNT = 0
RAISERROR('Nothing was done!', 11, 1)
END
GO
```

With the stored procedure altered, we would expect to see a lower error severity when no records are affected. An error is thrown but the severity is now showing as 11 (Figure 12.15).

```
EXEC SetEmployeeStatus 51, 'On Leave'
```

```
Messages
(0 row(s) affected)
Msg 50000, Level 11, State 1, Procedure SetEmployeeStatus, Line 7
Nothing was done!
                                                                    0 rows
```

Figure 12.15 The error severity is now showing level 11.

A severity of 11 is still an error. The text appearing in red indicates an error. Text in black, such as the "0 the row(s) affected" is just an informational message. We can test this a little further with an ALTER PROC statement that reduces the error severity level to 10. The following code will alter the stored procedure to throw a severity 10 message when no records are affected:

```
ALTER PROC SetEmployeeStatus @EmpID INT, @Status VARCHAR(20)
AS
BEGIN
UPDATE Employee SET [Status] = @Status
WHERE EmpID = @EmpID
IF @@ROWCOUNT = 0
RAISERROR('Nothing was done!', 10, 1)
END
GO
```

The SetEmployeeStatus sproc will throw a severity level 10 message. To test this, we will again try to update the nonexistent EmpID 51. Notice that we see no red text (Figure 12.16). There is no error displayed here but the message reads, "Nothing was Done!" Since severity levels 0-10 are not errors, the black printout "Nothing was done!" is an informational message (Figure 12.16). Levels 11 and higher are considered raised errors and thus are printed in red font.

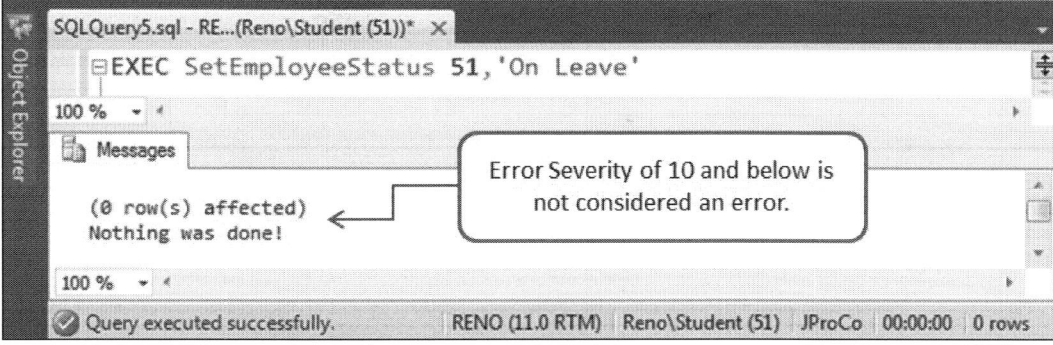

Figure 12.16 A severity of 10 or lower is not an error.

Using Error Message Variables

There are a few more options for programming your code to raise errors from within a stored procedure. We'll use the Grant table for our next example.

```
SELECT * FROM [Grant]
```

Figure 12.17 The Grant table has 4 fields and 13 records.

Suppose we occasionally have grant donors who contact us to let us know they want to increase the amount of their grant. To illustrate this, let's write a small program called AddGrantAmount. Run all of this code, and then we'll test our newly created sproc:

```sql
CREATE PROC AddGrantAmount @GrantID CHAR(3), @MoreAmount
MONEY
AS
BEGIN
UPDATE [Grant] SET Amount = Amount + @MoreAmount
WHERE GrantID = @GrantID
END
GO
```

We'll test AddGrantAmount by increasing GrantID 005 by $1,000. In Figure 12.18 we can see that the current amount of GrantID 005 is $21,000. If we were to add an additional $1,000 the new amount would become $22,000.

```sql
SELECT * FROM [Grant]
WHERE GrantID = '005'
```

	GrantID	GrantName	EmpID	Amount
1	005	BIG 6's Foundation%	4	22000.00

1 rows

Figure 12.18 The amount of GrantID 005 is $21,000.

Let's call on the AddGrantAmount stored procedure and pass in 005 for the GrantID and 90 for the amount. The following code will add 90 to GrantID 005:

```sql
EXEC AddGrantAmount '005', 90
```

A SELECT statement confirms that the amount for GrantID 005 has increased to $22,090 (Figure 12.19).

```sql
SELECT * FROM [Grant]
WHERE GrantID = '005'
```

	GrantID	GrantName	EmpID	Amount
1	005	BIG 6's Foundation%	4	22090.00

1 rows

Figure 12.19 The amount of GrantID 005 was increased to $22,090.

Now we'd like to alter our stored procedure to print an informational message whenever we run AddGrantAmount. We would like a customized message to show us the number of grants which have been increased. The severity level will be 10, which will print a notification message each time we run the AddGrantAmount sproc. In the next code example we have partially written the statement to raise the error and have chosen 10 for the second parameter. This will set the severity level to 10, which we know indicates an informational message printed in black font. The following code alters the AddGrantAmount sproc and reduces the severity of the message to 10:

```
ALTER PROC AddGrantAmount @GrantID CHAR(3), @MoreAmount MONEY
AS
BEGIN
UPDATE [Grant] SET Amount = Amount + @MoreAmount
WHERE GrantID = @GrantID
RAISERROR('Increased %i Grant records', 10, 1, @@ROWCOUNT)
END
GO
```

A notification message will print each time we run the AddGrantAmount stored procedure. There we included the global function @@ROWCOUNT to show the number of rows which have been affected by the stored procedure. The amount will be captured by the %i variable.

Including @@ROWCOUNT will show the number of rows affected by the sproc. Run the EXEC statement and notice the confirmation "Increased 1 Grant records" prints as a message, since the severity is below 11 (Figure 12.20).

```
EXEC AddGrantAmount '005', 90
```

```
Messages
(1 row(s) affected)
Increased 1 Grant records
                                                                    0 rows
```

Figure 12.20 Execute the revised stored procedure in order to see the new message printed.

The %i dynamically prints a 1 to display the count of rows affected. In Figure 12.21, we see the process flow for how this message is generated and displayed.

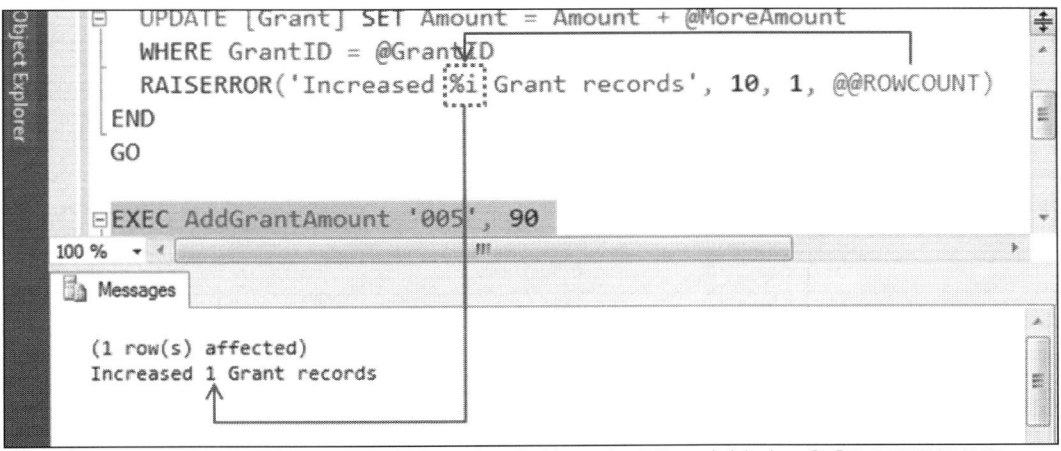

Figure 12.21 The 1 was printed from the value fed into the %i variable by @@ROWCOUNT.

Now let's evaluate the potential for an error by our sproc when we convert the GrantID field to an INT. Remember the GrantID is passed in as a char(3) data type. We will change the predicate to utilize this integer instead of the char data as seen in Figure 12.22. Why? Because we've been given a warning that the database team is going to convert the GrantID to an integer very soon. In fact, they said it should never have been created as character data. All stored procedures which depend on this field need to be prepared to use the integer version of this field.

```
ALTER PROC AddGrantAmount @GrantID CHAR(3), @MoreAmount MONEY
AS
BEGIN
    DECLARE @GrantINT INT
    SET @GrantINT = CAST(@GrantID AS INT)       -- 5 = CAST ('005')
    UPDATE [Grant] SET Amount = Amount + @MoreAmount
    WHERE GrantID = @GrantINT                    -- 5
    RAISERROR('Increased %i Grant records', 10, 1, @@ROWCOUNT )
END
GO
```

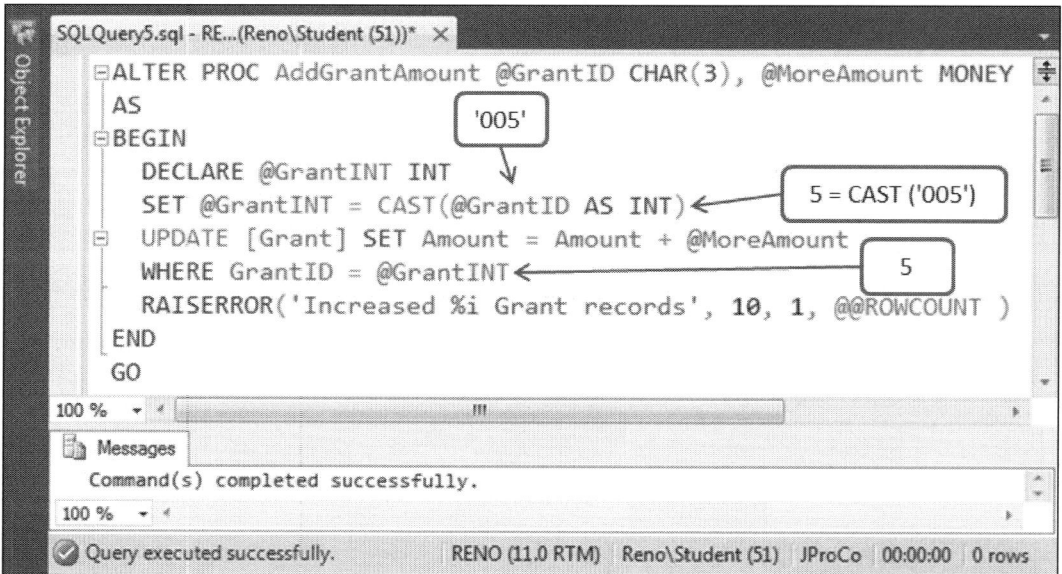

Command(s) completed successfully.

Figure 12.22 We will further error proof the sproc AddGrantAmount by converting the data type of the GrantID field to an INT.

Let's run an EXEC statement for AddGrantAmount (Figure 12.23). Notice we have the potential for an error if a user spells out "five" instead of using the numeral 5. Our CAST function will not be able to work with character data that has non-numeric values. A conversion error is generated. You can convert '005' into a 5, but the CAST function does not know how to handle 'Five'.

```
EXEC AddGrantAmount 'Five', 90
```

```
Messages
Msg 245, Level 16, State 1, Procedure AddGrantAmount, Line 5
Conversion failed when converting the varchar value 'Fiv' to data type int.

                                                                    0 rows
```

Figure 12.23 The sproc failed to convert VARCHAR "Five". to data type INT.

The CAST function failing with a conversion error means our RAISERROR code never gets a chance to run. The stored procedure terminates and the informational

Chapter 12. SQL Errors Messages

message is not displayed to the Messages tab. We see the conversion error but not the level 10 severity message, since the sproc terminates (Figure 12.24).

```sql
ALTER PROC AddGrantAmount @GrantID CHAR(3), @MoreAmount MONEY
AS
BEGIN
    DECLARE @GrantINT INT
    SET @GrantINT = CAST(@GrantID AS INT)
    UPDATE [Grant] SET Amount = Amount + @MoreAmount
    WHERE GrantID = @GrantINT
    RAISERROR('Increased %1 Grant records', 10, 1, @@ROWCOUNT )
END
GO

EXEC AddGrantAmount 'Five', 90
```

Messages
Msg 245, Level 16, State 1, Procedure AddGrantAmount, Line 5
Conversion failed when converting the varchar value 'Fiv' to data type int.

← No informational message was raised

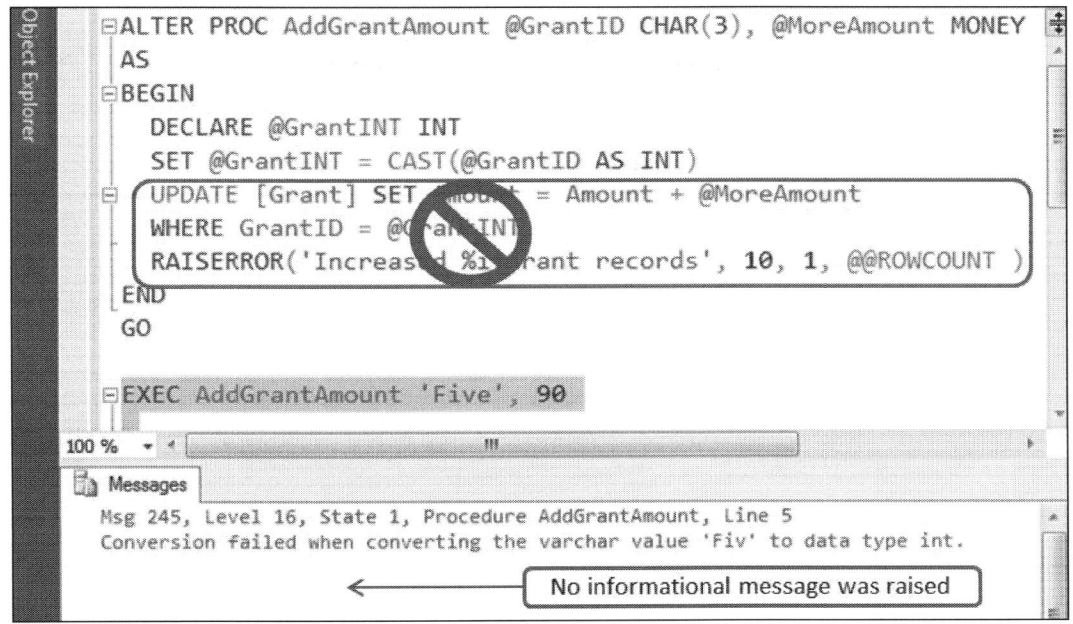

Figure 12.24 Our test input causes the CAST function to fail, and the stored procedure terminates.

Lab 12.1: SQL Server Error Messages

Lab Prep: Lab Prep: Each lab has one or more Skill Checks. Start with Skill Check 1 and proceed until reaching the Points to Ponder section.

Before beginning this lab, verify that SQL Server 2012 is properly installed and operating. Before running the lab setup script for resetting the database (SQLQueries2012Vol4Chapter12.1Setup.sql), please make sure to close all query windows within SSMS. An open query window pointing to a database context can lock that database preventing it from updating when the script is executing. A simple way to assure all query windows are closed, is to exit out of SSMS, then open a new instance of SSMS, and lastly run the setup script.

Skill Check 1: Create a stored procedure called SetGrantAmount which takes the variable @GrantID with CHAR(3) as the first parameter and @Amount MONEY as the second parameter. The procedure should update the Amount for the GrantID specified. The stored procedure should raise an error if no records are updated. Test this by trying to update GrantID 015. When done, your result should resemble Figure 12.25.

```
EXEC SetGrantAmount '015', 28000
```

```
Messages
(0 row(s) affected)
Msg 50000, Level 11, State 1, Procedure SetGrantAmount, Line 7
No grants were set!
                                                                0 rows
```

Figure 12.25 Skill Check 1 creates a sproc called SetGrantAmount and raises a user-defined error.

Skill Check 2: Alter the PayRates table so it has a BonusPoints field that takes an INT parameter. Start off by setting all values to zero.

```
ALTER TABLE PayRates
ADD BonusPoints INT
GO
```

Create a Stored Procedure called AddBonusPoint which takes an INT parameter named @EmpID and increments the BonusPoints field in the PayRates table. Raise an informational message with a level 10 severity which shows how many records were updated. Test your procedure with EmpID 2.

```
EXEC AddBonusPoint @EmpID = 2
```

Query your PayRates table to see that Employee 2 has a bonus point. Your result should look like Figure 12.26.

```
SELECT * FROM PayRates
```

EmpID	YearlySalary	MonthlySalary	HourlyRate	Selector	Estimate	BonusPoints
1	76000.00	NULL	NULL	1	1	0
2	79000.00	NULL	NULL	1	1	1
3	NULL	NULL	45.00	3	2080	0
4	NULL	6500.00	NULL	2	12	0
5	NULL	5800.00	NULL	2	12	0
6	52000.00	NULL	NULL	1	1	0

14 rows

Figure 12.26 Testing Skill Check 2.

Answer Code: The T-SQL code to this lab can be found in the downloadable files in a file named Lab12.1_SQL_ServerErrors.sql.

Points to Ponder - SQL Server Error Messages

1. Components of the SQL Server error message are:
   - Message Number – often referred to as Error number. This is the Message ID of the error. Message Numbers below 50,000 are system supplied errors. Message Numbers at or above 50,000 are user-defined errors.
   - Severity Level – ranging from 0 to 25. Levels 1-10 are informative, whereas 11 and higher are actual errors.
   - State – rarely used. If you raise the same error in several places, you can use this to mark the point at which the error was raised.
   - Procedure – this is the name of the stored procedure, trigger, or function where the error occurred. If you are just running code in a query window then "Procedure" will be blank.
   - Line – the line number in the procedure, function, trigger, or batch that contains the error.
   - Message Text – the actual message of the error telling you what went wrong.

2. The Sys.Messages table in the master database contains the list of all error messages.

3. If you want your procedure to raise an error defined by your own conditions, and this is not a system error, then you can call the RAISERROR() function. The first parameter can be a message number, text or a local @variable. The message number corresponds to the message_id column in the Sys.Messages table.

4. If you use RAISERROR and specify text without a message number, you will get a message number of 50,000.

5. If you specify the message number and not the text, then you will get the text belonging to the message as listed in the Sys.Messages table.

6. You can't manually raise errors below 13000. Those may be raised only by the system.

7. Error Severity of 10 or below is not really an error message at all. It is considered informational.

8. Errors of 20-25 result in connection termination. If you want to raise an error of 20 or higher, then you must be a sysadmin and provide them WITH LOG option.

SQL Error Actions

How does SQL Server react to an error? In other words, when SQL raises an error in one statement, should it stop or continue processing? Actually there are four different reactions SQL might take in response to an error.

Let's take the scenario in Figure 12.27 where a SQL client is going to execute a user stored procedure called usp_A. This stored procedure consists of two statements. The first statement is going to call usp_B and the second will call usp_C. Both usp_B and usp_C have three statements inside which could potentially throw an error.

Just how will SQL Server react when it encounters an error? This is known as a **SQL error action**. This section will discuss the possible reactions to errors in this hierarchy.

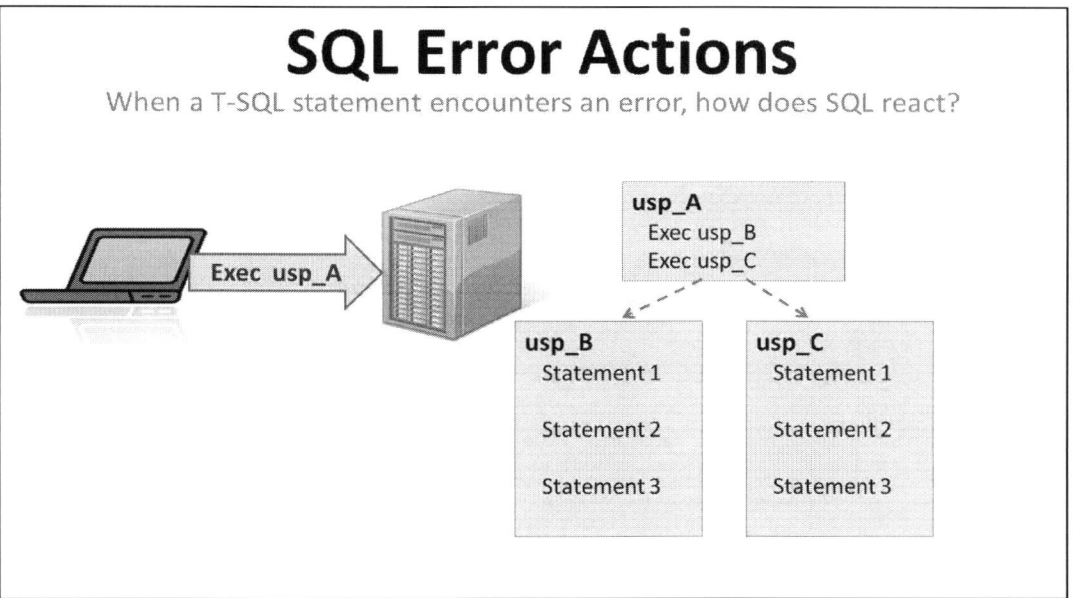

Figure 12.27 usp_A calls two stored procedures (usp_B and usp_C). Each sproc contains three statements.

Statement Termination

If an error is encountered in Statement 2 of usp_B, SQL might decide to proceed to Statement 3. This is the least disruptive reaction possible to an error; a single statement fails to run but all other statements continue operating as expected.

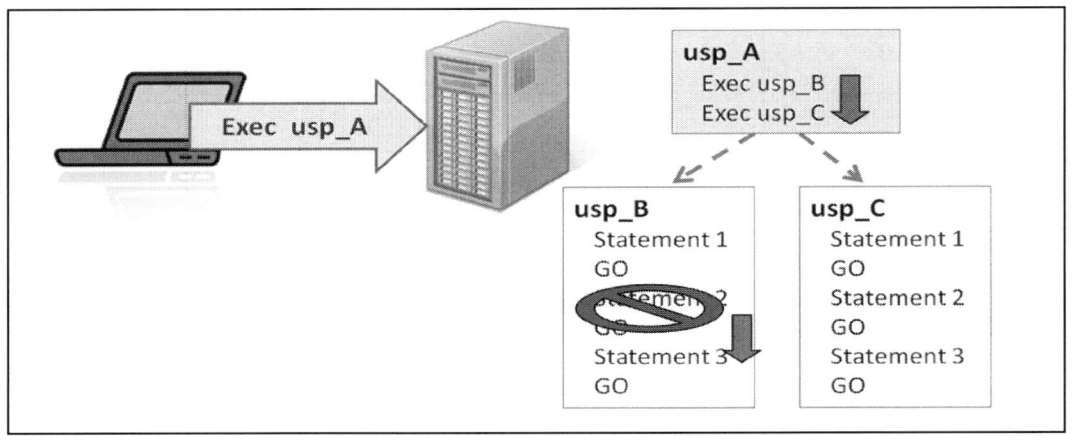

Figure 12.28 Statement Termination occurs when a single statement fails but execution of subsequent statements continues.

In Statement Termination there is no disruption to the calling code, and usp_A continues by running the rest of its code, including all the statements in usp_C.

Scope Abortion

In Scope Abortion, the failed statement causes the function or stored procedure to fail. While usp_B halts after one failed statement, the execution from usp_A will continue to run by calling on usp_C (Figure 12.29).

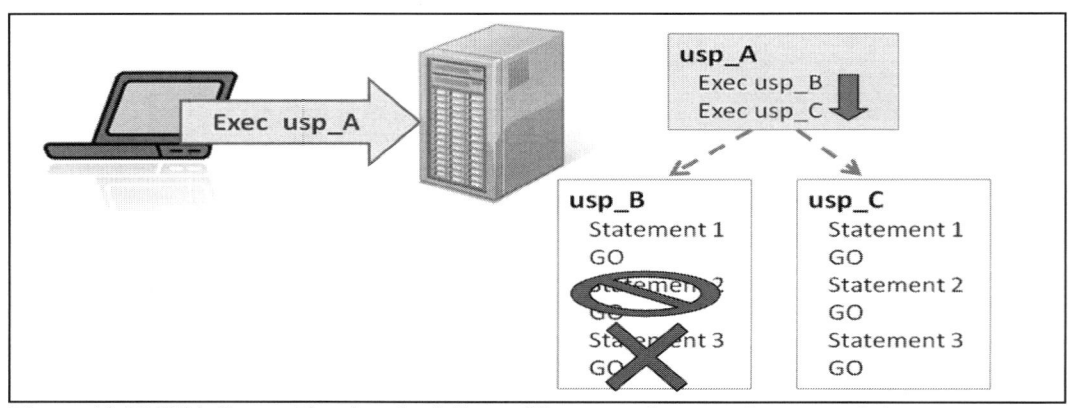

Figure 12.29 With Scope Abortion the failure of Statement 2 means Statement 3 does not get run.

Batch Abortion

With Batch Abortion, a failure in statement 2 will cause usp_B to fail and usp_A to return a failure to the calling code. The call to usp_C never takes place.

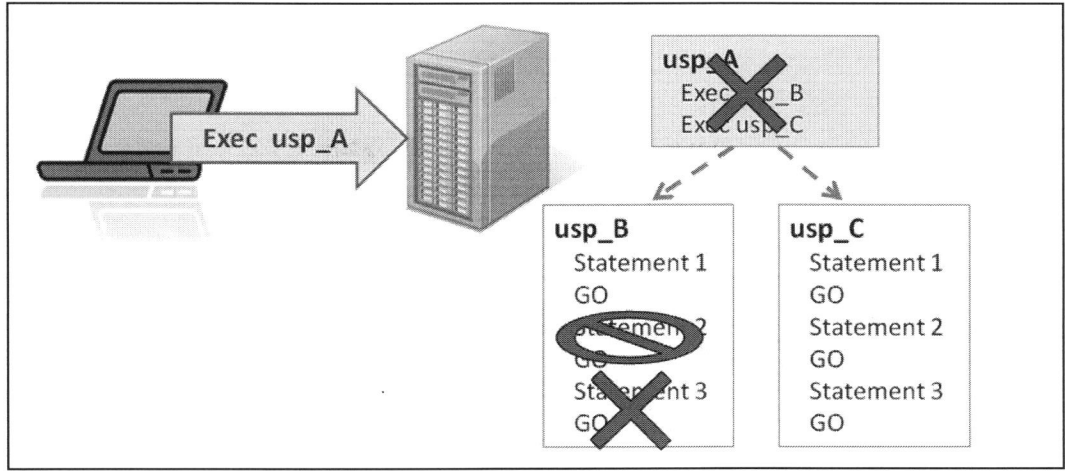

Figure 12.30 A failure in statement 2 will cause usp_B to fail and usp_A to return a failure to the calling code.

Connection Termination

In the most drastic of error scenarios, the connection from the client to the SQL Server database is severed. In Figure 12.31 we see an illustration where the connection from the client to the server is broken. This is usually due to an error with a severity greater than 20. *The typical 11-16 severity error will not cause a connection termination.*

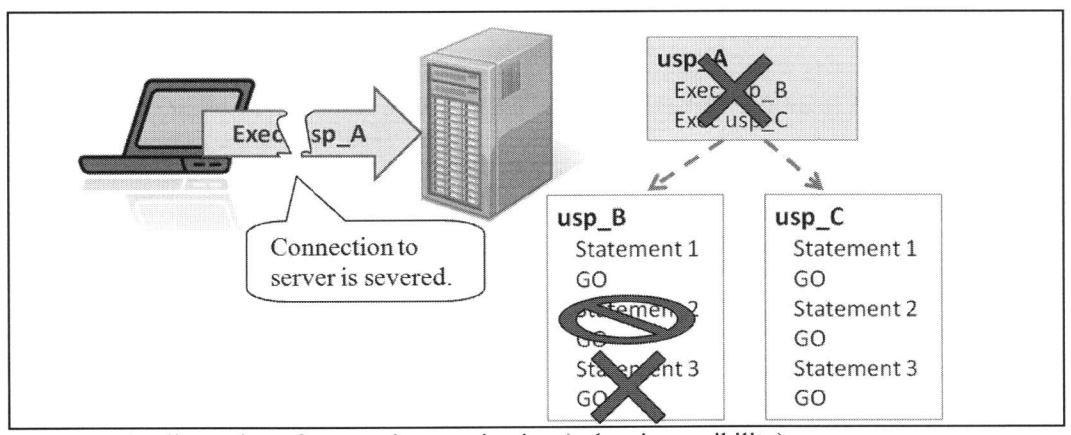

Figure 12.31 Illustration of connection termination (a drastic possibility).

Testing Error Actions

If you completed the last lab then you have a stored procedure called AddGrantAmount. This stored procedure takes two parameters: @GrantID and @Amount. Based on the GrantID, you will add the specified @Amount to the existing Amount value for that record. Inside the stored procedure is code which performs the update statement and then raises an informational message based on the number of grants which were updated.

You have another stored procedure called AddBonusPoint which, based on the employee ID (EmpID), will add one point to the employee's BonusPoint value contained in the PayRates table. Each of these stored procedures contains just one statement. The code for both stored procedures can be seen in this example:

```
CREATE PROC [dbo].[AddGrantAmount] @GrantID CHAR(3),
@MoreAmount MONEY
AS
BEGIN
DECLARE @GrantINT INT
SET @GrantINT = CAST(@GrantID AS INT)
UPDATE [Grant] SET Amount = Amount + @MoreAmount
WHERE GrantID = @GrantINT
RAISERROR('Increased %i Grant records',10,1,@@ROWCOUNT )

UPDATE em SET Em.LatestGrantActivity = CURRENT_TIMESTAMP
FROM Employee AS em INNER JOIN [Grant] AS gr
ON em.EmpID = gr.EmpID
WHERE GrantID = @GrantID
RAISERROR('Updated %i Employee records',10,1,@@ROWCOUNT)
END
GO

CREATE PROC [dbo].[AddBonusPoint] @EmpID INT
AS
BEGIN
UPDATE PayRates SET BonusPoints = BonusPoints + 1
WHERE EmpID = @EmpID
RAISERROR('Updated %i bonuses in PayRates table',10,1,@@ROWCOUNT)
END
GO
```

Notice that each of these stored procedures contains a single update statement. If you look at the Employee table, you'll notice a new field, LatestGrantActivity, which contains the timestamp of the latest change made to one of that employee's grants (Figure 12.32).

```
SELECT * FROM Employee
```

	EmpID	LastName	FirstName	HireDate	Loc...	Man...	Status	HiredOffset	TimeZone	LatestGrantActivity
1	1	Adams	Alex	2001-01-01...	1	4	On Leave	2001-01-01...	-08:00	NULL
2	2	Brown	Barry	2002-08-12...	1	11	Active	2002-08-12...	-08:00	2002-08-12 00:00:
3	3	Osako	Lee	1999-09-01...	2	11	Active	1999-09-01...	-05:00	1999-09-01 00:00:
4	4	Kinnison	Dave	1996-03-16...	1	11	Has Tenure	1996-03-16...	-08:00	1996-03-16 00:00:
5	5	Bender	Eric	2007-05-17...	1	11	Active	2007-05-17...	-08:00	2007-05-17 00:00:
6	6	Kendall	Lisa	2001-11-15...	4	4	Active	2001-11-15...	-08:00	NULL

Query executed successfully. RENO (11.0 RTM) | Reno\Student (51) | JProCo | 00:00:00 | 20 rows

Figure 12.32 A new field, LatestGrantActivity, has been added to the Employee table.

If an employee gets a new grant, or gets an update to an existing grant, then we want to update the LatestGrantActivity field (Figure 12.33). Immediately after the code block inside AddGrantAmount makes a change to a grant, we want to capture the current time and update the Employee table. This stored procedure will have two update statements run against two tables (Grant and Employee) see Figure 12.34.

```
CREATE PROC AddGrantAmount @GrantID CHAR(3), @MoreAmount Money
AS
BEGIN
    DECLARE @GrantINT INT
    SET @GrantINT = CAST(@GrantID AS INT)
    UPDATE [Grant] SET Amount = Amount + @MoreAmount
    WHERE GrantID = @GrantINT
    RAISERROR('Increased %i Grant records', 10, 1, @@ROWCOUNT)
END
GO
```
← 2nd update to dbo.Employee

Figure 12.33 A second update will capture the date and time of each change to the Grant table.

Here we see a second update statement which sets LatestGrantActivity to the current time for the employee who found that grant (Figure 12.34). Notice that we'll also want to include a RAISERROR statement to raise an informational (severity 10) message showing if any of the employee records gets updated. Recall that 0 employees may be updated if one of the grants has no employee associated with it.

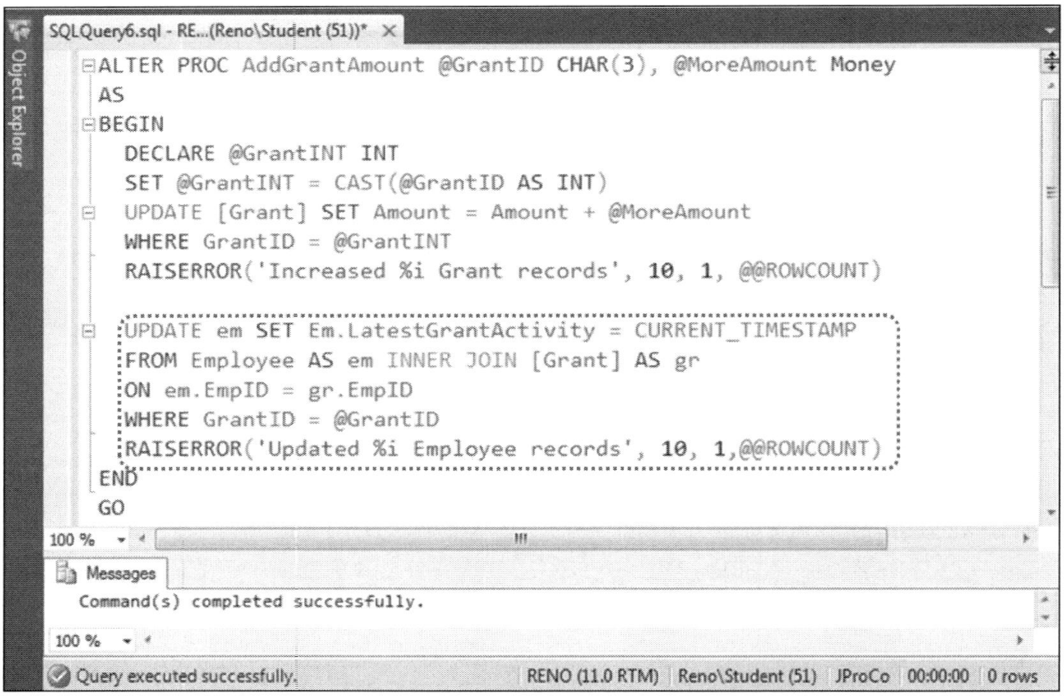

Chapter 12. SQL Errors Messages

```sql
ALTER PROC AddGrantAmount @GrantID CHAR(3), @MoreAmount Money
AS
BEGIN
    DECLARE @GrantINT INT
    SET @GrantINT = CAST(@GrantID AS INT)
    UPDATE [Grant] SET Amount = Amount + @MoreAmount
    WHERE GrantID = @GrantINT
    RAISERROR('Increased %i Grant records', 10, 1, @@ROWCOUNT)

    UPDATE em SET Em.LatestGrantActivity = CURRENT_TIMESTAMP
    FROM Employee AS em INNER JOIN [Grant] AS gr
    ON em.EmpID = gr.EmpID
    WHERE GrantID = @GrantID
    RAISERROR('Updated %i Employee records', 10, 1,@@ROWCOUNT)
END
GO
```

Messages
Command(s) completed successfully.

Figure 12.34 This code will make the second update described above and in Figure 12.33.

Consider the various inputs which could cause each update statement to fail. Notice how we utilize the @GrantID parameter versus the @GrantINT variable (Figure 12.35). We want to ensure there is zero chance of a conversion error in the second update statement.

Chapter 12. SQL Errors Messages

```
SQLQuery6.sql - RE...(Reno\Student (51))*  X
ALTER PROC AddGrantAmount @GrantID CHAR(3), @MoreAmount Money
AS                                    ↑
BEGIN
    DECLARE @GrantINT INT
    SET @GrantINT = CAST(@GrantID AS INT)   ← [CAST to INT]
    UPDATE [Grant] SET Amount = Amount + @MoreAmount
    WHERE GrantID = @GrantINT ← [INT]
    RAISERROR('Increased %i Grant records', 10, 1, @@ROWCOUNT)

    UPDATE em SET Em.LatestGrantActivity = CURRENT_TIMESTAMP
    FROM Employee AS em INNER JOIN [Grant] AS gr
    ON em.EmpID = gr.EmpID
    WHERE GrantID = @GrantID  ← [CAST to INT]
    RAISERROR('Updated %i Employee records', 10, 1,@@ROWCOUNT)
END
GO

Messages
Command(s) completed successfully.
```

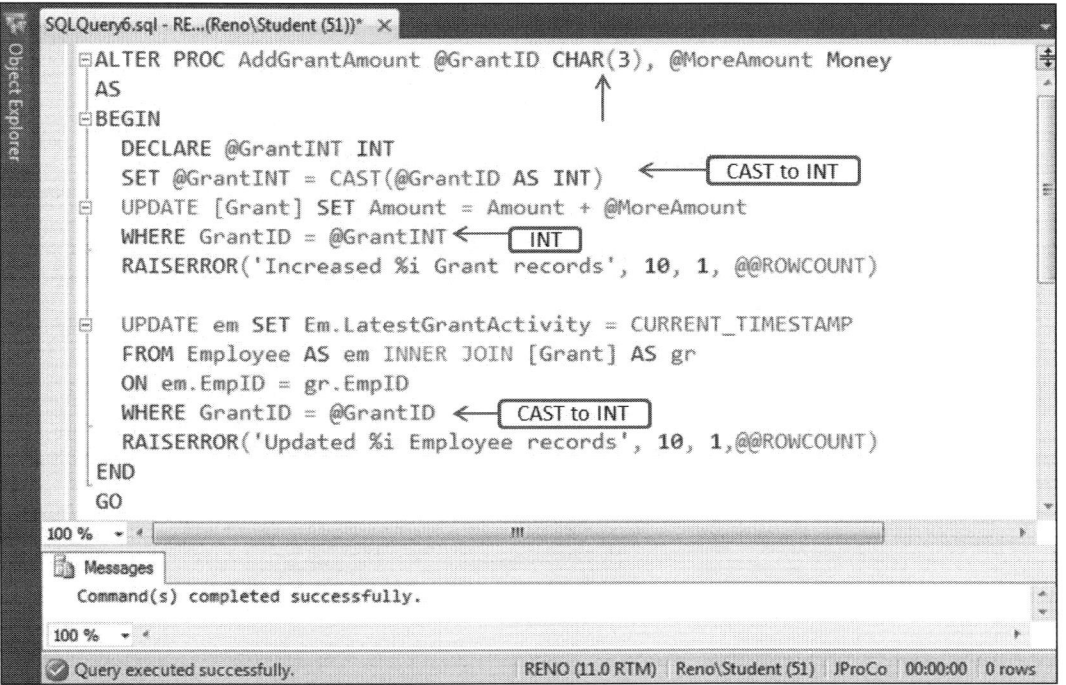

Figure 12.35 The second update is based on the CHAR(3) GrantID data instead of the INT GrantID.

Now let's attempt to alter just Grant 003 and increase its amount by $1000. Before we do that, let's first look at the current value of this grant's Amount.

```sql
SELECT * FROM [Grant] WHERE GrantID = '003'
```

	GrantID	GrantName	EmpID	Amount
1	003	Robert@BigStarBank.com	7	18100.00

Figure 12.36 GrantID '003' is $18,100 and was found by Employee 7 (David Lonning).

We see the record for Employee 7 (David Lonning) in the Employee table (Figure 12.37).

```sql
SELECT * FROM Employee WHERE EmpID = 7
```

	EmpID	LastName	FirstName	HireDate	Loc...	Man...	Status	HiredOffset	TimeZone	LatestGrantActivity
1	7	Lonning	David	2000-01-01...	1	11	On Leave	2000-01-01...	-08:00	2000-01-01 00:00

Figure 12.37 David Lonning's Employee record shows Jan 1, 2000 as the latest timestamp for the LatestGrantActivity field.

David Lonning's last Grant activity was in the year 2000. If we update one of his grants, then his LatestGrantActivity field will be updated to reflect the timestamp of the change. Now let's run the code to execute the sproc and increase Grant 003 by $1000. At the same time, we expect it to also update David Lonning's Employee record (Figure 12.38).

```
EXEC AddGrantAmount '003', 1000
```

```
Messages
(1 row(s) affected)
Increased 1 Grant records

                                                                   0 rows
```

Figure 12.38 This code increases Grant 003 by $1000 and updates David's Employee record.

Both statements included in the AddGrantAmount stored proc (shown earlier -- Figure 12.35) ran successfully. We can see the Amount of Grant 003 has increased by $1000 (Figure 12.39). The revised Amount value is now $19,100.

```
SELECT * FROM [Grant] WHERE GrantID = '003'
```

	GrantID	GrantName	EmpID	Amount
1	003	Robert@BigStarBank.com	7	19100.00

Query executed successfully.   RENO (11.0 RTM)   Reno\Student (51)   JProCo   00:00:00   1 rows

Figure 12.39 Grant 003 has been increased by $1000 (from $18,100 to $19,100).

When we re-check David's record in the Employee table, we see that the LatestGrantActivity field now shows a 2010 timestamp. It successfully reflects the update we just made to David's Grant 003 (Figure 12.38 through Figure 12.40).

```
SELECT * FROM Employee WHERE EmpID = 7
```

	EmpID	LastName	FirstName	HireDate	Loc...	Man...	Status	HiredOffset	TimeZone	LatestGrantActivity
1	7	Lonning	David	2000-01-01...	1	11	On Leave	2000-01-01...	-08:00	2012-10-07 17:50

Query executed successfully.   RENO (11.0 RTM)   Reno\Student (51)   JProCo   00:00:00   1 rows

Figure 12.40 David's updated Employee record has an updated LatestGrantActivity field.

Now let's consider errors which these statements could encounter. As illustrated by Figure 12.41, if the Grant table update statement failed, would we want the Employee table to still be updated?

```
DECLARE @Gr          INT
SET @Gran       = CA  T(@GrantID AS INT)
UPDATE [G  ant]  ET  mount = Amount + @MoreAmount
WHERE Gra   ID =      antINT
RAISERROR('I    sed %i Grant records', 10, 1, @@ROWCOUNT)

UPDATE em SE       LatestGrantActivity = CURRENT_TIMESTAMP
FROM Employ e A   em INNER JOIN [Grant] AS gr
ON em.EmpID =    .EmpID
WHERE GrantID     @GrantID
RAISERROR('Up   ted %i Employee records', 10, 1,@@ROWCOUNT)
```

Figure 12.41 If the first statement inside the stored procedure fails will the second statement run?

As we expected, the input of 'One Thousand' as the second parameter (Figure 12.42) produces a conversion error in the first update statement. The conversion error results in a batch abortion: the stored procedure terminates without running the rest of the statements.

```
ALTER PROC AddGrantAmount @GrantID CHAR(3), @MoreAmount Money
AS
BEGIN
    DECLARE @GrantINT INT
    SET @GrantINT = CAST(@GrantID AS INT)
    UPDATE [Grant] SET Amount = Amount + @MoreAmount
    WHERE GrantID = @GrantINT
    RAISERROR('Increased %i Grant records', 10, 1, @@ROWCOUNT)

    UPDATE em SET Em.LatestGrantActivity = CURRENT_TIMESTAMP
    FROM Employee AS em INNER JOIN [Grant] AS gr
    ON em.EmpID = gr.EmpID
    WHERE GrantID = @GrantID
    RAISERROR('Updated %i Employee records', 10, 1,@@ROWCOUNT)
END
GO
EXEC AddGrantAmount '003', 'One Thousand'
```

Messages
Msg 8114, Level 16, State 1, Procedure AddGrantAmount, Line 0
Error converting data type varchar to money.

Conversion failed here

Second statement did not run. (No 2nd message show here)

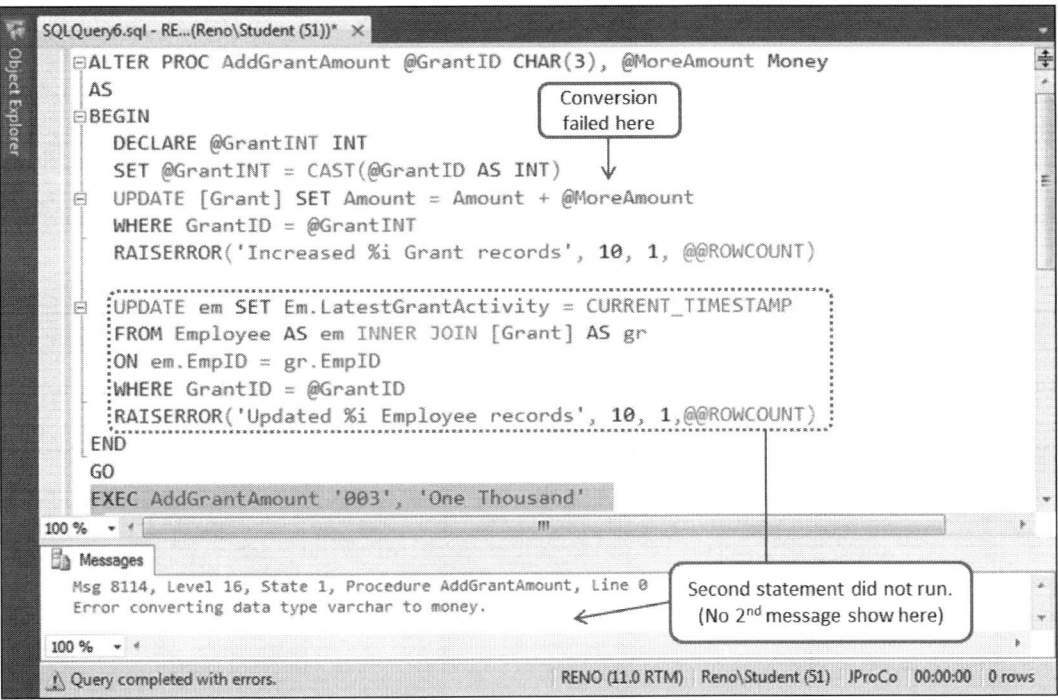

Figure 12.42 The conversion error results in a batch abortion where the stored procedure terminates without running the rest of the statements.

You can confirm that no record was updated in either the Grant table or the Employee table by using the following code:

```sql
SELECT * FROM [Grant] WHERE GrantID = '003'
SELECT * FROM Employee WHERE EmpID = 7
```

The results are the same as those seen in Figure 12.39 and Figure 12.40. So we clearly see that the conversion error in the first update of the stored procedure caused a **batch abortion** action by SQL Server.

Now let's attempt to generate another error by sending in a NULL value for the Amount (Figure 12.43). We expect this will produce an error, because the Amount field can't be NULL. We see this will cause a NULL conversion error on the first update statement. As expected, we get a Level 16 error saying that a NULL cannot be inserted into the Amount field. Look closely at the message pane and notice that the second statement ran and updated the Employee table. So we clearly see that a NULL inserted into a non-nullable field caused a **statement termination** action by SQL Server.

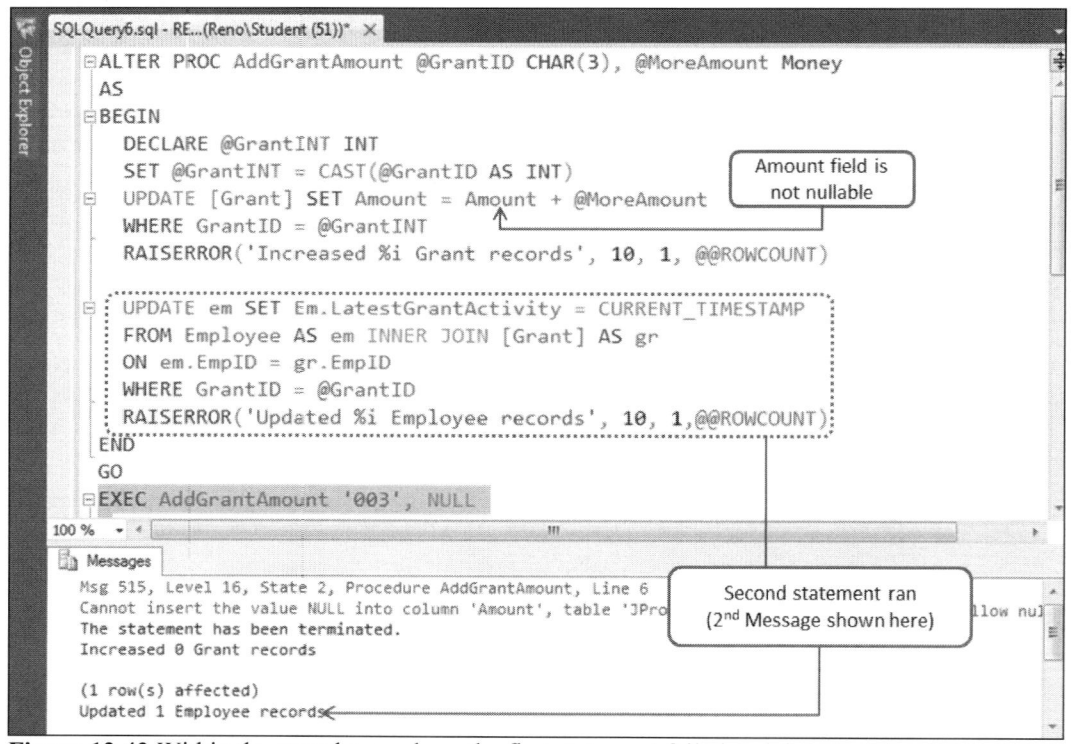

Figure 12.43 Within the stored procedure, the first statement failed and the second statement ran.

Since a NULL violation is considered less drastic, it generated only a single statement termination. The first statement didn't run, but the second statement did. The following process flow shows that the first statement threw an error but the stored procedure continued execution of the next statement (Figure 12.44).

```
DECLARE @GrantID INT
SET @GrantID = CAST(@GrantID AS INT)
UPDATE [Grant] SET Amount = Amount + @MoreAmount
WHERE GrantID = @GrantID
RAISERROR('Incremented %i Grant records', 10, 1, @@ROWCOUNT)

UPDATE em SET LatestGrantActivity = CURRENT_TIMESTAMP
FROM Employee AS em INNER JOIN [Grant] AS gr
ON em.EmpID = gr.EmpID
WHERE GrantID = @GrantID
RAISERROR('Updated %i Employee records', 10, 1,@@ROWCOUNT)
```

Figure 12.44 The first statement didn't run, but the second statement ran (see also Figure 12.45).

When we re-check the Employee table, we see that David Lonning's LatestGrantActivity field has been updated yet again (Figure 12.45).

```
SELECT * FROM Employee WHERE EmpID = 7
```

EmpID	LastName	FirstName	HireDate	Loc...	Man...	Status	HiredOffset	TimeZone	LatestGrantActivity
1	7	Lonning	David	2000-01-01...	1	11	On Leave	2000-01-01...	-08:00	2012-10-07 18:19:...

Figure 12.45 The LatestGrantActivity from EmpID 7 was updated again (Contrast with Figure 12.40).

XACT_ABORT

As introduced earlier in this section (Figure 12.18-Figure 12.30), the severity of the error dictates the action which SQL Server will take (e.g., single statement termination, batch abortion, or the most drastic step of client connection termination).

Recall our example where the Employee timestamp field (LatestGrantActivity) was updated, despite the corresponding Grant record not successfully updating. We might decide that in all cases of an error with our stored procedure it would be better to abort the entire batch. Otherwise, the timestamp field LatestGrantActivity will be out of sync with the updates which were actually made to an employee's grants.

In this case, we can use the SQL command **XACT_ABORT** ("transact abort"), which aborts the entire batch if any error is encountered (Figure 12.46). Activating XACT_ABORT means all errors with a severity 11 or greater will result in batch abortion. Compare Figure 12.46 to Figure 12.43 and notice this is the same stored procedure call. The big difference is that the second update did not run after the first error was encountered. With the XACT_ABORT setting on, any error of severity 11 or greater will result in batch abortion.

```
SET XACT_ABORT ON;
EXEC AddGrantAmount '003', NULL
```

```
Message
Msg 515, Level 16, State 2, Procedure AddGrantAmount, Line 6
Cannot insert the value NULL into column 'Amount', table 'JProCo.dbo.Grant';
column does not allow nulls. UPDATE fails.
                                                                        0 rows
```

Figure 12.46 Activating XACT_ABORT means all errors with a severity 11 or greater will result in batch abortion.

If you set XACT_ABORT to "OFF", then SQL will choose those errors which are drastic enough to fail an entire stored procedure or batch. In other words, SQL Server will pick the error action based on the error which was raised. In Figure 12.47 we see the effects of setting XACT_ABORT to OFF and using the same call to the AddGrantAmount stored procedure.

```
SET XACT_ABORT OFF;
EXEC AddGrantAmount '003', NULL
```

```
Messages
Msg 515, Level 16, State 2, Procedure AddGrantAmount, Line 6
Cannot insert the value NULL into column 'Amount', table 'JProCo.dbo.Grant';
column does not allow nulls. UPDATE fails.
The statement has been terminated.
Increased 0 Grant records

(1 row(s) affected)
Updated 1 Employee records
                                                                        0 rows
```

Figure 12.47 The syntax for deactivating XACT_ABORT.

Lab 12.2: SQL Error Actions

Lab Prep: Lab Prep: Each lab has one or more Skill Checks. Start with Skill Check 1 and proceed until reaching the Points to Ponder section.

Before beginning this lab, verify that SQL Server 2012 is properly installed and operating. Before running the lab setup script for resetting the database (SQLQueries2012Vol4Chapter12.2Setup.sql), please make sure to close all query windows within SSMS. An open query window pointing to a database context can lock that database preventing it from updating when the script is executing. A simple way to assure all query windows are closed, is to exit out of SSMS, then open a new instance of SSMS, and lastly run the setup script.

Skill Check 1: Create a stored procedure named UpdateGrantEmployee which calls on the AddGrantAmount and AddBonusPoint procedures. It should accept the parameters @GrantID (which is a CHAR(3)) and @Increase (Which is the MONEY data type). Call on this procedure by passing in grant 002 and an amount of 1000. The Messages tab should resemble Figure 12.48.

```
EXEC UpdateGrantEmployee '002',1000
```

```
Messages
(1 row(s) affected)
Increased
1 Grant records
(1 row(s) affected)
Updated 1 bonuses in the PayRates table
                                                         0 rows
```

Figure 12.48 Result produced by Skill Check 1.

Skill Check 2: Call on the UpdateGrantEmployee stored procedure and decrement $1,000 from Amount for Grant 003 to bring the value down from $18,100 (Hint: Pass in a negative number for the second parameter). When complete, your query of the Grant table should resemble the figure (Figure 12.49).

```
SELECT *
FROM [Grant]
WHERE GrantID = '003'
```

	GrantID	GrantName	EmpID	Amount
1	003	Robert@BigStarBank.com	7	17100.00

1 rows

Figure 12.49 Result produced by Skill Check 2.

Answer Code: The T-SQL code to this lab can be found in the downloadable files in a file named Lab12.2_SQL_ServerErrorActions.sql.

Points to Ponder - SQL Error Actions

1. There are 4 possible actions SQL Server will take when encountering errors:
   - **Statement Termination** – The statement with the procedure fails but the code keeps on running to the next statement. Transactions are not affected.
   - **Scope Abortion** – The current procedure, function or batch is aborted and the next calling scope keeps running. That is, if Stored Procedure A calls B and C, and B fails, then nothing in B runs but A continues to call C. @@Error is set but the stored procedure does not have a return value.
   - **Batch Abortion** – The entire client call is terminated.
   - **Connection Termination** – The client is disconnected and any open transaction is rolled back. This occurs when something really bad happens like a stack overflow or protocol error in the client library.

2. With the XACT_ABORT setting on, any error of severity 11-16 will result in batch abortion.

3. With the XACT_ABORT setting off, SQL Server will pick its error action.

Chapter Glossary

Batch abortion: the entire client call is aborted.

Connection termination: the client is disconnected and any open transaction is rolled back. This occurs when something really bad happened, such as a stack overflow or protocol error in the client library.

Informational notification: an error having an error level of 10, or lower, will simply produce an informational notification. Any code looking for errors will ignore severity levels of 10, or lower.

RAISERROR(): a function you can call if you want your procedure to raise an error defined by your own conditions, and not a system error.

Scope abortion: The current procedure, function or batch is aborted and the next calling scope keeps running. That is, if Stored Procedure A calls B and C, and B fails, then nothing in B runs but A continues to call B. @@Error is set but the stored procedure does not have a return value.

XACT_ABORT: pronounced "transact abort".

SET XACT_ABORT OFF: SQL will choose those errors which are drastic enough to fail an entire stored procedure. In other words, SQL Server will pick the error action based on what error was raised.

SET XACT_ABORT ON: Any error of severity 11-16 will result in batch abortion.

Severity Level: Ranging from 0 to 25. Levels 1-10 are informative, whereas 11 and higher are actual errors.

SQL error action: A response taken by SQL Server in response to an error it encounters.

Statement termination: The statement with the procedure fails but the code keeps on running to the next statement. Transactions are not affected.

Sys.Messages: A table in the Master database containing the list of all error messages.

User error: An error having a severity level between 11 and 16.

Review Quiz - Chapter Twelve

1.) Which SQL Server error action happens for errors with a severity of 11-16 when you set the XACT_ABORT setting to ON?

   O a. You will get Statement Termination.
   O b. You will get Scope Abortion.
   O c. You will get Batch Abortion.
   O d. You will get Connection Termination.
   O e. SQL Server will pick the error action.

2.) Which SQL Server error action happens for errors with a severity of 11-16 when you set the XACT_ABORT setting to OFF?

   O a. You will get Statement Termination
   O b. You will get Scope Abortion
   O c. You will get Batch Abortion
   O d. You will get Connection Termination
   O e. SQL Server will pick the error action

3.) You have many updates inside one transaction. You need to place an option at the top of the transaction that states if any errors in any updates are encountered, then the entire transaction should fail. Which option accomplishes this goal?

   O a. ARITHABORT
   O b. XACT_ABORT
   O c. ARITHIGNORE
   O d. DEADLOCK_PRIORITY
   O e. NOEXEC

4.) When does SQL Server always raise an error message? (Choose two)

   □ a. When a statement in SQL Server cannot run.
   □ b. When multiple records are updated in one table.
   □ c. When you issue a RAISERROR message.

5.) You have a function named FnValidate that returns a 1 if true and a 0 if false. If a 0 is returned then SQL should generate an error and the event should not be allowed to commit. How can you do this??

○ a. **CREATE TRIGGER** `trg_TEST`
   **FOR CREATE_TABLE,ALTER_TABLE AS`
   `IF FnValidate()=0`
   BEGIN
   `RAISERROR ('Must wait till next month.', 16, 5)`
   END
   GO

○ b. **CREATE TRIGGER** `trg_TEST` **ON DATABASE**
   FOR `CREATE_TABLE,ALTER_TABLE` **AS**
   `IF FnValidate()=0`
   BEGIN
   ROLLBACK
   `RAISERROR ('Must wait till next month.', 16, 5)`
   END
   GO

○ c. **CREATE TRIGGER** `trg_TEST`
   FOR `CREATE_TABLE,ALTER_TABLE` **AS**
   `IF FnValidate()=1`
   BEGIN
   `RAISERROR ('Must wait till next month.', 16, 5)`
   END
   GO

○ d. **CREATE TRIGGER** `trg_TEST` **ON DATABASE**
   FOR `CREATE_TABLE,ALTER_TABLE` **AS**
   `IF FnValidate()=1`
   BEGIN
   ROLLBACK
   `RAISERROR ('Must wait till next month.', 16, 5)`
   END
   GO

Answer Key

1.) Activating XACT_ABORT means all errors with a severity 11 or greater will result in batch abortion. With XACT_ABORT set to ON the entire transaction is terminated and rolled back when the statement raises an error, so (c) is the correct answer.

2.) If you set XACT_ABORT to "OFF", then SQL will choose those errors which are drastic enough to fail an entire stored procedure or batch XACT_ABORT may roll back the entire transaction or just the statement that raised the error, so (e) is the correct answer.

3.) ARITHABORT terminates a query when a mathematical error is encountered such as divide by zero. ARITHIGNORE determines whether mathematical errors return a message. Neither ARITHABORT nor ARITHIGNORE work with INSERT, UPDATE, or DELETE, so (a) and (c) are incorrect. DEADLOCK_PRIORITY determines the relative importance of whether or not to continue processing if the server is in deadlock with another session, so (d) is incorrect. When SET NOEXEC is ON it compiles every batch of SQL statements but does not execute them (e) is incorrect. Since XACT_ABORT terminates and roles back the transaction when a user level error is encountered (b) is the correct answer.

4.) Multiple records can be updated in a single table without error, so (b) is incorrect. When a statement in SQL Server cannot run and a RAISERROR message is issued will always raise an error, so (a)and (c) are correct.

5.) IF FnValidate raises a zero the transaction should be rolled back and error message raised, so (b) is correct since it raises an error and rolls back the transaction IF FnValidate equals zero.

Bug Catcher Game

To play the Bug Catcher game, run the file SQLQueries2012Vol4BugCatcher12.pps from the BugCatcher folder of the companion files found at www.Joes2Pros.com.

[THIS PAGE INTENTIONALLY LEFT BLANK.]

Chapter 13.   Error Handling

In everyday life, not everything you plan on doing goes your way. For example, recently I planned to turn left on Rosewood Avenue to head north to my office. To my surprise, the road was blocked because of construction. I still needed to head north, even though the signs told me that turning left was impossible. I could have treated the unexpected roadblock in the same way that SQL Server interprets a level 16 severity error. That is to say, I could have halted and simply abandoned my attempt to travel to the office. In the end, I came up with an alternate plan that was nearly as good. By using a detour route consisting of three right turns and traveling north on a parallel road, I was successfully able to avoid this unexpected disruption until the construction zone was cleared. When my Plan-A route didn't work, I tried and found a workable Plan-B.

Structured Error Handling in SQL Server is similar to the way we approach 'errors' in real life. When something does not go exactly as we expected, we adapt and find another way to accomplish our purpose. The job of a solution developer requires planning ahead and coding alternate pathways to keep our users and the application layer moving forward instead of stalling out when they encounter 'roadblocks.' As analysts and application users, we have come to expect that application architects anticipate the majority of errors which our input could generate. If a step we take within the application triggers a message or response from another program (e.g., from the underlying database program, from the operating system), then this is known as a bug – the developer has not adequately planned for this possibility and, as a result, the application appears broken to the user. Bugs which block the user from proceeding, or which force the user to exit and re-enter the application, are severe problems which should be caught and remedied during the test cycle. This chapter will demonstrate structured error handling techniques in SQL Server.

READER NOTE: *Please run the script SQLQueries2012Vol4Chapter13.0Setup.sql in order to follow along with the examples in the first section of Chapter 13. All scripts mentioned in this chapter may be found at **www.Joes2Pros.com***.

Structured Error Handling

SQL Server introduced new and improved options for error handling beginning with SQL Server 2005. Prior versions did not include structured error handling.

Up until now, all the errors which we've seen have raised an error message which the client code must handle. However, what if you prefer SQL Server (and not the client) to handle the error? With structured error handling, unexpected events can be treated entirely within SQL Server. The client either does not know there was an error or simply receives a message. In other words, the client layer never sees the SQL Server error, and the user is unaware that a SQL Server error was generated.

Anticipating Potential Errors

We'll begin with an example from the Grant table. We've just learned that our current spelling for Grant 001 is incorrect, as shown in the JProCo database. The donor was actually "92 Per-cents %% team", not "92 Purr_Scents %% team".

```
SELECT * FROM [Grant]
```

	GrantID	GrantName	EmpID	Amount	City	State
1	001	92 Purr_Scents %% team	7	4750.00	Seattle	WA
2	002	K-Land fund trust	2	16750.00	Seattle	WA
3	003	Robert@BigStarBank.com	7	18100.00	Seattle	WA
4	005	BIG 6's Foundation%	4	22180.00	Seattle	WA
5	006	TALTA_Kishan International	3	18100.00	Boston	MA
6	007	Ben@MoreTechnology.com	10	42000.00	Boston	MA
7	008	www.@-Last-U-Can-Help.com	7	26000.00	Seattle	WA

Figure 13.1 In the Grant table, the first Grant was made by "92 Purr_Scents %% team".

Let's first run an update statement correcting this GrantName. The following code changes the name of GrantID 001 to '92 Per-cents %% team':

```
UPDATE [Grant]
SET GrantName = '92 Per-cents %% team'
WHERE GrantID = '001'
```

The data types are the same, so our update runs just fine. The GrantName of Grant 001 was updated to "92 Per-cents %% team". Now we'll attempt to set a GrantName value to NULL. We expect to raise an error, since GrantName is a required field. The GrantName for Grant 001 fails to update to a value of NULL, since that field does not allow nulls.

```sql
UPDATE [Grant] SET GrantName = NULL
WHERE GrantID = '001'
```

```
Messages
Msg 515, Level 16, State 2, Line 1
Cannot insert the value NULL into column 'GrantName', table
'JProCo.dbo.Grant'; column does not allow nulls. UPDATE fails.
The statement has been terminated.
                                                           0 rows
```

Figure 13.2 The GrantName of NULL for Grant 001 fails to update, since that field does not allow nulls.

We can anticipate that updates might fail with an error. We can't prevent the occasional incorrect input from the client, but best practices require us to control or eliminate the error messaging and provide SQL Server instructions for how to behave when it receives incorrect input.

Let's next add code to our current example in order to catch these types of input errors. Structured error handling will help head off errors raised by incorrect inputs received from the client. We expect our users will send correct values and data types into the Grant table most of the time. However, for those few instances where a user attempts an incorrect value, seeing a message from anything besides the application or having to restart the application will not be comfortable experiences for our users. We will add code to deal with these types of errors and ensure that our users receive a message from the application layer (Preferably one which gives them a hint they've attempted an incorrect value and providing guidance as to what the correct input should be).

The TRY Block

The Try Block is where you place code which you think may raise an error. A Try Block is a code segment starting with a BEGIN TRY statement and ending with END TRY. If a statement sits inside a Try Block and raises an error, then the error gets passed to another part of SQL Server and not to the client. The Try Block is aware that there is code which may fail.

The code which is vulnerable to potentially receiving bad input from the client should be enclosed within the Try Block. Think of your TRY block as Plan-A. This is what you are hoping works on the first try. If Plan-A does not work, we can tell SQL Server to try Plan-B instead of reacting with an error message. Our code which will handle contingency steps (i.e., Plan-B) for bad input will be enclosed in what's known as a Catch Block. *Only one of these two blocks will run to completion.* Think of the Try Block as "Plan-A" and Catch Block as "Plan-B".

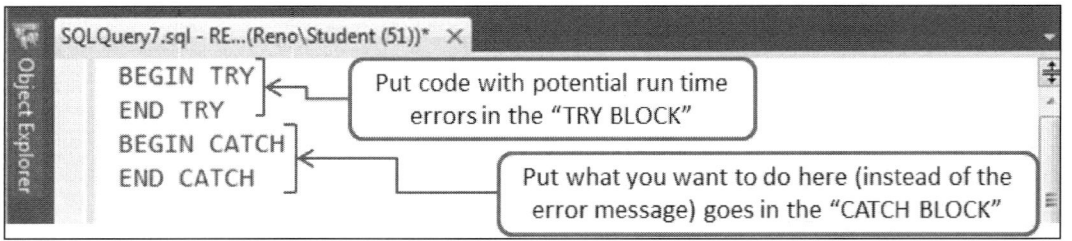

```
BEGIN TRY        ← Put code with potential run time
END TRY            errors in the "TRY BLOCK"
BEGIN CATCH
END CATCH        ← Put what you want to do here (instead of the
                   error message) goes in the "CATCH BLOCK"
```

Figure 13.3 The code you want to run goes in the Try Block. The Catch Block will not run unless the code in the Try Block raises an error.

The CATCH Block

The Catch Block serves as a contingency plan for failed code from the Try Block. In other words, if any statement raises a level 11 or higher severity in the Try Block, it will not show the error from the calling code. It will run the code you have set up in the Catch Block. In Figure 13.4 the Catch Block never runs, since the Try Block ("Plan-A") runs fine. In other words, if Plan-A works then there is no need to try Plan-B.

```
BEGIN TRY
UPDATE [Grant] SET GrantName = '92 Per-cents %% team'
WHERE GrantID = '001'
END TRY

BEGIN CATCH
PRINT 'No Change was made'
END CATCH
```

Messages

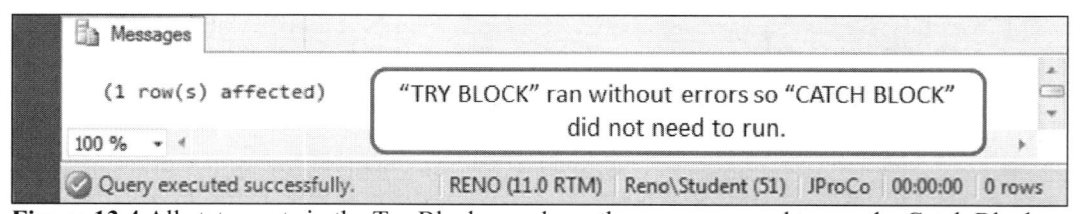

(1 row(s) affected)   "TRY BLOCK" ran without errors so "CATCH BLOCK"
                        did not need to run.

Query executed successfully.   RENO (11.0 RTM)   Reno\Student (51)   JProCo   00:00:00   0 rows

Figure 13.4 All statements in the Try Block ran ok, so there was no need to run the Catch Block.

Notice in Figure 13.4 the Catch Block never ran, since the Try Block ("Plan-A") ran without any error. Next let's observe an example where the Try Block will throw errors and not run successfully. Recall our previous example (refer back to Figure 13.2) where attempting to set GrantName to NULL threw an error. In using this same update statement, the Try Block encounters an error and thus will not run. The Catch Block will run instead.

```
BEGIN TRY
UPDATE [Grant] SET GrantName = NULL
WHERE GrantID = '001'
END TRY

BEGIN CATCH
PRINT 'No Change was made'
END CATCH
```

```
Messages

(0 row(s) affected)
No Change was made
```
"TRY BLOCK" encountered an error so the "CATCH BLOCK" ran instead.

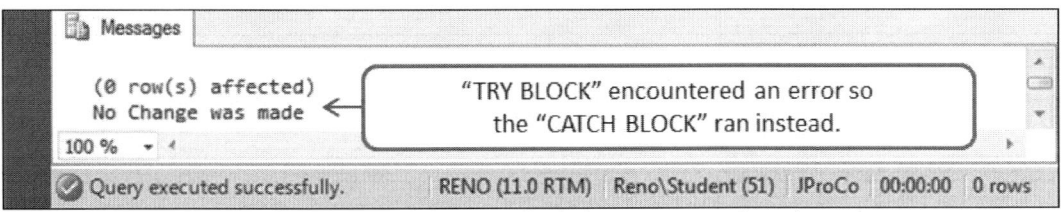

Figure 13.5 The Catch Block runs and the Try Block does not even show its error.

Let's review a few guidelines for getting the Catch Block to run. In general, the Catch Block will run if the Try Block encounters an error. However, there are some exceptions.

```
BEGIN TRY
END TRY
BEGIN CATCH
END CATCH
```
When does the "TRY BLOCK" hand over execution to the "CATCH BLOCK"

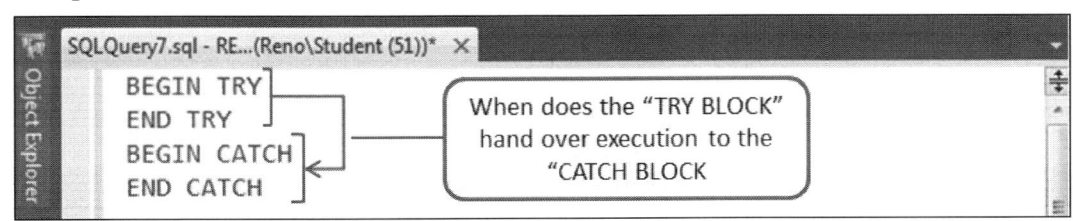

Figure 13.6 Under what conditions does the Try Block hand over execution to the Catch Block?

The Try Block in Figure 13.7 will always cause the Catch Block to run. Our RAISERROR function generates an error with severity level 16 and a state of 1. This means code in the Try Block encountered an error. When this happens, then the Catch Block runs. The Catch Block in Figure 13.7 prints the confirmation "Catch Ran".

Chapter 13. Error Handling

```
BEGIN TRY
    RAISERROR('Bad Stuff',16,1)
END TRY
BEGIN CATCH
    PRINT 'Catch Ran'
END CATCH
```

Messages
Catch Ran

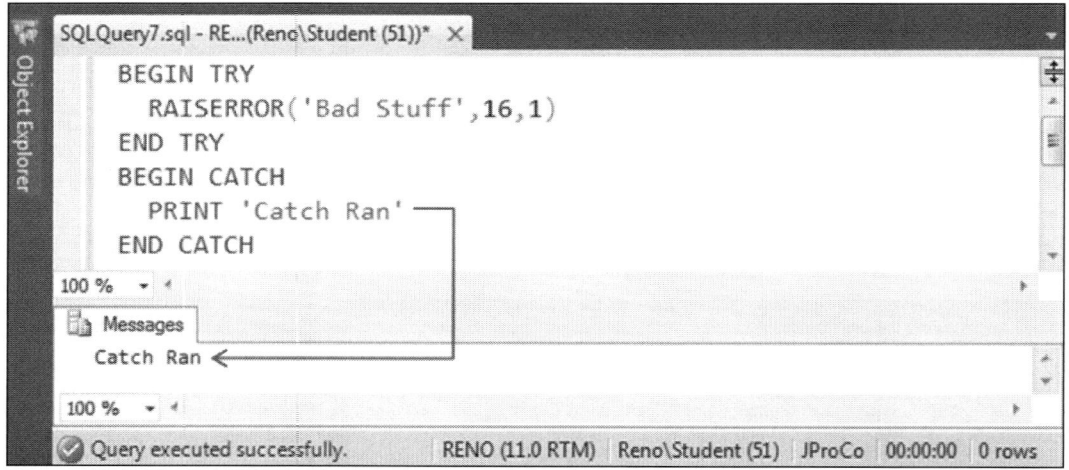

Figure 13.7 The RAISERROR function caused the Try Block to hand over execution to the Catch Block.

We can add another print statement which will allow us to see the error message displayed. When the Try Block passes execution to the Catch Block, the system is fully aware of why this has happened. For example, the error causing the Try Block to fail is captured in the ERROR_MESSAGE() system supplied function. In Figure 13.8 we have coded the Catch Block to print the error message generated by the Try Block.

```
BEGIN TRY
    RAISERROR('Bad Stuff',16,1)
END TRY
BEGIN CATCH
    PRINT 'Catch Ran'
    PRINT Error_Message()
END CATCH
```

Messages
Catch Ran
Bad Stuff

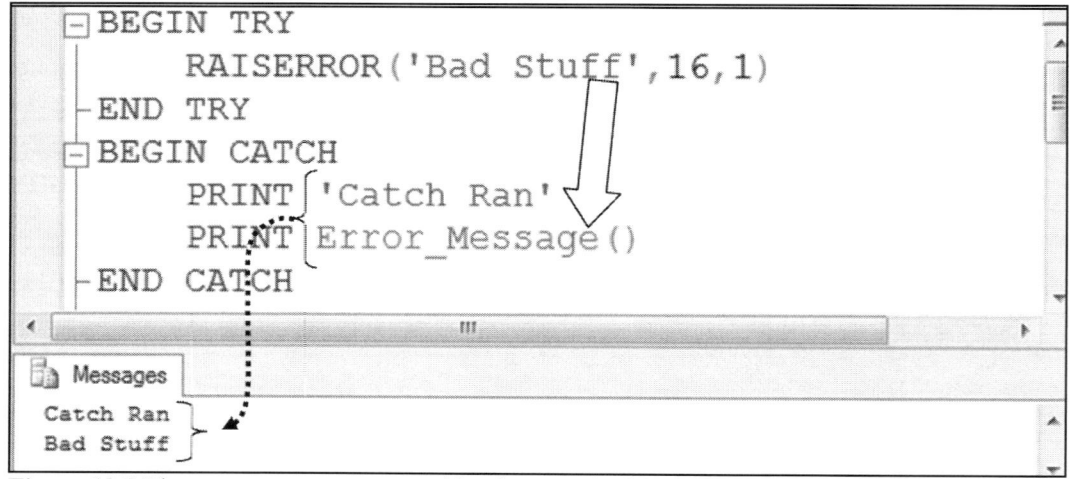

Figure 13.8 The error message generated by the Try Block is printed by the Catch Block.

We can extend this capability a bit further by capturing the severity of the error from the Try Block. By adding a print statement to display the severity level of the error, we see it in our Messages tab (Figure 13.9).

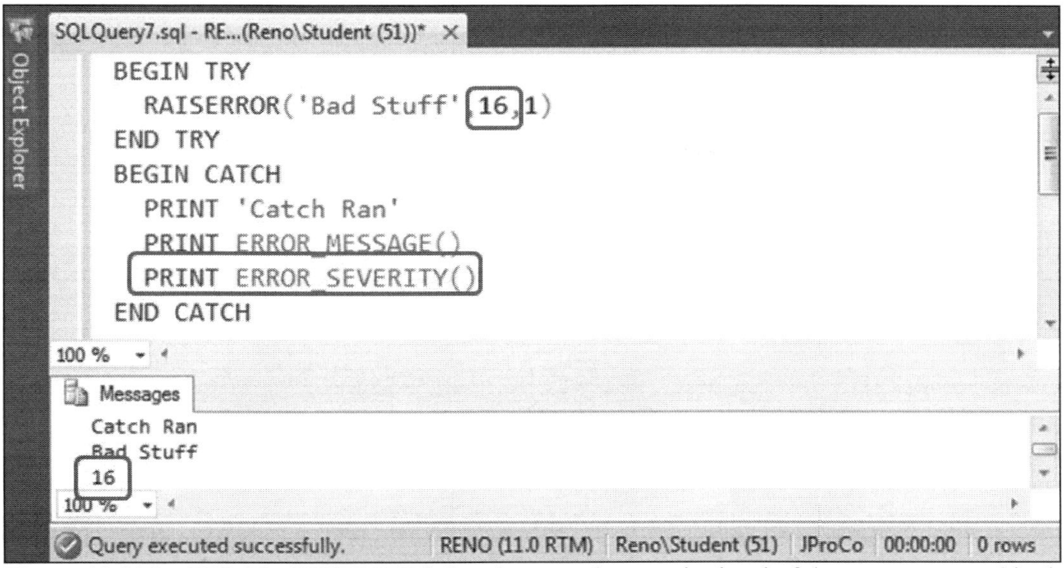

Chapter 13. Error Handling

```
SQLQuery7.sql - RE...(Reno\Student (51))*
    BEGIN TRY
        RAISERROR('Bad Stuff',16,1)
    END TRY
    BEGIN CATCH
        PRINT 'Catch Ran'
        PRINT ERROR_MESSAGE()
        PRINT ERROR_SEVERITY()
    END CATCH

Messages
Catch Ran
Bad Stuff
16
```

Figure 13.9 The ERROR_SEVERITY() function gets the severity level of the error generated in the Try Block.

Notice that we get the value 16 because that is the level of the error severity that is generated by the Try Block (Figure 13.9). In our next example, the Try Block has been changed to throw an error severity of 11 instead of 16 (Figure 13.10).

```
BEGIN TRY
RAISERROR('Sort of Bad Stuff',11,1)
END TRY

BEGIN CATCH
PRINT 'Catch Ran'
PRINT ERROR_MESSAGE()
PRINT ERROR_SEVERITY()
END CATCH
```

Message
Catch Ran
Sort of Bad Stuff
11

Figure 13.10 This severity 11 error causes the Catch Block to run.

The Try will only hand over execution to the Catch for errors with a severity level of 11 or higher. Note that in the last example, we saw a severity 11 error invoke the Catch. However, a severity 10 error will **not** cause the Catch to execute. SQL Server treats errors of severity 10 or lower simply as informational messages (Figure 13.11).

```
BEGIN TRY
RAISERROR('Trivial Stuff',10,1)
END TRY
BEGIN CATCH
PRINT 'Catch Ran'
PRINT ERROR_MESSAGE()
PRINT ERROR_SEVERITY()
END CATCH
```

Messages
Trivial Stuff
0 rows

Figure 13.11 This severity 10 error is just informational and does not cause the Catch Block to run.

The Try Block will pass execution to the Catch Block whenever it encounters execution errors of severity 11 or higher which do not close the database connection. If the severity is 10 or lower, then the Try Block will continue to run. Remember that it is just an informational message that is displayed when the severity is 10 or lower. Also, if the error severity is so high that it causes your database connection to close, then the Catch Block will never get the chance to run.

Structured Error Handling Summary

When you are using a Try Block together with a Catch Block to handle your errors, you are using what is known as "Structured Error Handling". The Try and Catch Blocks were introduced in SQL Server 2005 and are key tools for Structured Error Handling.

Transactions in Structured Error Handling

Our final topic will show error handling in the context of transactions, which use Begin Tran, Commit Tran, and Rollback Tran statements. Recall the stored procedure AddGrantAmount was used in Chapter 12. The code that created the AddGrantAmount sproc is as follows:

```sql
CREATE PROC AddGrantAmount @GrantID CHAR(3), @MoreAmount
MONEY
AS
BEGIN
DECLARE @GrantINT INT
SET @GrantINT = CAST(@GrantID as INT)
UPDATE [Grant] SET Amount = Amount + @MoreAmount
WHERE GrantID = @GrantINT
RAISERROR('Increased %i Grant records',10,1,@@ROWCOUNT)

UPDATE em SET Em.LatestGrantActivity = CURRENT_TIMESTAMP
FROM Employee as em INNER JOIN [Grant] as gr
ON em.EmpID = gr.EmpID
WHERE GrantID = @GrantID
RAISERROR('Updated %i Employee records',10,1,@@ROWCOUNT)
END
GO
```

The AddGrantAmount sproc from Chapter 12 contains two UPDATE statements. In Chapter 12, we saw that the second update statement sometimes runs, even if the first statement failed. This was a SQL error action called *Statement Termination*. In some cases we saw a failure of the first statement cause the stored procedure to fail and not run the second update statement. The behavior after an error in the first update statement in Figure 13.12 is somewhat unpredictable.

```
DECLARE @Grant
SET @GrantIN     CAST   GrantID as INT)
UPDATE [Gra   ] S   Am   nt = Amount + @MoreAmount
WHERE GrantI    = @G      INT
RAISERROR('Inc          %i Grant records',10,1,@@ROWCOUNT)

UPDATE em SET E       testGrantActivity = CURRENT_TIMESTAMP
FROM Employee   e   INNER JOIN [Grant] as gr
ON em.EmpID = gr     pID
WHERE GrantID =    rantID
RAISERROR('Update   %i Employee records',10,1,@@ROWCOUNT
```

Figure 13.12 Sometimes a failure on the first statement will not prevent execution of subsequent statements within a stored procedure.

For an example on Statement Termination, please see Figure 13.13. When we attempt to update Grant 003 with an Amount value of NULL, we see the first update statement fails and disallows the NULL (recall that Amount is a non-nullable field). However, we get a confirmation message showing that the second update statement ran anyway. Thus, our database information is inconsistent because the Employee table now shows an updated timestamp for the employee who found GrantID 003 even though no change was actually made.

```
ALTER PROC AddGrantAmount @GrantID CHAR(3), @MoreAmount MONEY
AS
BEGIN
  DECLARE @GrantINT INT
  SET @GrantINT = CAST(@GrantID as INT)
  UPDATE [Grant] SET Amount = Amount + @MoreAmount
  WHERE GrantID = @GrantINT
  RAISERROR('Increased %i Grant records',10,1,@@ROWCOUNT)

  UPDATE em SET Em.LatestGrantActivity = CURRENT_TIMESTAMP
  FROM Employee as em INNER JOIN [Grant] as gr
  ON em.EmpID = gr.EmpID
  WHERE GrantID = @GrantID
  RAISERROR('Updated %i Employee records',10,1,@@ROWCOUNT)
END
GO
EXEC AddGrantAmount '003', NULL
```

```
Messages
Msg 515, Level 16, State 2, Procedure AddGrantAmount, Line 6
Cannot insert the value NULL into column 'Amount', table 'JProCo.dbo.Grant'; col
The statement has been terminated.
Increased 0 Grant records

(1 row(s) affected)
Updated 1 Employee records
```

The second update statement ran even after the first update failed.

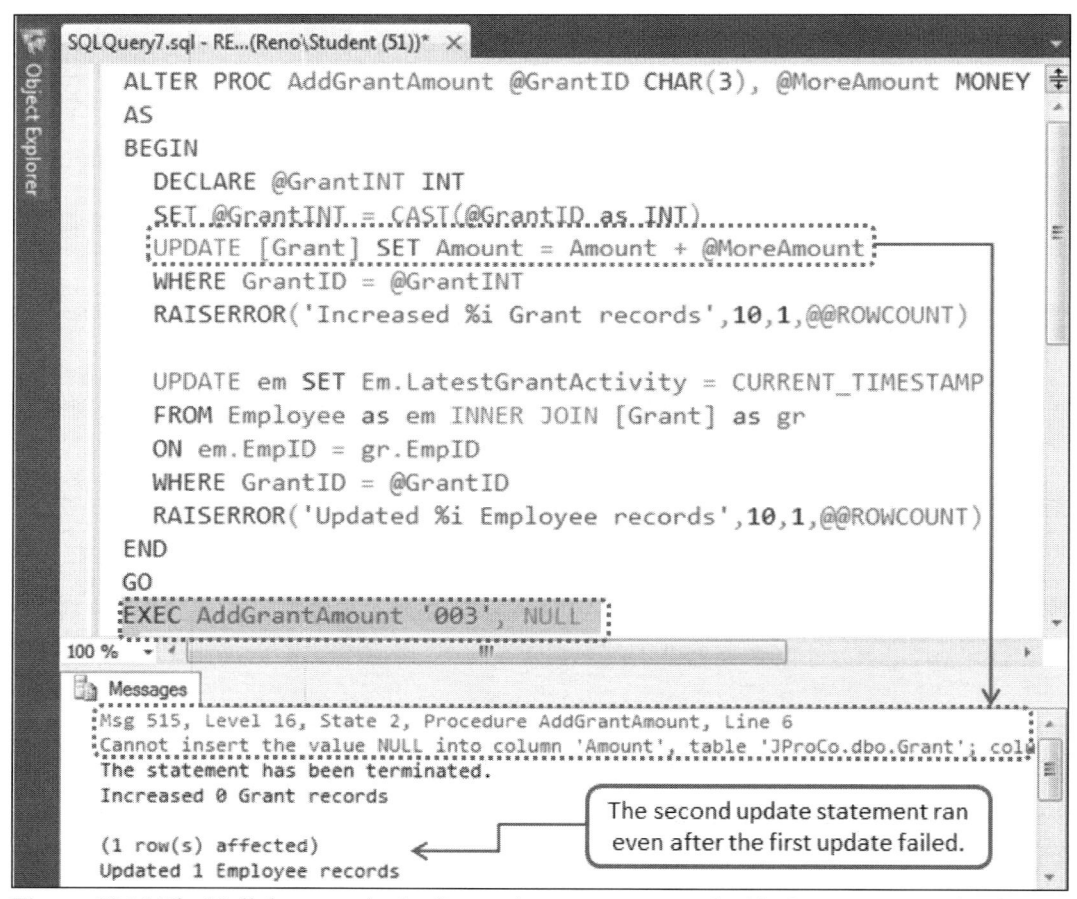

Figure 13.13 The Null data type in the first update statement resulted in Statement Termination.

Let's also recall the result produced by passing the sproc two valid parameters. The valid inputs in Figure 13.14 cause one Grant Amount to increase and the corresponding Employee record to be updated. This is the ideal situation we expect to see in nearly all cases.

EXEC AddGrantAmount '003', 1000

```
Messages
(1 row(s) affected)
Increased 1 Grant records

(1 row(s) affected)
Updated 1 Employee records
                                              0 rows
```

Figure 13.14 Calling on the AddGrantAmount stored procedure works with valid inputs.

Now we'll add the transaction keywords (BEGIN TRAN, COMMIT TRAN, and ROLLBACK TRAN) to enhance the robustness of our error handling. Previously in the *Joes 2 Pros* series (see *SQL Queries 2012 Joes 2 Pros 2012 Volume 1*, Chapter 9), we worked with updates and transactions which we wanted to either succeed or fail as a whole. If any part of the code failed, we wanted none of the changes to be committed. In Figure 13.15, we add a BEGIN TRAN and COMMIT TRAN statement at the beginning and end of our update code to put both statements into one transaction.

```sql
ALTER PROC AddGrantAmount @GrantID CHAR(3), @MoreAmount Money
AS
BEGIN
    BEGIN TRAN
    DECLARE @GrantINT INT
    SET @GrantINT = CAST(@GrantID as INT)
    UPDATE [Grant] SET Amount = Amount + @MoreAmount
    WHERE GrantID = @GrantINT
    RAISERROR('Increased %i Grant records',10,1,@@ROWCOUNT)

    UPDATE em SET Em.LatestGrantActivity = CURRENT_TIMESTAMP
    FROM Employee as em INNER JOIN [Grant] as gr
    ON em.EmpID = gr.EmpID
    WHERE GrantID = @GrantID
    RAISERROR('Updated %i Employee records',10,1,@@ROWCOUNT)
    COMMIT TRAN
END
GO
```

Figure 13.15 Both update statements are put inside of one transaction.

After running the stored procedure, we still seem to get an error on the first statement and an update on the second statement (Figure 13.16).

```sql
EXEC AddGrantAmount '003', NULL
```

```
Messages
Msg 515, Level 16, State 2, Procedure AddGrantAmount, Line 7
Cannot insert the value NULL into column 'Amount', table 'JProCo.dbo.Grant';
column does not allow nulls. UPDATE fails.
The statement has been terminated.
Increased 0 Grant records

(1 row(s) affected)
Updated 1 Employee records

                                                                    0 rows
```

Figure 13.16 The explicit transaction code inside the stored procedure did not change the statement termination error action.

Chapter 13. Error Handling

The query in Figure 13.17 confirms that no update was made to the Grant table, yet a new value shows in the LatestGrantActivity table in the Employee table.

```
SELECT * FROM [Grant] WHERE GrantID = '003'
SELECT * FROM Employee WHERE EmpID = 7
```

	GrantID	GrantName	EmpID	Amount						
1	003	Robert@BigStarBank.com	7	19100.00						

	EmpID	LastName	FirstName	HireDate	LocationID	ManagerID	Status	HiredOffset	TimeZone	LatestGrantActivity
1	7	Lonning	David	2000-01-0...	1	11	On Leave	2000-01-01 00:...	-08:00	2012-12-15 11:40:02.027

Figure 13.17 The update to the Grant table failed but the update to the Employee table succeeded.

While these statements are needed to change our code into a transaction, note that simply adding these statements doesn't produce a different result. This is because transactions ignore raised errors. In other words, before this code will accomplish our intended result, we first need to enclose all the code for our transaction within a Try Block. In Figure 13.18 we put the entire transaction inside its own Try Block. We then need to add a Catch Block just below it to react to the error.

```
BEGIN TRY
    BEGIN TRAN
    DECLARE @GrantINT INT
    SET @GrantINT = CAST(@GrantID AS INT)
    UPDATE [Grant] SET Amount = Amount + @MoreAmount
    WHERE GrantID = @GrantINT
    RAISERROR('Increased %i Grant records',10,1,@@ROWCOUNT)

    UPDATE em SET Em.LatestGrantActivity = CURRENT_TIMESTAMP
    FROM Employee AS em INNER JOIN [Grant] AS gr
    ON em.EmpID = gr.EmpID
    WHERE GrantID = @GrantID
    RAISERROR('Updated %i Employee records',10,1,@@ROWCOUNT)
    COMMIT TRAN
END TRY
```

Figure 13.18 Our transaction is placed inside of a Try Block.

What will we include in our Catch Block? Well if there is any error in the transaction, then we know there is a problem. We can simply have the Catch Block "Rollback Transaction", if the Try Block fails. The following code is contained in the ALTER PROC AddGrantAmount statement:

```
ALTER PROC AddGrantAmount @GrantID CHAR(3), @MoreAmount MONEY
AS
BEGIN
BEGIN TRY
BEGIN TRAN
DECLARE @GrantINT INT
SET @GrantINT = CAST(@GrantID AS INT)
UPDATE [Grant] SET Amount = Amount + @MoreAmount
WHERE GrantID = @GrantINT
RAISERROR('Increased %i Grant records',10,1,@@ROWCOUNT)

UPDATE em SET Em.LatestGrantActivity = CURRENT_TIMESTAMP
FROM Employee AS em INNER JOIN [Grant] AS gr
ON em.EmpID = gr.EmpID
WHERE GrantID = @GrantID
RAISERROR('Updated %i Employee records',10,1,@@ROWCOUNT)
COMMIT TRAN
END TRY
BEGIN CATCH
ROLLBACK TRAN
END CATCH
END
GO
```

Our Catch Block simply rolls back the transaction if the Try Block fails. After running all of the code in the ALTER PROC statement, observe that attempting to pass in the NULL parameter will have no effect on the database (Figure 13.19). Not only is the incorrect value disallowed by the Grant table, but the Employee table similarly does not get updated since the entire transaction is rolled back.

```
EXEC AddGrantAmount '003',NULL
```

Messages
(0 row(s) affected)
0 rows

Figure 13.19 When calling on the stored procedure creates an error, no records are affected.

Notice that passing in two valid parameters shows the result we expected to achieve: one Grant record was increased and one Employee record was updated (Figure 13.20). The amount of Grant 3 is now $20,100.

```
EXEC AddGrantAmount '003', 1000
```

```
Messages
(1 row(s) affected)
Increased 1 Grant records
(1 row(s) affected)
Updated 1 Employee records
                                                    0 rows
```

Figure 13.20 When no error is encountered, then all statements in the transaction complete.

Before proceeding to Lab 13.1, we will spend a few moments on this example which reviews transactions and foreign keys. We want to obtain a list of the products which have never been ordered. Since the SalesInvoiceDetail table contains sales invoice data, joining it to the CurrentProducts table on the ProductID field (using a left outer join) will show us the list of products that are not present in the SalesInvoiceDetail table and thus which have never been ordered. There are 426 products that have never been ordered (Figure 13.21). Any ProductID not listed in this result set has been ordered before.

```
SELECT * FROM CurrentProducts AS cp
LEFT OUTER JOIN SalesInvoiceDetail AS siv
ON cp.ProductID = siv.ProductID
WHERE siv.ProductID IS NULL
```

Figure 13.21 ProductID 1 is present in our query and thus has never been ordered.

Any product missing from this result set has already been ordered by a customer. For example, we know Products 7 through 12 have been ordered because they are missing from this result set.

Since Product 1 hasn't been ordered, we will delete it from the CurrentProducts table. SQL Server allows this deletion with the following code:

```
DELETE FROM CurrentProducts WHERE ProductID = 1
```

Since ProductID 1 has never been ordered, SQL Server allows deletion of this record. However, SQL Server will not allow us to delete Product 7, since there are invoice records which depend on ProductID 7. Here we see an error message (severity 16) which references a foreign key constraint, and we see the statement has been terminated (Figure 13.22).

```
DELETE FROM CurrentProducts WHERE ProductID = 7
```

```
Messages
Msg 547, Level 16, State 0, Line 1
The DELETE statement conflicted with the REFERENCE constraint
"FK_SalesInvoiceDetail_CurrentProducts_ProductID". The conflict occurred in
database "JProCo", table "dbo.SalesInvoiceDetail", column 'ProductID'.
The statement has been terminated.
                                                                    0 rows
```

Figure 13.22 Since ProductID 7 is listed in the SalesInvoiceDetail table, it can't be deleted.

After we delete Product 1, suppose that we receive an order for this product. Our query (Figure 13.23) attempts to insert a record reflecting this supposed order. Because Product 1 has been deleted, this INSERT Statement will fail and terminate.

```
INSERT INTO SalesInvoiceDetail
(InvoiceDetailID, InvoiceID, ProductID,
Quantity, UnitDiscount)
VALUES (6961, 1885, 1, 9, 0.00)
```

```
Messages
Msg 547, Level 16, State 0, Line 1
The INSERT statement conflicted with the FOREIGN KEY constraint
"FK_SalesInvoiceDetail_CurrentProducts_ProductID". The conflict occurred in
database "JProCo", table "dbo.SalesInvoiceDetail", column 'ProductID'.
The statement has been terminated.
                                                                    0 rows
```

Figure 13.23 Trying to insert an order for ProductID 1 fails since you deleted it earlier.

This brings us to the scenario described in the Lab 13.1 Skill Check. Suppose that at the same time you are deleting Product 2, a sales order is received for Product 2. This code would error out if you treat the insertion and deletion as two separate operations:

```
DELETE FROM CurrentProducts WHERE ProductID = 2

INSERT INTO SalesInvoiceDetail
(InvoiceDetailID, InvoiceID, ProductID, Quantity,
UnitDiscount)
VALUES (6961, 1885, 2, 9, 0.00)
```

Lab 13.1: Structured Error Handling

Lab Prep: Lab Prep: Each lab has one or more Skill Checks. Start with Skill Check 1 and proceed until reaching the Points to Ponder section.

Before beginning this lab, verify that SQL Server 2012 is properly installed and operating. Before running the lab setup script for resetting the database (SQLQueries2012Vol4Chapter13.1Setup.sql), please make sure to close all query windows within SSMS. An open query window pointing to a database context can lock that database preventing it from updating when the script is executing. A simple way to assure all query windows are closed, is to exit out of SSMS, then open a new instance of SSMS, and lastly run the setup script.

Skill Check 1: Take the code in Figure 13.24 and put all of it into one transaction. Wrap the transaction with a set of Try/Catch Blocks. Commit the transaction if there is no error and perform a rollback if there is an error. When done, check to see that no records have been deleted from the CurrentProducts table, nor have any records been added to the SalesInvoiceDetail table.

```
BEGIN TRANSACTION
INSERT INTO SalesInvoiceDetail
(InvoiceDetailID, InvoiceID, ProductID, Quantity,
UnitDiscount)
VALUES (6961,1885,2,9,0.00)
COMMIT TRANSACTION
```

```
Messages
(1 row(s) affected)
(0 row(s) affected)
                                                    0 rows
```

Figure 13.24 Starter code for Skill Check 1.

Answer Code: The T-SQL code to this lab can be found in the downloadable files in a file named Lab13.1_StructuredErrorHandling.sql.

Points to Ponder - Structured Error Handling

1. Until SQL Server 2005, there was no way to prevent SQL Server from raising error messages.

2. In SQL Server 2005 and beyond you can use the TRY-CATCH approach for all the error messages trapped by your catch handler. None of this was possible with the old RAISERROR process.

3. The catch block supports six functions:
    - ERROR_NUMBER()
    - ERROR_MESSAGE()
    - ERROR_SEVERITY()
    - ERROR_STATE()
    - ERROR_PROCEDURE()
    - ERROR_LINE()

4. A TRY CATCH construct catches all execution errors with a severity higher than 10 and which do not close the database connection.

5. GOTO statements cannot be used to enter a TRY or CATCH block.

6. In a trigger context, almost all errors result in batch abortion, except for errors which you raise yourself with a RAISERROR message.

7. Set XACT_ABORT to OFF. This sets your SQL Server instance back to the default set of rules for responding to errors.

8. Set XACT_ABORT to ON. This causes batch abortion on the first error (Except for errors you raise yourself with RAISERROR).

THROW

In a way you could say we learned most of what we need to know about THROW already and some people claim it is nearly the same as RAISERROR. It is true that RAISERROR will throw up an error if you set the severity to 11 or higher and therefore passes execution to the CATCH block if it is inside the TRY block. What happens if the RAISERROR is not inside the TRY block? Then the RAISERROR is thrown to the message window and you get the error message in red. It is also true the THROW will send the error message up to the CATCH (if it's in a TRY block) or to the message of the caller.

With both THROW and RAISERROR all you need is to set a time and place where SQL will throw or raise an error. There are some significant advantages to using THROW which is why Microsoft says RAISERROR will be deprecated and should not be used for future SQL development. This section will show demonstrations on exactly how to compare these two techniques.

Introduction to THROW

When we throw something we often hope someone is there to catch it. A few summers ago my friend was on a boat on the lake and as they were boating towards the dock they told me to catch their cell phone. They threw it to me and it slipped through my hands and landed in the lake. This resulted in an error and even some hard feelings. Had I caught the cell phone I could have then thrown it in the lake myself or kept it in my pocket.

In SQL when you THROW something it will either be caught or it will land on the message of the calling code. Another way of saying that is, it will land exactly where it was thrown unless someone catches it. We are aware of what the statement in Figure 13.25 does.

```
RAISERROR('Your bad!', 16, 1)
```

```
Msg 50000, Level 16, State 1, Line 1
Your bad!
                                                    0 rows
```

Figure 13.25 Result from explicit RAISERROR

The statement Figure 13.25 raises or throws an error. Is RAISERROR the only way to raise a specific error? Let's try this using THROW as seen in the following code:

```
THROW 50000, 'Your bad!', 1
```

```
Msg 50000, Level 16, State 1, Line 1
Your bad!
```
0 rows

Figure 13.26 The result from an explicit THROW.

As seen in Figure 13.26 we see that the THROW command delivered the same result as RAISERROR.

Using THROW with TRY/CATCH

In the game of dodge ball, when you throw the ball there are two outcomes. Someone will catch the ball or the ball will hit something (or someone). Just like in dodge ball where a ball is thrown and then caught, in SQL when we set this up it's called a TRY/CATCH block:

```
BEGIN TRY
END TRY
BEGIN CATCH
END CATCH
```

If the statement inside the TRY throws an error, the TRY then throws the error into the Catch block. The Catch block then has the option of performing an action other than raising the error as a message. We can run-through an example of this by writing an error prone INSERT Statement into the PayRates table that will violate the primary key. The following code will insert the pay for Employee 1, even though Employee 1 already has an existing yearly salary already in the PayRates table:

```
INSERT INTO PayRates (EmpID, YearlySalary, MonthlySalary,
HourlyRate, Selector, Estimate, BonusPoints)
VALUES (1, 50000, NULL, NULL, 1, 50000, 0)
```

The primary key ensures you can't enter the same record in a table twice. Doing so means the primary key will tell SQL to raise an error message. Running just the INSERT statement that tries to insert EmpID 1 a second time throws an error. This action without the TRY/CATCH block means it returns the error message as seen in Figure 13.27

```
Msg 2627, Level 14, State 1, Line 1
Violation of PRIMARY KEY constraint 'PK__PayRates__AF2DBA79157E27AA'. Cannot
insert duplicate key in object 'dbo.PayRates'. The duplicate key value is (1).
The statement has been terminated.
```
0 rows

Figure 13.27 Violation of PRIMARY KEY error message

What would happen to the process of the TRY/CATCH block if the insert ran successfully? Then all the code in the TRY block will continue to run until it's done. After the INSERT let's add more code to run. We will add the following PRINT statement that returns as a message with the successfully executed INSERT Statement.

```
PRINT 'After First Insert'
```

Let's also add the code into the CATCH block so when the INSERT statement in the TRY errors out it will pass into the CATCH block. In Figure 13.28 the CATCH block will then print "What is the error?" along with the actual error message.

```
BEGIN TRY
INSERT INTO PayRates (EmpID, YearlySalary, MonthlySalary,
HourlyRate, Selector, Estimate, BonusPoints)
VALUES (1, 50000, NULL, NULL, 1, 50000, 0)
PRINT 'After First Insert'
END TRY
BEGIN CATCH
PRINT 'What is the error?'
PRINT ERROR_MESSAGE()
END CATCH;
```

```
(0 row(s) affected)
What is the error?
Violation of PRIMARY KEY constraint 'PK__PayRates__AF2DBA79157E27AA'. Cannot
insert duplicate key in object 'dbo.PayRates'. The duplicate key value is (1).
                                                                        0 rows
```

Figure 13.28 Violation of PRIMARY KEY as information.

In Figure 13.28 you see that it returned the message "what is the error?" and the actual error message about the Violation of PRIMARY KEY. In this case the error message did not return in the normal "red" font for error messages since we showed this as pure information from the ERROR_MESSAGE() function.

Sometimes you want the error text and sometimes you will want the entire error. For the sake of error messages, why don't we use THROW to return whatever message is passed into the CATCH. In Figure 13.29 the CATCH block now has the error in its scope.

```
BEGIN TRY
INSERT INTO PayRates (EmpID, YearlySalary, MonthlySalary,
HourlyRate, Selector, Estimate, BonusPoints)
VALUES (1, 50000, NULL, NULL, 1, 50000, 0)
PRINT 'After First Insert'
END TRY
BEGIN CATCH
PRINT 'What is the error';
THROW
END CATCH;
```

```
(0 row(s) affected)
What is the error
Msg 2627, Level 14, State 1, Line 2
Violation of PRIMARY KEY constraint 'PK__PayRates__AF2DBA79157E27AA'. Cannot
insert duplicate key in object 'dbo.PayRates'. The duplicate key value is (1).
                                                                        0 rows
```

Figure 13.29 Violation of primary key from THROW command

In Figure 13.29 above, the statement to come out of the catch is the actual error. This is one way that the Catch can re-raise the error that it received from the TRY.

TRY/CATCH in Stored Procedures

At JProCo we have a couple of new employees, Gale Winds and Sue Fines. Their employee numbers are 20 and 21 respectively. When we query the Employee table we notice neither employee has pay information, nor are they present in the PayRates table.

It's possible that someone would accidentally try to insert employee information that already exists. It is also possible that someone will insert an employee that doesn't yet exist in the table, but should. This table has a primary key on the EmpID field to prevent duplicates. When inserting records there is a possibility for error and there is a possibility all will go smoothly. What we're going to do is create a stored procedure to handle either outcome. If we pass in the EmpID and YearlySalary for a new employee, it will then insert that data for you into the PayRates table. If there is an error during the insert (like a duplicate key value) then it will roll back the transaction. The following code will roll back any changes to the transaction if an error is encountered in the TRY block:

Chapter 13. Error Handling

```
CREATE PROC InsertYearlyPay @EmpID INT, @YrSalary MONEY
AS
BEGIN TRY
  BEGIN TRAN
  INSERT INTO [dbo].[PayRates] (EmpID, YearlySalary,
MonthlySalary, HourlyRate, Selector, Estimate, BonusPoints)
  VALUES (@EmpID, @YrSalary, NULL, NULL, 1, @YrSalary, 0)
COMMIT TRAN
END TRY
BEGIN CATCH
  ROLLBACK TRAN

END CATCH
GO
```

Notice in the previous code we start with the TRY block and if it runs successfully we added the COMMIT TRAN command at the end. If there is an error in the TRY BLOCK then execution will be handed off to the CATCH block. In this case the only statement to be run is where we added the ROLLBACK TRAN command. Once this CREATE PROC statement is run we will now have the stored procedure (InsertYearlyPay) that we can call on to insert data into the PayRates table. We know that Gale Winds is employee 20 from the Employee table and we need to give her a yearly salary of 50,000 dollars using the InsertYearlyPay stored procedure. In Figure 13.30 we insert Gale Winds (EmpID 20) and verify her new record as 50000.00 in the YearlySalary field in the PayRates table.

EXEC InsertYearlyPay 20, 1

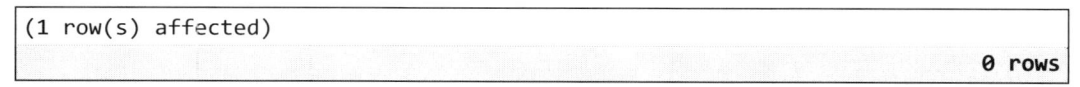

(1 row(s) affected)

SELECT * FROM PayRates

	EmpID	YearlySalary	MonthlySalary	HourlyRate	Selector	Estimate	BonusPoints
10	10	NULL	NULL	17.00	3	2080	NULL
11	11	150000.00	NULL	NULL	1	1	NULL
12	12	NULL	NULL	21.00	3	2080	NULL
13	13	72000.00	NULL	NULL	1	1	NULL
14	19	45000.00	NULL	NULL	1	1	NULL
15	20	50000.00	NULL	NULL	1	1	0

15 rows

Figure 13.30 PayRates table after stored procedure updated EmpID 20.

The work we needed to do to update Gale in the PayRates table is complete. However, all JProCo employees that have a salary are considered active and must be updated as such in the Employee table. Currently Gale is not listed as active in the Employee table. In Figure 13.31 we update her [status] to active to complete our work.

```
UPDATE Employee
SET [status] = 'Active'
WHERE EmpID = 20
SELECT * FROM Employee
```

	EmpID	LastName	FirstName	HireDate	LocationID	ManagerID	Status
15	15	Jones	Tess	2012-07-30…	1	11	Active
16	16	Biggs	Nancy	2012-07-30…	1	11	Active
17	17	Downs	Wendy	2012-07-30…	1	11	Active
18	18	Walker	Rainy	2010-01-01…	1	11	NULL
19	20	Winds	Gale	2010-03-25…	1	11	Active
20	21	Sue	Fines	2012-07-30…	1	4	NULL

20 rows

Figure 13.31 EmpID 20 updated to Active.

After you make both of these updates, the Employee table will now show EmpID 20 and the PayRates table shows the corresponding record having a YearlySalary of 50,000. We used a two-step process to give Gale her pay and make her active in two tables in the JProCo database.

Nesting Structured Error Handling

If you have ever watched a game of cricket or baseball you know it's the job of the players in the field (called fielders) to prevent the ball from going outside the fence line. Sometimes it gets really close. Right at the line, the fielder stops the ball and immediately throws the ball to another player in the direction of where the batsmen are running. Throwing a ball that far and that accurate is almost beyond the athletic ability of even the greatest athletes. Luckily there is another player who is much closer getting ready to receive the ball from the outfield. The player catches the ball and then re-throws it to the plate where the batsmen are running.

Why does the team intentionally throw the same ball twice on the same play? Sometimes the original THROW can't reach the execution point of where it needs to go unless it gets re-thrown.

In the previous section we added an employee's pay and updated her status in two steps. We updated the PayRates table by using the InsertYearlyPay stored procedure and then we directly updated the Employee Table. Many companies will have a policy where you're not supposed to directly update a table. This policy is meant to help avoid mistakes from ad hoc code. The company may want a stored procedure to update the Employee table for you. In the following code, we CREATE a stored procedure that will update the employee's salary in the PayRates table:

```
CREATE PROC MakeYearlyEmployeePay @EmpID INT, @YrSalary MONEY
AS
BEGIN TRY
  BEGIN TRAN
  UPDATE Employee
  SET [status] = 'Active'
  WHERE EmpID = @EmpID
  EXEC InsertYearlyPay @EmpID, @YrSalary
  COMMIT TRAN
END TRY
BEGIN CATCH
  ROLLBACK TRAN
END CATCH
GO
```

If you look closely you will see that in using the new MakeYearlyEmployeePay stored procedure, we also call on the InsertYearlyPay stored procedure. By doing this we change their status to Active in the Employee table and then update the PayRates table. Notice that we contained both of these actions in a TRY/CATCH block. If the entire TRY is successful then the instruction is to COMMIT the transaction. If either statement in the TRY block errors out then execution is sent to the CATCH block to ROLLBACK. After the ROLLBACK runs, the message from the error is shown.

The thinking is that since both actions are contained in the TRY, neither will commit unless both complete successfully. Let's try it out in a very good situation where we're going to insert an employee that we need. Sue Fines is an employee that is not yet listed in the PayRates table. Her employee number is 21 which does not yet exist in the PayRates table. Let's use our stored procedure to update her pay to 51,000 dollars in the YearlySalary field using the following code:

```
EXEC MakeYearlyEmployeePay 21, 51000
```

```
(1 row(s) affected)

(1 row(s) affected)
                                                                    0 rows
```

Figure 13.32 Stored procedure MakeYearlyEmployeePay ran successfully.

In Figure 13.32, notice one row was affected twice. One message for each table updated for EmpID 21. If you look at the Employee table in Figure 13.33 and the PayRates table in Figure 13.34 Employee 21's record was updated successfully in both tables. EmpID 21 is now set to active and also has a YearlySalary of 51000.

```
SELECT * FROM Employee
```

	EmpID	LastName	FirstName	HireDate	LocationID	ManagerID	Status
1	15	Jones	Tess	2012-07-30…	1	11	Active
2	16	Biggs	Nancy	2012-07-30…	1	11	Active
3	17	Downs	Wendy	2012-07-30…	1	11	Active
4	18	Walker	Rainy	2010-01-01…	1	11	NULL
5	20	Winds	Gale	2010-03-25…	1	11	Active
6	21	Sue	Fines	2012-07-30…	1	4	Active

20 ROWS

Figure 13.33 EmpID 15-21 of Employee table.

```
SELECT * FROM PayRates
```

	EmpID	YearlySalary	MonthlySalary	HourlyRate	Selector	Estimate
1	11	150000.00	NULL	NULL	1	1
2	12	NULL	NULL	21.00	3	2080
3	13	72000.00	NULL	NULL	1	1
4	19	45000.00	NULL	NULL	1	45000
5	20	50000.00	NULL	NULL	1	50000
6	21	51000.00	NULL	NULL	1	51000

16 rows

Figure 13.34 EmpID 11-21 of PayRates table.

What about a not so perfect situation? In the following code we will attempt to update EmpID 1. We can predict the outcome because we know EmpID 1 already exists. It will still update to active, but yearly pay won't work and therefore it should ROLLBACK the entire transaction.

```
EXEC MakeYearlyEmployeePay 1, 91000
```

```
(1 row(s) affected)
(0 row(s) affected)
Msg 3903, Level 16, State 1, Procedure MakeYearlyEmployeePay, Line 14
The ROLLBACK TRANSACTION request has no corresponding BEGIN TRANSACTION.

                                                                    1 rows
```

Figure 13.35 Partial fail of MakeYearlyEmployeePay stored procedure.

THROW the Calling Code

From our last example in Figure 13.35, notice the error message says "no corresponding BEGIN TRANSACTION". Keep in mind that the MakeYearlyEmployeePay sproc has two statements. The first statement is an update to the employee table and the second one is a call to the InsertYearlyPay sproc. If any one of these two statements fails throws an error then the CATCH block will run. We know the InsertYearlyPay sproc has failed but it is not throwing the error up. This means the MakeYearlyEmployeePay sproc does not detect any error and tries to run the commit.

This means the InsertYearlyPay sproc is rolling back the transaction. When the MakeYearlyEmployeePay sproc tries to commit the transaction that has already been rolled back we get the error message.

Our new directive is for the InsertYearlyPay sproc to not make any transaction decisions. It should just inform the calling sproc of MakeYearlyEmployeePay that an error has occurred. The THROW can pass the error up to the calling stored procedure.

Currently the rollback isn't throwing the error back up to the next stored procedure. Let's ALTER the stored procedure and add THROW and comment out the ROLLBACK command as seen in the following code.

```
ALTER PROC InsertYearlyPay @EmpID INT, @YrSalary MONEY
AS
BEGIN TRY
BEGIN TRAN
INSERT INTO [dbo].[PayRates] (EmpID, YearlySalary,
MonthlySalary, HourlyRate, Selector, Estimate, BonusPoints)
VALUES (@EmpID, @YrSalary, NULL, NULL, 1, @YrSalary, 0)
COMMIT TRAN
END TRY
BEGIN CATCH
THROW;
--ROLLBACK TRAN
END CATCH
GO
```

Once this procedure is run successfully let's call on it to test the outcome. In Figure 13.36 we are attempting to insert a pay of 11,000 for EmpID 1. Since EmpID 1 already exists in the PayRates table, this will raise an error from the InsertYearlyPay stored procedure. With the error thrown to the TRY block of MakeYearlyEmployeePay sproc we get an error. When a TRY block encounters an error then execution is passed to the CATCH block. The CATCH block of MakeYearlyEmployeePay rolls back the transaction and no changes to your data are made. Notice in Figure 13.36, you just get the message of Violation of PRIMARY KEY constraint.

```
EXEC MakeYearlyEmployeePay 1, 11000
```

(No column name)
Violation of PRIMARY KEY constraint 'PK__PayRates…

1 rows

Figure 13.36 Fail of the MakeYearlyEmployeePay stored procedure.

Lab 13.2: THROW

Lab Prep: Lab Prep: Each lab has one or more Skill Checks. Start with Skill Check 1 and proceed until reaching the Points to Ponder section.

Before beginning this lab, verify that SQL Server 2012 is properly installed and operating. Before running the lab setup script for resetting the database (SQLQueries2012Vol4Chapter13.2Setup.sql), please make sure to close all query windows within SSMS. An open query window pointing to a database context can lock that database preventing it from updating when the script is executing. A simple way to assure all query windows are closed, is to exit out of SSMS, then open a new instance of SSMS, and lastly run the setup script.

Skill Check 1: Take the AddGrantAmount sproc and make sure the CATCH block re-throws the error instead of rolling back the transaction. Doing it in this way, no rows will be affected. The error will show up in red in the message window. Test your work by opening another query window and issuing the following code in Figure 13.37

```
EXEC AddGrantAmount '003', NULL
```

```
Messages
(0 row(s) affected)
Msg 515, Level 16, State 2, Procedure AddGrantAmount, Line 8
Cannot insert the value NULL into column 'Amount', table 'JProCo.dbo.Grant';
column does not allow nulls. UPDATE fails.
                                                                      0 rows
```

Figure 13.37 Skill Check 1.

Skill Check 2: Take the AddBonusPoint sproc and alter it. Use a transaction with Structured Error Handling and the transaction should be started in the TRY block then committed at the end of the TRY block. The CATCH block should roll the transaction back. THROW the following error from the TRY block if the @EmpID value is null:

```
THROW 50000, 'Your bad!', 1;
```

Test your code as seen in Figure 13.38.

```
EXEC AddBonusPoint NULL
```

```
Message
Command(s) completed successfully.
                                                                      0 rows
```

Figure 13.38 Skill Check 2.

Skill Check 3: Take the AddBonusPoint Sproc from Skill Check 2 and use a transaction with Structured Error Handling. In the CATCH block re-throw the error.

```
EXEC AddBonusPoint NULL
```

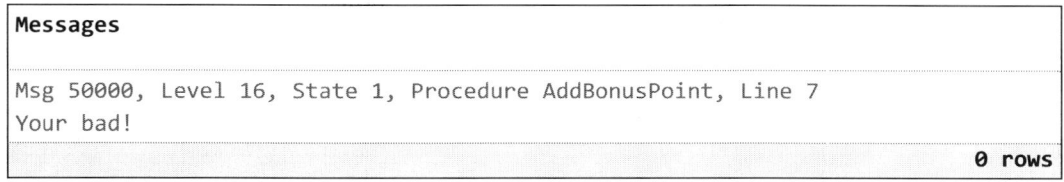

```
Messages
Msg 50000, Level 16, State 1, Procedure AddBonusPoint, Line 7
Your bad!
                                                                    0 rows
```

Figure 13.39 Skill Check 3.

Skill Check 4: Take the UpdateGrantEmployee sproc and use a transaction with Structured Error Handling. In the CATCH block DON'T throw the error but show the Error message from the calling code. Give it structured error handling with transactions where the CATCH rolls back the transaction.

```
EXEC UpdateGrantEmployee '001', NULL
```

```
Messages
(0 row(s) affected)
Cannot insert the value NULL into column 'Amount', table 'JProCo.dbo.Grant';
column does not allow nulls. UPDATE fails.
                                                                    0 rows
```

Figure 13.40 Skill Check 4.

Answer Code: The T-SQL code to this lab can be found in the downloadable files in a file named Lab13.2_THROW.sql.

Points to Ponder - THROW

1. SQL Server 2005 introduced structured error handling with BEGIN TRY...BEGIN CATCH blocks.
2. The RAISERROR command is often used inside of a BEGIN TRY...END TRY block to raise an exception which passes execution to the BEGIN CATCH...END CATCH block.
3. Sometimes we need to raise an error from the BEGIN CATCH...END CATCH block to send it to the calling code.
4. The THROW command is new to SQL 2012.
5. The THROW command reports the exact error number to the calling code.
6. When you re-throw an error with THROW, the original error number and line number is preserved but the RAISERROR gets overwritten.
7. RAISERROR will be deprecated and should not be used for future SQL development.
8. If you have a statement before the THROW it must be terminated with a semicolon.
9. You can THROW your own message with this syntax: THROW 50000, 'Your bad!', 1.
10. You can just re-throw the system error by not specifying any parameter with this syntax: THROW.
11. If the THROW statement does not specify any parameters then it can only be used inside a CATCH block.

Chapter Glossary

BEGIN CATCH END CATCH: The CATCH block; serves as a contingency plan for failed code from the Try Block.

BEGIN TRY END TRY: The TRY block; "Plan A" for what you would like your program to do. If the TRY block fails, it passes the attempted code to the CATCH block.

TRY CATCH: A construct which catches all execution errors with a severity higher than 10 and which does not close the database connection.

ERROR_NUMBER(): A SQL function that returns the error number of the error that caused the CATCH block to run.

ERROR_MESSAGE(): A SQL function similar to ERROR_NUMBER() but returns error text of the error that caused the CATCH block to run.

ERROR_SEVERITY(): A SQL function that returns the error's severity level of the error that caused the CATCH block to run.

ERROR_STATE(): A SQL function that returns the state number of the error that caused the CATCH block to run. If in two transactions you receive the same Error Number but the State Numbers are different each transaction error more than likely has a different cause.

ERROR_PROCEDURE(): A SQL function that returns the Stored Procedure's name that created an error and caused the CATCH block to run.

ERROR_LINE(): A SQL function that returns the line number of the piece of code that created an error and caused the CATCH block to run.

THROW: A SQL function that raises an exception in a TRY CATCH block and sends the execution to the CATCH block.

RAISERROR: A SQL function that does two things. It initiates error processing and generates an error message. The error message can be hard coded by the user or it can be generated dynamically.

Review Quiz - Chapter Thirteen

1.) You have tables named CurrentProducts and SalesInvoiceDetail. The CurrentProducts table has a foreign key relationship with the SalesInvoiceDetail table on the ProductID. All products in the CurrentProducts table are listed at least once in the SalesInvoiceDetail table. You use the following code:

```
BEGIN TRY
BEGIN TRANSACTION
DELETE FROM CurrentProducts WHERE ProductID = 1
INSERT INTO SalesInvoiceDetail VALUES (778,1,0,DEFAULT)
COMMIT TRANSACTION
END TRY
BEGIN CATCH
ROLLBACK TRAN
END CATCH
```

You need to know the results of this batch. What will happen?

- O a. 1 record is deleted from the CurrentProducts table and 1 record is added to the SalesInvoiceDetail table.
- O b. 1 record is deleted from the CurrentProducts table but no records are added to the SalesInvoiceDetail table.
- O c. No records are deleted from the CurrentProducts table but 1 record is added to the SalesInvoiceDetail table.
- O d. No records are deleted from the CurrentProducts table and no records are added to the SalesInvoiceDetail table.

2.) SQL Server has many error severity rating levels. You notice a severity of 9 ran inside your TRY block and did not pass control to the CATCH block. What level of severity is the minimum that will cause the TRY block to pass control to the CATCH block?

- O a. 11
- O b. 12
- O c. 16
- O d. 17

3.) You have code that counts the number of rows in a given table by using the following code:

```
BEGIN TRY
DECLARE @SQL Varchar(max)
'SELECT Count(*) FROM' + @TableName
EXEC (@SQL)
SET @Total = @@ROWCOUNT

--PUT CODE HERE

END TRY
BEGIN CATCH
PRINT ERROR_MESSAGE()
END CATCH
```

You want to insert a SQL statement right before the end of the TRY block that will send a notification and how many rows were affected. Which code do you use?

○ a. `RAISERROR ('Deleted %i records',10,1, @Total)`
○ b. `RAISERROR ('Deleted %i records',11,1, @Total)`
○ c. `RAISERROR ('Deleted %i records',16,1, @Total)`

4.) You are using a TRY...CATCH block in your structured error handling. You need to raise an error in the TRY block that will pass execution to the CATCH block. Which severity level will do this?

○ a. 0
○ b. 9
○ c. 10
○ d. 16

5.) You have written multiple DML statements to modify existing records in your CurrentProducts table. You have placed these DML updates into an explicit transaction. You know that some errors will cause SQL to abort the whole batch while other errors will encounter statement termination and continue to run the remaining code. You need to set an abort option and roll back all changes if any error in the transaction is encountered. Which option should you enable?

○ a. `SET NOEXEC`
○ b. `SET XACT_ABORT`
○ c. `SET TRANSACTION ISOLATION LEVEL`

6.) You have two tables named CurrentProducts and SalesInvoiceHeader. The CurrentProducts table has a foreign key relationship with the SalesInvoiceHeader table on the ProductID column. You are deleting ProductID 77 from the Product table and then trying to insert a sale for Product77 into the SalesInvoiceHeader table.

```
BEGIN TRY
BEGIN TRANSACTION
DELETE FROM CurrentProducts WHERE ProductID = 77;
BEGIN TRANSACTION
INSERT INTO SalesInvoiceHeader VALUES ( 95894, 77, 2 );
COMMIT TRANSACTION
COMMIT TRANSACTION
END TRY
BEGIN CATCH
ROLLBACK TRANSACTION
PRINT ERROR_MESSAGE();
END CATCH
```

What will be the outcome when you run this query?

O a. 1) The product will be deleted from the CurrentProducts table.
2) The order details will be inserted into the SalesInvoiceHeader table.

O b. 1) The product will be deleted from the CurrentProducts table.
2) The order details will not be inserted into the SalesInvoiceHeader table.

O c. 1) The product will not be deleted from the CurrentProducts table.
2) The order details will be inserted into the SalesInvoiceHeader table.

O d. 1) The product will not be deleted from the CurrentProducts table.
2) The order details will not be inserted into the SalesInvoiceHeader table.

7.) You have the following statement that raises an error:

```
RAISERROR('Your bad!', 16, 1)
```

You want to use alternate code to raise the same error message. What code will achieve this result?

O a. `THROW 50000, 'Your bad!', 1`
O b. `RETHROW 50000, 'Your bad!', 1`
O c. `RAISETHROW 50000, 'Your bad!', 1`

8.) You have the following code to create your stored procedure:

```
CREATE PROC TestQuestion @TestID INT, @TestName VARCHAR(50)
AS
BEGIN TRY
IF(@TestID IS NULL)
THROW
INSERT INTO dbo.Test VALUES (@TestID, @TestName)
END TRY
BEGIN CATCH
PRINT ERROR_MESSAGE();
THROW
END CATCH;
GO
```

You can't create the stored procedure and get an error message. Why?

O a. The THROW inside the TRY block must have parameters.

O b. The THROW inside the CATCH block must have parameters.

9.) What is one advantage to using THROW inside the CATCH block instead of RAISERROR?

O a. THROW can raise custom error messages where RAISERROR can only do system supplied error messages.

O b. THROW can raise system supplied error messages where RAISERROR can only do custom error message.

O c. When you re-throw an error with THROW, the original error number and line number is preserved but the RAISERROR overwrites the previous error.

O d. The THROW will not send the error to the calling code but the RAISERROR will.

Answer Key

1.) If any error is encountered in the explicit transaction of the TRY then all records will be rolled back. This means no records from any table were updated which is why (d) is the correct answer.

2.) The lowest error level that causes the TRY to send execution to the CATCH is level 11. Since we are looking for the lowest error number (b), (c) and (d) are too high. Therefore (a) is the correct answer.

3.) Error numbers below 11 are informational. Since we don't want to raise an error, (b) and (c) are too high and are incorrect. The correct answer is (a).

4.) If your error is 10 or below then the CATCH block will not run. Therefore (a), (b), and (c) are too low to pass the execution to the CATCH. This makes (d) the correct answer.

5.) If you want all statements to result to batch abortion to make an explicit transaction roll everything back then you need to use XACT_ABORT. This makes (b) the correct answer.

6.) If any error is encountered in the explicit transaction of the TRY then all records will be rolled back. This means no records from any table were updated which is why (d) is the correct answer.

7.) The two ways to create your own error in SQL 2012 is with RAISERROR or THROW. This makes (a) is the correct answer.

8.) If you are creating your own error from THROW it needs parameters. If you are using it to pass along an existing error then you don't need any parameters. A THROW in the CATCH is finding an existing error and does not need any parameters. In the TRY it would be generating and error. This means (a) is the correct answer.

9.) If you put a RAISERROR inside the CATCH then you are creating a new error to pass up and might not know the original error. The THROW will pass the original error up the stack. This makes (c) the correct answer.

Bug Catcher Game

To play the Bug Catcher game, run the file SQLQueries2012Vol4BugCatcher13.pps from the BugCatcher folder of the companion files found at www.Joes2Pros.com.

Chapter 14.   Dynamic SQL

Have you ever taken an oath? An oath is a promise calling upon someone or something that the oath maker considers sacred. As an example, the start of an oath may begin like this. "I *yourname,* swear to uphold the cause of education for my community". Now, if I were to read this oath it would say "I Rick Morelan, swear to uphold the cause of education for my community". This sentence changes based on the reader's name. This sentence is dynamic and adjusts to the current situation.

Humans use sentences to communicate and computers use statements. So what does a SQL statement look like? SELECT * FROM *YourTableName* is a pretty close example. Maybe the table is called Employee or Location. If the Employee table is chosen, the final statement would run as SELECT * FROM Employee. With dynamic SQL, a statement is placed inside a variable or fixed string and executed as a complete line of code. Using the SELECT * FROM *YourTableName* example, dynamic SQL would allow us to choose either the Employee or Location table on the fly. This chapter shows how to use dynamic SQL.

READER NOTE: *Please run the script SQLQueries2012Vol4Chapter14.0Setup.sql in order to follow along with the examples in the first section of Chapter 14. All scripts mentioned in this chapter may be found at **www.Joes2Pros.com**.*

Exec Dynamic SQL

The words "I want to" make very little sense without context. However the words "I want to have lunch with you" give context and the query makes sense. Just as incomplete sentences don't make sense in spoken languages, neither do partial SQL statements. The following statement is a complete statement for SQL to understand:

```
SELECT *
FROM MgmtTraining
```

This statement or SQL "sentence" will return the seven records from the MgmtTraining table. Before we dive into Dynamic SQL let's look at a simple SELECT Statement. If we select these two lines of code one at a time, the query does not run. SQL does not understand incomplete statements. This statement has two lines and we need both of these lines in order to run:

```
SELECT *
```

Will not run by itself and neither will:

```
FROM MgmtTraining
```

There is a big difference in the next two statements:

```
SELECT * FROM MgmtTraining
'SELECT * FROM MgmtTraining'
```

The first statement will run but the second will not. The single quotes around the second line make it a string and not a complete statement. If we could turn the string of the second statement into what it contains then we could execute the content as a SQL statement. One way to do this is by using the EXEC command. EXEC stands for execute and turns a string into running SQL code when the string is placed in a set of parentheses:

```
EXEC ('SELECT * FROM MgmtTraining')
```

Dynamic DML statements

This book has used variables before to change how a predicate is run. For example LastName = @LastName might get a different result set from the Employee table when the value for @LastName changes. We can also use variables to change what table we are going to query from.

Chapter 14. Dynamic SQL

Beginning with a simple query let's convert it to a Dynamic statement. Using the query from the first section of this chapter we will first declare the SELECT * and FROM MgmtTraining as @variables and set them equal to their corresponding lines of code. To see if we can reconstruct the query from variables we will add a print statement that concatenates the two variables into a message.

```
DECLARE @Select NVARCHAR(50) = 'SELECT * '
DECLARE @From NVARCHAR(50) = 'FROM MgmtTraining'
PRINT (@Select + @From)
```

MESSAGES
SELECT * FROM MgmtTraining
0 rows

Figure 14.1 Result from Print statement.

Figure 14.1 shows the same basic SELECT statement from the MgmtTraining table that we started with. The message is the same as the query. Our goal is to create dynamic SQL, so simply change the PRINT command to EXEC. Instead of just printing a message SQL executes the (@Select + @From) string as a SQL statement.

```
DECLARE @Select NVARCHAR(50) = 'SELECT * '
DECLARE @From NVARCHAR(50) = 'FROM MgmtTraining'
EXEC (@Select + @From)
```

	ClassID	ClassName	ClassDurationHours	ApprovedDate
1	1	Embracing Diversity	12	2007-01-01...
2	2	Interviewing	6	2007-01-15...
3	3	Difficult Negotiations	30	2008-02-12...
4	4	Empowering Others	18	2012-08-01...
5	8	Passing Certifications	13	2012-08-01...
6	9	Effective Communications	35	2012-08-01...
				7 rows

Figure 14.2 Result from querying MgmtTraining table.

The EXEC command took the two variables declared in lines one and two, concatenated them into the SELECT * FROM MgmtTraining statement and returned all the records from the MgmtTraining table (Figure 14.2). To query the Employee table we would replace the variable that holds MgmtTraining with Employee. This change to the variable value will be called on in the execute command. The EXEC command would then construct the 'SELECT * FROM Employee' statement and return the twenty records from the Employee table as seen in Figure 14.3.

Chapter 14. Dynamic SQL

```
DECLARE @Select NVARCHAR(50) = 'SELECT * '
DECLARE @From NVARCHAR(50) = 'FROM Employee'
EXEC (@Select + @From)
```

	EmpID	LastName	FirstName	HireDate	LocationID
1	1	Adams	Alex	2001-01-01 00:00:00.000	1
2	2	Brown	Barry	2002-08-12 00:00:00.000	1
3	3	Osako	Lee	1999-09-01 00:00:00.000	2
4	4	Kinnison	Dave	1996-03-16 00:00:00.000	1
5	5	Bender	Eric	2007-05-17 00:00:00.000	1
6	6	Kendall	Lisa	2001-11-15 00:00:00.000	4

20 rows

Figure 14.3 Result from querying Employee table.

Dynamic DDL statements

Dynamic SQL allows a single changed variable to completely alter what type of SQL statement runs as a result of that change.

Dynamic SQL is pretty cool, but it must be written correctly. It is fairly clear what we are trying to accomplish with these two statements:

```
SELECT * FROM MgmtTraining
SELECT * FROM 'MgmtTraining'
```

```
MESSAGES
Msg 102, Level 15, State 1, Line 1
Incorrect syntax near 'MgmtTraining'.
```
0 rows

Figure 14.4 SELECT * FROM 'MgmtTraining' returned an error message.

The first line queries SQL to return all the records from the management training table. The second line tries to SELECT all the fields FROM the string 'MgmtTraining'.(Figure 14.4). By this point we should all know that SELECT * FROM 'MgmtTraining' (as a string) is not going to work. We either need to put the entire statement into a string and execute it, or the statement needs to be object based like the first line.

To begin writing a dynamic SQL statement, take a look at the following code:

```
DECLARE @TableName NVARCHAR(50)
SET @TableName = 'MgmtTraining'
SELECT * FROM @TableName
```

We know SELECT * FROM @variable in an object based query will return an error message. To turn this into a dynamic statement there are a few more steps. There needs to be a variable to hold the SELECT * FROM part of the query. Let's declare @Query and set it to equal SELECT * FROM:

```
DECLARE @Query NVARCHAR(50)
DECLARE @TableName NVARCHAR(50)
SET @Query = 'SELECT * FROM '
SET @TableName = 'MgmtTraining'
```

We have our query set as @Query and our table set as @TableName. To combine them so they execute together use the familiar EXEC() command from earlier.

```
DECLARE @Query NVARCHAR(50)
DECLARE @TableName NVARCHAR(50)
SET @Query = 'SELECT * FROM '
SET @TableName = 'MgmtTraining'
EXEC (@Query + @TableName)
```

	ClassID	ClassName	ClassDurationHours	ApprovedDate
1	1	Embracing Diversity	12	2007-01-01...
2	2	Interviewing	6	2007-01-15...
3	3	Difficult Negotiations	30	2008-02-12...
4	4	Empowering Others	18	2012-08-01...
5	8	Passing Certifications	13	2012-08-01...
6	9	Effective Communications	35	2012-08-01...

7 rows

Figure 14.5 Result from querying the MgmtTraining table.

In Figure 14.5 the EXEC() command returned the MgmtTraining table records successfully with a Dynamic SQL statement.

Let's take what we know and create a stored procedure that queries any table we choose. For instance, if we pass in Employee, it will query the Employee table and if we pass in Location, the stored procedure will query from the Location table. As in all stored procedures we will start with a CREATE PROC command. Let's have it pass in any table we choose as the variable @TableName. We know that @TableName cannot be in an object based query because the entire statement has to be either executed entirely as a string or be entirely object based:

```
CREATE PROC GeneralQuery @TableName NVARCHAR(50)
AS
SELECT * FROM @TableName
GO
```

Since SELECT * FROM is object based and @TableName is a variable rather than a hard coded object it will not work. We have to create the stored procedure properly in order for an EXEC() command to run successfully. All parts of the query have to be within the string:

```
CREATE PROC GeneralQuery @TableName NVARCHAR(50)
AS
DECLARE @SQL NVARCHAR(1000)
SET @SQL = 'SELECT * FROM ' + @TableName
EXEC (@SQL)
GO
```

Notice we declared @SQL equal to 'SELECT * FROM' concatenated to @TableName. Then we set the action of the GeneralQuery stored procedure by adding the EXEC (@SQL) statement. Once this is run the only thing left to do is call on it:

```
EXEC GeneralQuery 'MgmtTraining'
```

	ClassID	ClassName	ClassDurationHours	ApprovedDate
1	1	Embracing Diversity	12	2007-01-01...
2	2	Interviewing	6	2007-01-15...
3	3	Difficult Negotiations	30	2008-02-12...
4	4	Empowering Others	18	2012-08-01...
5	8	Passing Certifications	13	2012-08-01...
6	9	Effective Communications	35	2012-08-01...

7 rows

Figure 14.6 Result from using stored procedure to query MgmtTraining table.

The GeneralQuery stored procedure executes just fine. The MgmtTraining table was passed in and its records returned as seen in Figure 14.6. This stored procedure can be executed passing in any table we choose. In Figure 14.7 the Location table was passed in and the same stored procedure now returned all the records from the Location table:

```
EXEC GeneralQuery 'Location'
```

	LocationID	street	city	state	Latitude	Longitude
1	1	111 First ST	Seattle	WA	47.455	-122.231
2	2	222 Second AVE	Boston	MA	42.372	-71.0298
3	3	333 Third PL	Chicago	IL	41.953	-87.643
4	4	444 Ruby ST	Spokane	WA	47.668	-117.529
5	5	1595 Main	Philadelphia	PA	39.888	-75.251
6	6	915 Wallaby Drive	Sydney	NULL	-33.876	151.315

6 rows

Figure 14.7 Result from using stored procedure to query the location table.

Lab 14.1: Exec Dynamic SQL

Lab Prep: Each lab has one or more Skill Checks. Start with Skill Check 1 and proceed until reaching the Points to Ponder section.

Before beginning this lab, verify that SQL Server 2012 is properly installed and operating. Before running the lab setup script for resetting the database (SQLQueries2012Vol4Chapter14.1Setup.sql), please make sure to close all query windows within SSMS. An open query window pointing to a database context can lock that database preventing it from updating when the script is executing. A simple way to assure all query windows are closed, is to exit out of SSMS, then open a new instance of SSMS, and lastly run the setup script.

Skill Check 1: You are given the following code:

```
CREATE PROC GeneralDatabase @DbName NVARCHAR(50)
AS
DECLARE @SQL NVARCHAR(1000)

--Put in Missing code here

EXEC (@SQL)
GO
```

In the JProCo database, you need the GeneralDatabase stored procedure to create a database. The new database will be named whatever you pass in to the @DbName parameter. Replace the comment with the correct dynamic SQL statement. Create the DropGeneralDatabase stored procedure and test it by creating the SkillCheck14 database. When you are done your screen should resemble Figure 14.8.

```
EXEC GeneralDatabase 'SkillCheck14'
GO
```

MESSAGES
Command(s) completed successfully
0 rows

Figure 14.8 Results of Skill Check 1.

Skill Check 2: You are given the follow code:

```
ALTER PROC DropGeneralDatabase @DbName NVARCHAR(50)
AS
DECLARE @SQL NVARCHAR(1000)
--Put in Missing code here
EXEC (@SQL)
GO
```

In the JProCo database, you need the DropGeneralDatabase stored procedure to drop a database if it exists based on the database name that you pass in to the @DbName parameter. Replace the comment with the correct dynamic SQL statement. Create the GeneralDatabase stored procedure and test by dropping the SkillCheck14 database. When you are done your screen should resemble Figure 14.9.

```
EXEC DropGeneralDatabase 'SkillCheck14'
GO
```

MESSAGES
Command(s) completed successfully
0 rows

Figure 14.9 Results of Skill Check 2.

Skill Check 3: You are given the follow code:

```
SET @SqlQuery = 'SELECT * FROM Employee WHERE EmpID IN ('+
@List + ')'
```

Declare the @List variable so it runs for Employee 1 and 2 and execute the @SqlQuery. When you are done your screen should resemble Figure 14.10.

```
EXEC (@SqlQuery)
```

	EmpID	LastName	FirstName	HireDate	LocationID	ManagerID	Status
1	1	Adams	Alex	2001-01-01…	1	11	On Leave
2	2	Brown	Barry	2002-08-12…	1	11	Active

2 rows

Figure 14.10 Results of Skill Check 3.

Answer Code: The T-SQL code to this lab can be found in the downloadable files in a file named Lab14.1_DynamicSQL.sql.

Points to Ponder - Exec Dynamic SQL

1. With dynamic SQL you can put a SQL statement inside a variable and execute it as a statement.
2. Build your SQL statement as a varchar first, and then execute that as a statement.
3. If you use dynamic SQL in your stored procedure there is no cached Execution Plan which can result in a loss of performance (Even if it's inside a stored procedure).

sp_executesql

We learned that EXEC can turn a string into a running SQL statement. This is true but is only one of the two ways to do this. Another way is to use the built in system stored procedure sp_executesql.

Before we dive into the sp_executesql system stored procedure let's do a quick recap. Look at following code:

```
SELECT * FROM Employee
DECLARE @SQL NVARCHAR(200) = 'SELECT * FROM Employee'
EXEC (@SQL)
```

We know that both of these queries do exactly the same thing. The first query uses object based code and the second query is using dynamic SQL. Both will return all the records from the Employee table.

Using sp_executesql

Let's use the same simple query as a starting point:

```
DECLARE @SQL NVARCHAR(200) = 'SELECT * FROM Employee'
EXEC (@SQL)
```

Instead of executing the @SQL directly we can call on the system stored procedure sp_executesql and pass in the variable @spSQL that represents the query:

```
DECLARE @spSQL NVARCHAR(200) = 'SELECT * FROM Employee'
EXEC sp_executesql @spSQL
```

	EmpID	LastName	FirstName	HireDate	LocationID
1	1	Adams	Alex	2001-01-01...	1
2	2	Brown	Barry	2002-08-12...	1
3	3	Osako	Lee	1999-09-01...	2
4	4	Kinnison	Dave	1996-03-16...	1
5	5	Bender	Eric	2007-05-17...	1
6	6	Kendall	Lisa	2001-11-15...	4

20 rows

Figure 14.11 Result using the sp_executesql to query the Employee table.

In Figure 14.11 the sp_executesql stored procedure returned all the records from the Employee table just as before. So far it appears that sp_executesql does the same thing as with the EXEC command but with more typing. The benefit of using sp_executesql in this example is not apparent, but as we dive deeper the advantages will become clear.

sp_executesql Parameters

A straight forward observation would be that not all queries are as simple as SELECT * FROM Employee. Sometimes seeing every employee is too much data. We may want to see just the employees with a LastName of Brown, Adams, or Smith:

```
SELECT * FROM Employee WHERE LastName = 'Brown'
SELECT * FROM Employee WHERE LastName = 'Adams'
SELECT * FROM Employee WHERE LastName = 'Smith'
```

Hard coding the LastName into the criteria is not efficient coding when there are constantly changing variable values for LastName. It would better to use a variable for LastName and set that variable to be used by the query. To return all the employees with a last name of Smith we are not going to hard code 'Smith', we will use the variable @EmpLastName. We can then change the way this query runs just by changing the value of the variable. The following code shows our idea but is not yet complete and will not run:

```
DECLARE @SQL NVARCHAR(200)
SET @SQL = 'SELECT * FROM Employee WHERE LastName = @EmpLastName'
```

Since there is the new variable @EmpLastName it would seem we should use a declare statement and set the value for use by the query. In this case we will call it @SQL as a NVARCHAR (30) data type. We will attempt to pass in the @EmpLastName value of Smith within the EXEC() command. The following example shows the EXEC statement did not accept the variable value and resulted in an error message (Figure 14.12).

```
DECLARE @SQL NVARCHAR(200)
SET @SQL = 'SELECT * FROM Employee WHERE LastName = @EmpLastName'
DECLARE @EmpLastName NVARCHAR(30)
EXEC (@SQL, @EmpLastName = 'Smith')
```

```
Messages
Msg 102, Level 15, State 3, Line 4
Incorrect syntax near ')'.
                                                                    0 rows
```

Figure 14.12 Error message. Dynamic SQL cannot swap variables without sp_executesql procedure.

The EXEC() command can only execute a concatenated string and is not capable of swapping variable values. Our goal is to execute the dynamic SQL, and swap out the @EmpLastName variable for a set value (such as 'Smith').

To swap out variables in real time, use the sp_executesql system stored procedure. Sp_executesql can swap out dynamic parameters right before execution. This code will execute the @SQL query and replace the @EmpLastName with Smith.

```
DECLARE @SQL NVARCHAR(200)
SET @SQL = 'SELECT * FROM Employee WHERE LastName = @EmpLastName'
EXEC sp_executesql @SQL, N'@EmpLastName NVARCHAR(50)', @EmpLastName = 'Smith'
```

	EmpID	LastName	FirstName	HireDate	LocationID	ManagerID	Status
1	11	Smith	Sally	1989-04-01...	1	NULL	Active
2	14	Smith	Janis	2009-10-18...	1	4	Active

2 rows

Figure 14.13 Result using sp_executesql to swap variables in dynamic code.

The sp_executesql stored procedure knows when a variable is passed in that the variable is being declared. Notice in the code (Figure 14.13) the DECLARE command is not present. The declaration is part of the parameter being passed in for the @EmpLastName variable. DECLARE is taken care of in the sp_executesql stored procedure. Also notice the "N" in this line of code. The "N" is Unicode and stands for "National Language Character Set" and lets the stored procedure know that an NCHAR, NVARCHAR or NTEXT value is being passed in rather than a CHAR, VARCHAR or TEXT. The "N" Unicode also helps the extended character sets fit into columns of database applications.

sp_executesql Performance

The contents of sp_executesql are compiled and saved as an Execution Plan resulting in a potential performance gain for stored procedures. Look at this next query from the first Joes2Pros book where we used the BETWEEN keyword to find a range of values.

```
DECLARE @Min MONEY = 15000
DECLARE @Max MONEY = 25000
SELECT * FROM [Grant] WHERE Amount BETWEEN @Min AND @Max
```

	GrantID	GrantName	EmpID	Amount
1	002	K-Land fund trust	2	16750.00
2	003	Robert@BigStarBank.com	7	18100.00
3	005	BIG 6's Foundation%	4	22180.00
4	006	TALTA_Kishan International	3	18100.00
5	009	Thank you @.com	11	22500.00
6	011	Big Giver Tom	7	19000.00

6 rows

Figure 14.14 The Grant table where amounts are between 15000 and 25000.

In Figure 14.14 we find all the grants between 15,000 and 25,000. Now let's turn this SELECT Statement with these two variables into dynamic SQL. The sp_executesql stored procedure can handle many variables. Start by declaring the @SQL string as an NVARCHAR(200) and set it equal to the exact same query in Figure 14.14. Set each of the variables as a MONEY type and pass in their values.

```
DECLARE @SQL NVARCHAR(200)
SET @SQL = 'SELECT * FROM [Grant] WHERE Amount BETWEEN @Min AND @Max'
EXEC sp_executesql @SQL, N'@Min MONEY, @Max MONEY', @Min = 15000, @Max = 25000
```

	GrantID	GrantName	EmpID	Amount
1	002	K-Land fund trust	2	16750.00
2	003	Robert@BigStarBank.com	7	18100.00
3	005	BIG 6's Foundation%	4	22180.00
4	006	TALTA_Kishan International	3	18100.00
5	009	Thank you @.com	11	22500.00
6	011	Big Giver Tom	7	19000.00

6 rows

Figure 14.15 Result using sp_executesql to query the Grant table.

Notice in Figure 14.15 the sp_executesql returned all six records that are between 15,000 and 25,000. How would you look for the records between 20,000 and 25,000? Simply change the variable values and then the sp_executesql stored procedure adapts to the new dynamic SQL and its values.

Lab 14.2: sp_executesql

Lab Prep: Lab Prep: Each lab has one or more Skill Checks. Start with Skill Check 1 and proceed until reaching the Points to Ponder section.

Before beginning this lab, verify that SQL Server 2012 is properly installed and operating. Before running the lab setup script for resetting the database (SQLQueries2012Vol4Chapter14.2Setup.sql), please make sure to close all query windows within SSMS. An open query window pointing to a database context can lock that database preventing it from updating when the script is executing. A simple way to assure all query windows are closed, is to exit out of SSMS, then open a new instance of SSMS, and lastly run the setup script.

Skill Check 1: Turn this query into dynamic SQL that runs from the sp_executesql:

```
DECLARE @ClassTime INT = 12
SELECT *
FROM MgmtTraining
WHERE ClassDurationHours > @ClassTime
```

The body of the code should be in the @SQL variable and the code you pass into the sp_executesql stored procedure should be called @ClassTime.

	ClassID	ClassName	ClassDurationHours	ApprovedDate
1	3	Difficult Negotiations	30	2008-02-12…
2	4	Empowering Others	18	2012-08-28…
3	6	Passing Certifications	13	2012-08-28…
4	7	Effective Communications	35	2012-08-28…
5	8	Story Presentations	19	2012-08-28…

5 rows

Figure 14.16 Skill Check 1.

Chapter 14. Dynamic SQL

Skill Check 2: Turn this query into dynamic SQL that runs from the sp_executesql:

```
DECLARE @MgrID INT = 11
DECLARE @Pay MONEY = 25000
SELECT em.*, pr.YearlySalary
FROM Employee AS em
INNER JOIN PayRates AS pr
ON em.EmpID = pr.EmpID
WHERE em.ManagerID = @MgrID
AND pr.YearlySalary > @Pay
```

The body of the code should be in the @SQL variable and the two parameters you pass into the sp_executesql stored procedure should be called @MgrID and @Pay.

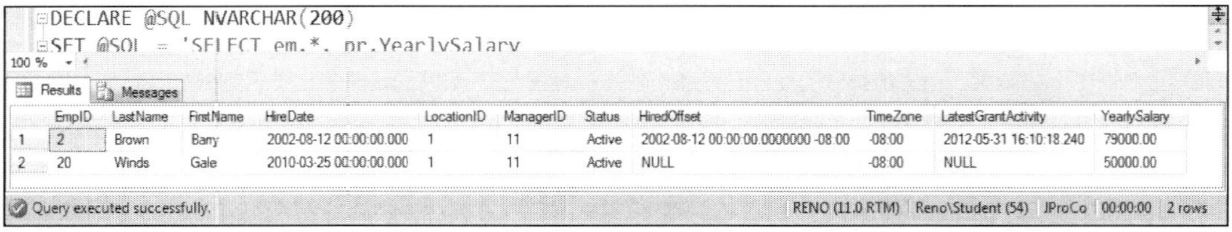

Figure 14.17 Skill Check 2.

Answer Code: The T-SQL code to this lab can be found in the downloadable files in a file named Lab14.2_sp_executeSql.sql.

Points to Ponder - sp_executesql

1. sp_executesql is a system stored procedure that executes your dynamic SQL similarly to that of the "exec" command.
2. In sp_executesql, the first parameter is the SQL statement followed by the list of parameters separated by commas.
3. sp_executesql parameters must be entered in a specific order or an error message will occur.
4. The contents of sp_executesql are compiled and saved as an Execution Plan resulting in a potential performance gain for stored procedures.
5. The "N" is Unicode and stands for "National Language Character Set".

Dynamic Admin Tasks

Queries are not the only thing that can be automated with dynamic SQL. There are administrative tasks that should be automated as well. One of the most common uses of Dynamic SQL is to perform administrative tasks. This book is on development and assumes readers have minimal exposure to the skills in the SQL Admin series. To be fair we are going to dedicate the first half of this section to introducing the BACKUP DATABASE command and make sure its process is understood. Once the backup process becomes easy, then we will introduce the options for automating the backup process with dynamic SQL. For now let's get a good start with foundational knowledge.

Let's start by looking at some basic administration tasks. The most common is backing up the database. Most of us have learned this lesson through the pain of losing family photos, or important documents that were stored on the computer and not backed up. Backing up a database to a file is very important to protect it from both computer and human error. Being able to access a backup file and to restore a database gives the programmer security and potentially saves the company they are working for a lot of money.

We should start with backing up the JProCo database into the Joes2Pros folder on the C: drive. This is where the Sql2012Vol4CompanionCD should have been downloaded from the Joes2Pros web site as seen in Figure 14.18.

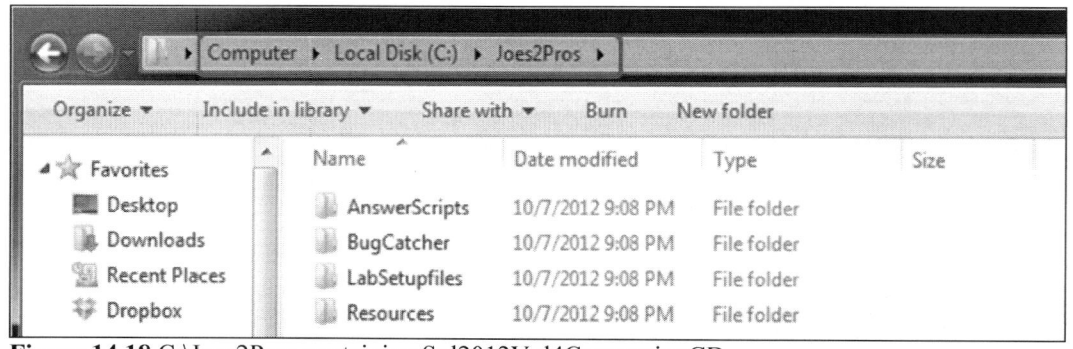

Figure 14.18 C:\Joes2Pros containing Sql2012Vol4CompanionCD

Let's open SQL Server Management Studio and a new query window and backup the JProCo database to our C: drive using the BACKUP DATABASE command. To finalize this process, create a path to C:\Joes2Pros and a file name of JProCo using the .bak extension.

```
BACKUP DATABASE JProCo TO DISK = 'C:\Joes2Pros\JProCo.bak'
GO
```

```
Messages
Processed 672 pages for database 'JProCo', file 'JProCo' on file 1.
Processed 9 pages for database 'JProCo', file 'JProCo_log' on file 1.
BACKUP DATABASE successfully processed 681 pages in 1.374 seconds (3.869
MB/sec).
                                                                   0 rows
```

Figure 14.19 JProCo database backed up successfully.

In Figure 14.19 the message tells us some information about the number of pages processed, that it was successfully processed and that it took 1.374 seconds to run.

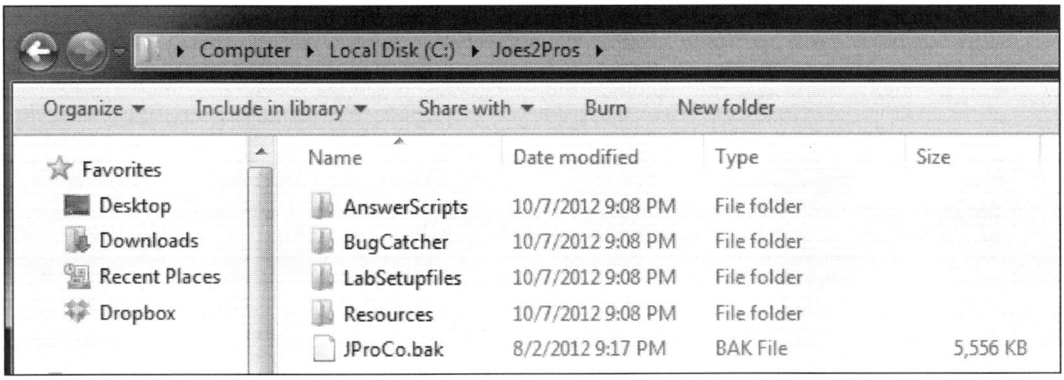

Figure 14.20 you will see the backup file (JProCo.bak) in the Windows Explorer. We now have the JProCo.bak file with a saved (modified) date of 8/2/2012 which is about 5.6MB.

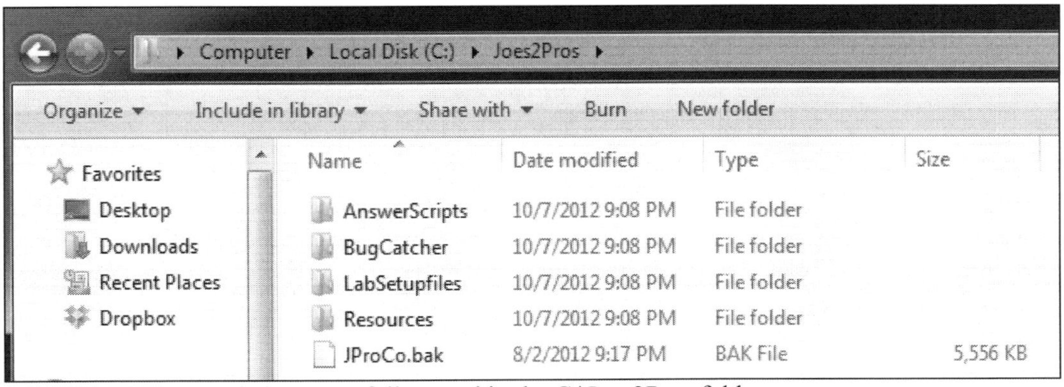

Figure 14.20 JProCo.bak successfully saved in the C:\Joes2Pros folder.

A new day has arrived and we need to do nightly backups. Today is August 3rd, yesterday was the 2nd. What happens if we run this backup statement using the exact same filename from Figure 14.19? Are we going to destroy the data from August 2nd? A good way to back up data is in a series or history of backups. Give

547

www.Joes2Pros.com

each backup a unique name like JProCo802.bak and JProCo803.bak for 08/02 and 08/03 respectively. In this next example however we kept the same backup name. What is your prediction? Do we wipe out the old data from August 2nd? Let's take the exact same code from yesterday, (Figure 14.19) and run it now that it is August 3rd.

```
BACKUP DATABASE JProCo TO DISK = 'C:\Joes2Pros\JProCo.bak'
GO
```

```
Messages
Processed 672 pages for database 'JProCo', file 'JProCo' on file 2.
Processed 2 pages for database 'JProCo', file 'JProCo_log' on file 2.
BACKUP DATABASE successfully processed 674 pages in 0.553 seconds (9.521 MB/sec).

                                                                    0 rows
```
Figure 14.21 JProCo successfully backed up into the same JProCo.bak file from the previous day.

In Figure 14.21 we see JProCo was successfully processed. It didn't give us a warning, so what happened to the file? In Figure 14.22 Windows Explorer shows there is still just one JProCo.bak file and it was modified on 8/3/2012 at 9:22pm but now it is twice as big from 5.6MB to 11MB.

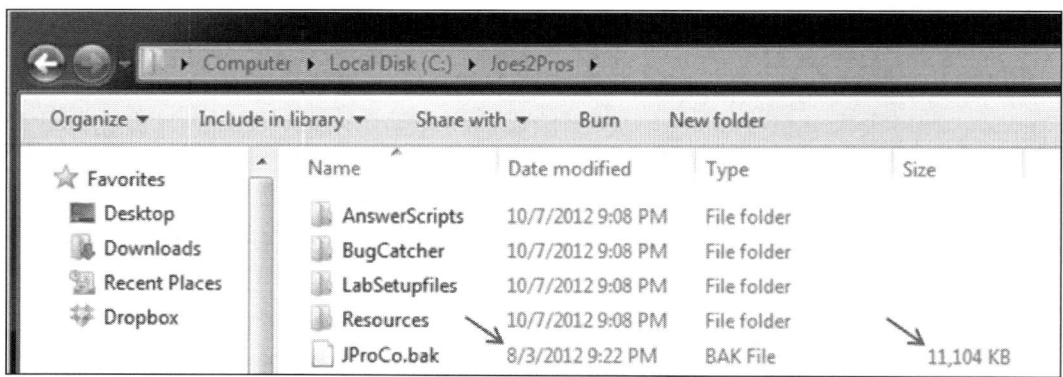

Figure 14.22 The JProCo.bak file is now twice as big.

By running the backup twice with the same filename it packaged two backup sets into one file. This is perfectly valid, although it can be confusing if you need to restore from a specific point. A better idea is to make one backup set with each file having a unique filename.

Database Backup Statement

Have you ever copied a file to a disk or USB drive? Most of the time we do this using Windows Explorer with a drag and drop operation. We may also be aware that we can use the command line utility (which looks like DOS) to copy that same file to your disk or USB drive. Either way we choose to do this, the same end results are our file was copied.

A database backup is a file that contains all your tables, relations, constraints and data into one neat little packaged file. From this file you can restore your database after disaster strikes.

Many say that this is the most important role as a database professional to ensure there are adequate backups on hand. In times of a disaster companies can rebuild applications, web, and database servers. On the other hand if they can't recover the data, it is nearly impossible to recreate it.

By following a step-by-step approach you will see the functionality of the code develop. To begin creating dynamic SQL to perform the backup function let's start with this simple statement.

```
DECLARE @DbName VARCHAR(100)
SET @DbName = 'dbBasics'
SELECT @DbName
```

(No column name)
1 dbBasics

1 rows

Figure 14.23 Variable @DbName displayed as dbBasics.

In Figure 14.23 we declare a variable, we set the variable and show the variable. This very straight forward code shows us exactly what we set. To run this as dynamic SQL we will have to make a path such as C:\Joes2Pros\. Then declare that path variable to be a VARCHAR type and set the variable to equal to the path of C:\Joes2Pros.

```
DECLARE @DbName VARCHAR(100)
SET @DbName = 'DbBasics'
DECLARE @Path VARCHAR(100) = 'C:\Joes2Pros\'
SELECT @Path
```

(No column name)
1 C:\Joes2Pros\

1 rows

Figure 14.24 Declared @Path and displayed it as c:\Joes2Pros.

In the next step of this progression, let's associate the path with the dbBasics database. By concatenating the @DbName onto the path, dbBasics will become part of the path as seen in Figure 14.25.

Chapter 14. Dynamic SQL

```sql
DECLARE @DbName VARCHAR(100)
SET @DbName = 'dbBasics'
DECLARE @Path VARCHAR(100) = 'C:\Joes2Pros\' + @DbName
SELECT @Path
```

(No column name)
C:\Joes2Pros\DbBasics

1 rows

Figure 14.25 @DbName is added to the path and displayed as dbBasics.

Look at the result in Figure 14.25 and compare it to the path in the code we wrote earlier in this chapter:

```sql
BACKUP DATABASE JProCo TO DISK = 'C:\Joes2Pros\JProCo.bak'
```

We now have a path to the C:\Joes2Pros folder but are backing up dbBasics instead of the JProCo database to that location. What is missing from our path in Figure 14.25? The only thing left now for the path to be complete is to concatenate the .bak extension to the end of the path.

```sql
DECLARE @DbName VARCHAR(100)
SET @DbName = 'dbBasics'
DECLARE @Path VARCHAR(100) = 'C:\Joes2Pros\' + @DbName + '.bak'
SELECT @Path
```

	(No column name)
1	C:\Joes2Pros\DbBasics.bak

1 rows

Figure 14.26 .bak is concatenated to the @Path variable.

Now we see in Figure 14.26 our path is complete. To turn the code we are building into dynamic SQL add a SELECT statement that concatenates BACKUP DATABASE dbBasics TO DISK = to the @Path variable.

```sql
DECLARE @DbName VARCHAR(100)
SET @DbName = 'dbBasics'
DECLARE @Path VARCHAR(100) = 'C:\Joes2Pros\' + @DbName + '.bak'
SELECT ('BACKUP DATABASE dbBasics TO DISK = ' + @Path)
```

	Messages
1	BACKUP DATABASE dbBasics TO DISK = C:\Joes2Pros\dbBasics.bak

1 rows

Figure 14.27 Print returned a message similar to functional backup code.

Copy the message from Figure 14.27 into SQL Server Management Studio and compare it to the backup code we wrote for the JProCo database earlier in this section:

```
BACKUP DATABASE dbBasics TO DISK = C:\Joes2Pros\dbBasics.bak
BACKUP DATABASE JProCo TO DISK = 'C:\Joes2Pros\JProCo.bak'
```

Notice the path portion of the statement we copied isn't a string. How do we get dynamic SQL to embed single quotes around the path portion of the statement? In *SQL Queries 2012 Joes 2 Pros Volume 1* we had an exercise in querying Irish names like O'Haire and O'Neil. Those names have single quotes embedded in them. Two single quotes in a row returns one single quote. So we'll add a pair at the beginning and end of the path.

```
DECLARE @DbName VARCHAR(100)
SET @DbName = 'dbBasics'
DECLARE @Path VARCHAR(100) = '''C:\Joes2Pros\' + @DbName + '.Bak'''
PRINT 'BACKUP DATABASE dbBasics TO DISK = ' + @Path
```

Messages
1 BACKUP DATABASE dbBasics TO DISK = 'C:\Joes2Pros\dbBasics.Bak'
1 rows

Figure 14.28 Single quotes added to code string.

One more side-by-side comparison of the result in Figure 14.28 to our original backup statement syntax style shows that they are identical:

```
BACKUP DATABASE dbBasics TO DISK =
'C:\Joes2Pros\dbBasics.bak'
BACKUP DATABASE JProCo TO DISK = 'C:\Joes2Pros\JProCo.bak'
```

All that is needed to run a backup using dynamic SQL is to execute this code instead of printing it:

```
DECLARE @DbName VARCHAR(100)
SET @DbName = 'dbBasics'
DECLARE @Path VARCHAR(100) = '''C:\Joes2Pros\' + @DbName +
'.bak'''
EXEC ('BACKUP DATABASE dbBasics TO DISK = ' + @Path)
```

```
Messages
Processed 288 pages for database 'dbBasics', file 'dbBasics' on file 1.
Processed 4 pages for database 'dbBasics', file 'dbBasics_log' on file 1.
BACKUP DATABASE successfully processed 292 pages in 0.574 seconds (3.974
MB/sec).
                                                                    1 rows
```

Figure 14.29 dbBasics successfully backed up with Dynamic SQL.

In Figure 14.29 we see that our dynamic SQL ran successfully. Open Windows Explorer to verify the backup file for the dbBasics database was created in the Joes2Pros folder on the C:\ drive of the computer.

Figure 14.30 dbBasics.bak saved in the C:\Joes2Pros\ dbBasics.bak file.

We have already backed up the dbBasics and JProCo databases. The Joes2Pros practice company has several more databases that need to be backed up. We need to also backup the dbMovie database. This dynamic SQL could be even more flexible. What if we SET the @DbName variable value equal to dbMovie:

```
DECLARE @DbName VARCHAR(100)
SET @DbName = 'dbMovie'
DECLARE @Path VARCHAR(100) =
'''C:\Joes2Pros\' + @DbName + '.Bak'''
EXEC ('BACKUP DATABASE dbBasics TO DISK = ' + @Path)
```

This is not going to work. Although we have changed the value of the @DbName variable, we have not changed the 'BACKUP DATABASE dbBasics' statement to use the @DbName variable. It will simply back up the dbBasics database under the name "DbMovie". Changing the @DbName variable will only change the path. Take a look at the following statement:

```
EXEC ('BACKUP DATABASE dbBasics TO DISK = ' + @Path)
```

Let's simplify the EXEC() command by declaring a new variable called @Command and make it a VARCHAR(100). Our goal here is to replace the hardcoded dbBasics with the @DbName variable.

```
DECLARE @DbName VARCHAR(100)
SET @DbName = 'dbMovie'
DECLARE @Path VARCHAR(100) = '''C:\Joes2Pros\' + @DbName + '.Bak'''
DECLARE @Command VARCHAR(100) = 'BACKUP DATABASE '+ @DbName + ' TO DISK = ' + @Path
EXEC (@Command)
```

```
Messages
Processed 272 pages for database 'dbMovie', file 'dbMovie' on file 1.
Processed 7 pages for database 'dbMovie', file 'dbMovie_log' on file 1.
BACKUP DATABASE successfully processed 279 pages in 0.656 seconds (3.322 MB/sec).
                                                                    1 rows
```

Figure 14.31 dbMovie successfully backed up in the C:\Joes2Pros\dbMovie.bak file.

Figure 14.32 dbMovie successfully backed up in the C:\Joes2Pros\dbMovie.bak file.

Figure 14.31 shows that the dbMovie database was successfully backed up and Figure 14.32 shows us in Windows Explorer that the dbMovie backup and dbBasics backup are different sizes and not the same backup.

Dynamic Date Stamps

In this chapter we backed up the JProCo database on August 2nd and then again on August 3rd however, since we used the same name both backups are contained in the same 11MB file. It is now August 4th and it is time to backup JProCo again. Since we have made this backup process somewhat dynamic let's finish it and make it completely dynamic. We can do this by adding one more variable in the path called @Date. DECLARE it as a VARCHAR(100) and set it equal to 2012August04.

```
DECLARE @DbName VARCHAR(100)
SET @DbName = 'JProCo'
DECLARE @Date VARCHAR(100) = '2012August04'
DECLARE @Path VARCHAR(100) = '''C:\Joes2Pros\' + @DbName +
@Date +'.Bak'''
DECLARE @Command VARCHAR(100) = 'BACKUP DATABASE '+ @DbName
+ ' TO DISK = ' + @Path
EXEC (@Command)
```

Messages
Processed 688 pages for database 'JProCo', file 'JProCo' on file 1.
Processed 3 pages for database 'JProCo', file 'JProCo_log' on file 1.
BACKUP DATABASE successfully processed 691 pages in 0.909 seconds (5.938 MB/sec).
1 rows

Figure 14.33 JProCo database successfully backed up with a unique filename.

Figure 14.33 shows the JProCo database backed up successfully and when we open Windows explorer we see the JProCo2012August04.Bak file with a modified date of 8/4/2012 at 9:33pm and is 5.6MB (Figure 14.34). From now on when we run this dynamic SQL we merely change the @DbName to the correct database and the @date variable to the correct date and run the back up.

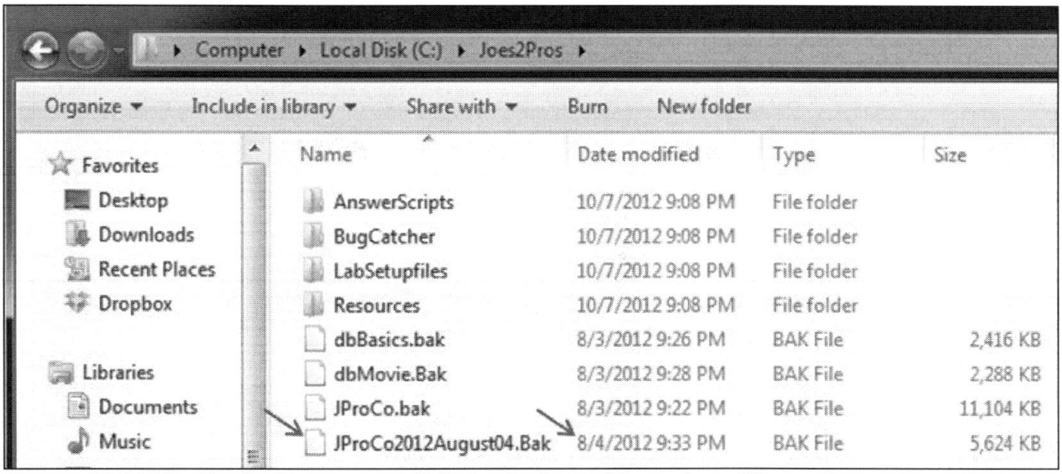

Figure 14.34 JProCo database successfully backed up with a unique filename.

Exec Dynamic SQL Drawbacks

There are two main drawbacks to dynamic SQL. One drawback is security and the other is performance. Let's talk about the security risk first with SQL Injection. We will then talk about dynamic SQL in stored procedures and its effect on performance.

SQL Injection

Pretend you hate to eat broccoli. If simply asked, do you like broccoli?, then your answer would be no. If asked, do you like broccoli or does 1=1? What would be the honest answer? The answer is NO for liking broccoli but is YES for does 1=1. With an OR in your criteria only one question has to be true for a "yes" answer. If a speaker asks his audience for everyone to stand whose last name is either Smith or Not Smith everyone would stand. This is an important concept for understanding SQL injection. In very simple terms, the WHERE clause looks for a YES answer to show you each record. With that in mind look at these two queries:

```
SELECT *
FROM Employee
WHERE EmpID = 1
```

Figure 14.35 This query shows the record for EmpID 1.

```
SELECT *
FROM Employee
WHERE EmpID = 1 OR 1 = 1
```

Figure 14.36 Since one equals one with every record, every record is returned. There was no record that caused 1 to not equal 1.

The WHERE clause in the query from Figure 14.35 looked at each record and asked is the EmpID is equal to 1. If the answer is true it returns that record, if false it does not. Only one record in Figure 14.35 has an EmpID equal to 1. The WHERE clause in Figure 14.36 looked at each record and asked is the EmpID equal to 1 or does 1 equal 1. Since 1 will always equal 1 the query returned every record.

Let's use a very innocent looking example of a dynamic SQL statement that puts together a simple query with the SELECT, FROM and WHERE clauses. The code in Figure 14.37 will query all records with EmpID of 1 from the Employee table.

```
DECLARE @Select NVARCHAR(50) = 'SELECT * '
DECLARE @From NVARCHAR(50) = 'FROM Employee '
DECLARE @Where NVARCHAR(50) = 'WHERE EmpID = 1'
EXEC (@Select + @From + @Where)
```

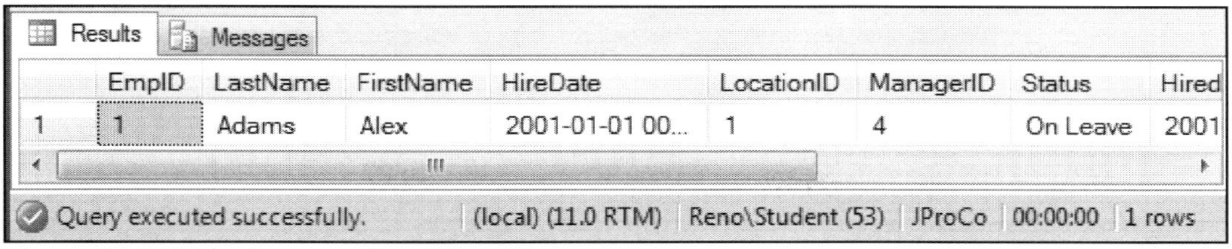

	EmpID	LastName	FirstName	HireDate	LocationID	ManagerID	Status	Hired
1	1	Adams	Alex	2001-01-01 00...	1	4	On Leave	2001

Figure 14.37 This shows we found EmpID one.

It is likely that more than employee one will need to be queried. Perhaps we want this to be more flexible. The following code is set up to allow a user to select the employee number. We only intend to show one employee record at a time and this appears to work.

```
DECLARE @Select NVARCHAR(50) = 'SELECT * '
DECLARE @From NVARCHAR(50) = 'FROM Employee '
DECLARE @Where NVARCHAR(50) = 'WHERE EmpID = '
DECLARE @UserSelection NVARCHAR(50) = '1'
EXEC (@Select + @From + @Where + @UserSelection)
```

	EmpID	LastName	FirstName	HireDate	LocationID	ManagerID	Status	Hired
1	1	Adams	Alex	2001-01-01 00...	1	4	On Leave	2001

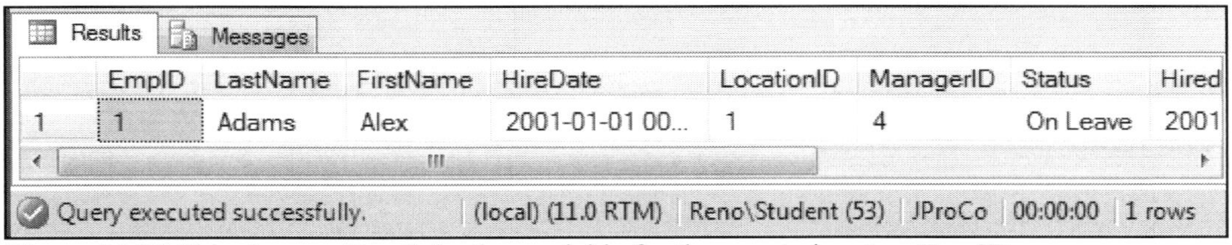

Figure 14.38 This shows a UserSelection variable for the user to input an EmpID

Let's say for the sake of this example that the EmpID is input for the @UserSelection variable through a website or other SQL data channel. And instead of entering an actual EmpID we are going to hack the system and enter a code fragment that changes the query such as "1 or 1=1". Now here is the trick to watch out for. With character data you can answer any way you want. If we input our employee number as '1 OR 1 = 1' then we get all the records.

```
DECLARE @Select NVARCHAR(50) = 'SELECT * '
DECLARE @From NVARCHAR(50) = 'FROM Employee '
DECLARE @Where NVARCHAR(50) = 'WHERE EmpID = '
DECLARE @UserSelection NVARCHAR(50) = '1 OR 1 = 1'
EXEC (@Select + @From + @Where + @UserSelection)
```

	EmpID	LastName	FirstName	HireDate	LocationID	ManagerID	Status
1	1	Adams	Alex	2001-01-01 00:0...	1	4	On Leave
2	2	Brown	Barry	2002-08-12 00:0...	1	11	Active
3	3	Osako	Lee	1999-09-01 00:0...	2	11	Active
4	4	Kinnison	Dave	1996-03-16 00:0...	1	11	Has Tenure
5	5	Bender	Eric	2007-05-17 00:0...	1	11	Active
6	6	Kendall	Lisa	2001-11-15 00:0...	4	4	Active

Query executed successfully.   (local) (11.0 RTM)   Reno\Student (53)   JProCo   00:00:00   20 rows

Figure 14.39 This shows all the records of the employee table were returned.

The intent is to only give information to the employee based on the assumption they have to know their EmpID. In this example the database could be hacked using SQL injection such as adding "1 or 1=1" for the user selection. In Figure 14.39 the query returned every record by "tricking" the query into having every record complying with the WHERE clause.

SQL injection is a technique where someone makes an entry that causes SQL to execute statements that compromise database security. SQL injection is possible with many dynamic SQL statements.

Dynamic SQL Performance

Every query in SQL Server needs a query Execution Plan. If one does not exist then SQL takes the time to create one. When you run a query the first time, SQL Server builds the query Execution Plan before it runs the query. If you run the same query again time is saved because SQL Server stores the query Execution Plan in memory. Re-used query Execution Plans save query execution time. If you use dynamic SQL in your stored procedure there is no cached Execution Plan which can result in a loss of performance (even if it's inside a stored procedure).

Dynamic SQL with Stored Procedures

One giant advantage to using stored procedures is they are not vulnerable to SQL injection. Another advantage of using stored procedures is the query Execution Plan is stored in memory for re-use.

For database security and accuracy of records returned, user input should never feed directly into the construction of ad-hoc query syntax. The user input should instead be taken as a parameter. The following two queries both find the record with an EmpID of one using the EXEC command.

```
DECLARE @SQL NVARCHAR(50) = 'SELECT * FROM Employee WHERE EmpID = '
DECLARE @UserSelection NVARCHAR(50) = '1'
EXEC (@SQL + @UserSelection)
```

	EmpID	LastName	FirstName	HireDate	LocationID	ManagerID	Status	Hired
1	1	Adams	Alex	2001-01-01 00...	1	4	On Leave	2001

Figure 14.40 Using EXEC with a SQL string we were able to query for EmpID one.

```
DECLARE @SQL NVARCHAR(200)
SET @SQL =
'SELECT * FROM Employee WHERE EmpID = @UserSelection'
DECLARE @UserSelection VARCHAR(30)
EXEC sp_executesql @SQL, N'@UserSelection VARCHAR(30)',
@UserSelection = '1'
```

	EmpID	LastName	FirstName	HireDate	LocationID	ManagerID	Status	Hired
1	1	Adams	Alex	2001-01-01 00...	1	4	On Leave	2001

Figure 14.41 Using EXEC with the sp_executesql stored procedure we queried for EmpID one.

The first query used EXEC with a SQL string and the second used EXEC with a system stored procedure. Both queries run fine and return only the record from the Employee table with the specified EmpID of 1 (Figure 14.40, Figure 14.41). Now let's try to hack the database using a basic SQL injection against both queries.

We will add the user input to become '1 or 1=1' to get all the records from the employee table. This technique does indeed get all the records out from the first query (Figure 14.42). The second query will get the same '1 or 1=1' passed in as a parameter to the sp_executesql stored procedure.

```
DECLARE @SQL NVARCHAR(50) = 'SELECT * FROM Employee WHERE EmpID = '
DECLARE @UserSelection NVARCHAR(50) = '1 OR 1 = 1'
EXEC (@SQL + @UserSelection)
```

Chapter 14. Dynamic SQL

	EmpID	LastName	FirstName	HireDate	LocationID	ManagerID	Status
1	1	Adams	Alex	2001-01-01 00:0...	1	4	On Leave
2	2	Brown	Barry	2002-08-12 00:0...	1	11	Active
3	3	Osako	Lee	1999-09-01 00:0...	2	11	Active
4	4	Kinnison	Dave	1996-03-16 00:0...	1	11	Has Tenure
5	5	Bender	Eric	2007-05-17 00:0...	1	11	Active
6	6	Kendall	Lisa	2001-11-15 00:0...	4	4	Active

Query executed successfully. (local) (11.0 RTM) Reno\Student (53) JProCo 00:00:00 20 rows

Figure 14.42 This shows using SQL injection allowed us to hack the Employee database.

```
DECLARE @SQL NVARCHAR(200)
SET @SQL = 'SELECT * FROM Employee WHERE EmpID = 
@UserSelection'
DECLARE @UserSelection VARCHAR(30)
EXEC sp_executesql @SQL, N'@UserSelection VARCHAR(30)',
@UserSelection = '1 OR 1=1'
```

```
Messages
Msg 245, Level 16, State 1, Line 1
Conversion failed when converting the varchar value '1 OR 1=1' to data type
int.
                                                                    0 rows
```

Figure 14.43 This shows the sp_executesql stored procedure did not accept the SQL injection as a valid data type.

The first query in Figure 14.42 was easily hacked. The attempted SQL injection of the second query in Figure 14.43 was stopped in the stored procedure due to an invalid data type.

Lab 14.3: Dynamic Admin Tasks

Lab Prep: Lab Prep: Each lab has one or more Skill Checks. Start with Skill Check 1 and proceed until reaching the Points to Ponder section.

Before beginning this lab, verify that SQL Server 2012 is properly installed and operating. Before running the lab setup script for resetting the database (SQLQueries2012Vol4Chapter14.3Setup.sql), please make sure to close all query windows within SSMS. An open query window pointing to a database context can lock that database preventing it from updating when the script is executing. A simple way to assure all query windows are closed, is to exit out of SSMS, then open a new instance of SSMS, and lastly run the setup script.

Skill Check 1: Create a stored procedure called BackupDatabase from the following code:

`'BACKUP DATABASE '+ @DbName + ' TO DISK = ' + @Path`

Make sure it takes the @DbName parameter and the @Date parameter as VARCHAR(100) fields that backup up the database to the C:\Joes2Pros\ location. When you are done your screen should resemble Figure 14.44.

```
EXEC BackupDatabase 'dbBasics', '2012June01'
```

```
Messages
Processed 296 pages for database 'dbBasics', file 'dbBasics' on file 1.
Processed 8 pages for database 'dbBasics', file ' dbBasics_log' on file 1.
BACKUP DATABASE successfully processed 304 pages in 0.299 seconds (7.925 MB/sec).
                                                                    0 rows
```

Figure 14.44 Skill Check 1.

Answer Code: The T-SQL code to this lab can be found in the downloadable files in a file named Lab14.3_DynamicAdminTasks.sql.

Points to Ponder - Dynamic Admin Tasks

1. A Common use of dynamic SQL is to perform database administrative and maintenance tasks.

2. One of the benefits of dynamic SQL is the ability to develop code that provides flexible paths to retrieve and manage information.

3. A database backup file contains all your tables, relations, constraints and data into one packaged file. From this file you can restore your database after disaster strikes.
4. Running a backup twice with the same filename packages two backup sets into one file.
5. Using a dynamic date stamp will help ensure that your backup process is neat and each backup file has a unique file name.

Chapter Glossary

Dynamic SQL: A string of character data that is evaluated as TSQL code at runtime.

sp_executesql: A system stored procedure that can turn a string into a running SQL statement much like the EXEC command.

SQL Injection: When malicious or unauthorized code is inserted into a string or strings through a SQL data channel that are then passed to an instance for parsing and execution by SQL Server.

N: N is Unicode and stands for "National Language Character Set The Unicode N allows your query to return international characters in the result set.

Review Quiz - Chapter Fourteen

1.) Which is the only dynamic SQL statement that will run?

   ○ a. **EXEC(**'SELECT * FROM' + MgmtTraining**)**
   ○ b. **EXEC(SELECT * FROM** + 'MgmtTraining'**)**
   ○ c. **EXEC(**'SELECT * FROM' + 'MgmtTraining'**)**
   ○ d. **EXEC(**'SELECT * FROM ' + 'MgmtTraining'**)**

2.) You have the following code:

   ```
   CREATE PROC GeneralQuery @TableName NVARCHAR(50)
   AS
   SELECT *
   FROM @TableName
   GO
   ```

   When you call on the stored procedure with a proper variable it always errors out. What change must you make to get this stored procedure to run correctly?

   ○ a. **ALTER PROC** GeneralQuery @TableName **NVARCHAR(50)**
   AS
   DECLARE @SQL **NVARCHAR(1000)**
   SET @SQL = 'SELECT * FROM ' + @TableName
   EXEC (@SQL)
   GO

   ○ b. **ALTER PROC** GeneralQuery @TableName **NVARCHAR(50)**
   AS
   DECLARE @SQL **NVARCHAR(1000)**
   SET @SQL = 'SELECT * FROM ' + @TableName
   EXEC (@SQL + @TableName)
   GO

Chapter 14. Dynamic SQL

3.) What is a true statement about the following code?

```
CREATE PROC GeneralDatabase @DbName NVARCHAR(50)
AS
EXEC ('CREATE DATABASE ' + @DbName)
GO
```

- O a. This stored procedure will always throw an error.
- O b. This stored procedure will work if you pass in a database name that exists in the database.
- O c. This stored procedure will work if you pass in a database name that does not exist in the database.

4.) What is one advantage of using the sp_executesql to run your dynamic SQL that EXEC does not do?

- O a. The contents of sp_executesql are compiled and saved as an Execution Plan resulting in a potential performance gain for stored procedures.
- O b. The contents of sp_executesql can be a concatenation of string expressions whereas EXEC can only come from one original string.

5.) Which dynamic SQL string can only be run using sp_executesql and will not run by using the EXEC statement?

- O a. `SET @SQL = 'SELECT * FROM [Grant] WHERE Amount >' + @Min`
- O b. `SET @SQL = 'SELECT * FROM [Grant] WHERE Amount > @Min'`
- O c. `SET @SQL = 'SELECT * FROM [Grant] WHERE Amount > 1000'`
- O d. `SET @SQL = 'SELECT * FROM ' + @Table + ' WHERE Amount > 1000'`

6.) Assuming you have a JProCo database and a folder on your C drive named C:\Joes2Pros with proper permissions set up, which dynamic SQL code will run correctly?

○ a.
```
DECLARE @DbName VARCHAR(100)
SET @DbName = 'dbBasics'
DECLARE VARCHAR(100) @Path
SET @Path = 'C:\Joes2Pros\' + @DbName + '.Bak'
EXEC ('BACKUP DATABASE dbBasics TO DISK = ' + @Path)
```

○ b.
```
DECLARE @DbName VARCHAR(100)
SET @DbName = 'dbBasics'
DECLARE VARCHAR(100) @Path
SET @Path = '''C:\Joes2Pros\''' + @DbName + '''.Bak'''
EXEC ('BACKUP DATABASE dbBasics TO DISK = ' + @Path)
```

○ c.
```
DECLARE @DbName VARCHAR(100)
SET @DbName = 'dbBasics'
DECLARE VARCHAR(100) @Path
SET @Path = '''C:\Joes2Pros\' + @DbName + '.Bak'''
EXEC ('BACKUP DATABASE dbBasics TO DISK = ' + @Path)
```

○ d.
```
DECLARE @DbName VARCHAR(100)
SET @DbName = '''dbBasics'''
DECLARE VARCHAR(100) @Path
SET @Path = 'C:\Joes2Pros\' + @DbName + '.Bak'
EXEC ('BACKUP DATABASE dbBasics TO DISK = ' + @Path)
```

Answer Key

1.) Queries can be object based or they can be dynamically run from strings. Mixing strings to be concatenated with actual keywords does not work, so (a) and (b) are wrong. Both (c) and (d) are using concatenated strings but with (c) there is no space between the 'SELECT * FROM' and the 'MgmtTraining' which throws an error. Therefore only (d) is the right answer.

2.) Dynamic SQL turns a string value into a running SQL statement. Both answers do this but one uses the same table name twice, making (b) incorrect. So (a) is the correct answer.

3.) Dynamic SQL must be executed from a string and the syntax inside the string must be a valid SQL statement. If you forget a database name or create one that already exists then it will error out which is why (a) and (b) are wrong. This means that (c) would be the correct answer.

4.) What is different between EXEC and sp_executesql? They both can concatenate string, so (b) is incorrect. Only sp_executesql can store Execution Plans, making (a) the correct answer.

5.) If the variable is inside the string then only sp_executesql can run the dynamic SQL statement. This means (b) would be the correct answer.

6.) When you need a single quote inside the string you use three single quotes in a row. For our backup database we need the single quotes around the path (not inside the path), so (b) is wrong. There are no triple single quotes in the path for (a) and (d) so they are wrong. The path for the backup is correct in (c), making it the correct answer.

Bug Catcher Game

To play the Bug Catcher game, run the BugCatcher_Chapter14.pps from the BugCatcher folder of the companion files. You can obtain these files from the www.Joes2Pros.com web site.

[THIS PAGE INTENTIONALLY LEFT BLANK.]

Chapter 15.   Cursors

Have you ever read a good book and used a yellow highlighter to bring attention to key points? When the highlighter is used it does not change the information stored in the book. The highlighter just marks one point of the book to make it easy to find. Think of the book by itself as a table in a database (just data). Think of a book with a yellow highlighter as a Cursor. A Cursor is basically a table with one of its records highlighted (or active).

Sometimes you want to see many records at once when reporting and sometimes you want to see just one record at a time for other processes. This chapter will show you how to use Cursors which are sets of records that allow SQL to fetch one row at a time until all the records have been covered.

READER NOTE: *Please run the script SQLQueries2012Vol4Chapter15.0Setup.sql in order to follow along with the examples in the first section of Chapter 15. All scripts mentioned in this chapter may be found at **www.Joes2Pros.com**.*

Using Cursors

We all understand the parallel between a cursor and a book with a highlighter. Once the book is marked with the highlighter those marks can never be removed or erased. There are better examples to use for our cursors.

Have you ever seen those re-stick-able flags you get at the office supply store? They are used to reference a page in a book or line within a page. Then when something else catches your attention you can remove the flag and put it in a new location. If you've ever purchased a house or signed a large contract in an attorney's office you are very familiar with the re-stick-able flags. Once your signature is in place that flag can be removed. After all, there is no reason to sign or initial any one line of a contract twice.

What good is it to have a bunch of records and only one active? Well if you have 10 records in your table and you have processed 6 of them then you have 4 to go right? Which 4 are left? The simple answer is any record that SQL has not yet fetched or marked as fetched. The cursor keeps track of which records have already been fetched and therefore makes a great checklist for you by presenting only the remaining records, one at a time.

As we have learned in the previous chapter there are several databases that need to be backed up each week. It is important to keep track of databases that need to be a part of this weekly maintenance. So, we're going to create a table named WeeklyBackups. This table will only have one field and will contain the names of the three databases that need to be backed up each week. The following code will create the WeeklyBackups table and populate it with the three records. When the code is run you will see that three rows were affected in Figure 15.1.

```
CREATE TABLE WeeklyBackups
(DatabaseName VARCHAR(100) PRIMARY KEY)
GO
INSERT INTO WeeklyBackups VALUES ('JProCo'), ('dbBasics'),
('RatisCo')
```

```
Messages
(3 row(s) affected)
                                                                    0 rows
```

Figure 15.1 Creating the WeeklyBackups table.

To verify the records were inserted, use a SELECT * FROM statement to see all the records in the WeeklyBackups table as in Figure 15.2.

```
SELECT * FROM WeeklyBackups
```

	DatabaseName
1	dbBasics
2	JProCo
3	RatisCo

3 rows

Figure 15.2 Records from the WeeklyBackups table.

Figure 15.2 shows us the three databases that need to be backed up each week. To do this we can use the BackupDatabase stored procedure that we created earlier in this book. Now let's reference the WeeklyBackups table and create an Execute command for each database that needs to be backed up as seen in the following code:

```
EXEC BackupDatabase 'dbBasics', '2012June05'
EXEC BackupDatabase 'JProCo', '2012June05'
EXEC BackupDatabase 'RatisCo', '2012June05'
```

This runs just fine and will back up all three databases. Using the WeeklyBackups table as a reference to run a maintenance task on every record is convenient but can be done in a more efficient manner.

Automation Challenges

It is possible to automate this process. In general, the more automated the process is, the more efficient it will become and increase the procedures resistance to human error. With automation you often run the same task over and over many times in a given period of time. For example you might want to back up your database every night. But you don't want the backup to run the exact same time each night. Maybe you have a list of three databases that must have a nightly back up. Another challenge may be that the backup for the database is at the same time each night and to the same location but each database must have its own unique name.

So although you are running the BACKUP DATABASE statement many times, each time it changes slightly. The following code shows the three statements which repeat the backup database process and uses a different name for each database:

```
BACKUP DATABASE JProCo TO DISK = 'C:\Joes2Pros\JProCo.bak'
BACKUP DATABASE RatisCo TO DISK = 'C:\Joes2Pros\RatisCo.bak'
BACKUP DATABASE dbBasics TO DISK = 'C:\Joes2Pros\dbBasics.bak'
```

Automating Tasks from a Table

You might want the backup yesterday to be JProCoAugust8 and the backup tonight to be called JProCoAugust9.

The top record in the WeeklyBackups table is dbBasics as seen in Figure 15.3

```
SELECT TOP (1) DatabaseName
FROM WeeklyBackups
```

	DatabaseName
1	dbBasics

1 rows

Figure 15.3 Top (1) from the WeeklyBackups table.

The first thing we will need to do is declare a couple variables. First we should declare @DbName and @TimeStamp and let SQL know they are each going to be a VARCHAR (100). We can set the @TimeStamp variable equal to '2012August09' and set the @DbName variable equal to the query SELECT TOP (1) of the DatabaseName in the WeeklyBackups table.

```
DECLARE @DbName VARCHAR(100)
DECLARE @TimeStamp VARCHAR(100) = '2012August09'
SELECT TOP (1) @DbName = DatabaseName
FROM WeeklyBackups
EXEC BackupDatabase @DbName, @TimeStamp
```

```
Messages
Processed 288 pages for database 'dbBasics', file 'dbBasics' on file 1.
Processed 4 pages for database 'dbBasics', file 'dbBasics_log' on file 1.
BACKUP DATABASE successfully processed 292 pages in 0.650 seconds (3.509 MB/sec).

0 rows
```

Figure 15.4 dbBasics database successfully backed up.

Figure 15.4 shows dbBasics backed up successfully. To back up the rest of the databases we replace the (1) and SELECT TOP (2) For JProCo, and TOP (3) for RatisCo. The problem with using TOP like TOP (3) for RatisCo is that it not only returns the third record but it also returns TOP (1) and TOP (2) as seen in Figure 15.5.

```
SELECT TOP (3) DatabaseName
FROM WeeklyBackups
```

	DatabaseName
1	dbBasics
2	JProCo
3	RatisCo

3 rows

Figure 15.5 Top (3) from the WeeklyBackups table.

TOP (3) will backup RatisCo but SQL has to do extra processing because dbBasics and JProCo were also passed through. We can use TOP (3) to get the third database. The SELECT Statement is actually going to assign the variable value three times and finally repopulate it with RatisCo. After running the code from Figure 15.4 with TOP (1), TOP (2), and TOP (3) we can open Windows Explorer and see that all three data bases were backed up successfully:

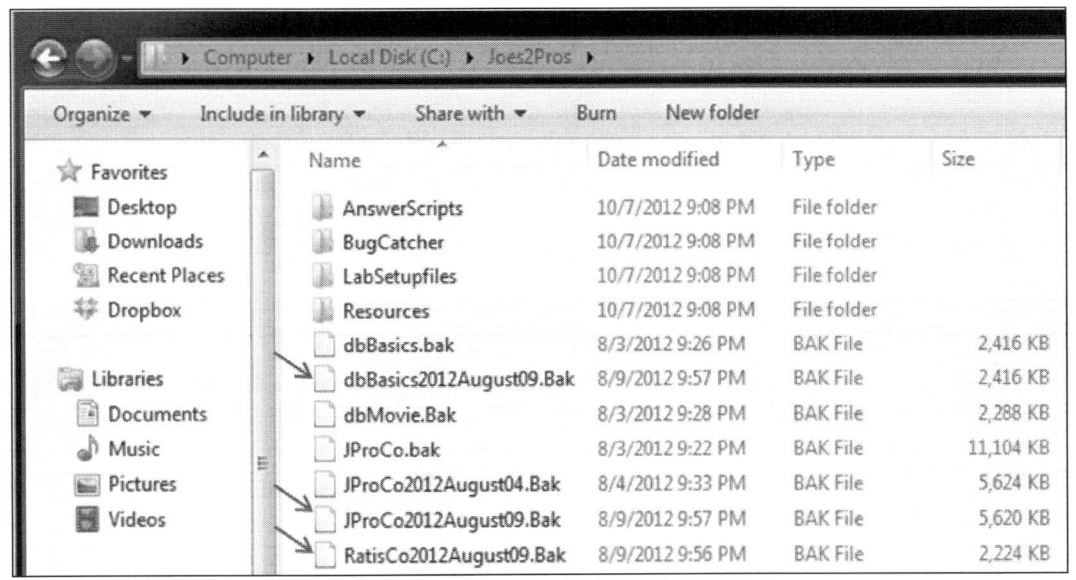

Figure 15.6 2012August09.bak files successfully saved in C:\Joes2Pros.

Using Cursors

The solution worked great for those three databases. But, what if there were four, five or perhaps 10 databases? Using SELECT TOP (10) causes SQL to process much more data than necessary for just one value to populate a variable. A better solution is to use cursors. Before we implement cursors with the SELECT TOP (1) solution we need to understand the function of cursors. Think of a cursor as the little yellow highlighter flag that can point to any chosen record in a table. The table can have many records but only one is highlighted or active at a given time. For us to discover what cursors can do we will declare a cursor for the WeeklyBackups table and run it.

```
DECLARE crsWeek CURSOR
FOR SELECT * FROM dbo.WeeklyBackups
```

Messages
Command(s) completed successfully.
0 rows

Figure 15.7 crsWeek cursor successfully created.

Now that the crsWeek cursor has been declared, it needs to be opened using the OPEN crsWeek command.

```
OPEN crsWeek
```

Messages
Command(s) completed successfully.
0 rows

Figure 15.8 crsWeek cursor successfully opened.

We see command(s) completed successfully in Figure 15.8. So far we have declared the crsWeek cursor for the WeeklyBackups table and opened it. By opening the cursor, what SQL has done, is placed a flag or made active the first record of the WeeklyBackups table. For us to see the record we must fetch it from the cursor as seen in Figure 15.9.

```
FETCH NEXT FROM crsWeek
```

	DatabaseName
1	dbBasics
	1 rows

Figure 15.9 First record fetched from crsWeek.

When we queried the WeeklyBackups table earlier Figure 15.3 showed the first record is dbBasics. The first time we fetched from the crsWeek cursor, it returned dbBasics. The second record in the WeeklyBackups table is JProCo. If we fetch the next record from the crsWeek cursor what would we predict it would return?

```
FETCH NEXT FROM crsWeek
```

	DatabaseName
1	JProCo
	1 rows

Figure 15.10 Second record fetched from crsWeek.

If JProCo was the prediction then the prediction is correct. The RatisCo database is the third and final record in the WeeklyBackups table. If we were to FETCH NEXT from the crsWeek cursor one more time, it would return RatisCo in the result set. Since there is no fourth database, the cursor has run its course and we can CLOSE the cursor and use the DEALLOCATE command to make sure the cursor is not reserving any more memory.

```
CLOSE crsWeek
DEALLOCATE crsWeek
```

```
Messages
Command(s) completed successfully.
                                                                    0 rows
```

Figure 15.11 CLOSE and DEALLOCATE completed successfully.

@@FETCH_STATUS

The lifecycle of the cursor is to declare the cursor as a SELECT Statement that will retrieve records one at a time from the table. Then the cursor opened so it can start fetching each of the records in order until the cursor has returned as many records from the table as is needed. The cursor is then closed and deallocated to keep it from reserving memory. As seen in the following code:

```
DECLARE crsWeek CURSOR
FOR SELECT * FROM dbo.WeeklyBackups
OPEN crsWeek
FETCH NEXT FROM crsWeek
Close crsWeek
DEALLOCATE crsWeek
```

How can we find out if the FETCH command has activated a record or has reached the end of the table and run its course. There is a way to do this using the following code:

```
SELECT @@FETCH_STATUS
```

We have already deallocated the crsWeek cursor so before we can fetch status we have to declare, open, and fetch next from crsWeek cursor as seen in Figure 15.12.

```
DECLARE crsWeek CURSOR
FOR SELECT * FROM dbo.WeeklyBackups
OPEN crsWeek
FETCH NEXT FROM crsWeek
```

	DatabaseName
1	dbBasics

1 rows

Figure 15.12 Cursor crsWeek returned the first record.

And we can now check the fetch status as seen in Figure 15.13.

```
SELECT @@FETCH_STATUS
```

	(No column name)
1	0

1 rows

Figure 15.13 @@FETCH_STATUS returned a 0 indicating an active record.

If we fetch next again crsWeek will return JProCo and then RatisCo. How do we know if it has run its course? Each time crsWeek fetches a record the SELECT @@FETCH_STATUS statement will return a 0 in its result set. After RatisCo, run the FETCH NEXT FROM crsWeek command one more time and in Figure 15.14 we see it returns no records.

```
FETCH NEXT FROM crsWeek
```

	DatabaseName

0 rows

Figure 15.14 crsWeek returned no record on fourth FETCH.

SELECT @@FETCH_STATUS returned a 0 when Fetched returned dbBasics, JProCo and RatisCo. The fourth time we run the fetch command, it returned no records. What is the @@FETCH_STATUS when the cursor returns nothing?

```
SELECT @@FETCH_STATUS
```

	(No column name)
1	-1

1 rows

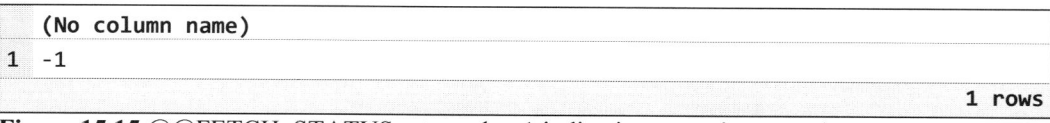

Figure 15.15 @@FETCH_STATUS returned a -1 indicating no active record.

In Figure 15.15 we see the status is -1. Each time the Fetch command retrieves a record the status will be 0, and when no record is returned or the fetch next cursor has run its course the status will be -1.

Capturing a Variable from a Cursor

READER NOTE: before doing the code samples coming up we will need to close and deallocate the crsWeek cursor each time.

The middle of the cursor lifecycle is the FETCH NEXT FROM crsWeek command. How can we use the middle of the lifecycle to satisfy a variable? Let's use the BackupDatabase stored procedure to demonstrate the process. We need to set up the entire lifecycle of the cursor:

```
DECLARE crsWeek CURSOR
FOR SELECT * FROM dbo.WeeklyBackups
OPEN crsWeek
FETCH NEXT FROM crsWeek
Close crsWeek
DEALLOCATE crsWeek
```

The name of the database path returned from the crsWeek cursor has to pass into the BackupDatabase stored procedure. BackupDatabase requires two variables; @DbName and @TimeStamp. The crsWeek cursor will satisfy the @DbName variable. To set this up, declare the variable as a VARCHAR(100) and set the fetch statement to return the result INTO the @DbName variable. Finally to check this lets add a SELECT @DbName statement to the end of our code.

```
DECLARE crsWeek CURSOR
FOR SELECT * FROM dbo.WeeklyBackups
OPEN crsWeek
DECLARE @DbName VARCHAR(100)
FETCH NEXT FROM crsWeek INTO @DbName
SELECT @DbName
```

	(No column name)
1	dbBasics

1 rows

Figure 15.16 SELECT statement shows crsWeek was successfully fetched into @DbName.

Figure 15.16 shows the SELECT @DbName returned dbBasics that was passed in from the crsWeek cursor.

Automating Tasks with a Cursor

READER NOTE: before doing the code samples coming up we will need to close and deallocate the crsWeek.

To automate our backup procedure using the cursor, we only have two more steps. The @TimeStamp variable needs to be declared and set and we need to execute the BackupDatabase stored procedure that was created in the previous chapter's Skill Check.

```sql
DECLARE crsWeek CURSOR
FOR SELECT * FROM dbo.WeeklyBackups
OPEN crsWeek
DECLARE @DbName VARCHAR(100)
DECLARE @TimeStamp VARCHAR(100) = '2012Aug14'
FETCH NEXT FROM crsWeek INTO @DbName
EXEC BackupDatabase @DbName, @TimeStamp
```

```
Messages
Processed 288 pages for database 'dbBasics', file 'dbBasics' on file 1.
Processed 2 pages for database 'dbBasics', file 'dbBasics_log' on file 1.
BACKUP DATABASE successfully processed 290 pages in 0.710 seconds (3.191 MB/sec).
                                                                      0 rows
```

Figure 15.17 dbBasics was successfully backed up.

Figure 15.17 shows the cursor successfully backed up dbBasics. In Figure 15.18 and Figure 15.19 we only run the last four lines and see it backs up JProCo and RatisCo.

```sql
--DECLARE crsWeek CURSOR
--FOR SELECT * FROM dbo.WeeklyBackups
--OPEN crsWeek
DECLARE @DbName VARCHAR(100)
DECLARE @TimeStamp VARCHAR(100) = '2012Aug14'
FETCH NEXT FROM crsWeek INTO @DbName
EXEC BackupDatabase @DbName, @TimeStamp
```

```
Messages
Processed 688 pages for database 'JProCo', file 'JProCo' on file 1.
Processed 2 pages for database 'JProCo', file 'JProCo_log' on file 1.
BACKUP DATABASE successfully processed 690 pages in 1.162 seconds (4.639 MB/sec).
                                                                      0 rows
```

Figure 15.18 JProCo successfully backed up.

```
--DECLARE crsWeek CURSOR
--FOR SELECT * FROM dbo.WeeklyBackups
--OPEN crsWeek
DECLARE @DbName VARCHAR(100)
DECLARE @TimeStamp VARCHAR(100) = '2012Aug14'
FETCH NEXT FROM crsWeek INTO @DbName
EXEC BackupDatabase @DbName, @TimeStamp
```

Messages
Processed 264 pages for database 'RatisCo', file 'RatisCo' on file 1.
Processed 2 pages for database 'RatisCo', file 'RatisCo_log' on file 1.
BACKUP DATABASE successfully processed 266 pages in 0.538 seconds (3.862 MB/sec).
0 rows

Figure 15.19 RatisCo successfully backed up.

What happens if we run this a fourth time even though there are no more records in the cursor?

```
--DECLARE crsWeek CURSOR
--FOR SELECT * FROM dbo.WeeklyBackups
--OPEN crsWeek
DECLARE @DbName VARCHAR(100)
DECLARE @TimeStamp VARCHAR(100) = '2012Aug14'
FETCH NEXT FROM crsWeek INTO @DbName
EXEC BackupDatabase @DbName, @TimeStamp
```

Messages
Command(s) completed successfully.
0 rows

Figure 15.20 Backup ran successfully but no database was backed up.

When the cursor has run its course and there are no more records, Figure 15.20 shows we receive the Command(s) completed successfully message and no database was backed up. The final step will be to close and deallocate the cursor as shown in Figure 15.21.

```
CLOSE crsWeek
DEALLOCATE crsWeek
```

Messages
Command(s) completed successfully.
0 rows

Figure 15.21 CLOSE and DEALLOCATE were completed successfully for cursor crsWeek.

Looping with @@FETCH_STATUS

There is a way to automate this procedure even more. As it's written we must remember that there are three records in the WeeklyBackups table and therefore it should be run three times. What if someone else updates the WeeklyBackups table and there are four records? Backing up databases would require a lot of diligence to check and re-check the WeeklyBackups table.

Let's put a fourth record in the weekly backups table.

```
INSERT INTO dbo.WeeklyBackups
VALUES ('dbMovie')
```

Messages
(1 row(s) affected) |如

0 rows

Figure 15.22 dbMovie was successfully added to WeeklyBackups table.

```
SELECT *
FROM dbo.WeeklyBackups
```

	DatabaseName
1	dbBasics
2	dbMovie
3	JProCo
4	RatisCo

4 rows

Figure 15.23 Results from WeeklyBackups table.

Figure 15.23 shows there is now a fourth database that needs to be backed up. There is a handy way to automate the process using the SELECT @@FETCH_STATUS command. The fetch status global variable indicates whether there is an active record or not. By using fetch status we tell our procedure to keep running as long as there is an active record in the cursor.

READER NOTE: *We will soon run the code sample from Figure 15.24 but need build the code in stages. Don't run the code until you get to Figure 15.24.*

In order for the cursor to pass it into the stored procedure each time we produce a new value we need to separate out the execute command with a BEGIN and END command:

```
DECLARE crsWeek CURSOR
FOR SELECT * FROM dbo.WeeklyBackups
OPEN crsWeek
DECLARE @DbName VARCHAR(100)
DECLARE @TimeStamp VARCHAR(100) = '2012Aug14'
FETCH NEXT FROM crsWeek INTO @DbName

BEGIN
EXEC BackupDatabase @DbName, @TimeStamp
END

CLOSE crsWeek
DEALLOCATE crsWeek
```

All we have to do from this point is tell the EXEC command when to begin and when to end and continue to the CLOSE and DEALLOCATE commands. Before the BEGIN statement ad:

```
WHILE @@FETCH_STATUS = 0
```

The WHILE modifier lets the procedure know to begin executing only while the fetch status equals 0. Once the fetch status equals -1 then the execute command will end and SQL will move to CLOSE and DEALLOCATE the cursor. Once SQL enters the BEGIN it will stay there until it is time to END. We need to add the fetch statement after the EXEC and before the END. We are going to set the date for a new day August 15th and take a look at the entire procedure in Figure 15.24.

```
DECLARE crsWeek CURSOR
FOR SELECT * FROM dbo.WeeklyBackups
OPEN crsWeek
DECLARE @DbName VARCHAR(100)
DECLARE @TimeStamp VARCHAR(100) = '2012Aug15'
FETCH NEXT FROM crsWeek INTO @DbName
WHILE @@FETCH_STATUS = 0

BEGIN
EXEC BackupDatabase @DbName, @TimeStamp
FETCH NEXT FROM crsWeek INTO @DbName
END

CLOSE crsWeek
DEALLOCATE crsWeek
```

```
Messages
Processed 288 pages for database 'dbBasics', file 'dbBasics' on file 1.
Processed 2 pages for database 'dbBasics', file 'dbBasics_log' on file 1.
BACKUP DATABASE successfully processed 290 pages in 0.506 seconds (4.477
MB/sec).
Processed 272 pages for database 'dbMovie', file 'dbMovie' on file 1.
Processed 7 pages for database 'dbMovie', file 'dbMovie_log' on file 1.
BACKUP DATABASE successfully processed 279 pages in 0.663 seconds (3.287
MB/sec).
Processed 688 pages for database 'JProCo', file 'JProCo' on file 1.
Processed 2 pages for database 'JProCo', file 'JProCo_log' on file 1.
BACKUP DATABASE successfully processed 690 pages in 1.483 seconds (3.634
MB/sec).
Processed 264 pages for database 'RatisCo', file 'RatisCo' on file 1.
Processed 2 pages for database 'RatisCo', file 'RatisCo_log' on file 1.
BACKUP DATABASE successfully processed 266 pages in 0.584 seconds (3.551
MB/sec).
                                                                    0 rows
```

Figure 15.24 Four databases were successfully backed up.

Figure 15.24 shows that all four databases from the WeeklyBackups table were successfully backed up. Figure 15.25 shows all the backed up files from this chapter including the August 15th backups listed in the C:\JProCo folder in Windows Explorer.

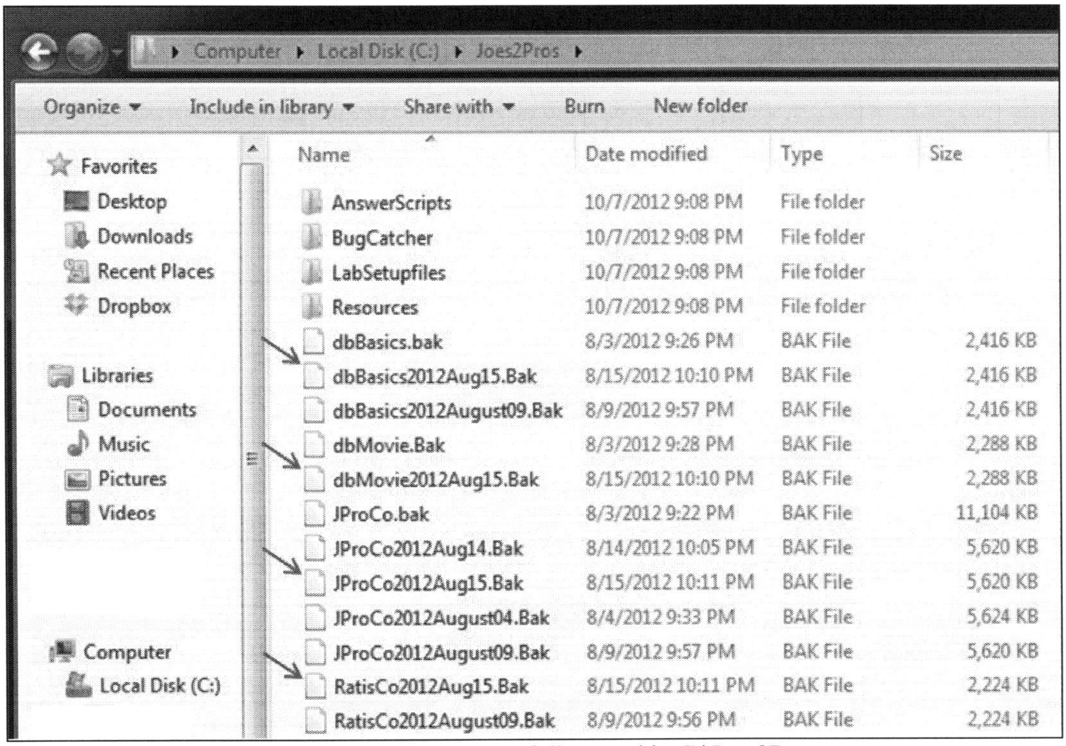

Figure 15.25 Four 2012Aug15.Bak files successfully saved in C:\Joes2Pros.

Lab 15.1: Using Cursors

Lab Prep: Lab Prep: Each lab has one or more Skill Checks. Start with Skill Check 1 and proceed until reaching the Points to Ponder section.

Before beginning this lab, verify that SQL Server 2012 is properly installed and operating. Before running the lab setup script for resetting the database (SQLQueries2012Vol4Chapter15.1Setup.sql), please make sure to close all query windows within SSMS. An open query window pointing to a database context can lock that database preventing it from updating when the script is executing. A simple way to assure all query windows are closed, is to exit out of SSMS, then open a new instance of SSMS, and lastly run the setup script.

Skill Check 1: In JProCo create a new table named NewCatalogs that has one field called DatabaseName. The DatabaseName field should be a VARCHAR(100) and it should be the primary key of the table.

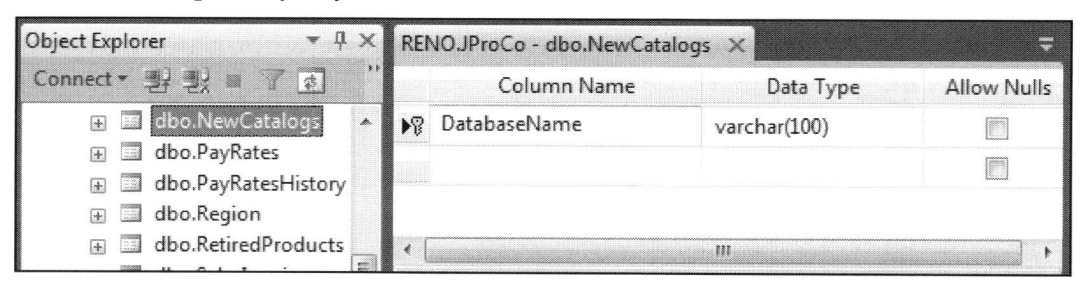

Figure 15.26 Skill Check 1.

Insert the three records you see in Figure 15.27.

```
SELECT * FROM NewCatalogs
```

	DatabaseName
1	Acme
2	DooDad
3	Widget

3 rows

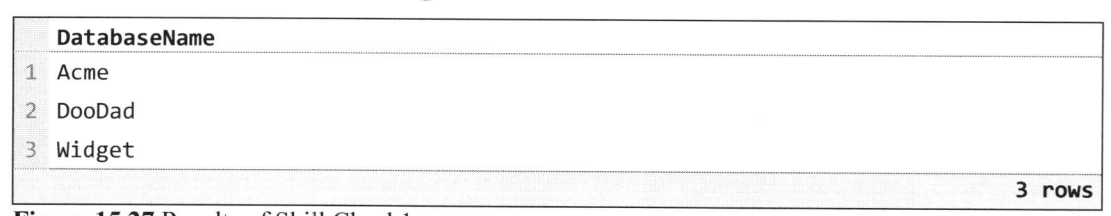

Figure 15.27 Results of Skill Check1.

Skill Check 2: Create three databases from the NewCatalogs table by iterating through a new Cursor called crsDatabases that calls on the BackupDatabase stored procedure.

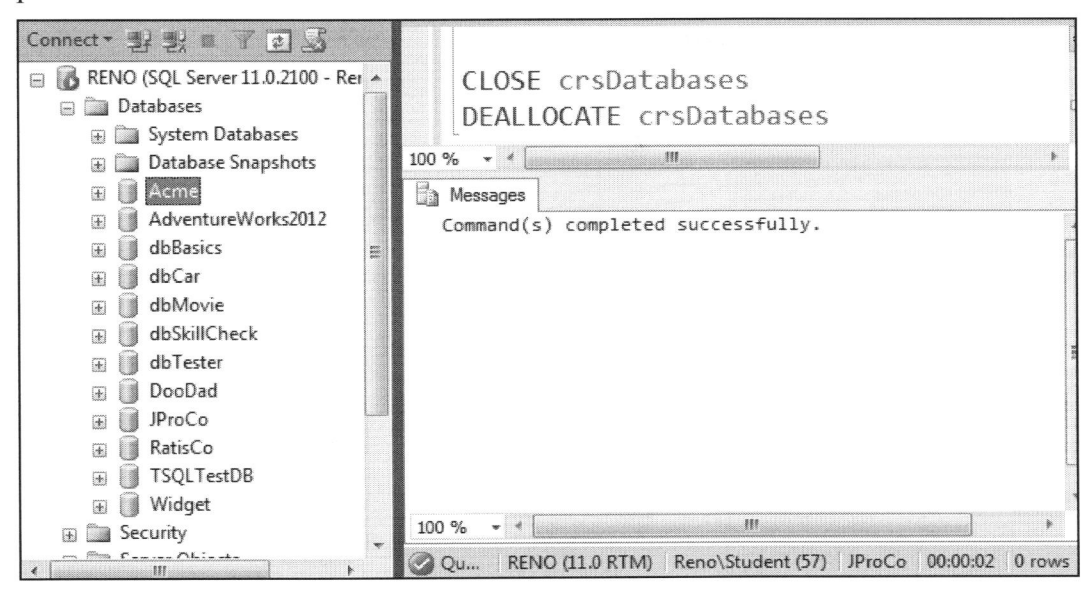

Figure 15.28 Results of Skill Check 2

Skill Check 3: Delete the three databases from Skill Check 2 by iterating through a new Cursor called crsDatabases and calling the DropGeneralDatabase stored procedure. When you are done your three databases from Skill Check 2 should be gone as you see in Figure 15.29.

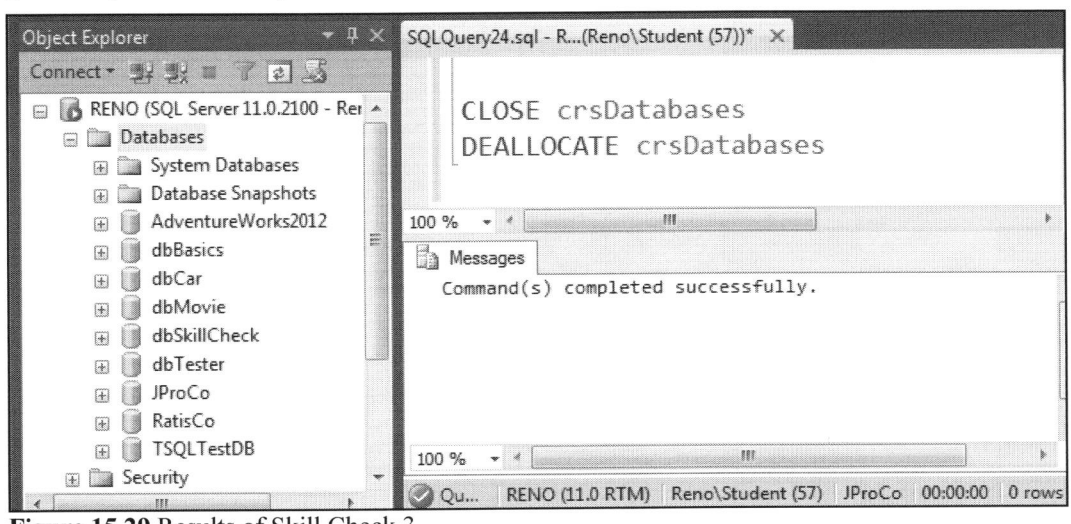

Figure 15.29 Results of Skill Check 3.

Answer Code: The T-SQL code to this lab can be found in the downloadable files in a file named Lab15.1_UsingCursors.sql.

Points to Ponder - Using Cursors

1. Cursors are used mainly in stored procedures with many statements to make the data of a result set available to subsequent statements.
2. The sp_describe_cursor shows the characteristics of a cursor.
3. The @@FETCH_STATUS is updated to reflect the status of the last fetch.
4. The fetched row is also known as the current row.
5. @@FETCH_STATUS returns a zero if a record was found and a -1 if no record was found.
6. Lifecycle Steps of a Cursor are:
    - Declare Cursor for a query
    - Open Cursor
    - Fetch Next from Cursor as many times as you need
    - Close Cursor
    - Deallocate cursor

Cursor Types

When you buy a new car you get choices about features. The more features you choose the more it costs. The same car with fewer features is less expensive but you might go without something you need later.

In the world of cursors there are very simple ones that are small and fast but only do one thing. Then there are cursors with more features. They may scroll up and down a table and even store copies of your data. Conventional wisdom is to use the simplest cursor that does just what you need. This section will show you the different types of cursors and the features and options they come with as well as some drawbacks. To start we should take a moment and familiarize ourselves with the Employee table of JProCo seen if Figure 15.30.

```
SELECT * FROM dbo.Employee
```

	EmpID	LastName	FirstName	HireDate	LocationID
1	1	Adams	Alex	2001-01-01 00:00:00.000	1
2	2	Brown	Barry	2002-08-12 00:00:00.000	1
3	3	Osako	Lee	1999-09-01 00:00:00.000	2
4	4	Kinnison	Dave	1996-03-16 00:00:00.000	1
5	5	Bender	Eric	2007-05-17 00:00:00.000	1
6	6	Kendall	Lisa	2001-11-15 00:00:00.000	4

20 rows

Figure 15.30 First six records from the Employee table.

FORWARD_ONLY and SCROLL Cursors

Let's start by reviewing the cursor we are familiar with.

```
DECLARE crsEmployee CURSOR
FOR SELECT * FROM dbo.Employee
OPEN crsEmployee
FETCH NEXT FROM crsEmployee
```

	EmpID	LastName	FirstName	HireDate	LocationID	ManagerID
1	1	Adams	Alex	2001-01-01 0:00:00.000	1	4

1 rows

Figure 15.31 crsEmployee returned the first record.

Figure 15.31 shows us Alex Adams. If we run it again we will get Barry Brown. The next record in the Employee table is Lee Osako. What if we want to go backwards, instead of fetching the next record we want to fetch the prior . Instead of going from

Barry Brown to Lee Osako we want the cursor to seek back up the list to Alex Adams. To do this we should try and fetch the prior record.

FETCH PRIOR FROM crsEmployee

```
Message
Msg 16911, Level 16, State 1, Line 1
fetch: The fetch type prior cannot be used with forward only cursors.
                                                              0 rows
```

Figure 15.32 FETCH PRIOR threw an error when run on the forward only cursor.

Even though this is a valid statement we get an error message. Figure 15.32 shows us that the fetch type PRIOR cannot be used with cursors. Forward only is the default CURSOR. There is no difference between the following two lines of code. They are interchangeable and run exactly the same:

DECLARE crsEmployee **CURSOR**
DECLARE crsEmployee **CURSOR FORWARD_ONLY**

Cursor forward only allows you to move sequentially, one record at a time from first to last. As I am sure you have guessed there are other types of cursors that will allow you to move in reverse order within a table. We should try the same code again with one change. We will write it using the CURSOR SCROLL syntax.

DEALLOCATE crsEmployee

DECLARE crsEmployee **CURSOR SCROLL**
FOR SELECT * **FROM** dbo.Employee
OPEN crsEmployee
FETCH NEXT FROM crsEmployee

	EmpID	LastName	FirstName	HireDate	LocationID	ManagerID
1	1	Adams	Alex	2001-01-01...	1	4

1 rows

Figure 15.33 crsEmployee CURSOR SCROLL returned the first record.

Figure 15.33 shows us that it returned record 1, Alex Adams. And when we run the FETCH NEXT statement again we get Barry Brown just as we did before. And a third time returns Lee Osako. With the default cursor we were given an error message when we utilized the FETCH PRIOR. The last record we returned was Lee Osako let's see if we can get Barry Brown.

```
FETCH PRIOR FROM crsEmployee
```

	EmpID	LastName	FirstName	HireDate	LocationID	ManagerID
1	2	Brown	Barry	2002-08-12…	1	11

1 rows

Figure 15.34 FETCH PRIOR returned the second record.

Figure 15.34 shows us that SQL was able to move back up the list just fine using the CURSOR SCOLL syntax. To go back to the first employee we can run FETCH PRIOR or we can use another form of FETCH called FIRST.

```
FETCH FIRST FROM crsEmployee
```

	EmpID	LastName	FirstName	HireDate	LocationID	ManagerID
1	1	Adams	Alex	2001-01-01	1	4

1 rows

Figure 15.35 FETCH FIRST returned the first record.

As you can see, in Figure 15.35 the FETCH FIRST command will always bring you to the first record in the table. There is also a FETCH LAST which will return the last record in a table as seen in Figure 15.36.

```
FETCH LAST FROM crsEmployee
```

	EmpID	LastName	FirstName	HireDate	LocationID	ManagerID
1	21	Sue	Fines	2012-08-14 16:52:13.310	1	4

1 rows

Figure 15.36 FETCH LAST returned the last record.

FETCH LAST does fetch the last record. The cursor scroll allows you to move from top to bottom with FETCH NEXT, from bottom to top with FETCH PRIOR and using FIRST and LAST jump straight to the first or last record in the table.

Dynamic Cursors

What happens if you create a cursor from a table and before you fetch all the records, the underlying table that you created it from changes? To explore this let's create and open a cursor:

```
DEALLOCATE crsEmployee
DECLARE crsEmployee CURSOR
FOR SELECT * FROM dbo.Employee
OPEN crsEmployee
```

We know 20 records from the employee table went into making the crsEmployee cursor. Alex Adams, Barry Brown, and Lee Osaka are the first three records. If we fetch the next record we are going to get Alex Adams as shown in Figure 15.37.

```
DEALLOCATE crsEmployee
DECLARE crsEmployee CURSOR
FOR SELECT * FROM dbo.Employee
OPEN crsEmployee

FETCH NEXT FROM crsEmployee
```

EmpID	LastName	FirstName	HireDate	LocationID	ManagerID
1	Adams	Alex	2001-01-01 0:00:00.000	1	4

1 rows

Figure 15.37 crsEmployee returned the first record.

And when we run the Fetch next query again we will get Barry Brown. The third employee is Lee Osako and has EmpID of 3. We want to see if CURSOR is dynamic. Will the result change if the record changes after the cursor was declared and opened but before it was fetched?

```
SELECT *
FROM Employee
WHERE EmpID = 3
```

EmpID	LastName	FirstName	HireDate	LocationID	ManagerID
3	Osako	Lee	1999-09-01 00:00:00.000	2	11

1 rows

Figure 15.38 Record three from the Employee table.

Figure 15.38 shows us the third record as it was when the crsEmployee cursor was created and opened. It has not yet been fetched so now we will update that record by changing the last name from Osako to Osaka.

```
UPDATE Employee
SET LastName = 'Osaka'
WHERE EmpID = 3
```

Message
(1 row(s) affected)

0 rows

Figure 15.39 Record 3 of the Employee table successfully updated.

Osako; has been changed to Osaka. When we captured this cursor it was Osako. When we run the FETCH NEXT statement for a third time as you can see in Figure 15.40 it captured the latest record and returned Lee Osaka.

```
FETCH NEXT FROM crsEmployee
```

	EmpID	LastName	FirstName	HireDate	LocationID	ManagerID
1	3	Osaka	Lee	1999-09-01…	2	11

1 rows

Figure 15.40 Dynamic cursor crsEmployee returned updated record.

Static Cursor

There may be an instance when we don't want the cursor to change when the underlying data changes. Once the cursor captures the values, we need it to remain in memory or static regardless of what changes are made from that point. The table can change but the cursor will return results from the table as it was when the cursor was created. The syntax for the static cursor is CURSOR STATIC as seen if in the following code:

```
DEALLOCATE crsEmployee

DECLARE crsEmployee CURSOR STATIC
FOR SELECT * FROM dbo.Employee
OPEN crsEmployee
```

We can run this and notice the command(s) completed successfully. Go ahead and fetch the first record which we know is Alex Adams. If we were to run it again immediately we would expect to get Barry Brown, but before we do this we should check the record and see.

```sql
SELECT *
FROM Employee
WHERE EmpID = 2
```

	EmpID	LastName	FirstName	HireDate	LocationID	ManagerID
1	2	Brown	Barry	2002-08-12 00:00:00.000	1	11

1 rows

Figure 15.41 Record two of the Employee table.

Figure 15.41 shows us that employee 2 is Barry Brown. We have already created crsEmployee as a static cursor and wish to return the record as it was in the table at that moment. However, a memo came to the office that employee 2's name should be Barry White.

```sql
UPDATE Employee
SET LastName = 'White'
WHERE EmpID = 2
```

Message
(1 row(s) affected)

0 rows

Figure 15.42 Record two of the Employee table successfully updated.

```sql
SELECT *
FROM Employee
WHERE EmpID = 2
```

	EmpID	LastName	FirstName	HireDate	LocationID	ManagerID
1	2	White	Barry	2002-08-12 00:00:00.000	1	11

1 rows

Figure 15.43 Updated record from the Employee table.

Figure 15.43 shows that employee 2 has been changed from Barry Brown to Barry White. The big question is will the FETCH NEXT statement with a static cursor return the new or old record.

```sql
FETCH NEXT FROM crsEmployee
```

	EmpID	LastName	FirstName	HireDate	LocationID	ManagerID
1	2	Brown	Barry	2002-08-12 00:00:00.000	1	11

1 rows

Figure 15.44 Static cursor maintained original record.

Figure 15.44 shows that a static cursor will retain the original record from the time of its creation. Even though Barry Brown was changed to Barry White the static cursor returned the original record.

Cursor Variables

Cursors can also be captured into variables. This next bit of code should be starting to look very familiar. Capturing cursors into variables starts like every other cursor:

```
DEALLOCATE crsEmployee

DECLARE crsEmployee CURSOR
FOR SELECT * FROM dbo.Employee
OPEN crsEmployee
```

Once the OPEN crsEmployee runs successfully we want to run the Fetch command from a variable. To do this we need to declare a variable which we will call @MyCurs as a CURSOR and then set it to equal the crsEmployee cursor.

```
DECLARE @MyCurs CURSOR
SET @MyCurs = crsEmployee
FETCH NEXT FROM @MyCurs
```

	EmpID	LastName	FirstName	HireDate	LocationID	ManagerID
1	1	Adams	Alex	2001-01-01...	1	4

1 rows

Figure 15.45 FETCH returned record one using variable @MyCurs.

Figure 15.45 shows the @MyCurs variable returned the first record set into the crsEmployee cursor. If we run it again we will get record two, Barry White as seen if Figure 15.46.

```
DECLARE @MyCurs CURSOR
SET @MyCurs = crsEmployee
FETCH NEXT FROM @MyCurs
```

	EmpID	LastName	FirstName	HireDate	LocationID	ManagerID
1	2	White	Barry	2002-08-12 00:00:00.000	1	11

1 rows

Figure 15.46 FETCH returned record two using variable @MyCurs.

Lab 15.2: Cursor Types

Lab Prep: Lab Prep: Each lab has one or more Skill Checks. Start with Skill Check 1 and proceed until reaching the Points to Ponder section.

Before beginning this lab, verify that SQL Server 2012 is properly installed and operating. Before running the lab setup script for resetting the database (SQLQueries2012Vol4Chapter15.2Setup.sql), please make sure to close all query windows within SSMS. An open query window pointing to a database context can lock that database preventing it from updating when the script is executing. A simple way to assure all query windows are closed, is to exit out of SSMS, then open a new instance of SSMS, and lastly run the setup script.

Skill Check 1: Create a cursor called crsGrant from all the records and fields of the Grant table. Create the type of cursor that will allow you to show the Last, Prior, Next and First records from the cursor.

```
FETCH LAST FROM crsGrant
FETCH PRIOR FROM crsGrant
FETCH NEXT FROM crsGrant
FETCH FIRST FROM crsGrant
```

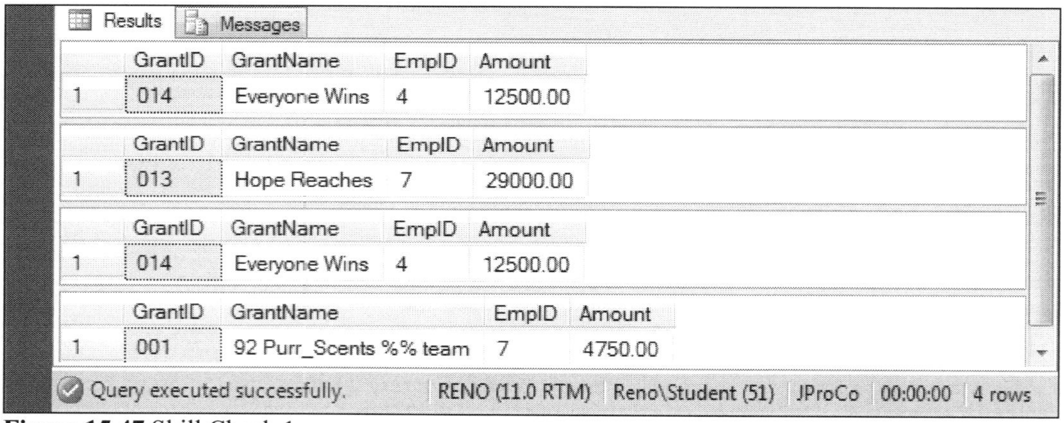

GrantID	GrantName	EmpID	Amount
014	Everyone Wins	4	12500.00

GrantID	GrantName	EmpID	Amount
013	Hope Reaches	7	29000.00

GrantID	GrantName	EmpID	Amount
014	Everyone Wins	4	12500.00

GrantID	GrantName	EmpID	Amount
001	92 Purr_Scents %% team	7	4750.00

Figure 15.47 Skill Check 1.

Answer Code: The T-SQL code to this lab can be found in the downloadable files in a file named Lab15.2_CursorTypes.sql.

Points to Ponder - Cursor Types

1. The scrolling behavior of cursors depends on the type of cursor you declare.
2. With a FORWARD_ONLY cursor you enable only sequential forward only reading.
3. SCROLL cursor enables you to move freely forward and backward which requires more resources.
4. If you only need to go forward (and not prior) then a FORWARD_ONLY cursor is much better for performance than a SCROLL cursor.
5. STATIC cursors loop over a copy of the data, not over the original data, hence it doesn't support any updates. Creating a copy of data is very resource-intensive.
6. DYNAMIC cursor immediately reflects any changes made to underlying tables.
7. If a cursor variable is set to a cursor type you can use the variable instead of the cursor name.
8. To fetch the second row from a scroll cursor use this syntax:
   - FETCH ABSOLUTE 2 FROM contact_cursor;
9. To fetch the row that is three rows after the current row:
   - FETCH RELATIVE 3 FROM contact_cursor;

Chapter Glossary

@@FETCH_STATUS: A SQL function that returns the status of the current row to determine if the last fetch action returned a record. If no records were returned then -1 is the returned value. @@FETCH_STATUS returns a zero if a record was found and a -1 if no record was found.

Cursor: A SQL tool that allows you to define a set of data rows and perform a SQL function on data set row by row.

Dynamic Cursors: A type of cursor that immediately reflects any changes made to the underlying tables.

Static Cursors: A type of cursors that creates a copy of the data, not over the original data, hence it doesn't support any updates. Static Cursors will not reflect updates to the underlying table once the cursor has been declared.

FORWARD_ONLY: A type of cursor that can only fetch subsequent rows not prior rows.

SCROLL: A type of cursor that enables you to move freely forward and backward to retrieve both prior and subsequent rows, which requires more resources.

Review Quiz - Chapter Fifteen

1.) You have the following code that does not run:

```
DECLARE crsWeek CURSOR
FOR SELECT * FROM dbo.WeeklyBackups
DECLARE @DbName VARCHAR(100)
FETCH NEXT FROM crsWeek INTO @DbName
SELECT @DbName
CLOSE crsWeek
DEALLOCATE crsWeek
```

What is wrong with that code?

O a. You can't use FETCH NEXT with a default cursor.
O b. You can't use variables to capture a cursor value.
O c. You can't fetch until you open the cursor.
O d. You must run DEALLOCATE before CLOSE.

2.) Your dbo.WeeklyBackups table has 3 records in it and you run the following code:

```
DECLARE crsWeek CURSOR
FOR SELECT * FROM dbo.WeeklyBackups
OPEN crsWeek
SELECT @@FETCH_STATUS
FETCH NEXT FROM crsWeek
SELECT @@FETCH_STATUS
FETCH NEXT FROM crsWeek
SELECT @@FETCH_STATUS
FETCH NEXT FROM crsWeek
SELECT @@FETCH_STATUS
FETCH NEXT FROM crsWeek
SELECT @@FETCH_STATUS
FETCH NEXT FROM crsWeek
```

Which is the first @@FETCH that will return a -1 value?

O a. The first SELECT @@FETCH_STATUS.
O b. The last SELECT @@FETCH_STATUS.
O c. The second SELECT @@FETCH_STATUS.
O d. The fourth SELECT @@FETCH_STATUS.
O e. None of them.

3.) A @@FETCH_STATUS of zero means what?

- O a. The last fetch found a value or record.
- O b. The next fetch found a value or record.
- O c. The last fetch did not find a value or record.
- O d. The next fetch did not find a value or record.

4.) What is the only type of cursor that will not change its values or records even if the underlying table is updated?

- O a. FORWARD_ONLY cursor
- O b. SCROLL cursor
- O c. DYNAMIC cursor
- O d. STATIC cursor

5.) You want to create a cursor that will support this statement. What type of cursor will do this?

`FETCH PRIOR FROM crsGrant`

- O a. FORWARD_ONLY cursor
- O b. SCROLL cursor
- O c. DYNAMIC cursor
- O d. STATIC cursor

Answer Key

1.) All cursors can do FETCH NEXT, so (a) is incorrect. The main way to capture values from cursors is with a variable, making (b) wrong. DEALLOCATE always comes after CLOSE, so (d) is wrong. You need to open the cursor before you can do any fetching, so (c) is the right answer.

2.) If you have three records in your cursor then you will get a @@FETCH_STATUS of zero after three fetches. Not until the 4th fetch will you get the -1 status. Notice the 5th @@FETCH_STATUS comes after the 4th FETCH. This means (b) is the correct answer.

3.) The @@FETCH_STATUS reflects the last fetched record (not the upcoming record), making (b) and (d) wrong. This means (a) is the correct answer.

4.) All cursors get their records in real-time from the underlying table except for the static cursor, so (d) is the correct answer.

5.) All cursors can fetch next but only the scroll cursor can fetch the prior record, making (b) the correct answer.

Chapter 15. Cursors

Bug Catcher Game

To play the Bug Catcher game, run the file SQLQueries2012Vol4BugCatcher15.pps from the BugCatcher folder of the companion files found at www.Joes2Pros.com.

Chapter 16. Summary of Volume 4

While working in the garage, I saw that one of our shelves was falling down. I decided to fix it, and noticed that in the very corner a small screw was missing. I found the screw and with a screwdriver tried to put it back. But the screwdriver and screw size didn't match. I found a bigger screwdriver, but now it was too big for the screw. Even though it looked like a simple task, I ended up having to use my fingers to tighten the screw and put the shelf back together. The next day I noticed that the shelf was falling down again. The same screw had fallen out. I ended up having to go out to buy the right size of screwdriver at a local hardware store. I used all the force I could to turn the screw back into the shelf. The next day when I checked the shelf, it was holding strong. The last few turns of that screw that I could not complete with my fingers had been the most important for the structural integrity of the shelf.

This simple thing inspired me. No matter how much we have learned, if we don't know the key thing, we can easily fail. Success needs more than hard work, it also needs to be done appropriately. You need the right tools for the right tasks. This book was all about using the right object for the needed task.

Some people will tell you never to use cursors. They should tell you never to use them if another object will complete your task better. There are times when cursors are the appropriate tool. In the last chapter we learned when and how to use cursors appropriately.

Here is a technical example of making sure to use the right object: a column was being updated, but no one knew why. After various audits, it was found that the column was being updated because of a trigger. No one knew it was there, it was done by a developer in the early stages of the application. The trigger was there because the application originally needed seven items updated. Six were now updated with a stored procedure, but the seventh one was missed. The developer had been afraid to go back and modify the stored procedure to update all seven fields, so he created the trigger. What he missed was that when the procedure executed, the trigger was fine. But the trigger was firing after every update was made to the table and not just updates from the stored procedure. These updates were often not needed. There were two times the trigger was firing: first when the stored procedure fired and the complete logic was correct; and the second was when the column was manually updated. At the end of the day, the table was updated twice – once correctly and once incorrectly. In this example, was the trigger incorrect? It was definitely not the right place for this scenario. The developer should have used this update logic in the stored procedure instead of adding it to the trigger.

And the end of this book, we have the proper knowledge of views, objects, triggers, and functions. Some functions reduce performance; others are absolutely needed regardless of their effect on performance. We have learned how to use objects properly. Where do we go now?

What's next

We understand the right usage of objects and how to use them in performance. Now we need to expand that knowledge. Assume a simple technical scenario. There is a heterogeneous system, a system that shares the same type of data back and forth. This system shares data in XML. XML is popular because we use it to standardize data. Once we receive the XML we have a problem. First, we have to decide if it is valid data, what its attributes are, and what kind of data it is. We also need to decide how to search in XML. We can store it in a table, but then we have to convert it back to XML before returning it to the previous system. Sometimes it makes sense to convert the data to a table and other times we need our data as XML.

XML is very popular, so we will be learning how to take our knowledge to the next level. We will learn how to share XML and write XML queries and indexes. If we keep it in XML, we then face the problem of how to get part of the data out or verify the existence of a value. For XML queries we can create XML indexes. We will be covering all these topics next in Volume 5. By combining our knowledge from Volumes 4 and 5 we will reach a state where we know most everything about SQL Server queries and how to use XML features to enhance learning of the subject.

Nowadays, a true SQL Pro will know about SQL's interoperability with .NET, XML, and PowerShell. The final book in this SQL certification preparation track series covers SQL Server's usage and interaction with other programming languages, such as C#, ADO.net, and XML. Beginning with SQL Server 2005, Microsoft has significantly enhanced SQL Server's ability to utilize and deliver data using these other programming languages. *Congratulations* to those who have made it all the way through this book's lessons on programming, a vital leg on your journey to becoming a SQL Pro!

Best wishes for your continued progress in the realm of SQL Server databases!!

Rick Morelan

Chapter 16. Summary of Volume 4

[THIS PAGE INTENTIONALLY LEFT BLANK]

Index

@

@@FETCH_STATUS, 575, 576, 579, 580, 581, 586, 595, 597, 598

A

About the Authors, 11
    Pinal Dave, 11
    Rick Morelan, 11
About this Book
    Downloadable Companion Files, 15
    Introduction, 13
    Skills Needed, 14
    Videos as a Companion, 16
    What this Book is Not, 17
Altering Views. *See DDL Statements*
Analytic Funcions
    PERCENTILE_CONT(), 409, 410, 411, 412, 414, 416, 417
Analytic Functions
    CUME_DIST(), 401, 402, 416, 417
    FIRST_VALUE(), 403, 404, 416, 417
    LAG(), 405, 407, 408, 416, 417
    LAST_VALUE(), 403, 416, 417
    LEAD(), 405, 406, 407, 416, 417
    PERCENT_RANK(), 401, 403, 416, 417

B

BACKUP DATABASE, 546, 547, 548, 550, 551, 552, 553, 554, 562, 566, 571, 572, 578, 579, 582
Batch Abortion. *See Error Actions*
BEGIN END Block, 84, 92, 94, 95, 101, 103, 104, 116, 117, 119, 120, 128, 134, 135, 136, 137, 139, 146, 148, 149, 215, 273, 423, 425, 428, 429, 433, 447, 448, 452, 463, 464, 466, 467, 476, 490, 495, 496, 497, 499, 500, 501, 503, 505, 511, 512, 513, 514, 516, 518, 519, 522, 523, 524, 525, 526, 527, 580, 581

C

CASE. *See Logical Functions*
Catalog Views, 188
CATCH Block, 495, 496, 497, 498, 499, 500, 504, 505, 509, 510, 511, 512, 513, 514, 516, 518, 519, 520, 521, 522, 523, 524, 525, 526, 527, 528
CHARINDEX(), 138, 139
Check Constraint, 23, 24, 25, 26, 27, 30, 31, 50, 51, 67, 70, 71, 72, 74, 75, 76
CHECK OPTION. *See WITH*
COALESCE(). *See Logical Functions*
Connection Termination. *See Error Actions*
CONSTRAINT, 21, 26, 33, 34, 35, 40, 42, 44, 59, 62, 68, 70, 72
Conversion Functions
    CAST(), 136, 137, 139, 317, 318, 319, 362, 426, 427, 428, 429, 468, 469, 476, 501, 505
    CONVERT(), 324, 325, 326
Creating Views. *See DDL Statements*
CUME_DIST. *See Analytical Functions*
Cursor Types
    Dynamic Cursors, 589, 595
    FORWARD_ONLY, 587, 588, 595, 596, 598
    SCROLL, 587, 588, 595, 596, 598
    STATIC, 591
Cursors, 569, 570, 573, 574, 576, 577, 584, 585, 586, 587, 588, 591, 593, 594, 595, 598, 600

D

Data Types
    Character
        CHAR, 67, 69, 317, 466, 467, 470, 476, 479, 485, 501, 505, 541
        NCHAR, 74, 453, 541
        NVARCHAR, 34, 35, 74, 76, 291, 294, 324, 325, 326, 531, 532, 533, 534, 536, 537, 539, 540, 541, 542, 556, 557, 559, 561, 564, 565
        TEXT, 38, 541
        VARCHAR, 32, 35, 38, 68, 70, 118, 136, 137, 139, 146, 255, 267, 275, 282, 284, 285, 286, 291, 294, 295, 296, 298, 301, 317, 318, 319, 362, 441, 463, 464, 468, 527, 541, 549, 550, 551, 552, 553, 554, 559, 561, 562, 566, 570, 572, 577, 578, 581, 584, 597
    Numeric
        FLOAT, 273, 307, 308, 427, 428, 429

Index

INT, 67, 68, 70, 74, 118, 134, 137, 139, 251, 253, 256, 258, 259, 260, 261, 262, 263, 264, 265, 266, 267, 270, 271, 272, 273, 274, 275, 285, 286, 291, 294, 295, 296, 301, 307, 308, 385, 386, 394, 400, 422, 423, 425, 428, 429, 463, 464, 468, 470, 476, 501, 505, 514, 516, 519, 527, 543, 544

MONEY, 275, 291, 296, 307, 308, 448, 466, 467, 470, 476, 485, 501, 505, 514, 516, 519, 542, 544

SMALLINT, 146

SMALLMONEY, 18, 19, 298

XML, 38, 136, 138, 187, 601

Date/Time

DATEFROMPARTS(), 365, 366, 367, 370, 374, 376, 377

DATETIME, 70, 271, 272, 273, 274, 291, 294, 295, 318, 322, 376, 380, 381

DATETIMEFROMPARTS(), 370, 374, 375, 376, 377

EOMONTH(), 371, 372, 373, 376, 377, 380

GETDATE(), 112, 118, 119, 141, 148, 151, 197, 228, 229, 230, 231, 232, 243, 294, 295, 300, 301, 329, 345, 350, 351, 352, 354, 358, 359, 362, 364, 365, 377, 378, 379, 380, 381, 421, 445, 446

Time Calculation Functions

DATEADD(), 359, 360, 361, 363, 364, 377

DATEPART(), 355, 356, 357, 358, 362, 364, 377, 421

TIMEFROMPARTS(), 367, 368, 370, 376, 377

DDL Statements

ALTER

FUNCTION, 429, 433, 448

PROCEDURE, 257, 259, 265, 271, 273, 277, 284, 285, 286, 463, 464, 467, 504, 505, 519, 564

TABLE, 21, 24, 26, 31, 33, 34, 35, 39, 40, 42, 44, 45, 48, 59, 62, 72, 82, 86, 87, 109, 111, 132, 470

VIEW, 167, 176, 178, 179, 180, 183, 184, 187, 188, 216, 224, 225, 228, 230, 231, 232, 233, 234, 236

CREATE

FUNCTION, 422, 423, 425, 428, 433, 435, 447

PROCEDURE, 249, 251, 253, 255, 257, 258, 261, 263, 268, 270, 276, 277, 282, 300, 301, 307, 466, 476, 501, 514, 516, 527, 533, 534, 536, 537, 564, 565

TABLE, 39, 68, 69, 70, 72, 80, 118, 133, 134, 135, 137, 138, 139, 146, 458, 570

TRIGGER, 84, 92, 94, 95, 101, 104, 110, 112, 116, 117, 119, 120, 134, 135, 146, 147, 148, 149, 150, 151, 215, 490

TYPE, 298, 301

VIEW, 141, 159, 161, 162, 165, 166, 170, 175, 176, 179, 180, 188, 189, 190, 198, 207, 222, 228, 231, 237, 242, 244, 245, 444, 446, 448

DROP

CONSTRAINT, 26, 62

PROCEDURE, 146, 257, 277

TABLE, 68, 70, 134, 135, 139, 181, 183, 184, 186

VIEW, 187

TRUNCATE, 99, 110

DECLARE, 137, 139, 251, 259, 260, 261, 262, 263, 264, 265, 266, 267, 271, 272, 274, 275, 284, 285, 286, 291, 294, 295, 298, 299, 301, 304, 305, 380, 385, 386, 394, 422, 423, 425, 428, 429, 447, 448, 476, 501, 505, 525, 531, 532, 533, 534, 536, 537, 539, 540, 541, 542, 543, 544, 549, 550, 551, 552, 553, 554, 556, 557, 559, 561, 564, 566, 572, 574, 575, 576, 577, 578, 581, 587, 588, 590, 591, 593, 597

Default Constraints, 39, 44, 45, 46, 48

Deterministic function, 241, 452

DML Statements

DELETE, 21, 59, 64, 72, 87, 90, 91, 92, 93, 94, 95, 96, 97, 98, 99, 110, 111, 113, 116, 117, 120, 121, 124, 128, 131, 132, 142, 144, 146, 147, 150, 152, 193, 194, 200, 204, 205, 206, 379, 433, 491, 506, 507, 524, 526

EXECUTE, 249, 257, 276, 422

INSERT, 31, 33, 41, 42, 43, 44, 45, 48, 58, 60, 62, 71, 72, 82, 83, 84, 85, 86, 89, 90, 92, 99, 110, 111, 118, 119, 120, 122, 123, 124, 125, 126, 128, 129, 130, 131, 142, 144, 193, 194, 197, 200, 204, 205, 282, 284, 285, 286, 295, 298, 299, 300, 301, 304, 307, 379, 433, 491, 507, 508, 511, 512, 513, 514, 519, 524, 526, 527, 570, 580

MERGE, 110

UPDATE, 21, 22, 23, 24, 25, 26, 27, 31, 48, 51, 54, 72, 90, 99, 100, 101, 102, 104, 105, 106, 109, 110, 111, 112, 113, 118, 120, 124, 132, 142, 143, 144, 146, 150, 151, 193, 194, 195, 199, 200, 202, 204, 206, 207, 208, 209, 210, 211, 212, 213, 214, 215, 217, 220, 258, 259, 350, 351, 433,

Index

463, 464, 466, 467, 476, 484, 491, 494, 495, 496, 497, 501, 503, 505, 515, 516, 520, 521, 591, 592
WITH
CHECK OPTION, 124, 216, 217, 218, 220, 242, 243, 244, 245, 246
ENCRYPTION, 176, 178, 179, 187, 188, 189, 191, 242, 244, 246, 257
LOG option, 472
Schemabinding, 183, 184, 188, 189, 190, 191, 224, 228, 230, 231, 232, 233, 234, 236, 237, 242, 244, 245, 444, 446, 448
Domain Integrity, 49, 50, 51, 52, 55, 56
Dynamic Cursors. *See* **Cursor Types**
Dynamic SQL, 529, 530, 532, 533, 536, 538, 540, 546, 552, 555, 558, 563, 567

E

ENCRYPTION. *See WITH*
END. *See BEGIN END Block*
Entity Integrity, 49, 51, 52, 54, 55, 56
Error Actions
Batch Abortion, 474, 487, 489
Connection Termination, 475, 487, 489
Scope Abortion, 474, 487, 489
Statement Termination, 473, 474, 487, 489, 501, 502
Testing Error Actions, 475
XACT_ABORT, 483, 484, 487, 488, 489, 490, 491, 509, 525, 528
Error Messages, 456, 457, 460, 463, 465, 470, 472, 473, 485, 487, 493, 500, 508, 509, 515, 520, 521, 523, 527, 540
ERROR_LINE(), 509, 523
ERROR_MESSAGE(), 498, 499, 500, 509, 512, 523, 525, 526, 527
ERROR_NUMBER(), 509, 523
ERROR_PROCEDURE(), 509, 523
ERROR_SEVERITY(), 499, 500, 509, 523
ERROR_STATE(), 509, 523
EVENTDATA(), 136, 137, 138, 139, 142, 147, 152

F

FIRST_VALUE. *See Analytical Functions*
FLOAT. *See Numeric*
Foreign Key, 49, 50, 56, 57, 58, 59, 60, 61, 62, 63, 65, 66, 67, 70, 75, 77, 132, 145, 507, 524, 526
FORWARD_ONLY. *See Cursor Types*

G

GOTO, 509

I

IIF. *See Logical Functions*
INT. *See Numeric*
ISMSSHIPPED, 339, 340, 342, 343
ISNULL. *See Logical Functions*

L

LAG. *See Analytical Functions*
LAST_VALUE(). *See Analytic Functions*
LEAD. *See Analytical Functions*
LOG option. *See WITH*
Logical Functions
CASE, 389, 390, 391, 400, 417, 418, 419
COALESCE(), 391, 392, 393, 394, 400, 417, 418, 419
IIF, 394, 395, 396, 417, 419
ISNULL, 385, 386, 387, 388, 389, 397, 400, 413, 417, 418, 419, 429

M

Manipulating Data
Inserting Records, 61, 62, 63, 64, 67, 73, 244, 245
Mathmatic
AVG(), 189, 190, 277, 311, 312, 426, 427, 428, 429
MAX(), 277, 311
MIN(), 277, 311
SUM(), 154, 174, 175, 176, 179, 277
Memory resident tables, 110
Metadata, 20, 59, 61, 161, 188, 310, 334, 335, 336, 344
Metadata Functions
OBJECTPROPERTY(), 339, 340, 342, 343, 344
SCOPE_IDENTITY(), 281, 284, 285, 286, 287, 288, 292, 305, 306, 307
SERVERPROPERTY(), 334, 335, 343, 344, 346
MONEY. *See Numeric*

N

N (Unicode), 385, 386, 541, 542, 545, 559, 561, 563
Nesting Views, 167

605
www.Joes2Pros.com

Index

NOCHECK. *See WITH*
Non-deterministic function, 241
Numeric
    INT, 294, 427, 468, 479

O

OUTPUT, 91, 110, 271, 272, 273, 274, 275, 276, 277, 379, 381

P

PERCENT_RANK. *See Analytical Functions*
PERCENTILE_CONT. *See Analytic Functions*
Primary Keys, 19, 21, 22, 24, 28, 29, 31, 32, 33, 38, 49, 51, 52, 53, 54, 55, 56, 57, 67, 68, 71, 72, 77, 78, 80, 81, 82, 146, 205, 223, 341, 511, 513, 584
PRINT, 117, 134, 135, 136, 137, 258, 260, 262, 263, 277, 284, 285, 286, 288, 289, 291, 496, 497, 499, 500, 512, 513, 525, 526, 527, 531, 551

R

RAISERROR(), 149, 463, 464, 467, 468, 472, 476, 477, 487, 489, 490, 491, 497, 498, 499, 500, 501, 505, 509, 510, 511, 522, 523, 525, 526, 527, 528
READONLY, 301, 304, 305, 307
Referential Integrity, 49, 53, 55, 56, 58, 60, 65, 67, 74, 78
RETURN, 259, 261, 262, 263, 265, 269, 271, 276, 277, 284, 285, 286, 423, 425, 428, 429, 435, 442, 447, 448
ROLLBACK, 95, 104, 105, 116, 138, 139, 148, 149, 151, 215, 490, 503, 505, 514, 516, 517, 518, 519, 524, 526

S

Scalar Results, 254, 255, 260, 290, 423, 425, 427, 428, 453, 455
Scalar Stored Procedure, 254, 267
SCHEMABINDING. *See WITH*
Scope Abortion. *See Error Actions*
SCOPE_IDENTITY. *See Metadata Functions*
SELECT DISTINCT, 220
SELECT INTO, 80, 81, 110
Severity Level, 457, 463, 464, 466, 488, 497, 498, 499, 523, 525

SMALLINT. *See Numeric*
sp_executesql. *See System Stored Procedures*
sp_helptext. *see System Stored Procedures*
SQL Injection, 555, 559, 563
Statement Termination. *See Error Actions*
STATIC CURSOR. *See Cursor Types*
Stored Procedure
    Capturing Return Data
        @@IDENTITY, 287, 288, 292, 305, 306, 307
        @@ROWCOUNT, 259, 289, 290, 292, 305, 463, 464, 467, 476, 501, 505, 525
        IDENT_CURRENT(), 289, 292, 305
    Execution Options, 281
    String Functions, 310
        CONCAT(), 323, 324, 333, 345, 346
        FORMAT(), 324, 326, 327, 328, 329, 330, 333, 345, 346
        LEFT(), 236, 312, 313, 322, 343, 344, 346, 421, 444, 454
        LEN(), 310, 311, 312, 314, 322, 343, 344, 346
        LOWER(), 314, 315, 316, 322, 343, 421
        LTRIM(), 315, 322, 343
        REPLACE(), 315
        RIGHT(), 312, 313, 322, 343, 344, 346, 421
        SUBSTRING(), 312, 313, 314, 322, 343, 344, 346, 421
        UPPER(), 314, 315, 322, 343, 421, 450
    String Functions()
        RTRIM(), 315, 322, 343
    System Stored Procedures
        sp_executesql, 539, 540, 541, 542, 543, 544, 545, 559, 561, 563, 565, 567
        sp_helptext, 160, 161, 166, 173, 176, 178, 179, 180, 185, 187, 188, 190, 191, 197, 207, 227, 228, 231, 241
        sp_spaceused, 238, 241

T

Table-Valued Parameter, 296, 299, 301, 307
Testing Error Actions. *See Error Actions*
THROW, 510, 511, 512, 513, 515, 518, 519, 520, 521, 522, 523, 526, 527, 528
Triggers, 79, 80, 81, 84, 85, 86, 87, 88, 89, 90, 91, 92, 93, 94, 95, 96, 97, 98, 99, 100, 101, 102, 103, 104, 105, 106, 107, 109, 110, 111, 112, 113, 115, 116, 117, 119, 120, 121, 122, 123, 124, 125, 126, 127, 128, 129, 130, 131, 132, 133, 134, 135, 136, 137, 138, 139, 140, 141, 142, 143, 144, 145, 146, 147, 150, 151, 152, 153, 157, 183, 193, 214, 215, 216, 220,

Index

242, 245, 246, 258, 288, 292, 454, 455, 472, 509, 600
TRY Block, 495, 496, 497, 499, 500, 505, 509, 510, 511, 512, 513, 514, 516, 519, 520, 522, 523, 524, 525, 526, 527, 528

U

Unicode, 541, 545, 563
Unique Constraints, 32, 33, 34, 35, 36, 37, 38, 49, 50, 51, 52, 53, 67, 68, 72, 74, 76, 77, 78

V

Views, 154
    Altering. *See DDL Statements*
    Creating. *See DDL Statements*
    Creating an Index, 221
    Deleting Data, 205
    Encrypting, 176
    Indexed, 188, 193, 198, 221, 224, 226, 227, 229, 230, 232, 233, 234, 235, 237, 238, 239, 240, 241, 243, 246, 421, 445, 454, 455
    Inserting Data, 204
    Manipulating Data, 194
        Inserting Records, 196
        Selecting Data, 194
        Updating Records, 195
    Materialized, 193, 226, 241, 277
    Partitioned, 241
    Rules, 174
    Schemabinding, 179
    Standard, 241
    Updating Data, 206
    Using Check Option, 211

W

WITH. *See DML Statements*

X

XACT_ABORT. *See Error Actions*

Made in the USA
San Bernardino, CA
21 December 2012